Fundamentals of Human Resource Management

Edition

David A. DeCenzo

Coastal Carolina University
Conway, SC

Stephen P. Robbins

San Diego State University
San Diego, CA

Susan L. Verhulst, PHR

Des Moines Area Community College
Ankeny, IA

WILEY

VICE PRESIDENT & EXECUTIVE PUBLISHER	George Hoffman
EXECUTIVE EDITOR	Lisé Johnson
DEVELOPMENTAL EDITOR	Susan McLaughlin
PROJECT EDITOR	Brian Baker
ASSOCIATE DIRECTOR OF MARKETING	Amy Scholz
MARKETING MANAGER	Kelly Simmons
MARKETING ASSISTANT	Marissa Carroll
SENIOR PRODUCT DESIGNER	Allison Morris
MEDIA SPECIALIST	Ethan Bernard
SENIOR PRODUCTION AND MANUFACTURING MANAGER	Janis Soo
ASSOCIATE PRODUCTION MANAGER	Joel Balbin
PHOTO DEPARTMENT MANAGER	Hilary Newman
PHOTO RESEARCHER	Susan McLaughlin
DESIGN DIRECTOR	Harry Nolan
SENIOR DESIGNER	Wendy Lai
COVER PHOTO CREDIT	©Onne van der Wal/Corbis Images
BACKGROUND WAVE PATTERN CREDIT	©Roman Okopny/iStockphoto

This book was set in 10/12 Kepler Std by Aptara Corp, Inc. and printed and bound by Courier/Kendallville. The cover was printed by Courier/Kendallville.

This book is printed on acid free paper.

Copyright © 2013, 2010, 2007, 2005, 2002 John Wiley & Sons, Inc. All rights reserved.

No part of this publication may be reproduced, stored in a retrieval system or transmitted in any form or by any means, electronic, mechanical, photocopying, recording, scanning or otherwise, except as permitted under Sections 107 or 108 of the 1976 United States Copyright Act, without either the prior written permission of the Publisher, or authorization through payment of the appropriate per-copy fee to the Copyright Clearance Center, Inc. 222 Rosewood Drive, Danvers, MA 01923, website www.copyright.com. Requests to the Publisher for permission should be addressed to the Permissions Department, John Wiley & Sons, Inc., 111 River Street, Hoboken, NJ 07030-5774, (201)748-6011, fax (201)748-6008, website http://www.wiley.com/go/permissions.

To order books or for customer service please, call 1-800-CALL WILEY (225-5945).

Library of Congress Cataloging-in-Publication Data
DeCenzo, David A.
  Fundamentals of human resource management / David A. DeCenzo, Stephen P. Robbins, Susan L. Verhulst. -- 11th ed.
     p. cm.
  Includes index.
  ISBN 978-0-470-91012-2 (paper/website) 1. Personnel management. I. Robbins, Stephen P., 1943- II. Verhulst, Susan L. III. Title.
  HF5549.D396 2013
  658.3--dc23
                            2012030735

ISBN 978-0-470-91012-2 (Main Book)
ISBN 978-1-118-37968-4 (Binder-Ready Version)

Printed in the United States of America

10 9 8 7 6 5 4 3 2 1

Brief Contents

Contents

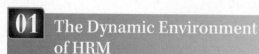

Part 2 THE LEGAL AND ETHICAL CONTEXT OF HRM

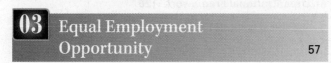

03 Equal Employment Opportunity **57**

04 Employee Rights and Discipline 91

Part 3 STAFFING THE ORGANIZATION

05 Human Resource Planning and Job Analysis 119

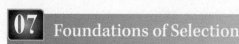

09 Managing Careers   221

Part 5 MAINTAINING HIGH PERFORMANCE

12 Employee Benefits 301

13 Ensuring a Safe and Healthy Work Environment 331

Part 6 LABOR-MANAGEMENT ENVIRONMENTS

14 Understanding Labor Relations and Collective Bargaining   359

Preface

The sailing crews on the cover face many of the same goals and challenges as any organization in an unpredictable business environment. Success, and possibly survival, depend on a well-designed boat with a carefully selected and thoroughly trained crew that understands the strategy of the race. They must be able to quickly adjust the sails, rigging and rudder to keep moving forward and somehow gain a competitive advantage in order to win the race. External factors may be visible and predictable, but invisible factors like the wind and waves may be unpredictable and require minor adjustments or a major change in strategy.

When organizations face challenges they depend on thoroughly trained professionals who react quickly to the changes in the environment and create strategies for success. Human Resource Management (HRM) is responsible for carefully selecting and training people with the necessary skills to pursue the strategy effectively. Some external factors can be predicted; others, such as the collapse of large banks and insurance companies, can seemingly come out of nowhere. The challenges have been coming fast and furious recently as organizations struggle to adjust strategy in the face of an unpredictable stock market, a sluggish economic recovery, an increasingly global environment, instability in the Eurozone and other global economies, changes brought by elections worldwide, and technology that has made social networking a mainstream tool for business—just to name a few!

> Like a crew sailing an ocean race, success and possibly survival depend on a good crew that understands the strategy and can adapt quickly to the unpredictable environment.

Welcome to the eleventh edition of *Fundamentals of Human Resource Management*. It is truly an exciting time to be studying Human Resource Management. We appreciate that you are taking time to read this preface to get a better understanding of the text and the resources for learning it includes.

About the Book

Students taking an HRM class are very likely to be taking it either as an elective or a first class toward an HRM major. Both of these groups need a strong foundation book that provides the essential elements of HRM and relevant applications of HR principles as well as a clear understanding of how HRM links with business strategy. It is becoming increasingly important for employees on every level of the organization to understand HRM elements such as recruitment, training, motivation, retention, safety, and the legal environment. These fundamentals will not create experts in HRM, yet for those who wish to become experts, this book will provide that strong foundation upon which additional coursework in HRM can be built. The objectives and content in this text have been created to be compatible with the content areas and curriculum templates developed and suggested by the Society of Human Resource Management (SHRM). The minimum HR content areas as identified by SHRM include:

- Compensation, benefits, and total rewards
- Employee and labor relations
- Employment law
- History of HR and its role
- HR and globalization
- HR and mergers and acquisitions
- HR and organizational strategy

- Human resource information systems (HRIS)
- Measuring HR outcomes and the bottom line
- Occupational health, safety, and security
- Performance appraisal and feedback
- Recruiting and selection
- Workforce planning and talent management

The content of the text has been developed to provide a background in the functional areas identified by the HR Certification Institute (HRCI) for the exams for certification for Professional in Human Resources (PHR), Senior Professional in Human Resources (SPHR), and Global Professional in Human Resources (GPHR). Our goal has been to produce a text that addresses these critical foundations of HRM, yet provides the most current reference possible for the dynamic present and unpredictable future environment of HRM. All research has been updated, and examples have been kept as current as possible, considering the timeline necessary for publishing a textbook. Some examples will undoubtedly change quickly and unexpectedly. Please consider this an opportunity to research how and why these changes took place and their implications for HRM. Many sources for research and updates have been included in the chapter content and HRM Workshop learning activities.

Several Content Topics New in This Edition

Ninety percent of the chapters begin with new opening vignettes to add interest and application of concepts as well. End-of-chapter case applications that challenge a student's understanding of the chapter's material are also included. Updates and additions to research, current examples, and assignments are too numerous to mention. New topics and other substantial additions to the text include:

- Suggested service learning activities designed to make a positive difference in the world, while increasing students' ability to apply HR functions and student employability.
- Examination of the impact of social media in recruiting, selection, employee rights, and discipline.
- The impact on the economy and economic recovery on HR including rebuilding a workforce.
- Updates on HR as a career including pay and employment opportunities.
- Updated coverage of Global HR practices.
- Major revisions to Chapter 3 on Equal Employment Opportunity focuses on the increasingly complex application of discrimination laws including retailiation.
- New discussion on slackers in the workplace—how to reduce, eliminate, or not hire them in the first place.
- Updated discussion of flexible work scheduling.
- New look at executive compensation and benefits.
- Americans with Disabilities Act coverage has been updated.
- New discussion of changes to employee health plans and evolving healthcare legislation.
- Significant overhaul of Chapter 13 on safety and OSHA.
- Updates on unions, labor relations, mediation, and scrutiny of public employee unions

New to Chapter 1: New chapter opener on how HR handles natural disasters and global upheaval. New feature on the future of Global HR, updated treatment on labor shortages, new end of chapter case on HR in the Navy.

New to Chapter 2: Updated explanation of Strategic HR, expanded coverage of Shared Services, new end of chapter case on how organizational mission and strategy are linked to job design at Frito-Lay.

New to Chapter 3: Extensively revised to include a new opener on Retaliation, new section on the protections in Title VII of the Civil Rights act, updated coverage of EEOC role and most common claims filed, updated examples for age discrimination, expanded coverage of the Lilly Ledbetter Fair Pay Act, added coverage of ADA Amendments Act of 2008, expanded coverage of FMLA, and a new section on Genetic Information Nondiscrimination Act (GINA).

New to Chapter 4: New chapter opener on unique employee discipline issues. Updated coverage of laws that protect employee rights in the workplace, extensive coverage of Social Media in Current Issues section, new Contemporary Connection box concerning managers who are insecure about using discipline policies.

New to Chapter 5: New opener on NASA changes and how they affect HR, new Ethical Issues on Green Jobs and how they are defined, update on HRIS technology and Saas (Software as a Service), new feature on hard to fill jobs, new Contemporary Connection feature on non-traditional schedules.

New to Chapter 6: Extended coverage of online recruiting efforts, new coverage of recruiting effectiveness, new section on using social media to the job seeker's advantage.

New to Chapter 7: New chapter opener on employee selection procedures at Bon Ton Department Stores. New Contemporary Connection feature on professionalism on the phone, expanded and updated coverage of I-9 forms and Employment Eligibility Verification, expanded coverage of Negligent Hiring,

New to Chapter 8: New chapter opener on a unique and successful Welfare-to-Work program. New features on the best practices in onboarding new employees and orientation checklists. New section on training methods.

New to Chapter 9: Increased coverage of internships. New learning activities and new case on career development at Newell Rubbermaid.

New to Chapter 10: New student-centered examples, expanded coverage of unethical practices and discrimination during performance appraisals, new Workplace Issues on HR movement to eliminate traditional appraisals in favor of better communication and frequent feedback, and Millenials' need for constant feedback. New Case Application that outlines the issues an organization encounters when the performance appraisal process is neglected.

New to Chapter 11: Updated coverage of the Lilly Ledbetter Fair Pay Act, new Workplace Issues on unpaid internships, updated coverage of Executive Compensation and Golden Parachutes. New coverage on hardship differentials in compensation for expat employees. New Case Application that focuses on a company that realigns compensation to fit organizational strategy with mixed results.

New to Chapter 12: Coverage of Michelle's Law updated to show influence on the Affordable Care Act, Social Security and Silver Tsunami discussions updated, and new section on employer efforts to cut healthcare costs.

New to Chapter 13: New Contemporary Connection feature on the Triangle Shirtwaist Factory Fire in 1911 and its continuing impact on employee safety. Expanded coverage of the General Duty Clause and its importance. Coverage of OSHA top ten violations, workplace violence, smoke free environment coverage, and cyberloafing updated.

New to Chapter 14: New chapter opener on public opinion of unions and the rights of public sector unions. Railway Labor Act section expanded, union organizing efforts coverage updated and expanded, new section on unions in China, two new learning activities added. New Case Application that looks at issues employers encounter when workers are considering talking to union organizers.

Features to Encourage Learning

Our experience has shown us that students are more likely to read a text when the reading is straightforward and conversational, the topics flow logically, and the authors make extensive use of examples to illustrate concepts. Students also remember and understand the concepts and practices most clearly when they are illustrated through examples, so we've used a wealth of examples to clarify ideas and build interest. The last year has provided unusual challenges to providing current examples. The U.S. Presidential election, political challenges to the Affordable Care Act (Obamacare), and the political and economic future of several countries including Greece, Italy, Spain, Ireland and Egypt are among the issues that remain unsettled as this text goes into print. You will probably discover that the circumstances of a particular company have changed dramatically since the text was published. Please consider it an opportunity to research and learn why the change occurred and the role HR has in the change.

We have also tried to write this edition in a clear, concise, and conversational style. Students taking the class online may appreciate a text that is more conversational since they usually do not have regular face-to-face interaction with faculty or classmates. These factors guided us in developing this text as a highly effective learning tool. Let's take a look as some of the features of the text that facilitate learning:

Learning Outcomes

Learning outcomes identify what the reader should gain after reading the chapter. These outcomes are designed to focus students' attention on major topics within each chapter. Each outcome is a key learning component for our readers. Learning outcomes were carefully examined and updated for this eleventh edition.

Chapter Summaries

Just as outcomes tell the readers where they are going, chapter summaries remind readers where they have been. Each chapter of the book concludes with a concise summary linked to the learning outcomes identified at the beginning of each chapter.

Key Terms

Throughout the chapter, key terms are highlighted where they first appear in the text and are defined in the margin as well as in the Glossary section in the back of the book. Key terms are also listed at the end of each chapter as a reminder of the major terms defined in the material just read.

Review and Discussion Questions

Every chapter in this book contains a set of review and discussion questions. If students have read and understood the concepts of the chapter, they should be able to answer the review questions. These reading-for-comprehension questions are drawn directly from the chapter material. The discussion questions go beyond comprehension. They're designed to foster higher order thinking skills by requiring readers to apply, integrate, synthesize, or evaluate an HRM concept. The Linking Concepts to Practice discussion questions will allow students to demonstrate that they not only know the facts in the chapter, but they can also use those facts to deal with more complex issues. They also make great "lecture break" discussion questions for small or large groups.

HRM Workshop

It's not enough to just know about Human Resource Management. Students entering HRM today need a variety of skills for career success. The HRM Workshop sections at the end of each chapter are designed to help students build analytical, diagnostic, team-building, investigative, presentation, communication, and writing skills. We address these skill areas in several ways. "Making a Difference: Service Learning Activities" is a new addition to the HRM Workshop for the 11th edition. Suggestions are included with the hopes that students will develop and participate in activities that make a difference in their community or the world. They require application of human resource management concepts and have the added benefit of enhancing students' resume and employability. A section called "Developing Diagnostic and Analytical Skills" consists of current case studies of real companies with questions designed to build critical thinking and decision-making skills along with diagnostic and analytical skills. "Working with a Team" includes thought-provoking scenarios for team discussions in class or team projects outside of class. A section called "Learning an HRM Skill" is comprised of skill-building activities that concentrate on the personal competencies necessary for HRM career success as identified by the Society of Human Resource Management (SHRM). Finally, "Enhancing Your Communication Skills" includes activities that develop important research, writing, and presentation skills. Many of these activities include writing short research papers or creating class presentations using presentation software or short videos found online.

PowerPoint

One piece of feedback we received was that many of professors were using PowerPoint slides and students were spending considerable time copying the slides. Students requested that we help them take better notes by including copies of the slides on our website. Accordingly, we've provided these PowerPoint slides that accompany each chapter on the student companion site.

Supplemental Material

This book is supported by a comprehensive learning package that helps instructors create a motivating environment and provides students with additional instruments for understanding and reviewing major concepts. The following resources can be found on the instructor and student companion sites at www.wiley.com/college/decenzo.

Instructor's Resource Guide

This includes a chapter overview, description of additional features within the chapter, chapter outline, additional lecture and activity suggestions, answers to class exercises, answers to case applications, and additional review and discussion questions for each chapter.

PowerPoint

A robust set of PowerPoint slides developed to help enhance your lectures are provided for each chapter. An image bank, containing all of the illustrations from the text, is also provided for inclusion in PowerPoint presentations. The slides have also been provided in handout form on the student companion site.

Test Bank

This resource contains approximately eighty questions per chapter, including multiple choice, true/false, matching, and completion questions.

Computerized Test Bank

This test bank, powered by Diploma, allows instructors to customize quizzes and exams for each chapter.

Video Package

A DVD has been developed for this course that contains a selection of video clips that relate to various topics throughout the text. These can be used to introduce topics, provide group activities during class, or provide background for class discussion. A learning guide for the videos is available on the instructor companion website.

Student Web Quizzes

Online quizzes, varying in level of difficulty, are designed to help students evaluate their individual chapter progress. Here, students will have the ability to test themselves with fifteen questions per chapter.

Acknowledgments

Getting a finished book into a reader's hands requires the work of many people. The authors do their part by efficiently developing an outline, thoroughly researching topics, writing about the topics, and developing learning activities. We would like to recognize just a few of the people who contributed to this text.

First are our reviewers. Authors cannot survive without good feedback from reviewers. Ours were outstanding, and we appreciate the feedback they gave us. We do recognize that the book before you is better because of the insight they provided. We'd like to recognize reviewers of this edition: Denise H. Barton, Wake Technical Community College;

Mary Anne Edwards, College of Mount Saint Joseph; Laurie Giesenhagen, California State University-Fullerton; Kelly Anne Grace, Georgia Institute of Technology; Jennie Johnson, University of Texas-Brownsville; Gundars Kaupins, Boise State University; Margaret Rechter, University of Pittsburgh, Greensburg; Valerie L. Robinson, Bakersfield College; Andrea Smith-Hunter, Siena College; Gary Stroud, Franklin University; Peter Szende, Boston University; Kostas Voutsas, Dickinson State University.

A book doesn't simply appear automatically on bookstore shelves. It gets there through the combined efforts of many people. For us, this is the outstanding publishing team at John Wiley & Sons, consisting of George Hoffman, Publisher; Lisé Johnson, Acquisitions Editor; Susan McLaughlin, our very gifted and patient editor; Brian Baker, Project Editor; Melissa Solarz, Editorial Assistant; and Joel Balbin, Associate Production Manager. Brenda Moorehead also deserves a special thanks for generously sharing experience and knowledge that was woven into many chapters, especially the thoroughly revised Chapter 13. The management and human resource management students of Des Moines Area Community College also deserve a big thank you for their endless supply of issues, examples and suggestions.

Last, we want to acknowledge a few people individually.

From Dave: To my wife, Terri, for all her support and love—and for simply putting up with me. And to my children—Mark, Meredith, Gabriella, and Natalie—thank you for all you do. It gives me great pride to say I am your father. You each have made me very proud in your own special way by the person you have become. You continue to be the "light of my life."

From Steve: To Laura for all that she brings to my life.

From Susan: To my endlessly supportive husband John, my amazingly talented daughter Katie, and my wonderful Mom. I love you all more than I can say.

About the Authors

DAVID A. DECENZO received his Ph.D. from West Virginia University. He is the president at Coastal Carolina University. His major teaching and research interests focus on the general areas of human resource management, management, and organizational behavior. He has published articles in such journals as *Harvard Business Review, Business Horizons, Risk Management, Hospital Topics,* and *Performance and Instruction.*

Dr. DeCenzo has spent the past two-plus decades writing textbooks. His books include *Supervision Today* and *Fundamentals of Management* with Stephen Robbins; *Human Relations* with Beth Silhanek; *Essentials of Labor Relations* (1992) with Molly Bowers; and *Employee Benefits* (1990) with Stephen Holoviak. These books are used widely at colleges and universities in the United States, as well as schools throughout the world.

Dr. DeCenzo also has industry experience as a corporate trainer, and has served as a consultant to a number of companies. He also serves on the Board of Directors of the AVX Corporation.

Courtesy of Costal Carolina University

STEPHEN P. ROBBINS received his Ph.D. from the University of Arizona. He previously worked for the Shell Oil Company and Reynolds Metals Company and has taught at the University of Nebraska at Omaha, Concordia University in Montreal, the University of Baltimore, Southern Illinois University at Edwardsville, and San Diego State University. Dr. Robbins's research interests have focused on conflict, power, and politics in organizations; behavioral decision making; and the development of effective interpersonal skills. His articles on these and other topics have appeared in such journals as *Business Horizons, California Management Review, Business and Economic Perspectives, International Management, Management Review, Canadian Personnel and Industrial Relations,* and *Journal of Management Education.*

Dr. Robbins is the world's number one selling textbook author in the areas of management and organizational behavior. His books have sold in excess of six million copies; are currently used by students in more than 1,500 U.S. colleges and universities; and have been translated into nineteen languages.

Dr. Robbins also actively participates in masters' track competition. Since turning fifty in 1993, he has set numerous indoor and outdoor age-group world sprint records; and won eighteen national championships and twelve world titles. In 2005, he was inducted into the Masters Track & Field Hall of Fame.

Courtesy of Stephen P. Robbins

SUSAN L. VERHULST, PHR received her M.B.A. from Drake University. She is a Professor of Management at Des Moines Area Community College where she has received the "Distinguished Teaching Award." Susan teaches human resource management and management classes and has researched, developed, and taught online courses in management and human resource management. Her previous work with John Wiley & Sons includes being a contributing author to *Fundamentals of Human Resource Management* 10th edition and instructor's guides in the areas of management and organizational behavior. She is a member of the Society of Human Resource Management and has achieved Professional in Human Resources (PHR) certification through the HR Certification Institute.

Courtesy of Paul Blaser, Blaser Photography

To: **Our Readers**

From: **Dave DeCenzo, Steve Robbins, and Susan Verhulst**

Subject: **How to Get the Most Out of This Text**

All authors of a textbook generally include a preface that describes why they wrote the book and what's unique about it, and then thank a lot of people for the role they played in getting the book completed. Well, we're no different. We just did that, too. But it has become crystal clear to us that two things are common about a book's preface. First, it's usually written for the professor, especially one who's considering selecting the book. Second, students usually don't read the preface. That's unfortunate because it often includes information that students would find useful.

As authors, we do listen to our customers. And many of ours have told us that they'd enjoy some input from us. So we've written this memo. Our purpose is to provide you with our ideas about the book, how it was put together, and more important how you can use it to better understand the field of HRM and do better in this class!

This book was written to provide you with the foundations of HRM. Whether you intend to work in HRM or not, most of these elements will affect you at some point in your career. How? Take, for example, the performance appraisal. Although you might not currently be in a position to evaluate another individual's work performance, if you are working, you're more than likely to have your performance appraised. For that matter, each time you take an exam in a class, your performance is being evaluated. Consequently, it's important for you to have an understanding of how it should work, and the potential problems that may exist.

We begin Part 1 of this book with an emphasis on providing you with an overview of the ever-changing world of work and the effect it is having on HRM. With that as a foundation, we then proceed to introduce you to HRM, its approach, the link to organizational strategy, and the different roles HR plays. In Part 2, we turn our attention to the laws that affect HRM activities. Much of how HRM operates is guided by legislation and court decisions that prohibit practices that adversely affect certain groups of people. Without a good understanding of these laws, an organization's performance can suffer, and the organization can be vulnerable to costly lawsuits. Part 2 ends with a discussion of several areas focusing on employee rights.

Parts 3 through 5 provide coverage of the fundamental activities that exist in HRM. Part 3 explores the staffing function, with discussions on employment recruiting and selection. Part 4 addresses means for socializing, training, and developing employees. Part 5 looks at how organizations encourage high performance by evaluating, paying, and rewarding its employees. Much of the discussion in Parts 2 through 5 reflects typical activities in an organization that is not unionized. When a union is present, however, many of these practices might need modification to comply with another set of laws. As such, we reserved the final chapter for dealing with labor-management relations.

While we are confident that completing the fourteen chapters contained in this book will provide the fundamentals of HRM, a text has to offer more. It should not only cover topics (we hope, in an interesting and lively way), it should also assist in the learning process. It should be written in such a way that you can understand it, it keeps your attention, and it provides you an opportunity for feedback. We think we've met each of these goals. Of course, only you can be the judge of our claim. But let's look at how we arrived at our conclusion.

To be understandable and lively means that we need to communicate with you. We make every attempt in this text to have it sound as if we were in front of your class speaking with you. Writing style is important to us. We use examples whenever possible—real companies, so you can see that what we talk about is happening in the real world. In the past, people using our books have indicated that our writing style does help hold their attention. But although good communication is critical, is only half of the equation. The ultimate tests for you are: Does the book help you do well on exams? Does it help prepare you for a job?

We start every chapter with learning outcomes. We view these as the critical learning points. They present a logic flow from which the material will be presented. If you can explain what is proposed in each learning objective, you'll be on the right track to understanding the material. But memory sometimes fools us. We read the material, think we understand it, see how the summaries directly tie the learning outcomes together, then take the exam and receive a grade that is not reflective of what we knew we knew. We have given a lot of thought to that issue, and think we've come up with something that will help—putting a feedback test on www.wiley.com/college/decenzo, the website that supports our book!

The typical textbook ends each chapter with a set of review questions. Sometimes, your tests look much like these types of questions. But exams also have a tendency to emphasize multiple-choice questions. So we've included sample test questions on our website (www.wiley.com/college/decenzo) to help you prepare for exams in this class. These questions are actual questions that we've used to test our students' understanding of the material. If you can correctly answer these questions, then you're one step closer to enhancing your understanding of HRM. Recognize, of course, that these are only a learning aid. They help you to learn but don't replace careful reading or intensive studying. And don't assume that getting a question right means you fully understand the concept covered. Why? Because any set of multiple-choice questions can only test a limited range of information. So don't let correct answers lull you into a false sense of security. If you miss a question or don't fully understand why you got the correct response, go back to the material in the chapter and reread the material.

Learning, however, goes beyond just passing a test. It also means preparing yourself to perform successfully in tomorrow's organizations. You'll find that organizations today require their employees to work more closely together than at any time in the past. Call it teams, horizontal organizational structures, matrix management, or something similar, the fact remains that your success will depend on how well you work closely with others. To help model this group concept for you, we have included class exercises in this text. Each of these team experiential learning efforts is designed to highlight a particular topic in the text and give you an opportunity to work in groups to solve the issue at hand.

One last thing before we close: What can you take out of this course and use in the future? Many business leaders have complained about how business schools train their graduates. Although business schools have made many positive accomplishments, one critical component appears lacking—practical skills. The skills you need to succeed in today's business environment are increasing. You must be able to communicate (both verbally and in a written format), think creatively, make good and timely decisions, plan effectively, and deal with people. In HRM, we have an opportunity to build our skills bank. As you go through this text, you'll find a dozen or more practical skills that you can use on your job. We hope you give them special attention, practice them often, and add them to your repertoire. We've also included suggestions for writing and presentation assignments that cover an important aspect of the chapter's material. Look at these as a learning tool, not as an assignment that you have to do. We think you'll find working on these will help prepare you for dealing with the kinds of writing requests you get on the job.

Finally, if you'd like to tell us how we might improve the next edition of this book, we encourage you to write Dave DeCenzo at Coastal Carolina University, P.O. Box 261954, Conway, SC 29528; or email him at ddecenzo@coastal.edu. To those of you who have done so in the previous editions, we appreciate you taking the time to write us. Thanks for helping us out.

(Source: Mark Schiefelbein/©AP/Wide World Photos)

LEARNING OUTCOMES

After reading this chapter, you will be able to

1. Discuss how cultural environments affect human resource management (HRM) practices.

2. Describe how technology is changing HRM.

3. Identify significant changes that have occurred in workforce composition.

4. Describe the HRM implications of a labor shortage.

5. Describe how changing skill requirements affect HRM.

6. Explain why organizational members focus on quality and continuous improvements.

7. Describe work process engineering and its implications for HRM.

8. Identify who makes up the contingent workforce and the HRM implications.

9. Define employee involvement and list its critical components.

10. Explain the importance of ethics in an organization.

The Dynamic Environment of HRM

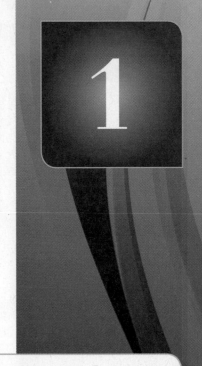

1

Disaster has struck your community. The power is out, phone lines are down, and you are having trouble getting to your company headquarters. Roads are blocked with debris and the streets are flooded. When you finally arrive, you cannot enter the building because the power is out and electronic key cards won't work. It may be days before you're able to return to your office. As the company HR director, you wonder where your employees are, if they are safe, and how you will manage to pay them in the midst of a disaster.

This scenario has been played out in many communities worldwide during recent disasters including tornadoes, flooding, hurricanes, earthquakes, tsunamis, economic meltdowns, and overthrown governments. These disasters have a ripple effect and are challenging not only for local employers, but also for a host of multinational companies that have interests in the country affected. The role of the HR professional can vary widely depending on the magnitude of the disaster and the size of the company. In a large organization, HR may work with the risk management, security, communications, and PR departments to coordinate a comprehensive response. This may include providing employees with protection, communication, shelter, food, and possibly even evacuation. HR professionals in smaller organizations may find themselves with the central role of meeting the immediate needs of employees and their families.

The devastating Japanese earthquake and tsunami, for example, provided challenges for the many Japanese and multinational companies with interests in the region. The U.S.-based insurance company Aflac Inc. had a disaster plan in place, but the extent of the devastation from the earthquake, tsunami, and resulting nuclear reactor failure tested the limits of even their well-thought-out plan. Food and personal supplies were brought to employees who were encouraged to stay at Aflac's Tokyo headquarters until they felt it was safe to return home.

FedEx also has extensive operations in Japan, including one facility that was wiped out by the tsunami. Although all employees survived the initial disasters, FedEx employed a radiation health physicist to help with future decisions regarding their Japanese operations.[1] HR departments at other Japanese companies provided employee services ranging from counseling to handing out potassium iodide tablets for protection from the health risks of exposure to radiation.

Natural disasters are only part of the complex environment faced by HR professionals operating in a global environment. Political unrest can also put employees in peril. In countries like Egypt, Libya, Yemen, and Syria, HR professionals have had to track down missing or kidnapped employees or arrange to evacuate employees to safety by ferry or chartered aircraft.[2]

The complicated scenarios involved in managing a worldwide workforce will only multiply as more businesses have global interests and multinational corporations continue to grow. Welcome to the dynamic environment of Human Resource Management in our changing world. Fasten your seat belts, you're in for a wild ride.

Looking Ahead

How have environmental factors such as technology, the economy, or natural disasters affected your work experience already?

Introduction

Most of the disasters discussed in the chapter opener occurred with little or no warning. The impact on the people and businesses affected has been profound and lasting. When disaster strikes a community, affecting the workplace, employees often turn to their employers for support, stability, and safety. This places enormous pressure on Human Resource Management (HRM) to anticipate and prepare for the unexpected, whether it is a natural disaster, technological change, or economic volatility. Fortunately, the majority of environmental changes faced in global business are not of the life-or-death variety. Businesses must recognize forces in our business environment that affect the expectations of employees as well as customers.

HRM is a subset of the study of management that focuses on how to attract, hire, train, motivate, and maintain employees. Strong employees become a source of competitive advantage in a global environment facing complex and rapid changes. As part of an organization, HRM must be prepared to deal with the effects of these changes. This means understanding the implications of globalization, global economies, technology changes, workforce diversity, labor shortages, changing skill requirements, continuous improvement initiatives, the contingent workforce, decentralized work sites, company mergers, offshore sourcing of goods and services, and employee involvement. Let's look at how these changes are affecting HRM goals and practices in organizations functioning in a global environment.

Understanding Cultural Environments

globalization
A process of interaction and integration among the people, companies, and governments of different nations, driven by international trade and investment, accelerated by information technology.

As part of the rapidly changing environment, organizational members face the **globalization** of business. Organizations are no longer constrained by national borders in producing goods and services. For example, BMW, based in Germany, builds cars in South Carolina. Similarly, Walmart is rapidly expanding their retail operations in China, and General Electric expects to receive 60 percent of its revenue growth from developing countries in the next ten years.[3] Toyota makes cars in Kentucky; Mercedes sport utility vehicles are made in Alabama.[4] Quintessentially American company John Deere makes farm equipment in Illinois to ship to Russia, makes equipment in China to ship to the Middle East, and its German-and Indian-made tractors to the United States. Tractors made in the United States are assembled with parts received from twelve countries and are shipped to over 110 countries.[5] These examples illustrate the extent of globalization's effect on manufacturing and labor. To be effective in this boundless world, organizational members and HRM professionals need to adapt to cultures, legal systems, and business practices in many different countries.

International businesses have been with us for a long time. For instance, Siemens, Remington, and Singer were selling their products in many countries in the nineteenth century. By the 1920s, some companies, including Fiat, Ford, Unilever, and Royal Dutch/ Shell, had gone multinational. Not until the mid-1960s, however, did **multinational corporations (MNCs)** become commonplace. These corporations, which maintain significant operations in two or more countries simultaneously but are based in one home country, initiated the rapid growth in international trade. Today, companies such as Ford, Walmart, Procter & Gamble, Apple, Disney, and Coca-Cola are among a growing number of U.S.-based firms that derive significant portions of their annual revenues from foreign operations.[6] The rise of multinational and transnational corporations[7] places new requirements on human resource managers. For example, human resource departments must ensure that employees with the appropriate mix of knowledge, skills, and cultural adaptability are available and ready to handle global assignments.

multinational corporations (MNCs)
Corporations with significant operations in more than one country.

Every country is different. The extreme variety of values, ethics, religious practices, customs, economic environments, and political and legal systems in the world puts enormous pressure on HR professionals to understand the circumstances of each country in its own context. For example, status is perceived differently in different countries. In France, status is often the result of factors important to the organization, such as seniority and education. This emphasis is called *ascribed status*. In the United States, status is more a function of what individuals have personally accomplished, also known as *achieved status*.

Countries That Value Individualism and Acquiring Things	Countries That Value Collectivism, Relationships, and Concern for Others
United States	Japan
Great Britain	China
Australia	Pakistan
Canada	Singapore
Netherlands	Venezuela
New Zealand	Philippines

Exhibit 1-1
Cultural Values
Countries differ greatly on the emphasis they place on the individual versus the collective. Organizations that plan to enter the global environment need to do their homework to understand the culture and workers.

Human resource managers need to understand societal issues, such as status, that might affect operations in another country. Countries also have different laws. For instance, in the United States, laws guard against an employer taking action against an employee solely on the basis of an employee's age. Not all countries have similar laws. Organizations that view the global environment from any single perspective may be too narrow and potentially problematic. A more appropriate approach is to recognize the cultural dimensions of a country's environment. Although it is not our intent here to provide the scope of cultural issues needed for an employee to go to any country, we do want to recognize that some similarities do exist (see Exhibit 1-1).

Research findings allow us to group countries according to such cultural variables as status differentiation, societal uncertainty, and assertiveness.[8] These variables indicate a country's means of dealing with its people and how the people see themselves. For example, in an *individualistic society* such as the United States, people are primarily concerned with their own family. In a *collective society* (the opposite of an individualistic one) such as that in Japan, people care for all individuals who are part of their group. A strongly individualistic U.S. employee may not work well if sent to a Pacific Rim country where collectivism dominates. Accordingly, flexibility and adaptability are key components for employees going abroad. To make this a reality, human resource managers must have a thorough understanding of the culture of the areas around the globe to which they send employees. HRM must also develop mechanisms that will help multicultural individuals work together. As background, language, custom, or age differences become more prevalent, employee conflict is likely to increase. HRM must make every effort to acclimate different groups to each other, finding ways to build teams and thus reduce conflict.

It's important to note that not all HRM theories and practices are universally applicable to managing human resources around the world. This is especially true in countries where work values differ considerably from those in the United States. Human resource managers must take cultural values into account when trying to understand the behavior of people *from* different countries as well as those *in* different countries. In every chapter of this text we will examine how globalization affects HRM practices.

Many organizations have explored expansion to other countries to find new markets and labor sources. McDonald's started expanding internationally in 1967. They now have over 30,000 restaurants in 118 countries. *(Source: Uriel Sinai/Getty Images, Inc.)*

The Impact of Technology

Think about the technology you've used today. Did you use a smart phone to check voicemail or Facebook? Check driving directions on a GPS? Check your e-mail? Use a wireless Internet connection on a laptop or iPad? Take a digital picture on a camera or phone? Maybe you're even taking this class online. It's hard to imagine daily life without these, but they are all on CNN's list of the top twenty-five innovations of the last twenty-five years.[9]

The Internet was the clear winner in CNN's reader poll of the most influential innovations of the last quarter century. The influence of the Internet on our lives, employers, the way we work, and the economy was on the mind of Thomas Friedman, a Pulitzer Prize-winning *New York Times* author, as he explored the foundations of globalization in his best-selling book, *The World Is Flat.*

Friedman contends that there are three eras of globalization, the first driven by transportation, the second by communication, and the third by technology. The first is called Globalization 1.0 and extends from Columbus's 1492 discovery of the new world to 1800. During this time, countries tried to establish their place in the world by conquering or collaborating with other countries and territories. The emphasis was national identification and economic domination. During this era, the world shrank from a size large to a size medium.

Globalization 2.0 began in 1800 and ended in 2000. Multinational companies emerged, seeking labor and markets for the goods of the industrial revolution. Expansion was fueled by lower costs and increased speed of transportation and communication, shrinking the world from a size medium to a size small.

Globalization 3.0 arrived around 2000 as countries, companies, and individuals were able to compete on an almost level playing field, aided by cheap, instantaneous communication via fiber optics and the Internet. Fast, inexpensive transportation of people and goods aided this transition of power that further shrank the world from a size small to a size tiny. Individuals are now empowered to compete globally regardless of country of origin. Friedman projects that world economies will be dominated by empowered individuals, creating a business environment that is more diverse and less dominated by organizations in Western countries.

You've already experienced the impact of Globalization 3.0. A shift has taken place in geographic labor supply and demand. Just as the industrial revolution changed national economies by shifting jobs from craftsmen to mass manufacturing, Globalization 3.0 has shifted demand for manufacturing and services such as customer service to low-cost providers in Mexico, India, and China.

Friedman points out that these forces can't be turned back and will only grow in their impact. Organizations operating in this global environment recognize that this diverse world includes many different nationalities, languages, and cultures. HR professionals need to be prepared for the challenge in welcoming diversity and adapting training.[10]

What Is a Knowledge Worker?

Technology has been a good news/bad news proposition for workers. While technology has reduced the demand for manufacturing jobs through automation and increased competition with other countries, it has also generated an increase in the demand for service producing and technology positions. Employment in information technology is expected to be among the fastest growing job sectors in the next decade, along with Internet publishing and wireless telecommunications.[11]

> Knowledge-work jobs are designed around the acquisition and application of information.

knowledge workers
Individuals whose jobs are designed around the acquisition and application of information.

Peter Drucker, the late management scholar and consultant, held that the key to the productivity of **knowledge workers** depends on the ability to use technology to locate and use information for decision making.[12] Knowledge workers include professionals such as registered nurses, accountants, teachers, lawyers, and engineers. It also includes technologists—people who work with their hands and with theoretical knowledge—commonly referred to as *information technologists*. Computer programmers, software designers, and systems analysts are examples of jobs in this category. Knowledge workers as a group—individuals in jobs designed around the acquisition and application of information—currently make up about a third of the U.S. workforce.

How Technology Affects HRM Practices

Technology has had a positive effect on internal operations for organizations, but it has also changed the way human resource managers work. HRM professionals have become the primary source of information in many organizations. Information can be communicated quickly and easily via company websites and intranets, e-mail, Facebook, and Twitter.

Human Resource Information Systems (HRIS) allow HRM professionals to better facilitate human resource plans, make decisions faster, clearly define jobs, evaluate performance, and provide cost effective benefits that employees want. Technology helps to strengthen communications with both the external community and employees. How? Let's look at some specific examples.

Recruiting Contacting a pool of qualified applicants is one of the most critical aspects of recruiting. Word of mouth, newspaper advertisements, and college visits have largely been replaced by job postings on the Internet. Posting jobs on company websites, or through specific job-search websites such as careerbuilder.com and Monster.com, help human resource managers reach a larger pool of potential job applicants and assist in determining if an applicant possesses basic technology skills. Additionally, rather than ask for a paper copy of a résumé, many organizations are asking applicants to submit an electronic résumé—one that can be quickly scanned for "relevance" to the job in question.

Employee Selection Hiring good people is particularly challenging in technology-based organizations because they require a unique brand of technical and professional skills. Employees must be smart and able to survive in the demanding cultures of today's dynamic organizations. In addition, many such "qualified" individuals are in short supply and may be offered a number of opportunities for employment. Once applicants have been identified, HRM must carefully screen final candidates to ensure they fit well into the organization's culture. Many Internet tools make background searches of applicants quick and easy. The realities of organizational life today may focus on an informal, team-spirited workplace, one in which intense pressure to complete projects quickly and on time is critical, and a 24/7 work mentality dominates. HRM selection tools help to "select out" people who aren't team players, can't handle ambiguity and stress, or are a poor fit with company culture. Companies like Southwest Airlines and Four Seasons Resorts recruit employees who convey a positive attitude, which to them is a better indicator of job success and fit with company culture than experience.

Training and Development Technology is also dramatically changing how human resource managers orient, train, and develop employees and help them manage their careers. The Internet has provided HRM opportunities to deliver web-based training and development to employees on demand, whenever the employee has the time to concentrate on the material. Four Seasons Resorts, for example, has discovered the advantages of delivering language training and management development classes online. Teleconferencing technology allows employees to train and collaborate in groups regardless of their location. Organizations that rely heavily on technology find an increased need for training. Online training and teleconferencing also allow HR departments to deliver cost effective training that helps stretch the HR budget.

Wireless Internet and smart phones help companies maximize productivity and effectiveness of workers regardless of their location. Mobile workers need access to the same applications and corporate data that they have in the office. *(Source: Masterfile)*

Ethics and Employee Rights Electronic surveillance of employees by employers is an issue that pits an organization's desire for control against an employee's right to privacy. The development of increasingly sophisticated surveillance software only adds to the ethical dilemma of how far an organization should go in monitoring the behavior of employees who work on computers (see Ethical Issues in HRM). One major example is our increased reliance on technology, providing a good news/bad news situation in the workplace. As mentioned earlier, technology is a valuable resource for knowledge workers, yet it provides ample opportunity for misuse and nonproductive work behaviors. The American Management Association reports that 66 percent of employers monitor employee's Internet use and 28 percent have fired employees for e-mail misuse.[13] We will take an extensive look at the privacy rights of employees in Chapter 4, and we will study the ethics of HRM throughout this book.

Motivating Knowledge Workers What are some of the unique challenges in motivating knowledge workers in organizations? Knowledge workers appear more susceptible to distractions that can undermine their work effort and reduce their productivity. Employers often believe they must monitor what employees are doing because employees are hired to work, not to surf the web checking stock prices, placing bets at online casinos, or shopping for presents for family or friends. "Cyber Monday," or the Monday after Thanksgiving, as a day to do personal holiday shopping has increased dramatically in recent years, and recreational on-the-job web surfing costs over a billion dollars in wasted computer resources and billions more in lost work productivity annually. That's a significant cost to businesses in terms of time and money.

Paying Employees Market Value It's becoming more difficult today for organizations to find and retain technical and professional employees. Many companies have implemented an extensive list of attractive incentives and benefits rarely seen by non-managerial employees in typical organizations: for instance, signing bonuses, stock options, cars, free health club memberships, full-time on-site concierges, and cell phone bill subsidies. These incentives may benefit their recipients, but they have downsides. One is the perception of inequity if they are not offered to all employees. Another is the problem created by offering stock options as a benefit to employees. While they look good when a firm is growing and the stock market is performing favorably on the company's future, stock options can reduce employee motivation when market conditions reduce the value of the stock. Pay plans and employee benefits will be addressed in depth in Chapters 11 and 12.

Communications Technology allows employees to communicate with any individual directly without going through traditional channels. Instantly, anytime, with anyone, anywhere. These open communication systems break down historical organizational communication pattern flows. They also redefine how meetings, negotiations, supervision, and watercooler talk are conducted. For instance, Facebook, LinkedIn, Twitter, and other social media allow employees to keep in close contact regardless of position or location. Moreover, it's now easier for employees in Baltimore and Singapore to covertly share company gossip than for offline employees who work two cubicles apart.

Decentralized Work Sites For human resource managers, much of the challenge regarding decentralized work sites revolves around training managers to establish and ensure appropriate work quality and on-time completion. Decentralized work sites remove traditional "face time," and managers' need to "control" the work must change. Instead, greater employee involvement will allow workers the discretion to make decisions that affect them. For instance, although a due date is established for the work assigned to employees, managers must recognize that offsite employees (or telecommuters) will work at their own pace. Instead of focusing work efforts over an eight-hour period, the individual may work two hours here, three hours at another time, and another three late at night. The emphasis, then, will be on the final product, not on the means by which it is accomplished. Working from home may also require HRM to rethink its compensation policy. Will it pay workers by the hour, on a salary basis, or by the job performed? More than likely, jobs such as claims processing that can be easily quantified and standardized will earn pay for actual work done.

Skill Levels What are the skill implications of this vast spread of technology? For one, employees' job skill requirements will increase.[14] Workers will need the ability to read and comprehend software and hardware manuals, technical journals, and detailed reports. Another implication is that technology tends to level the competitive playing field.[15] It provides organizations, no matter their size or market power, with the ability to innovate, bring products to market rapidly, and respond to customer requests. Remember that Globalization 3.0 allows individuals to compete worldwide in purchasing or providing services. Many companies have found that services in technology, programming, radiology, and financial analysis can be provided by skilled employees in India as easily as an employee in the United States.

A Legal Concern Every organization needs a clear policy that thoroughly explains what is appropriate and inappropriate use of company Internet use, e-mail, and social media. Employees need to understand that there is no privacy when they use e-mail, blogs, and social media, and that personal comments and photos are often grounds for discipline if they can be interpreted as discriminatory, harassing, or defamatory. We will address employee privacy rights further in Chapter 4.

ETHICAL ISSUES IN HRM

Invasion of Privacy?

Technological advances have made the process of operating an organization much easier, but these advancements have also provided employers with a means of sophisticated employee monitoring. Although most of this monitoring is designed to enhance worker productivity, it could become, and has been, a source of concern over worker privacy. These advantages have also brought with them difficult questions regarding what managers have the right to know about employees and how far they can go in controlling employee behavior both on and off the job. What can your employer find out about you and your work? You might be surprised by the answers! Consider the following:

- The mayor of Colorado Springs, Colorado, reads the e-mail messages that city council members send to each other from their homes. He defended his actions by saying he was making sure that their e-mails to each other were not being used to circumvent his state's "open meeting" law that requires most council business to be conducted publicly.
- The U.S. Internal Revenue Service's internal audit group monitors a computer log that shows employee access to taxpayers' accounts. This monitoring activity allows management to see what employees are doing on their computers.
- American Express has an elaborate system for monitoring telephone calls. Daily reports are provided to supervisors that detail the frequency and length of employee calls, as well as how quickly incoming calls are answered.
- Employers in several organizations require employees to wear badges at all times while on company premises. These badges contain a variety of data that allows employees to enter certain locations in the organization. Smart badges, too, can transmit where the employee is at all times!

Just how much control should a company have over the private lives of its employees? Where should an employer's rules and controls end? Does the boss have the right to dictate what you do on your own free time and in your own home? Could, in essence, your boss keep you from riding a motorcycle, skydiving, smoking, drinking alcohol, or eating junk food? Again, the answers may surprise you.

Employer involvement in employees' off-work lives has been going on for decades. For instance, in the early 1900s, Ford Motor Company sent social workers to employees' homes to determine whether their off-the-job habits and finances were deserving of year-end bonuses. Other firms made sure employees regularly attended church services. Today, many organizations, in their quest to control safety and health insurance costs, are once again delving into their employees' private lives.

Although controlling employees' behaviors on and off the job may appear unjust or unfair, nothing in our legal system prevents employers from engaging in these practices. Rather, the law is based on the premise that if employees don't like the rules, they have the option of quitting. Recently, companies with policies that prohibit employees smoking off the job have been supported in the courts after firing employees that were found to be smoking.

Managers typically defend their actions in terms of ensuring quality, productivity, and proper employee behavior. For instance, an IRS audit of its southeastern regional offices found that 166 employees took unauthorized peeks at the tax returns of friends, neighbors, and celebrities.

Ethical Questions:

When does an employer's need for information about employee performance cross over the line and interfere with a worker's right to privacy? Is any employer's action acceptable as long as employees are notified ahead of time that they will be monitored? What about the demarcation between monitoring work and non-work behavior? When employees engage in work-related activities at home during evenings and weekends, does management's prerogative to monitor employees remain in force? What's your opinion?

CONTEMPORARY CONNECTION

We Are Now Entering the Blogosphere

Technology continues to change the way many people communicate with one another. Blogs have become a way to express personal thoughts and political viewpoints and have become popular throughout corporate America—proving to be both a valuable tool as well as a potential means of disaster. Let's look at both sides.

On the positive side, blogs enable companies to discuss ideas among organizational members and allow consumers a means of easy feedback. It's a quick and efficient means of advertising a company's products, as well as a way to provide softer, more believable public relations information. Blogs also offer opportunities for employees to discuss "good things" that are happening to them—personalizing the "faceless" company to readers.

But not all blogs are advantageous. Disgruntled employees, dissatisfied customers, and the like can also use blogs to write about anything that they don't like. For example, consider an employee who doesn't like the organization's policies and practices. Rather than discuss his discontentment with someone in the organization, he vents his frustration on a blog he's created. In another example, as a prank, an employee posts sexually explicit short stories on a blog for all to see. Are these permissible, given they were written when the employee was not at work? More than likely, they are.

Organizations should have a policy in place on the use of blogs. For example, an employee needs to understand that confidential company information is not to be placed in a blog. Even blogging about what one does on the job could provide competitive intelligence to another organization interested in finding out how a competitor designs a certain product. A recent study by Forrester Research found that 19 percent of companies surveyed had disciplined employees for communicating proprietary or confidential information online in violation of company policy, and 9 percent had fired employees for these infractions.

As blogging has grown in popularity for both individuals and organizations, companies such as Coca-Cola, IBM, and Marriott have created their own blogs with the goal of improving communication with employees and customers. It's simply another communications tool that organizations, and HRM, must be aware of and constantly monitor to ensure that the positive aspects of blogs are achieved.[16]

Consider this:

Why do employees blog? Can a culture that encourages employee communication and participation reduce negative employee blogs? Should employers monitor employee blogs? Would you consider disciplining an employee for saying something negative about you?

Workforce Diversity

In the past, organizations took a "melting-pot" approach to diversity, assuming that people would somehow automatically assimilate into the existing culture. But today's managers have found that employees do not set aside their cultural values and lifestyle preferences when they come to work. The challenge, therefore, is to make organizations more accommodating to diverse groups of people by addressing different lifestyles, family needs, and work styles. The melting-pot assumption is being replaced by recognition and celebration of differences. Interestingly, those organizations that do celebrate differences are finding their profits to be higher.[17]

> Organizations that celebrate worker diversity are finding that their profits are increasing.

The Workforce Today

Much workforce change is attributed to the passage of U.S. federal legislation in the 1960s prohibiting employment discrimination, which will be discussed in detail in Chapter 3. Based on such laws, avenues began to open up for minority and female applicants. These two groups have since become the fastest growing segments in the workforce, and accommodating their needs has become a vital responsibility for managers. Furthermore, during this time, birth rates in the United States began to decline. The baby boom generation had already reached its apex in terms of employment opportunities, which meant that as hiring continued, the pool of **baby boomers** dwindled. Also, as globalization became more pronounced, increased numbers of Hispanic, Asian, and other immigrants came to the United States and sought employment.

baby boomers
Individuals born between 1946 and 1965.

DIVERSITY TOPICS

Chief Diversity Officer

Deborah Dagit stands just four feet tall, but casts a large shadow over the history of acceptance of diversity and disabilities in the workplace. She played a key role in the passing of the Americans with Disabilities Act, has held diversity management positions with several tech companies, and is currently the chief diversity officer at pharmaceutical giant Merck & Co.

She was born with osteogenesis imperfecta, or brittle bone disease, which is responsible for her short stature, sixty broken bones, and twenty-five operations. "I have a lot of hardware in my legs," states Dagit, but she has clearly never allowed the disease to hold her back. She demonstrates by example that disability accommodations are no different from flexible work arrangements for single mothers, long-distance commuters, or members of other groups with individual needs.[18]

When Merck was recognized in 2011 by DiversityInc. as one of the top 50 companies for diversity practices, Dagit noted, "At Merck we recognize that good intentions are insufficient to address the need for fair representation and equal opportunity for everyone, regardless of race, gender, ethnicity, sexual orientation, religious beliefs, military service, or age. We must create and sustain innovative workplace solutions that ensure inclusion for all to achieve a fully engaged and customer-focused workforce."[19]

(Source: Courtesy Deborah Dagit, Merck & Co., Inc.)

Things to think about:
How can a policy of inclusion similar to Merck's help achieve a "fully engaged and customer-focused workforce," as Dagit claims?

Projecting into the future is often an educated guess at best. Trying to predict the exact composition of our **workforce diversity** is no exception, even though we know it will be a heterogeneous mix of males and females, whites and people of color, LGBT (lesbian, gay, bisexual, transgender), heterosexuals, many ethnic and religious groups, the disabled, and the elderly. The now-aging baby boom population has had a significant impact on the workforce. Commonly referred to as the "graying of the workforce," more individuals are working past the traditional retirement age.[20] Brought about by a need for greater income to sustain current living standards or a desire to remain active, more individuals over the age of fifty-five are expected to remain in the workforce, with more than 80 percent of the baby boom generation indicating that they expect to work past age sixty-five. Coupled with the fact that many employers actively recruit this age group for their experience and work ethic, we can expect our workforce to continue to age, with seventy- to eighty-year-old workers no longer uncommon.

Multiculturalism is another diversity issue shaping the labor pool. Because globalization has reduced barriers to immigration, the proportion of U.S. residents of Hispanic, Asian, Pacific Island, and African origin has increased significantly over the past two decades. This trend will continue. Moreover, multiculturalism is not just a U.S. phenomenon. Countries such as Great Britain, Germany, and Canada are experiencing similar changes. Canada, for example, has large populations of recent immigrants from Hong Kong, Pakistan, Vietnam, and Middle Eastern countries. These newcomers are making Canada's population more diverse and its workforce more heterogeneous.

Of course, the problem of illegal immigration complicates the issue of worker diversity. HR professionals need to be diligent in understanding and enforcing immigration laws and worker documentation. We will discuss this further in Chapter 7, "Foundations of Selection."

workforce diversity
The varied personal characteristics that make the workforce heterogeneous.

How Diversity Affects HRM

As organizations become more diverse, employers have been adapting their human resource practices to reflect those changes.[22] Many organizations today, such as Bank of America and Merck Pharmaceuticals, have workforce diversity programs. These programs are established to hire, promote, and retain minorities; encourage vendor

DIVERSITY TOPICS

Valuing a Diverse Workplace

The workforce is changing, and anyone insensitive to diversity issues had better stop and check his or her attitude at the door. Today, people of color, women, and immigrants account for nearly 85 percent of our labor force. People are a company's number one asset—not the computers, not the real estate—the people. To waste people is to waste assets, and that is not only bad business, it is the kind of thinking that today, in our competitive marketplace, will put a company out of business. Management must realize that legal requirements simply are not enough to meet the needs of our changing workforce, to improve our workplace culture and environment, or to fully utilize the skills of all employees, thereby increasing a company's competitiveness. To fully maximize the contributions of minorities, management must commit to voluntarily focusing on opportunities to foster mutual respect and understanding. This can be done by valuing our differences, which enrich our workplace, not only because it's the law, or because it's morally and ethically the right thing to do, or because it makes good business sense, but also because when we open our minds and hearts, we feel better about ourselves. And decency is hard to put a price tag on.

What can companies and organizations do to facilitate diversity? Here are a few suggestions:[21]

- Enlist leadership from all levels to accomplish diversity goals.
- Identify goals, barriers, obstacles, and solutions, and develop a plan to meet goals and overcome obstacles.
- Develop awareness through training, books, videos, and articles. Use outside speakers and consultants, as well as internal resources, to determine how to motivate and maximize the skills of a diverse workforce.
- Establish internally sanctioned employee support systems, networks, or groups.

- Challenge each employee to question his or her beliefs, assumptions, and traditions, and assess how they impact their relationships and decisions.
- Modify existing policies or create diversity policies and communicate them to all current and future hires.
- Hold managers accountable and reward them for developing, mentoring, or providing awareness training.
- Build in accountability through surveys and audits to measure progress as diligently as you would increase production quotas or maintain zero loss-time accidents. Then communicate the results and repeat the process. Continuous improvement applies to diversity as well as to production.

(Source: Masterfile)

diversity; and provide diversity training for employees.[23] Some, like Coca-Cola, IBM, and FedEx, actually conduct cultural audits to ensure that diversity is pervasive in the organization (see Exhibit 1-2).

Workforce diversity requires employers to be more sensitive to the differences that each group brings to the work setting. For instance, employers may have to shift their philosophy from treating everyone alike to recognizing individual differences and responding to those differences in ways that will ensure employee retention and greater productivity. They must recognize and deal with the different values, needs, interests,

Exhibit 1-2
FedEx Corporation Diversity Mission Statement

FedEx has created a mission statement that specifically addresses a commitment to diversity in the way the organization treats employees, customers, and suppliers.

Our diverse workforce, supplier base, and supporting culture enable FedEx to better serve our customers and compete more effectively in the global marketplace. We value the contributions and perspectives of all employees regardless of race, gender, culture, religion, age, nationality, disability, or sexual orientation. We will strive in our workplace practices to deal with our employees, customers, and suppliers in a fair and ethical manner.

Source: www.fedex.com/us/supplier/diverse/

CONTEMPORARY CONNECTION

2020 Vision

What will the typical global company look like in 2020? What changes will we see and how will they affect HRM?

The Society of Human Resource Management recently commissioned a study to answer these tough questions. They surveyed nearly 500 senior executives worldwide and found that many current trends will continue, including larger and more global companies, with better flow of information and less centralization. Let's take a look at some of the key findings:

- More contingent workers will populate the workplace, outnumbering permanent employees.
- More companies will enter foreign markets, increasing the need for cultural understanding and foreign language skills.
- Management will become more international in scope as companies choose to hire local managers rather than send ex-pat managers overseas.
- There will be increased outsourcing of labor and automation. ·
- Increasing workforce diversity will require management with a global outlook.

- Talented young people will choose employment based on the international opportunities provided.
- Soft skills such as interpersonal and problem solving skills will become more important than technical skills for successful employees.
- The use of information technology and social networking tools to recruit and hire talented employees globally will increase.

To be successful in the future, HR managers will need to build and maintain a strong collaborative corporate culture that creates a sense of community. This will be difficult in view of the increased global reach and diversity of the findings. The secret may be to establish strong core values and allow local managers some autonomy in establishing culture and developing talent rather than imposing the biases of the home market.[25]

Things to think about:

Are you open to changes in your workplace? What are you doing to prepare for the changes coming your way?

---

and expectations of employees. They must avoid any practice or action that can be interpreted as being sexist, racist, homophobic, or offensive to any particular group and, of course, must not illegally discriminate against any employee. Employers also must find ways to assist employees in managing work/life issues.[24]

What Is a Work/Life Balance?

Recruiting and hiring the best employees is a priority for all organizations, but it's only half of the equation for keeping fully staffed. Employers must retain employees who increasingly demand flexibility. Research shows that over half of working mothers prefer part-time work as a way to fulfill their family responsibilities and contribute to family income. Many Gen Xers (born 1965–1980) and Gen Yers (born 1982–early 2000s), while passionate about their careers, won't sacrifice family and leisure for their career.[26] This becomes a difficult balance for employers to maintain as the lines between employee work and personal lives blur in the face of a demanding competitive environment.

First, the expansion of global organizations means their world never sleeps. At any time and on any day, for instance, thousands of Citigroup's 266,000 employees are working somewhere. The need to consult with colleagues or customers eight or ten time zones away means that many employees of global firms are "on-call" twenty-four hours a day. Second, communication technology allows employees to work at home, in their cars, or even on the beach. Many people in technical and professional jobs can work any time and from any place. Third, organizations are asking employees to put in longer hours. It's not unusual for employees to work more than forty-five hours a week, and some work much more than fifty. Finally, organizations realize that today's married employee is typically part of a dual-career couple. This makes it increasingly difficult for married employees to find the time to fulfill commitments to home, spouse, children, parents, and friends.

DIVERSITY TOPICS

Glass Ceiling Still a Barrier for Women Globally

As women and minority groups struggle to break through the glass ceiling into the executive ranks of U.S. businesses, it's interesting to compare how women in other countries are progressing. A recent survey found that women in Thailand are world leaders, holding 45 percent of senior management positions. How are U.S. women doing? Check the chart below[30]:

Thailand	45%	Hong Kong	35%	Canada	28%	United States	15%
Georgia	40%	Philippines	35%	France	21%	India	9%
Russia	36%	Mainland China	34%	Mexico	19%	Global Average	20%

Employees increasingly recognize that work is cutting into their personal lives, and they're not happy about it. For example, an employee's relationship with her manager used to be the number one reason for leaving an organization; now the reason most cited is lack of employer work schedule flexibility.[27] In addition, the next generation of employees is likely to have similar concerns.[28] A majority of college and university students say that attaining a balance between personal life and work is a primary career goal. They want "a life" as well as a job! Organizations that fail to help their people achieve work/life balance will find it increasingly hard to attract and retain the most capable and motivated employees.[29]

The Labor Supply

If you're less than handy with tools around the house and have tried to find a skilled home-repair person, you may have experienced something that many businesses are also experiencing. Skilled trades are tough positions to fill and the shortage is worldwide. World-wide job staffing company Manpower reported that their Talent Shortage Survey found that employers in six of the world's ten largest economies ranked skilled trades as their toughest hiring challenge.[31] This includes electricians, carpenters, cabinetmakers, and welders. Some businesses have been unable to expand because they can't fill openings for skilled trades.

Do We Have a Shortage of Skilled Labor?

When economists announced in 2010 that the recession had ended, many were left wondering why unemployment was still so high if the economy had begun to recover. The answer is that a complicated economic environment and changing demand for job skills have made it difficult to predict how long the economic recovery will take. While HR professionals are left with a surplus of workers in some areas, they are experiencing a shortage of workers in others.

At the heart of the problem is the declining demand for workers with certain skills, yet increasing demand for workers with other skills. Many manufacturing jobs have moved abroad in the last decade; many other jobs have been automated, and the demand for unskilled production workers is not expected to rebound. At the same time, productivity per worker is on the increase, reducing the number of workers required to produce the same amount of output, further reducing demand.

It would seem that the retirement of the Baby Boom generation (born between 1946 and 1965) would create job opportunities, but like many other aspects of the economic recovery, it's complicated. The uncertain economic outlook has prompted many older workers to remain in the workforce, making it difficult to predict when they will leave the workforce. Further complicating the picture, many of these older workers hold positions in the skilled trade areas where looming shortages exist. The baby boom generation will eventually retire, leaving a smaller workforce available for existing jobs. Immigration is expected to fill in some of the gap, resulting in an even more diverse workforce.[32]

The jobs being created increasingly demand highly skilled workers with math and science skills. Unfortunately, young workers worldwide are not choosing to prepare for skilled trades, creating a shortage in many areas. In fact, a survey by Manpower states that fewer than 10 percent of American teenagers, 12 percent of Italian, and 8 percent of Japanese, choose to prepare for the skilled blue-collar work needed to meet demand and grow the economy.[33] The Manpower report found that their choice may be the result of an image problem or lack of available training. These factors combined are leading researchers to predict shortages of skilled professionals such as butchers, electricians, plumbers, masons/bricklayers, cabinet makers, and welders by 2018.

When organizations cannot fill their open positions with home-grown workers, they look to workers in other countries. A recent survey by the Society of Human Resource Management (SHRM) discovered that 25 percent of U.S. and 35 percent of Canadian companies that recruit foreign nationals do so because of their inability to attract local workers with necessary skills.[34]

In times of labor shortage, good wages and benefits aren't always enough to hire and retain skilled employees. Human resource managers need sophisticated recruitment and retention strategies, and need to understand human behavior. In tight labor markets, managers who don't understand human behavior and fail to treat their employees properly risk having no one to manage.

> The need for skilled workers with math and science skills is increasing, and shortages of qualified workers exist.

Why Do Organizations Lay Off Employees during Shortages?

Even before the recession that began in 2008, most Fortune 500 companies made significant cuts in their overall staff. Thousands of employees have been cut by organizations such as GM, Citigroup, Bank of America, Verizon, and the U.S. Postal Service. This **downsizing** phenomenon is not unique to the United States. British banking firm HSBC announced a plan to cut 30,000 jobs worldwide by 2013[35].

Why this trend of downsizing? Organizations are attempting to increase their flexibility in order to better respond to change. Quality-emphasis programs are creating flatter structures and redesigning work to increase efficiency. The result is a need for fewer employees. Are we implying that big companies are disappearing? Absolutely not! But they are changing how they operate. Big isn't necessarily inefficient. Companies such as PepsiCo and Home Depot manage to blend large size with agility by dividing their organization into smaller, more flexible units.

Downsizing as a strategy is here to stay. It is part of a larger goal of balancing staff to meet changing needs. When organizations become overstaffed, they will likely cut jobs. At the same time, they are likely to increase staff in other areas if doing so adds value to the organization. A better term for this organizational action, then, might be **rightsizing.** Rightsizing involves linking staffing levels to organizational goals.[36] Rightsizing promotes greater use of outside firms for providing necessary products and services—called **outsourcing**—in an effort to remain flexible and responsive to the ever-changing work environment.

How Do Organizations Balance Labor Supply?

Thousands of organizations have decided they can save money and increase their flexibility by converting many jobs into temporary or part-time positions, giving rise to what is commonly referred to as the **contingent workforce** (see Exhibit 1-3).[37] Today, temporary workers can be found in secretarial, nursing, accounting, assembly-line, legal, dentistry, computer programming, engineering, marketing, education, publishing, and even senior management positions.[38]

downsizing
An activity in an organization aimed at creating greater efficiency by eliminating certain jobs.

rightsizing
Linking employee needs to organizational strategy.

outsourcing
Sending work "outside" the organization to be done by individuals not employed full time with the organization.

contingent workforce
The part-time, temporary, and contract workers used by organizations to fill peak staffing needs or perform work not done by core employees.

Exhibit 1-3
The Contingent Workforce

Contingent workers have become an important resource as HR struggles to balance the supply of workers available, yet maintain cost control. Part-time, temporary, and contract workers are valuable to many organizations.

Part-Time Employees	Part-time employees are those who work fewer than forty hours a week. Generally, part-timers are afforded few, if any, employee benefits. Part-time employees are generally a good source of workers for organizations to supplement their staff during peak hours. For example, the bank staff that expects its heaviest clientele between 10 A.M. and 2 P.M. may bring in part-time tellers for those four hours. Part-time employees may also be a function of job sharing, where two employees split one full-time job.
Temporary Employees	Temporary employees, such as part-timers, are generally employed during peak production periods. Temporary workers also act as fill-ins when some employees are off work for an extended time. For example, a secretarial position may be filled using a "temp" while the secretary is off work during his twelve-week unpaid leave of absence for the birth of his daughter. Temporary workers create a fixed cost to an employer for labor "used" during a specified period.
Contract Workers	Contract workers, subcontractors, and consultants (who may be referred to as freelancers) are contracted by organizations to work on specific projects. These workers, typically highly skilled, perform certain duties. Often their fee is set in the contract and paid when the organization receives particular deliverables. Contract workers are used because their labor cost is fixed and they incur none of the costs associated with a full-time employee population. Additionally, some contract arrangements may exist because the contractor can provide virtually the same good or service in a more efficient manner.

Why the organizational emphasis on contingent employees? Organizations facing a rapidly changing environment must be ready to quickly adjust their workforce. Having too many permanent, full-time employees limits management's ability to react.[39] For example, an organization that faces significantly decreased revenues during an economic downturn may have to cut staff. Deciding whom to lay off and how layoffs will effect productivity and the organization as a whole is extremely complex in organizations with a large permanent workforce (see Exhibit 1-4). On the other hand, organizations that rely heavily on contingent workers have greater flexibility because workers can be easily added or taken off projects as needed. In addition, staffing shortages, opportunities to capitalize on new markets, obtaining someone who possesses a special skill for a particular project, and the like, all point to a need for the organization to swiftly adjust its staffing level.[40]

Issues Contingent Workers Create for HRM

Temporary workers and the flexibility they foster present special challenges for human resource managers. Each contingent worker may need to be treated differently in terms of

Exhibit 1-4
Are Layoffs Justified?

The cast of characters in Scott Adam's *Dilbert* comic strip frequently mirror the concerns and frustrations of workers everywhere.

(*Source:* DILBERT: © Scott Adams/Dist. by United Features Syndicate, Inc.)

practices and policies. Human resource managers must also make sure that contingent workers do not perceive themselves as second-class workers. Because they often do not receive many of the amenities—such as training, health, and paid-leave benefits—that full-time **core employees** do (see Exhibit 1-5), contingent workers may tend to view their work as not critically important. Accordingly, they may be less loyal, less committed to the organization, or less motivated on the job than are permanent workers. That tendency may be especially relevant to individuals forced to join the temporary workforce. Today's human resource managers must recognize their responsibility to motivate their entire workforce—full-time and temporary employees—and to build their commitment to doing good work!

Additionally, when an organization makes its strategic decision to employ a sizable portion of its workforce from the contingency ranks, other HRM issues come to the forefront. These include having these "virtual" employees available when needed, providing scheduling options that meet their needs, and making decisions about whether benefits will be offered to the contingent workforce. No organization can make the transition to a contingent workforce without sufficient planning. As such, when these strategic decisions are made, HRM must be an active partner in the discussions. After all, it is HRM's responsibility to locate these temporary workers and bring them into the organization. Just as HRM played an integral role in recruiting full-time employees, so too will it play a major part in securing needed just-in-time talent.

core employees
An organization's full-time employee population.

One issue that arises in hiring contingent workers revolves around the definition of an employee. This distinction is important because it has federal income, Social Security, and Medicare tax implications for the organization. Although the debate continues as to what precisely an employee is versus an independent contractor, the IRS guidelines below generally focus on three major categories—behavioral control, financial control, and the relationships of the parties. Remember, these are only guidelines, not "absolutes" from the IRS.

Facts that provide evidence of the degree of control and independence fall into three categories:

Behavioral	Does the company control or have the right to control what the worker does and how the worker does his or her job?
Financial	Are the business aspects of the worker's job controlled by the payer? (These include things such as how the worker is paid, whether expenses are reimbursed, who provides tools/ supplies, etc.)
Type of Relationship	Are there written contracts or employee-type benefits (i.e., pension plan, insurance, vacation pay, etc.)? Will the relationship continue, and is the work performed a key aspect of the business?

Businesses must weigh all of these factors when determining whether a worker is an employee or an independent contractor. Some factors may indicate that the worker is an employee, while other factors indicate that the worker is an independent contractor. There is no magic or set number of factors that makes the worker an employee or an independent contractor, and no one factor stands alone in making this determination. In addition, factors that are relevant in one situation may not be relevant in another.

So, is the person an employee or independent contractor?

Independent Contractor The general rule is that an individual is an independent contractor if you, the person for whom the services are performed, have the right to control or direct only the result of the work and not the means and methods of accomplishing the result.

Employee Under common-law rules, anyone who performs services for you is your employee if you can control what will be done and how it will be done. This is so even when you give the employee freedom of action. What matters is that you have the right to control the details of how the services are performed.

Exhibit 1-5
Employee vs. Independent Contractor

The difference between employees and independent contractors is an important yet frequently difficult distinction to make. The Internal Revenue Service (IRS) published guidelines for employers.

Source: Internal Revenue Service, "Independent Contractor or Employee." www.irs.gov (January 2012).

As temporary workers are brought in, HRM will also have the responsibility of quickly adapting them to the organization. Although orientation for full-time employees is more detailed, the contingent workforce, nonetheless, must be made aware of the organization's personality. Along this line, too, some training may be required. Even a network analyst brought in to work on a specific intranet problem must quickly be brought up to speed on the organization's unique system.

HRM must also give some thought to how it will effectively attract quality temporaries. As this becomes more prominent in business, there will be significant competition for the "good" talent. Accordingly, HRM must reexamine its compensation philosophy. If temps are employed solely as a cost-cutting measure, the pay and benefits offered to contingent workers might differ from those offered to other workers hired part-time as a result of restructuring and work process engineering. HRM, then, must discover specifically what these employees want. Is it flexibility in scheduling, autonomy, or the control over one's career destiny that such situations afford that attracts them? Or has bad luck or a poor economy forced them into this situation?

Finally, HRM must be prepared to deal with potential conflicts between core and contingent workers. The core employees may become envious of the higher pay rates and flexibility in scheduling that the contingent workers receive. The core employees' salaries include benefits, or "in-kind" pay, but they may forget to factor in benefits when comparing their pay to that of contingent workers. For example, paying a training consultant $4,000 for presenting a two-day skills-training program might cause some conflict with core HRM trainers, although the HRM trainer may not have the time or resources to develop such a program. If the consultant offers twenty of these two-day programs over the year, earning $80,000 in consulting fees, a $50,000-a-year company trainer might take offense. Consequently, HRM must ensure that its communication programs anticipate some of these potential conflicts and address them before they become detrimental to the organization—or worse, provide an incentive for core employees to leave.

Exhibit 1-6
Continuous Improvement Programs

Organizations that pay attention to improving the quality of products and the customer experience see big rewards.

© 1999 Ted Goff

"Courtesy, up 25%. Effort, up 25%. Quality, up 25%. Customer retention, up 250%."

(*Source:* © 1999 Ted Goff)

Continuous Improvement Programs

quality management
Organizational commitment to continuous process of improvement that expands the definition of customer to include everyone involved in the organization.

continuous improvement
Organizational commitment to constantly improving quality of products or services.

kaizen
The Japanese term for an organization's commitment to continuous improvement.

A quality revolution continues in both the private and the public sectors. The generic terms that describe this revolution are **quality management** and **continuous improvement**. The revolution was inspired by a small group of quality experts—individuals such as Joseph Juran and the late W. Edwards Deming.[41] For our discussion, we'll focus our attention primarily on Deming's work. An American who found few managers in the United States interested in his ideas, Deming went to Japan in 1950 and began advising many top Japanese managers on ways to improve their production effectiveness. Central to his management methods was the use of statistics to analyze variability in production processes. A well-managed organization, according to Deming, was one in which statistical control reduced variability and resulted in uniform quality and predictable quantity of output. Deming developed a fourteen-point program for transforming organizations.[42] Today, Deming's original program has been expanded into a philosophy of management driven by customer needs and expectations[43] (see Exhibit 1-7). Quality management expands the term *customer* beyond the traditional definition to include everyone involved with the organization—either internally or externally—encompassing employees and suppliers as well as the people who buy the organization's products or services. The objective is to create an organization committed to continuous improvement or, as the Japanese call it, **kaizen**[44]—one that leads to achieving an effective and lean workplace.

1. Intense focus on the customer. The customer includes not only outsiders who buy the organization's products or services, but also internal customers (such as shipping or accounts payable personnel) who interact with and serve others in the organization.

2. Concern for continuous improvement. Continuous improvement is a commitment to never being satisfied. "Very good" is not good enough. Quality can always be improved.

3. Improvement in the quality of everything the organization does. Continuous improvement uses a broad definition of quality. It relates not only to the final product but also to how the organization handles deliveries, how rapidly it responds to complaints, how politely the phones are answered, and the like.

4. Accurate measurement. Continuous improvement uses statistical techniques to measure every critical variable in the organization's operations. These are compared against standards, or benchmarks, to identify problems, trace them to their roots, and eliminate their causes.

5. Empowerment of employees. Continuous improvement involves the people on the line in the improvement process. Teams are widely used in continuous improvement programs as empowerment vehicles for finding and solving problems.

Exhibit 1-7
Components of Continuous Improvement

These components of the continuous improvement process help employers determine what factors to consider when facing change.

Work Process Engineering

Although continuous improvement methods are useful innovations in many organizations, they generally focus on incremental change. Such action—a constant and permanent search to make things better—is intuitively appealing. Many organizations, however, operate in an environment of rapid and dynamic change. Consider the changes the auto industry faces as new technology makes electric cars a reasonable alternative, or the changes that aerospace contractors face as NASA shuts down the space shuttle program and moves to other types of space exploration. Incremental change simply won't do. As the elements around an organization quickly change, a continuous improvement process may actually keep them behind the times.

Work process engineering, also called work process reengineering, goes beyond incremental change and requires an organization to face the possibility that what the organization may really need is radical or quantum change.[45] Work process engineering is more radical than continuous improvement and may be a response to game-changing developments in technology, competition, or the economy. It usually entails rethinking or redesigning processes used to accomplish organizational goals with the objective of dramatic improvements in efficiency and competitiveness. These actions will ultimately require many changes that will involve human resource professionals.

work process engineering Radical, quantum change in an organization.

How HRM Can Support Improvement Programs

HRM plays an important role in implementing continuous improvement programs. Whenever an organization embarks on any improvement effort, it introduces change into the organization.

Responsibility falls on HRM to prepare the organization and the affected individuals for the coming changes. This requires clear and extensive communication of why the changes will occur, what is expected, and the effects on employees. Improvement efforts may change work patterns, operations, and even reporting relationships. Because change and fear are often associated, employees may create barriers to change. HRM must be ready to help affected employees overcome their resistance.

HRM must be ready to help affected employees overcome barriers to change.

Looking for better ways of working often results in new ways of doing things. Consequently, HRM must be prepared to train employees in these new processes and help them attain new skill levels that may be associated with improved operations.

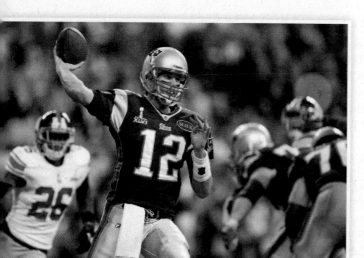

Tom Brady's success on the football field has been recognized with awards and achievements, including his record for the most completed touchdown passes in a season, yet each of those passes had to be caught by a teammate. Winning doesn't depend solely on the talents of superstars like Brady. The strength of successful teams requires the efforts of many individuals—coaches, specialized position players, and a field general (the quarterback) who becomes one of the team's biggest cheerleaders. *(Source: Sportschrome/NewsCom)*

How HRM Assists in Work Process Engineering

If we accept the premise that work process engineering will change how we do business, it stands to reason that our employees will be directly affected. As such, the gains that work process engineering offers will not occur unless we address the people issues.

First of all, work process engineering may involve changes that leave employees, at least the survivors, confused and angry. Although a preferred method of "change" would involve employees throughout the process, we need to recognize that work process engineering may leave some employees frustrated and unsure of what to expect. As change is implemented, some may lose jobs, survivors may need retraining, and stress levels may be magnified. Accordingly, HRM must have mechanisms in place to give employees appropriate answers and direction for what to expect, as well as assistance in dealing with conflicts that may permeate the organization.

Although the emotional aspect is difficult to resolve, work process engineering will generate benefits of improved efficiency and competitiveness only if HRM trains its employee population. Whether it's a new process, a technology enhancement, working in teams, or adding decision-making authority, employees will need to learn new skills. Consequently, HRM must be ready to offer the skills training necessary in the "new" organization. Even the best process will fail if employees lack the requisite skills to perform as the process task dictates.

Furthermore, as many components of the organization are redefined, so too will be many HRM activities that affect employees. For example, if redesigned work practices change employee compensation packages (for example, bonus/incentive pay), employees need to know. Likewise, they must understand performance standards and how they will be evaluated.

Employee Involvement

Whenever significant changes occur in an organization, subsequent changes in work methods must also occur. With respect to work process engineering and continuous improvements, many companies today require their employees to do more, faster and better, with less. Involving employees means different things to different organizations and people, but by and large for today's workers to be successful, a few necessary employee involvement concepts appear to be accepted. These are delegation, participative management, work teams, goal setting, and employer training—the empowering of employees.

How Organizations Involve Employees

Succeeding when facing multiple tasks, often on a number of projects, requires more employees at all levels to delegate some activities and responsibilities to other organizational members. This means that employees need certain amounts of authority to make decisions that directly affect their work. Even though delegation was once perceived as something that managers did with lower levels of employees, today delegation is required at all levels of the organization—in essence, it is peer delegation, or using influence without authority.

In addition to taking on more responsibilities, employees are expected to make decisions without the benefit of tried-and-true past decisions. Because all employees become part of the process, the need is greater for them to contribute to the decision-making process. In most organizations, the days of autocratic management are over. To facilitate customer demands and fulfill corporate expectations, today's employees must be more involved. Group decision making gives employees more input into the processes and greater access to needed information. Such actions are also consistent with work environments that require increased creativity and innovation.

Work teams are also an effective way to increase employee involvement. The bureaucratic structure of yesterday—where clear lines of authority existed and the chain of command was paramount—is not appropriate for many of today's companies. Workers from different specializations in an organization work together to successfully complete complex projects. As such, traditional work areas have given way to more team effort, building and capitalizing on the various skills and backgrounds that each member brings to the team. Consider, for example, what kind of group it takes to put together a symphony. One musician could not possibly play all the various instruments at one time. To blend the music of the orchestra, symphonies have string sections, brass instruments, percussion, and the like. At times, however, a musician may cross over these boundaries, such as the trombonist who also plays the piano. These work teams are driven by the tasks at hand. Involving employees allows them to focus on the job goals. With greater freedom, employees are in a better position to develop the means to achieve the desired ends. In the case of a symphony, the result is, hopefully, a harmonious concert.

Employee Involvement Implications for HRM

We have addressed some components of employee involvement; for an organization, however, addressing them is not enough. Useful employee involvement requires demonstrated leadership as well as supportive management. Additionally, employees need training, and that's where HRM can make a valuable contribution. Employees expected to delegate, to have decisions made within a group, to work in teams, or to set goals cannot do so unless they know and understand what they are supposed to do. Empowering employees requires extensive training in all aspects of the job. Workers may need to understand new job design processes. They may need training in interpersonal skills to make participative management and work teams function properly. In the future, we can anticipate much more involvement from HRM in all parts of the organization.

> Tomorrow's organizations will have an even greater emphasis on teams.

Other HRM Challenges

The challenges to HRM are in the headlines every day. Issues like recessions, offshoring, mergers, bankruptcies, layoffs, workplace violence, and unemployment lead the broadcast, print, and online news, and enter our daily conversation. As you study human resource management, make a point of following current events as they affect employment. These issues will continue to evolve, and HRM will need to find ways to manage the changes as they affect employees. We will examine a few here, but you will find many more if you stay informed of current events.

Recession

Throughout this chapter, we've discussed the impact of the recession that began in 2008 on the workforce and HRM. Certainly, layoffs top the list of difficult HR tasks during this time, but this is not the only challenge. Morale suffers as employees who survive layoffs feel fear and resentment. Retraining becomes necessary as retained workers assume increased responsibilities. Benefits may need to change to save money, and key employees may be difficult to retain as they begin to look for employment with another firm they consider to be more stable.

It's not all bad news for HR in a recession, however. Higher unemployment makes it possible to attract and hire better qualified people when openings do occur.

Offshoring

The pictures and headlines are compelling and heartbreaking. Families that have worked the line at a manufacturer for generations stand next to a shuttered factory and wonder what they will do next. When Maytag closed its 100-year-old Newton, Iowa, factory, 700 workers were left unemployed in this small town. The North American Free Trade Agreement (NAFTA) certainly played a role in the closure, as Maytag had already moved

offshoring
The process of moving jobs out of one country and in to another country.

much manufacturing to Mexico before its sale to Whirlpool, but many will admit that the problems weren't that simple.

Economists estimate that no more than 3 percent of all mass layoffs are due to **offshoring**, or the process of moving jobs to another country for economic reasons. Instead, many manufacturing jobs are lost to more efficient production methods such as robotics and computerized tooling.[46]

Manufacturing jobs are not the only ones to be sent overseas. Many employers see offshoring as a necessity in order to compete in a global economy and find necessary skills, lower labor costs, and reduced costs of distribution. Some employers estimate that as much as 15–20 percent of their jobs will eventually be sent overseas, but this does not necessarily mean that the United States will see a reduction in overall employment. A quarter of employers who have sent jobs overseas were able to create a greater number of better paying jobs here in the United States. Jobs frequently offshored include services that can be delivered electronically, such as an overseas radiologist reading X-rays e-mailed in the middle of the night or an accountant in India doing work to help a busy C.P.A. firm in the United States during tax season. Other types of jobs that are seeing offshore growth include computer programmers, software developers, systems analysts, and … get ready … human resources.[47]

Mergers

merger
Joining ownership of two organizations.

acquisition
The transfer of ownership and control of one organization to another.

Banking, telecommunications, and airlines have all seen increases in **mergers** and **acquisitions**, and many of us have had to get used to our banks or wireless carriers changing names in recent years. The recent financial crisis has necessitated mergers between such financial giants as Wells Fargo and Wachovia, the mergers of Northwest and Delta Airlines or Continental and United Airlines. If you or someone you know was affected by a merger or acquisition, you've probably experienced firsthand the uncertainty, change, loss of jobs, and differences in culture that are almost inevitable when companies combine. The number of mergers in recent years has steadily increased worldwide[48] and presents new challenges to HR professionals.

Mergers are a common way for businesses to enter new or global markets, acquire new technology, or gain a financial advantage by achieving economies of scale. Many mergers, possibly as many as three out of four, fail to achieve their objectives for financial or strategic gain. Many of the reasons for those failures can be traced to the lack of attention to the human resource function in the merger process. For example, when Hewlett Packard merged with Compaq, customers were lost as employees became more focused on keeping their jobs rather than serving their customers.[49]

HR professionals can assist employees in the merger process by providing a well-planned communication strategy. Employees want honest, current information that includes the goals of the merger, anticipated benefits, and a preliminary timeline for the planned changes. Multiple methods of communication are necessary, including meetings, Internet updates, newsletters, and question and answer sessions.

A Look at Ethics

ethics
A set of rules or principles that defines right and wrong conduct.

Ethics commonly refers to a set of rules or principles that define right and wrong conduct. Right or wrong behavior, though, may be difficult to determine. Most recognize that something illegal is also unethical, but what about the questionable "legal" areas such as the trips and bonuses authorized by AIG following their taxpayer bailout? The actions of BP in response to the oil spill in the Gulf of Mexico, shortsighted decisions affecting product safety at Toyota, and the financial misdealings at Countrywide Mortgage and Lehman Bros. that contributed to the financial crisis have led many to examine whether regulation is necessary to prevent organizations from making unethical decisions that affect millions. What executives at these companies did may be questionable, or even illegal, but the larger issue is the implications that such actions have created. For many, these corporate scandals have created a lack of trust of management. People are questioning how such unethical actions could have gone unnoticed if proper controls were in place in the organization. Moreover, the public is now examining the unethical cultures pervasive in these organizations.[50]

In the wake of the ethical failures that had a huge economic impact on employees and investors alike, Congress passed the Sarbanes-Oxley Act of 2002, also called SOX.

Several provisions of the act require compliance monitoring, which is left to HR professionals in many organizations. The intent of the law was to add accountability to the actions and financial transactions of people in organizations in order to discourage or detect ethical misconduct. Recent research indicates that despite the new SOX regulations, when misconduct does occur, employees are no more likely to report violations of company ethical standards than they were before the law was enacted.[51]

Understanding ethics may be difficult, depending on your view of the topic (see Learning an HRM Skill—Guidelines for Acting Ethically, p. 27). People who lack a strong moral sense, however, are much less likely to do wrong if they feel constrained by rules, policies, job descriptions, or strong cultural norms that discourage such behaviors. For example, someone in your class has stolen the final exam and is selling a copy for $50. You need to do well on this exam or risk failing the course. You expect that some classmates have already bought copies, and that could affect any possibility of the exam being curved by the professor. Do you buy a copy because you fear that without it you'll be disadvantaged, do you refuse to buy a copy and try your best, or do you report your discovery to your instructor?

The example of the final exam illustrates how ambiguity about what is ethical can be a problem for managers. **Codes of ethics** are an increasingly popular tool for attempting to reduce that ambiguity.[52] A code of ethics is a formal document that states an organization's primary values and the ethical rules it expects managers and employees to follow. Ideally, these codes should be specific enough to guide organizational personnel in what they are supposed to do, yet loose enough to allow for freedom of judgment. Although SOX may not yet have drastically changed employee behavior, most agree that a company with a pervasive culture of ethical behavior will benefit. Companies that have strong ethical cultures with ethical education programs see a 75-percent decrease in all unethical behavior.[53]

In isolation, ethics codes are unlikely to be much more than window dressing; Enron had a code of ethics statement. The effectiveness of ethics codes depends heavily on whether management supports them, and ingrains them into the corporate culture, and on how individuals who break the codes are treated.[54] If all managers, including those in HRM, consider ethics codes to be important, regularly reaffirm their content, follow the rules themselves, and publicly reprimand rule breakers, then such codes can supply a strong foundation for an effective corporate ethics program.[55]

code of ethics
A formal document that states an organization's primary values and the ethical rules it expects organizational members to follow.

Summary

(This summary relates to the Learning Outcomes identified on page 2.) After having read this chapter you should be able to:

1. **Discuss how cultural environments affect HRM practices.** Globalization is creating a situation where HRM must search for mobile and skilled employees who can succeed at their jobs in a foreign country. These employees must, therefore, understand the host country's language, culture, and customs.

2. **Describe how technology is changing HRM.** Technology is having a major impact on HRM. It's giving all employees instant access to information and changing the skill requirements of employees. Technological changes have required HRM to address or change its practices when it deals with such activities as recruiting and selecting employees, motivating and paying individuals, training and developing employees, and handling legal and ethical matters.

3. **Identify significant changes in workforce composition.** The workforce composition has changed considerably over the past thirty-five years. Once characterized as having a dominant number of white males, the workforce of the new millennium is comprised of a mixture of ethnic backgrounds, religious affiliations, citizenship statuses, global locations, physical abilities, sexual orientations, and gender.

4. **Describe the HRM implications of a labor shortage.** It is estimated that there will be a shortage of skilled labor in the United States over the next ten years. The primary reasons for this shortage are birthrates and labor participation rates of different generations, and the increasing demand for skilled labor. For HRM, the labor shortage means that human resource managers will need sophisticated recruitment and retention strategies, and must have a better understanding of human behavior.

5. **Describe how changing skill requirements affect HRM.** Changing skill requirements means HRM has to provide extensive employee training. This training can be in the form of remedial help for those who have skill deficiencies or specialized training dealing with technology changes.

6. **Explain why organizational members focus on quality and continuous improvements.** Organizational members focus on quality and continuous improvements for these reasons: Today's educated consumers demand it, and quality improvements have become strategic initiatives in the organization. HRM is instrumental in quality initiatives by preparing employees to deal with the change and training them in new techniques.

7. **Describe work process engineering and its implications for HRM.** Continuous incremental improvements focus on enhancing the quality of a current work process. Work process engineering focuses on major or radical change in the organization.

8. **Identify who makes up the contingent workforce and its HRM implications.** The contingent workforce includes part-time, temporary, consultant, and contract workers who provide as-needed services to organizations. The HRM implications of a contingent workforce include attracting and retaining skilled contingent workers, adjusting to their special needs, and managing any conflict that may arise between core and contingent workers.

9. **Define employee involvement and list its critical components.** Employee involvement can be best defined as giving each worker more control over his or her job. To do this requires delegation, participative management, developing work teams, goal setting, and employee training. If handled properly, involving employees should lead to developing more productive employees who are more loyal and committed to the organization.

10. **Explain the importance of ethics in an organization.** Ethics refers to rules or principles that define right or wrong conduct. Due to the recent ethical lapses of several organizations, ethics has become a focal point of proper organizational citizenship.

Demonstrating Comprehension

QUESTIONS FOR REVIEW

1. How has globalization contributed to the need for diversity awareness in our organizations?
2. Describe how technology has influenced workforce skills and the role of human resource managers.
3. Explain the concept of diversity. How will diversity create new demands on HRM?
4. How can human resource managers help employees deal with work/life issues?
5. What is a knowledge worker? What HRM changes can be expected in dealing with knowledge workers with respect to recruiting, selection, motivation, and work/life issues?
6. Explain the roles HR plays in dealing with current employment challenges such as mergers, offshoring, the recession and economy.
7. What is the purpose of a continuous improvement program? What role does HRM play in assisting continuing improvements?
8. What are the necessary ingredients for a successful empowerment program?
9. What are ethics and why are they important for organizations?

Key Terms

acquisition	ethics	outsourcing
baby boomers	globalization	quality management
code of ethics	kaizen	rightsizing
contingent workforce	knowledge workers	work process engineering
continuous improvement	merger	workforce diversity
core employees	multinational corporations (MNCs)	
downsizing	offshoring	

HRM Workshop

Linking Concepts to Practice   DISCUSSION QUESTIONS

1. How can HRM ensure that it is properly preparing the organization for dealing with globalization?
2. "Workforce diversity is nothing new. We need only look back to the early 1900s when thousands of immigrants came to the United States, understand how we handled them, and then implement similar practices again." Do you agree or disagree with this statement? Explain.
3. What can HRM do to help ensure the highest ethics in an organization?
4. Discuss the implications of hiring contingent workers from both the organizational and contingent worker perspective.
5. Training organizational members how to be coaches and how to empower employees will be a major HRM activity in the next decade. Do you agree or disagree with this statement? Explain.

Making a Difference   SERVICE LEARNING PROJECTS

Can an HR class assignment actually help you get a better job when you graduate? Certainly! Combine a community service project with an HR-related activity. It's called Service Learning.

Service learning projects put concepts from your textbook to use in your community. As you complete your service learning projects, you add community service and leadership activities to your résumé, giving you an advantage over other applicants for that first job. Service learning activities also allow you to build your professional network with important contacts to help you in your job search.

Consider viewing community service activities from the perspective of HR professionals. When accepting and screening résumés they look for motivated and enthusiastic applicants with proven organizational and leadership skills. One way to show that you possess these important traits is to add a strong service component to your résumé. All other things being equal, students with a strong background in service and volunteerism will have an advantage over other applicants. Résumés with community service indicate to the employer that the applicant is a team player, shows an interest in others, and is developing organization and leadership skills. Many organizations that have community involvement as a core value are looking to add new employees who share the same values. After you get that first job, leadership in community programs and projects is often a prerequisite to getting a promotion to further your career.

The HRM Workshop in each chapter of this text includes suggested activities that apply HR functions or concepts either directly or indirectly. Some are designed to build your teamwork, leadership, and organizational skills. Others are designed to provide a deeper understanding of how an HR concept applies in practice, give an appreciation of an unfamiliar circumstance, or a fresh perspective.

Like most college students, your time is precious. You may be tempted to undertake easy activities that require a minimal time commitment with organizations with which you're already familiar. You're going to get as much out of those activities as you put into them. They probably won't look as good on your résumé as those that allow you to stretch yourself by meeting new people and learning new skills. Maybe you were involved in service projects in the past, but during your college years you've been busy and haven't been as active. Remember that recent and continued experience looks better on a professional résumé than do one-time projects that were completed back in your high school years.

Who benefits from service learning activities? You, of course. You can build an impressive résumé with skills that your dream employer is looking for. Broaden your professional network with contacts that can help you in your job search and provide great references. Learn how HR concepts apply in the real world. Make a difference by helping your community and the world, and see how rewarding volunteering can be.

ARE YOU CONVINCED YET? GOOD. HERE ARE SOME SUGGESTED ACTIVITIES FOR CHAPTER 1:

Most colleges work with the same dynamic environmental challenges that affect businesses, including laws, regulations, the economy, downsizing, diversity, and technology. This gives you opportunities right on your campus to help the college and students to deal with important issues.

- Contact your college office for students with disabilities, international students, veterans, or other groups that may need assistance with their transition to college. Inquire about ways you may be able to volunteer. They may need help with communicating their services, assisting students with buying books and supplies, or getting around campus. You probably have a few ideas of your own.
- If you're good with technology, consider asking the college Information Technology department if you can assist them in helping students and faculty with technology issues.
- Take a look at other activities in other chapters that may need time to plan and organize.

As you put your service learning experience together, keep a journal of your activities, the time you spend, contact information for people you work with and your thoughts about the process. When you're finished, make a presentation to your class about the experience, highlighting what you learned. What concepts from Chapter 1 were you able to apply?

Developing Diagnostic and Analytical Skills

Case Application 1: A WAR FOR TALENT

The U.S. Navy may not be the first employer that comes to mind when you think of employers that are making efforts to help employees with work/life balance issues. However, the Navy has made improvements to maternity benefits, parental leave, and flexible work options with the goal of increasing retention and recruitment. Realizing that they are in competition for the most talented women and men in Generation Y, the Navy must be seen as competitive with the private sector on the issues that Generation Y values: flexibility and family over career and employer. In fact, Vice Admiral Mark Ferguson, Chief of Naval Personnel and Deputy Chief of Naval Operations, was recently quoted as saying, "The leadership at the very top of the Navy realizes that we are in a war for talent. We recruit a sailor, but we retain a family."[56]

You may be surprised to learn that the U.S. Navy has nearly all of the same HR functions and challenges that employers in the private sector face, although many of them are magnified greatly due to the size and responsibilities of the Navy. For starters, consider a recruiting goal that would challenge any HR department—the Navy's recruiting goal is over 37,000[57] new people annually and a total workforce of approximately 600,000. Next, train those employees/sailors for hundreds of specialized positions, help them achieve education goals, and manage their careers for the next four to six years. Finally, encourage them to serve beyond their initial commitment or to transition to reserve status or a civilian position within the Navy. Other traditional HR functions must be maintained including performance appraisal, compensation, discipline, dismissal, and retirement.

Beyond HR functions, the Navy faces many of the same challenges that private sector employers face. In recent years, the Navy has experienced extremely high retention rates. Between 2007 and 2010, retirements and separations dropped over 26 percent, creating a surplus of employees in several areas. The economy is likely a factor in the strong rate of retention. Another similarity with private industry is that the Navy is experiencing a shortage of qualified sailors in several areas, including cryptology, food service,

maintenance, electronics, information systems, machinist, and fire control. At the same time, there is a surplus of personnel in many other positions[58]. Many are offered the opportunity to retrain for another position, but many more may face "involuntary separation," which amounts to being fired.

The Navy generally gets good marks for diversity awareness with a strong diversity mission statement called "The Mission of the Navy Diversity Directorate"[59], and the establishment of "Affinity Groups" that allow minority and special interest groups to share concerns. The Navy's diversity mission also maintains a presence on Facebook and Twitter, outlining diversity initiatives and opportunities. Recently the Rand National Defense Institute announced a study that has found a reduction in the percentage of young black people enlisting in the Navy and an increase in the percentage of Hispanic recruits, further changing the diversity of the navy workforce.[60] Possibly the largest recent challenge of facilitating acceptance of a diverse workforce in the Navy has been the repeal of Don't Ask, Don't Tell, a policy that allowed homosexual members of the military to continue to serve as long as they were not openly homosexual. This change in policy has been approached with caution by the Navy and other branches of the military.

Questions:

1. Contrast the differences and similarities of the challenges of managing the human resource functions in the Navy from public sector employers.
2. How do the economic, technological, and cultural environments affect human resource management in the Navy and other branches of the armed forces?
3. What role does work/life balance play in recruiting and retention?
4. How is the Navy responding to changes in workforce composition?
5. How can the Navy more effectively address the changes in skill requirements necessary for its jobs?

Working with a Team   UNDERSTANDING DIVERSITY ISSUES

Workforce diversity has become a major issue for managers. Although similarities are common among individuals, obvious differences do exist. One way of identifying some of those differences is to get to know individuals from diverse groups. For this exercise, you will need to speak with a student at your school that is from a different country. If you don't know any, the office of your college responsible for coordinating international students can give you a list of names. Interview at least three people to ask such questions as:

1. What country do you come from?
2. What is your first language?
3. Describe your country's culture in terms of form of government, emphasis on individuals versus groups, roles of women

in the workforce, benefits provided to employees, and how employees are treated.
4. What were your greatest difficulties in adapting to this country's culture?
5. What advice would you give me if I had an HRM position in your country?

In groups of three to five class members, discuss your findings. Are there similarities in what each of you found? If so, what are they? Are there major differences? Describe them. What implications for managing in a global organization has this exercise generated for you and your group?

Learning an HRM Skill · GUIDELINES FOR ACTING ETHICALLY

About the skill: Making ethical choices can be difficult for human resource managers. Obeying the law is mandatory, but acting ethically goes beyond mere legal compliance. It means acting responsibly in those "gray" areas where right and wrong are not clearly defined. What can you do to enhance your abilities in acting ethically? We offer some guidelines.

1. Know your organization's policy on ethics. Company policies on ethics, if they exist, describe what the organization perceives as ethical behavior and what it expects you to do. This policy will help you clarify what is permissible and what discretion you will have. This becomes your code of ethics to follow.

2. Understand the ethics policy. Just having the policy in your hand does not guarantee that it will achieve what it is intended to. You need to fully understand it. Behaving ethically is rarely a cut-and-dried process, but the policy can act as a guide by which you will act in the organization. Even if no policy exists, you can take several steps before you deal with a difficult situation.

3. Think before you act. Ask yourself, "Why am I going to do what I'm about to do? What led up to the problem? What is my true intention in taking this action? Is my reason valid, or are ulterior motives behind it, such as demonstrating organizational loyalty? Will my action injure someone? Would I disclose to my boss or my family what I'm going to do?" Remember, it's your behavior and your actions. Make sure that you are not doing something that will jeopardize your role as a manager, your organization, or your reputation.

4. Ask yourself what-if questions when you think about why you are going to do something. The following questions may help you shape your actions: "What if I make the wrong decision? What will happen to me? To my job? What if my actions were described, in detail, on the local TV news, or in the newspaper, or posted on Facebook? Would it bother or embarrass me or those around me? What if I get caught doing something unethical? Am I prepared to deal with the consequences?"

5. Seek opinions from others. If you must do something major about which you are uncertain, ask for advice from other managers. Maybe they have been in a similar situation and can give you the benefit of their experience. Or maybe they can just listen and act as a sounding board for you.

6. Do what you truly believe is right. You have a conscience, and you are responsible for your behavior. Whatever you do, if you truly believe it was the right action to take, then what others say or what the "Monday-morning quarterbacks" say is immaterial. Be true to your own internal ethical standards. Ask yourself, "Can I live with what I've done?"

Enhancing Your Communication Skills

1. Visit a human resource management department of a local organization or visit their website. Research the organization in terms of its human resource activities. For example: What do they do to recruit new workers? What initiatives do they take to train, develop, and motivate current workers? Explore how their human resource department uses technology, including their website. Give a five- to ten-minute presentation of your findings to your class using three to five slides.

2. Research the effect of technology on the human resource aspects of a technology-based business (for example, Barnes and Noble, Verizon, Facebook, Apple, Netflix). Determine how the business has had to change its HRM practices to accommodate technology changes, and the benefits that have accrued or that are anticipated. Present your findings in either a three- to five-page paper, or a three- to five-slide presentation to your class.

3. Go to www.merck.com, and click on the "Podcasts" section of the website (it may be at the bottom of the home page). Select and listen to a podcast about a diversity topic. Search the Internet for a short video from a different company that outlines its diversity. Present the two to your class along with an explanation of the main points and any differences you notice in their policies and beliefs.

(Source: Steve Hasel/St. Petersburg Times/Zuma Press)

LEARNING OUTCOMES

After reading this chapter, you will be able to

1. Explain how HR practices align with organizational strategy.

2. Describe the importance of human resource management.

3. Identify the primary external influences affecting human resource management.

4. Characterize how management practices affect human resource management.

5. Discuss the effect of labor unions on human resource management.

6. Outline the components and the goals of the staffing, training, and development functions of human resource management.

7. List the components and goals of the motivation and maintenance functions.

8. Outline the major activities in the employment, training and development, compensation and benefits, and employee relations departments of human resource management.

9. Explain how human resource management practices differ in small businesses and in international settings.

Functions and Strategy

2

When the housing market entered a slump in early 2008, it took home improvement stores down with it. Home Depot responded to a drop in sales by laying off hundreds of workers. Since then, nearly 11,000 employees have been laid off from Home Depot operations in the U.S., Canada, and Mexico.[1] No division has been spared; in fact, Home Depot's human resource department made the shocking revelation that it was cutting itself in half, laying off as much as 50 percent of the HR staff.[2] The objective was to streamline HR processes and use the extra money to fortify the retail sales staff, something Home Depot calls "putting aprons on the floor," referring to the orange aprons worn by sales associates.

Why would HR offer to "take one for the team," cutting staff by nearly 1,200 people? The answer lies in how it aligned its strategy with Home Depot's organizational strategy. A little history helps put things in perspective.

Home Depot founders Arthur Blank and Bernie Marcus were advocates of an upside-down pyramid company structure. Customers were at the top, followed by store employees, and then by management who were encouraged to make their own decisions and focus on the customer and employees. HR strategy complimented the company strategy with recognition for sales performance and a compensation plan that included bonuses for top sales and stock benefits.

In 2001, Robert Nardelli became CEO and turned Home Depot into a traditional "topdown" structure with top managers firmly in charge. His prior experience at General Electric (GE) had taught him strict controls and measurement metrics. Cost cutting led to strong profits and sales, but customer satisfaction ratings were dismal and associate morale was low. HR's role turned to assistance by developing better controls and more efficient systems. Nardelli left in 2006 with a controversial severance package worth millions.

Current Chairman and CEO Frank Blake is in the process of turning the pyramid back upside-down with a renewed focus on customers and store associates. He announced the "aprons on the floor" initiative with the goal of increasing the quantity and quality of store associates. He also asked senior management to arrive at cost cutting strategies to raise the money necessary for the additional associates.

HR stepped up with a proposal to reduce staff by taking HR professionals out of the individual stores and combining the HR functions into district teams[3] that would oversee six to ten stores. These teams would consist of a district HR manager and three HR generalists with responsibility for staffing, development, associate relations, and performance management.[4] This is similar to the service centers that companies like Target and Walmart use for their HR functions.

Did HR at Home Depot hurt their role as partners in organizational strategy by cutting their staff? Probably not. Most of the positions eliminated were in the stores where strategy is administered, not set. HR demonstrated their commitment to company strategy by making the necessary sacrifices to gain more store associates. Will they weather the storm? Will they need more cuts? Stay tuned.

Looking Ahead

How have other organizations adjusted HR strategy in response to the recession?

Introduction

When you consider for a moment how HR at Home Depot reflects organizational strategy, it is important to note that achieving organizational goals cannot be done without human resources. What is Google without its employees? A lot of buildings, expensive equipment, and some impressive bank balances. Similarly, if you removed the employees from such varied organizations as Zappos, Facebook, the New York Yankees, Microsoft, Apple, Hallmark, Verizon, or the American Red Cross, what would you have left? Not much. People—not buildings, equipment, or brand names—make a company.

> People, not buildings, make a company successful.

This point is one that many of us take for granted. When you think about the millions of organizations that provide us with goods and services, any one or more of which will probably employ you during your lifetime, how often do you explicitly consider that these organizations depend on people to make them operate? Only under unusual circumstances, such as when you are put on hold for too long on a company's toll-free customer-service line or when a major corporation is sued for a discriminatory HRM practice, do you recognize the important role that employees play in making organizations work. But how did these people come to be employees in their organizations? How were they selected? Why do they come to work on a regular basis? How do they know what to do on their jobs? How does management know if the employees are performing adequately? And if they are not, what can be done about it? Will today's employees be adequately prepared for the technologically advanced work the organization will require of them in the years ahead? What happens in an organization if a union is present?

The answers of these many questions lie at the foundations of HRM. But, as we saw in Chapter 1, answers to these questions are affected by elements outside any organization's control. Make no mistake, globalization is changing the strategic nature of organizations, including HRM. For example, consider the shifting of jobs worldwide. Given the technology available for customer service, in what country the phone is answered makes no difference to the customer. Realistically, it's always 9-to-5 somewhere in the world. Routing customer service calls to different countries in different time zones can enable a company to provide 24/7 service without having to pay premium wages for work after "normal working hours." Remember "Globalization 3.0" from Chapter 1 and the book *The World Is Flat*?

We will discuss various elements as a set of activities to be accomplished by individuals, whether actual members or service providers for an organization. Regardless of the doer, certain actions must take place—actions that serve as the fundamentals of HRM. Yet the field of HRM cannot exist in isolation. Rather, it's part of the larger field of management.

management
The process of efficiently completing activities with and through people.

planning
A management function focusing on setting organizational goals and objectives.

organizing
A management function that deals with determining what jobs are to be done and by whom, where decisions are to be made, and how to group employees.

leading
A management function concerned with directing the work of others.

controlling
A management function concerned with monitoring activities to ensure that goals are met.

Why is HRM Important to an Organization?

Prior to the mid-1960s, personnel departments in organizations were often perceived as the "health and happiness" crews.[5] Their primary job activities involved planning company picnics, scheduling vacations, enrolling workers for health-care coverage, and planning retirement parties.

"Personnel Departments" evolved into Human Resource Departments as federal and state laws placed many new requirements on employers concerning hiring and employment practices. Jobs have also changed. They have become more technical and require employees with greater skills. Furthermore, job boundaries are becoming blurred. In the past, a worker performed a job in a specific department, working on particular job tasks with others who did similar jobs. Today's workers are just as likely, however, to find themselves working on project teams with various people from across the organization. Others may do the majority of their work at home and rarely see any of their coworkers.

And, of course, global competition has increased the importance of improving workforce productivity and looking globally for the best-qualified workers. Organizations need HRM specialists trained in leadership, motivation, employee training, organization and job design, and law.

Federal legislation requires organizations to hire the best-qualified candidate without regard to race, age, religion, color, sex, disability, or national origin. Many states and municipalities are adding extended protection to sexual orientation, making it necessary for the organization to stay current on the rights of all employees and applicants. Employees need to be trained to function effectively within the organization—and again, someone must oversee this as well as the continuing personal development of each employee. Someone must ensure that these employees maintain their productive affiliation with the organization. The work environment must be structured to encourage worker retention while simultaneously attracting new applicants. Of course, the "someones" we refer to, those primarily responsible for carrying out these activities, are human resource professionals.

Today, professionals in human resources are important elements in the success of any organization. Their jobs require a new level of sophistication. Not surprisingly, their status in some organizations has also been elevated. Even the name has changed. Although the terms *personnel* and *human resource management* are frequently used interchangeably, it is important to note that the two connote quite different aspects of the job. The human resource department head, once a single individual heading the personnel function, today may be a senior vice president sitting on executive boards and participating in the development of the overall organizational strategy.

Like many other companies, Starbucks has closed stores and laid off thousands of employees, yet unlike the others, they remain on *Fortune Magazine's* list of "Most Admired Companies." Why? The answer is simple—it's the people. From day one, Starbucks employees know exactly what's expected of them and how vital they are to the success of the business. As Starbucks says, it puts people before products. *(Source: Marc Asnin/Redux Pictures)*

The Strategic Nature

Effective projects begin with a plan. Whether you're embarking on a new business venture, a career, a vacation, or a diet, planning increases the odds of success. Strategic planning takes this concept and applies it to a business enterprise as a way to make a comprehensive analysis of an organization's goals for the future and establish the best way to achieve them. The role of HR in this process is to determine the best way to align the people in the organization so they are best able to assist the organization achieve those goals.

A typical HR department has responsibility for three major areas:

- **Transactional** work, which is administrative work on individuals, like payroll, and administering employee benefits, like insurance and retirement plans.
- **Tactical** work that involves developing solutions that benefit employee work groups, like resolving employee performance issues or work-group conflict.
- **Strategic** work that benefits the entire organization by aligning services that are linked to long term goals.

As part of the strategic HR responsibility, HR assists decision makers in evaluating where the organization currently stands, deciding where the organization wants to be in the future, developing a plan to achieve those goals, implementing the plan, and checking progress toward those goals. A successful plan will achieve a competitive advantage and efficiently utilize organizational resources, including human resources, in achievement of those goals. The advantage is that with a specific goal and a clear plan, the organization and the HR department can make better decisions regarding how to focus efforts on achieving the goal on a daily basis, resulting in less wasted effort and resources. Exhibit 2-1 describes how HR responds to four different strategic approaches.

TIPS FOR SUCCESS

Reviewing the Functions of Management

HRM is a subset of the field of management. For those who desire a quick review of management, please read on.

Management is the process of efficiently achieving the objectives of the organization with and through people. To achieve its objective, management typically requires the coordination of several vital components that we call functions. The primary functions of management that are required are:

Planning: Establishing goals

Organizing: Determining what activities need to be completed to accomplish those goals

Leading: Ensuring that the right people with appropriate skills are on the job, and motivating them to levels of high productivity

Controlling: Monitoring activities to ensure that goals are met

When these four functions operate in a coordinated fashion, we can say that the organization is heading in the correct direction toward achieving its objectives. Common to any effort to achieve objectives are three elements: goals, limited resources, and people.

In any discussion of management, one must recognize the importance of setting goals. Goals are necessary because activities undertaken in an organization must be directed toward some end. For instance, your goal in taking this class is to build a foundation of understanding HRM and, obviously, to pass the class. There is considerable truth in the observation, "If you don't know where you are going, any road will take you there." The established goals may not be explicit, but where there are no goals, there is no need for managers.

Limited resources are a fact of organizational life. Economic resources, by definition, are scarce; therefore, the manager is responsible for their allocation. This requires not only that managers be effective in achieving the established goals, but that they be efficient in doing so. Managers, then, are concerned with the attainment of goals, which makes them effective, and with the best allocation of scarce resources, which makes them efficient.

In summary, managers are those who work with and through people, allocating resources in the effort to achieve goals. They perform their tasks through four critical activities—planning, organizing, leading, and controlling.

Things to think about:

Which of the management functions does HR seem be most closely associated with? Is there one that seems to be least relevant to HR?

Source: For a comprehensive overview of management, see John R. Schermerhorn, *Management 12e* (2013), or *Exploring Management 3e* (2012), John Wiley and Sons, Inc.

Once the organizational structure has been implemented to fit the strategy, jobs need to be designed so that employees understand the relevance of their positions to the organizational strategy and the necessary *knowledge, skills, and abilities* (KSAs) to achieve success. Thought also needs to be given to the amount of autonomy, skill variety, and work pace the position needs. Hiring and recruitment policies must be examined to make sure that the proper sources are being contacted and people with the right skills are being selected.

Performance management also needs to support the organizational structure. HR needs to decide what the relevant job standards are and how to evaluate performance. Compensation needs to reward progress toward organizational goals. In short, **strategic human resource management** creates a clear connection between the goals of the organization and the activities of the people who work there. All employees should see the link between their daily tasks and achievement of a purpose or goal.

The HR functions of staffing, training, and development are important to supporting organization strategy through human capital related areas such as building, developing, and maintaining a productive and talented workforce.[7] Research has shown that companies that link strategy with human resources show increased profitability and shareholder value. Not only that, but the higher the emphasis on practices that value human capital, the more profitable they seem to be. Superior HR practices, including hiring the right people to support company strategy, seem to support productivity and profitability.[8]

strategic human resource management

Aligning HR policies and decisions with the organizational strategy and mission.

 The HRM Functions

HRM is the part of the organization concerned with the "people" dimension. HRM can be viewed in one of two ways. First, HRM is a staff or support function in the organization. Its role is to provide assistance in HRM matters to line employees, or those directly

Exhibit 2-1
Strategic HR Aligns with Organizational Strategy

Different organizational strategies call for tailor-made HR strategies. Staffing, training and development, motivation, and maintenance all must emphasize factors that support the strategy.

Strategy Type	What It Looks Like	Implications for HR
Cost Differentiation: Provide great value and low cost.	Emphasize acquiring low-cost materials, streamlining processes, reducing waste, maximizing efficiencies (e.g., Walmart, Hyundai).	**Structure** jobs and departments to maximize cross training, knowledge sharing. **Design** compensation programs to reward efficiency, cost savings.
Product Differentiation: Deliver product/service that is similar to competitors but incorporates a feature(s) that differentiates it.	Emphasize creativity and innovation. Consumers faced with multiple choices; identify those features that make the product/service stand out (e.g., Apple, Netflix, Aveda).	**Select** employees with versatile skill sets. **Design** compensation systems to reward creativity, innovation. **Educate** employees about product/service differentiating features. **Create** marketing campaign to promote special product features.
Customer Intimacy: Strong personal relationship between provider of product/service and customer.	Emphasize relationship between consumers and point person. Personalized service differentiates the product/service from competitors (e.g., local hair salon, Nordstrom, Hulu, Pandora).	**Recruit** and select job candidates with strong customer service and customer relations skills to help fortify the provider/consumer relationship. **Focus** reward strategies on customer attraction, satisfaction, and retention.
Customer/Market Focus: Unique target market characteristics.	Emphasize the needs of a specific target market, such as generational or lifestyle (e.g., Abercrombie & Fitch, Harley-Davidson, Urban Outfitters).	**Use** strong market research to drive recruitment and selection so employees have a strong understanding of the target market. **Emphasize** versatility and adaptability as products and services are subject to rapid change.[6]

involved in producing the organization's goods and services. Second, HRM is a function of every manager's job. Whether or not one works in a formal HRM department, the fact remains that to effectively manage employees, all managers must handle the activities we'll describe in this book. That's important to keep in mind!

Every organization is made up of people. Acquiring their services, developing their skills, motivating them to high levels of performance, and ensuring that they maintain their commitment to the organization are essential to achieving organizational objectives. This is true regardless of the type of organization—government, business, education, health, recreation, or social action. Hiring and keeping good people is critical to the success of every organization.

To look at HRM more specifically, we propose that it consists of four basic functions: (1) staffing, (2) training and development, (3) motivation, and (4) maintenance. In less academic terms, we might say that HRM is made up of four activities: (1) hiring people, (2) preparing them, (3) stimulating them, and (4) keeping them.

Even the smallest entrepreneurial organization with one or two employees must recognize responsibility for all four HR functions. In organizations that are too small for a formal human resource management department, these functions will be the responsibility of each line manager. Line managers will always have many of these responsibilities whether a formal human resources department exists or not. HR departments are generally responsible for assisting the line manager in these activities. Organizational strategy, structure, or culture may dictate that such activities, although supportive of line management, will be

staffing function
Activities in HRM concerned with seeking and hiring qualified employees.

more effective if handled in a more centralized fashion in the human resource department. For ease of clarity, we'll discuss the following functions as if they are the responsibility of an HRM department.

When one attempts to piece together an approach for HRM, many variations and themes may exist.[9] However, when we begin to focus on HRM activities as subsets of the four functions, a clearer picture arises (see Exhibit 2-2). Let's take a closer look at each component.

Staffing Function

Although recruiting is frequently perceived as the initial step in the **staffing function**, it has prerequisites. Specifically, before recruiting begins, the HR specialist must embark on employment planning. This area alone has probably fostered the most change in human resource departments in recent years. Organizations must have a well-defined reason for needing individuals who possess specific skills, knowledge, and abilities directly linked to specific jobs. After the organization's mission and strategy have been fully developed, human resource managers can begin to determine human resource needs that will support the strategic plan.[10]

Exhibit 2-2
Human Resource Management: Primary Activities

HRM goals are accomplished through the functions of staffing, training and development, motivation, and maintenance. External factors influencing the process are labor relations, management practices, government legislation, and globalization.

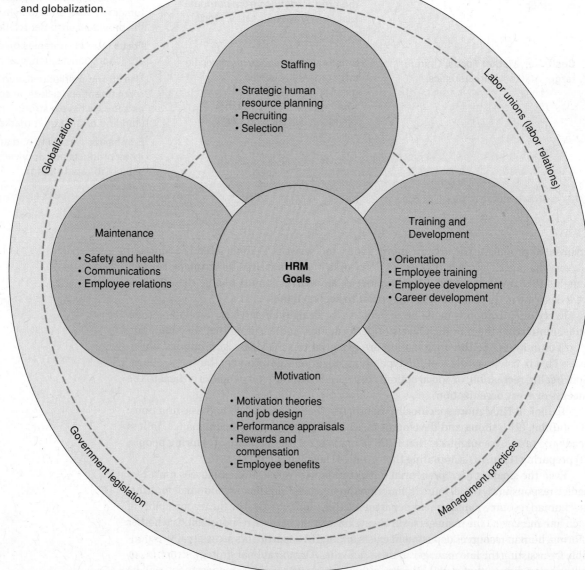

Specifically, when an organization plans strategically, it determines its goals and objectives for a given period of time. These goals and objectives often lead to structural changes in the organization, requiring changes in job requirements and reporting relationships. These new or revised structures will require HR professionals to direct recruiting efforts to find individuals with skills matching the organizational strategy. For example, an organization seeking a cost differentiation strategy may need to seek employees who are flexible and have a variety of skills in addition to their specific job description. It is these jobs that HRM must be prepared to fill.[11]

Many organizations are choosing to assist recruiting efforts by developing and promoting an employment "branding" strategy much the same way that consumer products have a distinct brand image. The image needs to fit the organizational strategy, mission, and values. Google, for instance, has promoted an employment brand that promotes their culture of creativity and innovation plus employee perks like free food, games, and lots of social interaction.[12] Branding assists candidates in selecting an employer that they perceive to be a good fit with their values, personality, and work ethic. Branding also allows candidates who do not feel that they would be a good fit with the organization to decide not to pursue employment.

As an organization's jobs are analyzed, specific skills, knowledge, and abilities are identified that the job applicant must possess to succeed. Through the job analysis process, HRM identifies the essential qualifications for a particular job and includes them in the job description. This accomplishes two objectives. First, prospective employees can see a clear connection between the job and the mission or strategy of the company. Second, it assures that the candidate is selected according to objective criteria and not politics or personal bias, hopefully reducing the chance that illegal discrimination may influence hiring.

Additionally, almost all activities involved in HRM revolve around an accurate description of the job. One cannot successfully recruit without knowledge of the critical skills required, nor can one appropriately set performance standards and pay rates or invoke disciplinary procedures fairly without this understanding. Once these critical competencies have been identified, the recruiting process begins. Armed with information from employment planning, HR can begin to focus on prospective candidates. When involved in recruiting, HR specialists should attempt to achieve two goals: to obtain an adequate pool of applicants, thereby giving line managers more choices, and simultaneously to provide enough information about the job to head off unqualified applicants. Recruiting then becomes an activity designed to locate potentially good applicants, conditioned by the recruiting effort's constraints, the job market, and the need to reach members of underrepresented groups such as minorities and women.

Once applications have come in, it is time to begin the selection phase. Selection, too, has a dual focus. It attempts to thin out the large set of applications that arrived during the recruiting phase and to select an applicant who will be successful on the job. To achieve this goal, many companies use a variety of steps to assess the applicants. The candidate who successfully completes all steps is typically offered the job, but that is only half of the equation. HRM must also ensure that the best prospect accepts a job offer. Accordingly, HRM must communicate a variety of information to the applicant, such as the organization culture, what is expected of employees, and any other information that is pertinent to the candidate's decision-making process.

The completed selection process ends the staffing function. The goals, then, of the staffing function are to locate competent employees and bring them into the organization. When this goal has been reached, HRM focuses its attention on the employee's training and development. We will cover these topics in depth in Chapters 6 and 7.

Google engineers energize by playing "Guitar Hero" at work. *(Source: Kate Lacey/The New York Times/Redux Pictures)*

> The goal of recruiting is to give enough information about the job to attract a large number of qualified applicants and simultaneously discourage the unqualified from applying.

Training and Development Function

training and development function
Activities in HRM concerned with assisting employees to develop up-to-date skills, knowledge, and abilities.

Whenever HRM embarks on the hiring process, it attempts to search for and secure the "best" possible candidate. And while HRM professionals pride themselves on being able to determine those who are qualified versus those who are not, the fact remains that few, if any, new employees can truly come into an organization and immediately become fully functioning, 100 percent performers. First, employees need to adapt to their new surroundings. Socialization is a means of bringing about this adaptation. While it may begin informally in the late stages of the hiring process, the thrust of socialization continues for many months after the individual begins working. During this time, the focus is on orienting the new employee to the rules, regulations, goals, and culture of the organization, department, and work unit. Then, as the employee becomes more comfortable with his or her surroundings, more intense training begins.

Employees often take months to adjust to their new organizations and positions. Although the job description may seem straightforward, employees need to learn the culture of the organization, how information is communicated, and how their position fits the organization's structure and strategy. HRM plays an important role in assimilating employees so they can become fully productive. To accomplish this, HRM typically embarks on four areas in the training and development phase: employee training, employee development, organization development, and career development. It is important to note that employee and career development is more employee centered, whereas employee training is designed to promote competency in the new job. Organization development, on the other hand, focuses on organizational changes. While each area has a unique focus, all four are critical to the success of the training and development phase. We have summarized these four in Exhibit 2-3.

The training and development function tends to be a continuous process. The goal of training and development is to have competent, adapted employees who possess the up-to-date skills, knowledge, and abilities needed to perform their current jobs more successfully. If that is attained, HRM turns its attention to finding ways to motivate these individuals to exert high energy levels.

motivation function
Activities in HRM concerned with helping employees exert themselves at high energy levels.

Motivation Function

The **motivation function** is one of the most important yet probably the least understood aspects of the HRM process. Human behavior is complex, and trying to figure out what motivates various employees has long been a concern of behavioral scientists. However, research has given us some important insights into employee motivation.

First of all, one must begin to think of motivation as a multifaceted process—one with individual, managerial, and organizational implications. Motivation is not just what the employee exhibits, but a collection of environmental issues surrounding the job.[13] It has been proposed that one's performance in an organization is a function of two factors:

Exhibit 2-3
Training and Development Activities

Training and development activities are a continuing process beginning with the first day on the job, building skills for high performance and high morale.

Employee Training	Employee training is designed to assist employees in acquiring better skills for their current job. The focus of employee training is on current job-skill requirements.
Employee Development	Employee development is designed to help the organization ensure that it has the necessary talent internally for meeting future human resource needs. The focus of employee development is on a future position within the organization for which the employee requires additional competencies.
Career Development	Career development programs are designed to assist employees in advancing their work lives. The focus of career development is to provide the necessary information and assessment in helping employees realize their career goals. However, career development is the responsibility of the individual, not the organization.
Organization Development	Organization development deals with facilitating system-wide changes in the organization. The focus of organization development is to change the attitudes and values of employees according to new organizational strategic directions.

ability and willingness to do the job.[14] Thus, from a performance perspective, employees need the appropriate skills and abilities to adequately do the job. This should be ensured in the first two phases of HRM by correctly defining the requirements of the job, matching applicants to those requirements, and training the new employee in how to do the job.[15] But another concern is the job design itself. If jobs are poorly designed, inadequately laid out, or improperly described, or if there does not seem to be a connection to the goals of the organization, employees will perform below their capabilities.

Consequently, HRM must ask if the latest technology has been provided to permit maximum work efficiency. Is the office setting appropriate (properly lit and adequately ventilated, for example) for the job? Are the necessary tools readily available for employee use? For example, imagine an employee who spends considerable time each day developing product designs. This employee, however, is struggling with outdated design software or a computer that is unable to accommodate the necessary sophisticated design software. Compared to another employee who does have access to such technology, the first individual is going to be less productive. Indeed, office technology and industrial engineering techniques must be incorporated into the job design. Without such planning, the best intentions of organizational members to motivate employees may be lost or significantly reduced.

Many organizations today recognize that motivating employees also requires a level of respect between management and the workers. This respect can be seen as involving employees in decisions that affect them, listening to employees, and implementing their suggestions where appropriate.

The next step in the motivation process is to set performance standards for each employee. While no easy task, managers must be sure that the performance evaluation system is designed to provide feedback to employees regarding their past performance, while simultaneously addressing any performance weaknesses the employee may have. A link should be established between employee compensation and performance: the compensation and benefit activity in the organization should be adapted to and coordinated with a pay-for-performance plan.[16] Performance management systems are covered in Chapter 10.

Throughout the activities required in the motivation function, the efforts all focus on one primary goal: to have highly productive, competent, and adapted employees, with up-to-date skills, knowledge, and abilities. Once that is achieved, it is time to turn the HRM focus to the maintenance function.

Maintenance Function

The last phase of the HRM process is called the **maintenance function**. As the name implies, this phase puts into place activities that will help retain productive employees. When one considers how employee job loyalty has declined in the past decade, it's not difficult to see the importance of maintaining employee commitment.[17] To do so requires some basic common sense and some creativity. HRM must ensure a safe and healthy working environment; caring for employees' well-being has a major effect on their commitment. HRM must also realize that any problem an employee faces in his or her personal life will ultimately be brought into the workplace. This calls for employee assistance programs that help individuals deal with stressful life situations such as substance abuse, child care, elder care, depression, and relationship problems. These programs provide many benefits to the organization while helping the affected employee.

In addition to protecting employees' welfare, HRM must operate appropriate **communications programs** in the organization. Such programs help employees know what is occurring around them and provide a place to vent frustrations. Employee relations programs should ensure that employees are kept well informed—through such things as the company's e-mail, voicemail, website, wiki, bulletin boards, town hall meetings, and videoconferencing—and foster an environment where employee voices are heard.[18] Time and effort expended in this phase help HRM achieve its ultimate goal of retaining highly productive, competent, and adapted employees, with up-to-date

maintenance function
Activities in HRM concerned with maintaining employees' commitment and loyalty to the organization.

communications programs
HRM programs designed to provide information to employees.

skills, knowledge, and abilities, who are willing to maintain their commitment and loyalty to the company. This process is difficult to implement and maintain, but the rewards should be such that the effort placed in such endeavors is warranted.

How External Influences Affect HRM

The four HRM activities are highly affected by what occurs outside the organization. It is important to recognize these environmental influences because any activity undertaken in each of the HRM processes is directly or indirectly affected by these external elements. For example, when a company downsizes its workforce in response to a downturn in the economy (sometimes referred to as rightsizing), does it lay off workers by seniority? Does the layoff affect an inordinate number of minority employees?

Although any attempt to identify specific external influences may prove insufficient, we can categorize them into four general areas: the dynamic environment, laws and regulation, labor unions, and current management practice.

The Dynamic Environment of HRM

Chapter 1 outlined many factors in the external environment that affect organizations and suggested how HR must respond. The factors mentioned in the chapter are by no means all-inclusive. HRM must prepare for the predictable changes as well as the unexpected. Some of the more obvious include globalization, technology, workforce diversity, changing skill requirements, continuous improvement, decentralized work sites, teams, employee involvement, and ethics.

Laws and Regulation

The legal environment of employment is constantly evolving. Recent changes in the legal environment of HR include expanded rights of the disabled, veterans, those needing leave from work to care for family members, minimum wage earners, as well as access to healthcare. HRM is constantly monitoring legislation and court cases for legal updates to employee and employer rights. For assistance, many turn to the Society of Human Resource Management (SHRM) for updates, trends, and training. Listed in Exhibit 2-4 are a few of the major laws that have had a tremendous effect on HRM in organizations. We'll explore the laws regarding employment discrimination in depth in Chapter 3 and the other major laws influencing compensation, employee rights, and labor unions in relevant chapters.

Labor Unions

In early 2012, dozens of workers who worked making Xbox 360 video game consoles assembled on the roof of a factory in China and threatened to jump to their deaths unless their employer, Foxconn, made good on a promise of severance pay. Strikes are illegal in China, unions are ineffective, and the workers felt they had no other way to force their employer to pay the money promised to employees who quit voluntarily rather than taking a transfer to another factory. Fortunately for workers in most of the rest of the world, **labor unions** exist to assist workers in dealing with the management of an organization. As the certified third-party representative, the union acts on behalf of its members to secure wages, hours, and other terms and conditions of employment.

Another critical aspect of unions is that they promote and foster what is called a grievance procedure, or a specified process for resolving differences between workers and management. In many instances, this process alone prevents management from making unilateral decisions. For instance, a current HRM issue is the debate over employers' ability to terminate employees whenever they want. When a union is present and HRM practices are spelled out in a negotiated agreement, employers cannot

labor union
Acts on behalf of its members to secure wages, hours, and other terms and conditions of employment.

Exhibit 2-4
Relevant Laws Affecting HRM Practices

Many laws protect the rights of employees in the workplace. These laws protect employee rights to union representation, fair wages, family medical leave, and freedom from discrimination due to conditions that are not related to job performance.

Year Enacted	Legislation	Focus of Legislation
1935	National Labor Relations Act (Wagner Act)	Prohibited unfair labor practices by management and protects unions.
1938	Fair Labor Standards Act	Provides minimum wage and overtime pay. Defines employee status.
1947	Taft-Hartley Act	Protects management rights and prohibits unfair labor practices by unions.
1959	Landrum-Griffin Act	Requires financial disclosure for unions.
1963	Equal Pay Act	Prohibits wage discrimination.
1964	Civil Rights Act Title VII	Prohibits discrimination in all employment decisions on basis of race, religion, ethnicity, sex, and national origin.
1967	Age Discrimination in Employment Act	Protects employees over 40 from discrimination.
1970	Occupational Safety and Health Act	Protects workers from workplace hazards.
1970	Fair Credit Reporting Act	Limits use of credit reports in employment decisions.
1974	Privacy Act	Permits employees to review personnel files.
1974	Employee Retirement Income and Security Act	Protects employee retirement funds.
1978	Mandatory Retirement Act	Raises mandatory retirement age from 65 to 70; uncapped in 1986.
1978	Pregnancy Discrimination Act	Protects from discrimination due to pregnancy.
1978	Uniform Guidelines of Employee Selection Procedures	Prohibits hiring policies that have an adverse impact on a race, sex, or ethnic group.
1986	Immigration Reform and Control Act	Requires verification of citizenship or legal status in the United States.
1986	Consolidated Omnibus Budget Reconciliation Act	Provides for benefit continuation when laid off.
1988	Drug Free Workplace Act	Requires some federal contractors to follow certain requirements to maintain a drug free workplace.
1988	Employment Polygraph Protection Act	Prohibits use of polygraphs in most HRM practices.
1989	Worker Adjustment & Retraining Notification Act (WARN)	Requires employers to give advance notice of plant closing or layoffs.
1990	Americans with Disabilities Act	Prohibits discrimination against those with disabilities.
1991	Civil Rights Act	Overturns several Supreme Court cases concerning discrimination.
1993	Family and Medical Leave Act	Permits employees to take unpaid leave for family matters.
1994	Uniformed Services Employment and Reemployment Rights Act	Protects the civilian employment of non-full-time military service members in the United States called to active duty.
1996	Health Insurance Portability and Accountability Act (HIPAA)	Establishes guidelines for protecting private personal information by employers, insurers, and healthcare providers.
2002	Sarbanes-Oxley Act	Establishes requirements for proper financial recordkeeping for public companies as well as penalties for noncompliance.
2008	Genetic Information Nondiscrimination Act (GINA)	Prevents discrimination based on genetic information about employees or their families.
2009	Lilly Ledbetter Fair Pay Act	Reinterprets timeframes available for employees to claim that they were victims of pay discrimination.

fire for unjustified reasons. Because of the complexities involved in operating with unionization and the special laws that pertain to it, we will defer that discussion until Chapter 14, when we will explore the unique world of labor relations and collective bargaining.

Management Thought

The last area of external influence is current **management thought**. Since the inception of the first personnel departments, management practices have played a major role in promoting today's HRM operations. Much of the emphasis has come from some of the early and highly regarded management theorists. Four individuals are regarded as the forerunners of HRM support: Frederick Taylor, Hugo Munsterberg, Mary Parker Follet, and Elton Mayo.

Frederick Taylor, often regarded as the father of **scientific management,** developed a set of principles to enhance worker productivity. By systematically studying each job and detailing methods to attain higher productivity levels, Taylor's work offered the first sense of today's human resource practices. For instance, Taylor advocated that workers needed appropriate job training and should be screened according to their ability to do the job (a forerunner of skill-based hiring).

What effect does the informal work group have on these workers' productivity? According to the Hawthorne studies, a significant amount. In fact, this classic research, which paved the way for the human relations movement, showed management that group standards and employee sentiments were the most important determinants of employee productivity—even more so than pay! (*Source: SUPERSTOCK*)

Hugo Munsterberg and his associates suggested improved methods of employment testing, training, performance evaluations, and job efficiency. Mary Parker Follet, a social philosopher, advocated people-oriented organizations. Her writings focused on groups, as opposed to individuals, in the organization. Thus, Follet's theory was a forerunner of today's teamwork concept and group cohesiveness. But probably the biggest advancement in HRM came from the works of Elton Mayo and his famous Hawthorne studies.

The **Hawthorne studies,** so named because they were conducted at the Hawthorne Plant of Western Electric just outside of Chicago, ran for nearly a decade beginning in the late 1920s. They gave rise to what today is called the human relations movement. The researchers found that informal work groups had a significant effect on worker performance. Group standards and sentiments were more important determinants of a worker's output than the wage incentive plan. Results of the Hawthorne studies justified many of the paternalistic programs that human resource managers have instituted in their organizations. The advent of employee benefit offerings, safe and healthy working conditions, and the concern of every manager for human relations stem directly from the work of Mayo and his associates at Hawthorne.

management thought
Early theories of management that promoted today's HRM operations.

scientific management
A set of principles designed to enhance worker productivity.

Hawthorne studies
A series of studies that provided new insights into group behavior and motivation.

In today's organizations, we can see the influence of management practice affecting HRM in a variety of ways. Motivation techniques cited in management literature, as well as W. Edwards Deming's influence on continuous improvement programs to enhance productivity, have made their way into HRM activities. Writers such as Tom Peters and Peter Drucker emphasize giving employees a say in what affects their work, teams, and work process engineering. Implementing these will ultimately require the assistance of HRM professionals.

Structure of the HR Department

Responsibility for the four HRM functions of staffing, training and development, motivation, and maintenance can be distributed many different ways in organizations. Company size, strategy, and structure will play a role in who handles the HRM functions. The proper fit can be individual to the organization, so describing all of the possible structures would be difficult in this textbook.

Realize, too, that more than half of all HR departments also offer administrative services to the organization. These might include operating the company's credit union,

Exhibit 2-5
Selected HR Salaries

HR salaries vary widely depending on the position, location, and industry.

Median Total Cash Compensation For Select HR Positions by U.S. Region					
	Northeast	**Southeast**	**North Central**	**South Central**	**West Coast**
HR Executive in Labor Relations	$340,500	$305,300	$302,300	$277,500	$276,000
HR Executive in Compensation and Benefits	$258,000	$204,400	$197,800	$204,700	$150,000
Human Resources Manager	$95,200	$90,900	$91,700	$93,500	$98,800
HR Generalist	$62,400	$60,200	$59,100	$60,200	$65,400
HR Assistant	$41,100	$39,400	$28,800	$28,300	$42,100

Source: Joseph Coombs, Shawn Fegley, "Best-Paying Specialties and Regions for HR Professionals," *HR Magazine,* (December 2010).

making child-care arrangements, providing security, or operating in-house medical or food services. Yet in spite of the different configurations, the typical nonunion HRM department usually includes four distinct areas: (1) employment, (2) training and development, (3) compensation/benefits, and (4) employee relations. Usually reporting to a vice president of human resources, managers in these four areas have specific responsibilities. Exhibit 2-5 is a simplified organizational representation of HRM areas, with some typical job titles and a sampling of what these job incumbents earn.[19]

Employment

The main thrust of the employment function is to promote staffing activities. Working in conjunction with position control specialists (in compensation, in benefits, or in a comptroller's office), the employment department embarks on the process of recruiting new employees.[20] This means correctly advertising the job to attract those with appropriate knowledge and abilities.

Entry level positions in companies with large HR departments frequently involve representing the company at job fairs and college campuses. Other positions include employment specialists who sort through résumés or applications (whether manually or electronically) and reject applicants who do not meet the job's requirements. The remaining applications and résumés are then typically forwarded to the line managers for review. The line manager may then instruct the employment specialist to interview the selected candidates. In many cases, this initial interview is another step in the hiring process. Understanding what the line manager desires in an employee, the employment specialist begins to further filter down the list of prospective candidates. During this phase, candidates who appear to "fit" the line area's need typically are scheduled to meet with the line manager for another interview. The recruiting and selection processes will be covered in detail in Chapters 6 and 7.

It is important to note that the employment specialist's role is not to make hiring decisions, but to coordinate efforts with line management. Once the line manager has selected a candidate, the employment specialist usually makes the job offer and handles the routine paperwork associated with hiring an employee.

Training and Development

The training and development section of an organization is often responsible for helping employees maximize their potential. Their focus is to enhance employees' personal qualities that lead to greater organizational productivity. More important, training and development members are often better known as the organization's internal change agents.

One employee benefit organizations have been providing is the on-site health club. Companies have found that giving employees a place to reduce their stress and enhance their overall well-being helps attract and retain employees. *(Source: © Kevin Wolf/AP/Wide World Photos)*

compensation and benefits
HRM function concerned with paying employees and administering the benefits package.

These change agents, or organizational development specialists, help organization members cope with change in many forms. Some examples of challenges in the dynamic environment that could trigger strategic changes in an organization are a change in government regulation; mergers; economic factors, such as the price of oil or gas; or a change in strategy by a major competitor. A change in the organization's strategy or structure can result in layoffs, new job assignments, team involvement, or a change in culture that would require new orientations for organizational members. There may also be changes in procedures or policies where employees must be informed and taught to deal with such occurrences. For instance, a growing concern of companies has been to implement policies to address an ethics violation. Employees must understand what constitutes an ethics violation. Training and education is often the best form of prevention. Training and development may also include career development activities and employee counseling to help people make better choices about their careers and to achieve their desired goals.

Compensation and Benefits

Work in **compensation and benefits**[21] is often described as dealing with the most objective areas of a subjective field. As the name implies, compensation and benefits is concerned with paying employees and administering their benefits package. These tasks are by no means easy ones. First of all, job salaries are not paid on a whim; rather, dollar values assigned to positions often come from elaborate investigations, surveys, and analyses. These investigations range from simple, logical job rankings (that is, the position of company president should pay more than the position of maintenance engineer) to extensive analyses.

Once these analyses are finished, job ratings are statistically compared to determine the job's relative worth to the company. External factors such as market conditions and limited supply of potential workers may affect the overall range of job worth. Organizational strategy may also dictate that the compensation system reward an important organizational goal such as efficiency, creativity, or customer service focus.[22]

Further analysis ensures internal equity in the compensation system. This means that as job rates are set, they are determined on such dimensions as skill, job responsibility, effort, and accountability—not by personal characteristics that may be suspect under employment law.

On the benefits side of the equation, much has changed over the past decade. As benefit offerings to employees have become significantly more costly, the benefits administrator (who may also have the title of risk manager) has the responsibility of piecing together a benefits package that meets employee needs and is cost-effective to the organization. As such, much effort is expended searching for lower-cost products, like health or workers' compensation insurance, while concurrently maintaining or improving quality. Additionally, various new products are often reviewed, such as flexible benefits programs and utilization reviews, to help in benefit cost containment. But benefits should not be viewed solely from a cost-containment perspective. Benefits are of a strategic nature in that they help attract and retain high-quality employees.[23]

The benefits administrator also serves as the resource information officer to employees regarding their benefits. This information may be provided through a variety of methods, including a company's intranet. Activities include helping employees prepare for their retirement, looking for various payout options, keeping abreast of recent tax law changes, or helping executives with their perquisites. The benefits administrator has a great deal of responsibility, but is also highly visible in the organization. We will discuss this in greater detail in Chapter 12.

Employee Relations

The final phase in our scheme of HRM operations is the **employee relations function**. Employee relations (ER) has several major responsibilities. Before we go further, however, we must differentiate between employee relations and labor relations. The two are structurally similar, but labor relations involve dealing with labor unions. As such, because other laws apply, some employee relations techniques may not be applicable. For instance, in a unionized setting, a specific grievance procedure might be detailed in the labor-management contract, and might involve the union, management, and the employee filing the grievance. In a nonunion environment, a similar procedure might exist or the grievance might be handled one-on-one. These may be subtle differences, but labor relations require a different set of competencies and understanding.

In the nonunion setting, we see employee relations specialists performing many tasks. As mentioned earlier, one of their key responsibilities is to ensure that open communications permeate the organization.[24] This entails fostering an environment where employees talk directly to supervisors and settle any differences that may arise. If needed, employee relations representatives intervene to assist in achieving a fair and equitable solution. ER specialists are also intermediaries in helping employees understand the rules. Their primary goal is to ensure that policies and procedures are enforced properly, and to permit a wronged employee a forum to obtain relief. As part of this role, too, comes the disciplinary process. These representatives see that appropriate disciplinary sanctions are used consistently throughout the organization.

What is the purpose of HRM communications? HRM communications programs are designed to keep employees informed of what is happening in the organization and knowledgeable of the policies and procedures affecting them. Whereas public relations departments keep the public informed of what an organization does, HRM communications focus on the internal constituents—the employees. Communication programs help increase employee loyalty and commitment by building into the corporate culture a systematic means of free-flowing, timely, and accurate information by which employees better perceive that the organization values them.[25] Such a system builds trust and openness among organizational members that helps withstand even the sharing of "bad news."

Building effective HRM communications programs involves a few fundamental elements. These include top management commitment, effective upward communication, determining what is to be communicated, allowing for feedback, and information sources. Let's look at each of these.

Top Management Commitment Before any organization can develop and implement an internal organizational communications program, it must have the backing, support, and "blessing" of the CEO. Employees must see any activity designed to facilitate work environments as being endorsed by the company's top management. These programs then receive priority and are viewed as significant components of the corporate culture. Just as it is critical for employees to see top management supporting communications, so, too, they must see communications operating effectively at all levels. Effective communications does not just imply that top management sends information down throughout the company. It also implies that information flows upward as well as laterally to other areas in the organization.[26]

Effective Upward Communication The upward flow of communication is particularly noteworthy because often the employees, the ones closest to the work, may have vital information that top management should know. For instance, let's take a situation that occurs in HRM. We've recognized the ever-changing nature of this field. Legislation at any level—federal, state, or local—may add new HRM requirements for the organization. Unless top management is made aware of the implications of these requirements, severe repercussions could occur. That information must filter up in the company.

A similar point could easily be made for any part of an organization. And in keeping with the spirit of employee empowerment,[27] as employees are more involved in making

employee relations function Activities in HRM concerned with effective communications among organizational members.

TIPS FOR SUCCESS

HRM Certification

Many colleges and universities are helping prepare HRM professionals by offering concentrations and majors in the discipline in addition to an accreditation process. The Society for Human Resource Management (SHRM) offers opportunities for individuals to gain a competitive advantage in the field. This is accomplished by achieving a level of proficiency predetermined by the Human Resource Certification Institute (HRCI) as necessary for successfully handling human resource management affairs. The American Society of Training and Development (ASTD) also offers certification for those wanting to specialize in Training and Development (see Learning an HRM Skill at the end of this chapter).

HRCI offers four certification areas for HR professionals:[29]

PHR°	Professional in Human Resources
SPHR°	Senior Professional in Human Resources
GPHR°	Global Professional in HumanResources
PHR-CA/SPHR-CA°	PHR with state certification in California and SPHR with state certification in California

Things to think about:
Is there an SHRM chapter in your area? Do they welcome students at meetings?

decisions that affect them, that information must be communicated up the ladder. Furthermore, it's important for top management to monitor the pulse of the organization regarding how employees view working for the company. Whether that information is obtained from walking around the premises, through formal employee suggestions, or through employee satisfaction/morale surveys, such information is crucial. In fact, on the latter point, advances in technology have allowed some employee satisfaction measures to be captured in almost real time at significantly reduced costs.[28] At IBM, for instance, such surveys are online, making them easier for the employees to use, more expedient in their analysis, and more timely for company use.

Determining What to Communicate At the extreme, if every piece of information that exists in our organizations were communicated, no work would ever get done; people would be spending their entire days on information overload. Employees, while wanting to be informed, generally are not concerned with every piece of information, such as who just retired, or was promoted, or what community group was given a donation yesterday. Rather, employees need pertinent information addressing what they should know in order to do their jobs. This typically includes where the business is going (strategic goals), current sales/service/production outcomes, new products or service lines, and human resource policy changes.

One means of determining what to communicate is through a "what-if, so-what" test. When deciding the priority of the information to be shared, HR managers should ask themselves, "What if this information is not shared?" (See Ethical Issues in HRM: Purposely Distorting Information.) Would employees be able to do their jobs as well as if it were shared? Would they be disadvantaged in some way by not knowing? If employees will not be affected one way or the other, then that may not be a priority item. Next, the so-what test: Will employees care about the information? Or will they see it as an overload of meaningless information? If the latter is the case, then that, too, is not priority information. That's not to say this information may never be exchanged; it only means that it's not important for employees to get the information immediately.

Allowing for Feedback HR managers cannot assume that their communication efforts are achieving their goals. Consequently, the HR department must develop both a means of assessing the flow of information and methods for fostering employee feedback. How that information is generated may differ from organization to organization. For some, it may be a casual word-of-mouth assessment. Others may use employee surveys to capture data, or provide a suggestion box for comments, or institute a formalized and systematic communications audit program.

No matter how the information is gathered, employees must be involved. Otherwise, not only will measurement of the communications program effectiveness be difficult, but it may also give the perception that employee commitment is unnecessary.

Information Sources   HRM communications should serve as a conduit in promoting effective communications throughout the organization. Although HRM plays an important role in bringing this to fruition, they are neither the only nor the main source of information. For that, we turn to employees' immediate supervisors. If successful programs can be linked to the immediate supervisor, then HRM must ensure that these individuals are trained in how to communicate properly. Even a health insurance premium change, if implemented, would likely result in questions for a supervisor. Thus, HRM must make every effort to empower these supervisors with accurate data to deal with the "frontline" questions.[30]

In addition to the communications role, the employee relations department is responsible for additional assignments. Typically in such a department, recruiting, employment, and turnover statistics are collected, tabulated, and written up in the company's affirmative action plan documentation. This material is updated frequently and made available to employees on request. Another part of department responsibility is to ensure safe and healthy work sites. This may range from casual work inspections to operating nursing stations and coordinating employee-assistance programs. The responsibilities vary, but the premise is the same—to focus on those aspects that help make an employee committed and loyal to the organization through fair and equitable treatment, and responding to employee feedback.

Last, there is the festive side of employee relations. This department is typically responsible for company outings, company athletic teams, and recreational and recognition programs. Whatever they do under this domain, the goal is to offer programs that benefit the workers and their families and make them feel part of a community.

Is a Career in HR for Me?

Maybe you've considered a career in Human Resource Management. That's a good decision, considering that the Bureau of Labor Statistics estimates that the need for HR professionals will grow faster than most career areas through 2017.[31] Exhibit 2-5 provides median annual salaries for several different HR positions in areas of the U.S.

Positions include:

- Assistant: provides support to other HR professionals
- Generalist: provides service to an organization in all four of the HR functions
- Specialist: is typically concerned with only one of the four functions
- Executive: reports directly to the organization's top management with responsibility for all HR functions and linking HR with organizational strategy

HR generalist
Position responsible for all or a large number of HR functions in an organization.

As in most business careers, HR professionals can expect to work their way up. An HR professional will frequently start as an **HR generalist** with many opportunities for employee contact including recruiting, hiring, training, evaluating, communication, administering benefits, disciplining, and, yes, possibly even firing employees. HR professionals know that much employee contact can be awkward and difficult, but proper training and skills can help.[32] Some of the skills that can pave your way to success in HR include strong interpersonal communication skills, drive and ambition, critical thinking skills, and a good background of business knowledge outside of HR.[33] Exhibit 2-6 illustrates key factors that HR professionals find important to career success.

> HRM is a function of every manager's job, not just those who work in human resources.

Does HRM Really Matter?

Is an organization better off with a properly functioning HRM department? Of course, most of us would say yes, but today's business environment requires any business function to justify its existence by its contribution to the bottom line. Fortunately, much research, including the Watson Wyatt's Human Capital Index (HCI), emphatically states that a fully functioning HR department makes a significant financial contribution.[35]

The HCI continuing study of North American and European companies indicates that good quality HRM services improved both the financial well-being of an organization

Exhibit 2-6
Advancing in Your HR Career

Factors that influence HR career success include important personal characteristics such as communication skills and ambition as well as experience.

What Does It Take To Get To The Top?

Key factors HR professionals said were very important in moving into or advancing in their careers:[34]

Interpersonal communication	80%
Drive/ambition	61
Reputation in the organization	56
Strategic/critical thinking skills	53
HR work experience	51
Leadership skills	51
Business acumen	30
HR generalist experience	30
Human Resource Certification Institute certification	30

Source: Kathy Gurchiek, "Survey: Key Skills Advance HR Career," *HR Magazine,* (April 2008).

and shareholder value. The companies studied by Watson Wyatt indicated that, over a five-year period, quality HRM "provided a 59 percent total return to shareholders . . . as compared to 11 percent return for companies with weaker HR practices."[36] In other words, organizations that spend the money to have quality HR programs perform better than those who don't. Accordingly, there is no chicken-and-egg syndrome here. It's not that HR practices are improved when financially viable, but rather by investing in HR up front, improved financial return followed.

Practices that go into superior HR services include rewarding productive work; creating a flexible, work friendly environment; properly recruiting and retaining quality workers; and maintaining effective communications. Many of the practices sometimes viewed as the latest HRM "fad," such as 360-degree appraisals, were not inherently problematic.

ETHICAL ISSUES IN HRM

Purposely Distorting Information

The idea of withholding information is an issue for all HRM professionals. Read the following two scenarios and think about what ethical dilemmas those in HRM might face relating to the intentional distortion of information.

Scenario 1 At the president's monthly executive staff meeting, you were informed of the past quarter's revenue figures. Moreover, you also were informed that the organization is going to more than double its quarterly expected numbers, and the value of your company's stock will likely surge. Your organization has a bonus plan that shares profits with employees. But this profit sharing is based solely on management's discretion and follows no systematic formula. If word gets out that profits are outstanding, employees might expect larger bonuses. The executive committee wants to share about half of the windfall with employees, reinvest most of the rest into capital equipment, and save some for less favorable times. Your staff and several employees from a cross section of departments are meeting with you tomorrow to begin the process of making profit-sharing decisions for the year. What do you tell them?

Scenario 2 An employee asks you about a rumor she's heard that some HR activities may be outsourced to a company in Des Moines, Iowa. You know the rumor to be true, but you'd rather not let the information out just yet. You're fearful that it could hurt departmental morale and lead to premature resignations. What do you say to your employee?

These two scenarios illustrate dilemmas that HRM managers may face relating to evading the truth, distorting facts, or lying to others. And here's something else that makes the situation even more problematic: it might not always be in a manager's best interest or that of his or her unit to provide full and complete information. Keeping communications fuzzy can cut down on questions, permit faster decision making, minimize objections, reduce opposition, make it easier to deny one's earlier statements, preserve the freedom to change one's mind, permit one to say "no" diplomatically, help avoid confrontation and anxiety, and provide other benefits that work to the advantage of the individual.

Ethical questions:

Is it unethical to purposely distort communications to get a favorable outcome? What about "little white lies" that don't really hurt anybody? Are these ethical? What guidelines could you suggest for those in HRM who want guidance in deciding whether distorting information is ethical or unethical?

Rather, they were implemented without a clear reason for implementation and without a link to the organization's strategic mission. As such, they lost their true potential benefits.

What does the HCI study tell us about HRM? Simply put, offer quality services to employees—but only after you confirm a direct linkage of those services to the overall strategy of the organization!

HR Trends and Opportunities

Although we have presented four generic areas of HRM, we must recognize the changing nature of HRM in today's organizations. As organizations change structures and strategy in response to changes in the dynamic environment, HR is a partner in developing structures that fit strategy. This often means that the structure of the HR department must also change. Let's take a look at some of the ways HRM has responded.

Outsourcing

HRM is not immune to the trend of **outsourcing** noncore business operations with the goal of saving money. In some organizations, top management has made a decision to outsource some, if not all, of the work HRM professionals once handled.[37] Human resource outsourcing (HRO) organizations have seen dramatic growth. A recent survey found that 53 percent of all companies outsource some portion of their HR functions.[38]

Outsourcing may be as simple as hiring a contractor to take responsibility for one HR function, such as benefit and pension administration. It's also possible to contract with a private staffing agency to perform the recruiting and selection activities, several consulting firms to provide training programs, and yet another financial organization to handle the majority of a company's benefits administration. American Airlines outsourced nearly all HR functions—including recruitment, staffing, training, and development—to IBM in partnership with Mercer, a company that handles administration of all benefits. American Airlines received improved employee access to and information about benefits and substantial cost savings from this $217 million, seven-year contract.[39] Other large companies that provide HR services include Accenture and ADP.

It is our contention that when much of HRM is outsourced, managers and employees still need to understand the basic HRM issues and activities. So, whether the activities we describe in this book fall to you, or to another company employee, or to someone external to your organization, you need some familiarity with these fundamental HRM practices.

outsourcing
Contracting with a company to handle one or more HR functions.

Professional Employer Organization (PEO)

A **professional employer organization** is a company that assumes all HR functions of a client company by hiring all of its employees and leasing them back to the company. This is also called employee leasing. The PEO gains economies of scale by negotiating for benefits for the employees of several organizations. This can be a very cost efficient way for a small- to medium-sized organization to provide benefits equal to those of larger organizations. The company pays the PEO a percentage of the gross wages. PEOs will account for most of the increase in money spent for HRM outsourcing.[40] Much of the attractiveness of using a PEO to a small- or medium-size business comes from the ability to attract stronger candidates with the benefits they could not have afforded without the bargaining power of the PEO. Another advantage is having the expertise of the PEO to handle confusing government regulation requirements.

professional employer organization
Assumes all HR functions of a client company by hiring all of its employees and leasing them back to the company.

Shared Services

In the strategic planning process, it may be necessary to re-evaluate the role of HR. This may involve restructuring the HR department to better align organizational resources in order to achieve strategic objectives. As described in the chapter opener, Home Depot experienced a decrease in demand for building and home improvement supplies during the economic downturn. The strategic objective turned to organizational survival which meant reducing staff positions, including HR, in order to put more "aprons on the floor" —line workers in customer contact. To establish the objective, HR resorted to cutting HR staff and moving to a **shared services**. This model restructures the HR department into three components that each report to HR executives at the company headquarters. The goal is to achieve cost savings by combining some HR functions, achieving economies of scale, eliminating duplicated services, and standardizing how some services are delivered. In a recent survey by the Society of Human Resource Management, 75 percent of HR managers reported using shared services to provide HR support within the organization.[41]

The format of shared services models varies depending on the needs of the organization. They may include:[42]

- **Centers of excellence** that handle a wide range of activities that may include staffing, training, benefits administration, employee relations, and diversity programs.
- **Service centers** that handle transactional HR duties such as payroll.
- **Business partners** who work directly with business unit managers in strategic roles like developing succession plans and compensation programs.

Depending on the organization's strategy and needs, some or all HR roles and responsibilities may be outsourced. Common HR activities that may be outsourced include those that are mostly transactional in nature and involve little contact with employees, such as benefit and flexible spending account administration, criminal background checks, and retirement planning. Organizations are less likely to outsource performance management, policy development, and compensation plan administration.

Large organizations that are geographically dispersed are finding it more cost-effective to share their HRM services among the divisions.[43]

shared services
Sharing HRM activities among geographically dispersed divisions.

HRM in a Small Business

The discussion about the four departments of HRM refers to situations with resources sufficient for functional expertise to exist. However, this is not always the case. In a small business, the owner-manager is often responsible for all HR activities.

In other situations, small-business human resource departments are staffed with one HR Generalist and possibly a full-time HR Assistant. Regardless of the unit's size, the same activities are required in small businesses, but on a smaller scale. These small-business HRM professionals must properly perform the four HRM functions and achieve the same goals that a larger department achieves. The main difference is that they are doing the work themselves without the benefit of a specialized staff.

There may be a tendency to use outside consultants to assist in or perform all HRM activities. For instance, in a small company, some benefits such as health insurance may be prohibitively expensive and benefit administration may be beyond the capability of the small business person. In that case, a Professional Employer Organization (PEO) may be able to provide more cost effective insurance benefits and benefit administration. HRM in a small business requires that individuals keep current in the field and associated legal issues. For example, the Family and Medical Leave Act of 1993 is applicable to those organizations that have fifty or more employees. Accordingly, the small business may be exempt from some laws affecting employment practices. Businesses with fewer than fifteen employees, for example, are not obligated to comply with the Americans with Disabilities Act. Being aware of this information can save the small business time and money.[44]

HRM in a Global Environment

As a business grows from regional to national to international in size, the HRM function must take on a new and broader perspective. As a national company expands overseas, first with a sales operation, then to production facilities and fully expanded operations, or to international joint ventures, or possibly a merger, the human resource function must adapt to a changing and far more complex environment.[45]

All basic functions of domestic HRM become more complex when the organization's employees are located around the world, and additional HRM activities that would be considered invasions of employee privacy in domestic operations become necessary. This is occurs partially because of the increased vulnerability and risk of terrorism or kidnapping that American executives sometimes experience abroad.

When a corporation sends its American employees overseas, that corporation takes on responsibilities that add to the basic HRM functions. For example, the staffing, training, and development functions take on greater emphasis.[46] Not only are organizations concerned about selecting the best employee for the job, they must also be aware of the entire family's needs. Why? Many individuals who take international assignments fail because their spouse or family can't adjust to the new environment. Furthermore, the relocation and orientation process before departure may take months of foreign language training and should involve not just the employee but the employee's entire family. Details must be provided for work visas, travel, safety, household moving arrangements, taxes, and family issues such as the children's schooling, medical care, and housing.[47] Administrative services for expatriate employees also must be available once they are placed in their overseas posts. All these additional functions make international HRM a very costly undertaking.

Sarbanes-Oxley Act
Established procedures for public companies regarding how they handle and report their finances.

HR and Corporate Ethics

We'll close this chapter by revisiting the topic of ethics. This time we're not defining ethics but rather discussing HRM's role in ensuring that ethics exist in an organization.

One of the primary changes related to corporate management scandals in the early years of the new millennium was legislation signed into law in July 2002. That legislation, called the **Sarbanes-Oxley Act** (SOX), established procedures for public companies regarding how they handle and report their financial picture. The legislation also established penalties for noncompliance. For example, SOX requires the following:[48]

- Top management (the CEO and CFO [chief financial officer]) must personally certify the organization's financial reports.
- The organization must have in place procedures and guidelines for audit committees.
- CEOs and CFOs must reimburse the organization for bonuses and stock options when required by restatement of corporate profits.
- Personal loans or lines of credit for executives are now prohibited.

The noncompliance penalty of SOX is catching executives' attention. Failure to comply with the stipulated requirements—such as falsely stating corporate financials—can result in the executive being fined up to $1 million and imprisoned for up to ten years.[49] Moreover, if the executive's action is determined to be willful, both the fine and the jail time can be doubled. What does any of this have to do with HRM?

Although Sarbanes-Oxley does not specifically identify HRM activities in the law, it does address items generally under HRM responsibility. For example, the act provides protection for employees who report executive wrongdoing (whistle-blowing). In 2011, Bank of America was found by the U.S. Department of Labor to be in violation of the whistle-blower provisions of SOX for retaliation against an employee that worked for Countrywide Financial Corp. before they merged with Bank of America. The employee was fired after presenting evidence of fraud involving Countrywide employees. The employee's whistle-blowing activity was protected and Bank of America was ordered to reinstate the employee and pay over $900,000 in back wages, interest, compensatory damages, and attorney fees.[50]

HRM must create an environment where employees can come forward with their allegations without fear of reprisal from the employer. This critical employee relations aspect is not limited solely to whistle-blowing under SOX, but the act does require that companies have mechanisms in place where the complaint can be received and investigated. Many companies are creating "organizational ombuds," HR professionals who will offer confidential help for employees and "handle

Running a multinational corporation takes a lot of energy and planning. Companies such as Costco need to ensure that their HRM practices are proper in whatever part of the world they operate. Here, Costco in Mexico needs to ensure that its policies and practices comply with the laws, social mores, and cultural aspects of the Mexican people. *(Source: Sarah Martone/Bloomberg News/Getty Images, Inc.)*

potentially unethical or illegal behavior" in the organization.[51] In some organizations, this job is called the corporate ethicist.

HRM also has other responsibilities. As keepers of corporate policies and employee documents, HRM must make sure that employees know about corporate ethics policies and train employees and supervisors on how to act ethically in organizations. Given the added responsibility that SOX places on CEOs and CFOs, HR must, when involved in hiring for either of these positions, provide the needed leadership to ensure that the individual hired understands the compliance issues. The bottom line is that organizations must hold themselves to high ethical standards. Employees and other stakeholders demand it. Although regulations signed into law attempt to legislate "proper" behavior, legislation alone cannot work. HRM must work with senior executives to establish the moral fabric of the organization, ensuring that it becomes part of the standard operating procedures of the enterprise.

Summary

(This summary relates to the Learning Outcomes identified on page 28.) After having read this chapter you can:

1. **Explain how HR practices align with organizational strategy.** HR works with organizational decision makers to evaluate and develop organizational strategy. HR also supports strategy building, developing and maintaining a productive and talented workforce to achieve strategic goals.

2. **Describe the importance of human resource management.** HRM is responsible for the people dimension of the organization. It is responsible for hiring competent people, training them, helping them perform at high levels, and providing mechanisms to ensure that these employees maintain their productive affiliation with the organization.

3. **Identify the primary external environmental influences affecting human resource management.** External environmental influences are factors that affect HRM functions. They include the dynamic environment of HRM, government legislation, labor unions, and management thought.

4. **Characterize how management practices affect human resource management.** Management practices affect HRM in various ways. As new ideas or practices develop in the field, they typically have HRM implications. Once these practices are implemented, they require support from HRM to operate successfully.

5. **Discuss the effect of labor unions on human resource management.** Labor unions affect HRM practices in a variety of ways. If a union exists, HRM takes on a different focus—one of labor relations as opposed to employee relations. Additionally, what occurs in the unionized sector frequently affects the activities in non-union organizations.

6. **Outline the components and goals of the staffing, training, and development functions.** The components of the staffing function include strategic human resource planning, recruiting, and selection. The goal of the staffing function is to locate and secure competent employees. The training and development function includes orientation, employee training, employee development, organization development, and career development. The goal of the development function is to adapt competent workers to the organization and help them obtain up-to-date skills, knowledge, and abilities for their job responsibilities.

7. **List the components and goals of the motivation and maintenance functions of human resource management.** The components of the motivation

function include motivation theories, appropriate job design, reward and incentive systems, compensation, and benefits. The goal of the motivation function is to provide competent, adapted employees who have up-to-date skills, knowledge, and abilities with an environment that encourages them to exert high energy levels. The components of the maintenance function include safety and health issues and employee communications. The goal of the maintenance function is to help these employees maintain their commitment and loyalty to the organization.

8. **Outline the major activities in the employment, training and development, compensation and benefits, and employee relations departments of human resource management.** The departments of employment, training and development, compensation and benefits, and employee relations support the components of the staffing, training and development, motivation, and maintenance functions, respectively.

9. **Explain how human resource management practices differ in small businesses and in an international setting.** In large HRM operations, individuals perform functions according to their specialization. Small-business HRM practitioners may instead be the only individuals in the operation and must operate as HRM generalists. In an international setting, HRM functions become more complex and typically require additional activities associated with staffing and training and development.

Demonstrating Comprehension

QUESTIONS FOR REVIEW

1. How is the role of HR demonstrated in each of the four management functions?
2. Explain the purpose of HRM in an organization.
3. What activities are involved in the staffing function of HRM?
4. Explain the goals of the training and development function of HRM.
5. Describe the primary goals of the motivation function of HRM.
6. In what ways can HRM meet its goals of the maintenance function?
7. What role does HRM play in the strategic direction of an organization?
8. What does a small business owner need to know about HRM?
9. Which of the HR functions seem to be most important and why?

Key Terms

communications programs	maintenance function	Sarbanes-Oxley Act
compensation and benefits	management	scientific management
controlling	management thought	shared services
employee relations function	motivation function	staffing function
Hawthorne studies	organizing	strategic human resource management
HR generalist	outsourcing	training and development function
labor union	planning	
leading	professional employer organization	

HRM Workshop

Linking Concepts to Practice   DISCUSSION QUESTIONS

1. "Motivation is the primary responsibility of line managers. HRM's role in motivating organizational employees is limited to providing programs that equip line managers with means of motivating their employees." Do you agree or disagree with the statement? Explain your position.
2. You have been offered two positions in HRM. One is a generalist position in a smaller business, and one is a recruiting position in a large corporation. Which of the two jobs do you believe will give you more involvement in a variety of HRM activities? Defend your answer.
3. "Few new employment laws have been passed in recent years. We've reached a point where workers have adequate protection of their rights." Do you agree or disagree with this statement? Explain your position.
4. "Employers only need to provide employees with enough information so they can effectively and efficiently get their jobs done. Beyond that, employees don't have a need to know." Do you agree or disagree with the statement? Defend your answer.

Making a Difference   SERVICE LEARNING PROJECTS

A good way to experience the strategic process is to develop and execute an activity of your own that is tailored to the needs of an existing non-profit organization.

- Research local non-profits that may need assistance with fundraising and develop an event that helps them achieve their goal. Activities may include planning and hosting a fundraising dinner or auction.
- Your college may welcome an event that raises money for scholarships or textbooks for needy students. Resist the

opportunity to sponsor a bake sale. It's one of those one-time activities that doesn't translate well to your résumé.

As you put your service learning experience together, keep a journal of your activities, the time you spend, contact information for people you work with and your thoughts about the process. When you're finished, make a presentation to your class about the experience and what you learned. What concepts from Chapter 2 were you able to apply?

Developing Diagnostic and Analytical Skills

Case Application 2: HUNGRY FOR PRODUCTIVITY: FRITO-LAY LINKS STRATEGY WITH JOB DESIGN

Frito-Lay knows you love your favorite snack foods, and the prospect of facing an empty shelf where your Doritos should be is just unthinkable. In fact, the Frito-Lay mission statement is "To be the world's favorite snack and always within arm's reach."[52]

In pursuit of their mission to have your beloved chips always at hand, Frito-Lay is constantly looking for ways to make sure their business practices match up with the goal. A few years ago, HR at Frito-Lay was put to the test when low productivity and high turnover of the route sales representatives (RSRs) made it increasingly difficult to meet sales and profitability targets. Line managers and HR were resorting to "cheerleading" in hopes of motivating the RSRs to meet sales goals. But turnover and low productivity continued to make it difficult to achieve, quarter after quarter. HR and line managers teamed up to formulate a cost-effective solution that would solve the problem for good, but first they needed to discover the causes at the heart of the high turnover, low productivity, and

morale problems. RSRs are responsible for all delivery of Frito-Lay products to store shelves. This method, called "direct store delivery" is a labor-intensive process. RSRs drive products from warehouses to retailers, stock the shelves, negotiate for more shelf space, take additional orders, and are paid a commission based on sales volume. Executives researched a list of factors that could be responsible for the productivity issues including compensation, training, a competitive retail environment, and rapidly increasing numbers of Frito-Lay products. In an effort to narrow down the possible causes, they contracted with researchers at the University of Southern California, Los Angeles, to study RSR recruitment, retention, motivation, and productivity. Job design was also studied by breaking the position into three major responsibilities: sales, driving and delivery, and merchandising.

Frito-Lay already knew that one key to increased sales volume was the ability to get additional display space in high traffic areas.

Securing additional shelf space was already an important part of RSR training. Frito-Lay had also created a highly structured job for RSRs that included carefully planned driving routes to minimize driving time, stocking procedures, and utilization of the truck. Routes were divided between low-volume routes that include convenience stores and drug stores using smaller trucks, and high-volume routes that service large grocery and discount stores with larger trucks. Predictably, low-volume routes required more driving time and contact with store managers. Research determined that RSR sales skills in securing additional display space was a bigger influence on increased sales in these low-volume routes. RSRs who had previous sales experience tended to be more successful that RSRs who did not.

On high-volume routes, the ability of the driver to stick to a tight delivery schedule and have shelves stocked with product earlier in the morning was critical to increased sales. Prior sales experience further enhanced the ability of the RSR in these high-volume routes.

HR used the information collected to link hiring and job training to organizational strategy and sales growth by:

- Putting more emphasis on recruiting and hiring individuals with prior sales experience.

- Increasing sales training for RSRs.
- Making hourly employees available to help the high-volume route RSRs with stocking duties, enabling them to focus on the tight driving, delivery schedules, and sales tasks.

HR was able to more successfully meet the organizational strategy by carefully analyzing the internal factors that were causing the problem. They were able to align, hire, train, and design jobs to meet organizational needs, resulting in happy snackers worldwide. Next time your favorite flavor of Doritos is in plentiful supply at your local retailer, remember Frito-Lay's mission and thank HR.[53]

Questions:

1. How are job design and organizational strategy at Frito-Lay linked? How does one influence the other?
2. What external environmental factors may have influenced the low productivity at Frito-Lay and how it was fixed?
3. If you were an RSR at Frito-Lay, which of the changes would you find most beneficial? Least?
4. Can all productivity problems be cured by better aligning job design with organizational mission? Why or why not?

Working with a Team   MAKING A LAYOFF DECISION

Every manager, at some point in his or her career, is likely to face the difficult task of managing the laying off of employees. Assume that you are the human resource director of a 720-member technology company. You have been notified by top management that you must permanently reduce your staff by two individuals. Below are some data about your five employees.

- **Shawana Johnson,** African American female, age 36. Shawana has been employed with your company for five years, all in HRM. Her evaluations over the past three years have been outstanding, above average, and outstanding. Shawana has an MBA from a top-25 business school. She has been on short-term disability the past few weeks because of the birth of her second child and is expected to return to work in twenty weeks.
- **Greg Oates,** White male, age 49. Greg has been with you for four months and has eleven years of experience in the company in systems management. He has a degree in computer science and master's degrees in accounting information systems. He's also a CPA. Greg's evaluations over the past three years in the systems department have been average, but he did save the company $150,000 on a suggestion he made to use electronic time sheets.
- **Carlos Rodriquez,** Hispanic male, age 31. Carlos has been with the company almost four years. His evaluations over the past three years in your department have been outstanding. He is committed to getting the job done and devotes whatever it takes. He has also shown initiative by taking job assignments that no one else wanted. Carlos has been instrumental in starting up your benefits administration intranet for employees.

- **Cathy Williams,** White female, age 35. Cathy has been with your company seven years. Four years ago, Cathy was in an automobile accident while traveling on business to a customer's location. As a result of the accident, she was disabled and is wheelchair-bound. Rumor has it that she is about to receive several million dollars from the insurance company of the driver who hit her. Her performance the past two years has been above average. She has a bachelor's degree in human resource management and a master's degree in human development. Cathy specializes in training, career, and organization development activities.
- **Rodney Smith,** African American male, age 43. Rodney just completed his joint MBA and law program and recently passed the bar exam. He has been with your department four years. His evaluations have been good to above average. Five years ago, Rodney won a lawsuit against your company for discriminating against him in a promotion to a supervisory position. Rumor has it that now, with his new degree, Rodney is actively pursuing another job outside the company.

Given these five brief descriptions, make a recommendation to your boss in which two employees will be laid off. Discuss any other options you might suggest to meet the requirement of downsizing by two employees without resorting to layoffs. Discuss what you will do to (1) assist the two individuals who have been let go and (2) assist the remaining three employees. Then, in a group of three to five students, seek consensus on the questions posed above. Be prepared to defend your actions.

Learning an HRM Skill   HR CERTIFICATION

About the skill: What skills and competencies lead to successful HRM performance? Although it is extremely difficult to pinpoint exactly what competencies will serve you best when dealing with the uncertainties of human behavior, we can turn to the certifying body in HRM for answers. Specifically, the Human Resources Certification Institute (HRCI) suggests that certified HR practitioners must have exposure to and an understanding in six specific areas of the field.[54] These include business management and strategy, workforce planning and employment, human resource development, compensation and benefits, employee and labor relations, and risk management. Let's briefly look at each of the testing areas for the Professional in Human Resources (PHR) and Senior Professional in Human Resources (SPHR) certifications, and relate these specifically to the part of this book where they are addressed.

Business Management and Strategy. As a subset of management, HRM practitioners must understand legal and regulatory processes, organizational strategy, the strategic planning process, environmental analyses, aligning HR policies and practices with organizational strategy, as well as how HRM contributes to the overall success of the organization. Specific references in this text: Chapters 1, 2, 3, 4, and 5.

Workplace Planning and Employment. HRM practitioners require an understanding of why and how jobs are filled and the various methods of recruiting candidates. Emphasis in this area is on understanding various staffing means and making good decisions about job candidates that use valid and reliable measures and are within the legal parameters. Interviewing technique is also a major component of this knowledge area. This section also covers voluntary and involuntary dismissal of employees. Specific references in this text: Chapters 3, 4, 6, and 7.

Human Resource Development. To be successful in an organization, employees must be trained and developed in the latest technologies and skills relevant to their current and future jobs. This means an understanding of adult learning methodologies, relating training efforts to organiza-

tional goals, and evaluating the effort via performance appraisals. Specific references in this text: Chapters 8, 9, and 10.

Compensation and Benefits. One of the chief reasons people work is to fulfill needs. One major need—compensation and benefits—is probably the most expensive with respect to the employment relationship. The HRM practitioner must understand the intricacies involved in establishing a cost-effective compensation and benefits package that supports the organization's strategic goals. Specific references in this text: Chapters 11 and 12.

Employee and Labor Relations. Working with employees requires an understanding of what makes employees function. A positive culture needs to be developed and maintained that supports the company strategy. Employees need to be kept informed and have a way to raise suggestions or complaints. When the case involves unionized workers, the HRM/labor relations practitioner must understand the various laws that affect the labor–management work relationship. Specific references in this text: Chapters 1, 2, and 14.

Risk Management. Occupational health, safety, and security support employees' needs to feel safe in the workplace. This means freedom from physical and emotional harm, including workplace violence. Mechanisms must be in place to provide a safe work environment for employees. Programs must permit employees to seek assistance for those things affecting their work and personal lives. Specific references in this text: Chapters 1 and 13.

If you intend to specialize in HRM and may be interested in taking the certification examination, we invite you to visit the Society of Human Resource Management's website at www.shrm.org, the website for the Human Resource Certification Institute at www.hrci.org, or the American Society of Training and Development website at www.astd.org. You can access information about certification, exams, sign up for a testing date, or even take the exam online.

Enhancing Your Communication Skills

1. Visit an HRM department, either on or off campus. During your meeting, ask an HRM representative what he or she does on the job. Focus specifically on the person's job title and key job responsibilities and why he or she is in HRM. After your appointment, provide a three- to five-page summary of the interview, highlighting how the information will help you better understand HRM practices.

2. Discuss how you believe the Hawthorne studies have influenced HRM. Find three examples of HRM applications that can be linked to these studies and illustrate them with presentation slides. Explain the benefits these applications provide to the organization in a short class presentation.

3. Go to the Society of Human Resource Management's website at www.shrm.org. Research the services they provide to their

membership and the different options for student membership. Find a contact for the SHRM chapter closest to you and ask if you can attend a meeting as a guest. Report your findings back to the class.

4. Go to the website for the Human Resource Certification Institute at www.hrci.org or ASTD's website at www.astd.org.

Research the types of certifications they offer and the process one must follow to prepare for the human resource certification exams. What are the benefits to those who achieve certification? Present your findings to your class with presentation slides.

(Source: Morgan Lane Studios/iStockphoto)

LEARNING OUTCOMES

After reading this chapter, you will be able to

1. Identify the groups protected under the Civil Rights Act, Title VII.

2. Discuss the importance of the Equal Employment Opportunities Act.

3. Describe affirmative action plans.

4. Define the terms *adverse impact*, *adverse treatment*, and *protected group members*.

5. Identify the important components of the Americans with Disabilities Act and ADAAA.

6. Explain the coverage of the Family and Medical Leave Act.

7. Explain business defenses for discrimination charges.

8. Specify the HRM importance of *Griggs v. Duke Power*.

9. Explain the different types of sexual harassment.

10. Discuss the term *glass ceiling*.

11. Identify legal issues faced when managing HR in a global environment.

Equal Employment Opportunity

I n your HR position in a small manufacturing company, you think you know most of the employees. But you were surprised when Ramona, a Quality Control Inspector, told you that her supervisor has been whispering comments in her ear about how good she looks in her uniform and wonders what she wears underneath it. "I've told him to knock it off a million times, but it's getting worse and I just dread going to work. Can you do something to help?" You feel awful for Ramona and want to protect her from further harassment while you investigate the complaint, so you ask her to work in the warehouse until further notice so you can deal with her supervisor.

Later, Harvey, a warehouse employee, is sent to your office after he breaks an expensive piece of equipment. He did this after learning he wouldn't receive any overtime because Ramona is now working in the warehouse. Harvey has a long history of discipline issues and gripes. He recently filed a complaint for age discrimination after his last performance appraisal warned him he was in danger of losing his job for performance deficiencies and insubordination. After a loud confrontation in your office about his behavior, you fire him. He shouts that it isn't over and you will pay for your mistake.

The problem is, you could possibly pay for two mistakes you made today. The actions you took with both Ramona and Harvey may be grounds for claims of retaliation, the largest category of claims made to the Equal Employment Opportunity Commission.

Retaliation is any action that an employer takes that causes the employee to feel that he or she wouldn't have filed the complaint if he or she would have known the action would be taken as a result. In Ramona's case, the warehouse position may be perceived as a demotion, causing her to file a claim of retaliation in addition the original sexual harassment claim. It doesn't matter if Ramona's original complaint had merit or not. Harvey may have decided to file a bogus age discrimination complaint when he learned he may be fired for poor performance. He may even file a retaliation claim after being fired, doubling your workload in investigating and responding to the complaint. Retaliation can be expensive, too. Hope Bailey-Rhodeman won $804,214 in a settlement for discrimination and retaliation against Xerox after she was demoted from sales manager to a sales position that paid $100,000 less per year after complaining that other sales managers were bullying her because of her race and gender. Bailey-Rhodeman continued to work at Xerox over the next five years while the complaint made its way through the courts.

The moral of the story is that HR needs to have clear discrimination policies and train managers and supervisors not only how to prevent discrimination and harassment, but how to handle complaints. It's possible to think you're doing the right thing, yet make the situation worse.[1]

Looking Ahead
Is it possible to eliminate discrimination in the workplace? Should employers be held accountable for discrimination even if it's unintentional?

Introduction

If you've ever experienced the adverse effects of favoritism in the workplace, you know that it can be very frustrating when a coworker receives favorable treatment, such as a better schedule, a raise, or promotion, for no justifiable reason. It doesn't seem fair to employees who are just as qualified and may even work harder than the person who management favors, yet don't have the same opportunities or rewards because of an employer bias. It doesn't seem to be a very wise business move either. Workers who are qualified and work hard have more to contribute to the organization than those who are hired or promoted simply because management likes them more. Certainly management needs to make hiring decisions based on who would be a better employee, but those decisions should be made by hiring or promoting the best employees based on their qualifications and how well they fit the job requirements, rather than irrelevant criteria or personal bias against a person's gender, color, age, religion, or any other protected status.

If you were to do a little research on the companies that have been sued for discrimination in the last couple of years, you would find a surprisingly long list that includes Walmart, Costco, Target, Walgreens, UPS, FedEx, Marriott, Disney, Abercrombie & Fitch, Microsoft, Apple, Google, Best Buy, Home Depot, and even the Equal Employment Opportunity Commission (EEOC). These organizations all claim to value diversity in race, gender, national origin, disability, religion, and sexual orientation, so what went wrong? The Equal Employment Opportunity Commission (EEOC) reports that charges of job discrimination are at an all time high, reaching nearly 100,000 every year.[2] This should serve as a warning to employers to update their knowledge of the laws protecting workers from discrimination, our focus in this chapter. Laws concerning other areas of HR, including pay, safety, benefits, and labor relations will be covered in the appropriate chapters throughout the book.

Keep in mind that our discussion will be mostly limited to federal employment legislation. State or municipal laws may go beyond what the federal government requires. For example, although the Civil Rights Act does not include sexual orientation as one of the protected classes, nearly half the states, plus over 180 cities and counties, protect employees from discrimination based on sexual orientation in the workplace.[3] Approximately sixteen countries around the world also have laws that protect gays, lesbians, and bisexuals from employment discrimination.[4] Many companies have gone beyond any legal requirements by voluntarily implementing policies that protect employees on the basis of sexual orientation. These include 94 percent of Fortune 500 companies, including most of the companies listed above.

Laws Affecting Discriminatory Practices

Illegal discrimination is the process of making employment decisions such as hiring, firing, discipline, pay, promotions, leaves, or layoffs based on criteria such as race, religion, gender, national origin, skin color, or any other criteria that has been identified as a protected category by equal employment laws or regulations. Discrimination is becoming an increasing concern as the U.S. workforce becomes more diverse. Let's take a look at the laws that define illegal discrimination in employment and the protection they provide.

Civil Rights Act of 1964
Outlawed racial segregation and discrimination in employment, public facilities, and education

Title VII
The most prominent piece of legislation regarding HRM, it states the illegality of discriminating against individuals based on race, religion, color, sex, or national origin.

The Importance of the Civil Rights Act of 1964

No single piece of legislation has had a greater effect on reducing employment discrimination than the **Civil Rights Act of 1964**. It was divided into parts called titles—each dealing with a particular type of discrimination. For HRM purposes, Title VII of the act is especially relevant.

Title VII prohibits discrimination in hiring, promotion, dismissal, benefits, compensation, or any other terms, conditions, or privileges of employment based on race, religion, color, gender, or national origin. Title VII also prohibits retaliation against an individual who files a charge of discrimination, participates in an investigation, or opposes any unlawful practice. Most organizations, both public and private, are bound by the law. The law, however, specifies compliance based on the number of employees in the organization. Any organization with fifteen or more employees is covered. This minimum number of employees serves as a means of protecting, or removing from the law, small, family-owned businesses. Let's take a closer look at the types of employment protection provided in Title VII.

> No single piece of legislation has had a greater effect on reducing employment discrimination than the Civil Rights Act of 1964.

Race and Color Discrimination The U.S. has come a long way since the fight for civil rights began in the 1950s, to the election of President Barack Obama in 2008. But evidence of employment discrimination based on race and color isn't hard to find. In fact, racial discrimination is one of the most common discrimination complaints filed with the Equal Employment Opportunity Commission. Racial and color discrimination involves treating an employee or applicant differently because of a personal characteristic that is related to race such as hair texture, skin color, or facial features. It may also arise from cultural characteristics like a person's name, attire, or accent. Employees need not belong to a racial minority to be protected. Employees that are subject to discrimination because they are married to a minority, or Caucasians working in a minority-owned organization may be protected as well.[5] Employees are even protected from discrimination if the employee and employer are of the same race or color. For example, people of the same racial or ethnic group may discriminate against each other because of lighter or darker skin tone.

Supermarket chain Albertson's paid $8.9 million in 2009 to resolve three race- and color-related lawsuits filed by 168 minority employees who were given harder work assignments and disciplined more severely than their Caucasian coworkers. The EEOC found that employees who complained about the discriminatory treatment were given harder job assignments, passed over for promotion, or fired.[6]

Religious Discrimination Claims of religious discrimination in the workplace increased sharply following the terrorist attacks of September 11, 2001. Many Muslim employees found themselves subject to suspicion and job discrimination. In one case, a woman was fired from Alamo Car Rental for refusing to remove her head scarf during the month of Ramadan. She was awarded $287,000 by a jury who found that she should not have been required to sacrifice her religious beliefs to keep her job.[7]

The U.S. is becoming more religiously diverse, requiring employers to understand how work practices may be discriminatory and establish policies that respect an employee's religion and protect employer and employee rights. Religious discrimination includes treatment of applicants or employees differently because of religious beliefs and how they are practiced. Traditional, organized religions such as Christianity, Buddhism, Hinduism, Islam, and Judaism are protected as well as atheism and smaller, less well-known religious groups. As long as the beliefs the employee holds and the practices he or she adheres to are "sincerely held," and his or her employer is informed of those beliefs, that employee cannot be discriminated against for religious reasons.

Employers are required to make reasonable accommodations in the workplace for employees unless doing so creates a burden on the operations of the business. This may include dress and appearance accommodations such as allowing religious head coverings for men and women, facial hair for men, or religious requirements to wear or not to wear certain articles of clothing. Employers do not need to make accommodations if safety is an issue, such as rules and regulations in the manufacturing industry. Tattoos may even be protected if required by religious belief.[8] There are situations in which scheduling accommodations can be made for employees whose religion requires that they do not work after sundown on Friday, on Saturday, or on Sunday, as long as it does not create an undue hardship on the employer. Employees may also

Civil Rights Act of 1964	Title VII prohibits employment discrimination in hiring, compensation, and terms, conditions, or privileges of employment based on race, religion, color, sex, or national origin.
Equal Pay Act	Requires equal pay for equal work regardless of gender.
Executive Order (E.O.) 11246	Prohibits discrimination on the basis of race, religion, color, and national origin by federal agencies as well as those working under federal contracts.
Executive Order 11375	Added sex-based discrimination to E.O. 11246.
Age Discrimination in Employment Act of 1967	Protects employees 40–65 years of age from discrimination. Later amended to age 70 (1978), then amended (1986) to eliminate the upper age limit altogether.
Executive Order 11478	Amends part of E.O. 11246, states practices in the federal government must be based on merit; also prohibits discrimination based on political affiliation, marital status, or physical handicap.
Equal Employment Opportunity Act of 1972	Granted the enforcement powers for the EEOC.
Age Discrimination in Employment Act of 1978	Increased madatory retirement age from 65 to 70. Later amended (1986) to eliminate the upper age limit.
Pregnancy Discrimination Act of 1978	Affords EEO protection to pregnant workers and requires pregnancy to be treated like any other disability.
Americans with Disabilities Act of 1990 and ADA Amendments Act of 2008	Prohibits discrimination against an essentially qualified individual, and requires enterprises to reasonably accommodate individuals
Civil Rights Act of 1991	Nullified selected Supreme Court decisions. Reinstates burden of proof by employer. Allows for punitive and compensatory damages through jury trials.
Family and Medical Leave Act of 1993	Permits employees in organizations of 50 or more workers to take up to 12 weeks of unpaid leave for family or medical reasons each year.
Uniformed Services Employment and Reemployment Rights act of 1994	Allows veterans the right to return to their job in the private sector when returning from military service
Genetic Information Nondiscrimination Act of 2008	Prohibits discrimination based on employee's genetic information.

Exhibit 3-1
Summary of Primary Federal
Laws Affecting Discrimination

Title VII of the Civil Rights Act of 1964 began a series of laws and Executive Orders that have attempted to eliminate discrimination in the workplace. Many of these laws prevent employers from making job related decisions on hiring, promotion, and pay on factors that are not related to the employee's ability to do the job, such as race, religion, gender, or disability.

request time and space for prayers during the work day. For extended time off during holidays when the business is open, employees may be required to take vacation or paid time off (PTO).

National Origin Discrimination National origin discrimination involves issues of citizenship and permanent residence status, and is often related to race or color discrimination. One example is when employers discriminate against employees because of their name, dress, or accent. Foreign accents should not be used in employment decisions unless it seriously interferes with job performance. For example, an employee who was fired after nine years of employment for failing to present a "positive, friendly, and enthusiastic image" to customers filed a complaint that she had been ridiculed for her accented English, instructed not to speak Spanish to anyone, even customers, unless the customer initiated the conversation in Spanish. A jury awarded her $500,000 because the discrimination was based on her national origin. Employers may only require English fluency if English is required to perform the essential job functions or for safe and efficient operation of the business.

Sex or Gender Discrimination In addition to Title VII of the Civil Rights Act, sex and gender discrimination are also defined and protected by other laws. These include the Equal Pay Act of 1963, the Pregnancy Discrimination Act of 1978, the Lilly Ledbetter Fair Pay Act of 2009, and more that will be covered further in this and other chapters. The U.S. Bureau of Labor Statistics reports that 59 percent of working-age women in the United States are in the labor force. This percentage has increased from 43 percent four decades ago.[9] Equality in the workplace for women has progressed in that time, yet the EEOC reports that gender discrimination accounts for approximately 30 percent of discrimination claims every year.[10] Some of these are large cases, such as *Dukes v. Walmart Stores*; which claimed systematic sexual discrimination against women at Walmart who sought training and promotions to management positions on behalf of over 1.6 million women. Some cases are as small as a female truck driver who filed a claim against her employer because she was fired after she failed a physical test that was not required of her male colleagues. Although the overwhelming majority of these discrimination situations involve women, some do involve men.

Sex or gender discrimination takes many forms. The wage gap between men and women in the U.S. shows that in spite of decades of attempts to create equity in pay, women still earn 77 cents for every dollar that men earn.[11] There are many possible reasons for the pay gap, including differences in education, experience, time in the workforce, and larger numbers of women in sales, clerical, and service jobs that traditionally pay less.[12] But when the earnings of women who work full time in salaried jobs were compared to the earnings of men by the U.S. Bureau of Labor Statistics, the women only moved up to 80 cents for every dollar that the men earned.[13] Time spent out of the workforce as a family caregiver and working in lower paying jobs may explain part of the wage gap, but women in the workforce still find that opportunities are not quite equal, and, therefore, pay isn't equal either.[14]

Ratio of women's to men's earnings, selected occupations, 2010

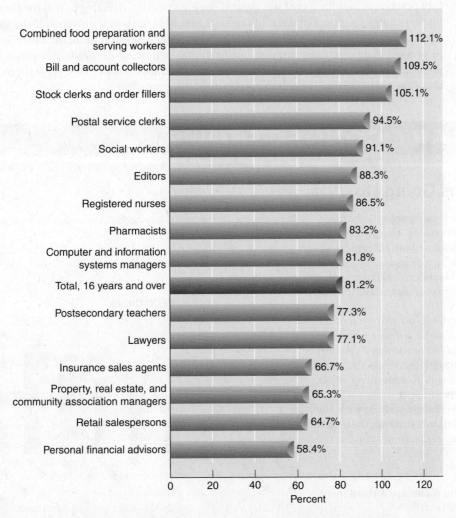

Occupation	Percent
Combined food preparation and serving workers	112.1%
Bill and account collectors	109.5%
Stock clerks and order fillers	105.1%
Postal service clerks	94.5%
Social workers	91.1%
Editors	88.3%
Registered nurses	86.5%
Pharmacists	83.2%
Computer and information systems managers	81.8%
Total, 16 years and over	81.2%
Postsecondary teachers	77.3%
Lawyers	77.1%
Insurance sales agents	66.7%
Property, real estate, and community association managers	65.3%
Retail salespersons	64.7%
Personal financial advisors	58.4%

Source: U.S. Bureau of Labor Statistics, http://www.bls.gov/spotlight/2011/women/

Exhibit 3-2
Ratio of women's to men's earnings in selected occupations

Equal pay for equal work has been the law of the land since 1963, yet in many professions, women have not closed the pay gap. The pay gaps between men and women in selected occupations are shown here.

Any job requirement that holds one sex to a different procedure, standard, or qualification than the other may be discriminatory. In addition to the pay issue discussed earlier, possible discriminatory practices include differences in policies regarding leaves of absence, benefits, unique job categories and promotions, dress codes, training opportunities, and more.

Equal Employment Opportunity Act (EEOA)
Granted enforcement powers to the Equal Employment Opportunity Commission.

Equal Employment Opportunity Commission (EEOC)
The arm of the federal government empowered to handle discrimination in employment cases.

EEOA/EEOC By 1972, after realizing that the Civil Rights Act left much to interpretation, Congress passed an amendment to the act called the **Equal Employment Opportunity Act (EEOA)**. This act provided a series of amendments to Title VII.[15] Probably the greatest consequence of the EEOA was the granting of enforcement powers to the **Equal Employment Opportunity Commission (EEOC)**, which was able to force employers who were reluctant to comply with the law. In addition, the EEOA also expanded Title VII coverage to include employees of state and local governments, employees of educational institutions, and employees of labor organizations with fifteen or more employees or members.

The EEOC is responsible for enforcing federal laws that make it illegal to discriminate against applicants and employees based on race, religion, color, sex, national origin, age, disability, or genetic information. The top priority for EEOC investigation is systemic discrimination, which means that the employer or industry has a pattern or practice that broadly discriminates against a protected group. This would include barriers to recruitment, hiring, or training that effectively limit the opportunities of a specific group. One example is an employer who rarely offers advancement or training to women beyond a certain level in an organization, similar to the plaintiff's claims in the *Dukes v. Walmart* class discrimination lawsuit.

If an investigation by the EEOC finds that an employer is engaging in a discriminatory practice, it may file a civil suit against the organization if unable to resolve discrimination charges within 120 days. Individuals may also file suit themselves if the EEOC declines to sue. In addition to investigating charges of discrimination, the EEOC works to prevent discrimination through outreach and education programs for employers, providing guidance to federal agencies to assure compliance with EEOC regulations and assistance with affirmative action employment programs.[16]

CONTEMPORARY CONNECTION

Discrimination Claims Going Up

Discrimination claims filed with the Equal Employment Opportunity Commission (EEOC) have increased sharply over the past five years, increasing the workload for both HR professionals and the EEOC. A combination of factors seem to be responsible, including difficult economic conditions resulting in high unemployment and a new online filing process, making it easier for employees to file claims.

Although all claims are investigated, over 80 percent are dismissed because they are found to be without merit, are duplicate claims, or are withdrawn. The remaining 20 percent are settled by awarding the em`ployee who made the claim back pay, promotion, or reinstatement of seniority or a job, totaling over $404 million in benefits.

The categories of claims are changing along with the increased numbers. Employer retaliation is currently the largest category of complaints, passing racial discrimination for the first time in 2010.[17]

Consider this:
Because an overwhelming number of claims are without merit, should the process be made more difficult?

Why do you think there has been an increase in retaliation claims?

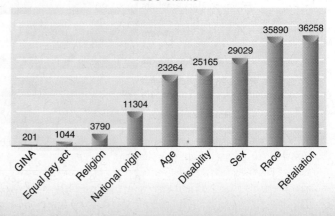

EEOC Claims

Category	Claims
GINA	201
Equal pay act	1044
Religion	3790
National origin	11304
Age	23264
Disability	25165
Sex	29029
Race	35890
Retaliation	36258

Relevant Executive Orders Executive Orders are issued by the president of the United States to provide guidance to government agencies on specific topics. Executive Order 11246 prohibits discrimination on the basis of race, religion, color, or national origin by federal agencies as well as by contractors and subcontractors who work under federal contracts. Executive Order 11375 added sex-based discrimination to the above criteria. Executive Order 11478 superseded part of Executive Order 11246 and states that employment practices in the federal government must be based on merit and must prohibit discrimination based on race, color, religion, sex, national origin, political affiliation, marital status, or physical disability.

These orders cover all organizations that have contracts of $10,000 or more with the federal government. Additionally, organizations with 50 or more employees and/or $50,000 in federal grants must have an active affirmative action program. The Office of Federal Contract Compliance Program (OFCCP) administers the order's provisions and provides technical assistance.

Why does the Age Discrimination in Employment Act permit certain exceptions, like requiring commercial airline pilots to retire upon reaching their 65th birthday? The rationale focuses on the potential for a pilot's skills to lessen after age 65. That, coupled with concern for air safety of traveling passengers, has resulted in an exception to the law. *(Source: © Digital Vision/Getty Images, Inc.)*

Age Discrimination in Employment Act of 1967 The Age Discrimination in Employment Act (ADEA) of 1967 prohibits the widespread practice of requiring workers to retire at age 65.[18] It also gives protected-group status to individuals between the ages of 40 and 65. Since 1967, this act has been amended twice—once in 1978, which raised the mandatory retirement age to 70, and again in 1986, where the upper age limit was removed altogether. People under 40 are not protected by the act, but some states have laws protecting younger workers from age discrimination.[19] Organizations with 20 or more employees, state and local governments, employment agencies, and labor organizations are covered by the ADEA.

Another area of concern involves pension benefits for older workers. In 1990, the ADEA was amended by the Older Workers Benefit Protection Act (OWBPA) to prohibit organizations from excluding employee benefits for older workers. However, the law does permit benefit reduction based on age so long as the cost of benefits paid by the organization is the same for older as it is for younger employees.[20] We'll look at employee benefits in greater detail in Chapter 12.

Like other types of discrimination previously discussed, age discrimination limits opportunities to workers. The EEOC reports that nearly 25 percent of the discrimination claims they receive concern age, and the percentage is increasing.[21] One likely reason is that as the baby boomer generation reaches retirement age, there are a larger number of older workers. Common types of age discrimination include policies that affect older workers more than younger workers, including physical fitness requirements that are not relevant to the position, and offering different health benefits or changing job requirements in order to convince older workers to quit and make room for younger employees. In addition, when a company needs to lay off workers in tough economic times, it's tempting to look to the highest paid workers first, and these tend to be more senior, and most likely older, workers. A layoff that targets older workers disproportionately is considered discriminatory. Older workers may also feel discriminated against if workers are allowed to use nicknames like "gramps," "geezer," "old lady," "hag," or even by celebrating landmark birthdays with an "over the hill" theme.

Some employers that offer early retirement packages to older workers have begun to require them to sign a document waiving the right to sue for age discrimination as a condition of accepting the package. Any waiver attached to retirement benefits must follow the requirements of the Older Workers Benefit Protection Act of 1990 (OWBPA),

Age Discrimination in Employment Act (ADEA)
This act prohibits arbitrary age discrimination, particularly among those over age 40.

Lilly Ledbetter sued her employer, Goodyear Tire & Rubber, after discovering that she was being paid less than coworkers with similar jobs. This photo shows Ledbetter directly behind President Obama as he signs the act into law.
(Source: Ron Edmonds/©AP/ Wide World Photos)

Pregnancy Discrimination Act of 1978
Law prohibiting discrimination based on pregnancy.

which prohibits discrimination in the types of benefits offered to older workers compared with younger workers.

In some circumstances, specialized employees such as commercial pilots may be required to leave their current positions because of strict job requirements. Pilots may no longer captain a commercial airplane when they reach the age of 65. This was increased from age 60 in 2007 for several reasons, including the fact that people are much healthier at age 65 now than when the rule was written in 1950. The FAA was also responding to a shortage of qualified pilots and foreign airlines that have higher age limits.[22]

Equal Pay Act The Equal Pay Act was enacted in 1963 with the intent of eliminating the practice of paying women lower wages for the same or similar jobs held by men. It was common practice to alter jobs slightly to justify higher pay for men because they had a family to support. The Equal Pay Act requires that as long as the jobs are substantially equal, the pay must also be equal. The job descriptions do not need to be identical if the jobs require "equal skill, effort, and responsibility, and . . . are performed under similar working conditions within the same establishment."[23]

Unfortunately, pay discrimination still exists in spite of specific laws designed to prevent it. One notable example is Lilly Ledbetter, who worked at Goodyear Tire & Rubber as an overnight production supervisor for nearly twenty years. When she was about to retire in 1998, she received an anonymous note informing her that she was earning substantially less than three male counterparts who held the same position. Ledbetter sued Goodyear, but the Supreme Court held that she was not entitled to compensation because her claim of discrimination needed to be filed within 180 days of the first discriminatory paycheck she received, which was twenty years before she discovered the discrimination. In response to the Supreme Court case, Congress passed the Lilly **Ledbetter Fair Pay Act** in 2009, allowing workers to file pay discrimination claims within 180 days (300 days in some states) of any discriminatory paycheck.

Pregnancy Discrimination Unbelievable as it sounds, it used to be common to ask women in job interviews or on applications if they were pregnant.[24] Employers were motivated by the desire to reduce work disruptions due to women who took time off for pregnancy complications, childbirth, or care of a newborn. In 1978, the **Pregnancy Discrimination Act** amended Title VII of the Civil Rights Act to prohibit sex discrimination on the basis of pregnancy. As a result, employers may not refuse to hire a pregnant woman because of the pregnancy or the perceptions of coworkers, clients, or customers who may be uncomfortable working with a pregnant woman. Pregnancy must be treated the same as any other health issue. It may not be excluded from health plans or disability leaves, and women must be allowed to work as long as they are able to perform their jobs.[25] When returning to work from leave, women are allowed to return to the same job. If the exact job she left is unavailable, a similar one must be provided. It is interesting to note that this law is highly contingent on other benefits the company offers. Should the organization not offer health or disability-related benefits such as sick leave to its employees, it is exempt from this part of the law. However, any type of health or disability insurance offered, no matter how much or how little, requires compliance. For instance, if a company offers a benefit covering 40 percent of the costs associated with any short-term disability, then it must include pregnancy in that coverage.

Employers are required to make reasonable accommodations to the work environment for pregnant workers, similar to the accommodations required by the Americans with Disabilities Act. Failure to do so amounts to discrimination, and a claim may be filed with the EEOC. For example, Yaire Lopez, a route driver delivering baked products to retail stores for Bimbo Bakeries USA Inc., was restricted from lifting more than twenty pounds when she became pregnant. Shortly after providing the written restriction to her supervisor, she was directed by the human resource manager to go home and use Family Medical Leave (FMLA). Lopez was then fired, even though she told her employer that she wanted to work. Lopez sued Bimbo for failing to accommodate her pregnancy, despite the availability of a work program for disabled employees. Lopez was awarded $2.34 million for wrongful firing and for failing to accommodate her pregnancy as other disabilities had been accommodated.[26]

The Americans with Disabilities Act of 1990 and The ADA Amendments Act of 2008 This act and its accompanying amendment prohibit employment discrimination on the basis of disability in employment for private employers, state and local governments, and labor organizations with fifteen or more employees. To be protected by the ADA, an individual with a disability must be qualified and able to perform the essential functions of the job with or without reasonable accommodations. An individual with a disability is defined by the ADA as a person who has a physical or mental impairment that substantially limits one or more major life activity, a person who has a history or record of such impairment, or a person who is perceived by others as having such impairment.

Several terms involved with the ADA require further definition.[27]

Qualified individuals must meet the basic skill, training, licensure, experience, education, or other job-related requirements for the position. For instance, an accountant applying for a position as a C.P.A. must have passed the C.P.A. exam.

Major life activities may include, but are not limited to, caring for oneself (showering, using the toilet), seeing, hearing, eating, walking, standing, lifting, bending, learning, speaking, breathing, concentrating, communicating, and working.

Years ago, an employee in a wheelchair may have had difficulty obtaining employment. However, with the passage of the Americans with Disabilities Act of 1990, employees cannot be discriminated against simply because of a disability or the perception of a disability. *(Source: John Lee/Age Fotostock America, Inc.)*

Essential job functions are required for the successful performance of the job. These need to be specified in job descriptions so applicants know what is required and employers can prove that they are necessary to the job and not arbitrarily applied.

Reasonable accommodations include activities or modifications to the work environment that allow the qualified individual to perform the work. They may be relevant to the size and financial position of the organization. For example, a small business may not be required to make expensive structural modifications like installing an elevator, yet it may be required of a large business. Examples of modifications may include purchase of modification equipment such as lifts or ramps, modified work schedules, reassignment to a vacant position, modifications to training and testing procedures, leaves of absence, hiring readers or interpreters, widening door frames and installing hand rails. Generally, these accommodations must be requested by the employee.[28]

It's important, however, to recognize that ADA doesn't protect all forms of disability. For example, illegal drug use is not included, but employees who no longer use drugs and have successfully participated in a supervised drug rehabilitation program may be included. Some psychiatric disabilities (like pyromania and kleptomania) may disqualify an individual from protection, but others may need minimal accommodations such as the ability to leave work early once a week to visit a therapist.[29] Correctable conditions such as poor eyesight or high blood pressure are not included.[30]

The **ADA Amendments Act of 2008 (ADAAA)** is intended to give broader protections for disabled workers and "turn back the clock" on court rulings that Congress deemed too restrictive. It is now easier for individuals to establish the existence of a disability, especially

The Americans with Disabilities Act of 1990
This act extends employment protection to most forms of disability status.

reasonable accommodations
Changes to the workplace that allow qualified workers with disabilities to perform their jobs.

"A worker knows immediately if she is denied a promotion or transfer, if she is fired or refused employment. And promotions, transfers, hirings, and firings are generally public events, known to coworkers. When an employer makes a decision of such open and definitive character, an employee can immediately seek out an explanation and evaluate it for pretext. Compensation disparities, in contrast, are often hidden from sight."
— Supreme Court Justice Ruth Bader Ginsberg, dissenting with the majority opinion that found Ledbetter's case was invalid, May 29, 2007[32]

Civil Rights Act of 1991
Employment discrimination law that nullified selected Supreme Court decisions. It reinstated burden of proof by the employer and allowed for punitive and compensatory damage through jury trials.

The Family and Medical Leave Act of 1993
Federal legislation that provides employees with up to 12 weeks of unpaid leave each year to care for family members or for their own medical reasons.

regarding impairments such as cancer, diabetes, epilepsy, HIV infection, and bipolar disorder. Major bodily functions are included such as cell growth, immune system function, digestive, bladder and bowel function, neurological and brain functions, respiratory and circulatory functions, and endocrine and reproductive functions. In Chapter 7, we will discuss the importance of understanding the ADA as it pertains to the employee selection process.

Obesity is an employment as well as a health concern in the American workplace. The Centers for Disease Control estimates that nearly 64 percent of Americans are overweight. Although obesity is not covered under the ADA, workers who are morbidly obese with a Body Mass Index (BMI) of 40 or above have successfully claimed that their obesity prevents them from performing one or more essential life functions. Although workers with a BMI under 40 are not protected, the state of Michigan and the District of Columbia have enacted laws to specifically protect workers from discrimination based on size or appearance.[31]

The Civil Rights Act of 1991 The Civil Rights Act of 1991 was passed to restore rights of employees who sued employers for discrimination after a series of Supreme Court decisions limited those rights. A number of other employment discrimination related issues were addressed, including prohibition of discrimination on the basis of race and racial harassment on the job. The act also returned the burden of proof that discrimination did not occur back to the employer and reinforced the illegality of employers who make hiring, firing, or promoting decisions on the basis of race, ethnicity, sex, or religion. Possibly the most drastic change was to allow discrimination victims who have been intentionally discriminated against under Title VII or the ADA to seek compensatory and punitive damages in a jury trial.

The Family and Medical Leave Act of 1993 (FMLA) The Family and Medical Leave Act of 1993 (FMLA) was passed in 1993 to provide workers an opportunity to balance family responsibilities and work. It allows unpaid leave for specific family related reasons like childbirth, adoption, the employee's own illness, or to care for a sick family member, with a guarantee of retaining an employee's job when he or she returns from leave. The FMLA benefits were extended in 2008 to include family members of military personnel who are on active duty. Employees who require a leave of absence from work in order to care for a wounded service member are also included. Several states already had laws in place similar to the new FMLA rules.[33]

Nearly 80 percent of all U.S. workers are covered under FMLA. The act allows workers of organizations that employ 50 or more workers within a 75-mile radius of the organization the opportunity to take up to 12 weeks of unpaid leave in a 12-month period for qualifying reasons.[34] Public agencies and schools are included regardless of the number of employees. To be eligible for these benefits, an employee must have worked for an employer for a total of 12 months (not necessarily consecutively) and must have worked for the organization for at least 1,250 hours in the past 12 months. Employees are generally guaranteed their current job or one equal to it on their return, and may retain employer provided healthcare coverage during the leave. If an organization can show that it will suffer significant economic damage by having a "key" employee out on FMLA leave, the organization may not be required to restore the employee to the previous position.[35] Employers are required to inform employees of their rights and responsibilities under the FMLA by posting notices such as the poster in Exhibit 3-3, including FMLA information in handbooks, and providing new employees with a copy of the notice.

Employees may use FMLA leave for one or more of the following reasons:[36]

- Birth or adoption of a child or placement of foster child
- Care for a spouse, son, daughter, or parent with a serious health condition
- Serious health condition of the employee
- Situations that arise because the employee's spouse, son, daughter, or parent is on active military duty such as deployment, welcome home ceremonies, counseling, or time to make necessary financial or legal arrangements because of deployment
- Caring for a spouse, son, daughter, parent, or next of kin who is a member of the armed forces with a serious injury or illness for up to 26 weeks

EMPLOYEE RIGHTS AND RESPONSIBILITIES
UNDER THE FAMILY AND MEDICAL LEAVE ACT

Basic Leave Entitlement

FMLA requires covered employers to provide up to 12 weeks of unpaid, job-protected leave to eligible employees for the following reasons:

- For incapacity due to pregnancy, prenatal medical care or child birth;
- To care for the employee's child after birth, or placement for adoption or foster care;
- To care for the employee's spouse, son or daughter, or parent, who has a serious health condition; or
- For a serious health condition that makes the employee unable to perform the employee's job.

Military Family Leave Entitlements

Eligible employees with a spouse, son, daughter, or parent on active duty or call to active duty status in the National Guard or Reserves in support of a contingency operation may use their 12-week leave entitlement to address certain qualifying exigencies. Qualifying exigencies may include attending certain military events, arranging for alternative childcare, addressing certain financial and legal arrangements, attending certain counseling sessions, and attending post-deployment reintegration briefings.

FMLA also includes a special leave entitlement that permits eligible employees to take up to 26 weeks of leave to care for a covered servicemember during a single 12-month period. A covered servicemember is a current member of the Armed Forces, including a member of the National Guard or Reserves, who has a serious injury or illness incurred in the line of duty on active duty that may render the servicemember medically unfit to perform his or her duties for which the servicemember is undergoing medical treatment, recuperation, or therapy; or is in outpatient status; or is on the temporary disability retired list.

Benefits and Protections

During FMLA leave, the employer must maintain the employee's health coverage under any "group health plan" on the same terms as if the employee had continued to work. Upon return from FMLA leave, most employees must be restored to their original or equivalent positions with equivalent pay, benefits, and other employment terms.

Use of FMLA leave cannot result in the loss of any employment benefit that accrued prior to the start of an employee's leave.

Eligibility Requirements

Employees are eligible if they have worked for a covered employer for at least one year, for 1,250 hours over the previous 12 months, and if at least 50 employees are employed by the employer within 75 miles.

Definition of Serious Health Condition

A serious health condition is an illness, injury, impairment, or physical or mental condition that involves either an overnight stay in a medical care facility, or continuing treatment by a health care provider for a condition that either prevents the employee from performing the functions of the employee's job, or prevents the qualified family member from participating in school or other daily activities.

Subject to certain conditions, the continuing treatment requirement may be met by a period of incapacity of more than 3 consecutive calendar days combined with at least two visits to a health care provider or one visit and a regimen of continuing treatment, or incapacity due to pregnancy, or incapacity due to a chronic condition. Other conditions may meet the definition of continuing treatment.

Use of Leave

An employee does not need to use this leave entitlement in one block. Leave can be taken intermittently or on a reduced leave schedule when medically necessary. Employees must make reasonable efforts to schedule leave for planned medical treatment so as not to unduly disrupt the employer's operations. Leave due to qualifying exigencies may also be taken on an intermittent basis.

Substitution of Paid Leave for Unpaid Leave

Employees may choose or employers may require use of accrued paid leave while taking FMLA leave. In order to use paid leave for FMLA leave, employees must comply with the employer's normal paid leave policies.

Employee Responsibilities

Employees must provide 30 days advance notice of the need to take FMLA leave when the need is foreseeable. When 30 days notice is not possible, the employee must provide notice as soon as practicable and generally must comply with an employer's normal call-in procedures.

Employees must provide sufficient information for the employer to determine if the leave may qualify for FMLA protection and the anticipated timing and duration of the leave. Sufficient information may include that the employee is unable to perform job functions, the family member is unable to perform daily activities, the need for hospitalization or continuing treatment by a health care provider, or circumstances supporting the need for military family leave. Employees also must inform the employer if the requested leave is for a reason for which FMLA leave was previously taken or certified. Employees also may be required to provide a certification and periodic recertification supporting the need for leave.

Employer Responsibilities

Covered employers must inform employees requesting leave whether they are eligible under FMLA. If they are, the notice must specify any additional information required as well as the employees' rights and responsibilities. If they are not eligible, the employer must provide a reason for the ineligibility.

Covered employers must inform employees if leave will be designated as FMLA-protected and the amount of leave counted against the employee's leave entitlement. If the employer determines that the leave is not FMLA-protected, the employer must notify the employee.

Unlawful Acts by Employers

FMLA makes it unlawful for any employer to:

- Interfere with, restrain, or deny the exercise of any right provided under FMLA;
- Discharge or discriminate against any person for opposing any practice made unlawful by FMLA or for involvement in any proceeding under or relating to FMLA.

Enforcement

An employee may file a complaint with the U.S. Department of Labor or may bring a private lawsuit against an employer.

FMLA does not affect any Federal or State law prohibiting discrimination, or supersede any State or local law or collective bargaining agreement which provides greater family or medical leave rights.

FMLA section 109 (29 U.S.C. § 2619) requires FMLA covered employers to post the text of this notice. Regulations 29 C.F.R. § 825.300(a) may require additional disclosures.

For additional information:
1-866-4US-WAGE (1-866-487-9243) TTY: 1-877-889-5627
WWW.WAGEHOUR.DOL.GOV

WHD★
U.S. Wage and Hour Division

U.S. Department of Labor | Employment Standards Administration | Wage and Hour Division   WHD Publication 1420 Revised January 2009

Exhibit 3-3
Family and Medical Act Poster

The U.S. Department of Labor provides employers with posters like this that inform employees of their rights. The Department of Labor website has posters available for free download at www.dol.gov. They also offer assistance in determining which posters you may be required to display in your business.

Source: U.S. Department of Labor

CONTEMPORARY CONNECTION

When Our Troops Come Home

Your small business supported employees who joined the National Guard. You participated in the community send-off when they were deployed. You displayed yellow ribbons while they were gone, helped their families when they were wounded, and celebrated when they came home.

What are your obligations now that they've returned? Do you have to hire them back when they return? About 17 percent of returning veterans have some service-related disability, 20 percent of those are quite serious.[38] What if they can't do their old jobs? You're just a small business with limited resources. Is help available for them? Is help available for you? Large companies may have experts that handle questions regarding veterans in the workplace, but often the small employer is left wondering what to do. Everyone wants to treat returning veterans fairly and should be educated about the state and federal regulations regarding their employment.

Anyone who has been absent from work because of service in the military is protected by the Uniformed Services Employment and Reemployment Rights Act (USERRA) and by the Veterans Benefits Improvement Act (VBIA). Veterans deployed less than 180 days must notify employers within two weeks of their return from the service that they intend to resume work. Those deployed over 181 days must notify employers within 90 days. In most situations, employers must re-employ the veteran within an additional two weeks.[39]

The Americans with Disabilities Act (ADA) provides additional protection for those veterans whose injuries require some type of accommodation in the workplace. The employer may be required to make reasonable accommodations, just as they would for any other qualified person with a disability. This may require modifying offices and restrooms, or acquiring

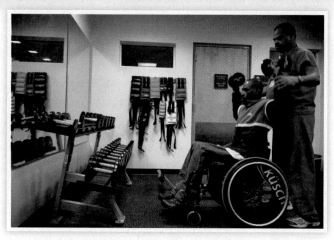

(Source: Jeff Hutchens/Getty Images, Inc.)

adaptive equipment such as lifts or voice recognition software. Veterans with post-traumatic stress disorder may need to modify work schedules and take time for visits with health care professionals.

Help is available for both the employer and veteran when a disability requires adjustment in the workplace. The U.S. Department of Veterans Affairs provides employer assistance including paying part of the cost of retraining a disabled veteran, tax credits for hiring veterans, and deductions for the cost of making the workplace accessible.[40]

Many employers find that veterans have learned valuable skills in the military that are helpful to civilian employers too.

Consider this:

Do you go to school or work with veterans? Are they aware of these rights? How do they feel about them?

Employees must give employers notice of intent to use FMLA leave in advance if possible. If it isn't possible to give advanced notice, the employer must be notified as soon as possible, usually within a day or two. Employers may require certification from a health care provider to authenticate that the condition is a serious health condition that qualifies for FMLA leave. Serious health conditions that qualify are illnesses or injuries that involve medical treatment overnight in a hospital, hospice care, or stay in a residential medical care facility. Illnesses or injuries that require absence from work of more than three days, pregnancy, or a serious or chronic illness also qualify.

Uniformed Services Employment and Reemployment Rights Act of 1994 (USERRA)
Clarifies and strengthens the rights of veterans to return to their jobs in the private sector when they return from military service.

Uniformed Services Employment and Reemployment Rights Act of 1994 (USERRA) The Act enacted to clarify and strengthen the rights of veterans who served in the Reserves or National Guard. Veterans have the right to return to their jobs in the private sector when they return from military service, and are entitled to the same seniority, status, and pay they would have attained during their military service. They may also retain their insurance benefits, although they may be required to pay for the premiums.

The USERRA also prohibits employers from discriminating or retaliating against a job applicant or employee based on prior military service. The process for filing a complaint against employers who do not comply with the act is also spelled out. In 2004, the Veterans' Benefits Improvement Act (VBIA) clarified the health insurance rights of veterans and required that employers display the USERRA poster along with other information notifying employees of their rights.[37]

Genetic Information Nondiscrimination Act (GINA) of 2008 Most employees wouldn't think a thing about their employer showing concern regarding a parent's serious illness such as breast cancer, heart disease, or Alzheimer's disease. Unfortunately, not all employers have such innocent motives. In 2001 it was discovered that Burlington Northern Santa Fe (BNSF) Railway was using genetic testing to determine if employees had a genetic predisposition to carpal-tunnel syndrome, a common reason for Workers Compensation claims for the railroad. Employees complained to the EEOC that their rights were being violated under the Americans with Disabilities Act, and the testing was stopped.[41]

The Genetic Information Nondiscrimination Act (GINA) was passed in 2008. GINA prohibits employers with fifteen or more employees from discriminating on the basis of genetic information when making any employment-related decisions, including insurance covered participation in wellness programs. Voluntary participation in health screenings is not covered. Fortunately the law makes an exception for employers who accidentally learn of relevant genetic information, but employers should be careful about discussing the health of employees and their family members. Since the law is relatively new and genetic research is evolving rapidly, HR managers should stay tuned for further developments and court cases.[42]

> **Genetic Information Nondiscrimination Act (GINA)**
> Prohibits employers from making employment decisions based on information about an employee's genetic information.

Preventing Discrimination

The number of laws and regulations makes it critical for HRM to stay informed on the best way to prevent discriminatory practices in the workplace and train managers and supervisors in the latest laws. The best prevention is an organizational culture that encourages equal employment opportunity, tolerance, acceptance, and good communication. Recall from our earlier discussion that employment discrimination may stem from any employment decision based on factors other than those relevant to the job. Should that occur frequently, the organization may face charges that it discriminates against some members of a protected group.

Uniform Guidelines on Employee Selection Procedures

In 1979, several government agencies with responsibilities for enforcing equal employment laws issued a document called Uniform Guidelines on Employee Selection Procedures. This document makes it clear that HR hiring policies and employee selection procedures must be tied to specific job-related factors and cannot be discriminatory. It also outlines the

TIPS FOR SUCCESS

Is a Problem Brewing?

HR managers often end up reacting to an event or, in the case of a discrimination charge, a legal matter. Although they usually have policies in place on how to handle such events, a more fundamental question arises. That is, are there signs that something is brewing? The answer is often yes—if HR managers are paying close attention to what's happening in the organization.

There may be a problem if:

- large numbers of employees (often individuals who share something in common—a personal characteristic, the same supervisor, etc.) ask for their personnel files;
- significant increases are witnessed in the use of the company's complaint procedure;

- a union campaign has just failed; or
- employees are using blogs to bash the organization.

Each of the above items might not always indicate a legal action is forthcoming, but should be considered warnings of potential problems, and HR needs take action. Being proactive—investigating things before they reach a fever pitch—is often the best defense.[44]

Things to think about:
What are the benefits of being proactive? Do you think employees appreciate management efforts to make things right before discrimination complaints are filed?

adverse impact
A consequence of an employment practice that results in a greater rejection rate for a minority group than for the majority group in the occupation.

adverse (disparate) treatment
An employment situation where protected group members receive treatment different from other employees in matters such as performance evaluations and promotions.

4/5ths rule
A rough indicator of discrimination, this rule requires that the number of minority members a company hires must equal at least 80 percent of the majority members in the population hired.

requirements necessary for employers to prove that hiring and employee selection practices observe equal employment laws. In addition, it addresses standards for employment testing that are not biased against or in favor of any particular group, and provides ways to determine if an employment test or qualification is valid. The Uniform Guidelines are not law, but are referenced by courts in cases of employment discrimination.[43]

Determining Potential Discriminatory Practices

Adverse impact can be described as any employment consequence that discriminates against employees who are members of a group protected by equal employment law. As an example of an adverse impact, many years ago, police departments had a height requirement that required applicants to be 5' 10" or greater. The requirement eliminated women and men of some ethnic groups at higher rates than Caucasian men, significantly reducing job opportunities for them. The courts found no evidence of tall officers being more effective at law enforcement than shorter colleagues. The concept of adverse impact results from a seemingly neutral, even unintentional consequence of an employment practice.[45]

Another issue differs from adverse impact but follows a similar logic. This is called **adverse (disparate) treatment**. Adverse treatment occurs when a member of a protected group receives less favorable outcomes in an employment decision than a nonprotected group member. For example, if a protected group member is more often evaluated as performing poorly or receives fewer organizational rewards, adverse treatment may have occurred.

The 4/5ths Rule One of the first measures of determining potentially discriminatory practices is called the **4/5ths rule**. Issued by the EEOC in its Uniform Guidelines on Employee Selection Procedures, the 4/5ths rule helps assess whether an adverse impact has occurred. Of course, the 4/5ths rule is not a definition of discrimination. It is, however, a quick analysis to help assess HR practices in an organization. Moreover, in applying the 4/5ths rule, the Supreme Court ruled in *Connecticut v. Teal* (1984) that decisions in each step of the selection process must conform to the 4/5ths rule.[46]

To see how the 4/5ths rule works, suppose there are two pools of applicants for jobs as management information systems analysts. The applicants' backgrounds reflect the following: 40 applicants are classified in the majority, and 15 applicants are classified as members of minority populations.[47] After the testing and interview process, 22 majority and 8 minority members are hired. Is the organization in compliance? Exhibit 3-4 provides the analysis. In this case, we find that the company is in compliance; that is, the

Exhibit 3-4
Applying the 4/5ths Rule

Although all the numbers may look intimidating, the concept of the 4/5ths rule is pretty simple. If the percentage of minority employees hired is 80 percent or more of the number of non-minorities hired, the company is in compliance the rule. If the percentage is under 80 percent, it indicates the company may have discriminated against minority applicants, and further research is indicated.

In Compliance						
Majority Group (Maj) = 40 Applicants			**Minority Group (Min) = 15 Applicants**			
Item	Number	Percent	Item	Number	Percent	%Min/%Maj
Passed test	30	75%	Passed test	11	73%	73%/75% = 97%
Passed interview	22	73%	Passed interview	8	72%	72%/73% = 98%
Hired	22	100%	Hired	8	100%	100%/100% =100%
Analysis	22/40 =	55%	Analysis	8/15 =	53%	
Ratio of minority/majority 53%/55% = 96%						

Not In Compliance						
Majority Group (Maj) = 40 Applicants			**Minority Group (Min) = 15 Applicants**			
Item	Number	Percent	Item	Number	Percent	%Min/%Maj
Passed test	30	75%	Passed test	11	73%	73%/75% = 97%
Passed interview	22	86%	Passed interview	4	36%	36%/86% = 41%
Hired	26	100%	Hired	4	100%	100%/100% = 100%
Analysis	26/40 =	65%	Analysis	4/15 =	26%	
Ratio of minority/majority 26%/65% = 40%						

ratio of minority to majority members is 80 percent or greater (the 4/5ths rule). Accordingly, even though fewer minority members were hired, no apparent discrimination has occurred. Exhibit 3-4 also shows the analysis of an organization not in compliance.

Remember, whenever the 4/5ths rule is violated, it indicates only that discrimination may have occurred. Many factors can enter in the picture. Should the analysis show that the percentage is less than 80 percent, more elaborate statistical testing must confirm or deny adverse impact. For instance, if Company A finds a way to keep most minority group members from applying in the first place, it need hire only a few of them to meet its 4/5ths measure. Conversely, if Company B actively seeks numerous minority group applicants and hires more than Company A, it still may not meet the 4/5ths rule.

Restricted Policy

A restricted policy occurs whenever HRM activities exclude a class of individuals. For instance, assume a company is restructuring and laying off an excessive number of employees over age 40. Simultaneously, however, the company is recruiting for selected positions on college campuses only. Because of economic difficulties, this company wants to keep salaries low by hiring people just entering the workforce. Those over age 39 who were making higher salaries are not given the opportunity to even apply for these new jobs. These actions may indicate a restricted policy. That is, through its hiring practice (intentional or not), a class of individuals (in this case, those protected by age discrimination legislation) has been excluded from consideration.

Geographical Comparisons

A third means of supporting discriminatory claims is through the use of a geographic comparison. In this instance, the characteristics of the potential qualified pool of applicants in an organization's hiring market are compared to the characteristics of its employees. If the organization has a proper mix of individuals at all levels in the organization that reflects its recruiting market, then the company is in compliance. Additionally, that compliance may assist in fostering diversity in the organization. The key factor here is the qualified pool according to varying geographic areas.

McDonnell-Douglas Test

Named for the ***McDonnell-Douglas Corp. v. Green*** 1973 Supreme Court case,[48] this test provides a guideline for the employee to establish a strong case of discrimination. Four components must exist:[49]

> *McDonnell-Douglas Corp. v. Green*
> Supreme Court case that led to a four-part test used to determine if discrimination has occurred.

1. The individual is a member of a protected group.
2. The individual applied for a job for which he or she was qualified.
3. The individual was rejected.
4. The employer, after rejecting this applicant, continued to seek other applicants with similar qualifications.

If these four conditions are met, the employee filing the complaint has established a prima facie (Latin for "at first sight") case of discrimination. At this point, the burden of proof shifts to the employer to prove that there was a legitimate reason for rejecting the applicant that was not discriminatory.

Affirmative Action Plans Affirmative Action

programs are instituted by an organization to correct past injustices in an employment process. Executive Order 11246 was established with the premise that as a matter of public policy and decency, minorities should be hired to correct past prejudice that kept them out. It was understood that many discriminatory practices were so well established that "Legal and social coercion [were] necessary to bring about the change."[50]

> **affirmative action**
> A practice in organizations that goes beyond discontinuance of discriminatory practices to include actively seeking, hiring, and promoting minority group members and women.

Affirmative action means that an organization must take certain steps to show that it is not discriminating. For example, the organization must analyze the demographics of its current workforce. Similarly, the organization must analyze the composition of the community from which it recruits. If the workforce resembles the community for all job classifications, then the organization may be demonstrating that its affirmative action program is working. If, however, there are differences, affirmative action also implies that the organization will establish goals and timetables for correcting the imbalance and have specific plans for recruiting and retaining protected group members. If it does not, it can lose the right to contract with the government for goods and services.

TIPS FOR SUCCESS

Suggestions for Recruiting Minorities and Women

An employer who has very few minority applicants may encounter discrimination claims even though he or she does not discriminate in the hiring process. It may be necessary to actively increase the number of qualified minorities who apply for employment. There are several ways to do this:

- Ask employees who are in an underrepresented group to help recruit.
- Participate in job fairs at colleges, universities, places of worship, social clubs, and community-based organizations where minorities are in a majority or in attendance.

- Advertise in community bulletins for clubs, sororities, fraternities, and places of worship where minorities are in a majority.
- Place job ads on television, radio, websites, and in newspapers and magazines that target a particular demographic.[51]

Things to think about:
Are there any organizations in your community that may need to make an effort to recruit underrepresented groups? What methods would be most effective?

Organizations that find an imbalance may actively search for qualified minorities by recruiting from places like predominantly African American or women's colleges, but need not necessarily hire these individuals under this process. However, as a result of affirmative action programs, an organization should be able to show significant improvements in hiring and promoting women and minorities or justify why external factors prohibited them from achieving their affirmative action goals.

Affirmative action programs have often been targets of criticism and lawsuits. Much of the criticism has focused on the realization that affirmative action bases employment decisions on group membership rather than individual performance. Giving certain groups of individuals (by race, sex, age) preference tugs at the heart of fair employment. As the argument goes, if it was wrong 50 years ago to give white males preference for employment, why is it right today to give other individuals preference simply because they possess certain traits?

Responding to an EEO Charge

If HRM practices have adversely impacted an employee group in an organization, the employer has a few remedies for dealing with valid allegations. First, the employer should discontinue the practice. Only after careful study should the practice, or a modified version, be reinstated. However, if enough evidence exists, an employer may choose to defend the disputed practice. Generally, three defenses can be used when confronted with an allegation of discrimination by adverse impact. These are job relatedness or business necessity, bona fide occupational qualifications, and seniority systems.

Business Necessity   An organization has the right to operate in a safe and efficient manner. This includes business practices necessary for the organization to survive. A major portion of business necessity involves job-relatedness factors, or having the right to expect employees to perform successfully. Employees are expected to possess the skills, knowledge, and abilities required to perform the essential elements of the job. Job-relatedness criteria are substantiated through the validation process. We'll return to this topic in Chapter 7.

bona fide occupational qualification (BFOQ)
Job requirements that are "reasonably necessary to meet the normal operations of that business or enterprise."

Bona Fide Occupational Qualifications   The second defense against discriminatory charges is a **bona fide occupational qualification** (BFOQ). Under Title VII, a BFOQ is permitted where such requirements are "reasonably necessary to meet the normal operation of that business or enterprise." As originally worded, BFOQs could be used only to support sex discrimination. Today, BFOQ coverage is extended to other categories such as religion. BFOQs cannot, however, be used in cases of race or color.

It is important to note that while BFOQs are "legal" exceptions to Title VII, they are narrowly defined. Simply using a BFOQ as the response to a charge of discrimination is not enough; it must be directly related to the job. Let's look at some examples.

Some employers tried to argue that a specific gender is a requirement to be a firefighter, police officer, or flight attendant for reasons such as physical strength or public perception. The courts, however, did not hold the same view. As a result, it is now common to see both sexes in nearly any career. Using gender as a job criterion is difficult to prove. However, under certain circumstances gender as a BFOQ has been supported. In some jobs like prison guards, washroom attendants, and health care, gender may be used as a determining factor to "protect the privacy interests of patients, clients, or customers."[52]

A religious BFOQ may have similar results. Religion may be used as a differentiating factor in ordaining a church minister, but a faculty member doesn't have to be Catholic to teach at a Jesuit college. Under rare circumstances, an organization may refuse to hire individuals whose religious observances fall on days that the enterprise normally operates if the organization demonstrates that it cannot reasonably accommodate these religious observances.[53] It's becoming harder to demonstrate an inability to make a reasonable accommodation, however.[54] For example, pizza delivery establishments cannot refuse to hire, or terminate, an employee who has facial hair—like that in the Hindu tradition. HRM managers must understand that some "traditional" policies may have to change to reflect religious diversity in the workforce. A policy that prohibits employees who have customer contact from having beards may be a violation of the Civil Rights Act. Accordingly, the company may have to change its policy to accommodate religious traditions.[55]

In terms of national origin, BFOQs have become rare. In some situations, organizations have been able to prove that a foreign accent or the inability to communicate effectively "materially interferes with the individual ability to perform" the job. An example would be a cab driver whose thick accent makes it extremely difficult for passengers to communicate with him. In that rare case, nationality can be used as a BFOQ.[56]

Our last area of BFOQ is age. With subsequent amendments to the Age Discrimination in Employment Act, age BFOQs are hard to support. As we mentioned in our discussion of age discrimination, age can sometimes be used as a determining factor when hiring new employees. However, aside from pilots and a select few key management executives in an organization, age as a BFOQ is limited.

Seniority Systems   Finally, the organization's bona fide **seniority system** can serve as a defense against discrimination charges. So long as employment decisions such as layoffs stem from a well-established and consistently applied seniority system, decisions that may adversely affect protected group members may be permissible. However, an organization using seniority as a defense must be able to demonstrate the appropriateness of its system. Although means are available for organizations to defend themselves, the best approach revolves around job-relatedness. BFOQ and seniority defenses are often subject to great scrutiny and, at times, are limited in their use.

seniority systems
Decisions such as promotions, pay, and layoffs are made on the basis of an employee's seniority or length of service.

Selected Relevant Supreme Court Cases

In addition to the laws affecting discriminatory practices, HRM professionals must be aware of Supreme Court decisions that affect the workplace. Many of these cases help further define HRM practices or indicate permissible activities. Although it is impossible to discuss every applicable Supreme Court case, we have chosen a few of the more critical ones to highlight what they have meant for the field.

Cases Concerning Discrimination

In the 1960s, Duke Power had a policy of requiring everyone to pass two different aptitude tests and have a high school diploma in order to work in any position other than a department called the Labor Department. The Labor Department was the lowest paying department at Duke Power and was almost exclusively staffed with African American employees. Willie Griggs filed a class action lawsuit on behalf of other African American employees, claiming that the requirement to pass the tests and have a high school

Does this employee need a high school diploma to do his job? According to the *Griggs v. Duke Power* case, if the organization cannot show how having a high school diploma relates directly to successful performance on the job, then a high school diploma cannot be required. To do so could be discriminatory.
(Source: Kari Goodnough/Bloomberg News/Getty Images, Inc.)

Griggs v. Duke Power Company Landmark Supreme Court decision stating that tests must fairly measure the knowledge or skills required for a job.

Albemarle Paper Company v. Moody Supreme Court case that clarified the methodological requirements for using and validating tests in selection.

diploma unfairly discriminated against African American employees who tended not to have the same education as other applicants.

In the 1971 ***Griggs v. Duke Power Company*** decision, the U.S. Supreme Court adopted the interpretive guidelines set out under Title VII: Tests must fairly measure the knowledge and skills required in a job in order not to discriminate unfairly against minorities. This action single-handedly made invalid any employment test or diploma requirement that disqualified African Americans at a substantially higher rate than whites (even unintentionally) if this differentiation could not be proven to be job related. Such action was said to create an adverse (disparate) impact.[57]

The Griggs decision had even wider implications. It called into question most intelligence and conceptual tests used in hiring without direct empirical evidence that the tests employed were valid. This crucial decision placed the burden of proof on the employer who must provide adequate support that any test used did not discriminate on the basis of non–job-related characteristics. For example, if an employer requires all applicants to take an IQ test, and test results factor in the hiring decision, the employer must prove that individuals with higher scores will outperform on the job those individuals with lower scores. Nothing in the Court's decision, however, precludes the use of testing or measuring procedures. What it did was to place the burden of proof on management to demonstrate, if challenged, that the tests used provided a reasonable measure of job performance.

Although companies began a process of validating these tests, requiring all job applicants to take them raised further questions. In 1975, the Supreme Court decision in the case of ***Albemarle Paper Company v. Moody*** clarified the methodological requirements for using and validating tests in selection.[58] In the case, four African American employees challenged their employer's use of tests for selecting candidates from the unskilled labor pool for promotion into skilled jobs. The Court endorsed the EEOC guidelines by noting that Albemarle's selection methodology was defective because:

- The tests had not been used solely for jobs on which they had previously been validated.
- The tests were not validated for upper-level jobs alone but were also used for entry-level jobs.
- Subjective supervisory ratings were used for validating the tests, but the ratings had not been done with care.
- The tests had been validated on a group of job-experienced white workers, whereas the tests were given to young, inexperienced, and often nonwhite candidates.

In addition to these two landmark cases, other Supreme Court rulings have affected HRM practices. We have identified some of the more important ones and their results in Exhibit 3-5. During the late 1980s, however, a significant change in the Supreme Court's perception of EEO became apparent. One of the most notable cases during this period was ***Wards Cove Packing Company v. Atonio*** (1989).[59] Wards Cove operated two primary salmon canneries in Alaska. The issue in this case stemmed from different hiring practices for two types of jobs. Noncannery jobs viewed as unskilled positions were predominately filled by nonwhites (Filipinos and native Alaskans). On the other hand, cannery jobs, seen as skilled administrative/engineering positions, were held by a predominately white group. Based on the ruling handed down in *Griggs v. Duke Power*, an adverse (disparate) impact could be shown by the use of statistics (the 4/5ths rule). However, in the decision, the Court ruled that statistics alone could not support evidence of discrimination.

Consequently, the burden of proof shifted from the employer to the individual employee. The Wards Cove decision had the effect of potentially undermining two decades of gains made in equal employment opportunities. This case could have struck a

Exhibit 3-5
Summary of Selected
Supreme Court Cases
Affecting EEO
These Supreme Court cases have
helped clarify the intent of Equal
Employment Laws.

Case	Ruling
Griggs v. Duke Power (1971)	Tests must fairly measure the knowledge or skills required for a job; also validity of tests.
Albemarle Paper Company v. Moody (1975)	Clarified requirements for using and validating tests in selection.
Washington v. Davis (1976)	Job-related tests are permissible for screening applicants.
Connecticut v. Teal (1984)	Requires all steps in a selection process to meet the 4/5ths rule.
Firefighters Local 1784 v. Stotts (1984)	Layoffs are permitted by seniority despite effects it may have on minority employees.
Wyant v. Jackson Board Education (1986)	Layoffs of white workers to establish racial or eth of balances are illegal; however, this case reaffirmed the use of affirmative action plans to correct racial imbalance.
United States v. Paradise (1986)	Quotas may be used to correct significant racial discrimination practices.
Sheetmetal Workers Local 24 v. EEOC (1987)	Racial preference could be used in layoff decisions only for those who had been subjected to previous race discrimination.
Johnson v. Santa Clara County Transportation Agency (1987)	Reaffirmed the use of preferential treatment based on gender to overcome problems in existing affirmative action plans.

significant blow to affirmative action. Despite that potential, businesses appeared unwilling to significantly deviate from the affirmative action plans developed over the years. Of course, it's now a moot point, as the Civil Rights Bill of 1991 discussed earlier nullified many of these Supreme Court rulings.

Cases Concerning Reverse Discrimination

Affirmative action programs are necessary to ensure continued employment possibilities for minorities and women, and programs to foster the careers of these two groups have grown over the decades. But while this voluntary action may have been needed to correct past abuses, some white males have found that affirmative action plans work against them, leading to charges of reverse discrimination. Let's take a look at a sample of cases involving reverse discrimination.

In 1978, the Supreme Court handed down its decision in the case of ***Bakke v. The Regents of the University of California at Davis Medical School.***[60] Allen Bakke applied to the Davis Medical School for one of 100 first-year seats. At that time, U.C. Davis had a self-imposed quota system to promote its affirmative action plan: that is, of the 100 first-year seats, 16 were set aside for minority applicants. Bakke's charge stemmed from those 16 reserved seats. His credentials were not as good as those gaining access to the first 84 seats, but were better than those of minorities targeted for the reserved seats. The issue that finally reached the Supreme Court was: Could an institution impose its own quota to correct past imbalances between whites and minorities? The Supreme Court ruled that the school could not set aside those seats, for doing so resulted in "favoring one race over another." Consequently, Bakke was permitted to enter Davis Medical School.

The Supreme Court's decision in the case of the ***United Steelworkers of America v. Weber*** (1979) appeared to have important implications for organizational training and development practices and for the larger issue of reverse discrimination.[61] In 1974, Kaiser Aluminum and the United Steelworkers Union set up a temporary training program for higher-paying skilled trade jobs, such as electrician and repairer, at a Kaiser plant in Louisiana. Brian Weber, a white employee at the plant who was not selected for the training program, sued on the grounds that he had been illegally discriminated against.

Wards Cove Packing Company v. Atonio
A notable Supreme Court case that had the effect of potentially undermining two decades of gains made in equal employment opportunities.

reverse discrimination
A claim made by white males that minority candidates are given preferential treatment in employment decisions.

Failure to document decisions on business necessity may lead to serious challenges.

He argued that African Americans with less seniority were selected over him to attend the training due solely to their race. The question facing the Court was whether it is fair to discriminate against whites to help African Americans who have been longtime victims of discrimination. The justices said that Kaiser could choose to give special job preferences to African Americans without fear of being harassed by reverse discrimination suits brought by other employees. The ruling was an endorsement of voluntary affirmative action efforts—goals and timetables for bringing an organization's minority and female workforce up to the percentages they represent in the available labor pool.

Despite the press coverage that both cases received, many questions remained unanswered. Just how far was a company permitted to go regarding preferential treatment? In subsequent cases, more information became available. In 1984, the Supreme Court ruled in ***Firefighters Local 1784 v. Stotts***[62] that when facing a layoff situation, affirmative action may not take precedence over a seniority system: that is, the last in (often minorities) may be the first to go. This decision was further reinforced in ***Wyant v. Jackson Board of Education*** (1986),[63] when the Supreme Court ruled that a collective bargaining agreement giving preferential treatment to preserve minority jobs in the event of a layoff was illegal. On the contrary, in ***Johnson v. Santa Clara County Transportation*** (1987) the Supreme Court did permit affirmative action goals to correct worker imbalances as long as the rights of nonminorities were protected. This ruling had an effect of potentially reducing reverse discrimination claims.

A more recent case, ***Ricci v. DeStefano***, involved a group of firefighters in New Haven, Connecticut who won a ruling from the U.S. Supreme Court in 2009 declaring that they were victims of reverse discrimination. In that case, a group of firefighters took an exam required for promotion and although care was taken to make sure the exam was fair and nondiscriminatory, no African American firefighters passed the exam. They threatened to sue the city, claiming disparate impact. In an effort to prevent a lawsuit, the city threw out the exam and didn't certify any firefighters for promotion. The white firefighters and two Hispanic firefighters who passed the test filed a complaint that they suffered reverse discrimination due to their race. The Supreme Court ruled that the city had indeed violated Title VII and that throwing out the results of the exam was discriminatory.

The implications of these cases may be somewhat confusing. The conclusion one needs to draw from these is that any HRM practice may be challenged by anyone. HRM must be able to defend its practices if necessary and explain the basis and the parameters on which the decisions were made. Failure to document or to base the decisions on business necessities may lead to serious challenges to the action taken.

Enforcing Equal Opportunity Employment

Two U.S. government agencies are primarily responsible for enforcing equal employment opportunity laws. They are the Equal Employment Opportunity Commission (EEOC) and the Office of Federal Contract Compliance Programs (OFCCP).

The Role of the EEOC

Any complaint filed against an employer regarding discrimination based on race, religion, color, sex, national origin, age, qualified disabilities, or wages due to gender falls under the jurisdiction of the EEOC. The EEOC is the enforcement arm for Title VII of the 1964 Civil Rights Act, the Equal Pay Act, the Age Discrimination in Employment Act, the Vocational Rehabilitation Act of 1973, the Americans with Disabilities Act, and the Civil Rights Act of 1991. The EEOC requires that charges typically be filed within 180 days of an alleged incident[64] and that these charges be written and sworn under oath. Once the charges have been filed, the EEOC may progress (if necessary) through a five-step process:[65]

1. The EEOC will notify the organization of the charge within 10 days of its filing and then begin to investigate the charge to determine if the complaint is valid. The company may simply settle the case here, and the process stops.

2. The EEOC will notify the organization in writing of its findings within 120 days. If the charge is unfounded, the EEOC's process stops, the individual is notified of the outcome, and the EEOC informs the individual that he or she may still file charges against the company in civil court (called a right-to-sue notice). The individual has 90 days on receipt of the right-to-sue notice to file his or her suit.

3. If there is justification to the charge, the EEOC will attempt to correct the problem through informal meetings with the employer. Again, the company, recognizing that discrimination may have occurred, may settle the case at this point.

4. If the informal process is unsuccessful, the EEOC will begin a formal settlement meeting between the individual and the organization (called a mediation meeting). The emphasis here is to reach a voluntary agreement between the parties.

5. Should Step 3 fail, the EEOC may file charges in court.

It's important to note that while acting as the enforcement arm of Title VII, the EEOC has the power to investigate claims, but it has no power to force organizations to cooperate. The relief that the EEOC tries to achieve for an individual is regulated by Title VII. If the allegation is substantiated, the EEOC attempts to make the individual whole. That is,

CONTEMPORARY CONNECTION

EEOC Reaches Out to Young Workers

Remember your first job? The one where you received your first real pay that wasn't from Mom and Dad? If you're like most young workers, there's a lot you probably didn't know about the world of work at that point. Many young workers are shy about even asking how much they will make per hour and find out only when they receive that first check.

(Source: Radius/SuperStock)

Unfortunately youth and inexperience makes young workers easy targets for sexual harassment and employment discrimination. Consider these situations:

■ A 16-year-old girl working at a Burger King franchise tried to complain when her 35-year-old manager made suggestive comments, rubbed up against her, and tried to kiss her. The manager became mad when she complained, fired her, re-hired her and continued the harassment. When the girl couldn't find a number to report the manager to the franchise owner, her mother went to the restaurant and discussed the situation with a shift supervisor. The manager

became angry and the girl was fired again. The courts found that the franchise owner made it difficult for the girl to find a number to report the abuse and found in favor of the girl.[70]

■ Three girls, including two 17-year-old high school students, employed at a Jiffy Lube franchise complained that supervisors and coworkers made lewd gestures and sexually explicit comments. The franchise was ordered to pay $300,000 to the three employees.[71]

■ Two young men were told that Walmart had no positions available for them because they were deaf. Five years after complaining to the EEOC, the young men were each awarded $66,250 in back pay, positions at the store, seniority from the time they originally applied, and a sign language interpreter for orientation, training, and meetings. Walmart was also ordered to pay legal fees and make many modifications to their hiring and training processes to accommodate people with disabilities.[72]

"Teens are particularly vulnerable because they are new to the workplace, they are impressionable, and are more likely than not to be at the bottom rung," says Jocelyn Samuels, Vice President for education and employment with the National Women's Law Center. "They feel less authorized to complain and they may not know that procedures are available to them."[73]

The EEOC has taken up the cause of young workers' rights with a website called "Youth At Work" at http://youth.eeoc.gov. The site includes information on employee rights using real cases and interactive self-quizzes.

Things to think about:

How can organizations effectively protect young workers from exploitation from discrimination and sexual harassment? Can you suggest other groups that are likely targets of discrimination and would benefit from increased communication from the EEOC?

> The EEOC prioritizes its cases to spend more time on those that have the greatest significance.

under the law, the EEOC attempts to obtain lost wages or back pay, job reinstatement, and other rightfully due employment factors (for example, seniority or benefits). The individual may also recover attorney fees. However, if the discrimination was intentional, other damages may be awarded. Under no circumstances may the enterprise retaliate against an individual filing charges—whether or not the person remains employed by the organization. The EEOC monitors that no further adverse action against that individual occurs.

The EEOC is staffed by five presidentially appointed commissioners and staff counsels. It is generally well known that the EEOC is quite understaffed in its attempt to handle more than 100,000 cases each year.[66] Consequently, the EEOC began prioritizing cases in the mid-1990s, attempting to spend more time on cases that initially appear to have merit. Furthermore, its enforcement plans are prioritized, with cases in which "alleged systematic discrimination has broad impact on an industry, profession, company, or geographic location" receiving the highest priority.[67] Under these new EEOC directions, it's more important than ever for HRM to investigate the complaints internally, communicate openly with the EEOC regarding the priority level of the complaint, and evaluate selecting and testing methods to ensure validity.

Office of Federal Contract Compliance Program (OFCCP)

In support of Executive Order 11246, the OFCCP enforces the provisions of this order (as amended), as well as Section 503 of the Vocational Rehabilitation Act of 1973 and the Vietnam Veterans Readjustment Act of 1974.[68] Provisions of the OFCCP apply to any organizations including universities that have a federal contract or act as a subcontractor on a federal project. The OFCCP operates within the U.S. Department of Labor. Similar to the EEOC, the OFCCP investigates allegations of discriminatory practices and follows a similar process in determining and rectifying wrongful actions. One notable difference is that the OFCCP has the power to cancel an enterprise's contract with the federal government if the organization fails to comply with EEO laws.[69]

Current Issues in Employment Law

As employment law evolves to respond to the dynamic environment of HRM, legal issues arise as employees seek to clarify and assert their rights. Let's take a look at several current legal issues including sexual harassment, comparable worth, English only laws, sexual orientation discrimination, and current trends in state and local laws.

Sexual Harassment

sexual harassment
Anything of a sexual nature that creates a condition of employment, an employment consequence, or a hostile or offensive environment.

quid pro quo harassment
Some type of sexual behavior is expected as a condition of employment.

hostile environment harassment
Offensive and unreasonable situations in the workplace that interfere with the ability to work.

Sexual harassment is a serious issue for both men and women in both public- and private-sector organizations. Nearly 12,000 complaints are filed with the EEOC each year; 16 percent of these are filed by males.[74] The good news is that the total number of complaints filed with the EEOC has dropped 20 percent in the last ten years.[75] Settlements in some of these cases incurred substantial litigation costs to the companies involved. At Mitsubishi, for example, the company paid out more than $34 million to 300 women for the rampant sexual harassment to which they were exposed.[76] But it's more than just jury awards. Sexual harassment results in millions lost in absenteeism, low productivity, recruiting problems, and turnover.[77]

Sexual harassment can be regarded as any unwanted activity of a sexual nature that affects an individual's employment. It can occur between members of the opposite or of the same sex, between organization employees or employees and nonemployees. Much of the problem associated with sexual harassment is determining what constitutes this illegal behavior.[78] In 1993, the EEOC cited three situations in which sexual harassment can occur. These are instances where verbal or physical conduct toward an individual

1. creates an intimidating, offensive, or hostile environment;
2. unreasonably interferes with an individual's work; or
3. adversely affects an employee's employment opportunities.

Two types of sexual harassment have been established. The first, **quid pro quo harassment**, is when some type of sexual behavior is expected as a condition of employment. The second, **hostile environment harassment**, is when a working environment is offensive and unreasonably interferes with an employee's ability to work.

Just what constitutes such an environment? The Supreme Court recognized in *Meritor Savings Bank v. Vinson* that Title VII of the Civil Rights Act could be used for hostile environment claims.[79] This case stemmed from a situation in which Ms. Vinson initially refused the sexual advances of her boss. However, out of fear of reprisal, she ultimately conceded. According to court records, it did not stop there. Vinson's boss continued to hassle Vinson, subjecting her to severe hostility, which affected her job.[80] In addition to supporting hostile environment claims, the Meritor case along with *Faragher v. City of Boca Raton* also identified employer liability: That is, in sexual harassment cases, an organization can be held liable for sexual harassment actions by its managers, employees, and even customers![81]

Is what you see in the picture sexual harassment? Perhaps. If the employee believes her supervisor's action interferes with her work and she has asked for the offensive behavior to stop and it hasn't, then she may be experiencing sexual harassment. Actions like this may be part of the reason why more than 20 percent of all working women have reported instances of sexual harassment at work. *(Source: Noel Hendrickson/ Masterfile)*

Although the Meritor case has implications for organizations, how do organizational members determine if something is offensive? For instance, does sexually explicit language in the office create a hostile environment? How about off-color jokes? Pictures of undressed women? It depends on the people in the organization and the environment in which they work. The point here is that we all must be attuned to what makes fellow employees uncomfortable—and if we don't know, we should ask. Smart employers are in tune with the culture and sensitivities of all employees. DuPont's corporate culture and diversity programs, for example, are designed to eliminate sexual harassment through awareness and respect for all individuals.[82] This means understanding one another and, most important, respecting others' rights. Similar programs exist at many companies including Quicken Loans, Verizon Wireless, and Walgreens.

If sexual harassment carries potential costs to the organization, what can a company do to protect itself (see Learning an HRM Skill, p. 88)?[83] The courts want to know two things: did the organization know about, or should it have known about the alleged behavior; and what did management do to stop it?[84] The judgments and awards against organizations today indicate an even greater need for management to educate all employees on sexual harassment matters and have mechanisms available to monitor employees. Victims no longer have to prove that their psychological well-being is seriously affected. The Supreme Court ruled in 1993 in the case of *Harris v. Forklift Systems, Inc.*, that victims need not suffer substantial mental distress to merit a jury award. In June 1998, the Supreme Court ruled that sexual harassment may have occurred even if the employee had not experienced any "negative" job repercussions. In this case, Kimberly Ellerth, a marketing assistant at Burlington Industries, filed harassment charges against her boss because he "touched her, suggested she wear shorter skirts, and told her during a business trip that he could make her job 'very hard or very easy.'" When Ellerth refused, the harasser never "punished" her. In fact, Kimberly even received a promotion during the time the harassment was ongoing. The Supreme Court's decision in this case indicates that "harassment is defined by the ugly behavior of the manager, not by what happened to the worker subsequently."[85]

Remember that the rights of the alleged harasser must be considered too. This means that no action should be taken against someone until a thorough investigation has been conducted. The results of the investigation should be reviewed by an independent and objective individual before any action against the alleged harasser is taken. Even then, the harasser should have an opportunity to respond to the allegation

If a sexual harassment claim goes to trial, courts want to know two things: did the organization know about, or should it have known about the alleged behavior; and what did management do to stop it?

ETHICAL ISSUES IN HRM

How Bad Does It Have to Be?

Sexually explicit language, joking, suggestive remarks, inappropriate touch, sharing a questionable e-mail or photo. Some employees would find some or all behaviors on that list offensive. The fact that some people are offended by some, or all of the above, can place those actions squarely under the heading of "sexual harassment."

Although offering or demanding sexual favors in return for rewards in the workplace clearly qualifies as sexual harassment or sex discrimination, a harder-to-recognize kind of harassment is defined by the EEOC. Such conduct "has the purpose or effect of unreasonably interfering with another employee's job performance or creating an intimidating, hostile, or offensive work environment." Title VII of the 1964 Civil Rights Act prohibits sexual harassment. Any behavior that may be perceived as harassment is prohibited. Suppose someone is told that keeping his or her job, or receiving a raise or plum assignment, depends on submitting to sexual advances or granting sexual favors; that's sexual harassment, pure and simple.

If it happens to you, report it immediately—to the ethics hotline, to your supervisor, or to another supervisor. The reverse situation—offering sexual favors for a job, an assignment, or a raise—can also be sexual harassment. When an employee gains job advantages in exchange for sex, it's considered discrimination against other employees, and that's illegal conduct as well. Everyone loses.

A hostile work environment is one where sexual conduct between coworkers is offensive to either one of them or to an observer, and that may include the actions on our list above. Sexual harassment can have negative effects on employees and on the company, and can lead to reduced productivity. An employee trapped in work areas where sexual harassment is tolerated is, most likely, under stress and may become less pro-

ductive. Customers may gain an unfavorable impression of the company if they think that harassment is being tolerated. Supervisors or coworkers must report any sexual harassment they observe, resulting in an investigation and discipline of those involved. Knowing what is and what is not acceptable and being sensitive to others' feelings is extremely important.

But what if you believe you are being harassed? A word to the offender might be enough. That person may be unaware of your sensitivity to the behavior. If that doesn't work, report the behavior to your supervisor or another manager, to labor or employee relations, or to the president of the company if you have to.

Education and training play an important role in cultivating an environment free of harassment.[86] Many company managers have received training in identifying and eliminating sexual harassment problems. Additional training in larger organizations is usually offered by human resources. Some people may fear that their complaints will be ignored or that reporting an incident will blemish their work record. Neither is the case. Companies must take all complaints of sexual harassment seriously and investigate each thoroughly and discreetly.[87] Both sides need to be considered, and disciplinary action should be taken against proven violators, as well as those who make false accusations.

Ethical questions:

What are your own limits concerning questionable language, jokes, or forwarding e-mails? Do you have the same standards in the workplace? What are your views of those whose standards are either more or less tolerant of questionable language or jokes? How might these differences in perspective cause problems?

---

and participate in a disciplinary hearing if desired. Additionally, an avenue for appeal should also exist for the alleged harasser, heard by someone in a higher level of management who is not associated with the case.

Comparable Worth and Equal Pay Issues

comparable worth
Equal pay for jobs similar in skills, responsibility, working conditions, and effort.

Previously, we discussed the pay gap between men and women. Women are gaining equality slowly, but still earn approximately 80 percent of men's salaries. **Comparable worth** addresses the issues of pay discrepancies of jobs and careers traditionally held by women as compared to those traditionally held by men. For instance, a nurse may be judged to have a comparable job to that of a police officer. Both must be trained, both are licensed to practice, both work under stressful conditions, and both must exhibit high levels of effort. But they are not typically paid the same; male-dominated jobs have traditionally been more highly paid than female-oriented jobs.

Under comparable worth, estimates of the importance of each job are used in determining and equating pay structures. The 1963 Equal Pay Act requires that workers doing essentially the same work must initially be paid the same wage. Later wage differences may exist due to performance, seniority, or merit systems. The act, however, is not directly applicable to comparable worth. Comparable worth proponents want to take the Equal Pay Act one step further. Under such an arrangement, factors present in each job (for example, skills, responsibilities, working conditions, effort) are evaluated. A pay structure is based solely on the presence of such factors on the job. The result is that dissimilar jobs equivalent in terms of skills, knowledge, and abilities are paid similarly.

The point of the comparable worth issue revolves around the economic worth of jobs to employers. If jobs are similar, even though they involve different occupations, why shouldn't they be paid the same? The concern here is one of pay disparities: women still earn less than men. While the disparity is lessening, the fact remains that despite significant progress in affirmative action for women, many may have reached a plateau in their organization. That is, laws may prohibit organizations from keeping qualified women out of high-paying positions, but a "glass ceiling" appears to be holding them down.

This is at the very heart of the largest class action lawsuit ever allowed by federal courts. ***Dukes v. Walmart*** represented more than two million women who have worked at any of the employer's 4,000 stores in the U.S. since 1998. This case alleged that Walmart discouraged the promotion of women into managerial positions. It also claimed that women have been paid less than men across all job categories. The lawsuit sought changes in Walmart's procedures of promoting and paying women, plus more than $1 billion in back pay and damages.[88] In 2011, the U.S. Supreme Court sided with Walmart, explaining that because the company was very large and gave wide discretion for decisions to the individual managers, the plaintiffs could not prove that a common pattern of discrimination was sanctioned by top management. Many of the women who were part of the class action lawsuit have vowed to pursue their cases against Walmart individually, but the Supreme Court decision made their quest more expensive and time consuming.[89]

The **glass ceiling** is an analogy explaining why women and minorities aren't more widely represented at the top of today's organizations. The expression depicts an image of a woman, minority, or other protected group, who can see the next step on the climb up the corporate ladder, but is unable reach it because there is a glass ceiling in the way. According to the Glass Ceiling Commission, it indicates "institutional and psychological practices, and the limited advancement and mobility of men and women of diverse racial and ethnic backgrounds."[90] It appears that despite significant gains by minorities and women in entry to organizations, women hold less than 15 percent of senior management positions in the United States.[91] Women in other parts of the world fare a little better. The percentage of women in senior managerial positions worldwide was approximately 20 percent in 2010, virtually unchanged from five years ago. Women in Thailand lead the world, holding 45 percent of senior management jobs, followed by 36 percent in Russia, Hong Kong, and the Philippines. The toughest country for women to gain a top management position? Japan, where only 10 percent of top management positions are held by women.[92]

To begin to correct this invisible barrier, the OFCCP is expanding its audit compliance reviews. In these reviews, the auditors look to see if government contractors do indeed have training and development programs operating to provide career growth to the affected groups. Should these be lacking, the OFCCP may take legal action to ensure compliance. For example, an audit of the Coca-Cola Company revealed several violations. Consequently, Coca-Cola, while admitting no wrongdoing, made several internal changes to improve the career opportunities of both women and minorities.[93] Beyond those organizations covered under the OFCCP, several are implementing policies and changing the organization's culture to enhance opportunities for women and minorities.

Dukes v. Walmart Stores
Lawsuit brought on behalf of 1.6 million women who have worked at Walmart since 1998 claiming discrimination in pay and promotions.

glass ceiling
The invisible barrier that blocks females and minorities from ascending into upper levels of an organization.

Exhibit 3-6
Equal Pay Issues
Women are gaining equality slowly, but still earn approximately 80 percent of men's salaries.

© 2009 Ted Goff

"We completely disregard gender when offering compensation. Unless you're the wrong gender."

(Source: © Ted Goff)

Sexual Orientation

Protection against discrimination because of an employee's sexual orientation or gender identity is not provided by federal law, but 21 states and the District of Columbia have laws prohibiting discrimination based on sexual orientation Federal employees are protected from sexual orientation discrimination by Executive Order 13087. A number of other states provide limited protection, and many cities and municipalities provide protection as well. In addition to the protection provided by state, city, and municipal governments for lesbian, gay, bisexual, and transgendered (LGBT) employees, corporate America is increasingly implementing policies that prohibit discrimination based on sexual orientation. A 2010 survey found, 69 percent of Fortune 100 companies and 41 percent of Fortune 500 companies had policies prohibiting discrimination based on gender identity. Insurance company Aetna added gender reassignment surgery as a benefit to employees and offered it to companies that contract with Aetna for insurance services.[94]

Although sexual orientation is not protected by federal law, claims for nontraditional workplace harassment, including same sex harassment, are on the increase. This may be the result of claims filed by employees who are victims of harassment because they do not fit traditional gender stereotypes for behavior or dress, and file claims based on gender discrimination.[95]

A related issue that may arise involves conflicts between sexual orientation discrimination and accommodation of religious beliefs of employees who do not approve of the lifestyle of another employee. Employees may cite religious beliefs as a refusal to work with LGBT employees or clients, or to participate in diversity training. Refusal to work with another employee because of sexual orientation may qualify as an undue hardship, especially if sexual orientation is protected by law in that state.[96]

English Only Laws and Policies

Can an organization require its employees to speak only English on the job? The answer is a definite "maybe."

Title VII protects employees from national origin discrimination, so employers must allow employees to converse in their native languages. On the other hand, employers may have the need to have a common language spoken at the work site during business hours.[97] Employers must be able to communicate effectively with all employees, especially when safety or productive efficiency matters are at stake.[98] This, they claim, is a business necessity.

Consequently, if it is a valid job requirement, the practice could be permitted. An employer's desire to have one language may stem from the fact that some workers may use bilingual capabilities to harass and insult other workers in a language they cannot understand. With today's ever-increasing concern with protecting employees, especially women, from hostile environments, English-only rules serve as one means of reasonable care.

A counterpoint to this English-only rule firmly rests with the workforce diversity issue. Workers in today's organizations come from all nationalities and speak different languages. More than 30 million workers in the United States speak a language other than English. What about these individuals' desire to speak their language, communicate effectively with their peers, and maintain their cultural heritage? To them, English-only rules are discriminatory in terms of national origin in that they create an adverse impact for non–English-speaking individuals.[99]

Appearance and Weight Discrimination

The statistics on pay differences leave little doubt that employers discriminate against people who are heavier than average. Heavy workers are paid an average of $1.25 an hour less than their average-size counterparts. Women who are slightly heavier than

ETHICAL ISSUES IN HRM

English-Only Rules

Central Station Casino in Colorado instituted an "English-Only" policy for their housekeeping department after a non-Spanish-speaking employee thought that other employees were talking about her in Spanish. The policy was defended as necessary for safety reasons. To enforce the policy, managers and non-Hispanic employees would shout "English, English!" at Hispanic employees when they encountered them in the halls of the hotel. Because of the embarrassment and distress this caused, the Hispanic employees filed a complaint with the Equal Employment Opportunity Commission.[100]

The EEOC settled the Central Station Casino complaint with a settlement of $1.5 million awarded to the Hispanic employees. Central Station Casino was directed to inform all employees that there was no English-only policy and provide training to ensure that discrimination does not occur.

Ethical questions:

Should employers be permitted to require that only English be spoken in the workplace? Would it make a difference if it were a family-owned Chinese restaurant? What if it is necessary for successful performance or to prevent a safety or health hazard? Should the Supreme Court view this as a discriminatory

practice, or render a decision that would create a single, nationwide standard on English-only? What do you think about this issue?

(Source: T. Ozonas/Masterfile)

average-weight women earn 6% percent less, and very heavy women make 24 percent less.[101] One study found that obese workers are perceived as less intelligent, so their ideas may not carry the same influence as average size workers, affecting hiring, pay, and promotion decisions. Discrimination based on weight and appearance isn't likely to end soon. Federal equal employment laws don't protect weight or appearance, and Michigan is the only state that has a law protecting workers from weight related discrimination. As mentioned in our discussion of adverse impact, weight and height requirements must be related to job performance, and employers may be concerned that excess weight may limit an applicant's ability to do the job.[102]

Workers with other appearance issues such as piercings and tattoos are having a little better luck, but very little. Piercings and tattoos are only protected if they worn for religious reasons, therefore protected by Title VII.[103]

HRM in a Global Environment

Does HRM face the same laws globally? In other words, are the laws presented above the same throughout the world? Absolutely not. Unfortunately, there are not enough pages in this text to adequately cover the laws affecting HRM in any given country. What we can do, however, is to highlight some of the differences and suggest that you need to know the laws and regulations that apply in your locale. To illustrate how laws and regulations shape HRM practices, we can highlight some primary legislation that influences HRM practices in China, Canada, India, Australia, and Germany.

Women in China rarely report discrimination or sexual harassment because of fears of retaliation by employers.
(Source: Lou Linwei/Alamy)

China

Equal Employment Laws in China resemble those in the U.S. in the 1950s. Applicants are commonly asked questions about age, height, weight, and parents' employment. In some cases, applicants are even asked their blood type, based on theories that it indicates personal characteristics, similar to the way people believe astrological signs indicate personality. The China Employment Promotion Law allowing workers to file discrimination lawsuits against employers was passed in 2008, but progress has been slow.[104]

Although China's first law against sexual harassment of women in the workplace was passed in 2007, at least 20 percent of women workers in China say that they have been victims of sexual harassment. Less than half of those women report the abuse for fear of losing their jobs and women who report harassment to authorities have a less than 30 percent chance of having the complaint ruled in their favor.[105]

Canada

Canadian laws pertaining to HRM practices closely parallel those in the United States. The Canadian Human Rights Act provides federal legislation that prohibits discrimination on the basis of race, religion, age, marital status, sex, physical or mental disability, or national origin. This act governs practices throughout the country. Canada's HRM environment, however, differs somewhat from that in the United States in that more lawmaking is done at the provincial level in Canada. For example, discrimination on the basis of language is prohibited nowhere in Canada except Quebec.

India

Over 26 percent of women workers in India report that they have been victims of sexual harassment.[106] India's Supreme Court recently declared sexual harassment to be illegal under a constitutional guarantee of the right to gender equity and requires all employers with more than 50 employees to have a sexual harassment prevention policy. These protections do not seem to be a match for a culture that doesn't take it seriously. Caste-based discrimination remains a barrier to equal employment in spite of legal and constitutional protection, reaffirming that ancient cultures are slow to change.

Australia

Australia's discrimination laws were not enacted until the 1980s. The laws that exist, however, generally apply to discrimination and affirmative action for women. Yet gender opportunities for women in Australia appear to lag behind those in the United States. In Australia, a significant proportion of the workforce is unionized. The higher percentage of unionized workers has placed increased importance on industrial relations specialists in Australia and reduced the control of line managers over workplace labor issues. In 1997, Australia overhauled its industrial labor relations laws with the objective of increasing productivity and reducing union power. The Workplace Relations Bill gives employers greater flexibility to negotiate directly with employees on pay, hours, and benefits. It also simplifies regulation of labor-management relations.

Germany

The General Equal Treatment Act was passed in 2006 to fulfill European Union guidelines. The act made it easier to prosecute employers for discrimination against women in the workplace. German women make 77 percent less than men and even under the new law, it's still difficult to take an employer to court because of a high burden of proof on the plaintiff. The wage gap hasn't changed much since the law was implemented, and the ratio of women to men in senior management positions remains low.

Summary

(This summary relates to the Learning Outcomes identified on page 56.) After having read this chapter you can now

1. **Identify the groups protected under the Civil Rights Act, Title VII.** The Civil Rights Act of 1964, Title VII, gives individuals protection on the basis of race, color, religion, sex, and national origin. In addition to those protected under the 1964 act, amendments to the act, as well as subsequent legislation, give protection to the disabled, veterans, and individuals over age 40. In addition, state laws may supplement this list and include categories such as marital status.

2. **Discuss the importance of the Equal Employment Opportunity Act.** The Equal Employment Opportunity Act of 1972 is an important amendment to the Civil Rights Act of 1964 as it granted the EEOC enforcement powers to police the provisions of the act.

3. **Describe affirmative action plans.** Affirmative action plans are good-faith efforts by organizations to actively recruit and hire protected group members and show measurable results. Such plans are voluntary actions by an organization.

4. **Define what is meant by the terms adverse impact, adverse treatment, and protected group members.** An adverse impact is any consequence of employment that results in a disparate rate of selection, promotion, or termination of protected group members. Adverse treatment occurs when members of a protected group receive different treatment than other employees. A protected group member is any individual who is afforded protection under discrimination laws.

5. **Identify the important components of the Americans with Disabilities Act and ADAAA.** The Americans with Disabilities Act of 1990 provides employment protection for individuals who have qualified disabilities. The act also requires organizations to make reasonable accommodations to provide qualified individuals access to the job. The ADAAA made it easier for individuals to establish the existence of a disability.

6. **Explain the coverage of the Family and Medical Leave Act.** The Family and Medical Leave Act grants up to 12 weeks of unpaid leave for family or medical matters.

7. **Explain business defenses for discrimination charges.** A business can protect itself from discrimination charges first by having HRM practices that do not adversely affect protected groups, through supported claims of job relatedness, bona fide occupational qualifications, or a valid seniority system.

8. **Specify the HRM importance of the *Griggs v. Duke Power case*.** *Griggs v. Duke Power* was one of the most important Supreme Court rulings that pertain to EEO. Based on this case, items used to screen applicants had to be related to the job. Additionally, post-Griggs, the burden was on the employer to prove that discrimination did not occur.

9. **Explain the different types of sexual harassment.** Sexual harassment is a serious problem existing in today's enterprises. Sexual harassment is defined as any verbal or physical conduct toward an individual that (1) creates an intimidating, offensive, or hostile environment; (2) unreasonably interferes with an individual's

work; or (3) adversely affects an employee's employment opportunities. These can be described as quid pro quo harassment that requires some type of sexual behavior as a condition of employment or hostile environment harassment that creates an offensive and unreasonable atmosphere that interferes with the ability to work.

10. Discuss the term "glass ceiling." The glass ceiling is an invisible barrier existing in today's organizations that prevents minorities and women from ascending to higher employment levels in the workplace.

11. Identify legal issues faced when managing HR in a global environment. International employment law differs widely, reflecting government and culture. Laws and wages in China are enforced loosely, and deceptive practices are widespread. Canadian laws are quite similar to U.S. laws. Australian employees are likely to be unionized and German employees are given more representation in company decisions than most countries.

Demonstrating Comprehension

QUESTIONS FOR REVIEW

1. What is the Civil Rights Act of 1964, and what groups does it protect?
2. What are the implications of the *Griggs v. Duke Power* case for HRM?
3. What is an adverse impact? How does it differ from adverse treatment?
4. What is meant by "reasonable accommodation" as it pertains to the Americans with Disabilities Act of 1990?
5. Explain why an employee might file a claim of retaliation and why retaliation claims are on the rise.
6. What job protection is offered to veterans?
7. In what ways do employment laws differ in a global environment?
8. Identify and explain how organizations can use BFOQs business necessity or seniority systems to defend charges of discrimination.
9. What is sexual harassment? Identify and describe the three elements that may constitute sexual harassment.
10. What is the purpose of the FMLA and who does it cover?

Key Terms

4/5ths rule
adverse (disparate) impact
adverse (disparate) treatment
affirmative action
Age Discrimination in Employment Act (ADEA)
Albemarle Paper Company v. Moody
Americans with Disabilities Act of 1990
Bakke v. Regents of the University of California at Davis Medical School
bona fide occupational qualification (BFOQ)

Civil Rights Act of 1866
Civil Rights Act of 1964
Civil Rights Act of 1991
comparable worth
Equal Employment Opportunity Act (EEOA)
Equal Employment Opportunity Commission (EEOC)
Family and Medical Leave Act of 1993
Genetic Information Nondiscrimination Act
glass ceiling
Griggs v. Duke Power Company

hostile environment harassment
McDonnell-Douglas Corp. v. Green
Pregnancy Discrimination Act of 1978
quid pro quo harassment
reasonable accommodation
reverse discrimination
seniority systems
sexual harassment
Title VII
Uniformed Services Employment and Reemployment Rights Act of 1994
Wards Cove Packing Company v. Atonio

Linking Concepts to Practice   DISCUSSION QUESTIONS

1. "Affirmative action does not work. When you're hired under an affirmative action program, you're automatically labeled as such and are rarely recognized for the value that you can bring to an organization." Do you agree or disagree with the statement? Defend your position.
2. "Since over half of all U.S. employees work for small businesses, equal employment laws shouldn't provide any exceptions for small employers." Do you agree or disagree with the statement? Defend your position.
3. "If all organizations would hire based solely on the ability to do the job, there would be no need for equal employment opportunity laws." Do you agree or disagree? Defend your position.
4. "Sexual harassment occurs between two people only. The company should not be held liable for the actions of a few wayward supervisors." Do you agree or disagree with this statement? Explain.

Making A Difference   SERVICE LEARNING PROJECTS

Equal employment based on purely on an individual's abilities is everyone's right, yet for many it isn't a well-understood concept. Chapter 3 offers many opportunities for you to apply EEO concepts in a service activity.

- Develop a presentation for high school or middle school students informing them about their rights in the workplace and how to defend themselves from discrimination or harassment. Other opportunities to inform that age group might include presentations to youth groups, after school programs, and church groups.
- Contact the office for veteran's affairs in your community or college and ask about opportunities to volunteer, to assist veterans, or to help with programs offered through the office.
- Contact the USO, National Guard, or any branch of the active military and ask about volunteer opportunities, including helping with local send off or welcome home ceremonies.

As you put your service learning experience together, keep a journal of your activities, the time you spend, contact information for the people you work with, and your thoughts about the process. When you're finished, make a presentation to your class about the experience and what you learned. What concepts from Chapter 3 were you able to apply?

Developing Diagnostic and Analytical Skills

Case Application 3-A: DIVERSITY IS FASHIONABLE

Carla Grubb was hired at Abercrombie and Fitch for what she believed was a job on the sales floor. Instead, she found herself dusting, cleaning windows, and vacuuming the store. "I was always doing cleaning—they said I was a good window washer," said Ms. Grubb, who happens to be black. "I should have received the same treatment as everyone else. It made me feel bad. No one should be judged by the color of their skin."[107]

The EEOC agreed with Grubb and filed suit against Abercrombie and Fitch for recruiting employees based on an image the company wanted to project and staffing their stores with sales people that were overwhelmingly white and athletic, just like their advertising and in-store photos. Minority applicants found themselves hired only to do low visibility and back-of-the-store jobs like stocking and cleaning up, often after retail hours. The company was also found to have refused to hire minority students with impressive work and school records. The percentage of minority managers at Abercrombie stores was far below industry averages.

Abercrombie settled the suit to the tune of $50 million.[108] They didn't admit any guilt, but did agree to do a better job of hiring and promoting minorities and depicting more minorities in their advertisements and catalogs.

1. Suggest several ways that Abercrombie and Fitch can increase their number of minority employees to an appropriate level.
2. How can employers maintain a certain "look" or "image" to their retail sales force and not violate EEOC regulations? Explain with examples.
3. Take a look at the Abercrombie and Fitch website (www.abercrombie.com) or visit an Abercrombie and Fitch store. What evidence do you see that they are making progress toward their diversity goals?
4. Are there other employers that you feel need to make a better effort at diversity? Can their lack of diversity be justified with bona fide occupational qualifications (BFOQ)?

Case Application 3-B: WHEN OVERSIGHT FAILS

What's in a job? For most workers, jobs entail specific and routine work activities. These work activities generally take place on the employer's premise where many different people come together to achieve certain goals. There should be, however, one common element to all work activities—whatever occurs in the office should be related to organizational efforts. Every once in a while, though, this concept evades some employers. When it does, it may be costly for the organization. Consider the lesson learned at Federal Express regarding an incident that happened in FedEx's Middletown, Pennsylvania, facility.[109]

Marion Shaub worked for FedEx at its Middletown facility. At the time of her employment, Shaub was the only female tractor-trailer driver at her facility. Although being the only female in this often male-dominated job initially brought about some gentle teasing, the jokes and actions by fellow employees gradually turned ugly. Shaub was often subjected to anti-female comments and questioned as to why she wanted to work a man's job. Shaub tried to ignore the comments directed toward her, but they became more pronounced and mean-spirited. Although she was attempting to do her job to the best of her abilities, the comments got nastier. She eventually saw them as threats against her. And that's where, in Shaub's mind, the line had been crossed.

Shaub reported to her supervisor that the "guys" were creating a threatening work environment for her. She had hoped that her male supervisor would speak to fellow employees and have such abuse stopped. But it didn't work out that way. Instead, after filing her complaint, Shaub was subjected to even more abuse, this time including the sabotage of the brakes of her truck. Moreover, as a general rule, when a package is over a certain weight, two FedEx employees are expected to handle the carton. When Shaub had such a package, she found that no one would help her.

To Shaub's dismay, FedEx officials in the Middletown facility did nothing to stop the harassment. Her complaints and requests for help fell on deaf ears. Finally, in desperation, she filed a suit against FedEx for sex discrimination and retaliation.

Under federal discrimination laws, it's the employer's responsibility to ensure that the workplace is safe and free from any form of discrimination. Regardless of employees' background, gender, age, and the like, individuals are not to be treated differently. But when discrimination occurs and management does little or nothing about it, the organization can be held liable.

For FedEx, Shaub's experiences proved to be a painful and expensive lesson. After conducting an investigation and finding her accusations to be factual, the EEOC awarded Shaub more than $3 million. This included monies for her lost wages, the pain and suffering she endured, and $2.5 million in punitive damages because FedEx didn't protect her civil rights as an employee.

Questions:

1. Where do you believe HR failed Marion Shaub in this case? Explain.
2. What do you believe FedEx must do differently to ensure that such an event does not occur again?
3. What effect on (a) corporate image and (b) attracting female employees to the organization do you believe this case has had on FedEx? Describe.

Working with a Team   WHAT'S YOUR PERCEPTION?

Could these situations demonstrate sexual harassment or prohibitive behaviors? Answer true or false to each question. Make whatever assumptions you need to make to form your opinion. Form into groups of three or four students and discuss each of your responses. Where differences exist, come to some consensus on the situation. You can then look at the footnote for suggested responses.[110]

1. A female supervisor frequently praises the work of a highly competent male employee.
2. A male employee prominently posts a centerfold from a female pornographic magazine.
3. A female employee voluntarily accepts a date with her male supervisor.
4. A male employee is given favored work assignments in exchange for arranging dates for his boss.
5. Male employees put rubber snakes, spiders, and mice in the lunch box of a female coworker because she screams when she is surprised by them. Male coworkers do not receive the same kind of teasing.

6. A client pressures a female salesperson for dates and sexual favors in exchange for a large purchase.
7. A female requests that her male assistant stay in her hotel room to save on expenses while out of town at a conference and holds acceptance as a job condition for continued employment.
8. A male has asked two female coworkers to stop embarrassing him by telling jokes of a sexual nature and sharing their sexual fantasies, but they continue, telling him a "real man wouldn't be embarrassed."
9. Although he has shared with his coworker that rubbing his shoulders and arms, calling him "Babe" in front of his coworkers, and pinching him is offensive, she continues to touch him in a way that makes him feel uncomfortable.
10. Al tells Marge an offensive joke, but when Marge says "Al, I don't appreciate your nasty jokes," Al responds, "I'm sorry, Marge, you're right, I shouldn't have told that one at work."

Learning an HRM Skill   INVESTIGATING A HARASSMENT COMPLAINT

About the skill: Harassment, sexual or otherwise, is a major issue for today's organizations. Given the rulings at all court levels, organizations can and should limit their liability. There are nine recommended steps.

1. **Issue a sexual harassment policy describing what constitutes harassment and what inappropriate behavior is.** Just stating that harassment is unacceptable at your organization is not enough. This policy must identify specific unacceptable

behaviors. The more explicit these identifications, the less chance of misinterpretation later on.

2. *Institute a procedure (or link to an existing one) to investigate harassment charges.* Employees, as well as the courts, need to understand what avenue is available for an employee to levy a complaint. This, too, should be clearly stated in the policy and widely disseminated to employees.

3. *Inform all employees of the sexual harassment policy.* Educate employees (via training) about the policy and how it will be enforced. Don't assume that the policy will convey the information simply because it is a policy. It must be effectively communicated to all employees. Some training may be required to help in this understanding.

4. *Train management personnel in how to deal with harassment charges and in what responsibility they have to the individual and the organization.* Poor supervisory practices in this area can expose the company to tremendous liability. Managers must be trained in how to recognize signs of harassment and where to go to help the victim. Because of the magnitude of the issue, a manager's performance evaluation should reinforce this competency.

5. *Investigate all harassment charges immediately.* All means all—even those that you suspect are invalid. You must give each charge of harassment your attention and investigate it by searching for clues, witnesses, and so on. Investigating the charge is also consistent with our societal view of justice. Remember, the alleged harasser also has rights. These, too, must be protected by giving the individual the opportunity to respond. You may also have an objective party review the data before implementing your decision.

6. *Take corrective action as necessary.* Discipline the harassers and "make whole" the harassed individual. If the charge can be substantiated, you must take corrective action, up to dismissing the individual. If the punishment does not fit the crime, you may be reinforcing or condoning the behavior. The harassed individual should also be given whatever was taken away. For example, if the sexual behavior led to an individual's resignation, making the person whole would mean reinstatement, with full back pay and benefits.

7. *Continue to follow up on the matter to ensure that no further harassment occurs or that retaliation does not occur.* One concern individuals have in coming forward with sexual harassment charges is the possibility of retaliation against them—especially if the harasser has been disciplined. Continue to observe what affects these individuals through follow-up conversations with them.

8. *Periodically review turnover records to determine if a potential problem may be arising.* (This may be EEO audits, exit interviews, and the like.) A wealth of information at your disposal may offer indications of problems. For example, if only minorities are resigning in a particular department, it may indicate that a serious problem exists. Pay attention to your regular reports and search for trends that may be indicated.

9. *Don't forget to privately recognize individuals who bring these matters forward.* Without their courageous effort, the organization might have faced with tremendous liability. These individuals took a risk in coming forward. You should show your appreciation for that risk. Besides, if others know that such risk is worthwhile, they may feel more comfortable in coming to you when any type of problem exists.

Enhancing Your Communication Skills

1. Research claims of discrimination against Walmart since the class action case was dismissed, and other current cases dealing with equal employment. How far have they progressed in the court system? What changes have the affected organizations made as a result of the complaints? Present your findings to your class with a visual aid such as presentation slides or a short, relevant video news clip.

2. Contact your local EEO office (may be called Human Rights Commission or Fair Employment Practice Agencies). Determine what equal employment opportunity laws exist in your state that go beyond those required under federal law. Provide a two- to three-page write-up of your findings.

3. Visit your college's EEO/Affirmative Action officer. Find out what specific EEO requirements on your campus affect students, faculty, and staff in matters such as recruiting, promotion, sexual harassment, and so on. Provide a two- to three-page write up of your findings.

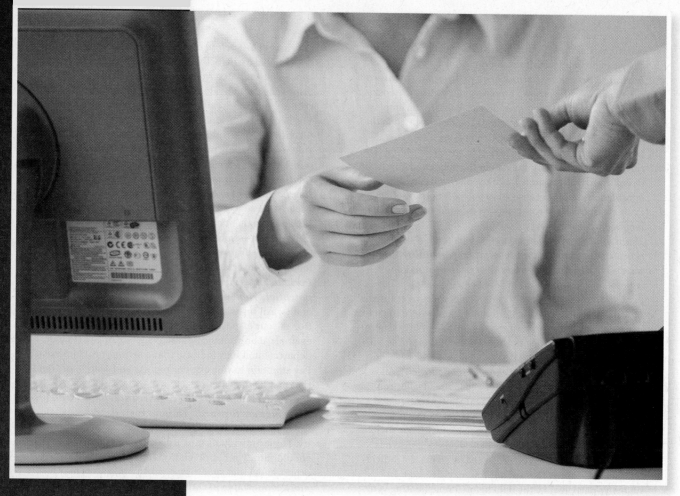

(Source: Masterfile)

After reading this chapter, you will be able to

1. Explain the intent of the Privacy Act, the Drug-Free Workplace Act, the Fair Credit Reporting Act, and their effects on HRM.

2. Explain employer concerns about social media use and the components of an effective social media policy.

3. Describe the provisions of the Worker Adjustment and Retraining Notification Act.

4. Identify the pros and cons of employee drug testing.

5. Discuss the benefits of using honesty tests in hiring.

6. Explain legal and ethical issues involved in monitoring employees.

7. Discuss the implications of the employment-at-will doctrine and identify the five exceptions to it.

8. Define discipline and the contingency factors that determine the severity of discipline.

9. Describe the general guidelines for administering discipline.

10. Explain the elements of the Hot Stove Rule and their application to discipline in the workplace.

11. Identify important procedures to follow when firing an employee.

Employee Rights and Discipline

4

Most HR professionals feel that their employee handbook and discipline policies are well thought out and comprehensive, thorough enough to cover nearly every situation and contingency... then along comes a situation that stumps even the most experienced HR managers. How would you have handled these actual situations?

- While on duty one night, a security guard was frightened by a group of ghosts. The guard claimed he was too frightened to continue working and called his supervisor asking to be excused from duty. The supervisor and another coworker were unable to see the ghosts that the guard was pointing out to them. The guard was fired for misconduct several hours later. When seeking unemployment benefits, the guard claimed that he was fired wrongfully. The administrative law judge agreed that seeing ghosts seems to make one unfit to be a security guard, yet ruled in the guard's favor and awarded him unemployment benefits, saying that the ghost sighting wasn't the type of misconduct that would disqualify him from receiving benefits.[1]

- A New York City police officer claimed his wife was angry about his decision against retiring after 20 years on the force, so she spiked his meatballs with "six marijuana doobies" in hopes that he would fail a drug test, forcing him to retire. Her plan worked... sort of. Upon failing a random drug test, he was fired and stripped of his pension and benefits. The cop fought the firing with the "meatball defense," claiming that his firing over one failed drug test was "arbitrary, capricious, unreasonable, and unconstitutional" because he didn't know he was eating the drug in his dinner. Evidence proved that the levels of marijuana found in the cop's hair samples were far beyond those that would be caused by eating his fill of marijuana-laced meatballs and his firing was upheld.[2]

- Two sanitation workers in Missouri were caught on video using a city truck to take 50–60 cases of expired Budweiser from the city landfill. The beer was part of a shipment of 1,500 cases sent to the landfill by a local Bud distributing company. The city HR Director said the beer became city property once delivered to the landfill, so the employees were stealing the beer. One worker quit, one worker faced disciplinary action, and the stolen beer was never recovered.[3]

- A Walmart greeter was "sacked" for greeting customers with a computer-generated photo of himself wearing only a carefully placed Walmart bag, telling customers that Walmart was cutting costs and the sack was the new uniform. His application for unemployment compensation was rejected. The administrative law judge said that "a reasonable person would know that showing a naked body wearing a Walmart sack would not be good for business."[4]

- A New York UPS worker was fired in 2008 after throwing a package at another employee, but kept showing up for work for two more years. In 2010, UPS filed suit to bar him from the facility claiming that his knowledge of the security system made him a risk.[5]

- The Norfolk, Virginia Community Services Board had the opposite problem when they discovered an employee who had never reported to work, yet collected a salary for twelve years. The woman collected an estimated $300,000 to $480,000 plus full benefits before being discovered in 2010 and subsequently fired.[6]

Looking Ahead

Is there any way an employer could have prevented these situations? How can employers help employees learn how to use good judgment?

Introduction

Both employees and employers have rights, and it's the responsibility of HR to sort them out when things don't go according to plan. In this chapter, we'll explore HR's role in protecting the rights of employees and employers alike. These rights are evolving as the workplace changes due to societal expectations, new technologies, and how the courts refine the way rights are applied.

Employee Rights Legislation and the HRM Implications

For starters, some laws have been created to give specific protection to employees. These laws include the Privacy Act, the Drug-Free Workplace Act, the Employee Polygraph Protection Act, and the Worker Adjustment and Retraining Notification Act. Let's briefly explore each of these.

The Privacy Act

Privacy Act
Requires federal government agencies to make information in an individual's personnel file available to him or her.

When an organization begins the hiring process, it typically establishes a personnel file for that person. The file is maintained throughout a person's employment. Any pertinent information, such as the completed application, letters of recommendation, performance evaluations, or disciplinary warnings, is kept in the file. Originally, the contents of these files were known only to those who had access to them—usually managers and HRM personnel. The **Privacy Act of 1974** sought to change that imbalance of information. This act, applicable only to federal government agencies, requires that an employee's personnel file be open for inspection.[7] This means that employees are permitted to review their files periodically to ensure that the information contained within is accurate. The Privacy Act also gives these federal employees the right to review letters of recommendation written on their behalf.

Even though this act applies solely to federal workers, state legislatures have passed similar laws giving similar rights to employees of state government and private businesses. These laws are often more comprehensive and include protection regarding how employers share information on past and current employees. For HRM, a key question is how employees should be given access to their files. Although the information contained within rightfully may be open for inspection, certain restrictions must be addressed. First, any information the employee has waived his or her right to review must be kept separate. For instance, job applicants often waive their right to see letters of recommendation written for them with the intent that the person writing the letter will be more objective. When that happens, human resources is not obligated to make that information available to the employee. Second, an employee can't simply demand to immediately see his or her file; there is typically a twenty-four-hour turnaround time. Consequently, organizations frequently establish special review procedures. For example, whether the employee can review the file alone or only in the presence of an HRM representative is up to each organization. In either case, personnel files generally are not permitted to leave the HRM area. And although an individual may take notes about the file's contents, copying the file often is not permitted.

The increasing use of Human Resource Information Systems (HRIS) systems means that many organizations now keep nearly all employee records on a computer or database. These records still need to be readily accessible and readable if requested by an employee, the Immigration and Naturalization Service (INS), the EEOC, Department of

Labor, or any other government agency that conducts an audit. Whether employee records are kept on paper or in computer files, access must be limited only to those with a "need to know." Paper files must be locked up and computer files must have restricted access to protect employee privacy.[8]

> Human Resource Information Systems (HRIS) are an important tool to store employee records and make them accessible.

The Fair Credit Reporting Act

Suppose you were in charge of hiring fifty new cashiers for the opening of a large new discount retail store. You're checking references and making criminal background checks, but just to be on the safe side, you would like to check their credit reports to make sure the applicants aren't in any financial trouble that may tempt them to be less than honest when handling cash. Can you do it? Do you need to tell anyone?

The answer to both questions is yes. Companies are held accountable to the **Fair Credit Reporting Act of 1971**, an extension to the Privacy Act that outlines procedures and responsibilities of organizations that use credit reports. The purpose of checking credit reports is to obtain information about the individual's "character, general reputation," and various other personal characteristics. Typically, companies can obtain this information by two approaches. The first is through a credit reporting agency, similar to the process in a loan application. In this instance, the employer must obtain permission from the individual to obtain a credit report from a credit bureau. If an applicant is rejected based on information in the report, the individual must be provided a copy of the credit report, as well as a means for appealing the accuracy of the findings. The second type of credit report is obtained through a third-party investigation. Under this arrangement, not only is the individual's credit checked, but the applicant's friends, neighbors, and associates are interviewed regarding the applicant's lifestyle, spending habits, and character. For an organization to use this type of approach, the applicant must be informed of the process in writing and, as with the credit report, must be notified of the report's details if the information is used to negatively affect an employment decision. Keep in mind, however, that how the information is used must be job relevant. If, for example, an organization denies employment to an individual who once filed for bankruptcy, and this information has no bearing on the individual's ability to do the job, the organization may be opening itself up to a challenge in the courts.

> Fair Credit Reporting Act
> Requires an organization to notify job candidates of its intent to check into their credit.

The Drug-Free Workplace Act

The **Drug-Free Workplace Act of 1988** was passed to help keep the problem of substance abuse from entering the workplace. Under the act, all individuals with federal contracts or grants and organizations with federal grants or contracts over $100,000[9] are required to actively pursue a drug-free workplace. In addition, the act requires employees who hold certain jobs in companies regulated by the Department of Transportation (DOT) and the Nuclear Regulatory Commission to be subjected to drug tests. For example, long-haul truck drivers, regulated by the DOT, are required to take drug tests.

Other stipulations address organizations covered under this act. For example, the organization must establish its drug-free work environment policy and disseminate it to its employees. This policy must spell out employee expectations in terms of being substance free and explain penalties for noncompliance. In addition, the organization must provide substance-abuse awareness programs to its employees.[10] No doubt this act has created difficulties for organizations. To comply with the act, they must obtain information about their employees. The whole issue of drug testing in today's companies is a major one, and we'll come back to its applications later in this chapter.

> Drug-Free Workplace Act
> Requires specific government-related groups to ensure that their workplace is drug free.

Can an organization use a polygraph in its HRM activities? Probably not, however, under certain circumstances (such as assisting in resolving an employee theft when a chief suspect has been identified) and for certain jobs *(such as those involving security), they can and do.* *(Source: Tek Image/Photo Researchers, Inc.)*

Polygraph Protection Act Prohibits the use of lie detectors in screening all job applicants.

Worker Adjustment and Retraining Notification (WARN) Act Specifies employers' notification requirements when closing down a plant or laying off large numbers of workers.

The Polygraph Protection Act

As a criminal investigation analyst applicant for the Federal Bureau of Investigation (FBI), you are asked to submit to a polygraph test as a condition of employment. Unsure of what will transpire, you agree to be tested. During the examination, you are asked if you have ever used the drug Ecstasy. You respond that you never have, but the polygraph records that you are not telling the truth. Because suspicion of illegal substance use is grounds for disqualification from the job, you are removed from consideration. Can this organization use the polygraph information against you? If the job involves security operations, it can!

The **Polygraph Protection Act** prohibits employers in the private sector from using polygraph tests (often referred to as lie-detector tests) in all employment decisions.[11] Based on the law, companies may no longer use these tests to screen all job applicants. In general, polygraph tests have been found to have little job-related value, which makes their effectiveness questionable.[12] However, the Employee Polygraph Protection Act did not eliminate their use in organizations altogether. The law permits their use, for example, when theft occurs in the organization, but this process is regulated, too. The polygraph cannot be used in a "witch hunt." For example, the Employee Polygraph Protection Act prohibits employers with a theft in the organization from testing all employees in an attempt to determine the guilty party. However, if an investigation into the theft points to a particular employee, then the employer can ask that employee to submit to a polygraph. Even in this case, however, the employee has the right to refuse to take a polygraph test without fear of retaliation from the employer. And in cases in which one does submit to the test, the employee must receive, in advance, a list of questions that will be asked. Furthermore, the employee has the right to challenge the results if he or she believes the test was inappropriately administered. Exhibit 4-1 contains the Department of Labor's Notice of Polygraph Testing explaining employee rights.

The Worker Adjustment and Retraining Notification Act

During their restructuring and eventual sale to Whirlpool, Maytag closed a factory in Galesburg, Illinois, putting 1,600 employees out of work and closed the original Maytag facility in Newton, Iowa, idling another 2,600 employees.[13] These small communities would have been economically devastated if they were not given advance notice of the closings and loss of jobs. The **Worker Adjustment and Retraining Notification (WARN) Act of 1988,**[14] sometimes called the Plant Closing Bill, places specific requirements on employers considering significant changes in staffing levels.

Under WARN, an organization employing one hundred or more individuals must notify workers sixty days in advance if it is going to close its facility or lay off fifty or more individuals.[15] The state officials with responsibility for displaced workers and local elected officials also must be notified. Should a company fail to provide this advance notice, the penalty is to pay employees a sum of money equal to salary and benefits for each day

EMPLOYEE RIGHTS

EMPLOYEE POLYGRAPH PROTECTION ACT

THE UNITED STATES DEPARTMENT OF LABOR WAGE AND HOUR DIVISION

The Employee Polygraph Protection Act prohibits most private employers from using lie detector tests either for pre-employment screening or during the course of employment.

PROHIBITIONS   Employers are generally prohibited from requiring or requesting any employee or job applicant to take a lie detector test, and from discharging, disciplining, or discriminating against an employee or prospective employee for refusing to take a test or for exercising other rights under the Act.

EXEMPTIONS   Federal, State and local governments are not affected by the law. Also, the law does not apply to tests given by the Federal Government to certain private individuals engaged in national security-related activities.

The Act permits polygraph (a kind of lie detector) tests to be administered in the private sector, subject to restrictions, to certain prospective employees of security service firms (armored car, alarm, and guard), and of pharmaceutical manufacturers, distributors and dispensers.

The Act also permits polygraph testing, subject to restrictions, of certain employees of private firms who are reasonably suspected of involvement in a workplace incident (theft, embezzlement, etc.) that resulted in economic loss to the employer.

The law does not preempt any provision of any State or local law or any collective bargaining agreement which is more restrictive with respect to lie detector tests.

EXAMINEE RIGHTS   Where polygraph tests are permitted, they are subject to numerous strict standards concerning the conduct and length of the test. Examinees have a number of specific rights, including the right to a written notice before testing, the right to refuse or discontinue a test, and the right not to have test results disclosed to unauthorized persons.

ENFORCEMENT   The Secretary of Labor may bring court actions to restrain violations and assess civil penalties up to $10,000 against violators. Employees or job applicants may also bring their own court actions.

THE LAW REQUIRES EMPLOYERS TO DISPLAY THIS POSTER WHERE EMPLOYEES AND JOB APPLICANTS CAN READILY SEE IT.

For additional information:

1-866-4-USWAGE ≋WHD
(1-866-487-9243)   TTY: 1-877-889-5627   U.S. Wage and Hour Division

WWW.WAGEHOUR.DOL.GOV

Scan your QR phone reader to learn more about the Employee Polygraph Protection Act.   U.S. Department of Labor | Wage and Hour Division

WHD 1462
Rev. Jan 2012

Exhibit 4-1
Employee Polygraph Protection Act Notification

The U.S. Department of Labor provides employers with free posters to inform employees of their rights. Employers may download this poster and many others at www.dol.gov.
Source: U.S. Department of Labor, Wage and Hour Division, http://www.wagehour.dol.gov.

Exhibit 4-2
Selected Laws Affecting
Employee Rights

Employees are entitled to their
privacy and to information about
employer actions such as
accessing credit information,
drug testing, or large layoffs.

Law	Effect
Fair Credit Reporting Act	Requires employers to notify individuals that credit information is being gathered and may be used in the employment decision.
Privacy Act	Requires government agencies to make information in an employee's personnel files available to him or her.
Drug-Free Workplace Act	Requires government agencies, federal contractors, and those who receive government monies to take steps to ensure that their workplace is drug free.
Employee Polygraph Protection Act	Prohibits the use of lie-detector tests in screening all job applicants. Permits their use under certain circumstances.
Worker Adjustment and Retraining Notification Act	Requires employers with one hundred or more employees contemplating closing a facility or laying off fifty or more employees to give sixty days' notice of the pending action.

notification was not given (up to sixty days). However, the law does recognize that under certain circumstances, advance notice may be impossible. Assume, for example, a company is having financial difficulties and is seeking to raise money to keep the organization afloat. If they fail and subsequently file for bankruptcy, WARN would not apply.

Plant closings, privacy of employee records, use of credit reports and drug testing are all concerns for human resource management. These laws have created specific guidelines for organizations to follow. They don't prevent the organization from doing what is necessary. Rather, the laws exist to ensure that whatever action the organization takes, it also protects employee rights. A summary of these laws is presented in Exhibit 4-2.

Current Issues Regarding Employee Rights

Recently, emphasis has been placed on curtailing specific employer practices, as well as addressing what employees may rightfully expect from their organizations. These basic issues are social media, drug testing, honesty tests, employee monitoring and workplace security, and workplace romance.

Social Media

Suppose you've had all you can take of an annoying and inept manager. On your personal Facebook account, you criticize the manager, calling her a "lunatic" along with a few other insults. Not wanting to leave any doubt as to how upset you are, you go on to call your workplace "toxic" and "oppressive." A couple of days later, your Facebook rant is discovered and you're fired. Can your company do that? The answer, similar to most answers to HR questions is, "it depends."

There is no protection for employees who post comments about employers on Facebook or blogs. A few have attempted to have disciplinary actions reversed by claiming that it was an unfair labor practice because the employer retaliated against them for "protected concerted activity." That means the employee was communicating with other employees about workplace issues. Read the cases below and see if you can guess if the National Labor Relations Board (NLRB) supported the employee or employer.

■ A bartender was fed up with his "redneck" customers and posted on a Facebook conversation with his sister that he hoped they would "choke on glass as they drove home drunk." No coworkers participated in the Facebook discussion. He was fired a few days later . . . via Facebook.

- A Walmart employee was so upset with his assistant manager that he called her a "puta" and said that her criticisms of his work were "retarded." He went on to tell Walmart to "kiss my royal white ass." Coworkers responded their approval of his comments. He was soon fired.
- A sales worker was fired from a BMW dealership after he made a Facebook post that mocked the management for serving hot dogs and bottled water from Sam's Club at an event promoting an expensive BMW model. He also expressed concern that sales commissions would suffer. Other employees joined the discussion expressing their concerns.
- An employee at an ambulance company complained on Facebook about her manager's incompetence, stating, "I love how the company allows a 17 to become a supervisor." "17" was company code for a psychiatric patient. The employer had a policy prohibiting employees from saying anything negative about the company online.[16]

The National Labor Relations Board (NLRB) denied the unfair labor practice claims of the bartender and the Walmart employee. The BMW sales worker and ambulance driver got better news. Their claims were upheld by the NLRB. What was the difference? They were seen as discussing the terms and conditions of their employment with other employees, which is protected, whereas the bartender and Walmart employee's posts were merely complaining to anyone who would pay attention. The NLRB has drawn a fine line and more complaints are expected. You can learn more about it on the NLRB Facebook page.

Laws regarding employee rights and use of **social media** sites like Facebook, LinkedIn, Twitter, MySpace, YouTube, and others are not keeping pace with the technology. Employers are often left making a "best guess" about employee and employer rights as lawmakers and courts get it sorted out. These social media sites provide ample opportunities for people to quickly make positive or negative comments to a global audience. If an impulsive angry rant includes a vague threat, it can reach employer and law enforcement agencies quickly with serious legal repercussions for the sender.

social media
Websites and mobile applications that facilitate interactive communication.

Use of social media at work also presents problems with productivity. Then why not just ban the use of social media at work entirely? It is a hotly debated topic with some feeling a ban would create morale problems and wouldn't be practical. Others have attempted to create restrictions and policies designed to prevent situations that can be embarrassing to the organization and avoid expensive legal problems. The risks are real. The reputation of people, products, and companies are at stake when a disgruntled employee airs the corporate dirty laundry online, opening the door to lawsuits for defamation. Even well-meaning employees can create problems. Consider a manager who posts a recommendation on his employee's LinkedIn site. If the employee is fired for poor performance in the future, this could cause problems for his or her manager.

Any number of laws may have an impact on the use of social media at work including:

- Stored Communications Act (SCA), which protects the privacy of electronic communications as they are being transmitted, like listening to a private phone call or reading un-opened e-mail. It does allow interception of communications with employee consent, and does not restrict accessing communication that is open to the public, like Facebook pages.
- Fair Credit Reporting Act (FCRA) requires employee permission for background checks and credit reports.
- Genetic Information Nondiscrimination Act (GINA) would be involved if an employee references health information on a social media page and lists things such as recruiting a team for a charity walk that benefits a disease that runs in the employee's family.

Employers need to craft Social Media policies that protect employers and employees by including:

- Information outlining the company's policy on monitoring Internet use.
- Explaining that employees have no expectation of privacy when using the Internet at work.[17]

- Reminding employees that comments need to be respectful of the company and clients.
- Explaining the possibility of legal repercussions from defamation.
- Reminding employees about privacy settings.
- Explaining the company's position on using the company name or photos depicting the company or employee with the company uniform.

Warner Bros. Entertainment social media policy prohibits employees, as a representative of the company, from giving recommendations for current or former coworkers on sites like LinkedIn. Personal testimonials that don't involve the employer are acceptable.[18]

Drug Testing

drug testing

The process of testing applicants/employees to determine if they are using illicit substances.

Previously in our discussion of the Drug-Free Workplace Act, we mentioned that the legislation is applicable to certain organizations. However, the severity of substance abuse in organizations has prompted many organizations not covered by this 1988 act to voluntarily begin **drug testing**. Why? It is estimated that a sizable percentage of the U.S. workforce may be abusing drugs and/or alcohol. Consider these frightening statistics:

- 75 percent of illicit drug users and 80 percent of heavy alcohol users are employed full-time.
- 60 percent of adults with a substance abuse problem are employed full-time.
- 17 percent of workers in hospitality and food service and 14 percent of workers in construction report illicit drug use.
- 13 percent of workers in arts, entertainment, and mining report being heavy users of alcohol.[19]

According to federal statistics, over 40 percent of full-time adult employees are tested at the time of hire, and an additional 29 percent are tested randomly.[20] It's difficult to find a major company today that doesn't do some form of drug testing. CVS, Costco, Toys R Us, Target, and Verizon are just a few that test all current employees as well as prospective employees. In fact, a recent survey by SHRM indicated that over 70 percent of the employers surveyed required at least some if not all job candidates to take a drug test.[21] Drug testing is designed to identify the abusers, either to help them overcome their problem (current employees) or to avoid hiring them in the first place (applicants). Other benefits exist, too. The SHRM survey also found that 20 percent of employers responding found increased productivity after implementing a drug testing policy.[22]

Although the Drug Free Workplace Act requires many employers to have policies against drug use, it doesn't require drug testing. Drug testing has been upheld by the Supreme Court in safety sensitive positions such as transportation and law enforcement, but the American Civil Liberties Union has repeatedly filed lawsuits to halt additional drug testing in the workplace. Their major concerns include problems with inaccurate testing and lack of proof that tests deter drug use.[23] The ACLU and other opponents of drug testing feel that drug testing in today's organizations should be conducted to eliminate illegal substance abuse in the workplace, not to catch those using them. For instance, drug testing may make better sense when there is a reason to suspect substance abuse or after a work-related accident. Although many might say that the same outcome is achieved, it's the process, and how employees view the process, that matters. In some organizations, individuals who refuse the drug test may be terminated immediately. Although this treatment appears harsh, the ill effect of employing a substance abuser is perceived as too great. But what if that person takes the drug test and fails it? Many organizations require individuals that fail drug tests to enter rehabilitation programs as a condition of continued employment. However, if they don't accept the help, or later fail another test, they will most likely be terminated.

Applicants, on the other hand, present a different story. If an applicant tests positive for substance abuse, that applicant is generally dropped from consideration. The company's liability begins and ends there—they are not required to offer those applicants

CONTEMPORARY CONNECTION

Why Organizations Conduct Drug Tests

Over two-thirds of all U.S. organizations use some form of drug testing—either as a pre-employment requirement, a random testing of current employees, or a required test after a workplace accident has happened. Why are companies likely to do this? Consider the following statistics. Substance abusers are:

- 10 times more likely to miss work
- 5 times more likely to file a workers' compensation claim
- 3.6 times more likely to be involved in a work-related accident
- 33 percent less productive than nonusers costing U.S. corporations nearly $100 billion annually

Utilizing tests that are administered using urine, blood, or hair samples, organizations most commonly look for such substances as marijuana, alcohol, amphetamines, cocaine, opiates such as heroin, and phencyclidine (PCP). Depending on the situation, organizations may also test for such substances as Valium, Ecstasy, LSD, and certain inhalants.[24]

Consider this:

In addition to jobs like transportation, law enforcement, and some federal agencies, what organizations should do drug testing? Can you think of any jobs where employees would not need to be tested?

---

any help. It is recommended that employers conduct applicant drug testing only after a conditional job offer is made. The actual job offer is only made after the applicant passes a drug test. Why require a drug test at this stage? To properly administer the test requires information about one's health and medication record and posing such questions before making a conditional offer may violate the Americans with Disabilities Act.

Most current and potential employees recognize why companies must drug test but expect to be treated humanely in the process; they also want safeguards built into the process to challenge false tests. And if a problem appears, many may want help, not punishment. Organizations can take several steps to create a positive atmosphere, and this is where HRM comes into play. HRM must issue its policies on substance abuse and communicate them to every employee. The policies must state what is prohibited, under what conditions an individual will be tested, consequences of failing the test, and how testing will be handled. Making clear what is expected, as well as what the company intends to do, can reduce the emotional aspect of this process. Where such policies exist, questions of legality and employee privacy issues are reduced.

Honesty Tests

How would you respond to the question: How often do you tell the truth? Would your answer be, "All the time"? What if the potential employer responded, "Sorry, we can't hire you because everyone has stretched the truth at some point in their lives. So you must be lying, and therefore are not the honest employee we desire." What if you answered, "Most of the time"? The employer might reply, "Sorry again! We can't afford to hire someone who may not have the highest ethical standards." Sound like a catch-22? Welcome to the world of **honesty tests** (sometimes referred to as integrity tests). Although polygraph testing has been significantly curtailed in the hiring process, employers have found another mechanism that supposedly provides similar information.

honesty test
A specialized question-and-answer test designed to assess one's honesty.

These integrity tests mostly entice applicants to provide information about themselves that otherwise would be hard to obtain. They tend to focus on two particular areas, theft and drug use, but are not simply indicators of what has happened; typically, they assess an applicant's past dishonest behavior and that individual's attitude toward dishonesty. One would anticipate that applicants would tailor their answers to these questions to avoid "being caught," or would even lie; however, research findings suggest otherwise. That is, individuals frequently perceive that being dishonest may be okay as long as you are truthful about your dishonesty. As such, applicants may discuss questions in such a way that the tests do reveal the information intended. These tests frequently are

Honesty tests typically focus on two areas: theft and substance abuse.

designed with multiple questions covering similar topic areas, to assess consistency. If consistency in response is lacking, the test may indicate that an individual is being dishonest.

The effectiveness of these tests, coupled with their costs, which are lower than other types of investigations, has prompted companies to use them in their selection process. In fact, it is estimated that several thousand organizations are using some variation of honesty tests to screen applicants, testing several million individuals each year.[25] Surprisingly, however, companies using these tests seldom reveal that they do. The large use of these tests has provoked questions about their validity and their potential for adverse impact. Research into the effectiveness of honesty testing to date is promising. Although instances have been recorded indicating that individuals have been wrongly misclassified as dishonest, other studies have indicated that they do not create an adverse impact against protected group members.[26]

Whistle-Blowing

Over the past few years, more emphasis has been placed on companies being good corporate citizens. Incidents like the BP oil spill in the gulf of Mexico, the Lehman Brothers collapse, and ethical lapses at AIG, Madoff Securities, and News Corporation have fueled interest in the area. One aspect of being responsible to the community at large is permitting employees to challenge management's practice without fear of retaliation. This challenge is often referred to as **whistle-blowing**.

whistle-blowing
A situation in which an employee notifies authorities of wrongdoing in an organization.

Whistle-blowing occurs when an employee reports the organization to an outside agency for what the employee believes is an illegal or unethical practice. In the past, these employees were often subjected to severe punishment for doing what they believed was right.

Employees of most private employers lack federal whistle-blower protection, but may be protected under individual state statutes. The federal government protects employees who report violations under the Sarbanes-Oxley Act, the Consumer Product Safety Act, Occupational Safety and Health Act, and many other federally regulated activities. The extent of state laws and how much protection they afford differ greatly. Many firms have voluntarily adopted policies to permit employees to identify problem areas. The thrust of these policies is to have an established procedure whereby employees can safely raise concerns and the company can take corrective action.

It is also important to note that passage of the Sarbanes-Oxley Act (see Chapter 2) gave employees protection for whistle-blowing activities if they perceive company wrongdoing. So long as the employee reasonably believes that some inappropriate or fraudulent activities exist in the organization, they are protected from employer retaliation. This is true whether or not the allegation is correct.[27]

Employee Monitoring and Workplace Security

Technology has revolutionized the way we work. It has allowed us to be more productive; to work smarter, not harder; and to bring about efficiencies in organizations impossible two decades ago. It has also provided a means of **employee monitoring**—what some would call spying on employees![28]

employee monitoring
An activity whereby the company keeps informed of its employees' activities.

Workplace security has become a critical issue for employers. Workplace security focuses on protecting the employer's property, inventory, data, and productivity.[29] Employee theft, excessive time spent surfing the Internet, revealing trade secrets to competition, online gambling, viewing online pornography, sending offensive or harassing e-mails, or using the company's customer database for personal gain could damage the company. But how far can this protection extend? Shouldn't we consider employees' rights, too? How do we create a balance?[30]

Consider the following cases:

- Arriving at work one morning, Callie notices her boss reading her e-mail. Although company managers verbally stated that e-mail messages were private, the company's written policy was different. Her employer contended that it owned the system and

CONTEMPORARY CONNECTION

By the Numbers

According to the Electronic Monitoring and Surveillance Survey conducted by the American Management Association and the ePolicy Institute, companies reported:[34]

- 83 percent inform workers that they monitor content, keystrokes, and time spent at the keyboard.
- 71 percent alert employees to e-mail monitoring.
- 66 percent monitor Internet use.
- 65 percent block connections to inappropriate websites.
- 52 percent use Smartcard technology to monitor building access.
- 48 percent use video monitoring of workers.
- 45 percent monitor time spent on the telephone and numbers called.

- 43 percent monitor e-mail.
- 33 percent fired workers for Internet misuse.
- 28 percent fired workers for e-mail misuse.
- 24 percent have had e-mail subpoenaed by courts.
- 16 percent record phone conversations.
- 12 percent monitor the blogosphere.
- 9 percent monitor voicemail.
- 2 percent use fingerprint scans.

Consider this:

What type of monitoring do you experience at work? Do you consider it necessary or an invasion of privacy?

---

accordingly had the right to see what was going on. And he was right! HR has the responsibility to communicate all policies clearly to all managers and employees.[31]

- A disgruntled artist at an animation studio checks around to be sure no coworkers are close enough to his cubicle to see what he's doing. He opens up his personal account and sends an e-mail to a rival movie studio with information about a top-secret movie project his employer is working on. What he didn't count on is that his employer has the ability to monitor any outgoing e-mail, even if it is not from the employer's e-mail accounts. The monitoring software is set up to filter for sensitive information. The animator is caught, sued, and probably won't ever be employed in the industry again.[32]
- The stepfather of a twelve-year-old girl put pictures of the girl on a child pornography website using his employer's Internet connection. The girl's mother sued the employer, alleging that the employer had a duty to monitor its systems and prevent misuse. The court found that there was a duty for the employer to guard against abuses and it would be liable for damages.[33]

With technology enhancements, companies can monitor many employee activities. Although some may feel this is intrusive, safety and liability issues almost mandate that employers ensure a safe and proper work environment.
(Source: Spencer Grant/PhotoEdit)

Part of the problem here goes back to the balance of security. Abuses by employees—using the company's computer system for gambling purposes, running their own businesses, playing computer games, or pursuing personal matters on company time—have resulted in companies implementing a more "policing" role.[35] This can extend, too, to Internet sites, ensuring that employees are not logging on to adult-oriented websites.[36] Further complicating the situation is the fact that companies issue laptops to log in to company servers remotely, or BlackBerry, iPhone, and other smart phones with Internet connections that blur the line between personal and business use. Employees may have an expectation of privacy in e-mail and Internet when taking company devices home or using them in remote locations.

As employee-monitoring issues become more noticeable, keep in mind that employers, as long as they have a policy regarding how employees are monitored, will continue to check on employee behavior. The American Management Association asserts that "Technology has provided a capability that we never had before to check up on employees like never before. It's within an organization's right to monitor just about anything you do during work time using work tools."[37]

Companies need to make clear what is acceptable and what's not acceptable, with examples if necessary. Policies need to be included in employee manuals, explained at employee orientation, even posted on computer log-in screens. Specifically targeted for this monitoring are the Internet, e-mail, and the telephone. In fact, it's estimated that most large companies and more than 76 percent of employers monitor their employees' e-mail and Internet usage.[38]

Employee movement can also be monitored with RFID (radio frequency identification). Boeing Co. uses RFID-embedded badges to track 150,000 employees in seventy countries. The company had to address employees' privacy concerns, including "will they track me in the bathroom," by listening to those concerns and by providing lots of communication.[39] RFID technology has caused such concern that two states have passed laws prohibiting the implantation of RFID chips in badges without an employee's consent. Odd as it sounds, at least one company has already offered implantation of RFID chips in the arms of employees who agree to the procedure.

Another developing controversy involves tracking employees. GPS tracking devices on company owned vehicles has been common practice for several years. Recently courts in New York and Missouri upheld employers' rights to secretly install tracking devices on an employee's personal vehicle to monitor their travels during working hours. Employees may also be tracked by company-issued cell phones. According to Lewis Maltby, president of the National Workrights Institute, "There are millions of company cell phones and smart phones out there, and all of them have GPS tracking, so now your boss can track you every minute of your private life. It's happening right now."[40]

As the opportunities for employee monitoring continue to grow, so too will the ethical debate. Organizations need to inform employees about their rights and responsibilities and be clear about the methods used to gather information and what will be done with the information.

Workplace Romance

workplace romance
A personal relationship that develops at work.

Workplace romance is common. When individuals close in age with similar interests meet at work and are together for forty hours a week or more, sometimes colleagues can turn into romantic partners. It's so common that a survey by Vault.com found that 47 percent of professionals admitted to having been involved in an office romance and another 19 percent have considered it. Furthermore, 11 percent said they had dated their boss or another superior in the organization.

Why should HR professionals be concerned? The problem is that these romances can lead to accusations of favoritism, breeches of ethics, low productivity, poor employee morale, and even workplace violence.[41] Concern over these complications has led some companies to implement fraternization policies that forbid relationships between all coworkers or between certain groups of coworkers such as employees in the same department. Other companies deal with the issue by asking affected employees to sign contracts stating that the relationship is consensual. These contracts often outline what the parties are expected to do if the relationship should cease to be consensual while reminding both parties of the company's sexual harassment policy. The purpose of these contracts is to:

What if your significant other is now your boss? Most organizations would find that situation unacceptable.

- reduce the risk of sexual harassment
- reduce the perception of favoritism
- provide an opportunity to discuss professional behavior in the workplace
- remind employees that the workplace does not provide privacy[42]

Romance at Work: It's More Than Loving Your Job!

Percentage of companies with a "no-fraternization" policy

- Written policy: 18 percent
- Verbal policy: 7 percent
- No policy: 72 percent

Restrictions on relationships in companies with a "no-fraternization" policy

- A supervisor and subordinate: 80 percent
- Employees in the same department: 24 percent
- Employees with significant rank difference: 16 percent
- Employees and customers: 13 percent

Consequences for violating company "no-fraternization" policy

- Employee transfers: 42 percent
- Formal discipline: 36 percent
- Termination: 27 percent

Outcomes of workplace romances

- Those involved get married: 62 percent
- Complaints of favoritism: 44 percent
- Divorce of married employees: 29 percent
- Decrease of productivity: 26 percent
- Diminished coworker morale: 25 percent
- Sexual harassment claims: 19 percent
- Stalking claims: 16 percent
- Complaints of retaliation: 15 percent

Source: SHRM 2006 Workplace Romance Poll.

Exhibit 4-3
No-Fraternization Policies

According to this survey by the Society of Human Resource Management (SHRM), some interesting statistics stand out: over 70 percent of companies do not have policies against workplace relationships; 80 percent of those relationships reported are between a supervisor and a subordinate; and over 60 percent ended up getting married!

Other issues that may be addressed include what would happen if one person in the relationship should be promoted over the other or moves on to work for a competitor. Exhibit 4-3 lists some interesting figures on workplace romance.

The Employment-at-Will Doctrine

The concept of the **employment-at-will doctrine** is rooted in nineteenth-century common law, which permitted employers to discipline or discharge employees at their discretion. The doctrine seeks to equalize the playing field. If employees can resign at any time they want, why shouldn't an employer have a similar right?

Under the employment-at-will doctrine, an employer can dismiss an employee "for good cause, for no cause, or even for a cause morally wrong, without being guilty of a legal wrong."[43] Of course, even then, an employer can't fire on the basis of race, religion, sex, national origin, age, or disability. Although this doctrine has existed for more than one hundred years, the courts, labor unions, and legislation have attempted to lessen its use. In these instances, jobs are compared to private property. That is, individuals have a right to these jobs unless the organization has specified otherwise. Employees today are challenging the legality of losing their jobs more frequently. When firing without cause occurs, employees may seek the assistance of the courts to address wrongful discharge. Most states permit employees to sue their employers if they believe their termination was unjust, claiming that through some action on the part of the employer, exceptions to the employment-at-will doctrine exist.

employment-at-will doctrine
Nineteenth-century common law that permitted employers to discipline or discharge employees at their discretion.

Exceptions to the Doctrine

Although employment-at-will thrives in contemporary organizations, five exceptions can support a wrongful discharge suit: contractual relationship, statutory considerations, public policy violation, implied contracts, and breach of good faith.[44] Let's take a closer look at these.

Contractual Relationship   A contractual relationship exists when employers and employees have a legal agreement regarding how employee issues are handled. Under such contractual arrangements, discharge may occur only if it is based on just cause. Where a distinct definition of just cause does not exist, just cause can be shown under guidelines derived from labor arbitration of collective-bargaining relationships (we'll look at discipline in labor-management relationships in Chapter 14):

- Was there adequate warning of consequences of the worker's behavior?
- Are the rules reasonable and related to safe and efficient operations of the business?
- Before discipline was administered, did a fair investigation of the violation occur?
- Did the investigation yield definite proof of worker activity and wrongdoing?
- Have similar occurrences, both prior and subsequent to this event, been handled in the same way and without discrimination?
- Was the penalty in line with the seriousness of the offense and in accord with the worker's past employment record?[45]

Statutory Considerations   In addition to this contractual relationship, federal legislation may play a key role. Discrimination laws such as those discussed in the previous chapter may further constrain an employer's use of at-will terminations. For example, an organization cannot terminate an individual based on his or her age just because such action would save the company some money.

Public Policy Violation   Another exception to the employment-at-will doctrine is the public policy violation. Under this exception, an employee cannot be terminated for failing to obey an order from an employer that can be construed as an illegal activity. Should an employee refuse to offer a bribe to a public official to increase the likelihood of the organization obtaining a contract, falsify time cards, or illegally dump hazardous waste, that employee is protected. Furthermore, employers cannot retaliate against an employee for exercising his or her rights (such as serving on a jury). Accordingly, employees cannot be justifiably discharged for exercising their rights in accordance with societal laws and statutes.

implied employment contract
Any organizational guarantee or promise about job security.

Implied Employment Contract   The fourth exception to the doctrine is the **implied employment contract.** An implied contract is any verbal or written statement made by members of the organization that suggests organizational guarantees or promises about continued employment.[46] These implied contracts, when they exist, typically take place during employment interviews or are included in an employee handbook. We'll look at employee handbooks in Chapter 8.

One of the earlier cases reaffirming implied contracts was *Toussaint v. Blue Cross and Blue Shield of Michigan.*[47] In this case, Toussaint claimed that he was discharged for unjust causes by the organization. He asserted that he was told he'd have a job in the company until he reached retirement age of sixty-five so long as he did his job. The employee handbook also clearly reinforced this tenure with statements reflective of discharge for just cause. Even if just cause arose, the discharge could occur only after several disciplinary steps. We'll look at the topic of discipline in the next section. In this case, the court determined that the discharge was improper because the organization implied that his job was permanent.

The issue of implied contracts is changing how HRM operates in several of its functions. For instance, interviewers are increasingly cautious, avoiding anything that could conjure up a contract. Something as innocent as discussing an annual salary may cause problems, for such a comment implies at least twelve months on the job. To avoid this, salaries are often communicated in terms of the amount of pay for each pay period. Many organizations that want to maintain an employment-at-will policy have disclaimers such as "This handbook is not a contract of employment," or "Employment in the organization is at the will of the employer," on the covers of their employee handbooks and manuals. Supervisors and interviewers still need to be careful not to make any statements that might override the printed words.

Breach of Good Faith   The final exception to the employment-at-will doctrine is the breach of good faith. Although this is the most difficult of the exceptions to prove, in some situations an employer may breach a promise. In one noteworthy case, an individual employed more than twenty-five years by the National Cash Register Company (NCR) was terminated shortly after completing a major deal with a customer.[48] The employee claimed that he was fired to eliminate NCR's liability to pay him his sales commission. The court ruled that this individual acted in good faith in selling the company's product and reasonably expected his commission. Although NCR had an employment-at-will arrangement with its employees, the court held that his dismissal and NCR's failure to pay commissions were breaches of good faith.

Discipline and Employee Rights

The exceptions to the employment-at-will doctrine may lead you to think that employers cannot terminate employees or are significantly limited in their action. We've all seen instances where an employer should have fired an employee who broke rules, was insubordinate, had a real attitude problem, or just didn't do a very good job. That can have a disastrous effect on productivity and morale. So why do employers refrain from firing these "bad apples"? Frequently it's because they don't know their rights as employers or don't understand how to discipline properly. HRM can help by establishing discipline policies and educating managers on their use.

What Is Discipline?

Discipline refers to a condition in the organization where employees conduct themselves in accordance with the organization's rules and standards of acceptable behavior. For the most part, employees discipline themselves by conforming to what is considered proper behavior because they believe it is the reasonable thing to do. Once they know what is expected of them, and assuming they find these standards or rules reasonable, they seek to meet those expectations.[49]

But not all employees will accept the responsibility of self-discipline. Some do not accept the norms of responsible employee behavior. These employees, then, require some degree of extrinsic disciplinary action. Managers don't always know how to effectively apply discipline, either. The following section covers how to establish discipline policies with appropriate consequences that so managers and employees all know what to expect.

discipline
A condition in the organization when employees conduct themselves in accordance with the organization's rules and standards of acceptable behavior.

Factors to Consider When Disciplining

Before we review disciplinary guidelines, we should look at the major factors to consider in having fair and equitable disciplinary practices.[50] The following seven contingency factors can help us analyze a discipline problem.

1. *Seriousness of the Problem* How severe is the problem? For example, dishonesty is usually considered a more serious infraction than reporting to work twenty minutes late.
2. *Duration of the Problem* Have there been other discipline problems in the past, and over how long a time span? The violation does not take place in a vacuum. A first occurrence is usually viewed differently from a third or fourth offense.
3. *Frequency and Nature of the Problem* Is the current problem part of an emerging or continuing pattern of disciplinary infractions? We are concerned with not only the duration but also the pattern of the problem. Continual infractions may require a different type of discipline from that applied to isolated instances of misconduct. They may also point to a situation that demands far more severe discipline to prevent a minor problem from becoming a major one.
4. *Extenuating Factors* Do extenuating circumstances relate to the problem? The student who fails to turn in her term paper by the deadline because of the death of her grandfather is likely to have her violation assessed more leniently than will her peer who missed the deadline because he overslept.
5. *Degree of Socialization* To what extent has management made an earlier effort to educate the person causing the problem about the existing rules and procedures and

TIPS FOR SUCCESS

What To Know Before Disciplining Employees

In a perfect world, there would be no disciplining, and no policies or procedures to misinterpret or ignore. Each employee would check his or her own work and contribute ways to cut costs, reduce waste, and improve quality and service to both internal and external customers. Lunch hours would never exceed agreed-on limits, and no personal business or phone calls would be conducted on company time or with company resources, equipment, or personnel. No one would blame computers, equipment, managers, the company, or "someone else" for work not completed or completed late or incorrectly. Managers would involve, train, and listen to employees, building teamwork through empowerment and trust. In a perfect world!

In a slightly less perfect but more exciting and challenging world, managers occasionally must discipline employees. Dealing with the effects of the mistakes and masking anger, resentment, disappointment, and disgust to create teaching moments can test even the most patient manager. The challenge is to keep employees focused on their behavior and how to correct or improve it, not on how they're being treated. Following these guidelines should help:

- *Cool off, but don't wait too long.* Even though you might like to ignore the problem and hope that it will go away, don't kid yourself. Any problem has a tendency to escalate from a minor to a major issue. It's not worth it. Become comfortable with positively confronting situations, mutually identifying problems, and agreeing on solutions and follow-up plans. Failing to address issues undermines your credibility and ability to do what you are paid to do: manage.
- *Think before you speak.* Stay calm. It may be tempting to sound off, but how you handle disciplining may be as important as the issue. Your goal should be to correct the situation, not to further impede the working relationship. You may wish to ask the employee to consider possible solutions and bring one or two to the meeting if appropriate.
- *Always discipline in private, on-on-one.* Consider using a conference room if added privacy is needed.
- *Follow company disciplinary procedures to ensure fairness and consistency.* If in doubt, take the time to check with the policy manual, your boss, or a personnel officer first. If you don't, you may be the next person in line to be disciplined for not following procedures.
- *Be prepared to hear a variety of both imaginative and worn-out excuses.* These can range from "I was stuck in traffic" to "Somebody made that up" to "The other department takes long lunches" to "Everybody else does it."

(Source: Josh Rinehults/iStockphoto)

- *Prepare to avoid nervousness.* No one likes to discipline, but it's part of the job. Before the meeting, think about possible objections or issues. Rehearse responses in your mind, outline your comments—whatever it takes to resolve the issue in a win-win manner.
- *Prepare by comparing the actual to the desired situation.* State what action is necessary, why it is necessary, and its impact.
- *Clarify expectations and contingencies for specific actions and timetables.* Make sure that the employee understands by asking for a summarization—something beyond just a grunt of agreement.
- *Ask employees for feedback.* How can you best help or support them in making the necessary changes? What suggestions do they have? How can problems be prevented in the future?
- *Let it go.* There is no need to ignore employees, stare at them, or use any other of a variety of cruel and unusual (and immature) punishments. Administer the appropriate consequence and try to resume a normal working relationship.

Imagine an environment that tolerated no mistakes because it tolerated no risks, no changes, and no tests. A less-than-perfect world looks good after all.

Things to think about:

How would the work atmosphere or organizational culture be affected if these suggestions were consistently followed? Would you add any suggestions?

---

the consequences of violations? Discipline severity must reflect the degree of knowledge that the violator holds of the organization's standards of acceptable behavior. The new employee is less likely to have been socialized to these standards than the twenty-year veteran. Additionally, the organization with formalized, written rules governing employee conduct is more justified in aggressively enforcing violations of these rules than is the organization whose rules are informal or vague.

6. *History of the Organization's Discipline Practices* How have similar infractions been dealt with in the past within the department? Within the entire organization? Has there been consistency in the application of discipline procedures? Equitable treatment of employees must take into consideration precedents within the unit where the infraction occurs, as well as previous disciplinary actions taken in other units within the organization. Equity demands consistency against some relevant benchmark.

7. *Management Backing* If employees decide to take their case to a higher level in management, will you have reasonable evidence to justify your decision? Should the employee challenge your disciplinary action, you need data to back up the necessity and equity of your action and to feel confident that management will support your decision. No disciplinary action is likely to carry much weight if violators believe that they can usually challenge and successfully override their manager's decision.

How can these seven items help? Consider the many reasons why we might discipline an employee. With little difficulty, we could list several dozen or more infractions that management might believe require disciplinary action. For simplicity's sake, we have classified the most frequent violations into four categories: attendance, on-the-job behaviors, dishonesty, and outside activities. We've listed the categories and potential infractions in Exhibit 4-4. Keep in mind that the same infraction may be considered minor or serious given the situation or the industry involved. For example, while concealing defective work when binding textbooks may be viewed as minor, the same action in an aerospace manufacturing plant is more serious. Recurrence and severity of the infraction will also play a role. Employees who commit their first minor offense might generally expect a minor reprimand. A second offense might result in a stronger reprimand, and so forth. In contrast, the first occurrence of a serious offense might mean not being allowed to return to work, the length of time being dependent on the circumstances surrounding the violation.

Type of Problem	Infraction
Attendance	Tardiness
	Unexcused absence
	Leaving without permission
On-the-job behaviors	Malicious destruction of organizational property
	Gross insubordination
	Carrying a concealed weapon
	Attacking another employee with intent to seriously harm
	Intoxicated on the job/substance abuse
	Sexually harassing another employee
	Failure to obey safety rules
	Defective work
	Failure to report accidents
	Loafing
	Gambling on the job
	Fighting
	Horseplay
	Sending text messages or using phone for personal use
Dishonesty	Stealing
	Deliberate falsification of employment record
	Clock-punching another's timecard
	Concealing defective work
	Subversive activity
Outside activities	Unauthorized strike activity
	Outside criminal activities
	Wage garnishment
	Working for a competing company

Exhibit 4-4
Specific Disciplinary Problems

Although this isn't a comprehensive list, this table outlines some of the more common types of disciplinary problems that managers encounter. HR professionals hold the responsibility for training managers and supervisors in the disciplinary process and frequently are also responsible for administering the consequences in the disciplinary process.

Can you imagine placing your hand on this hot stove? Clearly, if you did, you'd get burned. That's precisely the analogy used for disciplining employees. They have ample warning that it's hot; every time they touch it, they'll get burned—and whoever touches the stove will be burned regardless of who they are.
(Source: gwmullis/iStockphoto)

Disciplinary Guidelines

All human resource managers should be aware of disciplinary guidelines. In this section, we briefly describe them.

■ *Make disciplinary action corrective rather than punitive.* The object of disciplinary action is not to deal out punishment. The object is to correct an employee's undesirable behavior. Punishment may be a necessary means to that end, but one should never lose sight of the eventual objective.

■ *Use a progressive discipline approach.* Although the appropriate disciplinary action may vary depending on the situation, it is generally desirable for discipline to be progressive. Only for the most serious violations will an employee be dismissed after a first offense. Typically, **progressive discipline** begins with a written verbal warning and proceeds through a written warning, suspension, and, only in the most serious cases, dismissal.

■ *Follow the* **hot-stove rule**. Administering discipline can be viewed as similar to touching a hot stove.[51] Although both are painful to the recipient, the analogy goes further. When you touch a hot stove, you have an immediate response; the burn you receive is instantaneous, leaving no question as to cause and effect. You have advance warning; you know what happens if you touch a red-hot stove. Furthermore, the result is consistent: every time you touch a hot stove, you get burned. Finally, the result is impersonal; regardless of who you are, if you touch a hot stove, you will get burned. The comparison between touching a hot stove and administering discipline should be apparent, but let us briefly expand on each of the four points in the analogy.

 ■ *Immediate Response.* The impact of a disciplinary action fades as the time between the infraction and the penalty's implementation lengthens. The more quickly the discipline follows the offense, the more likely the employee is to associate the discipline with the offense rather than with the manager imposing the discipline. As a result, it is best that the disciplinary process begin within a reasonable time frame after the violation is noticed. Waiting too long may result in the employee not making a connection between the infraction and the consequence. In this case, the employee may feel that the punishment was made arbitrarily or because of a bias or prejudice. Of course, this desire for immediacy should not result in taking action before thinking it through. If all the facts are not in, managers may invoke a temporary suspension, pending a final decision in the case.

 ■ *Advance Warning.* The manager has an obligation to give advance warning prior to initiating formal disciplinary action. This means the employee must be aware of the organization's rules and accept its standards of behavior. Disciplinary action is more likely to seem fair to employees when they have a clear warning that a given violation will lead to discipline and what that discipline will be.

 ■ *Consistent Action.* Fair employee treatment also demands that disciplinary action be consistent.[52] When rule violations are enforced in an inconsistent manner, the rules lose their impact. Morale will decline, and employees will question the competence of management. Productivity will suffer as a result of employee insecurity and anxiety. All employees want to know the limits of permissible behavior, and they look to their managers' actions for such feedback. If, for example, Fatima is reprimanded today for an action that she took last week, about which nothing was said, these limits become blurry. Similarly, if Zachary and Tianna are both goofing off at their desks and Zachary is reprimanded while Tianna is not, Zachary is likely to question the fairness of the action. The point, then, is that discipline should be

progressive discipline
A system of improving employee behavior that consists of warnings and punishments that gradually become more severe.

hot-stove rule
Discipline, like the consequences of touching a hot stove, should be immediate, provide ample warning, be consistent, and be impersonal.

consistent. This need not result in treating everyone exactly alike because that ignores the contingency factors we discussed earlier, but it does put the responsibility on management to clearly justify disciplinary actions that may appear inconsistent or possibly discriminatory to employees.

- *Impersonal Application.* Penalties should be connected with a given violation, not with the personality of the violator.[53] That is, discipline should be directed at what employees have done, not the employees themselves. As a manager, you should make it clear that you are avoiding personal judgments about the employee's character. You are penalizing the rule violation, not the individual, and all employees committing the violation can expect to be penalized. Furthermore, once the penalty has been imposed, you as manager must make every effort to move past the incident; you should attempt to treat the employee in the same manner as you did prior to the infraction. Managers may be tempted to ignore small violations by longtime employees or employees who have been recognized in the past for outstanding or even heroic performance. New employees unfamiliar with these past glories may feel that this indicates a double standard, a discriminatory environment, or possibly that the employer will tolerate poor performance.

A final point needs to be made, and it revolves around whether an employee can be represented in a meeting where he or she may be subject to disciplinary action. Though one of the protections that unions offer is the opportunity to have a union representative present in such a meeting, that same protection has been afforded to nonunion employees, too. Based on the U.S. Supreme Court case *NLRB v. J. Weingarten, Inc.,* nonunion employees were permitted to have a fellow employee or other individual represent them at a disciplinary meeting. But in 2004, this changed. Based on a National Labor Relations Board decision, Weingarten rights no longer apply outside the union setting. But that's not to say that a nonunion employee cannot be represented. It's up to the company—although they are not obligated under law to do so, they may choose to allow a representative to be present.[54]

Disciplinary Actions

As mentioned earlier, discipline generally follows a typical sequence of four steps: written verbal warning, written warning, suspension, and dismissal[55] (see Exhibit 4-5). Let's briefly review these four steps.

Written Verbal Warning The mildest form of discipline is the **written verbal warning**. (Yes, the term is correct, even though it sounds like an oxymoron.) A written verbal warning is a temporary record of a reprimand that is placed in the manager's file on the employee. This written verbal warning should state the purpose, date, and outcome of the interview with the employee. This, in fact, is what differentiates the written verbal warning from the verbal warning. Because of the need to document this step in the process, the verbal warning must be put into writing. The difference, however, is that this warning remains in the hands of the manager; that is, it is not forwarded to HRM for inclusion in the employee's personnel file.

The written verbal reprimand is best achieved when conducted in a private and informal environment. The manager should begin by clearly informing the employee of the rule that has been violated and the problem that this infraction has caused.

written verbal warning
Temporary record that a verbal reprimand has been given to an employee.

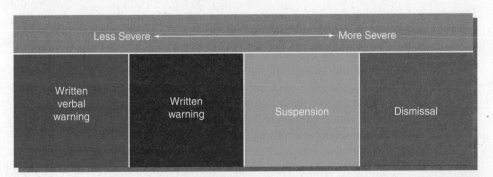

Exhibit 4-5
The Progressive Discipline Process

Progressive discipline begins with a written verbal warning and proceeds through increasingly severe written consequences.

For instance, if the employee has been late several times, the manager would reiterate the organization's rule that employees are to be at their desks by 8 A.M., and then proceed to give specific evidence of how violating this rule has increased work for others and lowered departmental morale. After the problem has been made clear, the manager should then allow the employee to respond. Is he aware of the problem? Are there extenuating circumstances that justify his behavior? What does he plan to do to correct his behavior?

After the employee has been given the opportunity to make his case, the manager must determine if the employee has proposed an adequate solution to the problem. If not, the manager should direct the discussion toward helping the employee figure out ways to prevent the trouble from recurring. Once a solution has been agreed on, the manager should ensure that the employee understands what, if any, follow-up action will be taken if the problem recurs.

If the written verbal warning is effective, further disciplinary action can be avoided. If the employee fails to improve, the manager will need to consider more severe action.

written warning
First formal step of the disciplinary process.

Written Warning The second step in the progressive discipline process is the **written warning**. In effect, it is the first formal stage of the disciplinary procedure. This is because the written warning becomes part of the employee's official personnel file. This is achieved by not only giving the warning to the employee but also sending a copy to HRM to be inserted in the employee's permanent record. In all other ways, however, the procedure for writing the warning is the same as the written verbal warning; that is, the employee is advised in private of the violation, its effects, and potential consequences of future violations. The only difference is that the discussion concludes with the employee being told that a formal written warning will be issued. Then the manager writes up the warning, stating the problem, the rule that has been violated, any acknowledgment by the employee that she will correct her behavior, and the consequences from a recurrence of the behavior, and sends it to HRM.

suspension
A period of time off from work as a result of a disciplinary process.

Suspension A **suspension** or layoff would be the next disciplinary step, usually taken only if the prior steps have been implemented without the desired outcome. Exceptions—where suspension is given without any prior verbal or written warning—occasionally occur if the infraction is of a serious nature.

A suspension may be for one day or several weeks; disciplinary layoffs in excess of a month are rare. Some organizations skip this step completely because it can have negative consequences for both the company and the employee. From the organization's perspective, a suspension means the loss of the employee for the layoff period. If the person has unique skills or is a vital part of a complex process, his loss during the suspension period can severely affect his department or the organization's performance if a suitable replacement cannot be located. From the employee's standpoint, a suspension can result in the employee returning in a more unpleasant and negative frame of mind than before the layoff.

Why would management consider suspending employees as a disciplinary measure? A short layoff is potentially a rude awakening to problem employees who didn't get the message from previous consequences. It may convince them that management is serious and may move them to accept responsibility for following the organization's rules. Organizations may choose to substitute a final warning for suspension in their discipline policy. Care must be taken to only make one final warning before moving to dismissal.

dismissal
A disciplinary action that results in the termination of an employee.

Dismissal Whether it's for poor performance or downsizing, managers frequently dread **dismissal** and often handle it poorly. Consider these examples:

- The President and CEO of Kia Motors America was fired between dinner and dessert during a meeting with Kia dealers at the Belagio Hotel in Las Vegas.[56]
- When Oracle purchased PeopleSoft, 5,000 packages were delivered to workers' homes on a Saturday, containing either a job offer or a severance package.[57]
- Yahoo CEO Carol Bartz didn't care for being fired over the phone, so she dashed off an e-mail to her employees stating: "I am very sad to tell you that I've just been fired over the phone by Yahoo's Chairman of the Board. It has been my pleasure to work with all of you and I wish you only the best going forward."

In spite of the organization's best efforts to train, coach, and raise the level of performance of employees, sometimes things just don't work out and HRM or managers with HRM assistance must fire an employee. Whether you call it a layoff, firing, dismissal, letting go, discharge, or outplacement, taking a job away from an employee is one of the most unpleasant tasks of HRM. A recent survey of small business owners found that 61 percent of owners found it difficult to fire employees and 78 percent admitted that they had kept an underperforming employee too long because they avoided the unpleasant task.[58] Reasons managers don't fire when they should include reluctance of admitting that they made a mistake in the hiring process, failure to document poor performance, not following the progressive discipline policy, fear of confrontation, worries about claims of discrimination and retaliation or concern about being short-staffed in the short term. Yet not firing someone who is underperforming or insubordinate sends the message that the employer accepts below-standard performance. It sends the message to high performing employees that their hard work doesn't really matter because the organization doesn't distinguish between their efforts and those of the mediocre employee.[59]

A dismissal decision should be given long and hard consideration. Have all efforts at coaching to improve performance been exhausted? Has HRM documented all substandard performance and communicated it to the employee? What replacement costs will the organization incur? Has the organization made all relevant documentation to avoid claims of discrimination? How are the courts likely to view any potential litigation?

© 1998 Ted Goff

"Define 'Fired.'"

Exhibit 4-6
Firing An Employee Can Be Difficult

Disciplinary actions can be difficult for employees to accept. Be very clear about the problem and action that will be taken.
(Source: © Ted Goff)

TIPS FOR SUCCESS

Are You Part of the Problem?

Progressive discipline and hot-stove rules are a proven way to help employees learn appropriate workplace behavior, but only if managers actually use them. New and inexperienced supervisors and managers don't automatically know the best way to handle problem employees who can often be menacing and may intimidate managers who have not been trained in how to enforce workplace rules. A common way managers handle the problem is to ignore it and hope it goes away. This rarely works and causes resentment, and morale and productivity problems with employees who follow the rules. HR needs to help develop new managers' supervisory skills, including training in the best ways to maintain a positive and productive workplace.
Are you part of the problem? Here are a few warning signs:[60]

- You are avoiding a problem employee.
- Employees accuse you of "playing favorites."
- You don't know how to handle an "out-of-control" employee.
- You ignore obvious problems or try to make them sound as though they're not serious.

- You fear employees will make claims of retaliation if you start to enforce the rules.
- You notice cliques forming to protect certain individuals.
- Individuals tell you they have been victims of pranks or horseplay.

The good news is it's never too late to do the right thing. If you or one of your managers needs to get back on track, one effective approach is to call a meeting and explain that you've seen the errors of your ways and that all rules and policies will now be enforced in a non-discriminatory manner. Take time to review those policies and the consequences for not following the rules. It's okay to ask employees for suggestions. They tend to remember rules and follow them better when they feel they had a chance to participate in their development.

Things to think about:
What can you do if employees resist your efforts to "take back" your authority and enforce workplace discipline?

Unless it's the result of downsizing, dismissal should be the last step and ultimate disciplinary consequence. Occasionally an offense is so serious that immediate dismissal is appropriate such as theft, sexual harassment, violence, plagiarism, or sabotage. These exceptions to the discipline policy should be spelled out in the employee manual.[61] When the decision is made, HRM needs to consider how the dismissal will be communicated. Terminations cause hard feelings, create economic hardship, and provoke lawsuits. Nearly 90 percent of discrimination charges filed with the Equal Employment Opportunity Commission are related to discharging employees.[62] There may be no way to prevent lawsuits, but there are certainly steps that employers can take to try to minimize them.

When firing an employee:

- *Review all facts.* Be very familiar with documentation such as performance appraisals, disciplinary actions, and productivity reports that led to this action.
- *Set the stage.* Call the employee into your office or another private setting. Have someone there as a witness. Darken your computer screen and silence your phones, as this deserves your full attention.
- *Be very clear.* Use language that leaves no doubt that the employee is being terminated. Consider making notes so you don't stray from your message. Review the performance problems and unsuccessful efforts to remedy the situation.
- *Allow a little dignity.* Suggest that the job may not have been the best match for the employee and express hope that things will work out better in a new job and under different circumstances.
- *Let the employee talk.* Give the person a chance to respond, regardless of how uncomfortable it is for you, but don't get drawn into an argument or back down. Try not to take employee comments personally. Harsh comments are likely to be made in frustration, hurt, or anger.
- *Give severance pay.* Providing severance pay slightly softens the blow, and is the decent way to behave. A good guideline is two weeks' pay plus one additional week's pay for every year of service.
- *Ask the person to sign an agreement waiving the right to sue for wrongful termination.* Consult your attorney. You may be allowed to make signing such an agreement a condition of the employee's receiving severance pay.
- *Immediately pay for any earned time.* In addition to any severance, you're responsible for any earned overtime and earned but unused vacation time or unused sick days.
- *Have the person leave that day.* It's unfair and uncomfortable for a terminated employee to continue to come to work. That would lower staff morale, and the possibility always exists that the person could do damage to your company.
- *Inform the person of any benefits.* Terminated employees will be grateful to learn about any benefits they're entitled to, such as unemployment payments or the ability to continue their medical insurance.
- *Take appropriate protective steps.* Immediately change passwords for any computer programs the employee had access to. Retrieve any keys they may have to premises.
- *Tell other employees that the employee has been terminated.* Other employees may need to know about the termination, but don't give any details. It's a private matter. At best, you might appear to be a gossip. At worst, it could lead to legal problems.

Summary

(This summary relates to the Learning Outcomes identified on page 90.) After having read this chapter, you can:

1. **Explain the intent of the Privacy Act, the Drug-Free Workplace Act, the Fair Credit Reporting Act, and their effects on HRM.** The Privacy Act of 1974 was intended to require government agencies to make available to employees information

contained in their personnel files. Subsequent state laws have afforded the same ability to nongovernment agencies. HRM must ensure that policies exist and are disseminated to employees regarding access to their personnel files. The Drug-Free Workplace Act of 1988 required government agencies, individuals with federal contracts, and organizations with federal contracts over $100,000 to take various steps to ensure that their workplace is drug free.

2. **Explain employer concerns about social media use and the components of an effective social media policy.** Social media such as Facebook, LinkedIn, Twitter, Myspace, and YouTube provide opportunities for employees to share their positive or negative feelings about employment on a global scale, endangering reputations and jobs. Productivity also suffers when employees use social media during work hours. Effective social media policies include information on how the employer monitors Internet use, warnings that there is no privacy when using the Internet at work, reminding employees to be respectful online, explaining legal repercussions of online defamation of character, privacy settings, and how company photos, names, and logos can be used.

3. **Describe the provisions of the Worker Adjustment and Retraining Notification Act.** The Worker Adjustment and Retraining Notification Act of 1988 requires employers with one hundred or more employees contemplating closing a facility or laying off fifty or more workers to provide sixty days advance notice of the action.

4. **Identify the pros and cons of employee drug testing.** Drug testing is a contemporary issue facing many organizations. The problems associated with substance abuse in our society, and our organizations specifically, lead companies to test employees. The costs of abuse in terms of lost productivity and the like support such action. On the other hand is the issue of privacy. Does the company truly have the right to know what employees do on their own time? Additionally, drug test validity as well as proper procedures are often cited as reasons for not testing.

5. **Discuss the benefits of using honesty tests in hiring.** Honesty testing in hiring has been used to capture the information unavailable from a polygraph in screening applicants. Many companies use these question-and-answer tests to obtain information on one's potential to steal from the company, as well as to determine whether an employee has stolen before. Validity of honesty tests has some support from research, and their use as an additional selection device appears reasonable.

6. **Explain legal and ethical issues involved in monitoring employees.** Employers have extensive rights to monitor employees in the workplace including use of phones, e-mail, and Internet. Technology available to track employee actions is increasing, including sophisticated computer use tracking, RFID, and GPS technology. Employee monitoring can save money and increase productivity for employers, however, employees often feel that their right to privacy is being violated. Concern over new technology that may track employees beyond the workplace is growing.

7. **Discuss the implications of the employment-at-will doctrine and identify the five exceptions to the doctrine.** The employment-at-will doctrine permits employers to fire employees for any reason, justified or not. Although based on nineteenth-century common law, exceptions to employment-at-will have curtailed employers' use of the doctrine. The five exceptions to the employment-at-will doctrine are: contractual relationships; statutory considerations; public policy violations; implied employment contracts; and breach of good faith by the employer.

8. **Define discipline and the contingency factors that determine the severity of discipline.** Discipline is a condition in the organization when employees conduct themselves in accordance with the organization's rules and standards of acceptable behavior. Whether to impose discipline and with what severity should reflect factors such as problem seriousness, problem duration, problem frequency and nature, the employee's work history, extenuating circumstances, degree of orientation, history of the organization's discipline practices, implications for other employees, and management backing.

9. **Describe the general guidelines for administering discipline.** General guidelines in administering discipline include making disciplinary actions corrective, making disciplinary actions progressive, and following the hot-stove rule—be immediate, provide ample warning, be consistent, and be impersonal.

10. **Explain the elements of the hot-stove rule and their application to discipline in the workplace.** The hot-stove rule consists of four elements: immediate response, advance warning, consistent action, and impersonal application. If employee disciplinary actions meet all of these elements every time discipline is applied, discipline will be seen as consistent, fair, and predictable. Employees will begin to regulate their own behavior out of their own self-interest.

11. **Identify important procedures to follow when firing an employee.** Review all facts; meet the employee in a private setting with witnesses; state the termination clearly; let the employee retain their dignity; pay salary and severance; ask the employee to sign an agreement not to sue; explain any benefits, such as insurance, that they have a right to; have the employee leave immediately; revoke their access by changing passwords and taking keys; and inform other employees of the termination.

Demonstrating Comprehension

QUESTIONS FOR REVIEW

1. What should an organization do to make employees' personnel files available to them?
2. What should be considered when developing a policy on employee use of social media?
3. What are the pros and cons of using honesty tests to screen job applicants?
4. What is employment-at-will? How does it affect employees? Employers?
5. Explain the potential advantages and disadvantages of having organizational policies that deal with workplace romance.
6. Define positive discipline.
7. Describe how positive discipline differs from the traditional disciplinary process.
8. What is the hot-stove rule?

Key Terms

discipline
dismissal
drug testing
Drug-Free Workplace Act of 1988
employment contract
employment-at-will doctrine
Fair Credit Reporting Act of 1971
honesty test

hot-stove rule
implied employment contract
Polygraph Protection Act of 1988
Privacy Act of 1974
progressive discipline
rule implied
social media
suspension

whistle-blowing
Worker Adjustment and Retraining Notification (WARN) Act of 1988
workplace romance
written verbal warning
written warning

HRM Workshop

Linking Concepts to Practice DISCUSSION QUESTIONS

1. "Employees should not be permitted to see their personnel files. Allowing them access to review the file constrains realistic observations by managers. Accordingly, as long as the information is not used against an employee, these files should be off limits." Do you agree or disagree with the statement? Explain.

2. "The goals of 'consistency' and having the 'punishment fit the crime' are incompatible with just-cause termination." Do you agree or disagree with the statement? Explain.

3. Do you believe drug testing is necessary for most organizations? Why or why not? Defend your position.

4. "Employees should not be allowed to make references to their employer online or on social media sites like Facebook or Twitter." Do you agree or disagree? Defend your position.

5. An employee is overheard telling a new worker, "Don't rush back from work. You'll make us look bad. Everyone takes an extra fifteen to thirty minutes. Every once in a while we get warned if the supervisor is in a bad mood, but he never does anything about it." Could the problem extend beyond long lunches? Explain.

Making a Difference SERVICE LEARNING PROJECTS

Effective communication is fundamental to helping employees understand policies and procedures that define rights and discipline in the workplace. These suggestions put your communication skills to work.

- Develop a social media campaign to assist a local non-profit organization in communicating its purpose or services.
- Contact a local organization that assists people living with or recovering from addictions and determine how you can assist them. Be sure to learn how the organization establishes rules and discipline for clients.

- Humane Societies and animal shelters often need volunteers to train and socialize pets before they can be adopted. Note the similarities between the hot-stove approach and teaching appropriate behavior to the animals.

As you put your service learning experience together, keep a journal of your activities, the time you spend, contact information for people you work with, and your thoughts about the process. When you're finished, make a presentation to your class about the experience and what you learned. What concepts from Chapter 4 were you able to apply?

Developing Diagnostic and Analytical Skills

Case Application 4-A: CASINO HAS NO SENSE OF HUMOR

David Steward wasn't planning on getting a lot of attention when he put up a *Dilbert* cartoon on the employee bulletin board at Catfish Bend Casino. He wasn't sure anyone saw him do it at all, but sure enough, a surveillance camera was watching.

Morale at Catfish Bend was pretty low when the company announced that the casino would be closing, and 170 workers would be laid off. Steward thought the *Dilbert* cartoon would cheer the workers up. In the strip, *Dilbert* had the following exchange with a garbage man:

DILBERT: Why does it seem as if most of the decisions in my workplace are made by drunken lemurs?
GARBAGE MAN: Decisions are made by people who have time, not people who have talent.
DILBERT: Why are talented people so busy?
GARBAGE MAN: They're fixing the problems made by people who have time.

Managers checked the surveillance tape, found that Steward had posted the offensive cartoon, and fired him. Steve Morley, human resource director at the casino, said that "upper management found

the cartoon to be very offensive". Morley went on to say, "Basically, he was accusing the decision makers of being drunken lemurs. We consider that misconduct when you insult your employers."

Steward tried to claim that the firing was wrong, and that he deserved unemployment pay, but the casino disagreed. *Dilbert* cartoonist Scott Adams tried to come to Steward's aid. "Most *Dilbert* comics don't come right out and call management a bunch of drunken lemurs," Adams said. "So I can see how this one might have been a tad over the line." Adams also said that Steward's dismissal might be the first confirmed instance of a worker being fired for posting a *Dilbert* strip. Adams published a follow-up comic:

BOSS: Our surveillance cameras caught you posting this anti-management comic on the wall.
BOSS: This comic compares managers to drunken lemurs.
BOSS: Do you think drunken lemurs are like managers?
DILBERT: No. Some lemurs can hold their liquor.

Management was not amused and still refused to pay jobless benefits. Steward appealed to an administrative law judge, claiming that putting the cartoon up was an error in judgment, not intentionally breaking any rules or being disrespectful. The judge found in Steward's favor.

Source: The Des Moines Register (December 19, 2007), pp. 1, 10.

Questions:

1. If you were the human resources director at the casino, what should you have done prior to firing Steward to be sure you had all of your bases covered?

2. Does the surveillance camera present any ethical or legal problems? Why or why not?

3. Explain any other legal issues regarding employee or employer rights that might apply.

4. Do you think the punishment was appropriate for posting the comic? Explain, using concepts from the chapter.

5. If you were the administrative law judge, would you award unemployment benefits to Steward? Why or why not?

Case Application 4-B: OFF-THE-JOB BEHAVIORS

Balancing the realities of protecting the organization and the rights of employees, both in and out of work, has become a major focal point for contemporary human resource managers. For example, by everyone's account, Peter Oiler was an outstanding employee. Oiler, a truck driver for Winn-Dixie Stores and a twenty-year employee, had an impeccable and unblemished work record.[63] He was punctual, trustworthy, and an exceptionally productive employee. Most coworkers viewed him as an asset to the organization. But none of that appeared to matter when Oiler was fired. The reason: Oiler was a cross-dresser. On his own time, Oiler changed his persona, becoming Donna, complete with wearing women's clothing, a wig, and makeup. Frequently out in public with his wife—in restaurants, at church—Donna maintained a dignified public appearance, bothering no one, and simply went on with his personal life as he chose.

Management at Winn-Dixie, however, saw things differently. Shortly after they learned of his cross-dressing behavior, Oiler was fired. This happened in spite of the realization that his out-of-work behavior had absolutely no adverse effect on his job performance. Rather, Winn-Dixie's position was that if he was seen in public by someone who recognized him as a Winn-Dixie employee, the company's image could be damaged.

Oiler sued the company for wrongfully terminating him on the basis of sex discrimination. He claimed that cross-dressing was nothing more than his "not conforming to gender stereotype as a man." During the trial, records reinforced that there was not one shred of evidence that any of Oiler's out-of-work activities affected his ability to work. Nonetheless, the court ruled in Winn-Dixie's favor, citing that there are no federal or state laws that protect the rights of "transgendered" employees. Although Winn-Dixie won at the trial, they experienced an aftermath that they were not expecting. Many coworkers rallied behind Oiler, wondering if the company could do this to him, what might they do next. Certainly people understood that a company can fire anyone for any legal reason, but how much latitude should a company have in defining a "legal" reason? Could they fire an employee who drinks alcohol outside of work, views an "inappropriate" movie, or visits adult websites? What if one is arrested? Does that result in an automatic termination? The answer is, it could—but there are consequences to this employer action. In such cases, companies have found that terminating an employee for outside-of-work activities brings negative publicity, lowers employee morale, and increases employee turnover.

Questions:

1. Do you believe Oiler's employee rights were violated? Explain your position.

2. What do you see as the consequences of organizations that punish employees for certain off-the-job behaviors? Explain.

3. Would you consider Winn-Dixie an organization that exhibits characteristics of progressive discipline or the hot-stove approach? Defend your position.

Working with a Team DEALING IN GRAY AREAS

Below are several scenarios and a number of alternatives. After reading each scenario, select the alternative you think best handles the situation. After completing the exercise, discuss your selections with a group of four to five students. Note where you agree on an alternative and where you differ. Where differences exist, describe the differences. Finally, as a group, reach consensus on an alternative.

1. A co-worker, Brad, invites you to share a pizza for lunch on the outside picnic tables the company recently installed. After eating pizza, Brad lights a marijuana cigarette and asks if you would like your own or a share of his. You know that having or consuming drugs at the work site is a violation of policy and law, and you must decide whether to:

   a. Inform Brad's supervisor, safety coordinator, or human resource manager of the incident.

   b. Tell Brad he shouldn't smoke pot at work and encourage him to seek help such as the employee assistance program in the human resource department.

   c. Say nothing, excuse yourself, and hope that when Brad returns to work, his reflexes aren't slowed, mental powers and perceptions aren't lessened, or that he won't become more forgetful and injure himself or someone else.

   d. Join Brad in prohibited behavior.

   e. Other (specify).

2. You are completing an honesty test for a potential employer. The question, "Have you ever knowingly stolen any item from an employer?" is a tough one because you remember the time when you were working as a cashier in a grocery store and at break you and other cashiers would eat pieces of fruit that did not meet quality requirements of store policy. You would

   a. Check yes.

b. Check no, rationalizing fruit consumption as an employee benefit.

c. Reconsider working for a company that asks such questions on tests.

d. Other (specify).

3. A coworker shares that she recently logged into the database, printed the customer mailing list, then sold it to various list subscribers for her "petty cash fund," because she didn't get the raise increase she deserved. You

a. Tell a human resources staff member.

b. Tell other coworkers.

c. Wish she hadn't told you and say nothing.

d. Other (specify).

4. You know that a coworker uses, sells, and distributes drugs to other coworkers. You

a. Tell human resources.

b. Call the company security or the local police.

c. Leave an anonymous message.

d. Other (specify).

In your group, in addition to considering these situations from the employee view, also consider management's perspective—that is, how management can lower the probability that these types of questionable employee behaviors would occur at work, and what actions management would like their employees to take if faced with any of these scenarios.

Learning an HRM Skill   GUIDELINES FOR COUNSELING EMPLOYEES

About the skill: Disciplinary meetings often involve counseling employees to achieve better performance. No one set procedure addresses counseling employees, but we offer the following nine guidelines that you should consider following when faced with the need to counsel an employee.[64]

1. **Document all problem performance behaviors.** Make note of specific job behaviors such as absenteeism, lateness, and poor quality in terms of dates, times, and what happened. This provides you with objective data.

2. **Deal with the employee objectively, fairly, and equitably.** Treat each employee similarly. Issues discussed should focus on performance behaviors.

3. **Confront job performance issues only.** Your main focus is on what affects performance. Even though it may be a personal problem, you should not try to psychoanalyze the individual. Leave that to the trained specialists! You can, however, address how these behaviors are affecting the employee's job performance.

4. **Offer assistance to help the employee.** Just pointing the finger at an employee serves little useful purpose. If the employee could "fix" the problem alone, he or she probably would have. Help might be needed—from both you and the organization. Offer this assistance where possible.

5. **Expect the employee to resist the feedback and become defensive.** It is human nature to dislike constructive or negative feedback. Expect that the individual will be uncomfortable with the discussion. Make every effort, however, to keep the meeting calm so that the message can get across. Documentation, fairness, focusing on job behaviors, and offering assistance help reduce this defensiveness.

6. **Make sure the employee owns up to the problem.** All things considered, the problem is not yours: it's the employee's. The employee needs to take responsibility for his or her behavior and begin to look for ways to correct the problem.

7. **Develop an action plan to correct performance.** Once the employee has taken responsibility for the problem, develop a plan of action designed to correct the problem. Be specific as to what the employee must do (for example, what is expected and when it is expected), and what resources you are willing to commit to assist.

8. **Identify outcomes for failing to correct problems.** You're there to help, not to carry a poor performer forever. Inform the employee of what the consequences will be if he or she does not follow the action plan.

9. **Monitor and control progress.** Evaluate the employee's progress. Provide frequent feedback on what you're observing. Reinforce good efforts.

Enhancing Your Communication Skills

1. Develop a two- to three-page report on how drug testing and drug information programs at work may discourage the sale and use of drugs in the workplace.

2. Conduct some research on employee monitoring. In a presentation with at least five presentation slides, describe ways that employers can monitor on-site employee behaviors. In your research, cite the benefits and drawbacks for companies from implementing such a practice.

3. In two to three pages, develop arguments for and against using honesty tests in hiring.

4. Provide an example where employee discipline was handled poorly. Explain what went wrong and write a scenario of how it could have been administered more appropriately. Consider presenting the "before" and "after" situations with role play or a short original video for your class.

(Source: NASA/NewsCom)

LEARNING OUTCOMES

After reading this chapter, you will be able to

1. Describe the importance of human resource planning.

2. Define the steps involved in the human resource planning process.

3. Explain what human resource information systems are used for.

4. Define the term *job analysis*.

5. Identify the six general techniques for obtaining job analysis information.

6. Describe the steps involved in conducting the job analysis.

7. Explain job descriptions, job specifications, and essential functions.

8. Identify elements of job enrichment that contribute to employee morale and productivity.

9. Describe how job analysis permeates all aspects of HRM.

10. Explain flexible scheduling alternatives.

Human Resource Planning and Job Analysis

It doesn't take a rocket scientist to figure out what to do when you have too many rocket scientists. It takes an HR manager.

When the space shuttle program ended in 2011, NASA and several of its contractors found themselves facing a change of mission for the space agency. The aging shuttle program had been ordered to close after thirty years of triumph and tragedy. Governmental and commercial interests were consulted as a new strategy for space exploration was developed for the United States.[1] The new goal was to develop a program that would send explorers to an asteroid by 2025 and Mars in the 2030s. In the meantime, U.S. astronauts would hitch rides into space with private spacecraft companies like SpaceX or with Russian astronauts.

This change in strategy was carefully planned. In 2009, an independent commission made up of astronauts, rocket scientists, NASA managers, NASA contractors, and academics worked together to develop a new direction for NASA. When the planning was complete, HR professionals at NASA needed to determine the staff changes necessary to implement the new strategy and keep the agency going. During the transition, a major challenge was keeping the workforce motivated and preventing employees from jumping ship before Atlantis flew the last shuttle flight in 2011. "Transition is a difficult time, especially for the people who are losing their jobs.... I am optimistic that what will emerge is a stronger, more robust program and agency, once the transition is worked through,"[2] reported Leroy Chiao, a commission member and former astronaut.

NASA's new space strategy involves outsourcing "low earth orbit" missions, like shuttling astronauts to the International Space Station, to "commercial space" companies with private spacecrafts. NASA will focus on missions that reach further into space, including the trips to Mars and a large asteroid. This change in strategy meant that NASA and its contractors didn't need all of the support people who ran the shuttle program. HR needed to determine the skills necessary for the employees that would fulfill the new missions, while making sure critical employees who had valuable knowledge and experience stayed with the organization. General Accountability Office official Christina Chaplain said, "I give NASA a lot of credit for trying to be very strategic and thoughtful in their planning. They've been mapping skills for the next program and figuring out how to translate those into people requirements and how they map back to the current workforce."[3]

Tracy Anania, NASA Director of Human Resources at the John F. Kennedy Space Center, was given the challenging task of determining who to keep and who would join the ranks of the unemployed. It was estimated that 7,800[4] would lose their jobs when the shuttle program ended. Since the number of employees that needed to be cut was beyond any amount that could be handled by attrition or early retirement, and the fact that NASA employees usually don't quit jobs in the space program, this was quite an undertaking. NASA reports that although 12 percent of employees are eligible to retire annually, only 3 percent retire each year.

Dave Nelson ran a shuttle simulator that trained astronauts for the last thirty years. During simulated lift offs and landings, Dave and his computers prepared astronauts for every emergency imaginable in order to sharpen their skills and avoid a catastrophe. Nothing in his job prepared him for the change in direction taken by the space agency that left him unemployed. NASA offered generous severance packages that included insurance benefits and assistance with job training and placement, but leaving a job he loved was still difficult for Nelson. "This has been my life for thirty years," said Nelson, "It's hard to believe it's coming to an end."[5]

How do you prepare for a life after NASA?

Looking Ahead

Strategy changes usually require adjustments in the size or composition of an organization's workforce. These changes aren't always negative. Are you aware of recent examples of organizations that have made strategic changes?

Introduction

The radical workplace changes necessary to close down the space shuttle program and shift emphasis to travel into deep space required NASA's HR planning to coordinate closely with organizational strategists. They realized early on that it's essential to have the right number of NASA scientists with the right skills in place in order to move the organization forward effectively.

Consider the results of making a decision without planning how to implement it. Think about the last time you took a vacation. For example, if you live in Frostburg, Maryland, and decide to go to a Florida beach for spring break, you need to decide which beach—Panama City or Daytona Beach, for example—you want to go to and the best route you can take. Will you drive or will you fly? Will you rent a hotel room or stay with a friend? This is what planning is all about—knowing where you are going and how you are going to get there. The same holds true for human resource management.

human resource planning
Process of determining an organization's human resource needs.

Whenever an organization is in the process of determining its human resource needs, it is engaged in a process we call **human resource planning**. Human resource planning is one of the most important elements in a successful HRM program because it is a process by which an organization ensures that it has the right number and kinds of people at the right place, at the right time, capable of effectively and efficiently completing those tasks that will help the organization achieve its overall strategic objectives.[6] Employment planning, then, ultimately translates the organization's overall goals into the number and types of workers needed to meet those goals.[7] Without clear-cut planning and a direct linkage to the organization's strategic direction, estimations of an organization's human resource needs are reduced to mere guesswork that may well fall short of the organization's actual needs.

This means that employment planning cannot exist in isolation. It must be linked to the organization's overall strategy.[8] Just a few decades ago, outside of the firm's top executives, few employees in a typical firm really knew about the company's long-range objectives. The strategic efforts were often no more than an educated guess in determining the organization's direction. But things are different today. Aggressive domestic and global competition, for instance, have made strategic planning virtually mandatory. Although it's not our intention to go into every detail of the strategic planning process in this chapter, senior HRM officials are required to understand it because they're playing a more vital role in the strategic process.[9] Let's look at a fundamental strategic planning process in an organization.

An Organizational Framework

The strategic planning process in an organization is both long and continuous.[10] At the beginning of the process, the organization's main emphasis is to determine what business it is in. This is commonly referred to as developing the **mission statement**. Defining the organization's mission forces key decision makers to identify the scope of its products or services carefully. For example, the business magazine *Fast Company* established its mission and set its sights "to chronicle the epic changes sweeping across business and to equip readers with the ideas, tools, and tactics that they need to thrive."[11]

mission statement
A brief statement of the reason an organization is in business.

The mission statement is important because it's the foundation on which every decision in the organization should be made. Take, for instance, Google's mission statement: "Organize the world's information and make it universally accessible and useful." The mission statement clarifies for all organizational members exactly what the company is about. A few years ago it would have seemed that producing entertainment programming and the devices on which to view it would be inconsistent with Google's mission, yet that's exactly what Google is working to develop. Technology and the way we use it has made it necessary for Google to change in order to fulfill its mission. Even though we assume that the world will change, the need to specifically define an organization's line of business is critical to its survival.

Mission statements are not written in stone, and at any time, after careful study and deliberation, they can be changed. For example, the March of Dimes was originally created to facilitate the cure of infantile paralysis (polio). When polio was essentially eradicated in the 1950s, the organization redefined its mission as seeking cures for children's diseases in general.

Kodak went from being one of the world's largest manufacturers of photographic film and processing to a leader in digital imaging. IBM went from being the world's largest producer of personal and mainframe computers to offering consulting, hosting, and business services.

After reaching agreement on what business the company is in and who its consumers are, senior management then begins to set strategic goals.[12] During this phase, these managers define objectives for the company for the next five to twenty years. These objectives are broad statements that establish targets the organization will achieve. After these goals are set, the next step in the strategic planning process begins—the corporate assessment. During this phase, a company begins to analyze its goals in terms of whether they can be achieved with the current organizational resources. Many factors are considered in the company's analysis: its current strategies, its external environment, its strengths and weaknesses, and its opportunities and threats. This is commonly referred to as a gap or **SWOT analysis** (strengths, weaknesses, opportunities, and threats). The company begins to look at what skills, knowledge, and abilities are available internally, and where shortages in terms of people skills or equipment may exist.

This analysis forces management to recognize that every organization, no matter how large and powerful, is constrained in some way by the resources and skills it has available. For example, although Walmart seems large enough to provide nearly any product or service, they are pretty unlikely to produce or sell cars any time soon. Their expertise and strength is in efficiently providing smaller consumer goods at a low cost. Cars would require different distribution channels and considerable investment in product development. Their business model is much better suited to providing automotive service, not the actual car itself.

The SWOT analysis should lead to a clear assessment of the organization's internal resources—such as capital, worker skills, patents, and the like. It should also indicate organizational departmental abilities, such as training and development, marketing, accounting, human resources, research and development, and management information systems. An organization's best attributes and abilities are called its **strengths**. And any of those strengths that represent unique skills or resources that can determine the organization's competitive

How did Facebook go from their launch in 2004 to having over 800 million active users? Maybe the answer lies in their mission statement: "Facebook's mission is to give people the power to share and make the world more open and connected." *(Source: Odilon Dimier/Altopress/NewsCom)*

SWOT analysis
A process for determining an organization's strengths, weaknesses, opportunities, and threats.

strengths
An organization's best attributes and abilities.

ETHICAL ISSUES IN HRM

Shades of Green

"Everybody wants to be green," exclaims one contractor who found new life in the "green" construction business. "It's a great selling feature for any business."[13] But what actually qualifies as a "green" job? As sustainability becomes a priority for consumers, communities, and investors, the definition is in question.

The Society of Human Resource Management (SHRM) defines green jobs as those that meet the need for environmentally responsible production and work processes and the development of green goods and services. This includes "reducing pollution or waste, reducing energy usage, and reducing use of limited natural resources."[14] Examples include jobs that involve: reducing pollution or waste, reducing energy usage, reducing use of limited natural resources, protecting wildlife or ecosystems, lowering carbon emissions, and developing alternative energy. In a 2010 survey, SHRM found that 81 percent of responding companies

were adding green duties to existing positions, but only 23 percent were adding completely new green positions. You've probably noticed consumer sentiment moving toward greener alternatives when they spend their "green." Businesses have noticed, too. Starbucks is rewarding coffee farmers who use environmentally and socially sound growing practices,[15] and McDonald's serves "Rainforest Alliance-certified" coffee and promotes sustainable fishing.[16]

Ethical Questions:

How far can employers stretch the "green jobs" label before it loses legitimacy? Does Starbucks or McDonald's policy of rewarding their coffee suppliers who use sustainable growing practices mean that they are green employers? How "green" do they need to be? Is the SHRM definition adequate?

Exhibit 5-1
The Strategic Direction—
Human Resource Linkage

The organization's mission guides all strategy and structure. The link between the mission and the work people do should be clear on every level.

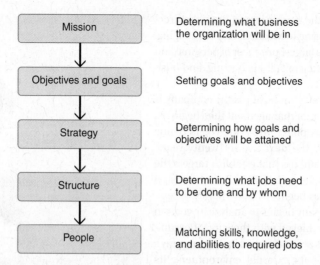

Mission	Determining what business the organization will be in
Objectives and goals	Setting goals and objectives
Strategy	Determining how goals and objectives will be attained
Structure	Determining what jobs need to be done and by whom
People	Matching skills, knowledge, and abilities to required jobs

core competency
Organizational strengths that represent unique skills or resources.

weaknesses
Resources an organization lacks or activities it does poorly.

opportunities
External environmental factors that can be used for the organization's advantage.

threats
External environmental factors that present challenges to the organization.

edge forms its **core competency**. On the other hand, if a firm lacks resources in a certain area or if there are some activities it performs poorly, these are considered **weaknesses**.

After examining the internal strengths and weaknesses, it's time for the organization to look outward at the opportunities and threats in the external environment. **Opportunities** are factors outside the organization that can be help gain an advantage including new technology, surplus of qualified applicants, weak competitors, and a strong economy. **Threats** in the external environment present challenges if not handled well, including a weak economy, government regulation, changes in employment laws, and new competitors.

This SWOT analysis phase of the strategic planning process cannot be overstated; it serves as the link between the organization's goals and ensuring that the company can meet its objectives—that is, establishes the direction of the company through strategic planning.

The company must determine which jobs need to be done and how many and what types of workers will be required for those jobs. In management terminology, we call this organizing. Thus, establishing the structure of the organization assists in determining the skills, knowledge, and abilities required of job holders. Only at this point do we begin to look at people to meet these criteria. And that's where HRM comes into play. To determine what skills are needed, HRM conducts a job analysis. Exhibit 5-1 is a simplistic graphic representation of the job analysis process. The key message in Exhibit 5-1 is that all jobs in the organization ultimately must be tied to the company's mission and strategic direction. Unless jobs can be linked to the organization's strategic goals, these goals become a moving target. It's no wonder, then, that employment planning has become more critical in organizations. Let's look at how human resource planning operates within the strategic planning process.

Linking Organizational Strategy to Human Resource Planning

To ensure that appropriate personnel are available to meet the requirements set during the strategic planning process, human resource managers engage in employment planning. The purpose of this planning effort is to determine what HRM requirements exist for current and future supplies and demands for workers.[17] For example, if a company has set as one of its goals to expand its international divisions over the next five years, such action will require that skilled employees be available to handle the jobs. After this assessment, employment planning matches the supplies and demands for labor, and supports the people component.

Assessing Current Human Resources

Assessing current human resources begins by developing a profile of the organization's current employees. This internal analysis includes information about the workers and the skills they currently possess. The rapidly increasing number of employers who use human resource information systems software (HRIS), makes it easier for most organizations to generate an effective and detailed human resources inventory report. The input to this report would be derived from forms completed by employees and checked by supervisors. Such reports would include a complete list of all employees by name, education, training, prior employment, current position, performance ratings, salary level, languages spoken, capabilities, and specialized skills. For example, if internal translators were needed for suppliers, customers, or employee assistance, a contact list could be developed. This would be extremely useful for HR at NASA as they look for specific skills when making decisions on which employees to retain.

From a planning viewpoint, this input is valuable in determining what skills are currently available in the organization. The inventory serves as a guide for supporting new organizational pursuits or in altering the organization's strategic direction. This report also has value in other HRM activities, such as selecting individuals for training and development, promotion, and transfers. The completed profile of the human resources inventory can also provide crucial information for identifying current or future threats to the organization's ability to successfully meet its goals. The organization can use the information from the inventory to identify specific variables that may have a particular relationship, for example, to training needs, productivity improvements, or succession planning. An inventory might reveal poor customer service skills— a threat that can adversely affect the organization's performance if it begins to permeate the entire organization.

How well trained are these workers for tomorrow's work? That's a question HRM must assess, as its answers will affect the need for human resources. HRM must ensure that employees are properly prepared to do the work needed so that organizational performance does not falter. *(Source: Manchan/Photodisc/ Getty Images, Inc.)*

Identifying employees and their skills is important, but one must also recognize that keeping them in the organization is crucial. Frequently called employee retention, HRM must lead the way to help managers understand that they play a critical role in retaining the best workers, and that their actions can go a long way to either stimulate or reduce employee turnover. It is estimated that about 75 percent of the reasons employees quit their jobs and leave organizations are within the control of managers, such as being honest with employees, giving them challenging work, and recognizing them for their performance.[18]

Human Resource Information Systems   To assist in the HR inventory, many organizations have implemented a **human resource information system (HRIS)**. The HRIS (sometimes referred to as a human resource management system [HRMS]) is designed to quickly fulfill the HRM informational needs of the organization. The HRIS is a database system that keeps important information about employees in a central and accessible location—even information on the global workforce. When such information is required, the data can be retrieved and used to facilitate employment planning decisions. Its technical potential permits the organization to track most information about employees and jobs and to retrieve that information when needed. In many cases, this information can help an organization gain a competitive advantage (see SWOT analysis discussed earlier in this chapter).[19] An HRIS may also be used to help track EEO data.

human resource information system (HRIS)
A computerized system that assists in the processing of HRM information.

HRISs have become valuable resources for HR professionals. This is essentially due to the recognition that management needs timely information on its people, and these systems can provide significant cost savings. Additionally, HRISs have become very user-friendly and provide quick and responsive reports—especially when linked to the organization's management information system. Moreover, systems today can streamline certain HRM processes, such as having employees select their employee benefits online during a period called open enrollment. Technology advances have created many competitive vendors of HRIS systems that fit any size of business and run on nearly any platform including smart phones and tablet computers like iPads. Employers have the choice of hosting the data themselves or using Software as a Service (SaaS), which delivers the necessary services over the Internet, usually for a contracted amount of time.[20]

At a time when quick analysis of an organization's human resources is critical, the HRIS is filling a void in the human resource planning process. With information readily available, organizations are in a better position to quickly move forward in achieving their organizational goals. Additionally, the HRIS is useful in other aspects of human resource management, such as providing data support for compensation and benefits programs, as well as providing a necessary link to corporate payroll.[21]

replacement chart
HRM organizational charts indicating positions that may become vacant in the near future and the individuals who may fill the vacancies.

Succession Planning In addition to the HRIS system, some organizations also generate a separate management inventory report. This report, typically called a **replacement chart**, covers individuals in middle- to upper-level management positions. In an effort to facilitate succession planning—ensuring that another individual is ready to move into a position of higher responsibility—the replacement chart highlights those positions that may become vacant in the near future due to retirements, promotions, transfers, resignations, or even upon the death of the incumbent. Organizations that rely heavily on the skills and leadership of the baby boom generation are likely to see skill gaps without effective succession planning.[22] Investors are increasingly demanding that large organizations develop and announce succession plans for top executives, hoping to avoid a crisis of leadership that could lead to financial problems if a CEO were to unexpectedly quit or die.[23]

Each individual manager's skills inventory is compared to the list of positions in order to determine if there is sufficient managerial talent to cover potential future vacancies. This "readiness" chart gives management an indication of time frames for succession, as well as helping spot any skill shortages.[24] Should skill shortages exist, HRM can either recruit new employees or intensify employee development efforts. At Intel, for example, succession starts shortly after an individual is hired. Employees marked for promotions are coached on management activities and are extensively trained to assume positions of greater responsibility.

Replacement charts look similar to traditional organizational charts. Incumbents are listed in their positions, and those individuals targeted to replace them are listed beneath with the expected time in which they will be prepared to take on the needed responsibility. We have provided a sample replacement chart in Exhibit 5-2.

Determining the Demand for Labor

Once an assessment of the organization's current human resources situation has been made and the future direction of the organization has been considered, it's time to develop a projection of future human resource needs. This means performing a year-by-year analysis for every significant job level and type. In effect, the result is a human resource inventory covering specified years into the future. These inventories are usually comprehensive and complex. Organizations typically require a diverse mix of people. That's because employees are not perfectly substitutable for one another within an organization. For example, in early 2008, Harley Davidson experienced labor shortages in critical fields such as engineers, material planners, marketing, and supply chain analysts, while at the same

Exhibit 5-2
Sample Replacement Chart

Individuals who have skills and experience to replace the company president are identified and evaluated for this replacement chart.

Carolyn Roberts
Current position: President
Age: 64
Expected replacement needed: 1 year
Education: Master's in taxation
Experience: 27 years of financial operations

Possible replacement	Potential	Ready in
Beth Harper	Medium	8 months
Carlos Hernandez	Medium	2.5 years
Gus Brame	High	14 months

Beth Harper
Current position: Vice President, Marketing
Expected replacement needed: 1 year
Experience: 17 years in marketing management

Possible replacement	Potential	Ready in
Rick Sapp	Low	2.5 years
Charese Singleton	Medium	3.0 years

Carlos Hernandez
Current position: Vice President, Human Resources
Expected replacement needed: 7 years
Experience: 18 years in human resources management

Possible replacement	Potential	Ready in
Bill McGregor	High	2.75 years
Eric Hayden	Medium	5.50 years

Gus Brame
Current position: Vice President and Corporate Counsel
Expected replacement needed: 11 months
Experience: 23 years as an attorney

Possible replacement	Potential	Ready
Kelly Williams	High	Immediately
No other candidate		

TIPS FOR SUCCESS

Where The Jobs Are

If you can't find a job or internship, you might find it hard to believe that some employers are having trouble finding qualified people for good jobs, but it's true! In a recent survey by ManpowerGroup, 52 percent of U.S. employers report having problems filling positions.

The reasons include applicants that do not have adequate technical skills, lack experience, or require more pay that the position offers. Manpower explains that over time jobs have changed, requiring different, and frequently more technical skills. The hardest to fill jobs include:[26]

- Skilled trades
- Sales representatives
- Engineers
- Drivers
- Accounting and finance staff
- Information technology staff
- Management/executives
- Teachers
- Secretaries/administrative assistants
- Machinist/machine operator

time experiencing an oversupply of production workers and a need to cut the overall workforce.[25] More recently, staffing agency Manpower reports that in spite of high unemployment in the U.S., companies are having a hard time filling openings for sales representatives, engineers, and skilled trade workers (see Tips For Success: Where The Jobs Are).

Accurate estimates of future demands in both qualitative and quantitative terms require additional information to determine that, for example, in the next twenty-four months, an organization will need to hire eighty-five additional individuals. It is necessary to know what types of employees, in terms of skills, knowledge, and abilities, are required. Remember, these skills, knowledge, and abilities are determined based on the jobs required to meet the strategic direction of the organization. Accordingly, our forecasting methods must allow for the recognition of specific job needs as well as the total number of vacancies.

Predicting the Future Labor Supply

Estimating changes in internal supply requires HRM to look at those factors that can either increase or decrease its employee base. As previously noted in the discussion on estimating demand, forecasting of supply must also concern itself with the micro, or unit, level. For example, if one individual in Department X is transferred to a position in Department Y, and an individual in Department Y is transferred to a position in Department X, the net effect on the organization is zero. However, if only one individual is initially involved—say, promoted and sent to another location in the company—only through effective human resource planning can a competent replacement be available to fill the position vacated by the departing employee. An increase in the supply of any unit's human resources can come from a combination of four sources: new hires, contingent workers, transfers in, or individuals returning from a leave of absence. The task of predicting these new inputs can range from simple to complex.[27]

> Forecasting methods must allow for the recognition of specific jobs as well as the total number of vacancies.

Decreases in the internal supply can come about through retirements, dismissals, transfers out of the unit, layoffs, voluntary quits, sabbaticals, prolonged illnesses, or deaths. Some of these occurrences are obviously easier to predict than others. The easiest to forecast are retirements, assuming that employees typically retire after a certain length of service and the fact that most organizations require some advance notice of one's retirement intent. Given a history of the organization, HRM can predict with some accuracy how many retirements will occur over a given time period. Remember, however, that retirement, for the most part, is voluntary. Under the Age Discrimination in Employment Act, an organization cannot force employees to retire, with the exception of airline pilots who must retire at age 65.

At the other extreme, voluntary resignations, prolonged illnesses, and deaths are difficult to predict. Although large organizations such as Verizon or General Motors can use probability statistics to estimate the number of deaths that will occur among its employee population, such techniques are useless for forecasting in small organizations or estimating the exact positions that will be affected in large ones. Voluntary resignations can also be predicted by utilizing probabilities when the population size is large. In a company like Microsoft, managers can estimate the approximate number of voluntary resignations during any given year. In a department consisting of two or three workers, however, probability estimation is meaningless. Weak predictive ability in small units is unfortunate, too, because voluntary resignations typically have the greatest impact on such units.

In between the extremes—transfers, layoffs, sabbaticals, and dismissals—forecasts within reasonable limits of accuracy can be made. All four of these types of action are controllable by management—that is, they are either initiated by management or are within management's veto prerogative—and so each type can be reasonably predicted. Of the four, transfers out of a unit, such as lateral moves, demotions, or promotions, are the most difficult to predict because they depend on openings in other units. Layoffs are more controllable and anticipated by management, especially in the short run. Sabbaticals, too, are reasonably easy to forecast, since most organizations' sabbatical policies require a reasonable lead-time between request and initiation of the leave. Surprises do happen, requiring HR to act quickly. For example, in 2008, Best Buy was forced to react quickly as the economic downturn dramatically reduced sales. They responded by offering a voluntary severance package to nearly all of the 4,000 employees at their Minneapolis area headquarters. The offer was accepted by 500 employees.

Dismissals based on inadequate job performance can usually be forecast with the same method as voluntary resignations, using probabilities where large numbers of employees are involved. Additionally, performance evaluation reports are usually a reliable source for isolating the number of individuals whose employment might have to be terminated at a particular point in time due to unsatisfactory work performance.

Where Will We Find Workers?

After organizations take a look at the people who are already within the organization, they consider the supply of workers preparing for jobs and those already in the job market. This includes high school and college graduates, as well as those who received highly specialized training through an alternative supplier of job skills training. Entrants to the workforce from sources other than schools may also include men and women seeking full- or part-time work, students seeking work to pay for their education or support themselves while in school, employees returning from military service, job seekers who have been recently laid off, and so on. Migration into a community may also increase the number of individuals seeking employment opportunities and represent another source for the organization to consider as potential additions to its labor supply.

The potential supply can be quite different than what a quick look at the traditional sources of supply would lead us to believe. For example, with additional training, a sales representative can become qualified to perform the tasks of a district sales manager; thus, an organization having difficulty securing individuals with skills and experience in sales management should consider those candidates who have had recent sales or similar experience and are interested in being managers. In similar fashion, the potential supply for many other jobs can be expanded.

Matching Labor Demand and Supply

The objective of employment planning is to bring together the forecasts of future demand for workers and the supply for human resources, both current and future. The result of this effort is to pinpoint shortages both in number and in kind, to highlight areas where overstaffing may exist

Layoffs have become a common way for companies to restructure in order to become profitable again, including Bank of America's 2011 announcement that they were cutting 30,000 jobs. *(Source: Oxford/iStockphoto)*

(now or in the near future), and to keep abreast of the opportunities existing in the labor market to hire qualified employees—either to satisfy current needs or to stockpile potential candidates for the future.

Special attention must be paid to determining shortages. Should an organization find that the demand for human resources could possibly increase in the future, it must be prepared to hire or contract with additional staff or transfer people within the organization, or both, to balance the numbers, skills, mix, and quality of its human resources. An often overlooked action, but one that may be necessary because of inadequate availability of human resources, is to change the organization's objectives. Just as inadequate financial resources can restrict the growth and opportunities available to an organization, the shortage of the right types of employees can also act as such a constraint, even leading to changing the organization's objectives.

When dealing with employment planning, it's also possible to have an oversupply of employees as NASA experienced once the space shuttle program came to an end. An organization may have too many employees or employees with the wrong skills. When this happens, HRM must undertake the difficult task of laying off workers. Layoffs might occur as a result of financial difficulty, mergers, plant closings, offshoring, changes in technology that replace workers, or organizational restructuring. It is estimated that over 50 percent of employees have experienced a layoff due to downsizing or restructuring at some point in their careers.[28]

The decision of who to dismiss is a difficult one. The decision may be based on seniority, job performance, or the position with the organization. If a union is present, there will usually be an agreement to make the decision based on seniority with the most recent hires being laid off first.

Downsizing is not without cost. In addition to severance package costs, the remaining employees may suffer low morale and productivity for many reasons:

- They may feel survivor guilt after their coworkers have lost their jobs.
- They may feel insecurity because of a belief they are next in line to go.
- Increased workload may result from the same amount of work being distributed to fewer employees.
- Valued employees may leave to seek opportunities at organizations they consider to be more stable.
- Organizational culture may suffer if fewer people within the organization are able to pass on "the way we do things here."

One company's loss may become another's hiring opportunity. During the same week 2,800 NASA employees received layoff notices, SpaceX listed over 200 openings on its career site including "Astronaut Safety Engineer" and "Space Suit Design Engineer." Financial services workers left jobless during the financial crisis have been hired by companies who value their transferable skills such as project management, IT, sales, and marketing. The downturn in the housing industry has been beneficial for companies like Home Depot that are able to hire construction and skilled trade workers with valuable construction expertise as sales associates.

Corporate strategic and employment planning are two critically linked processes; one cannot survive without the other. To perform both properly requires a blending of activities. We have portrayed these linkages in Exhibit 5-3.

Exhibit 5-3
Employment Planning and the Strategic Planning Process

The organizational mission is the guide for organizational strategy. HR analyzes the tasks to be done and figures out how to organize those tasks into jobs. The next step is to determine how many workers are necessary to fill those jobs and the skills they will need. If the supply of workers exceeds the number necessary, HR must "decruit" or reduce the number of workers. If the supply of workers is less than the number necessary, HR must recruit more workers to fulfill the organizational mission.

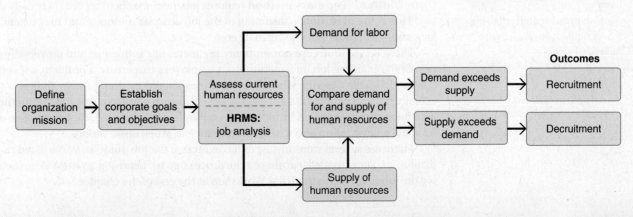

The Job Analysis Process

job analysis
Provides information about jobs currently being done and the knowledge, skills, and abilities that individuals need to perform the jobs adequately.

The philosophy behind the **job analysis** process is simple. The organization needs to know what every employee's job entails: what they do, how they do it, and what they need to know. It involves gathering data about the job and interpreting what it means about the tasks and responsibilities of the position. It encompasses tracking employee's tasks, observing and interviewing the employees that hold the position, and getting input from those who manage or work with the person in the position.[29]

Without a thorough job analysis and resulting job description, there could very well be a mismatch between the employee's skills and expectations and the reality of the day-to-day tasks required for the job. This can result in low morale, lack of motivation, and high turnover.

There are a variety of ways that a job analysis can be accomplished. The correct one really depends upon the type of job. Let's take a look.[30]

Job Analysis Methods

The basic methods by which HRM can determine job elements and the essential knowledge, skills, and abilities for successful performance include the following:

observation method
A job analysis technique in which data are gathered by watching employees work.

Observation Method Using the **observation method**, a job analyst watches employees directly or reviews films of workers on the job. Although the observation method provides firsthand information, workers rarely function most efficiently when they are being watched, and thus distortions in the job analysis can occur. This method also requires that the entire range of activities be observable, which is possible with some jobs, but impossible for many others—for example, most managerial jobs.

individual interview method
Meeting with an employee to determine what his or her job entails.

Individual Interview Method The **individual interview method** involves interviewing the employees who are actually doing the job. Their input and cooperation results in detailed and sometimes unexpected information about the position.

group interview method
Meeting with a number of employees to collectively determine what their jobs entail.

Group Interview Method The **group interview method** is similar to the individual interview method except that several people who hold the position are interviewed simultaneously. This may result in a more accurate picture of the position, but it's also possible that group dynamics distort the information.

structured questionnaire method
A specifically designed questionnaire on which employees rate tasks they perform in their jobs.

Structured Questionnaire Method The **structured questionnaire method** gives workers a specifically designed questionnaire on which they check or rate items they perform in their job from a long list of possible task items. This technique is excellent for gathering information about jobs. However, exceptions to a job may be overlooked, and opportunity may be lacking to ask follow-up questions or to clarify the information received.

technical conference method
A job analysis technique that involves extensive input from the employee's supervisor.

Technical Conference Method The **technical conference method** uses supervisors with extensive knowledge of the job, frequently called subject matter experts. Here, specific job characteristics are obtained from the experts. Although it is a good data-gathering method, it often overlooks the workers' perceptions about what they do on the job.

diary method
A job analysis method requiring job incumbents to record their daily activities.

Diary Method The **diary method** requires job incumbents to record their daily activities. This is the most time consuming of the job analysis methods and may extend over long periods of time—all adding to its cost.

These six methods are not mutually exclusive; nor is one method universally superior. Even obtaining job information from employees can create a problem, especially if these individuals describe what they think they should be doing rather than what they actually do. The best results are usually achieved with some combination of methods—with information provided by individual employees, their immediate supervisors, a professional analyst, or an unobtrusive source such as video observations.

There are several steps involved in conducting the job analysis. We've listed them in Exhibit 5-4. For extended learning on the process, go to "Learning an HRM Skill: Conducting the Job Analysis" in the HRM Workshop at the end of the chapter.

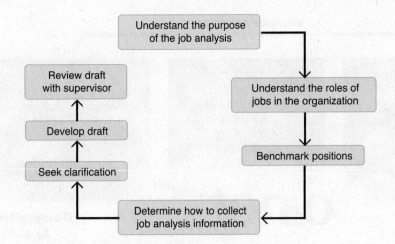

Exhibit 5-4
Steps in a Job Analysis

Job analysis begins with a clear understanding of the job and its link to organizational strategy. HR next determines the tasks necessary to successfully complete the job, and then determines the skills necessary to complete those tasks. Workers and supervisors need to be involved in the process.

Structured Job Analysis Techniques

Realizing now that job analysis data can be collected in several ways, and that we can follow a process to do the work, let us consider other notable job analysis processes. These are the Department of Labor's O*NET Content Model and the Position Analysis Questionnaire.

O*NET and the Department of Labor   Have you ever written a report on a potential career you are considering? You may have referenced the *Dictionary of Occupational Titles* (DOT), published by the U.S. Department of Labor or DOL. The Department of Labor recognized that the DOT and the job analysis and categories it used were based on stable workforce requirements and a foundation in manufacturing that didn't apply well to the service-based economy and emphasis on technical skills that emerged in the 1990s. They responded by replacing the DOT with the Occupational Information Network, or O*NET, in 1998. O*NET provides even more information to students needing career research to write reports and to HR professionals who want updated information on job requirements for job analysis.

The O*NET database contains information on hundreds of careers, and is continually updated and provided online at no cost. Careers are categorized using the Standard Occupational Classification (SOC), which is used by government and industry. These upgrades to the nation's database of job information were necessary because of new workforce requirements, including changes in technology, society, law, growth in the service sector, or business practices that are leading to new and emerging occupations such as those involved in new technology or global business.

The heart of O*NET is the Content Model (see Exhibit 5-5), which describes the different mix of knowledge, skills, and abilities necessary and the activities and tasks performed. These are categorized in six domains that describe the day-to-day aspects of the job, qualifications, and interests of the typical worker. These include:

Worker Characteristics that influence the ability to learn and perform the necessary tasks. These categories include abilities, occupational interests, work values, and work styles.

Worker Requirements describing the attributes workers need to acquire through experience and education, including basic skills, cross-functional skills, knowledge, and education.

Experience Requirements related to previous work experience and influencing work activities. These include experience and training, basic and cross-functional skills necessary for entry level, and licensing or certificates necessary.

Occupation-Specific Information that applies to the job such as tasks or necessary tools and technology.

Workforce Characteristics that describe the labor market, wages, and outlook for future employment opportunities.

Occupational Requirements that explain detailed occupational requirements such as general and detailed work activities or behaviors, descriptions of the type of organization that usually employs this occupation, or the context of the work.[31]

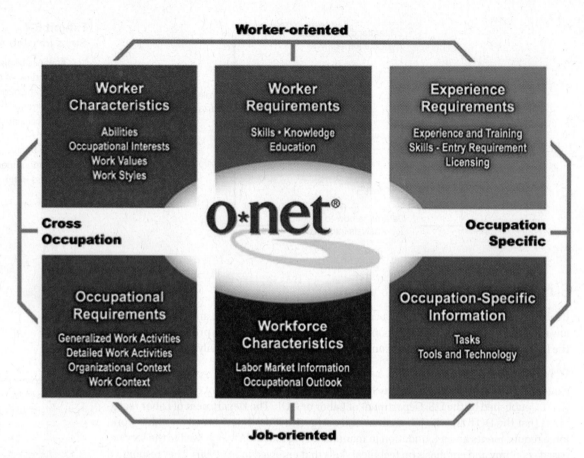

Exhibit 5-5
Department of Labor O*NET
Job Content Model

The O*NET Content Model
provides a detailed description of
the knowledge, skills, and abilities
that a worker will need to perform
the everyday tasks of a job. O*NET
replaced the popular Dictionary of
Occupational Titles (DOT).

Position Analysis Questionnaire Developed by researchers at Purdue University, the
Position Analysis Questionnaire (PAQ) generates job requirement information applicable to all types of jobs. In contrast to the DOL approach, the PAQ presents a more
quantitative and finely tuned description of jobs. The PAQ procedure involves "194 elements that are grouped within six major divisions and twenty-eight sections"[32] (see
Exhibit 5-6).

The PAQ allows HRM to scientifically and quantitatively group interrelated job elements into job dimensions. This, in turn, should allow jobs to be compared with each
other. However, research on the PAQ's usefulness is suspect. For the most part, it appears

Exhibit 5-6
PAQ Categories and Their
Number of Job Elements

The Position Analysis
Questionnaire is an alternative to
the O*NET Content Model.
The Position Analysis
Questionnaire provides a more
quantitative approach to
analyzing the knowledge, skills,
and abilities necessary to perform
a job on a day-to-day basis.

Category	Number of Job Elements
1. *Information input:* Where and how does the worker get the information he or she uses on the job?	35
2. *Mental processes:* What reasoning, decision making, planning, etc., are involved in the job?	14
3. *Work output:* What physical activities does the worker perform and what tools or devices are used?	49
4. *Relationships with other people:* What relationships with other people are required in the job?	36
5. *Job context:* In what physical and social contexts is the work performed?	19
6. *Other job characteristics:* What special attributes exist on this job (e.g., schedule, responsibilities, pay)?	41

Source: Reprinted with permission from the Position Analysis Questionnaire, Copyright 1969, Purdue
Research Foundation.

more applicable to higher-level, professional jobs, possibly because of the advanced reading level necessary to complete the questionnaire.

Position Analysis Questionnaire (PAQ)

A job analysis technique that rates jobs on elements in six activity categories.

Purpose of Job Analysis

No matter what method you use to gather data, the information collected and written down from the job analysis process generates three tangible outcomes: job descriptions, job specifications, and job evaluation. Let's look at them more closely.

Job Descriptions   A **job description** is a written statement of what the jobholder does, how the job is done, under what conditions, the essential functions, how the work is to be completed, what the purpose of the work is, and how it relates to the organizational mission (see Exhibit 5-7). It should accurately portray job content, environment, and conditions of employment. Although there is no standard format for job descriptions, a common format for a job description includes:

job description

A statement indicating what a job entails.

- **Date** the job description was written.
- **Job status** including whether the job is exempt or non-exempt under the FSLA and if it's full- or part-time.

Job Title: Benefits Manager
Job Code: 11-3041.00
Department: Human Resources
Reports to: Director, Human Resources
Job Summary: Manages employee benefits program for organization
Eessential functions:

Supervises: Staff of three
FLSA: Exempt
Effective Date: July 30, 2012

- Plans and directs implementation and administration of benefits programs designed to insure employees against loss of income due to illness, injury, layoff, or retirement;
- Directs preparation and distribution of written and verbal information to inform employees of benefits programs, such as insurance and pension plans, paid time off, bonus pay, and special employer sponsored activities;
- Analyzes existing benefits policies of organization and prevailing practices among similar organizations to establish competitive benefits programs;
- Evaluates services, coverage, and options available through insurance and investment companies to determine programs that best meet the needs of the organization;
- Plans modification of existing benefits programs, utilizing knowledge of laws concerning employee insurance coverage and agreements with labor unions, to ensure compliance with legal requirements;
- Recommends benefits plan changes to management and notifies employees and labor union representatives of changes in benefits programs;
- Directs performance of clerical functions such as updating records and processing insurance claims;
- May interview, select, hire, and train employees.

Job Specifications:

- Specialized Knowledge/Skills: General knowledge of policies and practices involved in human resource management functions—including recruitment, selection, training, and promotion regulations and procedures; compensation and benefits packages; labor relations and negotiations strategies; and human resource information systems. Excellent written and verbal communications skills as well as deductive and inductive reasoning skills are critical.
- Education/Experience: 2–4 years' experience in analysis, design, and/or administration of benefits. A bachelor's degree is preferred.
- Training/Equipment: Strong MS Office skills including Word, Excel, and PowerPoint will be useful. HRIS experience a plus, especially PeopleSoft.
- Work Environmdent/Physical Requirements: Fast-paced general office environment. Regular travel is not expected in this position.

Exhibit 5-7
Example of a Job Description

This job description details the duties, responsibilities, and necessary qualifications for a benefits manager in the human resources department. People holding the position and their supervisors were most likely consulted in the process of developing this job description.

- **Job title** usually describes the job and hints at the nature and duties of the job.
- **Job identification** section includes the department location of the job, who the person reports to, a job identification code, which is sometimes the O*NET code, and the date the description was last revised.
- **Objective** of the position or how it relates to other positions and the organizational mission.
- **Supervisor** to whom this position reports.
- **Job Summary** including an outline of the job responsibilities.
- **Job specifications or Minimum requirements** for education, experience, special skills, licenses, and certifications.
- **Essential functions** with a detailed list of tasks, duties, and responsibilities. This may be further divided into sections including essential mental functions and essential physical functions, major and minor. This section is particularly important because it helps the organization with ADA compliance.
- **Disclaimer** statement that indicates that the job description isn't an exclusive list of the activities the employee may need to perform. "Other duties as assigned" is a common part of the disclaimer.
- **Signatures** of top management, supervisor, and employee.

When we discuss employee recruitment, selection, and performance appraisal, we will find that the job description acts as an important resource for (1) describing the job to potential candidates (either verbally by recruiters and interviewers or in written advertisements), (2) guiding newly hired employees in what they are specifically expected to do, (3) developing criteria for evaluating performance of the individual holding that job, and (4) establishing the relative worth of the job for compensation. Furthermore, under the Americans with Disabilities Act, job descriptions have taken on an added emphasis in clearly identifying essential job functions and job specifications.

essential functions
Activities that are core to a position and cannot be modified.

Essential Functions are the duties an employee absolutely must be able to perform to successfully fill a position. The activities are core to performing the job and cannot be modified. For example, airline pilots need acceptable vision to fly a plane; firefighters need to be able to lift and carry heavy equipment or possibly even people; and receptionists must be able to greet people, answer phones, and use computers. The ADA requires employers to give equal consideration to applicants that can perform the **essential functions** of a position with "reasonable accommodation."[33] Employers who do not have job descriptions or with job descriptions that do not outline the essential functions may have difficulty explaining why a disabled candidate cannot fill the position.

job specification
Statements indicating the minimal acceptable qualifications incumbents must possess to successfully perform the essential elements of their jobs.

Job Specifications state the minimum acceptable qualifications that the incumbent must possess to perform the job successfully. Based on information acquired through job analysis, the **job specifications** identify pertinent knowledge, skills, education, experience, certification, and abilities. Individuals possessing the personal characteristics identified in the job specification should perform the job more effectively than those lacking these personal characteristics.[34] The job specification, therefore, is an important tool for keeping the selector's attention on the list of necessary qualifications and assisting in determining whether candidates are essentially qualified.

job evaluation
Specifies the relative value of each job in the organization.

Job Evaluations In addition to providing data for job descriptions and specifications, job analysis also provides valuable information for making job comparisons. If an organization is to have an equitable compensation program, jobs that have similar demands in terms of skills, knowledge, and abilities should be placed in common compensation groups. **Job evaluation** contributes by specifying the relative value of each job in the organization, which makes it an important part of compensation administration. In the meantime, keep in mind that job evaluation relies on data generated from job analysis.

The Multifaceted Nature of Job Analysis

One of the overriding questions about job analysis is whether it is conducted properly. The answer to this question varies, depending on the organization. Generally, most organizations do conduct some type of job analysis. This job analysis, however, extends

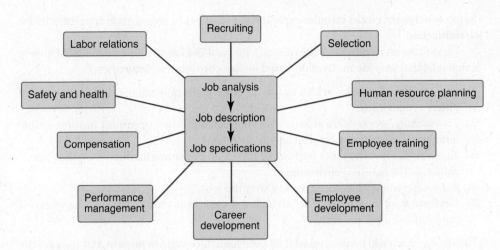

Exhibit 5-8
The Multifaceted Nature of
the Job Analysis
Job analysis is extremely
important to the organization. It
influences every aspect of human
resource functions.

beyond meeting the federal equal employment opportunity requirement. Almost everything that HRM does relates directly to the job analysis process (see Exhibit 5-8). Organizations frequently cite recruiting, selection, compensation, and performance appraisal as activities directly affected by the job analysis, among others. The job analysis process assists employee training and career development by identifying necessary skills, knowledge, and abilities. Where deficiencies exist, training and development efforts can help. Job analysis also aids in determining safety and health requirements and labor relations processes. Accordingly, the often lengthy and complex job analysis process cannot be overlooked.

We cannot overemphasize the importance of job analysis, as it permeates most of an organization's activities. If an organization doesn't do its job analysis well, it probably doesn't perform many of its human resource activities well. If employees in the organization understand human resource activities, they should understand the fundamental importance of job analysis. The job analysis, then, is the starting point of sound HRM. Without knowing what the job entails, the HRM activities covered in the following chapters may be merely an effort in futility.

Job Design

It's possible to conscientiously follow all of the steps we've described to analyze a job and create a thorough job description, yet create a job that is so mind-numbingly boring that employees grow to hate it and leave relatively quickly, creating motivation and turnover problems. If you've experienced one of these positions, you've been the victim of poor job design.

Job design refers to the way the position and the tasks within that position are organized. It describes what tasks are included; how and when the tasks are done; and any factors that affect the work, such as in what order the tasks are completed and the conditions under which the tasks are completed. Problems arise when employees don't feel a sense of accomplishment after completing the tasks. To prevent this, the job needs to be designed so that the tasks have a clear purpose and relate to the company mission. Too often, organizations take tasks that more senior employees consider unpleasant and load those into positions for new hires. Good job design incorporates tasks that relate to organizational goals and values into every job description.[35]

Job Enrichment

Frederick Herzberg suggested that the best way to motivate employees is through **job enrichment**. He suggested, "If you want people to do a good job, give them a good job to do."[36]

job design
Refers to the way the position and the tasks within that position are organized, including how and when the tasks are done and any factors that affect the work, such as in what order the tasks are completed and the conditions under which they are completed.

At the Toyota Avalon Plant in Kentucky, employees are grouped in work teams. Because these workers manage themselves, they need a different set of skills. The flexibility needed to achieve their team goals isn't always reflected in traditional job analysis processes. *(Source: © AP/Wide World Photos)*

job enrichment
Expanding job content to create more opportunities for job satisfaction.

His job enrichment model includes expanding job content to create more opportunities for job satisfaction.

Expanding on Herzberg's suggestions, J. Richard Hackman offered a model of how to design jobs that provide motivation based on five core job characteristics: [37]

1. *Skill variety:* allowing workers to use different skills and talents to do a number of different activities.
2. *Task identity:* workers are able to see a completed product or project or some visible outcome that creates a sense of accomplishment.
3. *Task significance:* the tasks performed have some meaningful impact on the organization, or the external environment.
4. *Autonomy:* worker has some control over the job.
5. *Feedback from the job itself:* the job includes some opportunity to show the worker if the tasks are done properly.

Not everyone will be motivated if all five characteristics are present, but they set the stage for employees who understand that their work is meaningful, feel responsible for the output, and actually know the results of their efforts.

CONTEMPORARY CONNECTION

Measuring Results, Not Face Time

In 2002, Best Buy discovered some disturbing trends at their Minneapolis area headquarters. They saw an increase in the number of people quitting and filing stress-related health claims. Employee surveys indicated that they didn't think their supervisors trusted them to do their work and that someone was always looking over their shoulders. They weren't happy or motivated.

The problem landed on the desk of Cali Ressler who managed Best Buy's work/life balance program. Ressler considered popular flexible work schedule options such as flextime and telecommuting, but decided, along with Jody Thompson who was working as a designated "Change Agent" at Best Buy, that the problem demanded a bigger solution. Ressler and Thompson created a way that workers at Best Buy's headquarters could be in control of their work and production. They devised a radical new program called "Results-Only Work Environment," or ROWE.[38] Employees who opt to sign on with ROWE are allowed to decide how, when, and where they work. They can work in the office, at home, in the park, a coffee shop, another country, wherever. Consider these examples:

- Employee relations manager Steve Hance participates in morning teleconferences from his fishing boat on a lake where he's been since dawn.
- Jason Dehne jogs to his local coffee shop and takes calls there.
- Marissa Plume does her best work at midnight in her home office.[39]

Clearly, this isn't an ordinary "work from home" program. It's more like a "work from anywhere, anytime" program. An obvious concern is whether anything would get done in such a flexible environment. The good news is yes, quite a bit gets done. Productivity at the headquarters has increased 41 percent and turnover has decreased 45 percent. Those savings are substantial considering the estimated per-employee cost of turnover is $120,000. Among the 2000[40] headquarters

employees who signed on for ROWE, surveys report that they have better relationships with family and friends, feel more loyalty to the company, have more control over their schedule, and are more focused and energized about their work.[41] Best Buy is so happy with the results that they are recommending the program to other companies. It is even working on implementing a modified version at its retail stores.

Steve Hance, the manager who takes conference calls on his fishing boat, understands why people are skeptical of ROWE. "Being able to take an extra-long lunch or get off work early if you wanted—it sounded like utopia, but could people really do this?" He says, "As it turned out, they could."[42]

(Source: Justin Sullivan/Getty Images, Inc).

Consider this:

Would a ROWE environment work in any organization's headquarters? Are there positions that should not be offered the kind of autonomy that ROWE allows?

Flexible Work Schedules

Employers have found that they can increase employee engagement and motivation through well-designed jobs. In addition, loyalty and retention are increased by allowing employees to do their jobs with more flexible work schedules. Although work schedules aren't part of the content of the job, they provide a context that is influential in the way workers perform their jobs. We'll look at some of the ways employers have adapted work schedules, including compressed workweeks, flexible schedules, job sharing, and telecommuting.

Compressed work week schedules allow employees to work longer days in exchange for longer weekends or other days off. The most typical is a 4/10 schedule, which allows employees to work four ten-hour days in exchange for a three-day weekend. Other alternatives include 9/8 schedules that allow employees to work nine-hour shifts for eight days, eight hours on the ninth day, and have one extra day off in a two-week period, or 3/12 schedule with three twelve-and-a-half hour days. Companies have started using compressed work weeks in response to customer demand for extended hours or employee demands for flexibility.

Flex time, also called flexible working hours, allows employees to schedule the time they begin their eight-hour working day within guidelines. For example, employees may choose from start times of 7, 8, or 9 A.M. and end their day eight hours later. The "core time" of 9:00 A.M. to 3:00 P.M. is shared by all workers.

Job sharing allows two people to share one job by splitting the work week and the responsibilities of the position. Most divide the five-day work week equally with a short overlapping time period for coordination, but unequal splits can be arranged. This is possibly the most complicated of the schedules discussed so far because there are so many variables. The two people splitting the job both need to be very cooperative and communicate well. Pay and benefits need to be determined as well as how to handle after-work or weekend obligations. Evaluating the position can also be a challenge for HR.

Telecommuting often conjures up images of people working from home in their pajamas, and that could possibly happen. It's also just as likely that employees use phone, Internet, and teleconferencing to accomplish their tasks while traveling, doing research, working at a branch office, or at the local coffee shop. Companies that have successfully implemented telecommuting programs list the following keys to success:[43]

- Planning is necessary before implementing a telecommuting program.
- Clear expectations are important; employees must understand the business goals that are to be met.
- Well-written policies and guidelines need to be developed as to who is eligible.
- Technology must be adequate to support remote workers.
- Employees must understand that the privilege may be revoked if the employee isn't performing to expectations.
- Senior management must be committed to promoting telecommuting and making it work.

Best Buy's ROWE, or Results-Only Work Environment discussed in *Workplace Issues*, goes beyond telecommuting to having no actual contact requirements other than holding employees responsible for meeting their goals. This solution won't work in every organization, but as technology makes mobile communication even more accessible, creative solutions such as ROWE are likely to develop in other organizations. Exhibit 5-9 lists several advantages and disadvantages of flexible scheduling.

compressed work week schedules
Employees work longer days in exchange for longer weekends or other days off.

flex time
An alternative to traditional "9 to 5" work schedules allows employees to vary arrival and departure times.

job sharing
Two people share one job by splitting the work week and the responsibilities of the position.

telecommuting
Using technology to work in a location other than the traditional workplace.

Job Design and Teams

We leave this chapter by revisiting the changing world of work, the importance of employment planning, and job design. Globalization, quality initiatives, flexible scheduling, and teams, for example, are requiring organizations to rethink job design. When jobs are designed around individuals, job descriptions frequently clarify employee roles. Jobs today often go beyond individual efforts, however, requiring the activities and collaboration of a team.

To be effective, teams need to be flexible and continually make adjustments. Effective work teams require competent individuals. Team members must have the relevant

Exhibit 5-9
Flexible Scheduling Advantages and Disadvantages

Flexible scheduling offers many alternatives to traditional scheduling. Each comes with advantages and disadvantages that must be considered carefully. Some of them are listed here.

Advantages and Disadvantages of Flexible Scheduling	
Advantages	**Disadvantages**
• Reduced commuting time	• Lack of supervision of employees
• Reduced costs of transportation	• Potential reductions in productivity
• Reduced childcare costs	• Increased turnover of employees who aren't productive
• Better work/life balance	• Employees feeling isolated from other employees
• Cost savings from fewer on-site employees	• Increased stress
• Increased retention of current employees	• Expensive technology
• Advantages in recruiting new employees	• Fair Labor Standards rules on overtime hours
• Reduced traffic at peak commuting	• Union contracts
• Increased morale	• Difficult to maintain "team atmosphere"

technical skills and abilities to achieve the desired corporate goals and the personal characteristics required to achieve excellence while working well with others. These same individuals must also be capable of readjusting their work skills—to fit the needs of the team. It's important not to overlook personal characteristics. Not everyone who is technically competent has the skills to work well as a team member. Accordingly, employment planning requires finding team members who possess both technical and interpersonal skills. As such, team members must have excellent communication skills. Team members must be able to both convey readily and clearly understood messages to each other. This includes nonverbal as well as spoken messages. Team members must be able to quickly and efficiently share ideas and feelings. Effective communication is also characterized by a healthy dose of feedback from team members and management. This helps guide team members and correct misunderstandings.

Summary

(This summary relates to the Learning Outcomes identified on page 118.) After reading this chapter, you should be able to:

1. **Describe the importance of human resource planning.** Employment planning is the process by which an organization ensures that it has the right number and kinds of people capable of effectively and efficiently completing tasks that directly support the company's mission and strategic goals.
2. **Define the steps involved in the human resource planning process.** The steps in the employment planning process include formulating a mission statement, establishing corporate goals and objectives, assessing current human resources, estimating supplies and demand for labor, and matching demand with current supplies of labor.
3. **Explain what human resource information systems (HRIS) are used for.** A human resource information system is useful for quickly fulfilling HRM information needs by tracking employee information and having that information readily available when needed.
4. **Define the term *job analysis*.** Job analysis is a systematic exploration of the activities surrounding and within a job. It defines the job's duties, responsibilities, and accountabilities.
5. **Identify the six general techniques for obtaining job analysis information.** The six general techniques for obtaining job information are observation method, individual interview method, group interview method, structured questionnaire method, technical conference method, and diary method.

6. **Describe the steps involved in conducting a job analysis.** The steps involved in conducting a job analysis include: (1) understanding the purpose of conducting the job analysis, (2) understanding the role of jobs in the organization, (3) benchmarking positions, (4) determining how to collect job analysis information, (5) seeking clarification wherever necessary, (6) developing the first draft of the job description, and (7) reviewing the draft with the job supervisor.

7. **Explain job descriptions, job specifications, and essential functions.** Job descriptions are written statements of what the jobholder does (duties and responsibilities); job specifications identify the minimum qualifications required to perform successfully on the job; essential functions are the major duties of the position.

8. **Identify elements of job enrichment that contribute to employee morale and productivity.** Skill variety, task identity, task significance, autonomy, and feedback all contribute to employees feeling that their work is meaningful.

9. **Describe how job analysis permeates all aspects of HRM.** Job analysis permeates all aspects of HRM in that almost everything HRM does relates directly to the job analysis process. Recruiting, selection, compensation, performance appraising, employee training and career activities, and safety and health requirements, for example, are affected by the job analysis, which identifies necessary skills, knowledge, and abilities.

10. **Explain flexible scheduling alternatives.** Compressed work weeks allow employees to work longer hours in a day and fewer days in a work week; flex time allows employees to schedule the time they begin and end their eight-hour working day as long as core hours are covered; job sharing allows two people to divide one job; and telecommuting enables employees to use information technology to work outside the office.

Demonstrating Comprehension

QUESTIONS FOR REVIEW

1. Define *human resource planning*. Why is it important to organizations?
2. What is involved in the human resource planning process?
3. How can an organization increase its human resource supply?
4. What is job analysis?
5. Identify the advantages and disadvantages of the observation, structured questionnaire, and diary job analysis methods.
6. Explain the terms *job description, job specification,* and *essential functions*.
7. Explain the importance of essential functions as they relate the Americans with Disabilities Act.
8. Identify how the five core job characteristics of job enrichment could be used to improve your job or a job of your choice.
9. Describe the human resource planning implications when an organization implements flexible scheduling.

Key Terms

compressed work week	individual interview method	observation method
core competency	job analysis	Position Analysis Questionnaire (PAQ)
diary method	job description	replacement chart
essential functions	job design	strengths
flex time	job enrichment	structured questionnaire method
group interview method	job evaluation	SWOT analysis
human resource information system (HRIS)	job sharing	technical conference method
	job specification	telecommuting
human resource planning	mission statement	weaknesses

HRM Workshop

Linking Concepts to Practice   DISCUSSION QUESTIONS

1. "More emphasis should be placed on the external supply of employees for meeting future needs because these employees bring new blood into the organization. This results in more innovative and creative ideas." Do you agree or disagree with this statement? Explain your response.

2. "Job analysis is just another burden placed on organizations through EEO legislation." Do you agree or disagree with this statement? Defend your position.

3. "Although systematic in nature, a job description is still at best a subjective process." Build arguments for and against this statement.

4. "Permanent layoffs should occur only as a last resort. Cutting staff affects morale, and, ultimately, the organization falters more. Organizations also have a social responsibility to their employees and owe it to them to find alternative ways to cut costs." Do you agree or disagree with the statement? Defend your position.

Making A Difference   SERVICE LEARNING PROJECTS

Planning and job analysis are fundamental to structuring any non-profit organization or community event.

■ Select a non-profit organization that needs help organizing a fund-raiser, celebration, or activity such as a parade or carnival. Volunteer to help plan, organize, and execute the event.

■ Contact a local food bank about organizing a food drive. Take responsibility for planning the event, determining what needs to be done and assigning responsibilities to volunteers.

■ Contact a local non-profit and inquire about any help they may need with cleaning (washing windows, cleaning vehicles,

shampooing carpets), moving, or painting. Take responsibility for raising money for the required materials, purchasing the materials, and completing the activity.

As you put your service learning experience together, keep a journal of your activities, the time you spend, contact information for people you work with, and your thoughts about the process. When you're finished, make a presentation to your class about the experience and what you learned. What concepts from Chapter 5 were you able to apply?

Developing Diagnostic and Analytical Skills

Case Application 5:   TURNOVER AND MORALE PROBLEMS AT TSA

Next time you go through security on your way through the airport, smile and say thank you to the screeners who help you send your bags through screening and wave you through the scanner. Low morale runs rampant through the screeners that work at the Transportation Safety Administration (TSA) and odds are that the screener you smile at is thinking about quitting.[44]

A recent government report revealed concerns that the low morale of the screeners may be a distraction to them on the job and may even cause them to be less focused on security and screening responsibilities. About one in five of the nation's 45,000 screeners quit every year due to low morale, low pay, discrimination and fear of retaliation if they complain.[45] Further complicating the morale problems are the "enhanced" pat down procedures added to screener's job responsibilities in 2010. Screeners report being called "molester, pervert, creep" and much worse by passengers who are understandably upset by being subjected to the pat downs after setting off metal detectors in some airports.

In an effort to gain more control over working conditions, TSA employees voted to allow the American Federation of Government Employees (AFGE) to represent them as a union in 2011.[46] TSA employees had a long list of issues they believed contributed to the low morale and turnover. At the top of the list was the TSA's pay-for-performance system called Performance Accountability and Standards System (PASS). It was widely viewed by employees as not fair, and discriminatory to older workers, minorities and women.[47] In 2012, the AFGE negotiated a collective bargaining agreement

designed to correct the working conditions that TSA employees found objectionable. Terms of the agreement include:

■ Replacing PASS with a performance appraisal process that puts increased emphasis on evaluating officer's performance based on supervisor observations rather than certification test scores.

■ Awards for attendance, outstanding service, leadership and performance will be offered. Additional awards may be established at individual airports based on their needs and challenges.

■ Changes in attendance policies, guidelines for tardiness and the process for approval of sick leave.

■ Revision of how employees bid for shifts, annual leaves, transfer policies and how employees may convert from part-time to full-time.

■ Changes in requirements for uniforms, personal appearance and subsidies for uniforms and parking.

■ Requirements for personal safety and comfort including workplace temperatures, lighting, ergonomic equipment and noise levels.

■ Revised dispute resolution process designed to provide fairness and due process for TSA officers including a revised appeal process for disciplinary actions.[48]

Kim Kraynak-Lambert of the AFGE was happy with the agreement, stating "TSOs (Transportation Safety Officers) come to work every day in the face of intense public and congressional scrutiny and, to the best of their ability, protect this nation from terrorist attack. Now we can look forward to new rights and new working conditions, and a chance to form a true labor-management partnership."[49]

Questions:

1. Do you think that the provisions of the new contract will increase morale and decrease turnover? Why or why not?
2. Choose a job analysis method or combination of methods to begin the process to redesign the TSA officer job descriptions. Why would this be the most appropriate method(s) to analyze the positions?
3. How might job enrichment concepts be used to increase morale and retention at TSA?
4. How do the elements of the collective bargaining agreement address job enrichment issues?
5. Can employers reduce the attractiveness of union representation by creating well designed jobs? Explain your response.

Working with a Team   JOB ANALYSIS INFORMATION

Research the technical and people skills and conceptual knowledge required to perform a human resources manager's tasks effectively. Describe your findings and compare them with the results of the members of your group.

You may obtain samples directly from a company's manager, with permission; interview a human resources manager; or use websites such as www.workforce.com and www.shrm.org. Discuss what values will be important for the human resources manager to personally possess and how these will be demonstrated in that role.

Finally, based on the information you've obtained, write a brief description of the job. What challenges did you experience in reaching consensus on job responsibilities and in choosing the correct words for inclusion in the job description?

Learning an HRM Skill   CONDUCTING THE JOB ANALYSIS

About the skill: Because the job analysis is the cornerstone of HRM activities, it's important to understand how the activity is performed. We suggest the following steps in conducting a job analysis (an elaboration of Exhibit 5-4).

1. *Understand the purpose of conducting the job analysis.* Before embarking on a job analysis, one must understand the nature and purpose of conducting the investigation. Recognize that job analyses serve a vital purpose in such HRM activities as recruiting, training, setting performance standards, evaluating performance, and compensation. In fact, nearly every activity in HRM revolves around the job analysis.
2. *Understand the role of jobs and values in the organization.* Every job in the organization should have a purpose. Before conducting the job analysis, one must understand the job's link to the organization's strategic direction. In essence, one must answer why the job is needed. If an answer cannot be determined, then maybe the job is unnecessary.
3. *Benchmark positions.* In a large organization, it would be impossible to evaluate every job at one time. Accordingly, by involving employees and seeking their input, selected jobs can be chosen based on how well they represent other, similar jobs in the organization. This information serves as a starting point in later analysis of other positions.
4. *Determine how you want to collect job analysis information.* Proper planning at this stage permits you to collect the desired data in the most effective and efficient manner. This means developing a process for collecting data.

Several methods should be combined, such as structured questionnaires, group interviews, and technical conferences. Select the ones that best meet your job analysis goals and timetables.

5. *Seek clarification, wherever necessary.* When the job analyst doesn't entirely understand some of the information collected, it's time to seek clarification from those who possess the critical information. This may include the employee and the supervisor. Clearly understanding and comprehending the information will make the next step in the job analysis process—writing the job description—easier and more productive.
6. *Develop the first draft of the job description.* Although job descriptions follow no specific format, most include certain elements. Specifically, a job description contains the job title, a summary sentence of the job's main activities, the job's level of authority and accountability, performance requirements, and working conditions. The last paragraph of the job description typically includes the job specifications, or those personal characteristics the job incumbent should possess to be successful on the job.
7. *Review draft with the job supervisor.* Ultimately, the supervisor of the position being analyzed should approve the job description. Review comments from the supervisor can assist in determining a final job description document. When the description is an accurate reflection, the supervisor should either sign off or approve the document.

Enhancing Your Communication Skills

1. Develop a two- to three-page response to the following statement: "Formal employment planning activities reduce flexibility and may hinder success." Present both sides of the argument and include supporting data. Conclude your paper by defending and supporting one of the two arguments you've presented.
2. Investigate how well different organizations align their job descriptions with the company mission or vision statement by visiting several businesses in person and asking for copies of their mission or vision statements and a job description. Some will have them readily available, and some will not know what you are talking about. Write a two- to three-page summary of the experience, analyzing the reactions you received, drawing any conclusions about the size of the organization, and your observations of how well the organization seems to be informing employees of the mission and how well their jobs seem to be aligned with that mission.
3. Select a job (or position in an organization) in which you have an interest. Visit the O*NET Online website (www.onet-center.org) and locate all relevant information about the position. Write a two- to three-page analysis of what the job entails, highlighting the job description and job specification data.

(Source: David Brewster/Minneapolis Star Tribune/Zuma Press)

LEARNING OUTCOMES

After reading this chapter, you will be able to

1. Define the term *recruiting*.

2. Identify the dual goals of recruiting.

3. Explain what constraints a human resource manager encounters when determining recruiting sources.

4. Identify the principal sources involved in recruiting employees.

5. Describe the advantages and disadvantages of employee referrals.

6. Identify three important variables that affect response rates to job advertisements.

7. Explain what distinguishes a public employment agency from a private employment agency.

8. Describe the benefits of online recruiting.

9. Explain the concept of employee leasing and the organizational benefits of such an arrangement.

Recruiting

6

The "Great Recession" has been hard on recruiters. As many employers have downsized, they have also cut back on their recruiting efforts or brought them to a screeching halt. Some companies, like The Container Store, have weathered the recession better than others. In fact, company founder and CEO Kip Tindell credits their constant recruiting efforts with the company's success.

Employees at The Container Store are encouraged to make recruiting a priority. They constantly have their eye on customers who would fit the unique culture, and frequently approaching a good candidate right on the sales floor. In fact, 34 percent of the applicants to The Container Store are referred by employees.

And it isn't hard to persuade people to apply. The Container Store has been a fixture on the Fortune Magazine list of top employers for ten years. The company pays better wages than most retailers and provides health benefits for part-time employees. During the recession, they did not layoff any employees, although matching employee 401k contributions were suspended until profits started to climb in 2011. Tindall reports that the company culture was a positive factor in strong employee acceptance of the cuts. "They were happy to help save their fellow coworker's jobs," reported Tindell in an interview on CBS.

Tindell opened the first Container Store in Dallas, Texas, in 1978. From the start, he created a culture that valued the employee. Tindell claims that if "you take care of the employee better than anyone else, they'll take care of the customer better than anyone else. When you're selling empty boxes, you've got to have great people." He goes on to say, "We're not just being nice, it's a successful profit strategy as well."

It is the responsibility of every employee at The Container Store, from Tindell on down, to recruit employees. These efforts are so effective that advertising for applicants is rarely necessary. That's because as customers enter the store, a trained sales associate talks up the benefits of working for The Container Store and all that the company offers. If the individual applies and is hired, the sales associate is given a $500 reward for successful recruiting ($250 if the person is hired on a part-time basis).

The application process might be easy, but getting hired isn't. Applicants go through as many as nine interviews, and only 3 percent of applicants are hired. Once hired, employees enjoy the job and company culture so much they just don't leave. The Container Store has one of the lowest rates of employee turnover in the industry. Whereas similar stores have annual turnover upward of 70 percent, The Container Store has a full-time turnover just under 10 percent a year, and it's less than 35 percent for part-timers.

Does The Container Store worry about finding the next qualified applicant? With employees in their 49 stores always looking for the next best associate it's not likely to be an issue! What better way to recruit than by utilizing employees who love what they do![1]

Looking Ahead

Are other recruiting methods necessary if employees do a good job of sharing their enthusiasm to customers and friends? What recruiting methods would best complement the employees' efforts?

Introduction

Successful employment planning is designed to identify an organization's human resource needs. Once these needs are known, an organization will strive to meet them. The next step in staffing, then—assuming that demand for certain skills, knowledge, and abilities is greater than the current supply—is recruiting. The company must acquire the people necessary to achieve the goals of the organization. Recruiting is the process of discovering potential candidates for actual or anticipated organizational vacancies. Or, from another perspective, it is a linking activity that brings together those with jobs to fill and those seeking jobs. Recruiting must be working at The Container Store as we observed in the chapter opener. Their 49 stores receive a total of 30,000 applications each year.[2]

In this chapter, we'll explore the activities surrounding the search for employees. We'll look at the fundamental activities and new developments in the recruiting process and provide insight and guidance in preparing a résumé and cover letter that may enhance your own chances of making it through this first step of the hiring process.

Recruiting Goals

recruiting
The process of seeking sources for job candidates.

recruiter
Represents employer to prospective applicants at colleges and job fairs.

Recruiting is frequently an entry-level position in human resources.
(Source: Jeff Greenberg/PhotoEdit)

Recruiting is a major human resource activity. Depending on the size of the company, HR departments estimate that they spend between 50 percent and 70 percent of their time on recruiting new employees each year.[3] Recruiting is quite often the entry-level HR position in organizations large enough to have HR departments. **Recruiters** essentially promote the organization to prospective applicants. Activities include participating in job fairs, visiting college campuses, and developing community or industry contacts.

An effective recruiting process requires a significant pool of diverse candidates to choose from. Achieving a satisfactory pool of candidates, however, may not be easy, and recruiters need to know the best places to recruit qualified candidates. This can be particularly challenging in times of economic growth that result in a tight labor market and overwhelming during difficult economic times, resulting in overqualified candidates or an overabundance of résumés. The first goal of recruiting, then, is to communicate the position in such a way that qualified job seekers respond. Why? The more applications received, the better the recruiter's chances for finding an individual who is best suited to the job requirements.

Simultaneously, however, the recruiter must provide enough information about the job so that unqualified applicants can select themselves out of job candidacy. For instance, when Ben & Jerry's was searching for a new CEO several years ago, someone with a conservative political view and a classical, bureaucratic perspective on management probably did not apply because that individual wouldn't fit the company's strong culture of social consciousness and liberal politics. Why is having a potential applicant remove themselves from the applicant pool important to human resource management? Typically, the company acknowledges applications received. That acknowledgment costs time and money. Then there are the application reviews and a second letter to send, this time rejecting failed applications. Again, this incurs costs. A good recruiting program should attract the qualified and discourage the unqualified. Meeting this dual objective will minimize the cost of processing unqualified candidates.

Factors That Affect Recruiting Efforts

Although all organizations will, at one time or another, engage in recruiting activities, some do so more than others. Obviously, size is one factor; an organization with 100,000 employees must recruit continually. So, too, must organizations with high turnover, such as fast-food firms, smaller service organizations, and firms that pay lower wages. Certain other variables will also influence the extent of recruiting.[5] Employment conditions in the local community influence how much recruiting takes place. The effectiveness of past recruiting efforts will show itself in the organization's historical ability to locate and keep people who perform well. Working conditions, salary, and benefit packages also influence

TIPS FOR SUCCESS

Something for Everyone

Even in tough economic times, organizations may need to hire employees to stay adequately staffed. Positions that require specialized or "in-demand" skills may be a challenge to fill. Competition, accordingly, is enhanced to recruit the best and the brightest of the applicant pool. But is treating everyone alike a means of putting an organization's best foot forward? Some research is suggesting not.

Consider that in today's organizations three distinct groups (or generations) are being sought. These include those classified as baby boomers, Gen Xers, and Millenials.

Millenials (workers born after 1980) are requiring recruiters to make the biggest changes in the way a workplace is promoted. Millenials are more likely to express a desire for a workplace that offers career development than high salary. They are likely to attend online job fairs and look at employment branding and ethical values to determine if the company is a good fit with their self-image. Internships are popular as a way to try the company

out before making a commitment. Recruiters also report that it's often necessary to take time to speak with the parents of recent graduates and keep them involved in the recruiting process.

Recruiting efforts may need to be tailored to address what each group may be interested in—something that reaches accord with their values and core beliefs. For instance, consider the following:[4]

What Do Groups Look For?

- Baby boomers are interested in the market leadership of the organization and the image it has, positive work ethic, and financial security.
- Gen Xers respond better to flexible work policies and programs designed to permit work/life balance.
- Millenials look for organizations that are technologically advanced, have value sustainability, and have a relaxed culture.

---

turnover and, therefore, the need for future recruiting. Organizations not growing, or those facing downsizing and layoffs, may find little need to recruit. On the other hand, growing organizations will find recruitment a major human resource activity.

Constraints on Recruiting Efforts

The ideal recruitment effort might bring in a satisfactory number of qualified applicants who want the job, but certain realities cannot be ignored. For example, a pool of qualified applicants may not include the best candidates, or the best candidate may not want to work for the organization. These and other **constraints on recruiting efforts** limit human resource recruiters' freedom to recruit and select a candidate of their choice. However, let us narrow our focus to five specific constraints.

> The more applications received, the better the recruiter's chances of finding an individual best suited to the job requirements.

Organization Image We noted that a prospective candidate may not be interested in pursuing job opportunities in the particular organization. The image of the organization can be a potential constraint. A poor image may limit its attraction to applicants. Many college graduates know, for example, that those in the top spots at Disney earn excellent salaries, receive outstanding benefits, and are greatly respected in their professions. Among most college graduates, Disney has a positive image. The hope of having a shot at one of its top jobs, being in the spotlight, and having a position of power means Disney has little trouble attracting college graduates into entry-level positions. But graduates can have negative or pessimistic views of some organizations.

constraints on recruiting efforts Factors that can limit recruiting outcomes.

In certain communities, local firms have a reputation for being in a declining industry; engaging in practices that result in a polluted environment; producing poor quality products; having unsafe working conditions; or being indifferent to employees' needs such as a work-life balance or an affordable health plan. Such reputations can and do reduce these organizations' abilities to attract the best personnel available. Many employers are putting considerable effort into developing a positive image or branding their employment experience, much the same way products and services are marketed to consumers. For more on this, see "Tips For Success: Employment Branding."

Job Attractiveness If the position to be filled is difficult, distasteful, or unattractive, recruiting a large and qualified pool of applicants will be difficult. In recent years, for

How important is corporate image? Just ask the HR people at Disney. It's critical for the organization to continue to attract and hire the best talent they can. (*Source: Brad Barket/Getty Images, Inc.*)

instance, many employers have been complaining about the difficulty of finding suitably qualified individuals for manual labor positions. For example, in the years immediately following Hurricane Katrina, qualified construction workers were in short supply in affected areas. In a job market where unemployment rates are low, and where a wide range of opportunities creates competition for these workers, a shortage results.[6]

Moreover, jobs viewed as boring, hazardous, anxiety creating, low paying, or lacking in promotion potential seldom attract a qualified pool of applicants. Even during economic slumps, people have refused to take many of these jobs. An example would be the difficulty that Midwest meat packing plants encounter in recruiting workers even in times of relatively high unemployment.

Internal Organizational Policies Internal organizational policies, such as "promote from within wherever possible," may give priority to individuals inside the organization. Such policies, when followed, typically ensure that all positions, other than the lowest-level entry positions, will be filled from within the ranks. Although this looks good once one is hired, it may reduce the number of applications.

Legal Influence The recruiting process needs to stay legal. An employer can no longer seek out preferred individuals based on non–job-related factors such as physical

TIPS FOR SUCCESS

Employment Branding

Employment branding makes the company name stand out when applicants are researching employers. Essentially, it's about marketing the company as an attractive employer in the same way that consumer products and services such as cars, beverages, and hotels have distinctive brand images. Employers want to be seen as a sought-after employer that people want to work for. Job branding is about making the job itself worthwhile. Top job candidates decide to take a position based on the work involved and what they'll learn, do, and become.[8]

Rich Floersch, executive vice president of worldwide human resources at McDonald's, takes the company's employment brand so seriously that he spent two weeks working at a McDonald's restaurant in Illinois (which included scrubbing bathroom floors!) to find out more about the company culture and what makes a good store manager or restaurant worker. "I really believe that the strongest employment brand that you can have is one where employees say they are proud to work for their companies," claims Floersch. "Our goal is to continue to build that sense of pride."[9]

When competition for talent gets more difficult, employers find that relying on their product brand isn't enough to attract the best candidates. They need to communicate the key aspects of the company culture that appeal to the candidate's image of a desirable employer. HGTV, the popular home and garden channel, takes branding seriously and incorporates key values in their mission statement, including Diversity, Clarity in Communication, Integrity, Compassion and Support, Shared Responsibility, Work/Life Balance, and Openness. Susan Packard, co-founder and former COO of HGTV, feels that "a solid brand instills discipline . . . it will keep you from trying to be all things to all people and will make it easier to communicate through words and symbols,"[10] including the HGTV logo with a roof on top and their catch phrase, "Start at Home."

Strong employment brands can be developed by HR or they may grow organically from a strong organizational mission or culture. Once established, an employment brand assists recruiting efforts by allowing recruiters to communicate not only what employment opportunities the company offers, but how it feels to work there.

Things to think about:

Identify other employers in your area that seem to have an "employment brand." Does that image help to recruit workers? How similar is employment branding to the image your college uses to recruit new students?

DIVERSITY TOPICS

Job Advertisements and EEO

Recall from Chapter 3 the discussion of adverse impact. In essence, an adverse impact occurs when protected group members are treated differently from others. Although most organizations will state that they are an equal employment opportunity employer, sometimes their actions may indicate differently. For instance, the following vignettes reflect job advertisements that ended up in the hands of the Equal Employment Opportunity Commission.

- An ad for a cashier in a grocery store: "Applicant must be young and energetic and be required to stand for long periods of time."
- A job posting for a position at an advertising firm: "Young-thinking, 'new wave' progressive advertising firm has openings for entry-level graphic artist with no more than three years' experience."
- An advertisement for a part-time laundromat employee: "Opening for a person seeking to supplement pension . . . retired persons preferred."

What's wrong with these ads? Let's take a look. In the first ad, the wording indicated a definite preference for someone young. Therefore, those forty and older might be deterred from applying for the job. The second ad, although not as clear-cut as the language in the first advertisement, implies that older workers might not be "young thinking." Furthermore, "with no more than three years' experience" also points to someone younger.

The third ad is somewhat unique. Indicating a retirement preference might be viewed as acceptable, but retirement usually comes after age fifty-five and more likely closer to age sixty-five. Although the ad focuses on older workers, individuals age forty to fifty-five (or sixty-five) might be excluded from this recruiting pool. Accordingly, an adverse impact may be occurring.

The primary lesson from these vignettes should be that, although an organization may hold itself as an equal opportunity employer, its choice of words in communications to the public may indicate otherwise. All communications must be carefully crafted so as to not have an adverse impact.

Your reaction

Have you ever seen an ad that seems to be discriminatory? How can you phrase an ad if you need someone that is energetic, strong, innovative or has mature judgment?

---

appearance, sex, or religious background. An airline that wants to hire only young, attractive females for flight attendant positions will find itself breaking the law if comparably qualified male candidates are rejected on the basis of gender—or if female candidates are rejected on the basis of age (see Diversity Topics: Job Advertisements and EEO).

Recruiting Costs The last constraint, but certainly not lowest in priority, centers on recruiting costs. Recruiting efforts are expensive—ranging from $2,000 for a retail position to $16,000 for a biotech position.[7] Sometimes budget restrictions put a time limit on searches. Accordingly, when an organization considers various recruiting sources, it considers effectiveness, such as maximizing its recruiting travel budget by first interviewing employees using conference calls or videoconferencing.

Recruiting Sources

Recruiting is more likely to achieve its objectives if recruiting sources reflect the type of position to be filled. For example, an ad in the business employment section of the *Wall Street Journal* is more likely to be read by a manager seeking an executive position in the $150,000- to $225,000-a-year bracket than by an automobile assembly-line worker seeking employment. Similarly, a recruiter trying to fill a management-training position who visits a two-year vocational school in search of a college graduate with undergraduate courses in engineering and a master's degree in business administration is looking for the right person in the wrong place. One area of recruiting that continues to evolve is online recruiting. Jobs at all levels are advertised on career websites and social media with instantaneous worldwide reach.

Certain recruiting sources are more effective than others for filling certain types of jobs. As we review each source in the following sections, we will emphasize their strengths and weaknesses in attempting to attract lower-level and managerial-level personnel.

The Internal Search

internal search
A promotion-from-within concept.

Many large organizations attempt to develop their own entry-level employees for higher positions. These promotions can occur through an **internal search** of current employees who have bid for the job, been identified through the organization's human resource management system, or even been referred by a fellow employee. Companies like UPS and McDonald's use these policies to develop candidates for promotion. In fact, 40 percent of the top fifty executives at McDonald's started out working in the restaurants.[11] The promote-from-within-wherever-possible policy has these advantages:

- promotes good public relations
- builds morale
- encourages individuals who are qualified and ambitious
- improves the probability of a good selection because information on the individual's performance is readily available
- is less costly than going outside to recruit
- helps with recruiting entry-level workers
- reduces orientation and training costs
- when carefully planned, can also act as a training device for developing middle and top-level managers.

There can be distinct disadvantages, however, to using internal sources. Promoting from within an organization creates problems if the organization uses less-qualified internal candidates only because they are there, when excellent candidates are available on the outside. However, an individual from the outside, in contrast with someone already employed in the organization, may appear more attractive because the recruiter is unaware of the outsider's faults. Internal searches also may generate infighting among rival candidates for promotion and decrease morale levels of those not selected.

The organization should also recognize that consistently using internal sources may not promote a diversity of people or ideas. New perspectives can broaden current ideas, knowledge, and enthusiasm, and productively question the "we've-always-done-it-that-way" mentality. As noted in the discussion of human resource inventories in Chapter 5, the organization's HRM files should provide information as to which employees might be considered for positions opening up within the organization. Most organizations can generate lists from computer databases of individuals who have the desirable characteristics to potentially fill the vacant position.

In many organizations, it is standard procedure to post any new job openings and to allow any current employee to apply for the position. This action, too, receives favorable marks from the EEOC. The posting notification can be communicated on a central "positions open" bulletin board in the plants or offices, in the weekly or monthly organization newsletter, or, in some cases, in a specially prepared posting sheet from human resources outlining those positions currently available. Even if current employees are not interested in the position, they can pass these notices on to other individuals who may seek employment within the organization—the employee referral.

Employee Referrals and Recommendations

employee referral
A recommendation from a current employee regarding a job applicant

One of the better sources for individuals who will most likely perform effectively on the job is a recommendation from a current employee. Why? Because employees rarely recommend someone unless they believe the individual can perform adequately. Such a recommendation reflects on the recommender, and when someone's reputation is at stake, we can expect the recommendation to reflect considered judgment. **Employee referrals** also may receive more accurate information about their potential jobs. The recommender often gives the applicant more realistic information about the job than could be conveyed through employment agencies or newspaper advertisements. This information reduces unrealistic expectations and increases job survival.

As a result of these preselection factors, employee referrals tend to be more acceptable applicants, who are more likely to accept an offer, and, once employed, have a higher job survival rate. Additionally, employee referrals are an excellent means of locating potential employees in those hard-to-fill positions. For example, difficulty in finding certain IT professionals, computer programmers, engineers, or nurses with specific skills has prompted some organizations to turn to their employees for assistance. Principal Financial Group, one of *Fortune* magazine's "100 Best Companies to Work For," gets at least 40 percent of new hires through employee referral. Wegmans, a regional grocery chain that is also on the "Best" list, reports that one in five of their employees are related to another Wegmans' employee.[12] Many of these organizations include a reward if an employee referral candidate is hired for these specifically identified hard-to-fill positions. Referral bonuses of $10,000 or more are not unusual in these fields. In doing so, both the organization and the employee benefit; the employee receives a monetary reward and the organization receives a qualified candidate without the major expense of an extensive recruiting search.

> Employee referrals are an excellent means of locating potential employees for hard- to-fill positions.

There are, of course, some potentially negative features of employee referral. For one, recommenders may confuse friendship with job performance competence. Individuals often like to have their friends join them at their place of employment for social and even economic reasons; for example, they may be able to share rides to and from work. As a result, a current employee may recommend a friend for a position without giving unbiased consideration to the friend's job-related competence. Employee referrals may also lead to nepotism, that is, hiring individuals related to persons already employed by the organization. Although such actions may not necessarily align with the objective of hiring the most qualified applicant, interest in the organization and loyalty to it may be long-term advantages. Finally, employee referrals may also minimize an organization's desire to add diversity to the workplace.

Employee referrals do, however, appear to have universal application. Lower-level and managerial-level positions can be, and often are, filled by the recommendation of a current employee. Higher-level positions, however, are more likely to be referred by a professional acquaintance rather than a close friend. Employees with jobs that require specialized expertise often participate in professional organizations that produce acquaintances with individuals they may think would make excellent contributions to their organizations.

External Searches

In addition to looking internally for candidates, organizations often open up recruiting efforts to the external community. These efforts include advertisements online job boards, employment agencies, schools, colleges and universities, professional organizations, and unsolicited applicants.

Advertisements Sign outside a construction location: "Now Hiring—Framers." Newspaper advertisement: "Telemarketing Sales. We are looking for someone who wants to assume responsibility and wishes to become part of the fast-growing wireless business. No previous sales experience required. Salary up to $45,000. For appointment, call Mrs. Brown: 1-800-555-0075." More sophisticated Internet job search engines can provide us with a richness of data about the job and the company and link us to several other websites that provide additional information.

Most of us have seen these kinds of advertisements. When an organization wishes to tell the public it has a vacancy, advertisement is one of the most popular methods used. The type of job often determines where the advertisement is placed. The higher the position in the organization, the more specialized the skills, or the shorter the supply of that resource in the labor force, the more widely dispersed the advertisement is likely to be. The search for a top executive might include advertisements in national publications—perhaps the *Wall Street Journal* or *New York Times*—or be posted on executive-search firm websites. On the other hand, advertisements of entry-level jobs usually appear in local daily newspapers, or on broad-based Internet job sites like Monster, CareerBuilder, Yahoo, HotJobs, and Craigslist.

Three important variables influence the response rate to advertisements: identification of the organization, labor market conditions, and the degree to which the advertisement includes specific requirements. Some organizations place a **blind-box ad**, one that

blind-box ad
An advertisement that does not identify the advertising organization

includes no specific identification of the organization. Respondents are asked to reply to a post office box number or to an employment firm acting as an agent between the applicant and the organization. Large organizations with a national reputation seldom use blind advertisements to fill lower-level positions; however, when the organization does not wish to publicize the fact that it is seeking to fill an internal position, or when it seeks to recruit for a position where there is a soon-to-be-removed incumbent, a blind-box advertisement may be appropriate.

Although blind ads can assist HRM in finding qualified applicants, many individuals may be reluctant to answer them. Obviously, there is the fear, sometimes justified, that the advertisement has been placed by the organization in which the individual is currently employed. Also, the organization itself is frequently a key determinant of whether the individual is interested; therefore, potential candidates may be reluctant to reply. Such advertisements also have a bad reputation because some organizations place ads when no position exists to test the supply of workers in the community, to build a backlog of applicants, or to identify those current employees who are interested in finding a new position. Others place ads to satisfy affirmative action requirements when the final decision, for the greater part, has already been made.

The job analysis process is the basic source for ad information. The ad can focus on descriptive elements of the job (job description) or on the applicant (job specification), a choice that often affects the number of replies received. If, for example, you are willing to sift through 1,000 or more responses, you might place a national ad in the *Los Angeles Times,* the *Chicago Tribune,* a regional newspaper's employment section, or on a website like Monster.com (see Exhibit 6-1). However, an advertisement in these locations that looks like Exhibit 6-2 might attract fewer than a dozen replies.

As you can see, Exhibit 6-1 uses more applicant-centered criteria to describe the successful candidate. Most individuals perceive themselves as having confidence and seeking high income. More important, how can an employer measure these qualities? The response rate should therefore be high. In contrast, Exhibit 6-2 calls for precise abilities and experience.

Employment Agencies Three different types of **employment agencies** exist to help employers and workers find each other. Public or state agencies, private employment agencies, and management consulting firms all provide valuable employment matching services. The major difference between them is the type of clientele served.

employment agencies
Assists in matching employees seeking work with employers seeking workers

Exhibit 6-1
Advertisement with General Information
This ad for an HR Generalist centers on candidate characteristics and should receive a large number of responses.

US-NY-New York-HR Generalist - Recruiter

Status: Full-Time Employee   **Salary:** from 50,000.00 per year   **Reference Code:** 294-036310

Job Location: NEW YORK 10028

Arts non-profit currently seeking an HR Generalist with a concentration in recruitment.

Qualifications:

Arts non-profit currently seeking an HR Generalist with a concentration in recruiting. This position requires a variety of generalist/administrative human resources functions in areas such as recruitment, employee relations, training and development, and benefits administration. Candidate must be comfortable working with management and staff on relevant corporate personnel practices, policies, and procedures. Prior recruiting experience is a must! Candidate must be a strategic and analytical thinker and thrive in a fast-paced environment. Excellent benefits offered. Salary commensurate with experience.

OfficeTeam is the world's leader in specialized administrative staffing offering job opportunities from Executive and Administrative Assistants to Office Managers and Receptionists. We have the resources, experience, and expertise to select companies and temporary to full-time positions that match your skills and career goals. We provide one of the industry's most progressive training, benefits and compensation packages. OfficeTeam is an Equal Opportunity Employer.

Principal Software Development Engineer, Ordering Systems 029162

Job Description

As one of the largest e-commerce companies in the world, we enable over 70 million customers to place orders globally using Amazon's technology each year. Orders are processed on behalf of thousands of merchants, including Amazon. Over the past decade, Amazon has become known across the globe as the most trusted company on the Internet. There is a tremendous amount of work behind the scenes to ensure that customers' experience on the website results in a successful delivery to their door or electronic devices.

The Principal Software Development Engineer for Ordering will have the unique opportunity to influence the direction of e-commerce solutions. In addition to driving innovation for the Shopping Cart, Checkout, and Your Account applications, the Principal SDE will drive the design and adoption of new workflow technology. The workflow systems will build on top of state-of-the-art ordering, payments, and fulfillment services. The solutions built will not only drive Amazon's ordering workflow, but can be used for custom merchant development.

Principal Engineers provide technical leadership at Amazon.com. They help establish technical standards and drive Amazon's overall technical architecture, engineer practices, and engineering methodologies. They work on our hardest problems, building high quality, architecturally sound systems that are aligned with our business needs. They think globally when building systems, ensuring Amazon.com builds high performing, scalable systems that fit well together. Principal Engineers are pragmatic visionaries who can translate business needs into workable technology solutions. Their expertise is deep and broad. They are hands on, producing both detailed technical work and high-level architectural designs.

Position Responsibilities

- Work effectively with other groups within Amazon in order to deliver ordering solutions and services that span multiple organizations, areas of business, and geographies.
- Lead in the design, implementation, and deployment of successful enterprise-level systems.
- Assist in the career development of others, actively mentoring individuals and the community on advanced technical issues, and helping managers guide the career growth of their team members.
- Exert technical influence over multiple teams, increasing their productivity and effectiveness by sharing your deep knowledge and experience.
- Contribute intellectual property through patents.

The ideal candidate will be a visionary leader, builder, and operator. He/she should have experience leading or contributing to multiple simultaneous product development efforts and/or IT projects and initiatives. The leader needs to balance technical leadership and savvy with strong business judgment to make the right decisions about technology choices. While constantly striving for simplicity, the Principal SDE must demonstrate significant creativity and high judgment.

Qualifications

- BS degree or higher in CS with 10 years of relevant, broad engineering experience required
- Experience managing complex projects, with significant bottom-line impact
- Experience leading development life cycle process and best practices
- Experience with Agile Management (SCRUM, RUP, XP), OO Modeling, working on Internet, UNIX, Middleware, and database related projects

Exhibit 6-2
Advertisement with Specific Information

This ad for a Software Development Engineer should receive fewer responses because of the very specific job qualifications.

Public and state agencies All states provide a public employment service. One major function of these agencies is assisting workers receiving unemployment benefits find employment. Many states have excellent and extensive employment services. The U.S. Department of Labor sponsors a site called CareerOneStop at www.careeronestop.org that offers career resources to job seekers, students, businesses, and workforce professionals along with

When hiring an executive for an organization, many companies turn to executive search firms for their network and other capabilities.
(Source: Masterfile)

executive search firms
Private employment agency specializing in middle- and top-management placements

links to job service listings in every state. In addition to matching employers with qualified workers, many public and state agencies assist employers with testing, job analysis, evaluation programs, and community wage surveys. Workers seeking employment can receive assistance with career guidance, job seeking skills, and training.

Private agencies How do private employment agencies, which charge for their services, compete with state agencies that give their services away? Private agencies collect fees from employers or employees for their matching services. The private employment agency's fee can be totally absorbed by either the employer or the employee, or it can be split. The alternative chosen usually depends on demand and supply in the community involved. Private agencies may also provide a more complete line of services than public agencies. They may advertise the position, screen applicants against the criteria specified by the employer, and often provide a guarantee covering six months or a year as protection to the employer should the applicant not perform satisfactorily. Some of the largest private agencies are Manpower, Addeco, and Kelly Services.

Management Consulting Firms Frequently called executive recruiters or "headhunters," these are actually specialized private employment agencies. They specialize in middle- and top-level executive placement, as well as hard-to-fill positions such as actuaries, IT specialists, or managers with international experience. In addition to the level at which they recruit, the features that distinguish executive search agencies from most private employment agencies are their fees, their nationwide contacts, and the thoroughness of their investigations. In searching for an individual of vice-president caliber, whose compensation package may far exceed $250,000 a year, the potential employer may be willing to pay a high fee to locate exactly the right individual to fill the vacancy: up to 35 percent of the executive's first-year salary is not unusual as a charge for finding and recruiting the individual.

Executive Search Firms **Executive search firms** canvass their contacts and do preliminary screening. They seek out highly effective executives who have the right skills, can adjust to the organization, and most important, are willing to consider new challenges and opportunities. Such individuals may be frustrated by their inability to move up quickly in their current organization, or they may have been recently passed over for a major promotion. The executive search firm acts as a buffer for screening candidates and, at the same time, keeps the prospective employer anonymous. In the final stages, senior executives in the prospective firm can move into the negotiations and determine the degree of mutual interest.[13]

Schools, Colleges, and Universities Educational institutions at all levels offer opportunities for recruiting recent graduates. Most educational institutions operate placement services where prospective employers can review credentials and interview graduates. Most also allow employers to see a prospective employee's performance through cooperative arrangements and internships. Whether the job requires a high school diploma, specific vocational training, or a bachelor's, masters, or doctoral degree, educational institutions are an excellent source of potential employees.

High schools or vocational-technical schools can prove to be a good source of part-time and entry-level employees. Community colleges along with other two- and four-year colleges and graduate schools can provide professional and managerial-level personnel. Although educational institutions are usually viewed as sources for inexperienced entrants to the workforce, it is not uncommon to find individuals with considerable work experience using an educational institution's placement service. They may be workers who have recently returned to school to upgrade their skills or former graduates interested in pursuing other opportunities.

Job Fairs Once thought to be a little old-fashioned and not very cost effective, **job fairs** are making a comeback as an effective recruiting tool. Often held on or near college campuses in the spring, they're a good opportunity to build a company's employment brand. They can also be staffed by employees, providing a great employee development tool. The primary purpose is to contact prospective employees and collect information and résumés, but it's not uncommon for online applications to double in the days following a job fair event. Most employers go out of their way to make sure that even unsuitable candidates leave the job fair with a favorable impression of the company. Many are counseled on the additional requirements and training they would need to be successful candidates. Employees staffing the events gain valuable leadership training and are often energized to promote the virtues of their employer long after the event.

A new twist on the concept is virtual job fairs. They have the same purpose and feel as traditional job fairs, but are held online. Some even include avatars—virtual online images of people—and virtual company recruiting booths. Candidates learn about the fairs from the "careers" section of company websites, Facebook, Twitter, or LinkedIn. Job seekers and recruiters meet online by logging into a specific website at a specified time. They may be held by a single company or group of employers. Sponsors have included Unisfair, CollegeGrad.com, and the National Association of Colleges and Employers, and participants have included Procter & Gamble, Citigroup, Boeing, Progressive, Amazon, and Safeway.[14] They can be highly targeted to specific groups such as Milicruit, which targets former military personnel. They are popular with tech-savvy Millenials seeking jobs because they don't involve expensive travel or the need to dress up.[15]

Professional Organizations Many professional organizations, including labor unions, operate placement services for the benefit of their members. Professional organizations serving such varied occupations as human resource management, industrial engineering, psychology, accounting, legal, and academia publish rosters of job vacancies and distribute these lists to members. It is also common practice to provide placement facilities at regional and national meetings where individuals looking for employment and companies looking for employees can find each other—building a network of employment opportunities.

Professional organizations, however, can also apply sanctions to control the labor supply in their discipline. For example, although the law stipulates that unions cannot require employers to hire only union members, the mechanisms for ensuring that unions do not break this law are poorly enforced. As a result, it is not unusual for labor unions to control supply through their apprenticeship programs and through their labor agreements with employers. Of course, this tactic is not limited merely to blue- collar trade unions. In professional organizations where the organization placement service is the focal point for locating prospective employers, and where certain qualifications are necessary to become a member (such as special educational attainment or professional certification or license), the professional organization can significantly influence and control the supply of prospective applicants.

job fairs
Events attended by employer representatives or recruiters with the goal of reaching qualified candidates.

Virtual Job Fair online sites provide contact between job seekers and prospective employers in real-time.
(Source: Courtesy InterCall)

Unsolicited Applicants Unsolicited applications, whether they reach the employer by letter, e-mail, online application, telephone, or in person, constitute a source of prospective applicants. Although the number of unsolicited applicants depends on economic conditions, the organization's image, and the job seeker's perception of the types of jobs that might be available, this source does provide an excellent supply of stockpiled applicants. Even if the company has no current openings, the application can be kept on file for later needs. Unsolicited applications made by unemployed individuals, however, generally have a short life. Those individuals who have adequate skills and who would be prime candidates for a position in the organization if it were available, usually find employment with some other organization that does have an opening. However, in times of economic stagnation, excellent prospects are often unable to locate the type of job they desire and may stay active in the job market for many months.

Online Recruiting

Newspaper advertisements and employment agencies may be on their way to extinction as primary sources for conveying information about job openings and finding job candidates, thanks to online recruiting. Most companies, both large and small, use the Internet to recruit new employees by adding a "careers" section to their website.[16] One recent survey indicates that 60 percent of employers report hiring new employees from online sources.[17]

Employer Websites Organizations like The Container Store that do a lot of recruiting often have a "Careers" section of their website specifically designed for recruitment. In addition to building the employment brand of the organization, they include the typical information you might find in an employment advertisement, such as qualifications sought, experience required, and benefits provided. They also showcase the organization's products, services, corporate philosophy, mission statement, testimonials from current employees, and some information about the benefits offered. This information should increase the quality of applicants, as those whose values don't mesh with the organization would not bother to apply.

Job Boards provide employers the opportunity to recruit for a wide variety of positions with worldwide exposure. Job seekers are able to search jobs by location, keywords, industry, level of education, salary, and any combination of these criteria. They also allow job seekers to post résumés and provide helpful services like career testing, and advice on conducting an effective job hunt. CareerBuilder.com and Monster.com are the two largest job board sites, with CareerBuilder reporting 25 million unique visitors to their website every month.[18] Employers pay these services per job post, which average about $400 per post. Craigslist is the most cost effective because it's free.

Social Media provides opportunities for companies like The Container Store, Walmart, and CareerBuilder to promote their business along with their employment brand and connect with potential applicants. Most include a "Careers" section on their Facebook page, promote employment on LinkedIn, and would love to add you to their list of followers on Twitter.

Specialized Job Boards narrow the focus of their postings to a specific career or set of job skills such as sales, medical, technology, or accounting. Others focus on characteristics of the job seeker such as interns, contractors, or part-timers. Some are even centered on ethnicity or age. Some specific examples of specialized job boards include:

Accountantsworld.com	Accounting
Dice.com	Technology
Miracleworkers.com	Healthcare
Jobsonthemenu.com	Restaurant
Careerrookie.com	Internships
Sologig.com	Contractors
Primecb.com	Baby boomers and Seniors
Hispanic-jobs.com	Hispanic
Blackcareers.com	African American

Many job candidates also use the Internet to their advantage by setting up their own web pages with **online résumés** to "sell" their job candidacy. When they learn of a possible job opening, they encourage potential employers to "check out my website." There, applicants have standard résumé information, supporting documentation, and sometimes a video where they introduce themselves to potential employers. Although résumés are frequently searched by recruiting firms that scan the Internet in search of viable job candidates, many employers are concerned that using video résumés in the initial screening process might make them vulnerable to claims of discrimination based on information they might infer by viewing the candidate's video.

Effective Recruiting

Determining the most effective recruiting method has become a real challenge. Employers need to understand the best method to contact prospective employees, much like marketers target prospective customers. Different methods are more effective for tech-savvy Millenials than for experienced professionals who may be older and not as connected to online sources. Most recent surveys of employers indicate that they agree with The Container Store; referrals are their leading source of external hires. Employers also report that online sources are growing as they expand their efforts to recruit online. Job boards CareerBuilder and Monster are the leading online suppliers of external recruits, with company career websites and social media sites such as LinkedIn, Facebook, Twitter, and even YouTube growing in importance. It's also fair to say that many recruits are exposed to more than one source of recruiting information, so tracking the effectiveness of any one recruiting source is becoming even more difficult.[19]

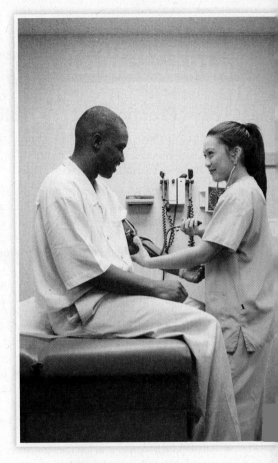

Recruitment Alternatives

Much of the previous discussion on recruiting sources implies that these efforts are designed to locate and hire full-time, permanent employees. However, economic realities that include employee layoffs, coupled with an increasing dependence on contingent workers, have created a slightly different focus. Recall, however, our discussion in Chapter 1 that temporary or contingent workers may raise some legal issues for employers—especially over the question as to whether or not an individual is, in fact, an employee.[20]

Temporary Help Services Organizations such as Kelly Services, Manpower, and Accountemps supply temporary employees. Temporary employees are particularly valuable in meeting short-term fluctuations in HRM needs.[21] Although traditionally developed in office administration, temporary staffing services have expanded to a broad range of skills. It is now possible, for example, to hire temporary nurses, computer programmers, accountants, librarians, drafting technicians, administrative assistants—even CEOs.

In addition to specific temporary help services, another quality source of temporary workers is older workers, those who have already retired or have been displaced by right-sizing in many companies.[22] An aging workforce and certain individuals' desire to retire earlier have created skill deficiencies in some disciplines. Older workers bring those skills back to the job. The reasons older workers continue to work vary,[23] but they bring several advantages: flexibility in scheduling, low absenteeism, high motivation, and mentoring abilities for younger workers.[24]

Employee Leasing **Leased employees** typically remain with an organization for longer periods than temporary employees. Under a leasing arrangement, individuals work for the leasing firm.[25] Organizations can use employee leasing companies to provide employees for specialized areas like human resources or accounting, or it can lease its entire staff. Employee leasing companies, called Professional Employee Organizations or PEOs, can provide substantial cost savings to organizations that lease employees rather than hire them, particularly for smaller employers. The PEO manages employees for many employers, so they can negotiate large group discounts for benefits such as health, life, vision, and dental insurance. They might also be able to offer a wider variety of benefits than a smaller employer.

Is this nurse a full-time employee of the hospital or an individual assigned to the hospital on a temporary basis? Temporary workers today can include nurses, computer programmers, accountants, librarians, even chief executives. *(Source: Andersen Ross/Photodisc Red /Getty Images, Inc.)*

online résumés
Résumés created and formatted to be posted on online résumé or job sites.

leased employees
Individuals hired by one firm and sent to work in another for a specific time.

TIPS FOR SUCCESS

"Best Practice" Ideas Applicable to Recruitment and Hiring

What are the EEOC-recognized best practices for private-sector organizations? Below are examples of what the "best of the best" do when recruiting.[26]

- Establish a policy for recruitment and hiring, including criteria, procedures, responsibilities, and applicability of diversity and affirmative action.
- Engage in short-term and long-term strategic planning.
- Identify the applicable barriers to equal employment opportunity.
- Ensure a communication network notifying interested persons of opportunities, including advertising within the organization and, where applicable, not only with the general media, but also with media aimed at minority people, disabled people, older people, and women.
- Communicate the competencies, skills, and abilities required for available positions.
- Communicate about family-friendly and work-friendly programs.
- Where transportation is an issue, consider arrangements with the local transit authority.
- Participate in career and job fairs and open houses.
- Work with professional associations, civic associations, and educational institutions with minorities, women, persons with disabilities, and/or older persons to recruit.

- Use recruiter, referral, and search firms with instructions to present diverse candidate pools to expand search networks.
- Partner with organizations that have missions to serve targeted groups.
- Use internship, work/study, co-op, and scholarship programs to attract interested and qualified persons and to develop potential candidates.
- Develop and support educational programs and become more involved with educational institutions that can refer a more diverse talent pool.
- Ensure that personnel involved in recruitment and hiring are well trained in their equal employment opportunity responsibilities.
- Explore community involvement options so the company's higher profile may attract more interested persons.
- Eliminate practices that exclude or present barriers to minorities, women, people with disabilities, older people, or any individual.
- Include progress in equal employment opportunity recruitment and hiring as factors in management evaluation.

Independent Contractors Another means of recruiting is the use of independent contractors. Often referred to as consultants, independent contractors are taking on a new relevance. Companies may hire independent contractors to do specific work at a location on or off the company's premises. For instance, claims processing or medical and legal transcription activities can easily be done at home and routinely forwarded to the employer. Online technology gives independent contractors the same access that telecommuters have.

Independent contractor arrangements benefit both the organization and the individual. Because the worker is not an employee, the company saves costs associated with full- or part-time personnel, such as insurance benefits, Social Security taxes, and workers' compensation premiums. Additionally, such opportunity is also a means of keeping talented and dependable individuals associated with your company. Suppose an employee wants to work but also be available to his or her school-age children, take care of elderly parents, or just wants a more flexible situation. Allowing the individual to work at home, on his or her time, can be a win-win solution to the problem.

Recruiting: A Global Perspective

The first step in recruiting for overseas positions is to define the relevant labor market. For international positions, however, that market is the whole world.[27] Organizations must decide if they want to send an American overseas, recruit in the host country, or overlook nationality and do a global search for the best person available. It's important to make an appropriate choice; the cost of failure in an international assignment can run high, sometimes in the six-figure range.[28]

This basic decision depends partly on the type of occupation and its requirements, as well as the stage of national and cultural development of the overseas operations and the economy. Although production, office, and clerical occupations are rarely filled beyond a local labor market, executive and sometimes scientific, engineering, or professional managerial candidates may be sought in national or international markets. If the organization is searching for someone with extensive company experience to launch a technical product in a new target country, it will probably want a home-country national. This approach is often implemented when a new foreign subsidiary is being established and headquarters wants to control all strategic decisions, but the plan requires technical expertise and experience. It is also appropriate where there is a lack of qualified host-country nationals in the workforce.

Other situations might benefit more from hiring a **host-country national (HCN)**, assuming this is a choice. For consumer products, corporate strategy may allow each foreign subsidiary to acquire its own distinct national identity.[29] Clothing, for example, has different styles of merchandising, and a company may feel that an HCN will most likely have a better handle on the best way to market the sweaters or jeans of an international manufacturer. Many companies are also finding that host-country nationals are increasingly better prepared for higher-level positions, particularly in India and China. Many companies are taking the initiative to partner with governments and universities to build relationships that create a pipeline of qualified candidates in emerging countries. For example, Infosys consults with colleges in India on curriculum that best prepares students for future employment and even helps with teacher training.[30]

Hiring choices may not be entirely left to the corporation. A few countries, including Saudi Arabia, place limits on expatriate workers. Using HCNs eliminates potential language problems, avoids problems of expatriate adjustment and the high cost of training and relocating an expatriate with a family. It also minimizes one of the chief reasons international assignments fail—the family's inability to adjust to their new surroundings. Even if companies pay a premium salary to lure the best local applicants away from other companies, employee-related costs are significantly lower then those incurred by sending an American overseas. In countries with tense political environments, a HCN may somewhat insulate the U.S. corporation from hostilities and possible terrorism.

The third option, recruiting regardless of nationality, develops a group of international executives with a truly global perspective. On a large scale, this type of recruiting may reduce managers' national identification with particular organizational units, creating a truly international organization that makes decisions for the good of the organization, regardless of location.

Companies like Enterprise Rent-A-Car have extensive overseas recruiting campaigns, establishing relationships with colleges all across Europe. Recruiters work with faculty, athletic departments, and campus clubs, promoting the company as a great place to work. (*Source: Joe Raedle/Getty Images, Inc.*)

host-country national (HCN)
A citizen of the host country hired by an organization based in another country.

expatriate
An individual who lives and works in a country of which he or she is not a citizen.

Your Own Job Search

You may have been reading this chapter from the perspective of a job seeker wondering how to make all this information work to your advantage in starting your career. The job seeking process is possibly one of the more stressful situations you will face. Do not expect the search to be quick and easy, particularly in times of high unemployment. In our society, we're conditioned to expect immediate results, and it's easy to get discouraged when rejection letters start to pile up. The job search process has been compared to a marathon rather than a sprint. Crossing the finish line takes training, commitment, endurance, and support.

Competition for most good jobs is fierce—even in times of low unemployment. You can't afford to wait until the last minute; your job hunt must start well in advance of when you plan to start work. So, for college seniors who plan to graduate in May, starting in the fall has two advantages. First, it shows that you are taking an interest in your career and that you are planning ahead. Not waiting until the last minute to begin reflects favorably

TIPS FOR SUCCESS

Posting Online Résumés

Many companies offer online help in developing your résumé and a few will help you post it online with your own unique Web address or URL. These companies merge and get bought out frequently, so you can't just put it out there and forget about it. Update your list of skills and the format frequently to keep it appearing current and fresh. Here are a few popular sites that offer tools for creating online résumés, managing Internet-based career portfolios, and sharing professional qualifications with employers.[32] Some do charge to develop or post your résumé, so compare prices and service.

- CareerBuilder
- Monster
- VisualCV.com
- Myresumeonline.org
- Pongoresume.com

on you. Second, starting in the fall coincides with many companies' recruiting cycles. If you wait until March to begin the process, some job openings are likely to already have been filled. For specific information regarding the company recruiting cycles in your area, visit your college's career development center.[31]

Preparing Your Résumé

All job applicants need to circulate information that reflects positively on their strengths and to send that information to prospective employers in a format that is understandable and consistent with the organization's hiring practices. In most instances, this requires a résumé.

No matter who you are or where you are in your career, you should have a current résumé, sometimes referred to as a CV or Curriculum Vitae (not necessarily just for education—it's Latin for "course of life"). Your résumé is typically a recruiter's primary information source in determining whether or not to grant you an interview. Therefore, your résumé must be a sales tool; it must give key information that supports your candidacy, highlights your strengths, and differentiates you from other job applicants. Make sure to include anything that distinguishes you from other applicants. Information to include is shown in Exhibit 6-3. Note that volunteer or community service, for example, shows that you are well rounded, committed to your community, and willing to help others.

It's valuable to pinpoint a few key themes regarding résumés that may seem like common sense but are frequently ignored. First, if you are making a paper copy of your résumé, it must be printed on a quality printer. The font style should be easy to read (for example, Arial or Times New Roman). Avoid any style that may be hard on the eyes, such as script fonts. A recruiter who must review one hundred or more résumés a day will look more favorably at those that make the job easier.

It is also important to note that many companies today rely on applicant tracking software to scan your application and résumé for keywords related to skill, training, degrees, job titles, and experience. This has created two important aspects for résumé writers to remember. Software matches key words in the job description, so use terminology similar to the job description.

Finally, regardless of whether your résumé is on paper or online, make sure it is carefully proofread. The résumé is your only representation to the recruiter, and a sloppy one can be deadly. If it contains misspelled words or is grammatically incorrect, your chances for an interview will be significantly reduced. Proofread your résumé several times, and if possible, let others proofread it.

Making Social Media Work For You

Most of us have been warned to be careful about the information posted on social media sites like Facebook, and we'll take another look at some guidelines for using those sites in

SHANE REYNOLDS
1820 North Avenue
Bentonville, AR 72712

CAREER OBJECTIVE: Seeking employment in an investment firm that provides a challenging opportunity to combine exceptional interpersonal skills and computer expertise.

EDUCATION:	University of Arkansas B.S., Business Economics and Computer Science (May 2012)
EXPERIENCE:	University of Arkansas
9/2011 to present	Campus Bookstore, Assistant Bookkeeper Primary Duties: Responsible for coordinating book purchases with academic departments; placing orders with publishers; invoicing, receiving inventory, pricing, and stocking shelves. Supervised four student employees. Managed annual budget of $125,000.
5/2011 to 12/2011	Student Intern Wal-Mart Corporation Primary Duties: Worked on team responsible for developing and maintaining a product tracking system for Southwest region. Presented concept to regional management and began process of implementation. Cited for outstanding work on the internship.
SPECIAL SKILLS:	• Experienced in Microsoft Excel, Word, Access, and PowerPoint presentation software. • Fluent in speaking and writing Chinese. • Certified in CPR.
SERVICE ACTIVITIES:	• Secretary/Treasurer, Student Government Association • President, Computer Science Club • Volunteer, Meals-on-Wheels
REFERENCES:	Available on request.

Chapter 7, but social networking sites can be used to your advantage in your job search. Providing employers with links to your profile on sites like LinkedIn or other professional networking sites is an opportunity to go beyond your résumé and share professional information. On these sites you can list accomplishments and links to your résumé along with recommendations from people in your network. You can also ask people in your network to help you in your job search. Be sure to check your profile often to make sure the information is accurate and up-to-date.[33] Use every advantage available to you. Remember, it's a marathon, not a sprint.

Exhibit 6-3
A Sample Résumé

There is no standard résumé format. The best format is the one that represents your strengths, skill, and qualifications most effectively. How would you evaluate this sample résumé?

Summary

(This summary relates to the Learning Outcomes identified on page 140.)
After reading this chapter, you should be able to:

1. **Define the term** *recruiting*. Recruiting is discovering potential applicants for actual or anticipated organizational vacancies. It involves seeking viable job candidates.
2. **Identify the dual goals of recruiting.** The two goals of recruiting are to generate a large pool of qualified applicants and to provide enough information for individuals to self-select out of the process.
3. **Explain constraints human resource managers face in determining recruiting sources.** Influences that constrain HRM in determining recruiting sources include image of the organization, attractiveness and nature of the job, internal policies, government requirements, and the recruiting budget.
4. **Identify the principal sources for recruiting employees.** The principal sources for recruiting employees include internal search, advertisements, employee referrals/recommendations, employment agencies, temporary leasing services, schools, colleges, universities, professional organizations, online recruiting, and casual or unsolicited applicants. Employee leasing, temporary employees, and independent contractors continue to be good sources of employees.

5. **Describe the advantages and disadvantages of employee referrals.** The advantages of employee referrals include access to individuals who possess specific skills, having job applicants with more complete job and organization information, and a universal application to all levels in the organization. The disadvantages of employee referrals include the potential of confusing friendship with job performance, nepotism, or for minimizing the organization's desire to add diversity to the organization's employee mix.

6. **Identify three important variables that affect response rates to job advertisements.** The three important variables are: identification of the organization; labor market conditions; and the degree to which specific requirements are included in the advertisement.

7. **Explain what distinguishes a public employment agency from a private employment agency.** The major difference between public and private employment agencies often lies in their image. Private employment agencies are believed to offer positions and applicants of a higher caliber. Private agencies may also provide a more complete line of services in that they advertise the position, screen applicants against the criteria specified by the employer, and provide a guarantee as protection to the employer should the applicant not perform satisfactorily. Public employment agencies are more closely linked to unemployment benefits. Accordingly, the image of most public agencies (not completely accurate) is that they tend to attract and list individuals who are unskilled or have had minimum training.

8. **Describe the benefits of online recruiting.** Internet recruiting provides businesses with low-cost and unprecedented access to potential employees worldwide. Online recruiting also helps increase diversity and finds people with unique talents.

9. **Explain the concept of employee leasing and the organizational benefits of such an arrangement.** Employee leasing refers to when individuals employed in an organization actually work for the leasing firm. One reason for the popularity of leasing is cost. The acquiring organization pays a flat fee for the employees and is not responsible for benefits or other costs it would incur for a full-time employee, such as Social Security payments.

Demonstrating Comprehension

QUESTIONS FOR REVIEW

1. What is the "dual objective" of recruiting?
2. Identify and describe factors that influence the degree to which an organization will engage in recruiting.
3. What specific constraints might prevent an HR manager from hiring the best candidate?
4. Present the advantages and disadvantages of recruiting through an internal search.
5. What are the pros and cons of using employee referrals for recruiting workers?
6. Describe the differences one may encounter when recruiting globally.
7. Explain the opportunities for promoting yourself online to potential employers.

Key Terms

blind-box ad	expatriates	online résumés
constraints on recruiting efforts	host-country national (HCN)	recruiter
employee referral	internal search	recruiting
employment agencies	job fairs	
executive search firms	leased employees	

HRM Workshop

Linking Concepts to Practice   DISCUSSION QUESTIONS

1. "A job advertisement that generates a thousand responses is always better than one that gets twenty responses." Build an argument supporting this statement and an argument refuting this statement.
2. "An organization should follow a promote-from-within policy." Do you agree or disagree with this statement? Explain.
3. When you go looking for a job after graduation, what sources do you expect to use? Why?
4. "The emphasis on leased or temporary employees in an organization will only lead to a decrease in employee morale. These employees come in, do their jobs, then leave it up to the full-timers to handle the details." Build an argument supporting this statement and an argument refuting this statement.

Making A Difference   SERVICE LEARNING PROJECTS

Organizations of all types need to recruit members and volunteers, including non-profits and your college. This important staffing function allows many opportunities for service activities.

- Ask your college placement office or local chapter of the Society of Human Resource Management (SHRM) if they need student volunteers to assist with career fairs on campus or off campus. This is a great opportunity to learn more about recruiting and make contacts with HR recruiting representatives.
- Contact your college recruiters about assisting with college recruitment efforts such as calling prospective students and giving campus tours.

- Community organizations often need help with events. Volunteer your services to recruit volunteers for parades, festivals, JDRF Walk to Cure Diabetes, Susan G. Komen Race for the Cure, or other community events.
- Create, organize, and recruit volunteer staff for a campus blood drive with the cooperation of your local blood bank or Red Cross chapter.

As you put your service learning experience together, keep a journal of your activities, the time you spend, contact information for people you work with, and your thoughts about the process. When you're finished, make a presentation to your class about the experience and what you learned. What concepts in Chapter 6 were you able to apply?

Developing Diagnostic and Analytical Skills

Case Application 6-A: POLICING PARADISE: HOW THE HONOLULU POLICE DEPARTMENT DEVELOPED ITS BRAND

For years, the chiefs of the Honolulu Police Department used *ohana,* the Hawaiian word for family, to describe the department. Family is important in Hawaiian culture and *ohana* is the reason why officers joined and stayed with the force.

Several years ago, the police family found itself in a staffing crisis. Like many other organizations, a large percentage of the officers were nearing retirement. Combined with other issues such as officers leaving for better paying jobs on the mainland and competition from other law enforcement agencies that went on hiring sprees after 9/11, the force found itself significantly short on officers with no reprieve in sight. Typically the department accepts only 3 percent of applicants into its six-month training class, and loses some before the training is complete. The situation called for lots of applicants . . . fast.

The department's leaders decided that a massive recruiting campaign built around their *ohana* family-style culture was in order; $60,000 was put into recruiting efforts that took many forms.

- Department image and culture was promoted as close knit and service oriented rather than the usual rough and tumble image of police departments.

- Women's recruitment seminars were held.
- Radio and TV ads were purchased.
- Print ads were published in a magazine developed for the launch of the new inter-island "Super Ferry."
- Physically fit young people were targeted with recruiting efforts at beach volleyball tournaments, college, and even high school athletic events.
- A police recruiting van was a visible presence at community events.
- People on the mainland with ties to Hawaii, such as prior military service, were targeted.
- A heavily promoted recruiting event in Portland, Oregon, drew people from as far away as New York and Florida.
- Officers who had left the force for departments on the mainland were contacted.

Although the downsides of working and living in Honolulu, Hawaii, primarily related to the high cost of living, were also explained, the numbers of recruits gradually climbed. Seven years of recruiting effort finally paid off in July of 2008 when the force reached zero vacancies according to HPD Recruiter, Officer Julie Kusuda.[34]

Questions:

1. How could the Honolulu Police Department have used other recruitment methods to accomplish their objectives?
2. How successful would their recruiting efforts have been without their branding campaign? Explain.

3. How would you handle the rejected applicants?
4. Take a look at the Honolulu Police Department Career Center at www.honolulupd.org. What suggestions can you make to improve their recruiting efforts?

Case Application 6-B: PRIORITY STAFFING

Imagine you work for a large global company in human resources. You are faced with some special staffing needs for a few of the departments that you serve. You know that the people you're looking for must be well trained and able to do the job immediately. So when staffing gets tough, you frequently turn to temporary staffing agencies for assistance. But today's challenge is a bit more complex.

You need an administrative assistant who is fluent in Spanish for one of the executives visiting from Spain. You also have a project for which you are providing HRM support that will require someone who is well versed in Hindi and Hindu culture. And your manufacturing vice president is asking for your help as she's preparing for a visit from a Korean client who doesn't speak English. What do you do? If you're in the New York area, the answer is simple. You contact Deborah Wainstein, founder of Priority Staffing Solutions, and ask for help.[35]

Priority Staffing Solutions is a temporary staffing agency in New York. Founded in 1999 by Wainstein, the organization provides multilingual temporary workers to organizations in the New York City area. Employing fifteen full-time individuals and more than five hundred part-time employees, the company places nearly seventy temporary employees daily as administrative assistants, computer graphics specialists, word processing operators, and legal office support staff. Serving the needs of approximately eighty

clients—such organizations as Revlon and RCN Corporation—Priority Staffing Solutions offers their clients "cost-effective strategies while distinguishing and responding to the ever-changing needs of each individual organization."

For Wainstein, her service is a wonderful help to her client organizations. She's helped them staff for peak periods, or find a particular skill needed for special projects. Through her service she's also assisted her clients in saving some HR-related costs, such as those associated with recruiting. In return, she's distinguished her company as a leading multilingual temporary staffing agency, resulting in the company generating several million dollars in annual revenues.

Questions:

1. What role does a temporary staffing agency such as Priority Staffing Solutions play in the recruiting efforts of an organization?
2. Does a surplus or a shortage of workers play a role in how organizations recruit? Discuss.
3. How does an organization such as Priority Staffing Solutions assist in filling "hard-to-recruit" jobs? Explain.
4. What effect, if any, does using a firm like Priority Staffing Solutions have on an organization's image? Defend your position.

Working with a Team   A QUESTION OF EFFECTIVE RECRUITING

Tommy Ford is an impatient, results-oriented, innovative, hardworking, focused entrepreneur. He likes working with aggressive, highly creative, skilled, focused team players who are flexible, change driven, informed, cutting-edge professionals much like himself in work ethic but from diverse groups. He believes that professionals with varied backgrounds contribute to better solutions and creativity. He wants only those who are as committed as he is to growing a company that produces the industry standard and benchmark in intranet and software technology. That means being willing to work sixty to ninety hours a week at High-5-Tech if the project requires, as well as dedication to and passion for customers, the firm, and the project team.

Ford may start people out with salaries slightly below industry average, but he rewards performance and tenure. He's reputed

to double a salary when a developer exceeds expectations. He also contributes his company's stock to the employees' benefit package, subject to their length of employment. At the current rate, a person might retire a millionaire if he or she can withstand the pace.

Interested? Discuss why or why not, comparing responses with your paired team member. Also, here are some guiding questions for you and your partner to consider:

1. What would be effective ways to recruit qualified professionals to work for Tommy?
2. How would you develop a recruiting brand for High-5-Tech to assist with recruiting efforts?

Learning an HRM Skill   WRITING A JOB ADVERTISEMENT

About the skill: How do you persuade individuals to pay attention to your job opening? Interest them in your organization? Give them enough information so that those who are not qualified do not respond? The answer to these questions lies in the job advertisement.[36] The more effective your advertisement, the more likely you will achieve the dual goal of recruiting.

1. *Tell enough about the job.* Provide enough information about the job so that potential applicants can determine whether they are interested or qualified.
2. *Give relevant information about the job.* Provide a job title and a description of job duties. This information should be drawn directly from the job description.

3. *List the minimum qualities a successful job incumbent needs.* Include specific requirements a job incumbent must possess. This may reflect educational levels, prior experience, and specific competencies or skills. Again, much of this information should be readily available from the job-specification component of the job description.

4. *Be specific about unique aspects of the job.* Disclose any pertinent information the job applicant should know. For example, if the job requires extensive traveling, state this information, as well as experience on specific equipment, technology applications, and so forth. Provide enough detail so that you comply with ADA requirements.

5. *Check the advertisement for correctness.* Make sure the advertisement is properly written, contains no grammatical or punctuation errors, and is easy to read. Whenever possible, avoid jargon and abbreviations that may be confusing. Review each word to ensure that no terms used may be deemed inappropriate or potentially create an adverse impact.

Enhancing Your Communication Skills

1. Using the job description of the benefits manager from Exhibit 5-7 (Chapter 5), write a job advertisement for this position to be placed on an online job board such as Career-Builder or Monster.

2. Develop a two- to three-page response to the following question: What are the pros and cons for an organization that uses temporary employees as a pool from which to select permanent employees? Are there benefits from the employee's standpoint?

3. Visit three different online job-recruiting sites or virtual career fairs. Explain the sites you visited. Describe the similarities and differences you noticed among the three. Which site did you prefer? Which seems most effective? Which has the most features for employers or employees? Explain your selections.

(Source: Masterfile)

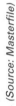

LEARNING OUTCOMES

After reading this chapter, you will be able to

1. Describe the selection process.

2. Identify the primary purpose of selection activities.

3. Discuss why organizations use application forms.

4. Explain the primary purposes of performance simulation tests.

5. Discuss the problems associated with job interviews and means of correcting them.

6. Specify the organizational benefits derived from realistic job previews.

7. Explain the purpose of background investigations.

8. List three types of validity.

9. Explain how validity is determined.

Foundations of Selection

7

Things were getting ugly in the cosmetic departments at Bon-Ton Department stores and something had to be done, fast. Beauty Advisors in their 277 stores were leaving the company at much higher rates than salespeople in other parts of the stores during their first few months on the job.[1]

It didn't make sense. Beauty advisors received more training and had higher income potential than most other selling associates in the Bon-Ton chain, yet turnover was much higher than all other selling positions in the store. Bon-Ton already had an assessment in place that was supposed to determine if an applicant was a good fit, but it clearly wasn't working for the Beauty Advisor position.

Bon-Ton HR started asking some tough questions about what it takes to be successful in a beauty sales position. Since cosmetic sales require getting up close and personal with customers, much more so than other sales positions, they wondered if a Beauty Advisor needed to have different personality traits than someone selling clothing or bedding.

Since the Bureau of Labor Statistics projected that demand for sales workers would grow at a faster rate than other professions, Bon-Ton couldn't afford to be constantly replacing sales workers, especially since they receive 30 hours of training in their first 60 days of employment. It was both time consuming and expensive.

Consultants interviewed hundreds of high performing Beauty Advisors and managers at Bon-Ton to try and determine the traits essential for job success. The results were surprising. Prior to the survey, managers assumed that friendly, customer-service oriented people who loved fashion and beauty were good candidates. Those factors certainly didn't hurt, but the most important traits turned out to be cognitive and problem solving ability. Successful Beauty Advisors, they found, are intelligent problem solvers as much as they are sales people, as they help customers with very personal skincare, makeup, and fragrance needs.[2]

As a result, ten questions were developed for store managers to ask when interviewing applicants. A new assessment was also developed and validated for adverse impact and other discriminatory factors. All applicants for cosmetic sales associate positions are now required to take the 80 question assessment test—it takes around 20 minutes to complete—and the results have been encouraging. Cosmetic associates now remain with Bon-Ton stores 12 percent longer than they did before the assessment test was implemented and turnover is the lowest of any sales group in the store. New associates also achieve 2.1 percent more total sales per hour than associates hired before the assessment was developed.[3]

Looking Ahead

What attributes should be included in the Bon-Ton assessment? Are there traits that should not be included? Do you think the new assessment will work for other areas of the store?

Introduction

Consider this scenario. A recent international business school graduate went on her first interview in an organization with significant operations on four continents.[4] Not knowing what to expect, she prepared as best she could. She was exquisitely dressed in a new suit and carried her tasteful leather briefcase. As she entered the human resource management office, she encountered two doors. On the first door was the sign "International Business Majors." On the second was "All Other Majors." She entered door one, which opened up to two more doors. On door one was "3.55 or Better GPA"; door two, "All Other GPAs." Having graduated with a 3.78 GPA, she entered door one, and found herself facing yet two more choices. Door one stated, "Fluent in three languages," and door two, "Fluent in two or fewer languages." Because her education did not require language proficiency and she was fluent in only one language, she went through door two. Upon opening the door, she found a box with preprinted letters saying, "Your qualifications did not meet the expectations of the job. Thanks for considering our organization. Please exit to the right."

Of course, no selection activity is this impersonal or clear-cut. Successful selection activities entail a lot of careful planning. The selection process is composed of steps, each of which provides decision makers with information that will help them predict whether an applicant will be a successful job performer.[5] One way to conceptualize this is to think of each step in the selection process as a higher hurdle in a race. The applicant able to clear all the hurdles wins the race, and the job offer.

The Selection Process

Selection activities follow a standard pattern, beginning with an initial screening interview and concluding with the final employment decision. The selection process typically consists of eight steps: (1) initial screening interview, (2) completion of the application form, (3) pre-employment tests, (4) comprehensive interview, (5) conditional job offer, (6) background investigation, (7) medical or physical examination, and (8) job offer. Each step represents a decision point requiring affirmative feedback in order for the process to continue. Each step in the process seeks to expand the organization's knowledge about the applicant's background, abilities, and motivation, and it increases the information that decision makers use to make their predictions and final choice. However, some steps may be omitted if they do not yield useful data, or if the cost of the step is unwarranted. Applicants should also be advised of any specific screening, such as credit checks, reference checking, and drug tests. The flow of these activities is depicted in Exhibit 7-1. Let's take a closer look at each.

Initial Screening

initial screening
The first step in the selection process whereby job inquiries are sorted.

The first step in the selection process involves the **initial screening** of potential candidates. This initial screening is, in effect, a two-step procedure: (1) screening inquiries and (2) screening interviews. If the company's recruiting effort has been successful, they will have a pool of potential applicants. The organization can eliminate some of these respondents based on the job description and job specification. Perhaps candidates lack adequate or appropriate experience, or adequate or appropriate education. Other red flags include gaps in the applicant's job history, a listing of numerous jobs held for short periods of time, or courses and seminars listed instead of appropriate education.

The screening interview is also an excellent opportunity for HRM to describe the job in enough detail so the candidates can consider if they are actually serious about applying. Sharing job description information frequently encourages the unqualified or marginally qualified to voluntarily withdraw from candidacy with a minimum cost to the applicant or the organization. Phone interviews are efficient ways to hold screening interviews.

HRM needs to remember to keep the phone screening interview short. Discuss the candidate's relevant experience as submitted on the application form and résumé.

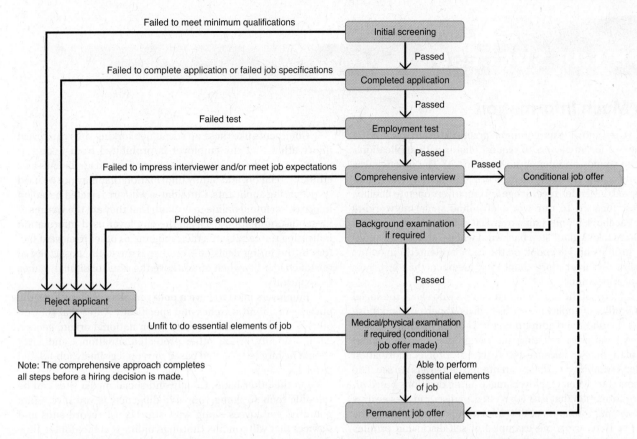

Note: The comprehensive approach completes all steps before a hiring decision is made.

Exhibit 7-1
The Selection Process

From advertising an opening to offering a job, HRM and the applicant may go through many steps. Not all employers use every step, but the comprehensive approach used by many employers is illustrated here.

Listen for energy and enthusiasm in their voice, and remember to project the company culture or employment "brand." The candidate is evaluating you and the organization, too. Be sure to tell them when the next step will occur and what to expect. Do not offer an official job interview during the phone screening interview.

Many organizations are replacing telephone screening interviews with online video screening. Skype or Apple's FaceTime may be utilized for online interviews with candidates, but several vendors offer online interviewing platforms tailored to the employer's specific needs. For example, specialized software allow employers to send prospective employees an e-mail link. When the candidate clicks on the e-mail link, they are recorded on a web cam as they answer a list of questions. The video is a one-way conversation between the candidate and the camera, providing scheduling convenience for the candidate and the HR department.

Another important point during the initial screening phase is to identify a salary range. Most workers are concerned about their salaries, and even if a job opening sounds exciting, a low salary may drive away excellent talent. During this phase, if proper HRM activities have been conducted, you should not need to mask salary data.

Completing the Application Form

After the phone screening interview, applicants may be asked to complete the organization's **application form**. In general terms, the application form includes the applicants' contact information, education, experience, skills, accomplishments, and references. Applications may also obtain other job-related information the company wants and needs in order to make a proper selection. Completing the application also serves as another hurdle. If the application requires following directions and the individual fails to do so, that is a job-related reason for rejection. Finally, applications require a signature attesting to the truthfulness of the information given and giving permission to check references. If, at a later point, the company finds out the information is false, it can justify immediate dismissal.

application form
Company-specific employment form used to generate specific information the company wants.

Key Issues   The Civil Rights Acts of 1964 and 1991 and subsequent amendments, executive orders, court rulings, and other legislation have made it illegal to discriminate on

TIPS FOR SUCCESS

Too Much Information

Many years ago it was common practice to put photos on résumés, or for employers to request photos with applications. The idea sounds antiquated now, doesn't it? The practice was stopped because the appearance of using the photos to discriminate based on gender, race, or age left employers open to liability.

Fast forward to our world of online social networking where Facebook alone claims over 800 million active users. Do employers take a giant step backward when they look up applicants' profiles on Facebook or the career-oriented LinkedIn? Such sites reveal far more about their members than just their physical appearances.

Estimates of the number of employers who check the social media profiles of applicants are as high as 80 percent, and those are just the ones who admit doing it. Looking up candidates is not illegal and privacy settings on user profiles have eliminated much of the liability because users can easily protect information they don't want the world (or parents and employers) to see. The problems start when employers make hiring decisions based on online information that isn't job related, or discriminates against the applicant in violation of EEO laws. Candidates don't help the situation. Here are some examples of self-disclosing profiles on Facebook:

- A candidate discloses that he kicked a drug habit, got out of rehab, and is getting on with his life.
- "My Ritalin level must be down today," writes a young prospective employee.
- Another candidate posts the comment, "The turning point in my life: attending a college course on 'under-represented minorities and the continuing plight of African Americans in the white community.'"
- A job applicant writes, "Nothing is more important to me than the values I have learned from being a Seventh Day Adventist."[6]

Comments like these on social networking sites can reveal information that the employer is prohibited from asking or using in an interview, and photos can reveal an applicant's age, ethnicity, religion, and family information that may not be used in evaluating applicants. Candidates who are rejected based on information found online may claim that they are the victims of illegal discrimination because the employer used information indicating the candidate's race, religion, or other irrelevant factors in the hiring decision. Another issue is the possibility of mistaken identity when others have the same or similar names to applicants.[7]

Employers need to have a policy in place that outlines the purpose of online searches and specifically states that they do not base any decisions on race, color, national origin, gender, faith, disability, or any other protected situation. Candidates should be hired or rejected based only on legitimate job-related criteria.

On the other hand, Google and social media sites can be valuable tools in doing your due diligence as you investigate potential employees along with state court record sites and services that will conduct thorough online searches for employers. If you choose to use social media sites like Facebook and LinkedIn, it's a little safer to use it after a face-to-face interview so the employer cannot be accused of using non-job-related criteria as a way to screen applicants.

Things to think about:
What are your thoughts on the issue? As an employer, would you check an applicant's online profiles before or after an interview? As job candidate, would you consider "cleaning up" your personal online presence during your job hunt?

---

the basis of sex, race, color, religion, national origin, disability, and age. The only major exceptions to these guidelines involving age, sex, and religion are those rare cases where these criteria are bona fide occupational qualifications (BFOQ) as discussed in Chapter 3. Any question listed on a job application form or asked in an interview must be job related. Management has a responsibility to demonstrate that information supplied by applicants is job related, and items that fail that test should be omitted.[8]

In addition to these changes in application forms, one important aspect has been added. Applications typically include a statement giving the employer the right to dismiss an employee for falsifying information. They also typically indicate that employment is at the will of either party (the employer or the employee can end the work relationship) and that the employee understands that employment is not guaranteed. Furthermore, the applicant gives the company permission to obtain previous work history. Of course, an applicant has the right not to sign the application. In that event, however, one's application may be removed from consideration.

weighted application form
A special type of application form that uses relevant applicant information to determine the likelihood of job success.

Weighted Application Forms **Weighted application forms** offer excellent potential in helping recruiters differentiate between potentially successful and unsuccessful job performers.[9] To create such an instrument, individual form items, such as years of schooling, months on last job, salary data for all previous jobs, and military experience, are validated against performance and turnover measures and given appropriate weights. Let's assume, for example, that HRM is interested in developing a weighted application form that would predict which applicants for the job of accountant, if hired, would stay with the company. They would select from their files the application forms from each of two groups of previously hired accountants—a group that had short tenure with the organization (adjusters who stayed, say, less than one year), and a group with long tenure (say, five years or more). These old application forms would be screened item by item to determine how employees in each group responded.

In this way, management would discover items that differentiate the groups and weigh them relative to how well they differentiate applicants. If, for example, 80 percent of the long-tenure group had a college degree, possession of a college degree might have a weight of 4. But if 30 percent of the long-tenure group had prior experience in a major accounting firm, compared to 30 percent of the short-tenured, this item might have a weight of only 1. Note, of course, that this procedure would have to be done for every job in the organization and balanced against the factors of those that do not fall into the majority category. For example, although 80 percent of the long-tenure individuals had a college degree, HRM would need to factor into the weighting scheme those who had a college degree and were successful on the job, but had only short tenure with the company.

Items that predict long tenure for an accountant might be totally different from items that predict long tenure for an engineer or even a financial analyst. As discussed in the chapter opener, Bon-Ton Department Stores discovered that their screening for traits for successful sales people worked well in most departments, but not for the Beauty Advisor position in the cosmetics departments. Additional and specific research may be necessary to determine relevant traits for job success.

Successful Applications Application forms have been very successful as a tool in the selection process for a wide range of jobs. Many companies including Bon-Ton and Target stores provide the opportunity to complete applications online. This allows them to go "green" or "paperless" as they pursue sustainability goals as well as collect relevant information on applicant qualifications. Some employers have found that this expedites application form analysis. In one study, seven items on the application were highly predictive of successful performance as measured by job tenure.[10] Evidence that the application form provides relevant information for predicting job success is well supported across a broad range of jobs. Care must be taken to ensure that application items are validated for each job, and that the privacy and security of personal data is protected. Additionally, since their predictive ability may change over time, the items must be continuously reviewed and updated.

Employers who have switched to online applications have found that in addition to helping eliminate the use of paper, online applications provide significant cost savings and help HRM with compliance issues through the use of electronic forms such as an online I-9 form.[11] A major consideration is the possibility that the application information given is erroneous. A background investigation can verify most data.

Pre-employment Testing

In the chapter opener, we took a look at how pre-employment tests were developed by Bon-Ton Stores to reduce turnover among cosmetic sales consultants. It is estimated that more than 60 percent of all organizations use some type of employment test.[12] Tests like the one administered by Bon-Ton are quite helpful in predicting who will be successful on the job.[13] There are a wide variety of tests available to HR professionals. They can measure intellect, spatial ability, perception skills, mechanical

How can an organization like Lowe's ensure that it has the right person handling the checkout counter? Using work sampling as part of the selection process, the organization can determine which candidate has the requisite skills to perform the job.
(Source: © Ric Feld/AP/ Wide World Photos)

comprehension, motor ability, or personality traits.[14] Employers recognize that the investment in time and cost of these tests, combined with other selection tools and a well-thought-out hiring process, results in better quality hires. We'll cover a few of the most commonly used tests.

Performance Simulation Tests To avoid criticism and potential liability from using psychological, aptitude, and other types of written tests, the interest in **performance simulation tests** has been increasing. The single identifying characteristic of these tests is that they require the applicant to engage in specific behaviors necessary for performing the job successfully. As a result, performance simulation tests should more easily meet the requirement of job relatedness because they evaluate actual job behaviors.

performance simulation tests
Work sampling and assessment centers evaluate abilities in actual job activities.

Work Sampling **Work sampling** creates a miniature replica of a job. Applicants demonstrate that they possess the necessary talents by actually doing the tasks. Carefully devised work samples based on job analysis data determine the knowledge, skills, and abilities needed for each job. Then, each work sample element is matched with a corresponding job performance element. For example, a work sample for a customer service representative at Wells Fargo Bank may involve keyboard computation: the applicant performs computations during a customer transaction. At Lowe's, a potential check-out clerk is screened for a job that requires scanning the prices of a customer's purchases quickly and accurately. Most candidates first go through a similar work- sampling session where supervisors demonstrate how to scan accurately, ensuring that the product did indeed ring up. Then the candidate is given an opportunity to show that he or she can handle the job. Work sampling, then, reflects hands-on experience.

work sampling
A selection device requiring the job applicant to perform a small sampling of actual job activities.

The advantages of work sampling over traditional pencil-and-paper tests should be obvious. Because work samples are essentially identical to job content, work sampling should be a better predictor of short-term performance and should minimize discrimination. Additionally, the nature of their content and the methods used to determine content help ensure that well-constructed work sample tests easily meet EEOC job-related requirements. The main disadvantage is the difficulty in developing appropriate work samples for each job. Furthermore, work sampling is not applicable to all levels of the organization. The difficulty in using this method when screening for managerial jobs lies in creating a work sample test that can address the full range of managerial activities and responsibilities.

Assessment Centers A more elaborate set of performance simulation tests, specifically designed to evaluate a candidate's managerial potential, are administered in **assessment centers**. Assessment centers use procedures that incorporate group and individual exercises. Applicants go through a series of these exercises and are appraised by line executives, practicing supervisors, and/or trained psychologists as to how well they perform. As with work sampling, these exercises are designed to simulate the work of managers and tend to be accurate predictors of later job performance. In some cases, however, the assessment center also includes traditional personality and aptitude tests.[15]

assessment center
A facility where performance simulation tests are administered. These include a series of exercises used for selection, development, and performance appraisals.

Testing in a Global Arena Many of the standard selection techniques described in this text do not easily transfer to international situations. When recruiting and employing host-country nationals, typical American testing works in some countries but not in others. For example, handwriting or graphology tests, sometimes used in the United States, are frequently used in France. In Great Britain, most psychological tests such as graphology, polygraph, and honesty tests are rarely used in employment.[16] Accordingly, whenever American corporations prepare to do business abroad, their practices must adapt to the cultures and regulations of the country in which they will operate.

Comprehensive Interviews

Applicants who pass the initial screening, application form, and required tests typically receive a **comprehensive interview**. The applicant may be interviewed by HRM interviewers, senior managers within the organization, a potential supervisor, colleagues, or some variation. The comprehensive interview is designed to probe areas not easily addressed by the application form or tests, such as assessing a candidate's motivation,

comprehensive interview
A selection device used to obtain in-depth information about a candidate.

DIVERSITY TOPICS

Interview Questions

There are no interview questions that are actually illegal, but the EEOC does look with "extreme disfavor" on questions about age, color, disability, national origin, race, religion, gender, or veteran status. Interviewees are becoming increasingly savvy about their rights, and an employer that is careless about interview questions that may lead to illegal discrimination could find themselves in court. For example, in 2012, Pepsico had to pay $3.1 million to more than 300 black applicants who were adversely affected because of a company policy that would not allow them to hire applicants who had been arrested, yet never convicted. The EEOC has long held that arrest records are not a valid screening tool unless the arrests are relevant to the position because of their adverse impact against some groups. Pepsico agreed to revise their criminal background check process and affirmed their commitment to diversity and inclusion in the workplace as a result of the suit.[17]

Remember that beyond EEO laws, many specific state fair employment laws expressly forbid certain types of questions. The following is a representative list of unacceptable questions that may lead to direct or indirect discrimination because of the "adverse impact" of how the answer may affect protected groups. Acceptable questions are listed if there is an acceptable alternative. This list is NOT all-inclusive.[18]

Topic	Unacceptable	Acceptable
Reliability and Attendance	Number of children? Who is going to baby-sit? Do you observe Yom Kippur/Ramadan/ Christmas? Do you have preschool age children at home? Do you have a car?	What hours and days can you work? Are there specific times that you cannot work? Do you have responsibilities other than work that will interfere with specific job requirements such as traveling?
Citizenship and National Origin	Where are you from originally? Where are your parents from? What is your maiden name?	Are you legally eligible for employment in the United States? Have you ever worked under a different name?
Arrest and Conviction	Have you ever been arrested?	Have you ever been convicted of a crime? If so, when, where, and what was the disposition of the case?
Disabilities	Do you have any job disabilities?	Can you perform the duties of the job you are applying for?
Credit Record	Do you own your own home? Have your wages ever been garnished? Have you ever declared bankruptcy?	Credit references may be used if in compliance with the Fair Credit Reporting Act of 1970 and the Consumer Credit Reporting Reform Act of 1996.
Military Service	What type of discharge did you receive? Are you in the National Guard or Reserves?	What type of education, training, and/or work experience did you receive while in the military?
Language	What is your native language? How did you acquire the ability to read, write, or speak a foreign language?	What languages do you speak and write fluently? (If the job requires additional languages.)
Organizations	Which clubs, societies, and lodges do you belong to?	Are you a member of an organization that is relevant to your ability to perform the job?
Race or Color	Include a recent photograph.	No acceptable alternative.
Worker's Compensation	Have you ever filed for worker's compensation? Have you had any prior work injuries?	No acceptable alternatives.
Religious Faith	Inquiry into applicant's religious denomination, religious affiliations, church, parish, pastor, or religious holidays observed.	No acceptable alternatives unless there is a bona fide occupational qualification.
Gender	Do you wish to be addressed as Mr.?, Mrs.?, Miss?, or Ms.?	No acceptable alternative.
Education	When did you graduate from high school or college?	Do you have a high school diploma or equivalent? Do you have a university or college degree?
Personal	What color are your eyes, hair? What is your height and weight?	No acceptable alternative unless there is a bona fide occupational qualification.

values, ability to work under pressure, attitude, and ability to "fit in" with the organizational culture.[19] Fit cannot be overstated. Ironically, in many cases, employees are hired based on their competencies and how likely they are to be successful performers. The majority of those who fail do so because they cannot fit in with the organization's culture. Accordingly, skills and aptitudes may get candidates in the door, but how well they adapt to the organization frequently determines how long they'll stay.[20] Many organizations are adopting the philosophy of Southwest Airlines and Four Seasons resorts, "Hire for Attitude, Train for Skill." They recognize that getting to know the applicant's personality is crucial. An employee's knowledge can change, but most likely, their personality will not.

It is also believed that the interview offers the greatest value as a selection device in determining an applicant's organizational fit, level of motivation, and interpersonal skills. This is particularly true of senior management positions. Accordingly, candidates for these positions often go through many extensive interviews with executive recruiters, company executives, and even board members before a final decision is made. Similarly, where teams hire their own members, often each team member interviews the applicant.

Interview Effectiveness   The interview has proven an almost universal selection tool—one that can take numerous forms.[21] It can be a one-on-one encounter between the interviewer and the applicant (the traditional interview) or involve several individuals who interview an applicant at once (the panel interview). Interviews can follow a predetermined pattern that identifies both questions and expected responses (a situational

TIPS FOR SUCCESS

Steps for Effective Interviewing

Inexperienced managers can benefit from a little training on how to interview applicants. These steps are a good start:

- **Review the job description and job specification.** Reviewing pertinent information about the job provides valuable information on how you will assess the candidate. Furthermore, knowledge of relevant job requirements helps eliminate interview bias.

- **Prepare a structured set of questions** to ask all applicants. A set of prepared questions ensures that the information the interviewer wishes to elicit is attainable. Furthermore, if you ask them all similar questions, you can better compare candidates' answers against a common base.

- **Review the application form and résumé** before meeting a candidate. Doing so helps you create a complete picture of the candidate in terms of what the résumé or application says and what the job requires. You will also begin to identify areas to explore in the interview. That is, areas not clearly defined on the résumé or application but essential for the job will become a focal point of your discussion with the candidate. It also shows a respect for the candidate if you are prepared. You expect the candidate to be prepared; you should be prepared too.

- **Open the interview** by putting the applicant at ease and providing a brief review of the topics to be discussed. Keep in mind that interviews are stressful for job candidates. By opening with small talk (for example, the weather) you give the candidate time to adjust to the interview setting. Providing a preview of topics gives the candidate an agenda with which to begin framing his or her responses to your questions. First interviews for entry-level positions usually last between thirty and forty minutes. For higher-level positions, they should be longer, around sixty to ninety minutes.

- **Ask your questions and listen carefully** to the applicant's answers. Select follow-up questions that naturally flow from the answers given. Focus on the responses as they relate to information you need to ensure that the candidate meets your job requirements. Any uncertainty you may still have requires a follow-up question to probe further for the information.

- **Take a few notes.** You may be interviewing several candidates, and you'll be surprised how quickly the details of your conversations get confused.

- **Close the interview** by telling the applicant what is going to happen next. Applicants are anxious about the status of your hiring decision. Be honest with the candidate regarding others who will be interviewed and the remaining steps in the hiring process. If you plan to make a decision in two weeks or so, let the candidate know what you intend to do. In addition, tell the applicant how you will let him or her know about your decision.

- **Write your evaluation** of the applicant while the interview is still fresh in your mind. Don't wait until the end of your day, after interviewing several candidates, to write your analysis of a candidate. Memory can fail you. The sooner you complete your write-up after an interview, the better chance you have for accurately recording what occurred in the interview.

REAL HR ENCOUNTERS

Interview Headaches

Roger Jans: HR Professional at Ramapo College in Mahwah, NJ

Finding a great candidate for your vacancy is vital to an organization's success, but it can be extremely difficult to do. On one recent search for a Nurse Practitioner, an applicant came in for an interview. Upon meeting the applicant, I extended my hand and welcomed the interviewee. To my surprise and puzzlement, she placed a little white pill in my hand. I asked the applicant what was in my hand. The response was: "It's an aspirin! All your headaches are now over!" I replied, "Over, or just beginning?"

She then realized a critical mistake had been made: The attempt to be clever had failed.

HR professionals look at the applicant's knowledge, skills, and abilities (KSA's). Candidates who focus and successfully demonstrate their KSA's are the ones hired. What organizations want in this very competitive global market place are people who are passionate about their work, and who are committed to making a real and meaningful contribution to the organization's mission. Leave the props to show business.

---

interview). The interview can also be designed to create a difficult environment in which the applicant is "put to the test" to assess his or her confidence levels. This is frequently referred to as the stress interview (see Ethical Issues in HRM).

Interviewing is often the responsibility of managers with little experience or training in how to interview or what to look for in an interview. Entrepreneurs, managers in retail, or small businesses often find themselves without an HR department to handle the process or give advice. Too often this results in a hiring decision that is a poor fit. There may not be a job description, and inexperienced interviewers may ask off-topic questions or spend more time talking than listening. They may like an applicant so much that they skip reference checks. And an employer may be so eager to fill the position that they hire someone they know isn't completely qualified and hope for the best. Managers and HR professionals need to learn all they can about effective interviewing to increase the odds of a successful hiring decision. Let's take a look at some factors that can help managers interview applicants more effectively.

First Impressions "You never have a second chance to make a first impression" is good advice, and you've probably heard it over and over again. Applicants are trying to make a good impression on the interviewer, and the interviewer is probably trying to impress the applicant as well. A couple of factors will help avoid making any false assumptions about the applicant before qualifications are considered objectively.

Impression Management **Impression management** is directly related to the applicant's actions. It refers to an applicant's attempt to project an image that will result in a favorable outcome.[22] If an applicant can say or do something the interviewer approves of, that person may be viewed more favorably for the position.[23] For example, suppose you find out that the interviewer values workers who are willing to be available via smartphone 24/7/365. Accordingly, you make statements of being a workaholic, which conform to this interviewer's values and may create a positive impression.

Interviewers often have remarkably short and inaccurate memories. In one study of an interview simulation, a twenty-minute videotape of a selection interview was played for a group of forty interviewers. Following this, the interviewers were given a twenty-question test. Although the questions were straightforward and factual, the average number of wrong answers was ten—half of the questions! The researchers concluded that even in a short interview, the average interviewer remembers only half of the information. However, taking notes during an interview has been shown to reduce memory loss. Note-taking—while possibly disconcerting for the interviewee—helps the interviewer retain accurate information and develop a clearer understanding of the applicant's fit by allowing follow-up questions.[24]

impression management
Influencing performance evaluations by portraying an image desired by the appraiser.

ETHICAL ISSUES IN HRM

The Stress Interview

Your interview day has finally arrived. You have researched the company, and are dressed for success, ready to make an excellent first impression. You finally meet Ms. Prince; the HR Hiring Manager. She shakes your hand firmly and invites you to be comfortable. Your interview has started! This is the moment you've waited for.

The first few moments are mundane enough. The questions, in fact, seem easy. Your confidence is growing. That little voice in your head keeps telling you that you are doing fine—just keep going. Suddenly, the questions become tougher. Ms. Prince leans back and asks about why you want to leave your current job—the one you've been in for only eighteen months. As you explain that you wish to leave for personal reasons, she begins to probe more. Her smile is gone. Her body language changes.

All right, you think, be honest. You tell Ms. Prince that you want to leave because you think your boss is unethical and you don't want your reputation tarnished through association with this individual. You've already had several public disagreements with your boss, and you're tired of dealing with the situation. Ms. Prince looks at you and replies, "If you ask me, that's not a valid reason for wanting to leave. It appears to me that you should be more assertive about the situation. Are you sure you're confident enough and have what it takes to make it in this company?"

How dare she talk to you that way! Who does she think she is? You respond with an angry tone in your voice. Guess what, you've just fallen victim to one of the tricks of the interviewing business—the stress interview.

Stress interviews are becoming more common in today's business.[26] Every job produces stress, and every worker has an occasional horrendous day, so stress interviews become predictors of how you may react at work under less-than-favorable conditions. Interviewers want to observe how you'll react under pressure—as well as your values and ethics in stressful conditions.[27] Those who demonstrate the resolve and strength to handle stress indicate a level of professionalism and confidence, the characteristics being assessed. Individuals who react to the stress interview in a more positive manner indicate that they will probably be more able to handle day-to-day irritations at work.

On the other hand, these are staged events. Interviewers deliberately lead applicants into a false sense of security—the comfortable interaction—then they abruptly change the pace or tone of the interview. They verbally attack and it's usually a personal affront that focuses on a weakness they've uncovered about the applicant. It's possibly humiliating; at the very least it's demeaning.

Ethical Questions:

Should companies use stress interviews? Should interviewers be permitted to assess professionalism, confidence, and how one reacts to the everyday nuisances of work by putting applicants into a confrontational scenario? Does becoming angry in an interview indicate a propensity toward outbursts or violence under work stress? Should HRM advocate the use of an activity that could possibly slip out of control?

---

interviewer bias
Image created by reviewing materials such as the résumé, application, or test scores prior to the actual interview.

Interviewer Bias Seeing the candidate's résumé, application form, test scores, or appraisals from other interviewers may introduce **interviewer bias**.[25] In such cases, the interviewer no longer relies on data gained in the interview alone. Data received prior to the interview creates an image of the applicant. Much of the early part of the interview, then, becomes an exercise wherein the interviewer compares the actual applicant with the image formed earlier.

behavioral interview
Observing job candidates not only for what they say but for how they behave.

The Behavioral Interview A modification to interviews that is becoming popular in contemporary organizations is the **behavioral interview** or situation interview.[28] In this type of interview, candidates are observed not only for what they say but also for how they fit the competencies of the position or organizational culture.

Organizations have found that past performance in similar environments and situations is a much better indicator of future success than any other factor. If the position is analyzed and its competencies identified, by questioning the candidate as to how he or she has dealt with these situations the organization can see whether the candidate has the necessary qualities and behaviors to succeed in their organizational environment. Candidates are presented with open-ended questions or situations that may include complex problems. These questions may sometimes involve role playing, including a discussion of how they have dealt with a situation in the past, using relevant examples, or how they would go about dealing with the role-play situation. This type of interview can also provide an opportunity for interviewers to evaluate communication skills, problem-solving skills, and sense of humor. Proponents of behavioral interviewing indicate such a process is much more indicative of a candidate's performance than simply having the candidate tell the

TIPS FOR SUCCESS

Professionalism on the Phone

HR Professionals spend a bit of time on the phone, so it's a good idea to learn the basics of phone etiquette at the beginning of your career. A few simple tips will help you make a more professional impression whether you are calling an applicant or if you're the one receiving the long awaited call about your own interview or promotion:

- **Reduce the distractions**. Focus on the conversation. Ignore your computer screen, e-mail notifications, and any other phones such as a personal cell phone. The listener can tell that you're not fully engaged in the conversation.

- **Speak clearly**. Make yourself easy to understand. Sit up straight so you can breathe adequately. Practice an appropriate volume and pace so you aren't shouting or talking too fast for the speaker to listen well. If you're conducting a screening interview, the applicant may be too intimidated to ask you to repeat yourself and you won't get an accurate or appropriate answer to your question. Avoid saying things like "yup" and "uh huh." Standard English makes a better impression.

- **Introduce yourself**. Begin by saying your name and the name of your company before asking, "May I speak to . . ." Be ready to give a short explanation of the reason for your call. If you get a receptionist or voicemail, give your name, reason for the call, and a number where you can be reached. Be sure to repeat the number. Accuracy is important.

- **Answer the phone**. "Hello" is a start, but in a business environment, you need to go on to identify your employer or place of business and then say your name. A good example would be "Human Resources, this is Benjamin Wu speaking. How may I help you?"

- **Set up your own voicemail**. Whether at work, home, or your personal cell phone, your voicemail message needs to be clear and professional. At work, the best option is to tell the caller your name, the date, whether you're in the office that day, and when the caller can expect you to return the call. On your personal phone, remember that the caller may be a prospective employer, so resist the temptation to leave a cute or funny message.

- **Make sure you understand**. Don't be afraid to ask the person on the phone to repeat something if you're not sure you understand. Cell phones and speaker phones sometimes have a momentary gap after someone speaks that result in two people talking at the same time. Just saying "I'm sorry, would you please repeat that?" is a lot better than wondering if you got the information you need correctly.

- **Hold on**. If you must put someone on hold, be sure to ask permission to do it and wait for the answer. It's possible that they would rather call back another time. Make sure you know how to use the hold feature on your phone.

- **Call back**. If you've said you'll call back at a certain time, do it. If that becomes impossible for some reason, call them as soon as possible.

Things to think about:
Have you encountered other issues that made phone contact ineffective or left a bad impression? What other suggestions would you add?

interviewer what he or she has done. In fact, research in this area indicates that behavioral interviews are nearly eight times more effective for predicting successful job performance.[29]

One final issue revolves around when the interviewer actually makes the decision. Early studies indicated that interviewers made their choice to hire or not hire a candidate within the first few minutes of the interview. Although that belief was widely held, subsequent research does not support it.[30] In fact, initial impressions may have little effect, unless that is the only information available for an interviewer to use.

Realistic Job Previews

Most of us have approached a new job brimming with enthusiasm based on the glowing description of endless possibilities, only to leave, dejected and discouraged when the job turned out to be completely different from our expectations. Occasionally, recruiters or advertisements paint a rosy picture of a job that doesn't live up to the hype. For example, an organization where salespeople make large numbers of "cold" or unsolicited sales calls might emphasize the excellent benefits and high earning potential for "self starters," but fail to mention that on average only one out of one hundred calls leads to a sale. Such bait and switch recruitment creates large numbers of job applicants and new hires. It also increases replacement costs due to the large turnover when disillusioned employees quit after training, and makes recruiting more difficult when former employees spread the news.

The primary purpose of any selection device is to identify individuals who will be effective performers. But it is also in an interviewer's best interest to hire qualified candidates and retain them after incurring the expense of hiring and training. Therefore, part of selection should be concerned with reducing voluntary turnover and its associated costs. One device to achieve that goal is the **realistic job preview (RJP)**.[31] Realistic job previews address the theory that unmet expectations of new employees can cause them to be dissatisfied in the job and quit. RJP may include brochures, online videos, plant tours, work sampling, or a short script that includes realistic statements that accurately describe the job. The key element in RJP is that unfavorable as well as favorable information about the job is shared before the applicant makes a decision.[32] RJP has been used by call centers, police recruiters, nursing homes, and organizations that work with the handicapped. For example, applicants may have an idealized image of police work from watching crime dramas on television or movies. Law enforcement professionals use realistic job previews to show applicants that law enforcement can be quite challenging emotionally and physically, and that crimes are not solved as quickly as they are on TV! Although the RJP is not normally treated as a selection device, it should take place during the interview.

Applicants who receive a realistic job preview (as well as a realistic preview of the organization) hold lower and more realistic expectations about the job they will be doing and are better prepared for coping with the position and its potentially frustrating elements.[33] Most studies demonstrate that giving candidates a realistic job preview before offering them the job reduces turnover without lowering acceptance rates. Of course, exposing an applicant to RJP may also result in the hiring of a more committed individual.

realistic job preview (RJP)
A selection device that allows job candidates to learn negative as well as positive information about the job and organization.

Conditional Job Offers

If a job applicant has passed each step of the selection process so far, a **conditional job offer** is usually made. Conditional job offers typically come from an HRM representative. In essence, the conditional job offer implies that if everything checks out—such as passing a certain medical, physical, or substance abuse test—the conditional nature of the job offer will be removed and the applicant will be offered the job.

conditional job offer
A tentative job offer that becomes permanent after certain conditions are met.

background investigation
The process of verifying information job candidates provide.

Background Investigation

The next step in the process is to conduct a **background investigation** of applicants who are potential employees. Background investigations, or reference checks, are intended to verify that information on the application form is correct and accurate. Sometimes just notifying applicants that the firm will check all references and former employers is enough to keep them from falsifying any information. HRM must always remember to ask the candidate to sign a waiver giving the organization permission to check court records, references, former employers, and education.[34] Common sources of background information include:

- *References* are provided by the applicant and are usually very positive. Even applicants with very poor work records can find someone to agree to be a reference; often it may be a friend or relative. When speaking with references, be sure to ask what their relationship to the applicant is. HRM should also ask for specific instances where the reference has had the opportunity to observe the applicant in a work environment or demonstrating work skills.
- *Former employers* should be called to confirm the candidate's work record and to obtain their performance appraisal. Frequently, you will encounter employers who will be hesitant to provide detailed information and will only provide the dates of employment. This is usually due to a company policy in place to prevent defamation lawsuits from former employees or the mistaken belief that

Exhibit 7-2
Background Investigation

A simple online search can turn up some interesting information about a job candidate.
(*Source:* © Ted Goff)

"I looked you up on the web. Those photos of you dancing on your desk in a clown suit sure were funny."

providing more information is illegal. Many states have passed laws protecting employers from civil liability when providing employment verification. Sometimes HRM can coax more information from former employers by asking them to rate the employee on a "scale of one to ten." If all else fails, HRM should ask them if they would rehire the worker. If they say no, it should serve as a red flag.

- *Educational accomplishments* can be verified by asking for transcripts.
- *Legal status to work in the United States* via the Employment Eligibility Verification, I-9 Form; see Exhibit 7-3. Employers need to check current guidelines on the acceptability of documents that support an employee's verification of eligibility to work legally. As of May 2011, employers may accept only unexpired documents. E-Verify is an online system used by nearly 300,000 employers in the U.S. that checks information provided on the I-9 form to data from the Department of Homeland Security and Social Security Administration. Employers in a few states and some with federal contracts are required to use E-Verify, but for most employers it's voluntary.[35]
- *Credit references,* if job related, subject to legal requirements in Chapter 4.
- *Criminal records* can be checked by third-party investigators. Most states also have easy to use websites where you can search public records of criminal records.
- *Background checks* are conducted by third-party investigators.[36]
- *Online searches* as simple as a "Google" search of a candidate can turn up information on press releases or news items about a candidate that was left off the application or résumé. Social networking sites such as Facebook, Twitter, YouTube, and LinkedIn also provide professional as well as personal information. They also may provide more information than the employer wants, such as references to age, religious affiliation, race, or disability. Employers need to be careful only to consider job-related information. See "Tips for Success: Too Much Information."

Why do this? Documentation supports the premise that a good predictor of an individual's future behavior is his or her past behavior, as well the fact that many—in some studies nearly half—of all applicants exaggerate their backgrounds or experiences.[37] Organizations also need to be aware of negligent hiring liability, which occurs when an employer or employment agency has failed to properly investigate an employee's background and that employee is later involved in wrongful conduct.[38]

Failure to investigate applicants can be costly at best, in the worst case it can be tragic as these examples illustrate:

- A small advertising agency in Chicago, Illinois, hired a temporary bookkeeper through Robert Half International, a large employment agency. By the end of her first year, the bookkeeper had embezzled $70,000 by forging checks on the agency's account. A complete background check would have uncovered the fact that prior to being placed at the advertising agency, she had pled guilty to stealing $192,873 from another employer and was currently serving four years' probation.[39]
- Within two weeks of being hired, a security guard at a Rite Aid Pharmacy in California sexually assaulted a 13-year-old girl. He continued to work after receiving a suspension while the complaint was investigated. During this "working suspension," he accused a 14-year-old girl of shoplifting. He handcuffed and locked her in an interview room and sexually assaulted her. The employer did not complete a thorough background check, which would have disclosed that the guard had previously been convicted of sexual assault. Rite Aid settled a lawsuit with the young victims for over $2 million.[40]
- A truck driver for a hazardous waste company caused an accident that killed a man in Texas. A jury found that the employer failed to adequately check his background for drug use and his driving record and awarded the victim's estate $20.7 million.[41]

Negligent hiring assumes that a proper background check would have uncovered information about the candidate, resulting in the candidate not being hired. For instance, any individual who works with children—in a school or day care, for instance—must not have been accused or convicted of abusing children. An organization that fails to check if

Exhibit 7-3
Employment Eligibility Verification

All employees are required to complete an I-9 form and provide documents like a driver's license, passport, or Social Security card to prove they are eligible to work legally. For a list of acceptable documents, go to the website of the Department of Homeland Security, U.S. Citizenship and Immigration Service.

(*Source*: Department of Homeland Security, U.S. Citizenship and Immigration Services, http://www.uscis.gov/files/form/i-9.pdf.)

OMB No. 1615-0047; Expires 08/31/12

Department of Homeland Security
U.S. Citizenship and Immigration Services

Form I-9, Employment Eligibility Verification

Read instructions carefully before completing this form. The instructions must be available during completion of this form.

ANTI-DISCRIMINATION NOTICE: It is illegal to discriminate against work-authorized individuals. Employers CANNOT specify which document(s) they will accept from an employee. The refusal to hire an individual because the documents have a future expiration date may also constitute illegal discrimination.

Section 1. Employee Information and Verification *(To be completed and signed by employee at the time employment begins.)*

Print Name: Last | First | Middle Initial | Maiden Name

Address *(Street Name and Number)* | Apt. # | Date of Birth *(month/day/year)*

City | State | Zip Code | Social Security #

I am aware that federal law provides for imprisonment and/or fines for false statements or use of false documents in connection with the completion of this form.

I attest, under penalty of perjury, that I am (check one of the following):
- [ ] A citizen of the United States
- [ ] A noncitizen national of the United States (see instructions)
- [ ] A lawful permanent resident (Alien #) _____
- [ ] An alien authorized to work (Alien # or Admission #) _____
  until (expiration date, if applicable - *month/day/year*) _____

Employee's Signature | Date *(month/day/year)*

Preparer and/or Translator Certification *(To be completed and signed if Section 1 is prepared by a person other than the employee.)* I attest, under penalty of perjury, that I have assisted in the completion of this form and that to the best of my knowledge the information is true and correct.

Preparer's/Translator's Signature | Print Name

Address *(Street Name and Number, City, State, Zip Code)* | Date *(month/day/year)*

Section 2. Employer Review and Verification *(To be completed and signed by employer. Examine one document from List A OR examine one document from List B and one from List C, as listed on the reverse of this form, and record the title, number, and expiration date, if any, of the document(s).)*

List A	OR	List B	AND	List C
Document title:				
Issuing authority:				
Document #:				
Expiration Date *(if any)*:				
Document #:				
Expiration Date *(if any)*:				

CERTIFICATION: I attest, under penalty of perjury, that I have examined the document(s) presented by the above-named employee, that the above-listed document(s) appear to be genuine and to relate to the employee named, that the employee began employment on *(month/day/year)* _____ and that to the best of my knowledge the employee is authorized to work in the United States. (State employment agencies may omit the date the employee began employment.)

Signature of Employer or Authorized Representative | Print Name | Title

Business or Organization Name and Address *(Street Name and Number, City, State, Zip Code)* | Date *(month/day/year)*

Section 3. Updating and Reverification *(To be completed and signed by employer.)*

A. New Name *(if applicable)* | B. Date of Rehire *(month/day/year)* *(if applicable)*

C. If employee's previous grant of work authorization has expired, provide the information below for the document that establishes current employment authorization.

Document Title: _____ | Document #: _____ | Expiration Date *(if any)*: _____

I attest, under penalty of perjury, that to the best of my knowledge, this employee is authorized to work in the United States, and if the employee presented document(s), the document(s) I have examined appear to be genuine and to relate to the individual.

Signature of Employer or Authorized Representative | Date *(month/day/year)*

Form I-9 (Rev. 08/07/09) Y Page 4

a candidate has a record and hires the individual opens itself up to a negligent-hiring lawsuit. If the employee is ever involved in some wrongful conduct involving children, the organization can be held liable for its failure to properly hire.

Common sense dictates that HRM find out as much as possible about its applicants before the final hiring decision is made. Failure to do so can have a detrimental effect on the organization, both in financial cost and morale. Obtaining the needed information may be difficult, especially when there may be a question about invading privacy, but it's worth the effort.

Based on a concept of **qualified privilege**, some courts have ruled that employers must be able to talk to one another about employees. Additionally, about half of the states have laws that protect employers from "good-faith references." Accordingly, these discussions may be legal and may not invade one's right to privacy so long as the discussion is a legitimate concern for the business—and in some cases if the applicant has authorized the background investigation. For example, had a Midwest hospital learned that one of its anesthesiologist applicants lost his license in three states for substance abuse, it clearly would not have hired him. The information given, however, cannot be discriminatory, retaliate against a former employee, or "disclose confidential facts that constitute an invasion of privacy."[42]

qualified privilege
The ability for organizations to speak candidly to one another about employees or potential hires.

Medical/Physical Examination

The next-to-last step in the selection process may consist of having the applicant take a **medical/physical examination**. Physical exams can only be used as a selection device to screen out individuals who are unable to physically comply with the requirements of a job. For example, firefighters must perform activities that require a certain physical condition. Whether it is climbing a ladder, lugging a water-filled four-inch hose, or carrying an injured victim, these individuals must demonstrate that they are fit for the job. Jobs that require certain physical characteristics may entail a job-related physical examination. However, this includes only a small proportion of jobs today.

medical/physical examination
An examination to determine an applicant's physical fitness for essential job performance.

A company must show that any required medical clearance is job-related. Failure to do so may result in the physical examination creating an adverse impact, as explained in Chapter 3. The company must also keep the Americans with Disabilities Act in mind. Thus, even a valid physical examination may be required only after a conditional job offer. Having a physical disability may not be relevant to the hiring process for the position. As we mentioned in Chapter 3, companies may be required to make reasonable accommodations for disabled individuals. If an applicant is not selected for a position due to a disability, the employer must be able to show that the disability prevented the applicant from performing the job even if reasonable accommodations were made.

The selection process can be likened to a hurdle race. Similar to a runner, those who fail to clear a hurdle are out of the race. In selection, the hurdles may involve tests, interviews, reference checks, and background investigations.
(Source: Uli Deck/EPA/NewsCom)

Aside from its use as a screening tool, the physical exam may also show that an individual does not meet the minimum standards of health required to enroll in company health and life insurance programs. Additionally, a company may use this exam to provide base data in case of an employee's future claim of injury on the job. This occurs, however, after one has been hired. In both cases, the exam is paid for by the employer.

One last event fits appropriately under medical examination: the drug test. As we discussed in Chapter 4, many companies require applicants to submit to a drug test. Where in the hiring process that test occurs is somewhat immaterial; the fact remains that failing an employment drug test may be grounds for rejecting an applicant.

Job Offers

Individuals who perform successfully in the preceding steps are now considered eligible to receive the employment offer. Who makes the final employment offer depends on several factors. For administrative purposes (processing

Should firefighter candidates be expected to climb stairs, carry equipment, break through doors with sledgehammers, and carry 165 pound rescue dummies while wearing up to 75 extra pounds of weight? The answer is definitely, yes. The physical demands of the job require firefighters to perform numerous activities, often while under stress.
(Source: David McNew/Getty Images, Inc.)

comprehensive selection
Applying all steps in the selection process before rendering a decision about a job candidate.

salary forms, maintaining EEO statistics, ensuring a statement exists that asserts that employment is not guaranteed, etc.), the offer typically is made by an HRM representative. But that individual's role should be only administrative. The actual hiring decision should be made by the manager in the department where the vacancy exists. This is recommended for two reasons. First, the applicant will be working for this manager, which necessitates a good fit between boss and employee. Second, if the decision is faulty, the hiring manager has no one else to blame. Remember—as we mentioned in Chapter 6—finalists not hired deserve the courtesy of prompt notification.

The Comprehensive Approach

We have presented the general selection process as being comprised of multiple hurdles, beginning with a screening interview and culminating with a final selection decision. This discrete selection process is designed so that tripping over any hurdle puts one out of the race. This approach, however, may not be the most effective selection procedure for every job. If, for example, the application form shows that the candidate has only two years of relevant experience, but the job specification requires five, the candidate is rejected. Yet in many jobs, positive factors can counterbalance negative factors. Poor performance on a written test, for example, may be offset by several years of relevant job experience. This suggests that sometimes it may be advantageous to do comprehensive rather than discrete selection.

In **comprehensive selection**, all applicants complete every step of the selection process, and the final decision is based on a comprehensive evaluation of the results from all stages. The comprehensive approach overcomes the major disadvantage of the discrete method (eliminating potentially good employees simply because they receive an acceptable but low evaluation at one selection step). The comprehensive method is more realistic. It recognizes that most applicants have weaknesses as well as strengths. But it is also more costly because all applicants must go through all the screening hurdles. Additionally, the method consumes more of management's time and can demoralize many applicants by building up hope. Yet in those instances where job success relies on many qualities, and where finding candidates who are strong on all qualities is unlikely, the comprehensive approach is probably preferable to the typical discrete method.

No matter which approach you use or which steps you take, one critical aspect must be present: the devices used must measure job-related factors. That is, these devices must indicate how one would perform on the job. That's critical for business success, and it's necessary to defend and respond if there is an allegation that the hiring practices are discriminatory (see Tips for Success: Avoiding Hiring Mistakes).

Now It's Up to the Candidate

If the organization's selection process has been effective in differentiating between those individuals who will make successful employees and those who will not, the selection decision is now in the hands of the applicant. What can management do at this stage to increase the probability that the individual will accept an offer? Assuming that the organization has not lost sight of the process of selection's dual objective—evaluation and a good fit—we can expect that the potential employee has a solid understanding of the job being offered and what it would be like to work for the organization. Yet it might be of interest at this point to review what we know about how people choose jobs. This subject—job choice—represents selection from the perspective of the potential employee rather than the organization.

Research indicates that people gravitate toward jobs compatible with their personal orientation. Individuals appear to move toward matching their work and employer with their personality. Social individuals lean toward jobs in clinical psychology, foreign service, social work, and the like. Investigative individuals are compatible with jobs in biology, mathematics, and oceanography. Careers in management, law, and

TIPS FOR SUCCESS

Avoiding Hiring Mistakes

As an owner or manager, it may seem like your rights to hire, interview, retain, and terminate employees are diminishing. Learning too little too late is a continuing frustration and challenge as managers and entrepreneurs seek to work within legal limitations to obtain information about possible candidates. For example, a manager recently hired a seemingly outstanding applicant only to have the newly hired department head resign one week later after realizing his inability to fulfill the job's expectations. On closer investigation, it seemed the candidate had projected the right experience and credentials on paper—not falsifying, but embellishing in the name of a competitive job market.

In fact, the résumé and cover letter were the best the manager had seen, thanks to the candidate's outside professional assistance. Résumé writers may help project images on paper to secure employment, but it takes more than illusions to keep a job. Implying or exaggerating accomplishments is not only poor judgment; it's bad business.

As managers and entrepreneurs, we make hiring mistakes. We may not detect some situations, such as an exaggerated résumé, but we can prevent others by knowing our rights as employers—not only what we cannot do but what we can do. Here are some suggestions:

- Prior to interviewing applicants, update and prepare a list of job requirements, duties, and responsibilities so that you and the applicant will understand the expectations of the position. After all, the longer a position is open and the more desperate you are to fill it, the more likely you are to make the position fit the candidate—any candidate.
- Don't panic. Hire a temporary employee, contract or subcontract out some of the work, or ask others to assist during the transition rather than hiring the wrong person.
- Ask appropriate questions: What are your long- and short-range goals? Why are you interested in this position? What do you consider your greatest strengths and weaknesses? Why should I hire you? In what specific ways do you think you can make a contribution to the company? Do you have plans for continuing education?

- Before you extend an offer, check references, including several supervisors or managers—even if the candidate had an exemplary interview and a seemingly perfectly matched background. Because many companies allow only human resources to provide information about former employees, you may gain little information, but checking references is worthwhile. The answer to the question, "Would you rehire this individual?" may not provide all you need to know, but it's a start. Remember to also check education references.
- Obtain applicants' permission to check references with a signed release form saying that they agree to your calling their references to ask about their background and work performance. Ask for former supervisors or managers, and if the applicant cannot provide them as references, ask why not.
- Don't depend on letters that provide only partial information. Call and talk with someone, ask open-ended questions, and listen for content as well as hesitation and inflections. If you do not feel adept, ask your personnel or human resources manager to check references or hire a consultant or reference-checking service.
- Sample questions when checking references may include one or more of the following: Why didn't you persuade him or her to stay? How well did he or she take criticism or suggestions given in his or her last performance appraisal process? Go over the part of the résumé that relates to the reference and ask for comments.
- Avoid questions that indirectly or directly identify age; physical characteristics, such as height, weight, hair or eye color; religious affiliation; marital and family status; medical history; work absenteeism due to illness or physical limitations; or child- or adult-care obligations.

Things to think about:

This process takes time, effort, and patience, which may all be in short supply when you're short-staffed. In an emergency, you may be tempted to trust your instincts and hire someone quickly without going through all of the steps. What might be some possible consequences of shortening the process?

---

public relations appeal to enterprising individuals. This approach to matching people and jobs suggests that management can expect a greater proportion of acceptances if it has properly matched the candidate's personality to the job and to the organization.

Not surprisingly, most job choice studies indicate that an individual's perception of the company's attractiveness is important.[43] People want to work where their expectations are positive and where they believe their goals can be achieved. This, coupled with conclusions from previous research, should encourage management to ensure that those to whom they make offers can see the job's compatibility with their personality and goals. Candidates will be determining if the recruiting and interview process were consistent with the culture that was promoted as the "employment brand." If the candidate sees that the culture or "brand" is still a good fit with his or her image, the chances of a successful hire increase.

Before we leave this last step in the selection process, what about those applicants to whom we did not make an offer? Those involved in the selection process should carefully consider how they treat rejected candidates. What HR communicates and how HR communicates will have a central bearing on the image rejected candidates have of our organization. And that image may be carried for a lifetime. The young college graduate rejected for a position by a major computer manufacturer may, a decade later, be the influential decision maker for his or her current employer's computer purchases. The image formed many years earlier may play a key part in the decision.

Selection for Self-Managed Teams

Much of the discussion about selection devices thus far has assumed that HRM has full responsibility for the selection process. Today, however, that may not always be the case. Companies such as Perdue Farms, General Mills, Corning, Motherwear, Toyota, and Federal Express are more team oriented, and they empower their employees to take responsibility for the day-to-day functions in their areas. Accordingly, these employees may now work without direct supervision and take on the administrative responsibilities once performed by their supervisor. One aspect of this change has been a more active role in hiring their coworkers.[44]

CONTEMPORARY CONNECTION

What Were They Thinking?

Reality, in many cases, is stranger than fiction. And when it comes to employment selection, some things are just remarkable. Anyone who's ever worked in the screening process—especially when interviewing job candidates—has some fascinating stories to tell. Consider the following questions posed or comments made by interviewees during actual interviews.[47]

- Do you know of any companies where I could get a job I would like better than this one?
- I'm quitting my present job because I hate to work hard.
- I don't think I'm capable of doing this job, but I sure would like the money.
- My résumé might look like I'm a job hopper. But I want you to know that I never left any of these jobs voluntarily.
- I don't believe that anyone in my former organizations was as gifted as I was.
- Did you know my uncle is president of a competing organization?
- What job am I applying for anyway?
- I'm leaving my present job because my manager is a jerk; all managers are jerks.
- After being complimented on the his choice of college and GPA, the candidate remarked that he didn't actually attend that college—he just said so to get the company's attention.
- One candidate arrived at the airport for the start of his interview. As he got off the plane, he said it was too cold to

live and work in that city, and immediately left to find a return flight.

(Source: Masterfile)

Consider a time when you took a course that required a group project. How was your team formed? Did the professor assign you to a group, or were you permitted to form the group yourself? If you selected your own group, what did you look for in a potential group member? Other students who shared your values in finishing work on time and of high quality? Those whom you knew would pull their own weight and not let one or two in the group do all of the work? Well, that's the same premise behind self-managed work-team selection. In any organization, a critical link to success is how well employees perform their jobs. It is also understood that when those jobs require the interaction of several individuals or a team, coming together as a cohesive unit takes time. The length of that time, however, is a function of how the team views its goals and priorities and how open and trusting group members are. A good way to begin this team-building is to have the "personalities" involved actually making the hiring decision.[45]

Workers empowered to hire their coworkers bring to the selection process varied experiences and backgrounds. This better enables them to assess applicants' skills in their field of expertise.[46] They want to hire people they can count on to perform their duties and not let the others down. This means that they focus their attention on the job duties required and on the special skills and qualifications necessary for success. Although a more objective evaluation may result, that's not to say that there are no problems when self-managed work teams make hiring decisions. If these workers are unfamiliar with proper interviewing techniques or the legal ramifications of their hiring decisions, they too could experience many of the difficulties often associated with interviews.

It would be great if it was always this obvious that an applicant isn't going to work out, but unfortunately HR practitioners usually do not have clear-cut situations that allow them to make quick, decisive decisions about a candidate. Making selection determinations is often difficult. Yet all selection activities exist for the purpose of making effective selection decisions—seeking to predict which job applicants will be successful job performers if hired.

Key Elements for Successful Predictors

HR is concerned with selection activities that can help predict which applicants will perform satisfactorily on the job. In this section we explore the concepts of reliability, validity, and cut scores. For illustration purposes, we will emphasize these elements as they relate to employment tests, but they are relevant to any selection device. Tests must comply with the Uniform Guidelines on Employee Selection Procedures as discussed in Chapter 3. This means that any of the selection criteria needs to predict job performance. Employers need to be able to show that criteria are not discriminatory, including requirements that have an adverse impact on a protected group. The Office of Federal Contract Compliance has responsibility for monitoring compliance with these guidelines and in the last decade, the fines levied against employers whose testing was found to provide adverse impact have more than doubled. HRM can't be too careful when creating and validating selection criteria.

Reliability

Have you ever checked your height or weight and received results that just didn't seem right? The first thing you probably thought was that the scale must be off. You might have been at someone else's home or at a different fitness center and that is why the scale or height measurement is not the same. You probably decided to use the scale you always use for a more accurate comparison, because there's no way you could have gained that much weight or shrunk a whole inch!

Just like your bathroom scale, for any measure or predictor to be useful, the scores it generates must possess an acceptable level of **reliability** or consistency of measurement.

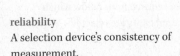

reliability
A selection device's consistency of measurement.

This means that the applicant's performance on any given selection device should produce consistent scores each time the device is used.[48]

Similarly, if an organization uses tests to provide input to the selection decision, the tests must give consistent results. If the test is reliable, any single individual's scores should remain fairly stable over time, assuming that the characteristic it is measuring remains stable. An individual's intelligence, for example, is generally a stable characteristic, and if we give applicants an IQ test, we should expect that someone who scores 110 in March would score close to 110 if tested again in July. If, in July, the same applicant scored 85, the reliability of the test would be highly questionable. However, if we were measuring an attitude or a mood, we would expect different scores on the measure, because attitudes and moods change.

Validity

validity
The proven relationship of a selection device to relevant criterion.

High reliability may mean little if the selection device has low **validity**, that is, if the measures obtained do not relate to a relevant criterion such as job performance. For example, just because a test score is consistent is no indication that it is measuring important characteristics related to job behavior. This is what Bon-Ton stores encountered when their criteria for successful sales associates didn't work as a good indicator for their Beauty Advisors. The selection device must also differentiate between satisfactory and unsatisfactory performance on the job. We should be aware of three specific types of validity: content, construct, and criterion related.

content validity
The degree to which test content, as a sample, represents all situations that could have been included, such as a typing test for a clerk typist.

Content Validity **Content validity** is the degree to which test content or questions about job tasks, as a sample, represent situations on the job. All candidates for that job receive the same test or questions so applicants can be properly compared. A simple example of a content-valid test is a typing test for a word processing position. Such a test can approximate the work; the applicant can be given a typical sample of typing, on which his or her performance can be evaluated. Assuming that the tasks on the test, or the questions about tasks, constitute an accurate sample of the tasks on the job (ordinarily a dubious assumption at best), the test is content valid.[49]

construct validity
The degree to which a particular trait relates to successful job performance, as in IQ tests.

Construct Validity **Construct validity** is the degree to which a test measures a particular trait related to successful performance on the job.[50] These traits are usually abstract in nature, such as the measure of intelligence, and are called constructs. Construct validity is complex and difficult. In fact, it is the most difficult type of validity to prove because you are dealing with abstract measures.

criterion-related validity
The degree to which a particular selection device accurately predicts the important elements of work behavior, as in the relationship between a test score and job performance.

Criterion-Related Validity **Criterion-related validity** is the degree to which a particular selection device accurately predicts the level of performance or important elements of work behavior. This validation strategy shows the relationship between some predictor (test score, for example) and a criterion (say, production output or managerial effectiveness). To establish criterion-related validity, either of two approaches can be used: predictive validity or concurrent validity.

predictive validity
Validating tests by using prospective applicants as the study group.

To give a test **predictive validity**, an organization would administer the test (with an unknown validity) to all prospective applicants. The test scores would not be used at this time; rather, applicants would be hired as a result of successfully completing the entire selection process. At some prescribed date, usually at least a year after being hired, the applicants' job performance would be evaluated by their supervisors. The evaluation ratings would then be compared with the initial test scores, which have been stored in a file over the period. At that time, an analysis would assess any relationship between test scores (the predictors) and performance evaluation (the measure of success on the job, or the criterion). If no clear relationship exists, the test may have to be revised. However, if the organization found statistically that employees who scored below some predetermined score, called a **cut score** (determined in the analysis), were unsuccessful performers, management could appropriately state that any future applicants scoring below the cut score would be ineligible for employment. Unsuccessful performers would be handled like any other employee who has experienced poor evaluations: training, transfer, discipline, or discharge.

cut score
A scoring point below which applicants are rejected.

The **concurrent validity** method validates tests using current employees as subjects. These employees take a proposed selection test experimentally. Their scores are immediately analyzed, revealing a relationship between their test scores and existing performance appraisal data. Again, if a relationship appears between test scores and performance, a valid test has been found.

Predictive validity is the preferred choice. Its advantage over concurrent validity is that it is demonstrated by using actual job applicants, whereas concurrent validity focuses on current employees. These validation strategies are similar, with the exception of whom they test and the time that elapses between gathering of predictor and criterion information (see Exhibit 7-4). Although the costs associated with each method are drastically different, predictive validation strategies should be used if possible. Concurrent validity, although better than no validity at all, leaves many questions to be answered.[51] Its usefulness has been challenged on the premise that current employees know the jobs already because a learning process has taken place. Thus, similarity may be lessened between the current employee and the applicant.

concurrent validity
Validating tests by using current employees as the study group.

Validity Analysis

Correlation coefficients used to demonstrate the statistical relationships existing between an individual's test score and his or her job performance are called validity coefficients. The correlation analysis procedure can result in a coefficient ranging from –1 to +1 in magnitude. The closer the validity coefficient is to the extreme (1), the more accurate the test;[52] that is, the test is a good predictor of job performance. For instance, individuals who score higher on the test have a greater probability of succeeding at their jobs than those who score lower. Based on this relationship, this test appears to be valid. When we have a valid test as determined by our correlation analysis, we may then identify the test score that distinguishes between successful and unsuccessful performers (the cut score).

Exhibit 7-4
Predictive vs. Concurrent Validation

HRM professionals might use testing to determine which applicants will perform the job well. Concurrent and predictive validity are two ways to determine if the tests used are good predictors of job performance.

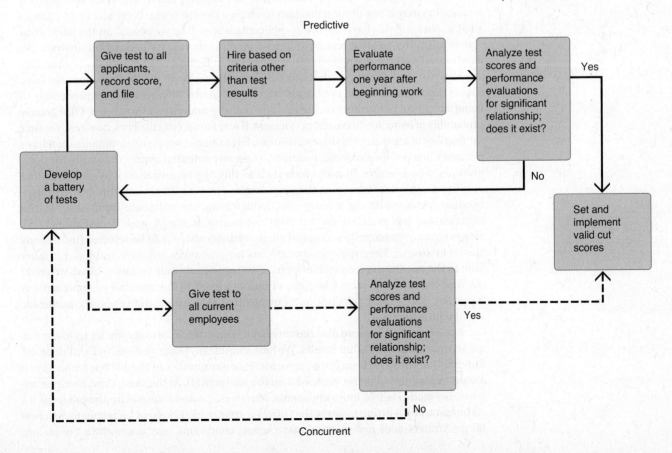

Exhibit 7-5
Validity Correlation Analysis
After Cut Score Is Raised

Here is a situation where
economic problems raise
unemployment and create a
surplus of applicants when job
openings occur. This "buyer's
market" allows HRM to raise cut
scores so that all but the most
qualified applicants are rejected.

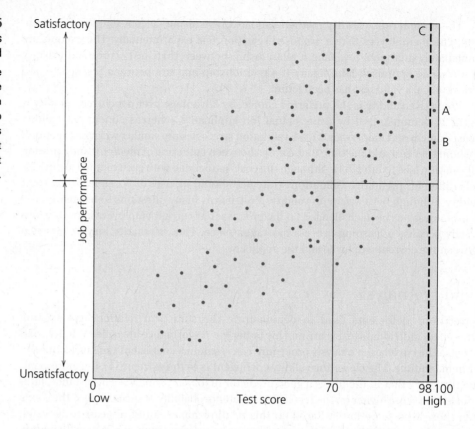

Cut Scores and Their Impact on Hiring

In this discussion, we have referred to test scores and their ability to predict successful job performance. By using our statistical analyses, we generate a scoring point, the cut score, below which applicants are rejected.[53] However, existing conditions (such as applicant availability) may cause an organization to change the cut score. If cut scores do change, what impact will this have on hiring applicants who will be successful on the job? Let us review again the positive relationship we found in our validity correlation analysis. We have reproduced the main elements in the graph in Exhibit 7-5. Let us assume that after our analysis, we determined that our cut score should be 70. At this cut score, we have shown that the majority of applicants who scored above 70 have a greater probability of being successful performers on the job, and that the majority scoring below 70, a greater probability of being unsuccessful performers. If we change our cut score, however, we alter the number of applicants in these categories. For example, suppose the organization faces a "buyer's market" for particular positions. The many potential applicants permit the organization to be selective. In a situation such as this, the organization may choose to hire only those applicants who meet the most extreme criteria. To achieve this goal, the organization increases its cut score to 98. By increasing the cut score from 70 to 98, the organization has rejected all but two candidates (areas A and B in Exhibit 7-5). However, many potentially successful job performers also would be rejected (individuals shown in area C). Here the organization has become more selective and has put more faith in the test than is reasonable. If out of 100 applicants only two were hired, we could say that the selection ratio (the ratio of number hired to the number of applicants) is 2 percent. A 2-percent selection ratio means that the organization is highly particular about who is hired.

Lowering the cut score also has an effect. Using the same diagram, let us lower our cut score to 50 and see what results. We have graphically portrayed this in Exhibit 7-6. By lowering the cut score from 70 to 50, we increase our number of eligible hires who have a greater probability of being successful on the job (area D). At the same time, however, we have also made eligible more applicants who could be unsuccessful on the job (area E). Although using a hiring process that offers a greater likelihood of engaging unsuccessful performers does not seem to make sense, conditions may necessitate the action.

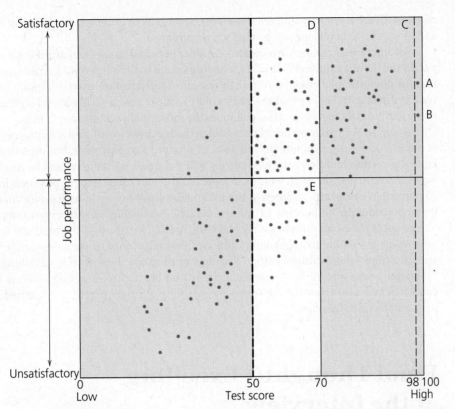

Exhibit 7-6
Validity Correlation Analysis
After Cut Score Is Lowered

This illustrates the situation many employers experienced prior to 2008. Unemployment was low and many employers had difficulty staying fully staffed. In such a "seller's market," HRM may lower cut scores to allow consideration of applicants with lower skill levels.

Labor market conditions may lead to a low supply of potential applicants who possess particular skills. For example, in some cities, finding home health aides or other health-care professionals may be difficult. Even in times of rising unemployment, the supply may be low, and demand high. Companies may hire individuals on the spot (more commonly referred to as an open-house recruiting effort). In this approach, the organization hires almost all the applicants who appear to have the skills needed (as reflected in a score of 50), puts them on the job, and filters out the unsuccessful employees at a later date. This may not appear effective, but the organization is banking on the addition of individuals in area D of Exhibit 7-6.

Validity Generalization

In the late 1970s, two researchers published a model that supported a phenomenon called validity generalization.[54] Validity generalization refers to a test valid for screening applicants for a variety of jobs and performance factors across many occupations.[55] For example, the Department of Labor's General Aptitude Test Battery (GATB) was shown to be valid for 500 jobs studied in terms of the test's ability to predict job performance and training success irrespective of race.[56] What distinguishes validity generalization is its use of a statistical technique called meta-analysis.[57] Through meta-analysis, researchers can determine correlations that may exist among numerous variables, and correct or adjust for any variances that may exist in predictor-criterion relationships.

Selection from a Global Perspective

The selection criteria for international assignments are broader in scope than those for domestic selection. To illustrate the point, in addition to such factors as technical expertise and leadership ability, an international assignment requires greater attention to personality and especially to flexibility in the design. The individual must have an interest in working overseas and a talent for relating well to all types of people. The ability to relate to different cultures and environments, sensitivity to different management styles, and a supportive family are often selection requirements.[58]

Not surprisingly, many corporations consider personal factors of maturity and age, as well as the "family situation factor," far more important in their international assignments than in domestic placements. Although not all expatriates are married, many human resource managers believe that marital stability reduces a person's likelihood of returning home early and in many countries enhances the individual's social acceptability.

American women have been successful in the business world, and it is unacceptable in our culture to discriminate on the basis of gender in employment, but organizations know that some Middle Eastern countries will not grant working papers to American women executives. Although women in Japan hold senior management positions in only 25 percent of companies, women in the Philippines lead the world with senior management positions in 97 percent of the companies. According to a recent survey, over 80 percent of the companies in China, Malaysia, Brazil, Hong Kong, Thailand, and Taiwan have women in senior management positions.[59] Past reluctance to assign women to overseas positions where culture rather than law once made them rare is vanishing, and American women are more often working in Asia and Latin America. Employers in other countries may also consider the social acceptability of single parents, unmarried partners, and blended families.

Final Thoughts: Excelling at the Interview

In the previous chapter we discussed some important elements of making your résumé look good to secure an interview. Interviews play a critical role in determining whether you are hired. Up to now, all the recruiter has seen is your well-polished cover letter and résumé (see Exhibit 6-4 and Exhibit 7-7). Remember, however, few individuals get a job without an interview. No matter how qualified you are for a position, if you perform poorly in the interview, you're not likely to be hired!

Interviews are popular because they help the recruiter determine if you are a good fit for the organization in terms of your level of motivation and interpersonal skills.[60] The following suggestions can help you make your interview experience a successful one.

Exhibit 7-7
The Interview

The interviewer's job can be a challenge at times, as illustrated in this comic.
(Source: © Randy Glasbergen, www.glasbergen.com)

First, do some homework. Search for the company on the Internet (or visit your library) and find as much information on it as possible. Develop a solid understanding of the company, its history, markets, financial situation, and the industry in which it competes. Also remember that the employer may do some homework on you, too. Make sure you clean up your presence on social media sites and check your privacy settings. You may even consider removing your profile until your job search is successful. Be sure you have an e-mail address that presents a professional image. Recent research shows that applicants with cutesy or inspirational e-mail addresses don't score as well on pre-employment assessments of professionalism as applicants with more appropriate addresses. It probably comes as no surprise that applicants with questionable or inappropriate e-mail addresses scored even lower.[61]

The night before the interview, get a good night's rest. As you prepare for the interview, keep in mind that your appearance will make your first impression. Dress appropriately. Incorrect attire can result in a negative impression. Arrive early, about fifteen minutes ahead of your scheduled

"**Unfortunately, you are overqualified. However, your résumé is full of misspelled words and grammatical errors so that tips the scales back in your favor.**"

interview. It's better to wait than to chance having the unexpected, such as a traffic jam, make you late. Arriving early also gives you an opportunity to survey the work environment and gather clues about the organization. Pay attention to the waiting room layout, the formality of the receptionist, and anything else that can give you insights into the organization.[62] As you meet the interviewer, give him or her a firm handshake. Make eye contact and maintain it throughout the interview. Remember, let your body language augment the impression you want an interviewer to pick up. Sit erect and maintain good posture. Although you will most likely be nervous, try your best to relax. Interviewers know that you'll be anxious, and a good one will try to put you at ease. Being prepared for an interview can also help build your confidence and reduce the nervousness. You can start building that confidence by reviewing a set of questions most frequently asked by interviewers, which are usually available at your college career center. Develop rough responses to these questions beforehand. This will lessen the likelihood that you'll be asked a question that catches you off guard. Our best advice, however, is to be yourself. Don't go into an interview with a prepared text and recite it from memory. Have an idea of what you would like to say, but don't rely on verbatim responses. Experienced interviewers will see through this over-preparedness and likely downgrade their evaluation.

Now's your chance. What you do and say in the next fifteen to thirty minutes will have a tremendous impact on whether you get the job. The more preparation you do, the more you anticipate interview question topics, the more successful you will be. *(Source: Masterfile)*

If possible, go through several practice interviews.[63] Universities often have career days on campus when recruiters from companies visit to interview students. Take advantage of them. Even if a job doesn't fit what you want, the practice will help you become more skilled at dealing with interviews. You can also practice with family, friends, career counselors, student groups, or your faculty adviser.

When the interview ends, thank the interviewer for his or her time and for the opportunity to talk about your qualifications, but don't think that selling yourself stops there. Send an immediate thank-you letter to the recruiter for taking the time to interview you and giving you the opportunity to discuss your job candidacy. Depending on the company culture, it may be appropriate to send the note via e-mail, but many employers still prefer U.S. mail. This little act of courtesy has a positive effect—use it to your advantage.

Summary

(This summary relates to the Learning Outcomes identified on page 162.) After reading this chapter, you now can:

1. **Describe the selection process.** The selection process includes the following: initial screening interview, completion of the application form, employment tests, comprehensive interview, background investigation, conditional job offer, physical or medical examination, and the job offer. In the discrete selection process, each step acts as a stand-alone predictor—failing to pass any of these discrete steps means disqualification from the job. In the comprehensive approach, candidates go through most of the steps before a final decision about them is rendered.

2. **Identify the primary purpose of selection activities.** Selection devices provide managers with information that helps them predict whether an applicant will prove to be a successful job performer. Selection activities primarily predict which job applicant will be successful if hired. During the selection process, candidates also learn about the job and organization. Proper selection can minimize the costs of replacement and training, reduce legal challenges, and result in a more productive workforce.

3. **Discuss why organizations use application forms.** The application form is effective for acquiring hard biographical data that can ultimately be verified.

4. **Explain the primary purposes of performance simulation tests.** Performance simulation tests require the applicant to engage in specific behaviors demonstrated to be job related. Work sampling and the assessment center, which are performance simulations, receive high marks for their predictive capability.

5. **Discuss the problems associated with job interviews and means of correcting them.** Interviews consistently achieve low marks for reliability and validity. These, however, are more the result of interviewer problems than problems with the interview. Interviewing validity can be enhanced by using a structured process.

6. **Specify the organizational benefits derived from realistic job previews.** Realistic job previews reduce turnover by giving the applicant both favorable and unfavorable information about the job.

7. **Explain the purpose of background investigations.** Background investigations are valuable when they verify hard data from the application.

8. **List three types of validity.** The three validation strategies are content, construct, and criterion-related validity.

9. **Explain how validity is determined.** Validity is determined either by discovering the extent to which a test represents actual job content, or through statistical analyses that relate the test used to an important job-related trait or to performance on the job.

Demonstrating Comprehension

QUESTIONS FOR REVIEW

1. Describe the eight-step selection process.
2. What is meant by a "reliable and valid" selection process?
3. Explain guidelines for developing effective interview questions that respect the legal rights of the applicant.
4. What is a weighted application form? How does it work?
5. Explain the advantages and disadvantages of searching social media as a screening tool for applicants.
6. What are the major problems of the interview as a selection device? What can HRM do to reduce some of these problems?
7. What effect should a realistic job preview have on a new hire's attitude and behavior?
8. What are the advantages of conducting background investigations on applicants and what do employees need to consider when conducting the investigations?
9. Define the concepts of reliability and validity. What are the three types of validity? Why are we concerned about reliability and validity?
10. What is the purpose of making a "conditional job offer"?

Key Terms

application form	construct validity	performance simulation tests
assessment center	content validity	predictive validity
background investigation	criterion-related validity	qualified privilege
behavioral interview	cut score	realistic job preview (RJP)
comprehensive interview	impression management	reliability
comprehensive selection	initial screening	validity
concurrent validity	interviewer bias	weighted application form
conditional job offer	medical/physical examination	work sampling

HRM Workshop

Linking Concepts to Practice   DISCUSSION QUESTIONS

1. What do you think of realistic job previews? Would you be more likely to choose a position where recruiters emphasized only the positive aspects of the job?
2. "I'm a pretty good judge of character, so I rarely call former employers. Besides, past employers have become really cautious about being candid with their comments." Do you agree or disagree with this statement? Explain.
3. "Untrained interviewers can make mistakes that are very costly to the organization." Discuss errors in perception and selection that interviewers can make and how to avoid them.
4. "When hiring a member of a team, each team member should have equal say in who is hired." Do you agree or disagree? Explain.

Making a Difference   SERVICE LEARNING PROJECTS

The selection process covers a broad range of skills and activities for both the employer and job seeker. Your service activity can focus on either group.

- Develop a presentation for middle school or high school students on getting a great summer or part-time job with an effective résumé and good interview skills.
- Contact local shelters about helping clients complete online job applications or teaching job interview skills.

- Help local non-profit organizations with their screening process for volunteers.

As you put your service learning experience together, keep a journal of your activities, the time you spend, contact information for people you work with, and your thoughts about the process. When you're finished, make a presentation to your class about the experience and what you learned. What concepts from Chapter 7 were you able to apply?

Developing Diagnostic and Analytical Skills

Case Application 7: TIMING OF THE JOB OFFER

Does it make a difference when a job offer is made? For many, the answer may be no, but then, in HRM things are rarely cut and dry. Consider the events that took place in early 2005 at American Airlines.[64]

In their quest to add flight attendants to their organization, company officials began a major recruiting effort. To deal with the numbers they anticipated, American representatives spent considerable time screening applicants through extensive phone interviews. Those who passed this initial screening were invited to Dallas, American's headquarters, for group and individual interviews. For expediency's sake and for competitive reasons, successful candidates were then given a conditional job offer—conditioned on passing a drug test, a background investigation, and a medical exam. These individuals were then taken to the company's on-site medical facility, where they were asked to complete a personal history questionnaire and give a blood sample. Shortly thereafter, the results were available, and three individuals had a questionable blood test result. After discussing the matter with them, American officials learned that the three were HIV positive. Consequently, the company withdrew the conditional offer. As a result, the three applicants sued.

The issue from American's perspective was that the three individuals did not fully disclose their medical situation on the questionnaire—thus they lied on their "application." American held that the conditional job offer was just that—conditional. They hadn't completed the entire hiring process—such as the background check—and only after all relevant information is in do they actually make a real or permanent job offer. They also cited that employment law requires individuals to be honest in disclosing their medical conditions, which in this case the individuals did not. The first court to look at this matter agreed and dismissed the case in favor of American.

But the three individuals persevered. They appealed, and on appeal the court ruled that American had, in fact, made a real job offer, and then fired them for reasons that violate the Americans with Disabilities Act. In its decision, the appellate court said that a conditional offer should be made only after all nonmedical factors have been evaluated. In this case, American had not done everything prior to requesting the medical examination, thus they did not follow the standard hiring process they had in place. As a result, the lower court's decision was overturned and the case was permitted to go to trial.

Questions:

1. Do you believe American Airlines has the right to rescind a conditional job offer? Why?

2. Is the fact that American Airlines did not follow their standard hiring process a problem here? Explain.

3. Do you believe American Airlines has the right to not hire someone who is HIV positive? Defend your position.

4. If you were the judge at the trial, given the facts presented above, who would you rule in favor of—American Airlines or the three individuals? Why?

Working with a Team   PREPARING FOR THE INTERVIEW

Using the job description for the benefits manager (Chapter 5, Exhibit 5-7) and the ad you wrote (Chapter 6, Learning an HRM Skill), develop a list of interview questions you'd ask of job candidates. In groups of two or three, compare your interview questions and reach consensus on the questions you'd ask. Based on those questions, develop a list of evaluation metrics (how you'll evaluate candidate responses). Share your team's responses with other teams in the class.

What similarities and differences did you note? If time permits, you may want to have a mock interview. One of you plays the role of the interviewer, one the job candidate, and one the observer. Ask the candidate your questions and evaluate the information obtained. The observer's job is to critique the interview. When you are finished, change roles and redo the mock interview.

Learning an HRM Skill   CREATING EFFECTIVE INTERVIEW QUESTIONS

About the skill: As an interviewer, you need to determine if the applicant has the aptitude, ability, and skills to perform the essential functions of the position. You also need to know if the applicant has "soft skills." Soft skills are those skills that make the person a good fit for the position and the organizational culture, including communication, teamwork, and problem-solving skills.

Individuals who infrequently interview job candidates often ask for guiding questions, that is, what they should ask to assess soft skills that are relevant to the job. Though questions may vary, here are some that you might find useful, as well as which soft skills they target.

Assessing Integrity

- In what business situations do you feel honesty would be inappropriate?
- What would you do if your boss asked you to do something unethical?

Assessing Personality

- What kinds of people bother you? Why?
- Describe a situation in which you had to take a risk.
- What motivates you most?
- What does your employer owe to you?

Past Mistakes

- The last time you were criticized, how did you deal with it?
- If you could change one decision you made in the past year, what would it be and why?
- Describe a situation where you blew it, and what you did to correct the problem.

Assessing Problem-Solving Ability

- What is the most difficult decision you had to make, and why?
- If you could change anything in the world, what would it be?
- Your colleague is talking to you about a problem and needs help. Your boss has just handed you a report with a lot of questions and needs it returned in the next hour. Your assistant tells you a customer is on the phone with a complaint. What do you do to handle these three things happening simultaneously?

Again, remember that asking the questions is the easy part. Listening to the responses and making sense of what is said is the critical part. You need to know what you're looking for and how what is said relates to successful performance on the job.

Source: Questions were adapted from Ceridian Abstracts, "General Interview Questions," (2005), available online at www.ceridian.com/www/content/10/12455/12487/12903/12909/041305_customer_query.htm

Enhancing Your Communication Skills

1. Develop a response to the following statement: "The social media profile of an applicant is not a valid selection device. Accordingly, it should not be used in determining whether or not to hire a job candidate." Present both sides of the argument with supporting data in a five- to ten-minute presentation with three to five presentation slides. Conclude your presentation by defending and supporting one of the two arguments you've presented.

2. Visit your college's career center and obtain a copy of their guide to job interviews. Obtain the same type of guide from another college's career center online resources. Compare the two. If your college does not have a job interview guide, create a pamphlet for them.

3. Research interview questions online, and obtain a list of the fifty most frequently asked interview questions. Reviewing the questions, which ones do you believe would pose the

greatest difficulty for you? Which ones would be easier for you? In a short video, discuss why the questions you've identified would be difficult for you, and what you can do to help overcome this difficulty.

4. Search the Internet for software packages that can assist HRM in the selection process. Identify three different software packages that can be purchased by the public. State the benefits of the software package to the HRM practitioner and the costs associated with purchasing the product. Based on your limited search, which of the three software packages would you recommend? Write a two-page memo to your boss requesting permission to purchase your selected software. Remember to include in your memo a comparison of the software packages and the reasons for your recommendation.

5. Search *YouTube* for short videos on job interviews. Use the video in a presentation to your class on job interviewing.

(Source: Blend Images/Masterfile)

LEARNING OUTCOMES

After reading this chapter, you will be able to

1. Define *socialization*.

2. Identify the three stages of employee socialization.

3. Identify the key personnel involved in orientation.

4. Describe the purpose of the employee handbook and explain what information should be included in the handbook.

5. Explain why employee training is important.

6. Define *training*.

7. Describe how training needs evolve.

8. Discuss the term *organizational development* and the role of the change agent.

9. Explain the term *learning organization*.

10. Describe the methods and criteria involved in evaluating training programs.

11. Explain issues critical to international training and development.

Socializing, Orienting, and Developing Employees

8

Cascade Engineering founder, Fred Keller visited a local mission and recruited unemployed people to work at Cascade Engineering, a manufacturing plant that makes automotive parts, garbage cans, wind turbines, and other environmentally friendly products in Grand Rapids, MI. By the end of the second week, Keller was surprised to discover that none of the workers recruited from the mission were still on the job.

Determined to develop a welfare-to-career program that worked, Keller then partnered with a local Burger King franchise. Welfare recipients would be offered jobs at Cascade if they successfully completed a six month stint at the Burger King with the hopes that they would develop good work habits and team skills. Again, none of the participants lasted the entire trial period.

Keller and his executives did some research to try and figure out why these welfare recipients weren't able to make the transition from the ranks of the unemployed to successful employment. They discovered that people from low-income backgrounds encountered cultural differences that made it difficult for them to move into the middle class. And they found that most hadn't had an opportunity to learn the skills and the rules of the game necessary in order to be successful in the workplace.

Potential employees coming off welfare often come from more than two generations of poverty, and may not understand middle class rules of behavior and etiquette. They may never have learned that it is necessary to call an employer when they are going to be late or absent. They may have additional challenges that interfere with work attendance, such as a lack of reliable transportation or childcare.

Cascade found an answer to the retention problems for "welfare-to-work" employees by revamping the onboarding process for new employees. Orientation was moved to the first days of employment. Trained company personnel discussed the company's culture, diversity awareness, the "rules" of middle-class culture, work ethics, and the range of services available to new hires. They were made aware of:

- The onsite caseworker available to assist employees during their transition.
- Company policy that includes sick children as an acceptable reason for absence from work.
- Convenient bus transportation and 90 days of free bus travel.
- Emergency $200 loans for unexpected expenses like a flat tire or utility shut-off notice.
- Money management skills classes for employees who use the Emergency Loans frequently.
- Annual $900 car repair benefit or a one-time $2,000 car purchase benefit.

Armed with an earlier orientation, benefits that removed barriers to work attendance and a new knowledge of the cultural expectations in the workplace, retention rates of the welfare-to-career workers soared to 95 percent in 2011. Cascade has seen benefits too, with an estimated five-year savings total of over $500,000 due to lower contracting costs, wage subsidies, and tax credits. And the savings to the government has exceeded $900,000 in lower welfare costs and higher tax receipts.[1]

Looking Ahead

What do you think? Would Mr. Keller's formula work in other communities or work environments?

Introduction

When we talk about socializing, orienting, training, and developing employees, we refer to a process of helping new employees adapt to their organizations and work responsibilities. These programs are designed to help employees understand what working is about in the organization and help them become fully productive as soon as possible. In essence, it's about learning the ropes! Research shows that when the socialization or onboarding process is done correctly, the results include higher employee job satisfaction, lower turnover, better performance, and lowered stress for new employees.[2]

In this chapter, we'll explore the arena of socializing, orienting, training, and developing employees. We'll first look at the socialization process and what organizations should do when employees first join them. We'll then explore training and development efforts designed to ensure a supply of highly skilled employees.

The Outsider–Insider Passage

socialization or onboarding
A process of adaptation that takes place as individuals attempt to learn the values and norms of work roles.

> Loneliness and a feeling of isolation are not unusual for new employees—they need special attention to put them at ease.

Socialization, frequently called **"onboarding,"** refers to the process of helping employees adapt to a new job and new organizational culture. It goes beyond new employee orientation. For instance, when you begin a new job, accept a lateral transfer, or are promoted, you must make adjustments. You adapt to a new environment that includes different work activities, a new boss, a different and most likely diverse group of coworkers, and probably a unique set of standards for what constitutes successful performance.

Although we recognize that this socialization will go on throughout people's careers—within an organization as well as between organizations—the most profound adjustment occurs when one makes the first move into an organization: the move from being an outsider to being an insider. The following discussion, therefore, is limited to the outsider–insider passage, or, more appropriately, organization–entry socialization. This is an important topic for HRM because failing to help new employees make a connection right away can result in costly turnover. For example, half of all hourly workers leave new jobs within the first 120 days.[3]

Socialization

Think back to your first day in college. What feelings did you experience? Anxiety over new expectations? Uncertainty over what was to come? Excitement at being on your own and experiencing new things? Fear based on everything friends said about how tough college courses were? Stress over what classes to take and with which professors? You probably experienced many of these—and maybe much more. Entry into a job is no different. Organizations can assist in the adjustment process if a few matters are understood. We'll call these the assumptions of employee socialization.

Assumptions of Employee Socialization

Several assumptions underlie the process of socialization: (1) socialization strongly influences employee performance and organizational stability; (2) new members suffer from anxiety; (3) socialization needs to be consistent with culture; and (4) individuals adjust to new situations in remarkably similar ways. Let's look a little closer at each of these assumptions.[5]

Socialization Strongly Influences Employee Performance and Organizational Stability   Your work performance depends to a considerable degree on knowing what you should or should not do. Understanding the right way to do a job indicates proper socialization. Furthermore, appraisal of your performance includes how well you fit into the organization. Can you get along with your coworkers? Do you have acceptable work habits? Do you demonstrate the right attitude and present appropriate behaviors?

Best Practices for Onboarding

Companies recognized for having effective onboarding programs have several things in common. Put yourself in the position of a new employee. What do you think would give you the tools you need to succeed? Here are a few principles for an effective onboarding program:[4]

- Have a written onboarding plan.
- Involve stakeholders at all levels in the planning process.
- Use a formal orientation program.
- Make the first day on the job special.
- Make sure the process explains and exhibits the organizational culture and mission.
- Clearly explain new employee expectations and responsibilities.
- Include opportunities for the new employee to participate.
- Monitor the program for results.
- Use technology to facilitate the process.
- Check with the employee at regular intervals: 30, 60, 90 days.
- Implement the program consistently.

Is there anything else you would add?

These qualities differ among jobs and organizations. For instance, on some jobs you will be evaluated higher if you are aggressive and indicate that you are ambitious. On others, or in other organizations, such an approach might be evaluated negatively. As a result, proper socialization becomes a significant factor in influencing both your actual job performance and how others perceive it.

Organizational Stability Also Increases through Socialization   When, over many years, jobs are filled and vacated with a minimum of disruption, the organization will be more stable.[6] Mission and culture transfer more smoothly as longtime employees help teach and reinforce the culture to new employees. Loyalty and commitment to the organization should be easier to maintain because the organization's philosophy and objectives appear consistent over time. Given that most managers value high employee performance and organizational stability, the proper socialization of employees should be important.

New Members Suffer from Anxiety   The outsider–insider passage produces anxiety. Stress is high because the new member feels a lack of identification—if not with the work itself, certainly with a new supervisor, new coworkers, a new work location, and new rules and regulations. Loneliness and a feeling of isolation are not unusual. This anxiety state has at least two implications. First, new employees need special attention to put them at ease. This usually means providing adequate information to reduce uncertainty and ambiguity. Second, tension can be positive in that it often motivates individuals to learn the values and norms of their newly assumed role as quickly as possible. The new member is usually anxious about the new role but motivated to learn the ropes and rapidly become an accepted member of the organization.

Socialization Needs to be Consistent with Culture   Learning associated with socialization goes beyond comprehending the formal job description and the expectations of human resources people or managers. Socialization is influenced by both subtle and not so subtle statements and behaviors offered by colleagues, management, employees, clients, and other people with whom new members come in contact. Employers need to make sure the new employee's experience is consistent with the culture or "employment brand" that was promoted in the recruiting process.

Individuals Adjust to New Situations in Remarkably Similar Ways   This holds true even though the content and type of adjustments may vary. For instance, as pointed out previously, anxiety is high at entry and the new member usually wants to reduce that anxiety quickly. Information obtained during recruitment and selection is always incomplete and

Research tells us that every individual new to an organization goes through the outsider–insider passage, a time of adjusting to the organization and learning what to do and what not to do. *(Source: nyul/iStockphoto)*

pre-arrival stage

This socialization process stage recognizes that individuals arrive in an organization with a set of organizational values, attitudes, and expectations.

encounter stage

The socialization stage where individuals confront the possible dichotomy between their organizational expectations and reality.

can be distorted. New employees, therefore, must clarify their understanding of their role once they are on the job. Adjustments take time—every new member goes through a settling-in period that tends to follow a relatively standard pattern.

The Socialization Process

Socialization can be conceptualized as a process made up of three stages: pre-arrival, encounter, and metamorphosis.[7] The first stage encompasses the learning the new employee has gained before joining the organization. In the second stage, the new employee gains a clearer understanding of the organization and deals with the realization that expectations and reality may differ. The third stage involves lasting change. Here, new employees become fully trained in their jobs, perform successfully, and fit in with the values and norms of coworkers.[8] These three stages ultimately affect new employees' productivity on the job, their commitment to the organization's goals, and their decision to remain with the organization.[9]

The **pre-arrival stage** explicitly recognizes that each individual arrives with a set of organizational values, attitudes, culture, and expectations. These may cover both the work to be done and the organization. In many jobs, particularly high-skilled and managerial jobs, new members will have considerable prior socialization in training and in school.[10] Part of teaching business students is to socialize them as to what business is like, what to expect in a business career, and what kind of attitudes professors believe will lead to successful assimilation in an organization. Pre-arrival socialization, however, goes beyond the specific job. Most organizations use the selection process to inform prospective employees about the organization as a whole. In addition, of course, selection interviews also help ensure that the right type of employee will be chosen—one who will fit the organization's culture and mission.

Once the best candidate has been selected, organizations would do well by not sitting back and waiting until she shows up for the first day of work. There may be other employers that are showing an interest in the new hire, particularly for tough to fill positions. It is important to keep the new hire interested by maintaining contact until she is completing employment forms on the first day. Ways to maintain contact and begin the onboarding process include mailing small gifts such as shirts or backpacks emblazoned with the company logo, inviting the employee for luncheons or tours of the new employer's facilities with other new hires, and/or establishing contact with a mentor that can answer questions and begin to teach the new employee about the company culture.

Upon entry into the organization, new members enter the **encounter stage**. Here, individuals confront the possible contrast between their expectations about jobs, coworkers, supervisors, and the organization in general, and reality. If expectations prove to have been more or less accurate, the encounter stage merely reaffirms perceptions generated earlier. However, this is not always the case. Where expectations and reality differ, new employees must be socialized to detach themselves from previous assumptions and replace these with the organization's pivotal standards.[11] Socialization, however, cannot solve all expectation differences. At the extreme, some new members may become totally disillusioned with the actualities of their jobs and resign. Proper selection, including realistic job previews and education about the company mission and culture, can significantly reduce this.

At Zappos, the online retailer recognized for exceptional customer service, the culture is based on the four week New Hire training foundation. Over a period of 10 days, up to an hour a day is spent teaching and reinforcing Zappos's Core Values. And all new hires spend two weeks in customer service training with call center employees taking customer calls. Throughout the four weeks of orientation and training, Zappos offers new employees $2,000 to quit if they feel they aren't a good fit with the company's culture. Zappos's founder and CEO, Tony Hsieh, says, "We want to make sure that employees are here

TIPS FOR SUCCESS

Orientation Checklist

The information that needs to be covered in new employee orientation will vary widely depending upon the size and type of organization. Once an organization determines what should be covered, a checklist should be created to make sure that regardless of who administers the orientation, all new employees will have access to information they need to get a good start. This checklist covers some of the basics:[15]

Introduction to the Organization

- Organizational mission
- Culture
- Organizational chart
- Tour of the workplace

HR Paperwork Requirements

- W-4 form
- I-9 form
- Personal information

- Pay
- Enroll in benefits
- Employee handbook and policies: non-discrimination, anti-harassment, phone, e-mail and online use, dress code, employment-at-will, leaves, discipline
- Security and access information

Working

- Meet supervisor and coworkers
- Discuss work standards and expectations
- Tools and supplies: business cards, e-mail accounts, keys, and access cards
- Etiquette issues: answering phones, personal items in the workplace
- Where to park, eat lunch, keep coats and purses
- Who and when to call in case of absence

for more than just a paycheck. We want employees that believe in our long term vision and want to be part of our culture."[12]

Finally, the new members must work out any problems discovered during the encounter stage. This may mean going through changes—this is called the **metamorphosis stage**. But what is a desirable metamorphosis? Metamorphosis is complete—as is socialization—when new members become comfortable with the organization and their work teams. They internalize coworker and organization norms, and they understand and accept these norms.[13] New members will feel accepted by their peers as trusted and valued individuals. They will feel competent to complete their jobs successfully. They will understand the organizational system—not only their own tasks but the rules, procedures, and informally accepted practices as well. Finally, they will know how they will be evaluated. That is, they've gained an understanding of what criteria will be used to measure and appraise their work. They'll know what is expected of them and what constitutes a good job. Consequently, successful metamorphosis should have a positive effect on new employees' productivity, the employee's commitment to the organization, and should reduce the likelihood that the employee will leave the organization any time soon.[14]

If HRM recognizes that certain assumptions hold for new employees entering an organization and that they typically follow a three-staged socialization process, they can develop a program to begin helping these employees adapt to the organization. Let's turn our attention, then, to this aspect of organizational life—socializing our new employees through the new-employee orientation process.

metamorphosis stage
The socialization stage during which the new employee must work out inconsistencies discovered during the encounter stage.

The Purpose of New-Employee Orientation

New-employee **orientation** covers the activities involved in introducing a new employee to the organization and to the individuals in his or her work unit. It expands on information received during the recruitment and selection stages and helps reduce the initial anxiety employees usually feel when beginning a new job.[16] For example, an

orientation
Activities that introduce new employees to the organization and their work units.

Zappos.com offers new employees $2,000 to quit any time during the four week orientation program if they feel they are not a good fit with Zappos's unique culture. Less than 1 percent of new hires have ever accepted the offer. *(Source: William Widmer/Redux Pictures)*

orientation program should familiarize the new member with the organization's objectives, history, philosophy, procedures, and rules; communicate relevant HRM policies such as work hours, pay procedures, overtime requirements, and company benefits; review the specific duties and responsibilities of the new member's job; provide a tour of the organization's physical facilities; and introduce the employee to his or her manager and coworkers.[17]

Who is responsible for orienting the new employee? This can be done by the new employee's supervisor, by the people in HR, through computer-based programs, or by some combination of methods. In many medium-sized and most large organizations, HRM takes charge of explaining such matters as overall organizational policies and employee benefits. In other medium-sized and most small firms, new employees will receive their entire orientation from their supervisor or be exposed to an orientation program on the company's intranet.[18] Of course, the new employee's orientation may not be formal at all. For instance, in many small organizations, orientation may mean the new member reports to her supervisor, who then assigns her to another employee who introduces her to her coworkers. This may be followed by a quick tour of the facilities, after which the new employee is shown to her desk and work begins. If orientation becomes the responsibility of the supervisor, there should be some training for that supervisor to ensure that the new employee has a thorough orientation that goes beyond where to park and when payday is. For instance, in today's dynamic organizations, new employees must understand the organization's culture.

Learning the Organization's Culture

We know that every individual has what psychologists have termed personality, a set of relatively permanent and stable traits. When we describe someone as warm, innovative, relaxed, or conservative, we are describing personality traits. An organization, too, has a personality, which we call the organization's culture. What do we

REAL HR ENCOUNTERS

HR's Role in Creating and Sustaining Culture

Janel Cerwick: Human Resources Business Partner, CIPCO, A Touchstone Energy Cooperative

An organization's culture develops, with or without a conscious effort on the part of its leaders. Changing unwanted aspects of a culture such as top-down decision making or limited communication is difficult, and imbedding new cultural attributes such as participative decision making and open communication takes time and persistence. Leaders of organizations who fail to intentionally develop and continually reinforce the desired culture, run the risk of a resulting cultural environment that undermines the day-to-day performance and financial success of the organization.

It is a key responsibility of HRM to assume ownership, along with the organization's leaders, to define the desired cultural elements such as how decisions are made at all levels of the organization, how employees will work with and communicate with one another, and how employee performance and associated rewards will be managed. All business and HR processes and policies must then be aligned to reinforce the desired attributes.

Creating and maintaining a strong and healthy culture is difficult to attain and sustain, and is easily lost without constant diligence on the part of HRM and the organization's leaders. Missteps in business decisions, communications, policies, and programs lead to employee skepticism, morale issues, and ultimately, increased turnover.

specifically mean by **organization culture**? We refer to a system of shared meaning.[19] Just as tribal cultures have totems and taboos that dictate how each member should act toward fellow members and outsiders, organizations have cultures that govern how their members should behave.[20] Every organization, over time, evolves stories, rituals, material symbols, and language.[21] These shared values determine, in large part, what employees see and how they respond to their world.[22]

An employee who has been properly socialized to the organization's culture, then, has learned how work is done, what matters, and which work-related behaviors and perspectives are or are not acceptable and desirable. In most cases, this involves input from many individuals.

> An employee who has been properly socialized to the organization's culture knows what acceptable behavior is and what it is not.

organization culture
The system of sharing meaning within the organization that determines how employees act.

The CEO's Role in Orientation

Many senior managers have become highly visible in their organizations, meeting and greeting employees and listening to employee concerns. For example, Tony Hsieh, of Zappos.com, has a cubicle just like other employees at Zappos's Las Vegas headquarters, allowing him to stay closer to employees and better understand their suggestions and concerns. As more successful companies have been cited in business literature for their leaders' involvement with the workforce, a question arises. If this connection works well for existing employees, what would it do for employees joining the organization?

One of the more stressful aspects of starting a new job is the thought of entering the unknown. Although conditions at a previous organization may have made you leave—such as lack of upward mobility—at least the conditions were familiar. Starting a new job is frightening. You may wonder if you made the right choice. Having the CEO present from day one, addressing you as a new employees, helps allay those fears. The CEO's first responsibility is to welcome new employees aboard and talk to them about what a good job choice they made.[23] In fact, this segment of new-employee orientation can be likened to a school pep rally. The CEO is in a position to inspire new employees by talking about what it is like to work for the organization. In addition, the CEO can begin to discuss what really matters in the company—an indoctrination to the organization's culture.

When a CEO is present, the company shows that it truly cares for its employees. Employee-satisfaction concepts are sometimes thrown around an organization to such an extent that they become nothing more than lip service to the idea.[24] But a senior company official's presence validates that the company really is concerned—the CEO's commitment to making the first day special is evidenced by his or her presence. When scheduling conflicts arise, some companies use previously prepared videos or other electronic means of carrying the same message.

HRM's Role in Orientation

In our introductory comments we stated that the orientation function can be performed by HRM, line management, or a combination of the two. Despite a preference for a combination strategy, we contend that HRM plays a major coordinating role in new-employee orientation, which ensures that the appropriate components are in place. In addition, HRM also serves as a participant in the program. Consequently, we should recognize what HRM must do. For example, in our discussion of making the job offer (Chapter 7), we emphasized that the offer should come from human resources to better coordinate administrative activities surrounding a new hire. The same holds true for new-employee orientation. Depending on the recruiting, a systematic schedule should guide employee entry into a company.

As job offers are made and accepted, HRM should instruct the new employee when to report to work. However, before the employee formally arrives, HRM must be prepared to handle some of the more routine needs of these individuals. For example, new employees typically have a long list of questions about benefits. More proactive organizations prepare a package for new employees. This package generally focuses on important decisions a new employee must make—choice of health insurance, setting up direct deposit of paychecks, and tax-withholding information. When HRM provides this information a few weeks before new hires start work, they have ample time to make a proper choice—quite possibly one affected by a working spouse's or partner's options.

HRM's second concern involves its role as a participant in the process. Most new employees' exposure to the organization thus far has been with HRM, but after the hiring process is over, HRM quickly drops out of the picture unless there is a problem. Therefore, HRM must spend some orientation time addressing what assistance it can offer to employees in the future. This point cannot be minimized. If HRM provides an array of services such as career guidance, benefit administration, or employee training, HRM cannot become complacent. They must let new employees know what else HRM can do for them in the future, particularly if many HRM services may be contracted out by departments, thereby lessening HRM's effect in the organization.[25]

It's All in Here: The Employee Handbook

The first few days on a new job are packed with learning skills, meeting coworkers, and becoming familiar with the organization's policies. It's no wonder that new employees sometimes fail to absorb all of the important information. Stressful situations aren't always the best place for listening and learning, and HRM realizes that although new employees may appear to absorb a lot, important information should be followed up with written reminders. Consequently, HRM usually provides a permanent reference guide. This reference guide for employees is called the employee handbook.

DIVERSITY TOPICS

Training, Development, and EEO

Much of our previous discussions of equal employment opportunity (EEO) have centered on the selection process. Undoubtedly, equal employment opportunities are most prevalent in the hiring process, but EEO's application to training and development cannot be overlooked. Remember that our definition of adverse impact includes any HRM activity that adversely affects protected group members in hiring, firing, and promoting. So how does training fall into the EEO realms?[28] Let's take a brief look.

Training programs may be required for promotions, job bidding (especially in unionized jobs), or salary increases. Regarding any of these, the organization must ensure that training selection criteria relates to the job. Furthermore, equal training opportunities must exist for all employees. Failure at something as simple as informing all employees of the schedule of training programs could raise suspicions regarding how fair the training programs are. Organizations should also pay close attention to training completion rates. If more "protected group" members fail to pass training programs than "majority group" members, this might indicate dissimilarities in the

training offered. Once again, organizations should monitor these activities and perform periodic audits to ensure full compliance with EEO regulations.

Employee development methods have come into question as well. An estimated 70 percent of companies don't have a clear strategy for employee development aimed at developing female leaders for the organization. Hurdles women face include lack of an executive sponsor or mentor, insufficient experience, and difficulty finding work/life balance. In addition to leadership development programs, flexible work arrangements, coaching, mentoring, diversity sourcing, and recruiting are identified as effective employee development methods for female leaders.[29]

The lack of programs and strategies for developing women is particularly confusing when paired with the fact that an estimated 70 percent of HRM professionals are women.[30]

Your Reaction:

Why hasn't there been more success in developing programs for women and minorities? Are these programs something you would look for in a potential employer?

Exhibit 8-2
A Sample Employee
Handbook Disclaimer
This excerpt from an employee
handbook makes it clear that
employment is not a permanent
relationship.

"This handbook is not a contract, expressed or implied, guaranteeing employment for any specific duration. Although [the company] hopes that your employment relationship with us will be long term, either you or the company may terminate this relationship at any time, for any reason, with or without cause or notice."

Why Use an Employee Handbook?

An employee handbook, when developed properly, serves both employees and the employer. A well-designed handbook gives employees a central source for such useful information as what the company is about, including its mission, history, policies, and employee benefits. The handbook, then, gives employees an opportunity to learn about the company and what benefits it provides, and to understand the information at their own pace. Such a readily available resource helps ensure quicker and easier answers to questions that may arise over such benefits as vacation accrual, matching contributions, and insurance.[26]

Employee handbooks also generate other benefits. They can help new employees understand the elements of organizational culture, which will, hopefully, build loyalty and commitment. By being thorough in its coverage, an employee handbook will address various HRM policies and work rules so employees understand what is expected. For example, the handbook may discuss discipline and discharge procedures and the appeals process should the employee believe that the procedure was administered unfairly. The handbook, then, serves to ensure that any HRM policy will be fair, equitable, and consistently applied.

Employers, too, can benefit from using an employee handbook. In addition to any benefits accrued from having a more committed and loyal workforce, handbooks are tools to educate, inform, and guide employees in the organization. But a word of caution is in order. In our earlier discussion in Chapter 4 on employment-at-will, we addressed the issue of implied contracts. Recall that an implied contract is anything expressed orally or in writing that may be perceived by the individual to mean that she or he can't be terminated. For example, telling an employee that as long as her performance is satisfactory, she will have a job until retirement could be construed as an implied contract. Over the years, the courts have ruled that various statements made in employee handbooks may be binding on the company. To prevent this from occurring, many legal advocates and HRM researchers recommend a careful choice of words in the handbook, and a disclaimer. We have reproduced a disclaimer from one business in Exhibit 8-2.

It is important to note that an employee handbook is of little use if employees don't read it. To facilitate that goal, it is recommended that first of all, the handbook should be pertinent to employees' needs. Handbooks that are wordy, unclear, or contain unnecessary information will discourage employees from reading them. Consequently, employers should establish feedback mechanisms to assess how useful employees find the employee handbook information, gather input, and make modifications where necessary. HRM should not assume that once developed and disseminated to employees, the employee handbook is final. Rather, it should be updated and refined on a continuous basis. Employers are finding that putting the employee handbook on the company's intranet is an effective way of making the materials available to employees and allows easy and quick revision when necessary.[27]

employee handbook
A booklet describing important aspects of employment an employee needs to know.

Employee Training

Every organization needs well-adjusted, trained, and experienced people to perform its activities. As jobs in today's dynamic organizations have become more complex, the importance of employee education has increased. On the whole, for example, planes usually don't cause airline accidents, people do. Nearly three-quarters of collisions, crashes, and other airline mishaps result from pilot or air traffic controller errors or inadequate maintenance. Weather and structural failures typically account for the remaining accidents.[31] We cite these statistics to illustrate the importance of training in the airline industry. These maintenance and human errors could be prevented or significantly reduced by better employee training.

employee training
Present-oriented training that focuses on individuals' current jobs.

Employee training is a learning experience: it seeks a relatively permanent change in employees to improve job performance. Thus, training involves teaching new skills, knowledge, attitudes, and/or behavior.[32] This may mean changing what employees know, how they work, or their attitudes toward their jobs, coworkers, managers, and the organization. Managers, possibly with HRM assistance, decide when employees need training and what form that training should take (see Diversity Issues in HRM).

For our purposes, we will differentiate between employee training and **employee development** for one particular reason: Although both are similar in learning methods, their time frames differ. Training is more present-day oriented; it focuses on individuals' current jobs, enhancing those specific skills and abilities needed to immediately perform their jobs. For example, suppose you enter the job market during your senior year of college, pursuing a job as a marketing representative. Despite your degree in marketing, you will need some training. Specifically, you'll need to learn the company's policies and practices, product information, and other pertinent selling practices. This, by definition, is job-specific training, or training designed to make you more effective in your current job.

employee development
Future-oriented training that focuses on employee personal growth.

Employee development, on the other hand, generally focuses on future jobs in the organization. As your job and career progress, you'll need new skills and abilities. For example, if you become a sales territory manager, the skills you need to perform that job may be quite different from those you used to sell products. Now you must supervise sales representatives and develop a broad-based knowledge of marketing and specific management competencies in communication skills, evaluating employee performance, and disciplining problem individuals. As you are groomed for positions of greater responsibility, employee development efforts can help prepare you for that day.

Determining Training Needs

Determining training needs typically involves generating answers to several questions (see Exhibit 8-3).[33] Recall from Chapter 5 that these types of questions demonstrate the close link between employment planning and determining training needs. Based on our determination of the organization's needs, the work to be done, and the skills necessary to complete this work, our training programs should follow naturally. Once we identify where deficiencies lie, we have a grasp of the extent and nature of our training needs.

The leading questions in Exhibit 8-3 suggest the kinds of signals that can warn a manager when training may be necessary. The more obvious ones relate directly to

Exhibit 8-3
Determining Training Needs

How does HR determine when training is necessary? These questions help make that determination.

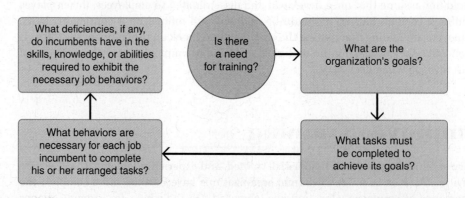

productivity. Indications that job performance is declining may include production decreases, lower quality, more accidents, and higher scrap or rejection rates. Any of these outcomes might suggest that worker skills need to be fine-tuned. Of course, we are assuming that the employee's performance decline is in no way related to lack of effort. Managers, too, must also recognize that a constantly evolving workplace may require training. Changes imposed on employees as a result of job redesign or a technological breakthrough also require training.

It is important to put training into perspective. Training may be costly, and it should not be viewed as a cure-all for what ails the organization. Rather, judge training by its contribution to performance, where performance is a function of skills, abilities, motivation, and the opportunity to perform. Managers must also compare the value received from performance increases attributable to training with the costs that training incurred.[34]

Once it has been determined that training is necessary, training goals must be established. Management should explicitly state its desired results for each employee.[35] It is not adequate to say we want change in employee knowledge, skills, attitudes, or behavior; we must clarify what is to change and by how much. These goals should be tangible, verifiable, timely, and measurable.[36] They should be clear to both the supervisor and the employee. For instance, a firefighter might be expected to jump from a moving fire truck traveling at fifteen miles per hour, successfully hook up a four-inch hose to a hydrant, and turn on the hydrant, all in less than forty seconds. Such explicit goals ensure that both the supervisor and the employee know what is expected from the training effort.

Training Methods

The old saying, "If the only tool you have is a hammer, then you tend to see every problem as a nail," is quite applicable to employee training. If you're familiar with one type of training, such as classroom lectures, it may seem to be a good way to deliver training for many types of topics. However, what works best for teaching one type of skill may not work well for another. For example, teaching employees computer skills necessary for a newly automated process would require much different training methods than teaching employees about the skills and attitudes necessary for better customer service, diversity training, or preventing sexual harassment. Fortunately, many different types of training methods are available.[37] For the most part, however, we can classify them as on-the-job or off-the-job training.

On-the-Job Training Methods For many situations, the most effective way to train an employee involves putting the employee in the workplace and providing training with a fellow employee or trainer. Examples include:

On-the-Job Training (OJT) is probably the oldest and most frequently used type of training. If you think back to your first job, you were probably trained on-the-job. It can be quite informal and involves the trainee working alongside more experienced employees or trainers in the actual work environment. Small organizations may use OJT as their primary or only training method because they may not know that there are other methods available. It's appropriate for many entry-level jobs, but there are other training tools that can be more effective. Employees who facilitate on-the-job training need to be trained themselves on the best way to model, teach, and reinforce the skills. Trainers also need to understand that they are representatives of the organizational culture as well as an expert in performing the task.

on-the-job training
Trainee works with more experienced employee in the actual work environment.

HRM needs to determine which training methods are the most appropriate for the skills needed and the employees. It may be necessary to combine several methods. For example, production employees may need classroom instruction in topics like safety, quality standards, math, and measurement before hands-on training can begin.

Job Rotation has long been considered a valuable tool to increase employee motivation. Job rotation involves lateral transfers that allow employees to work at different jobs and provides exposure to a variety of tasks. As with any training, HRM should take care to make sure the trainers not only know the job, but how to train others as well. Employers often move new hires through a rotation of different roles in the organization such as marketing, finance, and operations before they settle into a permanent position. This allows employees to develop a broad understanding of how jobs at the organization are interrelated and how one job may depend on the quality output from another.

apprenticeships
Combine instruction with coaching from an experienced mentor.

Apprenticeships are frequently used to combine classroom instruction in combination with working alongside a seasoned veteran, coach, or mentor. The combination of hands-on and classroom learning complement each other. Apprenticeships are frequently used in skilled trade or craft jobs such as building trades. The experienced worker provides support and encouragement in addition to training.

internships
Structured program for students to gain employment experience in their area of study.

Internships are opportunities for students in higher education to utilize their instruction and training in a chosen profession as part of their education. Internships vary from very unstructured to highly structured, and may include college credit. Organizations usually value internships as a way to reduce recruitment expenses without creating an obligation of regular employment. Interns also provide a valuable source of new ideas and creativity. Students participating in internships gain valuable real-world experience and greatly enhance their value to prospective employers, particularly in difficult economic times. Many HR departments offer internships to students who wish to pursue an HR career. Check the "Careers" section of organizational websites to check for internship opportunities. Society of Human Resource Management (SHRM.org), CareerBuilder.com, and Monster.com also list internships.

Off-the-Job Training Methods Some job skills require the trainee to spend some time developing a skill before he is ready for "prime time." This may be because accuracy is particularly important or because mistakes can be dangerous or costly. Other situations may require learning a great deal of information before being allowed to work unsupervised. These methods include:

classroom lectures
Training in a traditional classroom setting.

Classroom Lectures, probably don't need much explanation at this point of your education. But once you finish college, you may not have seen the inside of your last classroom. Many organizations use classroom instruction along with other methods to provide a great deal of information in a limited timeframe. Instructors need to understand the different learning characteristics of adult learners and the variety of types of instruction that create interest in the specific technical, interpersonal, or problem-solving skills they are teaching. Jobs that may require classroom lecture training include insurance agents or financial advisors, for example.

multimedia learning
Videos, simulations and games are used for learning and training.

Multimedia Learning, can demonstrate technical skills not easily presented by other training methods. This may include videos, simulations, and games that are offered on-site or online. The key advantage of online learning is the flexibility that allows employees, contractors, telecommuters, and temporary workers access to training whenever and wherever it is necessary. After UPS started using games to train new truck drivers, the number of drivers that failed training dropped from 30 percent to 10 percent.[38] Some research has shown, however, that employees who participate in online orientation don't understand the job or company as well as employees who participate in a traditional face-to-face orientation. This may indicate that a combination of online and face-to-face orientation is more effective than a completely online experience.

Simulations involve learning a job by actually performing the work (or its simulation). Simulation methods may include case analyses, experiential exercises, computer simulations, virtual reality, role playing, and group interaction. Computer simulations are particularly useful when training involves expensive or dangerous equipment.

vestibule training
using actual work tools or equipment in a training situation

Vestibule Training, facilitates learning by using the same equipment that one actually will use on the job, but in a simulated work environment. Vestibule training is used to deliver training for a variety of jobs from astronauts to cashiers, manufacturing machine operators, and bank tellers.

Employee Development

Employee development, as mentioned earlier, is future oriented and more concerned with education than with employee job-specific training. Goals may include increasing an employee's ability to understand and interpret knowledge or improving critical thinking or problem solving skills, rather than imparting a body of facts or teaching a specific set of motor skills. Development, therefore, focuses more on the employee's personal growth.[39] Successful employees who are prepared for positions of greater responsibility have developed analytical, human relations, conceptual, and specialized skills. Training cannot overcome an individual's inability to understand cause-and-effect relationships, to synthesize from experience, to visualize relationships, or to think logically. As a result, employee development tends to be predominantly an education process rather than a training process.

Consider one critical component of employee development: all employees, regardless of level, can be developed. Historically, development was reserved for potential management personnel. Although it is critical for individuals to be trained in specific skills related to managing—planning, organizing, leading, controlling, and decision making—time has taught us that nonmanagerial employees need to develop these skills as well.

The use of work teams, reductions in supervisory roles, allowing workers to participate in setting job goals, and a greater emphasis on quality and customer service has changed the way we view employee development. Accordingly, organizations now require new employee skills, knowledge, and abilities. As we go through the next few pages, note that the methods used to develop employees in general are the same as those used to develop future management talent.

Sprint Nextel may be the third largest wireless carrier, but it is leading the way in moving from instructor-led training to short videos that employees can access through the company's intranet, cutting training costs, and making the information available when managers need it.
(Source: The NYC Collection/ Alamy Limited)

Employee Development Methods

Some development of an individual's abilities can take place on the job. We will review several methods: three popular on-the-job techniques (job rotation, assistant-to positions, and committee assignments), and three off-the-job methods (lecture courses and seminars, simulation exercises, and adventure or outdoor training).

Job Rotation   **Job rotation** is used in employee development as well as training. Job rotation can be either horizontal or vertical. Vertical rotation is nothing more than promoting a worker into a new position. In this chapter, we will emphasize the horizontal dimension of job rotation, also known as a short-term lateral transfer.

Job rotation represents an excellent method for broadening an individual's exposure to company operations and for turning a specialist into a generalist. In addition to increasing the individual's experience and allowing him or her to absorb new information, it can reduce boredom and stimulate the development of new ideas. It can also provide opportunities for a more comprehensive and reliable evaluation of the employee by his or her supervisors.

Assistant-To Positions   Employees with demonstrated potential sometimes work under a seasoned and successful manager, often in different areas of the organization. Working as staff assistants, or in some cases, serving on special boards, these individuals perform many duties under the watchful eye of a supportive coach (see Contemporary

job rotation
Moving employees horizontally or vertically to expand their skills, knowledge, or abilities.

Connections: Training Expenditures). In doing so, these employees experience a wide variety of management activities and are groomed for assuming the duties of the next higher level.

Committee Assignment Committee assignments can allow the employee to share in decision making, to learn by watching others, and to investigate specific organizational problems. Temporary committees often act as a taskforce to delve into a particular problem, ascertain alternative solutions, and recommend a solution. These temporary assignments can be both interesting and rewarding to the employee's growth. Appointment to permanent committees increases the employee's exposure to other members of the organization, broadens his or her understanding, and provides an opportunity to grow and make recommendations under the scrutiny of other committee members.

In addition to the above on-the-job techniques, employees benefit from off-the-job development. We will briefly discuss three of the more popular means: lecture courses and seminars, simulations, and adventure or outdoor training.

Lecture Courses and Seminars Traditional forms of instruction revolve around formal lecture courses and seminars. These help individuals acquire knowledge and develop their conceptual and analytical abilities. Many organizations offer these in-house, through outside vendors, or both.

Technology is allowing for significant improvements in the training field. Online learning allows for employees to view a lecture or presentation live or view streaming video at any time or place. Courses or seminars are provided by employers, professional associations, or colleges. For example, websites of the Society of Human Resource Management (SHRM) and American Society for Training and Development (ASTD) provide members with extensive libraries of videos, podcasts, and webcasts on a variety of HR and training topics.

Many organizations offer incentives for employees to take college classes. Incentives can include increased potential for promotion, tuition reimbursement, or both. Classes can be taken toward a degree or continuing education. Either way, employees are taking the responsibility to advance their skills, knowledge, and abilities in an effort to enhance their value to their current or future employer.

simulation
Any artificial environment that attempts to closely mirror an actual condition.

Simulations While critical in training employees on actual work experiences, **simulations** are probably even more popular for employee development.[40] The more

---

CONTEMPORARY CONNECTION

Training Expenditures

How much do U.S. companies spend annually for employee training and development? How much does that add up to for each employee? How much is spent on classroom-based learning as opposed to technology-based learning? Let's take a look at the numbers, according to the American Society for Training and Development (ASTD).

■ $171.5 billion is spent annually on employee training. Nearly two-thirds of that was spent internally. The balance was spent on training by external organizations. With that large of an investment, you can see why managers want to be sure they're getting a good return on investment.

■ $1,228 was the average spent per employee in the United States. How do you think your employer spent that money training you?

■ Employees spend an average of nearly 32 hours a year in training, with 22 of those spent in a classroom, and nearly 9 of those hours spent online using self-paced or instructor-led online learning. Are you taking this class online? If so, you have a good idea of what online workplace training is like.

The amount of money spent using technology to train employees is increasing because of the cost savings. Cost advantages include the efficiency of online learning, the ability to reuse the learning tools without much additional expense, and the decreasing costs of developing online learning.[43]

Consider this:
How do you prefer to learn new skills on the job? Is there too much emphasis on online or computer based training? What skills would you prefer to more traditional face-to-face environment?

widely used simulation exercises include case studies, decision games, and role plays. Employee development through case-study analysis was popularized at the Harvard Graduate School of Business. Taken from the actual experiences of organizations, these cases represent attempts to describe, as accurately as possible, real problems that managers have faced. Trainees study the cases to determine problems, analyze causes, develop alternative solutions, select what they believe to be the best solution, and implement it. Case studies can provide stimulating discussions among participants, as well as excellent opportunities for individuals to defend their analytical and judgmental abilities. It appears to be a rather effective method for improving decision-making abilities within the constraints of limited information.

Simulated decision games and role-playing exercises put individuals in the role of acting out supervisory problems. Simulations, frequently played on a computer, provide opportunities for individuals to make decisions and witness the implications of their decisions for other segments of the organization. Airlines, for instance, find that simulations are a much more cost-effective means of training pilots— especially in potentially dangerous situations. Poor decisions typically have no worse effects on the learner than the need to explain why the choice was not a good one. Role playing allows participants to act out problems and deal with real people. Participants are assigned roles and are asked to react to one another as they would have to do in their managerial jobs.

The advantages of simulation exercises are the opportunities to "create an environment" similar to real situations managers face, without high costs for poor outcomes. Of course, the disadvantages are the reverse of this: it is difficult to duplicate the pressures and realities of actual decision making on the job, and individuals often act differently in real-life situations than they do in a simulated exercise.

Vestibule training, that occurs in a flight simulator, can be highly cost-effective. Computer programming allows trainers to present scenarios for pilots to handle that could be difficult or dangerous to replicate in a real aircraft. Make a mistake in the simulator, and you start over. Make a mistake at 35,000 feet, and starting over may not be an option.
(Source: Alvis Upitis/Getty Images, Inc.)

Adventure Training A recent trend in employee development has been the use of adventure (sometimes referred to as outdoor, wilderness, or survival) training. The primary focus of such training is to teach trainees the importance of working together, or coming together as a team.[41] Adventure training typically involves a major emotional and physical challenge. This could be white-water rafting, mountain climbing, paintball games, or surviving a week on a sailing adventure.

The purpose of such training is to see how employees react to the difficulties that nature presents to them. Do they face these dangers alone? Do they freak out? Or are they controlled and successful in achieving their goal? How cooperative are they under harsh circumstances? The reality is that today's business environment does not permit employees to stand alone. This has reinforced the importance of working closely with one another, building trusting relationships, and succeeding as a member of a group. Companies such as Wells Fargo, Whole Foods Markets, Microsoft, and Bank of America have embraced adventure training efforts.[42]

Organization Development

Although our discussion so far has related to the people side of business, it is important to recognize that organizations change from time to time. Changes with respect to continuous improvements, diversity, and work process engineering require the organization to move forward through a process we call **organization development (OD).** OD has taken on a renewed importance today. Whether brought about by globalization,

organization development (OD) The part of HRM that addresses system-wide change in the organization.

Are these people on an adventure vacation or an employee development activity? If they work for Wells Fargo, it might be a little of both.
(Source: Silvrshootr/iStockphoto)

challenging economic times, mergers, or continuous-improvement goals, many organizations have drastically changed the way they do business.[44]

No matter what role OD takes in an organization, it requires facilitation by an individual well versed in organization dynamics. In HRM terms, we call this person a **change agent**. Change agents are responsible for fostering the environment in which change can occur, and working with the affected employees to help them adapt to the change. Change agents may be either internal employees, often associated with the training and development function of HRM, or external consultants. Before we discuss specific aspects of organization development, let's look at this phenomenon we call change.

Change Is a Popular Topic

Change usually affects four areas of an organization: its systems, technology, processes, and people. No matter what the change, or how minor it may appear, understanding its effect is paramount for it to be supported and lasting.[45] OD comes into play with efforts designed to support the business's strategic direction. For instance, if work processes change, people need to learn new production methods, procedures, and possibly, new skills. OD becomes instrumental in bringing about the change. How so? The effects of change become organizational culture issues. Accordingly, OD efforts help ensure that all organizational members support the new culture and assist in bringing the new culture to fruition.

We often use two metaphors to clarify the change process.[46] The calm waters metaphor envisions the organization as a large ship crossing a calm sea. The ship's captain and crew know exactly where they are going because they have made the trip many times before. Change surfaces as the occasional storm, a brief distraction in an otherwise calm and predictable trip. The white-water rapids metaphor pictures the organization as a small raft navigating a raging river with uninterrupted white-water rapids. Aboard the raft are a half dozen people who have never worked together before, who are totally unfamiliar with the river, who are unsure of their eventual destination, and who, as if things weren't bad enough, are traveling in the pitch-dark night. In the white-water rapids metaphor, change is a natural state, and managing change is a continual process.

These two metaphors present widely differing approaches to understanding and responding to change. Let's take a closer look at each one.

The Calm Waters Metaphor Until recently, the calm waters metaphor dominated the thinking of practicing managers and academics. The prevailing model for handling change in calm waters is best illustrated in Kurt Lewin's three-step description of the change process (see Exhibit 8-4).[47]

According to Lewin, successful change requires unfreezing the status quo, changing to a new state, and refreezing the new change to make it permanent. The status quo can

Exhibit 8-4
Lewin's Change Process

In this illustration, movers assist an office relocation by disassembling the office in the unfreezing phase and moving equipment in the change phase. Office workers settle into their new location in the refreezing phase.

Moving

Unfreezing   Change   Refreezing

be considered an equilibrium state. Unfreezing, necessary to move from this equilibrium, is achieved in one of three ways:

- The driving forces, which direct behavior away from the status quo, can be increased.
- The restraining forces, which hinder movement from the existing equilibrium, can be decreased.
- The two approaches can be combined.

After unfreezing, the change itself can be implemented. However, the mere introduction of change does not ensure that it will take hold. The new situation, therefore, needs to be refrozen so that it can be sustained over time. Without this last step, the change will likely be short-lived, and employees will revert to the previous equilibrium state. The objective of refreezing, then, is to stabilize the new situation by balancing the driving and restraining forces.

Note how Lewin's three-step process treats change as a break in the organization's equilibrium state. The status quo has been disturbed, and change is necessary to establish a new equilibrium state.[48] This view might have been appropriate to the relatively calm environment that most organizations operated in when proposed by Lewin in the 1940s, but the calm waters metaphor doesn't seem appropriate now as businesses face change that seems constant and a future that seems more uncertain than ever.

The White-Water Rapids Metaphor This metaphor takes into consideration the fact that environments are both uncertain and dynamic. To understand what managing change while negotiating uninterrupted rapids might be like, imagine attending a college in which courses vary in length. When you sign up, you don't know whether a course will last for two weeks or thirty weeks. Furthermore, the instructor can end a course at any time, with no prior warning. If that isn't unsettling enough, the length of the class session changes each time—sometimes twenty minutes, other times three hours—and the time of the next class meeting is set by the instructor during the previous class. Oh, yes: The exams are unannounced; you must be ready for a test at any time. To succeed in this college, you would have to be incredibly flexible and able to respond quickly to every changing condition. Students too structured or slow on their feet would not survive.

A growing number of organizational members are accepting that their jobs are much like what students would face in such a college. The stability and predictability of calm waters do not exist. Disruptions in the status quo are not occasional and temporary, followed by a return to calm waters. Many of today's employees never get out of the rapids. They face constant change, bordering on chaos. These individuals must play a game they have never played before, governed by rules created as the game progresses.[49]

The white-water metaphor seems to be more applicable all the time, as environmental factors such as technology, the worldwide economy, consumer tastes and preferences change rapidly. Consider the issues faced by these companies:

- Kodak faces restructuring and bankruptcy as digital imaging technology nearly eliminates the need for most of their imaging products.
- Gannett, the newspaper and magazine publisher, faces restructuring as their core publishing business loses consumers and advertisers. Online sources of news and information are blamed for the decline in readership and advertising revenue.

change agent
Individual responsible for fostering the change effort and assisting employees in adapting to changes.

Just as white-water rafters deal with continuously changing water currents, organizational members facing rapid and uncertain change must adjust quickly and react properly to unexpected events. *(Source: Javier Pierini/Digital Vision/Getty Images, Inc.)*

■ Research in Motion (RIM), the maker of BlackBerry smart phones and tablet computers, encounters loss of market share and revenue as Apple iPhones and Android-based phones gain popularity with consumers who prefer the applications they provide.

Kodak, Gannett, Research in Motion, and many other organizations worldwide have struggled to keep market share and maintain their core business model as the world around them changes in rapid and unpredictable ways. Will they survive the trip through the white water?

OD Methods

Most organizational change that employees experience happens not by chance, but by a concerted effort to alter some aspect of the organization. Whatever happens—in terms of structure or technology—ultimately affects organizational members. Organization development assists organizational members with planned change.

Organization Development Organization development facilitates long-term organization-wide changes. Its focus is to constructively change attitudes and values among organizational members so that they can more readily adapt to and be more effective in achieving the new directions of the organization.[50] When they plan OD efforts, organization leaders, in essence, attempt to change the organization's culture.[51]

However, one fundamental issue of OD is its reliance on employee participation to foster an environment of open communication and trust.[52] Persons involved in OD efforts acknowledge that change can create stress for employees. Therefore, OD attempts to involve organizational members in the changes that will affect their jobs, and seeks their input about how the innovation is affecting them.

OD Techniques Any organizational activity that assists with implementing planned change can be viewed as an OD technique (see Ethical Issues in HRM). However, the more popular OD efforts in organizations rely heavily on group interactions and cooperation. These include survey feedback, process consultation, team building, and inter-group development.

ETHICAL ISSUES IN HRM

OD Intervention

Organization development interventions often produce positive change results. Interventions that rely on participation of organizational members can create openness and trust among coworkers and respect for others. Interventions can also help employees understand that the organization wants to promote risk taking and empowerment. "Living" these characteristics can lead to better organizational performance. However, a change agent involved in an OD effort imposes his or her value system on those involved in the intervention, especially when the intervention addresses coworker mistrust. The change agent may deal with this problem by bringing all affected parties together to openly discuss their perceptions of the dilemma.

Although many change agents are well versed in OD practices, sometimes they walk a fine line between success and failure. To resolve personal problems in the workplace, participants must disclose private, and often sensitive, information. An individual can refuse to divulge such information, but doing so may carry negative ramifications. For example, it could lead to lower performance appraisals, fewer pay increases, or the perception that the employee is not a team player.

On the other hand, active participation can cause employees to speak their minds. But this also carries risks. For instance, imagine that an employee questions a manager's competence. This employee fully believes the manager's behavior is detrimental to the work unit, but his or her reward for being open and honest could be retaliation from the boss. Although, at the time, the manager might appear receptive to the feedback, he or she may retaliate later. In either case—participation or not—employees could be hurt. Even though the intent was to help overcome worker mistrust, the result may be more back stabbing, more hurt feelings, and more mistrust.

Ethical Questions:

Do you think there is a risk of coworkers being too open and honest under this type of OD intervention? What do you think a change agent can do to ensure that employees' rights will be protected?

Survey feedback efforts assess employee attitudes about, and perceptions of, the change they are encountering. Employees generally respond to a set of specific questions regarding how they view organizational aspects such as decision making, leadership, communication effectiveness, and satisfaction with their jobs, coworkers, and management.[53] The data the change agent obtains helps clarify problems that employees may be facing. The change agent can consider actions to remedy the problems.

In process consultation, outside consultants help organizational members perceive, understand, and act on process events.[54] These might include, for example, workflow, informal relationships among unit members, and formal communications channels. It is important to recognize that consultants give organizational members insight into what is going on, but they are not there to solve problems. Rather, they coach managers in diagnosing interpersonal processes that need improvement. If organizational members, with consultants' help, cannot solve the problem, consultants will often help organizational members locate experts who do have the requisite knowledge (see Workplace Issues).

Organizations are made up of individuals working together to achieve goals. Because organizational members must frequently interact with peers, a primary function of OD is to help them become a team. Team building helps work groups set goals, develop positive interpersonal relationships, and clarify the role and responsibilities of each team member. There may be no need to address each area because the group may be in agreement and understand what is expected of it. Team building's primary focus is to increase each member's trust and openness toward one another.[55]

Whereas team building focuses on helping a work group become more cohesive, **intergroup development** attempts to achieve cohesion among different work groups. That is, intergroup development attempts to change attitudes, stereotypes, and perceptions that one group may have about another group. Doing so can build better coordination among the various groups.

The Learning Organization

The concept of a **learning organization** describes a significant organizational mindset or philosophy. A learning organization has the capacity to continuously adapt and change because all members take an active role in identifying and resolving work-related issues.[56] In a learning organization, employees practice knowledge management by continually acquiring and sharing new knowledge and willingly applying that knowledge to making decisions or performing their work.

In a learning organization, it's critical for members to share information and collaborate on work activities throughout the entire organization—across different functional specialties and even at different organizational levels. Employees are free to work together and collaborate in completing the organization's work the best way they can, and in the process, to learn from each other. This need to collaborate also tends to make teams an important feature of a learning organization. Employees work on activities in teams and make decisions about doing their work or resolving issues. Empowered employees and teams have little need for "bosses" to direct and control them. Instead, traditional managers serve as facilitators, supporters, and advocates for employee teams.

Learning can't take place without information. For a learning organization to learn, information must be shared among members; that is, organizational employees must engage in knowledge management. This means sharing information openly, in a timely manner, and as accurately as possible. The learning organization environment is conducive to open communication and extensive information sharing.

Leadership plays an important role as an organization moves toward become a learning organization. One of the most important leadership functions is to facilitate the creation of a shared vision for the organization's future, and to keep organizational members working toward that vision. In addition, leaders should support and encourage the collaborative environment critical to learning. Without strong and committed leadership

survey feedback
Assessment of employees' perceptions and attitudes regarding their jobs and organization.

> One of the fundamental issues behind OD is the need to foster an environment of communication and trust.

intergroup development
Helping members of various groups become a cohesive team.

learning organization
An organization that values continued learning and believes a competitive advantage can be derived from it.

throughout the organization, maintaining a learning organization would be extremely difficult.

Finally, the organizational culture is an important aspect of being a learning organization. A learning organization's culture is one in which everyone agrees on a shared vision and recognizes the inherent interrelationships among the organization's processes, activities, functions, and external environment. There is a strong sense of community, caring for each other, and trust. In a learning organization, employees feel free to openly communicate, share, experiment, and learn without fear of criticism or punishment. If you delve deeply into many of the learning organization's characteristics you may notice something startling: Many of these elements are parts of a fully functioning, effective HRM system in an organization.

Evaluating Training and Development Effectiveness

Any training or development implemented in an organizational effort must be cost-effective. The benefits gained must outweigh the costs of the learning experience. It is not enough to merely assume that any training an organization offers is effective; we must develop substantive data to determine whether the training effort is achieving its goals. Did the training correct the deficiencies in skills, knowledge, or attitudes management assessed as needing attention? Note, too, that training and development programs are expensive—in the billions of dollars annually in the United States alone. The costs incurred justify evaluating the effectiveness.

Evaluating Training

How will we determine if a training program is effective? This is easier if some output can be measured, such as an increase or decrease in costs, sales, production, employee turnover, or revenue. In these cases, HR can calculate a return on the investment (ROI) by determining the benefit of the training and dividing it by the training expense. For example, after training, a delivery driver is able to make five additional deliveries each day. Each of those deliveries represents $10 of the driver's time, so the benefit to the employer is $50 per day for each driver trained. Divide the benefit of the training by the cost of training, and we can determine the ROI of the training.

What if we're training managers on better communication skills or teaching English as a second language to employees? That's a little more difficult to evaluate. A different approach to determining the effectiveness of training is called the **Kirkpatrick's model**. This is a four-level approach that works well in determining the value of managerial training and any training that is difficult to assess in terms of ROI.

Level one measures the reactions of the participants toward the training and answers questions about whether the participants liked the training; felt they achieved their learning goals; how much they liked the trainers; and any suggestions they have for improving the training.

Level two measures how much the participants learned. This could be accomplished by pre- and post-testing the participants or by evaluating the participants against a control group that has not been trained.

Level three measures whether the training actually changes the employee's behavior when he or she returns to the job. This might be evaluated by the participants, supervisors, or trainer.

Level four measures whether the training benefited the employer or not. This could be done by determining ROI as we have above, or by evaluating a behavior against another standard, such as a benchmark.

Surprisingly, research indicates that nearly half of all training programs are not measured against any substantive outcome, such as employee retention, satisfaction,

Kirkpatrick's model
Evaluates the benefits of training for skills that are hard to quantify, such as attitudes and behaviors.

or productivity.[57] It would be ideal if all companies could boast the returns on investments in training that The Cheesecake Factory does. Their employee turnover rate is consistently below the industry average, and customer satisfaction rates and repeat visits are high.[58] Such a claim, however, is valueless unless training is properly evaluated.

The following approach for evaluating training programs can be generalized across organizations. Several managers, representatives from HRM, and a group of workers who have recently completed a training program are asked for their opinions. If the comments are generally positive, the program may receive a favorable evaluation and it will continue until someone decides, for whatever reason, it should be eliminated or replaced.

The reactions of participants or managers, though easy to acquire, are the least valid. Their opinions are heavily influenced by factors such as level of difficulty, entertainment value, or the personality characteristics of the instructor, all of which may have little to do with the training's effectiveness. Trainees' reactions to the training may, in fact, provide feedback on how worthwhile the participants viewed the training.[59]

Beyond general reactions, however, training must also be evaluated in terms of how much the participants learned, how well they use their new skills on the job, positive changes in behavior, and whether the training program achieved its desired results including reduced turnover, increased customer service, etc.[60]

Performance-Based Evaluation Measures

We'll explore three popular methods of evaluating training programs. These are the post-training performance method, the pre–post-training performance method, and the pre–post-training performance with control group method.

Post-Training Performance Method The first approach is the **post-training performance method**. Participants' performance is measured after attending a training program to determine if behavioral changes have been made. For example, assume we provide a week-long seminar for HRM recruiters on structured interviewing techniques. We follow up one month later with each participant to see if, in fact, attendees use the techniques addressed in the program, and how. If changes did occur, we may attribute them to the training, but we cannot emphatically state that the change in behavior is directly related to the training. Other factors, such as reading a current HRM journal or attending a local Society of Human Resource Management presentation, may have also influenced the change. Accordingly, the post-training performance method may overstate training benefits.

post-training performance method
Evaluating training programs based on how well employees can perform their jobs after training.

Pre–Post-Training Performance Method In the **pre–post-training performance method**, each participant is evaluated prior to training and rated on actual job performance. After instruction—of which the evaluator has been kept unaware—is completed, the employee is reevaluated. As with the post-training performance method, the increase is assumed to be attributable to the instruction. However, in contrast to the post-training performance method, the pre–post-training performance method deals directly with job behavior.

pre–post-training performance method
Evaluating training programs based on the difference in performance before and after training.

Pre–Post-Training Performance with Control Group Method The most sophisticated evaluative approach is the **pre–post-training performance with control group method**. Two groups are established and evaluated on actual job performance. Members of the control group work on the job but do not undergo instruction; the experimental group does receive instruction. At the conclusion of training, the two groups are reevaluated. If the training is really effective, the experimental group's performance will not only have improved but will be substantially better than the control group. This approach attempts to correct for factors, other than the instruction program, that influence job performance.

pre–post-training performance with control group method
Evaluating training by comparing pre- and post-training results with individuals.

Of the numerous methods for evaluating training and development programs, these three appear to be the most widely recognized. Furthermore, the latter two methods are preferred because they provide a stronger measure of behavioral change directly attributable to the training effort.

International Training and Development Issues

Important components of international human resource management include both cross-cultural training and a clear understanding of the overseas assignment as part of a manager's development.[61]

Cross-Cultural Training

Cross-cultural training is necessary for expatriate managers and their families before, during, and after foreign assignments.[62] It is crucial to remember that when the expatriates arrive, they are the foreigners, not the host population. Before the employee and family relocate to the overseas post, they need to absorb as much cultural and practical background as possible. Language training is essential for everyone in the family.

Although English is the dominant business language worldwide, relying on English puts the expatriate at a disadvantage. The expatriate will be unable to read local trade journals and newspapers, which contain useful business information, and must rely on translators, which slow down discussions and possibly create misunderstandings. Even if an expatriate manager is not fluent, a willingness to try communicating in the local language makes a good impression on the business community—unlike the insistence that all conversation be in English. Foreign-language proficiency is also vital for family members to establish a social network and accomplish the everyday tasks of maintaining a household. Americans may be able to go to the produce market and point at what they recognize on display, but if the shop has unfamiliar meats or vegetables, it helps to be able to ask what each item is, and it's even better to understand the answers!

Cross-cultural training is, of course, much more than language training. It should provide an appreciation of the new culture, including details of its history and folklore, economy, politics (both internal and its relations with the United States), religion, social climate, and business practices.[63] It is easy to recognize that religion is highly important in daily life in the Middle East, but knowledge of the region's history and an understanding of the specific practices and beliefs is important to avoid in advertently insulting business associates or social contacts.

All this training can be carried out through a variety of techniques. Language skills are often provided through classes and recordings, whereas cultural training utilizes many different tools. Lectures, books, videos, and movies are useful for background information, but cultural sensitivity is more often taught through role playing, simulations, and meetings with former international assignees and natives of the countries now living in the United States.

After the overseas assignment has ended and the employee has returned, more training is required for the entire family. All family members must reacclimate to life in the United States. The family faces changes with their extended family, friends, and even local events that have occurred in their absence. Teenagers find reentry particularly difficult, as they may be more sophisticated and mature than their local and less traveled friends. The employee also must adjust to organizational changes, including the inevitable promotions, transfers, and resignations that have taken place during his or her absence. Returnees are anxious to know where they fit in, or if they should change their career path.

Development

The current global business environment makes the overseas assignment a vital component in developing top-level executives. Many American managers return with broader experiences, having been relatively independent of headquarters. Particularly, mid-level managers experience greater responsibilities than others at their level and frequently acquire greater sensitivity and flexibility to alternative ways of doing things.

It is vital for the organization to make the overseas assignment part of a career development program.[64] In the absence of such a developmental program, two negative consequences often occur. First, the recently returned manager who is largely ignored or underutilized becomes frustrated and leaves the organization. This is extremely costly, as the company has lost the investment in developing this individual and the talent that will likely be recruited by a competitor, either at home or overseas.

Second, when overseas returnees are regularly underutilized or leave out of frustration, other potential expatriates become reluctant to accept overseas posts, inhibiting the organization's staffing ability. When the overseas assignment is completed, the organization has four basic options. First, the expatriate may be assigned to a domestic position, beginning the repatriation process. Hopefully, this new assignment will build on some of the newly acquired skills and perspectives. Second, the return may be temporary, with the goal of preparing for another overseas assignment. This might be the case where a manager has successfully opened a new sales territory and is being asked to repeat that success in another region. Third, the expatriate may seek retirement, either in the United States or in the country in which she or he spent the past few years. Finally, employment may be terminated, either because the organization has no suitable openings or because the individual has found opportunities elsewhere.

All of these options involve substantial expenses or a loss in human investment. A well-thought-out and organized program of employee development can make overseas assignments a part of the comprehensive international human resource management program.

Summary

(This summary relates to the Learning Outcomes identified on page 192.) After having read this chapter, you can

1. **Define *socialization*.** Socialization is a process of adaptation. Organization-entry socialization refers to the adaptation that takes place when an individual passes from outside the organization to the role of an inside member.

2. **Identify the three stages of employee socialization.** The three stages of employee socialization are the prearrival, the encounter, and the metamorphosis stages.

3. **Identify the key personnel involved in orientation.** The key people in orientation are the CEO and HRM representatives. The CEO welcomes the new employees, reaffirms their choice of joining the company, and discusses the organization's goals and objectives while conveying information about the organization's culture. Each function in HRM has a specific role in orientation to discuss what employee services they can offer in the future.

4. **Describe the purpose of the employee handbook and explain what information should be included in the handbook.** Handbooks serve as a source of information about company culture, policies, rules, and benefits.

5. **Explain why employee training is important.** Employee training has become increasingly important as jobs have become more sophisticated and influenced by technological and corporate changes.

6. **Define** *training.* Training is a learning experience that seeks a relatively permanent change in individuals that will improve their ability to perform on the job.

7. **Describe how training needs evolve.** An organization's training needs will evolve by seeking answers to these questions: (a) What are the organization's goals? (b) What tasks must be completed to achieve these goals? (c) What behaviors are necessary for each job incumbent to complete his or her assigned tasks? and (d) What deficiencies, if any, do incumbents have in the skills, knowledge, or attitudes required to perform the necessary behaviors?

8. **Discuss the term** *organizational development* **and the role of the change agent.** Organization development is the process of effecting change in the organization. This change is facilitated through the efforts of a change agent.

9. **Explain the term** *learning organization.* A learning organization continuously adapts and changes because all members take an active role in identifying and resolving work-related issues. In a learning organization, employees practice knowledge management by continually acquiring and sharing new knowledge, which they willingly apply.

10. **Describe the methods and criteria involved in evaluating training programs.** Training programs can be evaluated by post-training performance, pre–post- training performance, or pre–post-training performance with control group methods. The evaluation focuses on trainee reaction, what learning took place, and how appropriate the training was to the job.

11. **Explain issues critical to international training and development.** International issues in training and development include cross-cultural training, language training, and economic-issues training.

Demonstrating Comprehension

QUESTIONS FOR REVIEW

1. How can a socialization process benefit the organization and the employee?
2. What are the similarities and differences between training and development?
3. Describe the role HRM plays in orientation.
4. What are the purposes of the employee handbook?
5. What kinds of signals can warn a manager that employee training may be necessary?
6. Why is evaluation of training effectiveness necessary?
7. What types of training are critical for employees embarking on an overseas assignment?
8. How do the Calm Waters and White Water Rapids metaphors differ in their views of change?
9. How is organizational culture communicated to new employees?

Key Terms

apprenticeships	job rotation	post-training performance method
change agent	Kirkpatrick's model	prearrival stage
classroom lectures	learning organization	pre–post-training performance method
employee development	metamorphosis stage	pre–post-training performance with
employee handbook	multimedia learning	control group
employee training	on-the-job training	simulations
encounter stage	organization culture	socialization or onboarding
intergroup development	organization development (OD)	survey feedback
internship	orientation	vestibule training

HRM Workshop

Linking Concepts to Practice   DISCUSSION QUESTIONS

1. "Proper selection is a substitute for socialization." Do you agree or disagree with this statement? Explain.
2. Describe what a socialization program might look like if management desired employees who were innovative and individualistic.
3. Training programs are frequently the first items eliminated when management wants to cut costs. Why do you believe this occurs?
4. Explain the effects a learning organization may have on employees in today's organizations. What are the HRM implications of these effects?

Making A Difference   SERVICE LEARNING PROJECTS

The onboarding process may be even more important for new volunteers than for new employees. Without knowledge that they have an important role in accomplishing a worthwhile task, volunteers may not show up or stay. Many opportunities exist to volunteer in this process, including:

- Develop an onboarding process to help with new volunteer orientation and training at a nonprofit organization such as Goodwill or the Salvation Army.
- Volunteer to assist with new student orientation at your college.
- Explore the learning process by volunteering to help in local schools.

As you put your service learning experience together, keep a journal of your activities, the time you spend, contact information for people you work with, and your thoughts about the process. When you're finished, make a presentation to your class about the experience and what you learned. What concepts from Chapter 8 were you able to apply?

Developing Diagnostic and Analytical Skills

Case Application 8-A: THE UNDERRATED CHECKLIST: FIVE STEPS TO SAVE LIVES

Does the idea of having to go through a checklist in your job sound a little demeaning? That type of thinking is why Dr. Peter Pronovost of Johns Hopkins University School of Medicine ran into opposition when he proposed a five-step checklist that would not only save money, but also save lives.

In the United States, hospital-acquired infections affect 1 in 10 patients, killing 90,000 of them and costing as much as $11 billion each year.[65] Many of those infections are acquired when an IV line delivering medication becomes infected. Dr. Pronovost's checklist is simple and straightforward, and includes steps such as doctors and nurses washing their hands before inserting an IV, and cleaning the patient's skin with antiseptic at the point of the insertion. When Michigan hospitals put the checklist into practice, they not only saved over $175 million in eighteen months because they didn't have to treat infections, but they also saved nearly 1,500 lives!

Such impressive evidence would seem to convert even the toughest critics of checklists, but the hospitals found the same truth that many trainers face: employees don't always comply with rules that are for their own good, or for the good of others. They need to be convinced. It turns out that doctors are just as stubborn as production employees who refuse to wear safety goggles or a hard hat.

Dr. Pronovost found that doctors didn't like being told what to do. They especially resented being reminded of the checklist by the nurses who were put in charge of managing the checklists. The organizational culture of the hospitals, including the roles of doctors and nurses, got in the way of patient safety. Dr. Pronovost learned to overcome the resistance by bringing both doctors and nurses together in training and appealing to their common concern for patient health. He asked, "Would you ever intentionally allow a patient's health to be harmed in your presence?" They'd say, "Of course not." Then he would hit them with, "Then how can you see someone not washing their hands and let them get away with it?"[66]

Saving lives, saving money. It's all in the training.

Questions:

1. How can HR professionals overcome resistance to training?
2. What method should hospitals use to evaluate IV checklist training?
3. Develop a checklist that would make a process more efficient or safe for your employer or college.
4. What is the best way to train an employee to use your checklist? How would you evaluate your training?

Case Application 8-B: DELIVERING AT UPS

When it comes to training, UPS seems to have thought of everything. Employees are taught efficient procedures for safe driving, how to lift and carry packages, knock on doors, and even how to carry the keys to the big brown delivery vans. Procedures for how to effectively manage people, however, are not as clear-cut. UPS attempted to fix that with their Community Internship Program (CIP) that helps managers strengthen management skills and develop greater sensitivity toward UPS staff and customers.

UPS founder, James Casey, realized that many of the managers in his organization hadn't experienced and didn't really understand poverty and inequality. This sheltered perspective made it more difficult for these managers to deal with diversity in their workforce. Casey believed that if UPS employees were going to be most effective, they had to learn about and live with societal elements that were foreign to most of them. That did not mean, however, relaxing the rigid rules of UPS. Rather, it meant fitting the rigid rules to the diversity of the organization.[67]

The month-long program is designed to help managers understand the increasingly complex needs of a diverse workforce and customer base.[68] CIP builds on the understanding between managers and entry-level employees who are often minorities from low-income communities in New York City; Chicago; Chattanooga, Tennessee; McAllen, Texas; or San Francisco. During the thirty-day internship, UPS managers live among the area's poorest residents. They serve meals to the homeless, build homes, counsel recovering addicts, fix bikes in a community center, tutor individuals in prison, or aid migrant farmers. They spend time in the community attempting to find workable solutions to transportation, housing, education, or healthcare problems.

But most of all, the CIP was designed to develop the UPS manager's ability to listen and be empathetic toward their employees. For example, manager Mark Colvard recalled a situation in which he had to make a difficult decision. One of his drivers needed some time off from work to care for an ill family member. Under the rules that applied to this worker, he was not eligible for the leave. But Colvard made the decision to give the employee some time off—even though other drivers had an issue with this decision. But Colvard never second-guessed what he did. Even though Colvard took some flack over the two weeks the driver was out, the driver returned to work very appreciative of what Colvard had done. And Colvard retained a valuable employee.

What the CIP program does, in essence, is develop another aspect of UPS managers. Although the company's process and procedure training was thorough, UPS leaders came to realize that managers also must be sensitive to needs of today's workers. By developing employees in this manner, UPS is reinforcing a culture of what they believe is important, and provides its employees with the necessary tools to walk the walk. CIP coordinators admit they have no quantitative way to measure the program's success, but they point to retention numbers and personal contributions as proof that the system works. As one UPS manager stated, the program "made me a better person and a better manager. I've never been exposed to anything like it in my life." That's hard to put a price tag on.[69]

Questions:

1. How does the CIP at UPS foster a positive and inclusive culture in the organization?
2. What role can human resources play in ensuring success for this internship program?
3. What criteria would you use to determine who should participate in the program?
4. Explain how you would evaluate the CIP program to demonstrate that it's beneficial to the manager and the organization using Kirkpatrick's model or another method of evaluation.

Working with a Team   ORIENTING EMPLOYEES

1. Identify and then contact a human resource manager at your college or university, employer, a nonprofit organization, or a local company. Ask if you may observe part or all of an upcoming orientation or training program as part of a class assignment.
2. Summarize your orientation experience in a one- or two-page report, and then share your experience with your class or team.
3. What guidelines, policies, or standards did your organization practice regarding orientation?
4. Discuss your responses with your team. What similarities or differences did you find?

Learning an HRM Skill   COACHING EMPLOYEES

About the skill: Effective managers are increasingly described as coaches rather than bosses. Just like coaches, they're expected to provide instruction, guidance, advice, and encouragement to help team members improve their job performance.

Steps in the Coaching Skill

1. *Analyze ways to improve the team's performance and capabilities.* A coach looks for opportunities for team members to expand their capabilities and improve performance. We recommend the following coaching behaviors: Observe your team members' behavior on a day-to-day basis. Ask questions of them: Why do you do a task this way? Can it be improved? What other approaches might work? Show genuine interest in team members as individuals, not merely as employees. Respect them individually. Listen to each employee.

2. ***Create a supportive climate.*** It's the coach's responsibility to reduce barriers to development and to facilitate a climate that encourages personal performance improvement. Create a climate that contributes to a free and open exchange of ideas. Offer help and assistance. Give guidance and advice when asked. Encourage your team. Be positive and upbeat. Don't use threats. Ask, "What did we learn from this that can help us in the future?" Reduce obstacles. Assure team members that you value their contribution to the team's goals. Take personal responsibility for the outcome, but don't rob team members of their full responsibility. Validate the team members' efforts when they succeed. Point to what was missing when they fail. Never blame team members for poor results.

3. ***Influence team members to change their behavior.*** The ultimate test of coaching effectiveness is whether an employee's performance improves. You must encourage ongoing growth and development. Recognize and reward small improvements and treat coaching as a way of helping employees continually work toward improvement. Use a collaborative style by allowing team members to participate in identifying and choosing improvement ideas. Break difficult tasks down into simpler ones. Model the qualities you expect from your team. If you want openness, dedication, commitment, and responsibility from your team members, you must demonstrate these qualities yourself.

Enhancing Your Communication Skills

1. Search YouTube for short videos that illustrate or explain the culture of an organization. Prepare a ten-minute presentation that includes the video, an explanation of the culture, and how you would prepare a new employee for the culture.

2. Do an Internet search of articles on learning organizations. Summarize in a two- to three-page article how organizations become learning organizations and what benefits a learning organization provides for a company.

3. Write a two-page discussion of training program development costs. Discuss how companies may find ways to make training programs more cost effective.

4. Create a three- to five-minute presentation with at least three presentation slides that describes the type of organization culture in which you would prefer to work. In your presentation, describe how you anticipate locating such an organization with the type of preferred culture you've identified.

(Source: Ariel Skelley/Blend Images/Alamy Limited)

LEARNING OUTCOMES

After reading this chapter, you will be able to

1. Explain who is responsible for managing careers

2. Describe the term *career*.

3. Discuss the focus of careers for both organizations and individuals.

4. Describe how career development and employee development differ.

5. Explain why career development is valuable to organizations.

6. Identify the five traditional stages involved in a career.

7. List the Holland vocational preferences.

8. Describe the implications of personality typologies and jobs.

9. Identify several suggestions that you can use to manage your career more effectively.

Managing Careers

9

The ad read like an EEO nightmare, advertising "job openings for mothers of schoolchildren," and backed it up by offering part-time hours and summers off. Rather than being a current example of gender and age discrimination, it was quite the opposite. It was an ad for the Principal Financial Group from 1966, indicating an early interest in equal career opportunities for women.

Former Principal Financial Group CEO Barry Griswell stated, "It's been important to me to know that women have equal pay, equal access—all of the things that men have." His efforts have been so successful that the company boasts recognition as one of the Best Places to Work by the National Association of Female Executives, *Working Mother* magazine, *Fortune, Latina Style* magazine, and AARP. How does the company manage to earn so many awards? They do it by developing programs that support employees through the more vulnerable points in the employee's career cycle, hoping that by helping employees to manage their career, they'll be more likely to stay.

Examples include:

- Eight hours of paid time off to volunteer at a non-profit agency of the employee's choice, including their church or child's school.
- "No meeting Fridays" to allow employees to catch up on work, get organized, and decompress.
- Working Caregiver Leave, allowing employees to return to their job on a part-time schedule with full-time benefits for twelve weeks to care for a new baby or other loved one needing care after Family Medical Leave is exhausted.
- "Happy Returns"—a partnership with Manpower that allows retirees to work part-time while retaining retirement benefits.
- Offering older workers opportunities to work for several months in a nonprofit organization or overseas assignment.
- Leadership Development programs to employees over the age of fifty.

The company has developed a loyal and devoted employee base that reflects diversity in age, culture, ethnicity, and background on every level. Over two-thirds of the employees are women, and five of the eleven board members are women. Promotions are based on ability, often offered when an employee is working part-time, as was the case with Ellen Lamale, the company's chief actuary. Valarie Vest, a regional client service director was offered her promotion midway through her maternity leave. The programs have not only resulted in retention of employees at times when they were considering changes of careers or employers, they've also proven to be very profitable to the company.

Looking Ahead

Policies at Principal Financial Group clearly assist employees in managing their careers. In what ways does Principal benefit?

Introduction

Career development is important to us all, but the definition of career success takes on different meanings for just about everyone. Maybe you're one of the many who has had difficulties achieving your career goals. This reflects the new and unexpected complexities managers now confront in their efforts to mobilize and manage their employees. The historical beliefs that every employee will jump at the chance for a promotion, that competent people will somehow emerge within the organization to fill vacancies, and that a valuable employee will always be a valuable employee, are no longer true. Lifestyles, too, are changing. Organizations are increasingly aware of employees' different needs and aspirations. In order to have competent and motivated people to fill the organization's future needs, HRM representatives should be concerned with matching employee career needs with the organization's requirements.

It's important to note that although career development has been an important topic in HRM-related courses for several decades, there have been some drastic changes since the Principal Financial Group advertised "mother's hours" back in 1966. Downsizing, restructuring, work process engineering, globalization, contingent workers, and so forth have drawn us to one significant conclusion about managing careers: Although employers like the Principal Financial Group offer many opportunities for personal development, you, the individual, are responsible for your career.

> You, not the organization, are responsible for managing your career!

Workers cannot depend on employers to take responsibility for managing their careers. The environment of business is simply too unpredictable. In a recent example, the career plans of thousands of Bank of America employees vanished when the company announced that they would reduce their payroll by as many as 30,000 employees.[1] You must be prepared to continue to gain the skills necessary to advance your career, especially in turbulent economic times.

What, if any, responsibility does the organization have for career development in an unpredictable global economy? The organization's obligation is to build employee self-reliance and help employees maintain their marketability through continual learning.[2] The essence of a contemporary career development program is providing support so employees can continually add to their skills, abilities, and knowledge. This support includes:

- *Clearly communicating the organization's goals and future strategies.* When people know where the organization is headed, they're better able to develop a personal plan to share in that future.
- *Creating growth opportunities.* Employees should have opportunities for new, interesting, and professionally challenging work experiences.
- *Offering financial assistance.* The organization should offer tuition reimbursement to help employees keep current.
- *Providing the time for employees to learn.* Organizations should be generous in providing paid time off from work for off-the-job training. Additionally, workloads should not be so demanding that they preclude employees from having the time to develop new skills, abilities, and knowledge.

In this chapter we'll review some of the basics of career development, and HRM's current role in offering assistance. Throughout the chapter, remember that it's up to you to manage your career. If you don't, chances are no one else will!

What Is a Career?

career
The sequence of employment positions that a person has held over his or her life.

The term **career** has numerous meanings. In popular usage it can mean advancement ("He's moving up in his career"), a profession ("She's chosen a career in medicine"), or stability over time (career in the military).[3] For our purposes, we define career as "the pattern of work-related experiences that span the course of a person's life."[4] Using this definition, it is apparent that we all have or will have careers. The concept is as relevant to unskilled laborers as it is to engineers and physicians. For our purposes, therefore, any work, paid or unpaid, pursued over an extended time, can constitute a career. In addition to formal job work, careers can include schoolwork, homemaking, or volunteer work. Furthermore, career success is defined not only objectively, in terms of promotion, but also subjectively, in terms of satisfaction.

Individual versus Organizational Perspective

The study of careers takes on a different orientation depending on whether it is viewed from the perspective of the organization or of the individual. A key question in career development, then, is, "With whose interests are we concerned?" From an organizational or HRM viewpoint, career development involves tracking career paths and developing career ladders.[5] HRM seeks to direct information and monitor the progress of special groups of employees, and to ensure that capable professional, managerial, and technical talent will be available to meet the organization's needs. Career development from the organization's perspective is also called organizational career planning.

In contrast, individual career development, or career planning, focuses on assisting individuals to identify their major goals and how to achieve them. Note that this focuses entirely on the individual and includes his or her life outside the organization, as well as inside. Therefore, while organizational career development looks at individuals filling the needs of the organization, individual career development addresses each individual's personal work career and other lifestyle issues. For instance, an excellent employee, assisted in better understanding his or her needs and aspirations through interest inventories, life-planning analysis, and counseling, may even decide to leave the organization if it becomes apparent that career aspirations can be best achieved outside the employing organization. Both individual and organizational career approaches have value. However, because the primary focus of HRM is the organization's interest in careers, we will primarily emphasize this area. At the end of the chapter we will take a special look at how you can better manage your career.

Career Development versus Employee Development

Given our discussions in Chapter 8 on employee development, you may be wondering what, if any, differences there are between career development and employee development. These topics have a common element, but they have one distinct difference—the time frame.

Career development looks at the long-term career effectiveness and success of organizational personnel. By contrast, the kinds of development discussed in Chapter 8 focused on work effectiveness or performance in immediate or intermediate time frames. These two concepts are closely linked; employee training and development should be compatible with an individual's career development in the organization. But a successful career program, in attempting to match individual abilities and aspirations with the needs of the organization, should develop people for the long-term needs of the organization and address the dynamic changes that will take place over time.

Career Development: Value for the Organization

Assuming that an organization already provides extensive employee development programs, why should it need to consider a career development program as well? A long-term career focus should increase the organization's effectiveness in managing its human resources. More specifically, several positive results can accrue from a well-designed career development program. We'll examine them below.

Needed Talent Will Be Available Career development efforts are consistent with, and a natural extension of, strategic and employment planning. Changing staff requirements over the intermediate and long term should be identified when the company sets long-term goals and objectives. Working with individual employees to help them align their needs and aspirations with those of the organization will increase the probability that the right people will be available to meet the organization's changing staffing requirements.

The Organization's Ability to Attract and Retain Talented Employees Improves
Outstanding employees will always be scarce, and competition to secure their services
considerable. Such individuals may prefer employers who demonstrate a concern for
employees' futures and personal interests. These people may exhibit greater loyalty and
commitment to an organization that offers career advice.[6] Importantly, career development appears to be a natural response to the rising concern by employees for the quality
of work life and personal life planning. A survey of college students and recent graduates
by Manpower subsidiary Right Management found that they would be more likely to stay
put at an organization that offered the ability to grow from within, a workplace that offers
flexibility, and a culture where there is camaraderie and a good work/life balance.[7]

**Minorities and Women Have Comparable Opportunities for Growth and
Development** As discussed in previous chapters, equal employment opportunity legislation and affirmative action programs have demanded that minority groups and women
receive opportunities for growth and development that will prepare them for greater
responsibilities within the organization. The fair employment movement has served as a
catalyst to career development programs targeted for these groups. Legislation, such as
the Lilly Ledbetter Fair Pay Act of 2009, offers additional support for equality in the workplace. Furthermore, courts frequently look at an organization's career development
efforts with these groups when ruling on discrimination suits.

Reduced Employee Frustration Although the workforce educational level has risen,
so, too, have occupational aspirations. However, as periods of economic stagnation
increase organizations' efforts to reduce costs, they also reduce opportunities. This has
increased frustration in employees who often see a significant disparity between aspirations and actual opportunities. When organizations downsize to cut costs, employee
career paths, career tracks, and career ladders often collapse. Career counseling can produce realistic, rather than raised, employee expectations.

Enhanced Cultural Diversity The workforce in
the next decade will continue to reflect a more varied combination of race, nationality, gender, and
values in the organization. Effective organizational
career development provides access to all levels of
the organization for more employees. Extended
career opportunities make cultural diversity, and
the appreciation of it, an organizational reality.

Organizational Goodwill If employees think
their employing organizations care about their
long-term well-being, they tend to respond in
kind by projecting positive images of the organization into other areas of their lives (for example,
through volunteer work in the community). For
instance, employees at Principal Financial Group,
discussed in the chapter opener, are encouraged
to use eight hours of paid time off each year to
volunteer at a local nonprofit organization,
including their church or their child's school.
Employees who are happy with this arrangement
spread the word, making them effective recruiters for the company. One young mother who left
a teaching career to work for Principal said, "Friends who are working moms told me
about it. I didn't even look at positions at another company."[8]

Principal Financial Group
encourages employees to volunteer in their community with paid
time off. Employees make positive contributions to the community, promoting goodwill for the
company throughout the area.
(Source: Zoran Milich/Masterfile)

Career Development: Value for the Individual

Effective career development is also important for the individual. In fact, as we've previously mentioned, it is more important today than ever. Changing definitions of careers

and success have expanded the value of individual career development programs. Career success may no longer be measured merely by an employee's income or hierarchical level in an organization. It may now include using one's skills and abilities to face expanded challenges, or having greater responsibilities and increased autonomy in one's chosen profession. Employees are increasingly wanting more than just a salary and security from their jobs. They want intrinsic career development, or "psychic income," too. They want interesting and meaningful work, such as that derived from a sense of being the architect of one's own career.

Careers are both external and internal. The **external career** involves properties or qualities of an occupation or an organization.[9] For example, think of a career in business as a person's sequence of jobs or positions: undergraduate degree in business; sales representative for a construction supply house; graduate training in business; district manager in a do-it-yourself hardware chain; president of a small housing inspection and appraisal firm; retirement. External careers may also be characterized by career ladders within a particular organization (employment recruiter, employment manager, HRM director, vice president HRM).

> **external career**
> Attributes related to an occupation's properties or qualities.

The individual career encompasses a variety of individual aspects or themes: accumulation of external symbols of success or advancement (bigger office with each promotion); threshold definition of occupational types (that is, physicians have careers, dogcatchers have jobs); long-term commitment to a particular occupational field (such as a career soldier or teacher); a series of work-related positions; and work-related attitudes and behaviors.[10]

Careers are the pattern of work-related experiences that span the course of a person's life, but we must understand that both personal relationships and family concerns are also of intrinsic value to employees. You've probably learned in your management studies that individual motives are unique and complex. This means that what we value in a career is equally unique and complex. Career success can therefore be defined by internal personal, subjective value judgments as well as objective, external elements such as titles and income.

For example, if after five years at the same company you are promoted, and Chris, a colleague hired the same day you were for the same type of job, has not yet been promoted, you may view yourself as more successful than Chris, in both objective and external terms. The external definition also states that a certified public accountant is more successful than an animal control worker. However, if you consider the subjective, internal valuation of success, the story may be different. An animal control worker who defines his job as protecting children and others in the community from danger, who goes home proud at night because he has successfully and compassionately captured stray dogs that day, is successful in his career. Compare that to a CPA who works only to buy a new sports car so she can escape from the drudgery of her day-to-day office life of dealing with clients, accounting forms, and automated systems. Is she more or less successful than the dogcatcher?

This differentiation of internal from external is important to the manager who wants to motivate employees. Different employees may respond to different motivational tools. For instance, Jayden is working for you as a consultant, looking to earn enough money to purchase a time-share in a condo in Florida. Isabella, your newest software developer, joined the company with the expectation that within four years she will have obtained a master's degree and be in a supervisory position in the company. Would they respond equally to the opportunity to be trained in interpersonal skills? Would both of them be as likely to accept (or reject) a transfer to another city? Probably not, because they have different motivations. Thus, we can say that internal and external career events may be parallel but result in different outcomes. We have displayed these events in Exhibit 9-1, which discusses them in the context of career stages, the topic discussed in the next section.

Mentoring and Coaching

It has become increasingly clear over the years that employees who aspire to higher management levels in organizations often need the assistance and advocacy of someone

Exhibit 9-1
Internal and External Events and Career Stages

Not everyone will experience these traditional career stages in the same sequence. Many will find themselves starting over due to layoffs or career changes.

Stage	External Event	Internal Event
Exploration	Advice and examples of relatives, teachers, friends, and coaches	Development of self-image, what one might be, what sort of work would be interesting
	Actual successes and failures in school, sport, and hobbies	Self-assessment of own talents and limitations Development of ambitions, goals, motives, dreams
	Actual choice of educational path—vocational school, college major, professional school	Tentative choices and commitments, changes
Establishment	Explicit search for a job	Shock of entering the "real world"
	Acceptance of a job Induction and orientation	Insecurity around new tasks of interviewing, applying, being tested, being turned down
	Assignment to further training or first job Acquiring visible job and organizational	Making a real choice: to take a job or not, which job; first commitment
	membership trappings (ID card, parking sticker, uniform, organizational manual)	Fear of being tested for the first time under real conditions and not measuring up
	First job assignment, meeting the boss and co-workers	Reality shock—what the work is really like, doing the "dirty work"
	Learning period, indoctrination period of full performance—"doing the job"	Forming a career strategy, how to make it—working hard, finding mentors, conforming to an organization, making a contribution This is real, what one is doing matters
		Feeling of success or failure—going uphill, either challenging or exhausting
		Decision to leave organization if outlook isn't positive
		Feeling of being accepted fully by the organization, having made it—satisfaction of seeing "my project"
Mid-Career	Leveling off, transfer, and/or promotion Entering a period of maximum productivity	Period of settling in or new ambitions based on self-assessment
	Becoming more of a teacher/mentor than a learner	More feeling of security, relaxation, but danger of leveling off and stagnation
	Explicit signs from boss and co-workers that one's progress has plateaued	Threat from younger, better trained, more energetic, and ambitious persons—"Am I too old for my job?"
		Thoughts of new possibilities and challenges—"What do I really want to do?"
		Working through mid-life crisis toward greater acceptance of oneself and others
		"Is it time to give up on my dreams? Should I settle for what I have?"
Late Career	Job assignments drawing primarily on maturity of judgment	Psychological preparation for retirement Deceleration in momentum
	More jobs involving teaching others	Finding new sources of self-improvement off the job, new sources of job satisfaction through teaching others
Decline	Formal preparation for retirement Retirement rituals	Learning to accept a reduced role and less responsibility
		Learning to live a less structured life
		New accommodations to family and community

Source: Adapted from John Van Maanen and Edgar H. Schein, "Career Development," in *Improving Life at Work,* eds. J. Richard Hackman and J. Lloyd Suttle (Santa Monica, CA: Goodyear, 1977), pp. 55–57; and D. Levinson, *The Seasons of a Man's Life* (New York: Ballantine Books, 1986).

higher up in the organization. These career progressions often require the favor of the dominant in-group, which sets corporate goals, priorities, and standards.[11]

When a senior employee takes an active role in guiding another individual, we refer to this activity as **mentoring** or **coaching**. Just as baseball coaches observe, analyze, and attempt to improve the performance of their athletes, "coaches" on the job can do the same. The effective coach, whether on the diamond or in the corporate hierarchy, gives guidance through direction, advice, criticism, and suggestions in an attempt to aid the employee's growth.[12] These mentors provide a support system for junior employees by offering insight into how the organization operates, helping expand the junior employee's professional network, assisting in setting career development goals, and providing feedback when necessary.[13]

The technique of having senior employees coach individuals has the advantages of learning by doing, and provides opportunities for high interaction and rapid feedback on performance. Unfortunately, its two strongest disadvantages are (1) tendencies to perpetuate the current styles and practices in the organization and (2) heavy reliance on the coach's ability to be a good teacher. Just as we recognize that not all excellent Hall of Fame baseball players make outstanding baseball coaches, we cannot expect all excellent employees to be effective coaches. An individual can become an excellent performer without necessarily possessing the knack of creating a proper learning environment for others to do the same; thus, the effectiveness of this technique relies on the ability of the coach. Coaching of employees can occur at any level and can be most effective when the two individuals have no type of reporting relationship. In fact, having a boss for a mentor may have some real disadvantages when office politics develop into a rivalry, compromising loyalties.[14] In some cases, mentors are current coworkers[15]. In fact, coworker mentoring has been found to be extremely effective in organizations—more so than the traditional mentoring relationship of an experienced employee providing guidance to a newer, younger employee.[16] Mentoring relationships can be maintained online via e-mail, Facebook, or Twitter, as well as through traditional ways such as meeting for coffee or sharing a meal.

A mentor is a personal coach in the organization who assists the "next generation" of leaders in learning the organizational ropes. *(Source: Creatas/Age Fotostock America, Inc.)*

ETHICAL ISSUES IN HRM

Mentoring Programs for Women and Minorities

There have been many discussions recently regarding how more women and minorities, groups underrepresented in the top echelons of organizations, can break through the glass ceiling. Several reasons for the prevalence of the glass ceiling dilemma have been well documented. One centers on the issue of mentoring.

Constantly changing workforce composition, employment legislation, and changing societal views of women and minorities in the workplace have increased mentoring relationships for this group. Organizations such as Citigroup, Allstate Insurance, General Mills, and Verizon Wireless have developed special mentoring programs for women and minorities, creating a sort of "jump start" to the relationship. In some respects, this may be the best way at this time to help further advance these two groups. On the other hand, can a mentoring relationship be forced and regulated? The crux of these relationships is for an individual to become close to his or her protégé in an effort to further their career. Won't forcing two individuals together lead to a constrained relationship?[21] Given the degree of potential conflict between the two, more harm than good for the protégé's career may result.

Ethical questions:

Should women and minorities receive special treatment in the mentoring relationship by having organizational policies dictating who will mentor who, and how? Should special guidelines ensure mentoring for women and minorities? And what about the white male? Is he being left out? What do you think?

Recall from Chapter 3 our discussion on the glass ceiling. A main reason for its existence is that women previously had few role models at top levels in the organization who could help them maneuver through the system.[17] There is no excuse for this situation, but there may be some explanation. Mentors sometimes select their protégés on the basis of seeing themselves, in their younger years, in the employee.[18] Because men can rarely identify with younger women, many appeared unwilling to play the part of their mentor (see Ethical Issues in HRM). Of course, women have battled their way into the inner circle of organizational power with visible success. Additionally, organizations are beginning to explore ways of advocating cross-gender mentoring. This revolves around identifying the problems associated with such an arrangement,[19] deciding how to handle problems effectively, and providing organizational support.[20]

Traditional Career Stages

One traditional way to analyze and discuss careers is to consider them in stages or steps.[22] Progress from a beginning point through growth and decline phases to a termination point is typical in one's work life. Most of us begin to form our careers during our early school years. Our careers begin to wind down as we reach retirement age. We can identify five career stages typical for most adults, regardless of occupation: exploration, establishment, mid-career, late career, and decline. These stages are portrayed in Exhibit 9-2.

The age ranges for each stage in Exhibit 9-2 are intended only to show general guidelines. Although this model may seem overly simplistic, the key is to give primary attention to the stages rather than the age categories. For instance, someone who makes a dramatic change in career to undertake a completely different line of work at age forty-five will have many of the same establishment-stage concerns as someone starting at age twenty-five. However if the forty-five-year-old started working at twenty-five, he or she now has twenty years of experience, as well as interests and expectations that differ from those of a peer just starting a career at middle age. Of course, if the forty-five-year-old individual is a newly admitted college student who starts college once her children have grown, she will have more in common—regarding career stages—with the twenty-three-year-old sitting next to her than she will with the forty-five-year-old full professor teaching the class. So, don't get hung up on the age generalizations in Exhibit 9-2. They are simply points of reference.

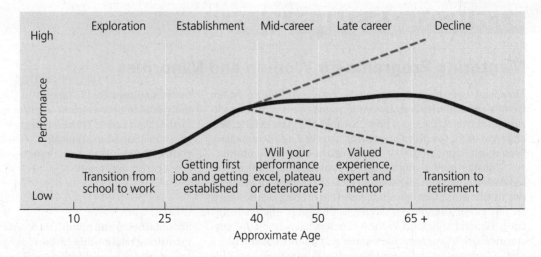

Exhibit 9-2
Career Stages

A traditional view of careers is to pass through five stages before reaching retirement.

Exploration

We make many critical choices about our careers before we enter the workforce for pay. What we hear from our relatives, teachers, and friends; what we see on television, in the movies, or on the Internet helps us narrow our career choices, and leads us in certain directions. Certainly, family careers, interests, aspirations, and our financial resources are heavy factors in determining our perception of what careers are available or what schools, colleges, or universities we might consider.

The **exploration period** ends for most of us as we make the transition from formal education programs to work. This stage has the least relevance to organizations because it occurs prior to employment. It is, of course, not irrelevant. During the exploration period we develop many expectations about our career, a number of them unrealistic. Such expectations may lie dormant for years and then pop up later to frustrate both employee and employer.

Successful career exploration strategies involve trying a lot of potential fields to see what you like or don't like. College internships and cooperative education programs are excellent exploration tools to help you see your future coworkers firsthand and to do, day in and day out, a "real" job. Some successful internships will even lead to job offers. From a career stage perspective, any internship that helps you realize you're bored to death with the work is also a successful one. In the exploration stage, we form our attitudes toward work (doing homework, meeting deadlines, taking or avoiding short-cuts, attendance), and our dominant social relationship patterns (easygoing, domineering, indifferent, likable, obnoxious). Therefore, exploration is important and necessary preparation for work.

exploration period
A career stage that usually ends in the mid-twenties as one makes the transition from school to work.

Establishment

The **establishment period** begins with the search for work and includes accepting your first job, being accepted by your peers, learning the job, and gaining the first tangible evidence of success or failure in the real world. It begins with uncertainties and anxieties, and is indeed dominated by two problems: finding a niche and making your mark.

Finding the right job takes time. In fact, you may know a thirty-seven-year-old who has held a series of seemingly unrelated jobs (for instance, after high school, clerk in a sporting goods store, three years; navy, six years; police dispatcher, four years; small business owner, three years; long-distance truck driver, now). This person has looked for a niche—or attempted to establish one—for nearly twenty years! Many people may not change jobs as frequently as the individual above, but your first real job probably won't be with the company from which you retire. Thorough career exploration helps make this part of establishment an easier step.

The second problem of the establishment stage, making your mark, is characterized by making mistakes, learning from those mistakes, and

establishment period
A career stage in which one begins to search for work and finds a first job.

> When you establish your career, you are trying to find your niche and make your mark.

REAL HR ENOUNTERS

Encouraging Managers

Roger Jans: HR Professional at Ramapo College, Mahwah, NJ

After the initial excitement of a promotion, new managers often find themselves buried in work and employee grief. They might wonder what they've gotten themselves in to!

During difficult economic times, workers will be pushed to their limits. They will be asked to sacrifice and must learn to cope with uncertainty about their own future with the company. Some will rise to the occasion, and others will despair. In order to motivate and help employees succeed, supervisors need to apply three very simple rules: be fair, be friendly, and be firm (the three Fs). Employees will, at one time or another, need a fair hand, a friendly ear, and a compassionate, but firm counselor to keep them focused on the company's strategic goals. In turn, remembering and applying the three Fs will keep supervisors grounded and focused so they can deliver on their expectations. As an added benefit employees will go the extra mile knowing that management cares about them.

assuming increased responsibilities. Individuals in this stage have yet to reach their peak productivity, though, and they rarely receive work assignments that carry great power or high status. As shown in Exhibit 9-2, this stage is experienced as "going uphill." Careers take a lot of time and energy, and often involve a sense of growth, expectation, or anticipation, such as a hiker feels when approaching the crest of a trail, waiting to see what lies on the other side. And, just as a hiker "takes" a hill when she stands at the crest, the establishment stage has ended when you "arrive" (make your mark). Of course, at this time you're considered a seasoned veteran.

Mid-Career

mid-career stage
A career stage marked by continuous improvement in performance, leveling off in performance, or beginning of deterioration in performance.

Many people do not face their first severe career dilemmas until they reach the **mid-career stage**. Here, individuals may continue their prior improvements in performance, level off, or begin to deteriorate. Therefore, although remaining productive at work after you're seasoned is a major challenge of this career stage, the pattern ceases to be as clear as it was for exploration and establishment. Some employees reach their early goals and go on to even greater heights. For instance, a worker who wants to be the vice president of HRM by the time he's thirty-five to forty years old might want to be CEO by the time he's fifty-five, if he has achieved the prior goal. Continued growth and high performance are not the only successful outcomes at this stage.

plateaued mid-career
Promotion beyond one's current job becomes less likely.

Maintenance, or holding onto what you have, is another possible outcome of the mid-career stage. These employees are plateaued, not failed. **Plateaued mid-career** employees can be highly productive.[23] They are technically competent—even though some may not be as ambitious and aggressive as the climbers. They may be satisfied to contribute a sufficient amount of time and energy to the organization to meet production commitments; they also may be easier to manage than someone who wants more. These employees are not deadwood, but good, reliable employees and "solid citizens." An example would be the same HRM vice president who decides at forty-five to not go for the next promotion, but to enjoy other aspects of his life—spending more time with his family and pursuing his hobbies—while still performing well on the job.

The third option for mid-career deals with the employee whose performance begins to deteriorate. This stage for this kind of employee is characterized by loss of both interest and productivity at work. Organizations are often limited to relegating such individuals to less conspicuous jobs, reprimanding them, demoting them, or severing them from the organization altogether. The same HRM vice president could become less productive if, by forty-six, he realizes that he will never be CEO and tries to "wait it out" for thirteen years until he can take early retirement. Smart organizations will realize that individuals can be reenergized by additional training, responsibilities, moving them to another position in the organization, or other development activities. This can boost their morale and their productivity.

Late Career

late-career stage
A career stage in which individuals are no longer learning about their jobs nor expected to outdo levels of performance from previous years.

Those who continue to grow through the mid-career stage often experience the **late-career stage** as a pleasant time with the luxury of relaxing a bit and enjoy playing the part of the elder statesperson, resting on one's laurels, and basking in the respect of less experienced employees. Late-career individuals frequently escape expectations of outdoing their previous performance. Their value to the organization typically lies heavily in their judgment, built up over many years and through varied experiences. They often teach others based on the knowledge they have gained.

Those who have stagnated or deteriorated during the previous stage, on the other hand, often realize late in their career that they will not have an everlasting impact or change the world as they once thought. Employees who decline in mid-career may fear for their jobs. It is a time when individuals recognize that they have decreased work mobility and may be locked into their current job. One begins to look forward to retirement and opportunities for doing something different. Mere plateauing is no more negative than it was during mid-career. In fact, it is expected at late career. The marketing vice president who didn't make it to executive vice president might begin delegating more to her next in line. Life off the job is likely to carry far greater importance than it did in earlier years, as time and energy, once directed to work, are now being redirected to family, friends, and hobbies.

Decline (Late Stage)

The **decline or late stage** in one's career is difficult for just about everyone, but ironically is probably hardest on those who have had continued successes in the earlier stages. After decades of continued achievements and high levels of performance, the time has come for retirement. These individuals step out of the limelight and relinquish a major component of their identity. For those who have seen their performance decline over the years, it may be a pleasant time; the frustrations associated with work are left behind. For the plateaued, it is probably an easier transition to other life activities.

decline or late stage
The final stage in one's career, usually marked by retirement.

CONTEMPORARY CONNECTION

Where Are the Jobs?

Many individuals who are at the beginning of a career search often ask the obvious question: Where are the jobs? Many factors influence that answer, including the economy, technology, and globalization. Although having a solid foundation of communications, technology, and people skills is critical, even these skills need to be focused on where the demand for jobs exists.

So, which fields have these jobs—and which ones are slowly and significantly declining? Let's look at what the research is telling us about specific jobs.[27]

Fastest Growing Occupations Projected through 2018 by the Bureau of Labor Statistics

- Biomedical engineers
- Network systems and data communications
- Personal and home care aides
- Financial examiners
- Medical scientists
- Physician assistants
- Skin care specialists
- Biochemists and biophysicists
- Athletic trainers
- Physical therapist aides

Occupations Showing the Biggest Declines through 2018 by the Bureau of Labor Statistics

- Farmers and ranchers
- Sewing machine operators
- Order clerks
- Postal service mail sorters and processors
- File clerks
- Shipping, receiving, and traffic clerks
- Telemarketers
- Office and administrative support workers
- Supervisors of production workers
- Packers and hand packagers

Athletic trainers are among the fastest growing careers through 2018, according to the Bureau of Labor Statistics.
(Source: Suprijono Suharjoto/iStockphoto)

Adjustments, of course, must be made, whether one is leaving a sparkling career or a hopeless job. The structure and regimentation that work provided is gone. Work responsibilities are generally fewer. It is a challenging stage for anyone to confront.

However, as we live longer, healthier lives, coupled with laws removing age-related retirement requirements, sixty-two, sixty-five, or sixty-seven ceases to be a meaningful retirement age demand. Some individuals shift their emphasis to other work—either paid or volunteer. Often, the key element in this decision is financial security. Those who have adequate funds to maintain their lifestyles in retirement are more likely to engage in activities that they desire. Unfortunately, those less financially secure may be unable to retire when they want, or find that they have to seek gainful employment in some capacity to supplement their retirement income.

An increasing number of workers are refusing to allow themselves to be phased out when they reach retirement age. Workers may choose to remain in the workforce indefinitely for a variety of reasons including income, keeping their company-sponsored health benefits, taking advantage of flexible work hours offered by their employers, or the desire to phase into retirement gradually. Many just enjoy the social aspects of working, or love their jobs and don't want to retire.[24] Employers are recognizing the experience and productivity that older workers bring. Mature workers have developed critical thinking skills necessary for uncertain and unstructured problems. Studies indicate that older workers use fewer sick days than younger workers and have lower healthcare costs because they do not have small children as dependents. Employers' healthcare costs are further reduced as older workers become eligible for Medicare at age 65.[25] Companies like CVS Pharmacies place a priority on hiring older workers, finding that their customer service is better. And their ability to relate to the drugstore chain's mature customers results in significant customer loyalty.[26]

Career Choices and Preferences

The best career choice offers the best match between what you want and what you need. Good career choice outcomes for any of us should produce a series of positions that give us an opportunity for good performance, make us want to maintain our commitment to the field, and give us high work satisfaction. A good career match lets us develop a positive self-concept and do work that we think is important.[28] Let's look at some of the existing research that can help you discover which careers may provide the best match for your skills.

Holland Vocational Preferences

Holland vocational preferences model
Represents an individual occupational personality as it relates to vocational themes.

One of the most widely used approaches to guide career choices is the **Holland vocational preferences model**.[30] This theory consists of three major components. First, Holland found that people have varying occupational preferences; we do not all like to do the same things. Second, his research demonstrates that if you do a job you think is important, you will be a more productive employee. Personality of workers may be matched to typical work environments where that can occur. Third, you will have more in common with people who have similar interest patterns and less in common with those who don't. For instance, Karen hates her job; she thinks it is boring to waste her time packing and unpacking trucks on the shipping dock of a manufacturing firm and would rather be working with people in the recruiting area. Pat, on the other hand, enjoys the routine of her work; she likes the daily rhythm and the serenity of loading and unloading the warehouse. Karen and Pat feel differently about the same job. Why? Their interests, expressed as occupational interests, are not compatible.

The Holland vocational preferences model identifies six vocational themes (realistic, investigative, artistic, social, enterprising, and conventional) presented in Exhibit 9-3. An individual's occupational personality is expressed as some combination of high and low scores on these six themes. High scores indicate that you enjoy those kinds of activities. Although it is possible to score high or low on all six scales, most people are identified

Realistic Rugged, robust, practical, prefer to deal with things rather than people. Prefers outdoor jobs with little paperwork. Best job matches are Agriculture, Nature, Adventure, Military, Mechanical.

Investigative Scientific, task-oriented, prefer abstract problems, prefer to think through problems rather than to act on them, not highly person-oriented, enjoy ambiguity. Corresponding jobs are Science, Mathematics, Medical Science, Medical Service.

Artistic Enjoy creative self-expression, dislike highly structured situations, sensitive, emotional, independent, original. Corresponding jobs are Music/Dramatics, Art, Writing.

Social Concerned with the welfare of others, enjoy developing and teaching others, good in group settings, extroverted, cheerful, popular. Corresponding jobs are Teaching, Social Service, Athletics, Domestic Arts, Religious Activities.

Enterprising Good facility with words, prefer selling or leading, energetic, extroverted, adventurous, enjoy persuasion. Corresponding jobs are Public Speaking, Law/Politics, Merchandising, Sales, Business Management.

Conventional Prefer ordered, numerical work, enjoy large organizations, stable, dependable. Corresponding job is Accountant, Actuary, Economist, Pharmacist.[29]

Exhibit 9-3
Holland's General Occupational Themes

These six types of work, environments as explained by Holland, help job seekers match their personality to a compatible profession. Many vocational preference tests are based on Holland's typology. Which look appealing to you? Which do you think best fits a career in human resource management?

by three dominant scales. The six themes are arranged in the hexagonal structure shown in Exhibit 9-4. This scale model represents the fact that some of the themes are opposing, while others have mutually reinforcing characteristics.

For instance, Realistic and Social are opposite each other in the diagram. A person with a realistic preference wants to work with things, not people. A person with a social preference wants to work with people, no matter what else they do. Therefore, they have opposing preferences about working alone or with others. Investigative and Enterprising are opposing themes, as are Artistic and Conventional preferences.

An example of mutually reinforcing themes is the Social-Enterprising-Conventional (SEC) vocational preference structure. Sophia, for example, likes working with people, being successful, and following ordered rules. That combination is perfect for someone willing to climb the ladder in a large bureaucracy. What about Ryan? He's Realistic-Investigative-Artistic, preferring solitary work to large groups, asking questions to answering them, and making his own rules instead of following someone else's. How does Ryan fit into a large bureaucracy? Some may think his preferred actions label him as a troublemaker. He might fit better in a research lab—both the scientist preference and the research lab environment are characterized by lack of human interruptions and concentration on factual material. That's consistent with the Realistic-Investigative-Artistic profile.

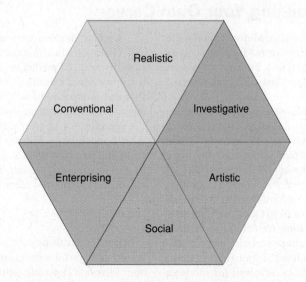

Exhibit 9-4
Structure of Holland's Themes

The Holland occupational themes are arranged so that themes that reinforce each other are next to each other, and themes that are not compatible are opposite.

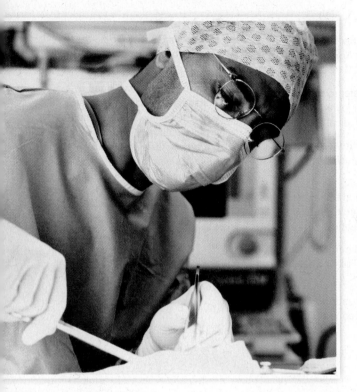

The Schein Anchors

Edgar Schein has identified anchors, or personal value clusters, that may be satisfied or frustrated by work. When the worker holds a particular combination of these personal value clusters (technical-functional competence, managerial competence, security-stability, creativity, and autonomy-independence) and the organization characteristically offers them, that person is "anchored" in that job, organization, or industry.[34]

Most people have two or three value clusters that are important to them. If an organization satisfies two out of three, that is considered a stable match. For instance, Aaron is a recent college graduate. He wants to use his human resources degree. His father was laid off when his organization downsized last year, and Aaron never wants to deal with that type of uncertainty. Schein would describe Aaron's anchors as technical competence and security-stability. His current job choices are marketing on a commission basis for a credit card company, or recruiting for an established and growth-oriented home health services firm. Which job should he take? Based on his combination of value clusters, the recruiting job currently appears to better match Aaron's preferences.

What vocational preferences might this surgeon have? According to Holland, this individual more than likely is investigative (scientific) with an artistic flare. Our preferences make certain careers appear more likely ones that we will enjoy, as well as be more productive in. (*Source: Lifesize/Getty Images, Inc.*)

The Myers-Briggs Typologies

One of the more widely used methods of identifying personalities is the Myers-Briggs Type Indicator (MBTI®).* The MBTI uses four dimensions of personality to identify sixteen different personality types based on responses to an approximately one hundred-item questionnaire (see Exhibit 9-5). More than two and a half million individuals each year in

*The Myers-Briggs Type Indicator and MBTI are registered trademarks of Consulting Psychology Press, Inc.

TIPS FOR SUCCESS

Entrepreneurship: Building Your Own Career

Think of someone who is an entrepreneur. Maybe it's someone you know personally or someone you've read about such as Mark Zuckerberg of Facebook, Richard Branson of Virgin Group, or Oprah Winfrey of Harpo, Inc. How would you describe this person's personality?

One of the more researched areas of entrepreneurship has been determining what, if any, psychological characteristics entrepreneurs have in common, what types of personality traits might distinguish them from nonentrepreneurs, and what traits among entrepreneurs might predict who will be successful.

Is there a classic entrepreneurial personality? Although pin-pointing specific personality characteristics that all entrepreneurs share is difficult, this hasn't stopped entrepreneurship researchers from searching for common traits.[31] Most lists of common personality characteristics of entrepreneurs include the following: high level of motivation, abundance of self-confidence, ability to be involved for the long term, high energy level, persistent problem solver, high degree of initiative, ability to set goals, and moderate risk taker.[32]

A recent development in defining entrepreneurial personality characteristics was the proposed use of a **proactive personality** scale to predict an individual's likelihood of pursuing entrepreneurial ventures. Proactive personality describes individuals more prone to take actions to influence their environment.[33] An entrepreneur is likely to exhibit proactivity as he or she searches for opportunities and acts to take advantage of those opportunities. Various items on the proactive personality scale appear to be good indicators of a person's likelihood of becoming an entrepreneur. These include education and having an entrepreneurial parent.

Things to think about:

Would you consider becoming an entrepreneur or working for one? Which of Holland's General Occupational Themes, Schein Anchors, or Myers-Briggs Typologies seem to best describe entrepreneurs? Which ones best describe you?

Exhibit 9-5

Characteristics Frequently Associated with Myers-Briggs Types

The Myers-Briggs Type Indicator or MBTI is used in many organizations to determine how employees will interact and solve problems.

		Sensing Types S		Intuitive Types N	
		Thinking T	**Feeling F**	**Feeling F**	**Thinking T**
Introverts I	Judging J	**ISTJ** Quiet, serious, dependable, practical, matter-of-fact. Value traditions and loyalty	**ISFJ** Quiet, friendly, responsible, thorough, considerate. Strives to create order and harmony.	**INFJ** Seek meaning and connection in ideas. Committed to firm values. Organized and decisive in implementing vision.	**INTJ** Have original minds and great drive for their ideas. Skeptical and independent, have high standards of competence for self and others.
Introverts I	Perceiving P	**ISTP** Tolerant and flexible. Interested in cause and effect. Value efficiency.	**ISFP** Quiet, friendly, sensitive. Likes own space. Dislikes disagreements and conflicts.	**INFP** Idealistic, loyal to their values. Seek to understand people and help them fulfill their potential.	**INTP** Seeks logical explanations. Theoretical and abstract over social interactions. Skeptical, sometimes critical. Analytical.
Extroverts E	Perceiving P	**ESTP** Flexible and tolerant. Focus on here and now. Enjoy material comforts. Learn best by doing.	**ESFP** Outgoing, friendly. Enjoy working with others. Spontaneous. Learns best by trying a new skill with other people.	**ENFP** Enthusiastic, imaginative. Wants a lot of affirmation. Relies on verbal fluency and ability to improvise.	**ENTP** Quick, ingenious, stimulating. Adept at generating conceptual possibilities and analyzing them strategically. Bored by routine.
Extroverts E	Judging J	**ESTJ** Practical, realistic, matter-of-fact, decisive. Focus on getting efficient results. Forceful in implementing plans.	**ESFJ** Warmhearted, cooperative. Wants to be appreciated for who they are and for what they contribute.	**ENFJ** Warm, responsive, responsible. Attuned to needs of others. Sociable, facilitates others, provides inspirational leadership.	**ENTJ** Frank, decisive, assumes leadership. Enjoys long-term planning and goal setting. Forceful in presenting ideas.

Source: Modified and reproduced by special permission of the publisher, Consulting Psychologists Press, Palo Alto, CA 94303 from *Introduction to Type*™, 6th edition by Isabel Briggs Myers. Copyright 1998 by Consulting Psychologists Press. All rights reserved. Further reproduction is prohibited without the publisher's written consent. Introduction to Type is a trademark of Consulting Psychologists Press, Inc.

the United States alone take the MBTI.[35] It's used in such companies as Apple, Honda, AT&T, Exxon, and 3M, as well as many hospitals, educational institutions, and the U.S. armed forces.

The sixteen personality types are based on the four dimensions noted in Exhibit 9-5. That is, the MBTI dimensions include extroversion versus introversion (EI), sensing versus intuitive (SN), thinking versus feeling (TF), and judging versus perceiving (JP). The EI dimension measures an individual's orientation toward the inner world of ideas (I) or the external world of the environment (E). The sensing-intuitive dimension indicates an individual's reliance on information gathered from the external world (S) or from the world of ideas (N). Thinking-feeling reflects one's preference of evaluating information in an analytical manner (T) or on the basis of values and beliefs (F). The judging-perceiving index reflects an attitude toward the external world that is either task completion oriented (J) or information seeking (P).[36]

How can the MBTI help managers? Proponents of the instrument believe that it's important to know these personality types because they influence the way people interact and solve problems. For example, if your boss is an intuitor and you are a sensor, you will each gather information in different ways. An intuitor prefers gut reactions, whereas a sensor prefers facts. To work well with your boss, you must present more than just facts about a situation; you must discuss how you feel. The MBTI has been used to

proactive personality
Describing those individuals who are more prone to take actions to influence their environment.

TIPS FOR SUCCESS

Internships: Experience at Work

Your dream job is out there. The trouble is, it probably requires more experience than you have right now. Getting the right type of experience is a little easier if you're open to being an intern. Many college programs either require or encourage internships in most career fields, including Human Resource Management. They typically run for at least three months and can last up to a year. During difficult economic times, internships have become increasingly populars as companies demand more of applicants.[38] College students and recent graduates are the most common internship candidates, but the recession has increased the number of workers over fifty who are seeking internships to change careers, update skills, or land a full-time job.[39]

Internships give job seekers a chance to demonstrate that they not only have experience, but relevant job skills. And interns can get references from supervisors who have seen them in action. Many employers have formal internship programs that not only train employees for jobs, but also incorporate career development programs with training in leadership and collaboration with the goal of hiring the intern at the end of

the internship or upon college graduation. Competition for the best internships can be fierce.

Campbell Mithun, an ising agency in Minneapolis, Minnesota requires applicants for their "Lucky 13" ten-week paid internship program to apply by submitting thirteen comments on Twitter over thirteen days.[40] Over 300 applicants submitted "tweets" for six available positions in 2011. HR Vice President Debbie Fischer is proud and pleased with the results of the search. "We've been wanting to shake up the process for some time,"[41] reports Fischer. Most Lucky 13 interns are offered full-time jobs at the agency that represents Famous Footwear, General Mills, SuperValu, Toro, and Hefty. Take a look at a summary of the tweets submitted by the selected interns on the Lucky 13 Internship Highlights Reel posted on YouTube.

Things to think about:

Although competition for the best internships is fierce, competition for the best interns is a challenge for HR, too. Campbell Mithun has created an innovative way to attract interest. How would you recruit the best internship candidates?

---

help managers match employees with jobs. For instance, a marketing position that requires extensive interaction with outsiders would be best filled by someone who has extroverted tendencies. Also, MBTI has also been found useful in focusing on growth orientations for entrepreneurial types.[37]

Taking Responsibility
For Building Your Career

Consider managing your career like an entrepreneur managing a small business. Think of yourself as self-employed, even if you work in a large organization. In a world where most of us are "free agents," the successful career requires you to maintain flexibility and keep skills and knowledge up to date. The following suggestions are consistent with the view that you, and only you, hold primary responsibility for your career (see Exhibit 9-6).

Exhibit 9-6
Suggestions for Managing Your Career

Careers are like any important activity in your life. They require preparation and monitoring.

Know yourself · Manage your reputation · Network contacts · Build and maintain → **SUCCESSFUL CAREER TIPS** ← Keep current · Balance your specialist and generalist competencies · Document your achievements · Keep your options open

■ *Know yourself.* Know your strengths and weaknesses. What talents can you bring to an employer? Personal career planning begins by being honest with yourself (see Learning an HRM Skill, p. 240).

■ *Manage your reputation.* Let others both inside and outside your current organization know about your achievements. Make yourself and your accomplishments visible. Clean up your online profile on social media sites like Facebook, Twitter, Tumbler, or Google+, and join more professional career sites like LinkedIn. Ask colleagues to post recommendations on LinkedIn.

■ *Build and maintain network contacts.* In a world of high mobility, you need contacts. Join national and local professional associations, attend conferences, and network at social gatherings. Organizations often want individuals who have some experience and show some initiative. One way of demonstrating these attributes is through an internship. Many universities today not only offer internships as part of their curriculum, they require some type of job experience to fulfill their degree pre-requisites. Internships offer you a chance to see what the work is really like, to better understand an organization's culture, and to see if you fit well into the organization. And although no guarantees are given, many organizations use internships as a means of developing their applicant pool—often extending job offers to outstanding interns.

Internships provide a wealth of experience for college students and give a taste of the world of work. This can be crucial in the transition from school to work. *(Source: Kei Uesugi/Taxi/Getty Images, Inc.)*

■ *Keep current.* Develop specific skills and abilities in high demand. Avoid learning only organization-specific skills that don't quickly transfer to other employers.

■ *Balance your specialist and generalist competencies.* Stay current within your technical specialty, but also develop general competencies that give you the versatility to react to an ever-changing work environment. Overemphasis in a single functional area or even in a narrow industry can limit your mobility.

■ *Document your achievements.* Employers are increasingly looking to what you've accomplished rather than the titles you've held. Seek jobs and assignments that provide increasing challenges and offer objective evidence of your competencies.

■ *Keep your options open.* Always have contingency plans prepared that you can call on when needed. You never know when your group will be eliminated, your department downsized, your project canceled, or your company acquired in a takeover. "Hope for the best but be prepared for the worst" may be a cliché, but it's still sound advice.[42]

Summary

(This summary relates to the Learning Outcomes identified on page 220.) After having read this chapter, you can:

1. **Explain who is responsible for managing careers.** The responsibility for managing a career belongs to the individual. The organization's role is to provide assistance and information to the employee, but it is not responsible for growing an employee's career.

2. **Describe the term *career.*** A career is a sequence of positions occupied by a person during the course of a lifetime.

3. **Discuss the focus of careers for both organizations and individuals.** Career development from an organizational standpoint involves tracking career paths and developing career ladders. From an individual perspective, career development focuses on assisting individuals in identifying their major career goals and in determining how to achieve these goals.

4. **Describe how career development and employee development differ.** The main distinction between career development and employee development lies in their time frames. Career development focuses on the long-range career effectiveness and success of organizational personnel. Employee development focuses more on immediate and intermediate time frames.

5. **Explain why career development is valuable to organizations.** Career development is valuable to an organization because it (1) ensures needed talent will be available; (2) improves the organization's ability to attract and retain high-talent employees; (3) ensures that minorities and women have opportunities for growth and development; (4) reduces employee frustration; (5) enhances cultural diversity; (6) assists in implementing quality; and (7) promotes organizational goodwill.

6. **Identify the five traditional stages involved in a career.** The five stages in a career are exploration, establishment, mid-career, late career, and decline.

7. **List the Holland vocational preferences.** The Holland vocational preferences are realistic, investigative, artistic, social, enterprising, and conventional.

8. **Describe the implications of personality typologies and jobs.** Typology focuses on personality dimensions including extroversion-introversion; sensing-intuition; thinking-feeling; and judging-perceiving. These four pairs can be combined into sixteen different combination profiles. With this information, job personality traits can be matched to individual personality traits.

9. **Identify several suggestions that can help you manage your career more effectively.** Some suggestions for managing your career include (1) know yourself, (2) manage your reputation, (3) build and maintain network contacts, (4) keep current, (5) balance your specialist and generalist competencies, (6) document your achievements, and (7) keep your options open.

Demonstrating Comprehension

QUESTIONS FOR REVIEW

1. What is a career?
2. Contrast employee development with career development. How are they alike? How are they different?
3. How might a formal career development program be consistent with an organization's affirmative action program?
4. Contrast the external and internal dimensions of a career. Which do you believe is more relevant in determining an employee's work behavior?
5. What are the five traditional career stages? Which of the five is probably least relevant to HRM? Defend your position.
6. Identify the Holland vocational preferences and explain the importance of this model.
7. What is a mentor and how do you go about finding one?

Key Terms

career	external career	mentoring or coaching
decline or late stage	Holland vocational preferences	mid-career stage
establishment period	model	plateaued mid-career
exploration period	late career stage	proactive personality

Linking Concepts to Practice   DISCUSSION QUESTIONS

1. Which career perspective is more relevant to HRM managers—the individual or the organizational? Defend your position.
2. Do you think a person's age and career stage evolve together? Why or why not?
3. Which of the sixteen Myers-Briggs typologies do you believe are most consistent with the behaviors needed for (a) a sales position, (b) a computer programmer, and (c) an HRM recruiter? Support your selections.
4. "Women and minorities require more career attention than do white males." Do you agree or disagree with the statement? Why or why not?

5. "Investments in career development do not provide an organization a viable return on its investment. It simply raises employee expectations, which, if not fulfilled, cause employees to leave. Accordingly, the organization has trained employees for its competitors." Take a position in support of this statement, and one against it.
6. After reviewing the chapter opener describing the efforts of Principal Financial Group to help employees manage their careers, explain which of the company's initiatives you feel is the most valuable and why.

Making A Difference   SERVICE LEARNING PROJECTS

Career management encompasses an employee's work experience from the first day until retirement, and sometimes beyond.

- Volunteer with an organization such as Big Brothers Big Sisters that establishes mentoring programs for youth.
- Volunteer as a peer mentor to freshmen or new students on campus.
- Contact your college HR department to see if they need student volunteers for HR tasks or assist with activities they have for retired employees.
- Start a clothing drive in association with local women's groups or SHRM chapter to collect professional clothing for

women in job training programs who are re-entering the workforce.
- Establish a relationship with a local senior citizens center and assist with their programs such as holiday parties or Veteran's Day observance.

As you put your service learning experience together, keep a journal of your activities, the time you spend, contact information for people you work with, and your thoughts about the process. When you're finished, make a presentation to your class about the experience and what you learned. What concepts from Chapter 9 were you able to apply?

Developing Diagnostic and Analytical Skills

Case Application 9-A: REDUCING TURNOVER AT THE TOP

If turnover isn't a human resource manager's worst enemy, it certainly makes the top ten list. And it's particularly painful when turnover involves executives recruited or promoted with high hopes for success. Atlanta-based Newell Rubbermaid found that 30 percent of the executives they recruited from outside and 23 percent of the executives who had been promoted from within the organization left the company after two years in their new position. After three years, up to half of all newly executives had left the company. Clearly career development was not meeting the expectations of the newly hired or promoted.

Newell Rubbermaid faced an uphill battle when replacing baby boom era executives who were approaching retirement. Newell Rubbermaid, a consumer products company with over 23,000 employees worldwide, estimates that more than 90 percent of U.S. households have at least one of their Rubbermaid, Graco, Calphalon, Goody,

Sharpie, or Levolor products. As the company planned to meet their goal of worldwide growth, they knew they needed young, upwardly mobile senior managers who had the ability to think globally.[43]

Their solution was to create a program to develop current employees for leadership positions rather than follow the trend of expensive executive recruitment that was often followed by a high failure rate. The program, called "Aspire," is limited to twelve participants at a time and includes four weeks of classroom instruction, on-the-job projects, readings, and activities spread out over the course of one year. The content of the Aspire program includes four modules: creating followership, leading global change, coaching employees, and developing "next generation" leaders. Participants are also paired with experienced executives within the organization who serve as personal coaches. These coaches help the participants apply concepts learned in the Aspire program to their jobs. To build the Aspire participant's knowledge of the differences between U.S. and foreign markets, they are sent to another country, most recently France, to better understand cultural differences, how they affect consumer preferences, and how particular products, such as Graco baby strollers, are used.

Retention has increased dramatically, with 80 percent of the participants in the first four groups who completed the program staying with the company. The number of executive vacancies filled internally increased from 58 percent in 2006 to 90 percent in 2010. Aspire graduate Laurel Hurd is one of many that rave about the program's benefits. Hurd was promoted from Vice President, Sales, at Calphalon to General Manager, North America, for Graco Children's Products after completing Aspire. Hurd states, "The fact that the company was going to spend that much time and energy to help develop me as a leader was inspiring." Andrea Lawson, Director of Global Learning and Development is happy with the results, too.

Lawson says, "We've seen some pretty amazing results from our work . . . We've promoted leaders into new positions and we've increased the commitment internally to leadership development."[44]

Questions:

1. Describe how you would establish an effective mentoring or coaching element for the Aspire program, including the characteristics of an effective mentor, and your expectations for a successful mentoring relationship.
2. How does the Aspire program provide value for the organization in addition to reducing turnover?
3. What value does Aspire provide for the individual in terms of career development?
4. Explain how employees in each of the traditional career stages could benefit from a program like Aspire. Explain which would benefit most and why.

Working with a Team   CAREER INSIGHTS

Imagine that you enter the elevator on your way to an interview for an entry-level job at your first-choice company. Two other individuals are also on the elevator. As you head to your floor, the elevator stalls, and it will be another twenty minutes before the mechanics can fix the elevator. You and the two other individuals begin to talk, introduce yourselves, and find that each of you is in the building for an interview. You decide to pose questions to one another.

Take turns responding to the following questions, noting similarities and differences in your responses.

- Who do you think is responsible for your career?
- What are your plans to continue your education?
- Why did you pick your chosen career?
- What phase of your career development are you in?
- How would you match what you want out of life and your career? Career goals? Job goals?
- What are your skills, interests, work-related needs, and values?
- What courses do you like best and least? Which are most challenging and most difficult?
- Have you ever had a mentor? Share that experience.

Learning an HRM Skill   MAKING A CAREER CHOICE

About the skill: Career planning can assist you in becoming more knowledgeable of your needs, values, and personal goals through the following three-step, self-assessment process.[45]

1. *Identify and organize your skills, interests, work-related needs, and values.* The best place to begin is by drawing up a profile of your educational record. List each school attended from high school on. What courses do you remember liking most and least? In what courses did you score highest and lowest? In what extracurricular activities did you participate? Did you acquire any specific skills? Have you gained proficiency in other skills? Next, begin to assess your occupational experience. List each job you have held, the organization you worked for, your overall level of satisfaction, what you liked most and least about the job, and why you left. It's important to be honest in covering each of these points.

2. *Convert this information into general career fields and specific job goals.* By completing step 1, you should now have some insights into your interests and abilities. Now look at how these can convert into organizational settings or fields of endeavor with which you will be a good match. Then become specific and identify distinct job goals. What fields are available? In business? In government? In nonprofit organizations? Break your answer down further into areas such as

education, financial, manufacturing, social services, or health services. Identifying areas of interest is usually far easier than pinpointing specific occupations. When you identify a limited set of occupations that interest you, you can start to align these with your abilities and skills. Will certain jobs require you to move? If so, would this be compatible with your geographic preferences? Do you have the educational requirements necessary for the job? If not, what additional schooling will you need? Does the job offer the status and earning potential that you aspire to? What is the long-term outlook for jobs in this field? Does the career suffer from cyclical employment? No job is without its drawbacks—have you seriously considered all the negative aspects? When you have fully answered questions such as these, you should have a relatively short list of specific job goals.

3. *Test your career possibilities against the realities of the organization or the job market.* The final step in this self-assessment process is testing your selection against the realities of the marketplace. Go out and talk with knowledgeable people in the fields, organizations, or jobs you desire. These informational interviews should provide reliable feedback as to the accuracy of your self-assessment and the opportunities in the fields and jobs that interest you.

Enhancing Your Communication Skills

1. Prepare a presentation on how the current world economy has influenced your career decisions and preparation. Use presentation software with three to five slides to illustrate your major points.

2. Using the material presented in the HRM Skills section, write a two- to three-page response to your skills, interests, work-related needs, and values.

3. Visit your college career planning center and ask to take a career guidance survey, or find an online career guidance survey at a career site like CareerBuilder.com or Monster.com. After completing the survey, write up a two- to three-page analysis of the results you received. End the paper with some insight into what the survey indicated to you.

4. Write a two- to three-page paper that focuses on where you see yourself in ten years. Describe how you intend to accomplish this and what you'll have to do to increase your chances of attaining this goal.

(Source: Ruaridh Stewart/Zuma Press)

LEARNING OUTCOMES

After reading this chapter, you will be able to

1. Identify the three purposes of performance management systems and whom they serve.

2. Explain the six steps in the appraisal process.

3. Discuss absolute standards in performance management systems.

4. Describe relative standards in performance management systems.

5. Discuss how management by objective (MBO) can be used as an appraisal method.

6. Explain why performance appraisals might be distorted.

7. Identify ways to make performance management systems more effective.

8. Describe the term *360-degree appraisal*.

9. Explain the criteria for a successful performance appraisal meeting.

10. Discuss how performance appraisals may differ in a global environment.

Establishing the Performance Management System

10

If you worked at the San Diego Zoological Society prior to 2006, you might have thought you were doing a great job at the San Diego Zoo or Wild Animal Park. Since performance appraisals were such a low priority, it wasn't uncommon to wait several years, even decades between reviews, and most employees didn't have a clue how management thought they were doing.

Employees and managers alike didn't turn in paperwork necessary to complete the appraisal process and there was no consequence for ignoring the procedures. Different versions of a one-page form were used to evaluate employees ranging from world-renowned scientists to teenage foodservice workers. Managers were paid annual cost of living raises that were not linked to performance. Doesn't sound like a recipe for success, does it?

That all changed when Director of Human Resources, Tim Mulligan, was given responsibility for developing processes to support the San Diego Zoological Society's new strategic plan. Mulligan decided that appraisals needed to be tied to the plan, stating, "It's hard to insist on accountability if there are no goals to hold anyone to."[1] The Zoological Society decided that an effective appraisal system should be easy to use, link employee goals to the Zoological Society's objectives, objectively measure performance and link it with compensation, keep appraisals on schedule, and allow employees to record their achievements on a year-round basis.

They decided on a Web-based system that did all that and then some. In addition, it provided a "comment helper" that assisted managers in writing relevant comments, automatically inserted the correct pronoun for the employee's gender, and checked language for "sensitivity." For example, the checker suggests replacing "old" with "overqualified." Since the system is Web-based, managers are able to write appraisals at home or any place they can access the Internet. It does not, however, allow managers to e-mail appraisals to employees. Appraisals must be printed and reviewed in person, ensuring face-to-face discussion of the performance review.

Did it work? Consider these results: the annual percentage of completed appraisals went from 50 percent to 100 percent.[2] Employees report being motivated to better performance when it is tied to compensation. Managers report increased employee motivation and higher morale. Employees like seeing managers held accountable for customer and employee satisfaction. Mulligan also reports an unexpected benefit, "What I found is that it's a recruiting tool."[3] Prospective employees like the idea of getting timely feedback on their goals and objectives and being paid for performance.

Looking Ahead

What are the benefits of the performance appraisal process for employees and employers? In your opinion, why don't more employers have an effective performance appraisal process?

Introduction

Every year, most employees experience an evaluation of their past performance. This may be a five-minute informal discussion between employees and their supervisors or a more elaborate, several-week process involving many specific steps. Employees generally see any such evaluations as having some direct effect on their work lives. They may lead to increased pay, a promotion, warnings about sub-standard performance, or assistance in personal development areas for which the employee needs some training. As a result, any evaluation of employees' work can create an emotionally charged event.

Because the performance evaluation is no longer a simple process, it is now more critical to perform one while simultaneously focusing on key job activities. For example, should an employee's body language when interacting with other employees and customers become part of the employee's performance evaluation? Should how well a manager serves as a mentor to her employees be considered? Moreover, should a supervisor's employees have input into their boss's effectiveness at work? Should employees' abilities to perform tasks in a timely and accurate manner matter in an evaluation of their work? Questions like these cannot be overlooked. If we want to know how well our employees are doing, we must measure their performance—not necessarily an easy task. Many factors go into the performance evaluation process, such as why we evaluate, who should benefit from the evaluation, what type of evaluation we should use, and what problems we might encounter.

Before beginning this chapter, however, recognize that no performance appraisal system is perfect. Organizations have good reasons for completing them properly, but sometimes that simply doesn't happen, perhaps through poor appraisal training or obsolete measures. It could also be the result of the dynamic environment in which employees work. That is, some jobs change so frequently that it's almost impossible to properly define what an employee should do over the next twelve months.

Regardless of potential problems, one can expect performance management systems to survive in some format. Accordingly, understanding the foundations of performance management systems, the way appraisals might be constructed, as well as the potential problems that one may encounter, benefits anyone involved in contemporary organizations—and helps executives know precisely how well the organization is progressing on meeting its strategic goals.[4]

Performance Management Systems

Performance management systems involve numerous activities. The performance appraisal is the most easily identifiable, but it's just part of a system that seeks to motivate employees to maximum performance by evaluating the employee's effort on the job, comparing it to standards, and using those results to help employees improve. Because it's an involved process that needs a clear understanding of the purpose of the performance management system, problems that may arise in its implementation. Let's take a look at both of these issues.

Purposes of a Performance Management System

You probably entered your Human Resource Management class with the intent of learning a lot and getting a good grade. In order to do that, you needed to know the learning goals or competencies for the course, the timeframe for accomplishing those goals, the method of evaluation to be used, and the level of competence you would need to achieve to get the grade you wish. How difficult would it be if your class had no learning goals, no timeframe for learning the material, no evaluation from the professor, and no grading scale? You might get frustrated by the lack of goals and feedback, and even be suspicious that the evaluation of your effort might be unfair or biased. Employees aren't much different. They start a job wanting to do well, but they need to know their performance goals, how long they have to accomplish those goals, how they will be evaluated, that the evaluation will be fair, and the level of competence they need to achieve. That's at the heart of the performance appraisal process.

A key piece of this process is the performance appraisal. Performance appraisals take the part of the evaluation instrument that conveys to employees how well they have progressed toward achieving their goals. Often these goals and performance measures are mutually set between the employee and the supervisor. Without the two-way feedback provided by the performance appraisal regarding an employee's effort and its effect on performance, we run the risk of decreasing his or her motivation. Employee development is an important part of the process as well.[5] By development, we are referring to those areas in which an employee has a deficiency or weakness, or an area that simply could be improved through an effort to enhance performance.[6] Going back to our example of your HR class, suppose a student does well on tests and case assignments, but just doesn't do a very good job of participating in class. If class participation is a part of the class grade, the student would benefit from some advice from the professor on how much participation is expected, how his current level of participation is affecting his grade, and how the student can improve on this aspect of the class goals.

The performance appraisal process also provides **documentation** of an employee's performance. This becomes important to prove that discipline or dismissal were the result of documented performance issues that were communicated to the affected employee. In Chapter 3, we discussed Equal Employment laws (EEO) and the need to make sure that all HRM decisions are job-related. Those job-related measures must be performance-supported when an HRM decision affects current employees. For instance, suppose a supervisor has decided to terminate an employee. Although the

Without proper two-way feedback about an employee's effort and its effect on performance, we run the risk of decreasing his or her motivation. (*Source: Jacob Wackerhausen/iStockphoto*)

documentation
A record of performance appraisal process outcomes.

CONTEMPORARY CONNECTION

Abolish Performance Appraisals?

There's no doubt that many managers dislike evaluating employees. In fact, one survey indicates that managers dread it as much as firing an employee. Does it make sense to eliminate appraisals altogether? But how would employees know how they are doing? How would raises be determined? How would slackers find out how they need to shape up? How would star performers be recognized?

It may sound extreme, but a growing number of critics are advocating the elimination of yearly evaluations. Critics claim that annual feedback isn't relevant to younger workers accustomed to frequent, nearly instant feedback via social media (see Contemporary Connection: The Feedback Fix). Furthermore, brain research indicates that workers process criticism emotionally rather than rationally, reducing the effectiveness of the feedback.[8,9]

Certainly some type of feedback is necessary. Apple Inc., Zappos, and SAS have all ditched traditional performance appraisals in favor of non-traditional evaluations that include increasing the role of the manager as coach and providing more frequent feedback. They've found success by emphasizing personal development and recognizing behaviors that embody core values or accomplish meaningful goals.[10] Focusing on these behaviors tends to increase intrinsic motivation, loyalty, and promotes better communication with managers more that comparing more quantifiable performance measures such as meeting sales goals or company profits.

Consider this:

What are your thoughts on the issue? Are performance reviews more trouble than they are worth? What would you use in their place?

supervisor cites performance matters as the reason for the discharge, a review of this employee's recent performance appraisals indicates that performance was evaluated as satisfactory for the past two review periods. Accordingly, unless this employee's performance signi-ficantly decreased (and assuming that proper methods to correct the performance deficiency were performed), personnel records do not support the supervisor's decision. This critique by HRM is absolutely critical to ensure that employees are treated fairly and that the organization is "protected."[7] Additionally, in our discussion of sexual harassment in Chapter 3, we addressed the need for employees to keep copies of past performance appraisals. If retaliation such as termination or poor job assignments occurs for refusing a supervisor's advances, existing documentation can show that the personnel action was inappropriate (see Ethical Issues in HRM).

Because documentation issues are important, HRM must ensure that the evaluation systems used support the legal needs of the organization. However, even though the performance appraisal process is geared to serve the organization, we should also recognize two other important players in the process: employees and their appraisers.

Through timely and accurate feedback and development, management can better serve employees' needs. In doing so, managers may also be in a better position to show the effort–performance linkage.

Next, supervisors should keep in mind the needs of the appraiser. If feedback, development, and documentation are to function effectively, appraisers must have a performance system appropriate for their needs—a system that facilitates giving feedback and development information to employees, and one that allows for employee input. For example, if appraisers are required to evaluate their employees using inappropriate performance measures, or to answer questions about employees that have little bearing on the job, the system may not provide the same benefits as one that avoids such negatives. Tailoring the evaluation process to the job analysis and the organization's and employee's goals is the difference between a satisfactory evaluation system and one that is an integral part of the HRM process.

To create the performance management system desired, however, management must recognize any difficulties in the process. Supervisors must look for ways to either overcome these difficulties or deal with them more effectively. Let's turn our attention to these challenges.

Difficulties in Performance Management Systems

Three stakeholders coexist in this process—employees, appraisers, and organizations—and coordinating the needs of each may cause problems. By focusing on the difficulties, we can begin to address them so as to reduce their overall consequence in the process. Let us address two primary categories of difficulties: (1) focus on the individual and (2) focus on the process.

Emotions may run high during a performance feedback session. However, a properly designed system and effective implementation (including appraiser training and continuous feedback) will help avoid emotional outbursts like this. *(Source: Altrendo Images/ Getty Images, Inc.)*

Focus on the Individual Do you remember the last time you received a graded test from a professor and believed that something was marked incorrect that wasn't wrong, or that your answer was too harshly penalized? How did you feel about that? Did you accept the score and leave it at that, or did you question the instructor? Whenever performance evaluations are administered (and tests are one form of performance evaluation), we run into the issue of people not seeing eye-to-eye on the evaluation. Appraising individuals is probably one of the more difficult aspects of a supervisor's job. Why? Because emotions are involved, and sometimes supervisors just don't like to do appraisals. We may think we are performing in an outstanding fashion, but that may be our perception. And although a boss recognizes our work is good, it may not be considered outstanding. Accordingly, in evaluating performance, emotions may arise.[11] And if these emotions are not dealt with properly, they can lead to greater conflict. What would happen if you confronted the professor in the previous example? Depending on the encounter, especially if it is aggressive, both of you may become defensive.[12] And because of the conflict, nothing but ill feelings may arise. The same applies for appraisers.

A difference on performance outcomes may lead to emotions overcoming both parties, a poor way for evaluations to be handled. A manager's first concern in the process is to remove the emotion difficulty from the process. When emotions stay calm in these meetings, employee satisfaction in the process may increase and carry over into future job activities, where both the employee and supervisor have opportunities for ongoing feedback in an effort to fulfill job expectations.

Focus on the Process Wherever performance evaluations are conducted, a particular structure must be followed. This structure exists to facilitate documentation that often allows for quantifiable evaluation. Additionally, HRM policies can dictate performance outcomes. For example, if a company ties performance evaluations to pay increases, consider the following potential difficulty: Sometime during the spring, the company's managers develop budgets for their units—budgets dictated and approved by upper management. Now, in this budget for the next fiscal year, each manager's salary budget increases by 3 percent. As the company enters the new fiscal year, the managers evaluate their employees. One employee in particular has done an outstanding job and is awarded a 6 percent raise. What does this do to the budget? To average 3 percent, some employees will receive less than the 3 percent salary increase.

ETHICAL ISSUES IN HRM

"That's Not Fair!" When Performance Appraisals Go Wrong

Used correctly, performance appraisals are a great tool for managers to provide feedback, and increase motivation and productivity. When their power is used for evil, however, good employees quit, or even worse, file a lawsuit against the organization.

Many things can go wrong in the appraisal process that can potentially violate Equal Employment Opportunity Act requirements or other employee rights. Some may be unintentional. Supervisors who are inadequately trained and evaluate employees poorly may do so because they don't understand the form or the process. Forms can also be part of the problem if they contain overly subjective ratings, vague descriptions of acceptable performance, or criteria that create disparate impact. Comments from coworkers who are either too critical or too flattering may be included by supervisors who are not aware of ongoing office politics.

Intentional distortion of employee appraisals can also occur. For example, what if a manager deliberately evaluates a favored employee higher than one he likes less, even though the latter is a better promotional candidate? Likewise, what if the supervisor avoids identifying areas of employee development for individuals, knowing that their likelihood of career advancement is stalemated without better skills?

Managers may use the process to discriminate, harass, or bully employees; create a hostile work environment; or retaliate against employees who file complaints.[16] Gary Namie of the Workplace Bullying Institute claims that the performance appraisal is a "very biased, error-prone, and abuse-prone system" that enables managers to become abusive and wreak emotional havoc with their employees.[17]

Supporters of properly functioning performance appraisals point to two vital criteria that managers must bring to the process: sincerity and honesty. Yet no legislative regulations, such as EEO laws, enforce such ethical standards. Hence, standards are frequently missing from the evaluation process.

Ethical Questions:

How can managers be trained to be sincere and honest when evaluating an employee's performance? Can organizations develop an ethical evaluation process? Should we expect companies to spend training dollars to achieve this goal? What do you think?

Evidence exists that managers who are poorly trained in the performance appraisal process show bias against women and minorities, but over time those biases tend to disappear as a result of training and practice. *(Source: Stígur Karlsson/iStockphoto)*

Consequently, company policies and procedures may present barriers to a properly functioning appraisal process.[13]

In order to balance these numbers, an appraiser focuses on negative rather than positive work behaviors of some employees. This can lead to a tendency to search for problems, which can ultimately lead to an emotional encounter. We may also find from the appraiser's perspective some uncertainty about how and what to measure, or how to deal with the employee in the evaluation process. Frequently, appraisers are poorly trained in how to evaluate an employee's performance. This lack of training may lead appraisers to make judgment errors or permit biases to enter into the process.

Because difficulties may arise, HRM should begin to develop the performance appraisal process so that maximum benefit can be achieved. This maximum benefit can translate into employee satisfaction with the process.[14] Such satisfaction is achieved by creating an understanding of the evaluation criteria used, permitting employee participation in the process, and allowing for development needs to be addressed.[15] To begin doing so requires us to initially understand the appraisal process.

Performance Management and EEO

Performance management systems are an integral part of most organizations. Properly developed and implemented, performance management processes can help an organization achieve its goals by developing productive employees without discrimination or bias. The many types of performance management systems, each with advantages and disadvantages, require us to be aware of the discriminatory practices and legal implications that may arise.

EEO laws require organizations to have bias-free HRM practices. HRM performance management systems must be objective and job related. That is, they must be reliable and valid. Under the Americans with Disabilities Act, performance management systems must also be able to measure "reasonable" performance success. Two factors assist in these matters: (1) the performance appraised must be conducted according to some established intervals, and (2) appraisers must be trained in the process.[18] The reasons for this become crystal clear when you consider that any employee action, such as promotion or termination, must be based on valid data prescribed from the performance management documentation. These objective data often support the legitimacy of employee actions.

Let's turn our attention now to a major component of the performance management system—the appraisal process.

The Appraisal Process

Establish Performance Standards

The appraisal process (Exhibit 10-1) begins with the establishment of performance standards in accordance with the organization's strategic goals. These should evolve out of the company's strategic direction—and, more specifically, the job analysis and the job description discussed in Chapter 5. These performance standards should also be clear and objective enough to be understood and measured. Too often, standards are articulated in ambiguous phrases that tell us little, such as "a full day's work" or "a good job." What is a full

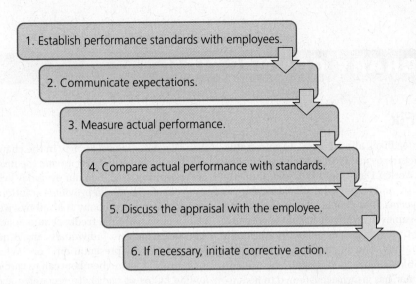

1. Establish performance standards with employees.

2. Communicate expectations.

3. Measure actual performance.

4. Compare actual performance with standards.

5. Discuss the appraisal with the employee.

6. If necessary, initiate corrective action.

Exhibit 10-1
The Appraisal Process

The appraisal process evaluates employee performance by measuring progress toward goals.

day's work or a good job? A supervisor's expectations of employee work performance must be clear enough in her mind so that she will be able to, at some later date, communicate these expectations to her employees, mutually agree to specific job performance measures, and appraise their performance against these established standards.

Communicate Expectations

Once performance standards are established, it is necessary to communicate these expectations; employees should not have to guess what is expected of them. Too many jobs have vague performance standards, and the problem is compounded when these standards are set in isolation and without employee input. Communication is a two-way street: mere information transfer from supervisor to employee is not successful communication.

Measure Actual Performance

The third step in the appraisal process is performance measurement. To determine what actual performance is, we need information about it. We should be concerned with how we measure and what we measure.

Four common sources of information frequently used by managers address how to measure actual performance: personal observation, statistical reports, oral reports, and written reports. Each has its strengths and weaknesses; however, a combination of them increases both the number of input sources and the probability of receiving reliable information. What we measure is probably more critical to the evaluation process than how we measure it. Selecting the wrong criteria can produce serious, dysfunctional consequences. And what we measure determines, to a great extent, what people in the organization will attempt to excel at. The criteria we measure must represent performance as it was mutually set in the first two steps of the appraisal process.

Compare Actual Performance with Standards

The fourth step in the appraisal process is the comparison of actual performance with standards. This step notes deviations between standard performance and actual performance. The performance appraisal form should include a list and explanation of the performance standards. It should also include an explanation of the different levels of performance and their degree of acceptability against the performance standard. This provides a valuable feedback tool as the manager moves on the next step, discussing the appraisal.

Discuss the Appraisal with the Employee

As we mentioned previously, one of the most challenging tasks facing appraisers is to present an accurate assessment to the employee. Appraising performance may touch on one of the most emotionally charged activities—evaluation of another individual's contribution and ability. The impression that employees receive about their assessment

CONTEMPORARY CONNECTION

The Feedback Fix

How long do you wait for feedback after you update your status on Facebook, upload a picture, or use Twitter to share your latest observations on life? Weeks? Days? Not likely. You probably get feedback within minutes and within a day it's old news.

We've developed, it seems, into people who are impatient for feedback. From video games that provide instant scores and standings, to schools that provide grades online immediately after tests are completed, to text messaging and social media sites like Facebook, Tumblr, Google+, and Twitter, the Millennial generation, in particular, has grown accustomed to instantaneous feedback. Author Dan Pink claims that "Millenials have lived their whole lives on a landscape lush with feedback, yet when they enter the workforce they find themselves in a veritable feedback desert . . . it's hard to get better at something if you receive feedback on your performance just once a year."[19]

What is HR to do? Most performance management systems are set up on a one year cycle, frustrating those who crave more frequent feedback. Condensing the process so the cycle repeats more than once a year may create a workload that gives nightmares to any conscientious HR department. Software programs that facilitate the process similar to the one used at the San Diego Zoological Society in the chapter opener would certainly help, but still don't provide the near immediate feedback we're growing used to in our everyday lives.

Can social media provide a solution? Possibly. Rypple is a social software company that allows work groups to provide continuous real-time feedback and coaching with team members and managers. Individuals can ask questions such as, "How did you like my presentation?" or, "What can I do differently next time?"[20] Team members can reward each other with public online kudos or badges to recognize accomplishments. Feedback can also be confidential and anonymous, which can be useful when constructive criticism is necessary. Even if performance management systems continue to be on a one year cycle, HR can access an archive of the Rypple activity, providing a comprehensive view of an employee's accomplishments and challenges for the full year.[21]

Consider this:

Would you appreciate having access to a system like Rypple as an employee? As a manager or HR manager? How about in your HR class?

---

has a strong impact on their self-esteem and, importantly, on their subsequent performance. Of course, conveying good news is considerably easier for both the appraiser and the employee than conveying bad news. In this context, the appraisal discussion can have negative as well as positive motivational consequences.

Initiate Corrective Action if Necessary

absolute standards
Measuring an employee's performance against established standards.

critical incident appraisal
A performance evaluation that focuses on key behaviors that differentiate between doing a job effectively or ineffectively.

The final step in the appraisal is the identification of corrective action where necessary. Corrective action can be of two types: one is immediate and deals predominantly with symptoms, and the other is basic and delves into causes. Immediate corrective action is often described as "putting out fires," whereas basic corrective action touches the source of deviation and seeks to adjust the difference permanently. Immediate action corrects problems such as mistakes in procedures and faulty training, and gets the employee back on track right away. Basic corrective action asks how and why performance deviated from the expected performance standard and provides training or employee development activities to improve performance. In some instances, appraisers may rationalize that they lack time to take basic corrective action and therefore must be content to perpetually put out fires. Good supervisors recognize that taking a little time to analyze a problem today may prevent the problem from worsening tomorrow.

Appraisal Methods

The previous section described the appraisal process in general terms. In this section we will look at specific ways in which HRM can actually establish performance standards and devise instruments to measure and appraise an employee's performance. Three approaches exist for doing appraisals: employees can be appraised against (1) absolute standards, (2) relative standards, or (3) outcomes. No one approach is always best; each has its strengths and weaknesses.[22]

Evaluating Absolute Standards

Our first group of appraisal methods uses **absolute standards**. This means that employees are compared to a standard, and their evaluation is independent of any other employee in a work group. This process assesses employee job traits and/or behaviors.[23] Included in this group are the following methods: the critical incident appraisal, the checklist, the graphic rating scale, forced choice, and behaviorally anchored rating scales. Let's look at each of these, focusing on their strengths and weaknesses.

Critical Incident Appraisal The **critical incident appraisal** focuses the rater's attention on critical or key behaviors that make the difference between doing a job effectively and doing it ineffectively. The appraiser writes down anecdotes describing employee actions that were especially effective or ineffective. For example, a police sergeant might write the following critical incident about one of her officers: "Brought order to a volatile situation by calmly discussing options with an armed suspect during a hostage situation, which resulted in all hostages being released, and the suspect being apprehended without injury to any individual." Note that with this approach to appraisal, specific behaviors are cited, not vaguely defined individual traits. A behavior-based appraisal such as this should be more valid than trait-based appraisals because it is clearly more job related. It is one thing to say that an employee is "aggressive," "imaginative," or "relaxed," but that does not tell us anything about how well the job is being done. Critical incidents, with their focus on behaviors, judge performance rather than personalities.

The strength of the critical incident method is that it looks at behaviors. Additionally, a list of critical incidents provides a rich set of examples that can be used to point out which employee behaviors are desirable and which ones call for improvement. Its drawbacks are that (1) appraisers must regularly write these incidents down and doing this on a daily or weekly basis for all employees is time-consuming and burdensome for supervisors; and (2) critical incidents suffer from the same comparison problem found in essays—they do not lend themselves easily to quantification. Comparison and ranking of employees may be difficult.

Checklist Appraisal In the **checklist appraisal**, the evaluator uses a list of behavioral descriptions and checks off behaviors that apply to the employee. As Exhibit 10-2 illustrates, the evaluator merely goes down the list and checks off "yes" or "no" to each question.

Once the checklist is complete, it is usually evaluated by the HRM staff, not the appraiser completing the checklist. The rater does not actually evaluate the employee's performance; he or she merely records it. An HRM analyst scores the checklist, often weighting the factors in relationship to their importance to that specific job. The final evaluation can either be returned to the appraiser for discussion with the employee, or someone from HRM can provide the feedback.

The checklist appraisal reduces some bias in the evaluation process because the rater and the scorer are different. However, the rater usually can pick up the positive and negative connections in each item—so bias can still be introduced. From a cost standpoint, too, this appraisal method may be inefficient and time-consuming if HRM must spend considerable time in developing individualized checklists of items for numerous job categories.

Graphic Rating Scale Appraisal One of the oldest and most popular methods of appraisal is the **graphic rating scale**.[24] An example of some rating scale items is shown in Exhibit 10-3. Rating scales can be

checklist appraisal
A performance evaluation in which a rater checks off applicable employee attributes.

graphic rating scale
A performance appraisal method that lists traits and a range of performance for each.

How would you evaluate this employee using a graphic rating scale? This employee's supervisor would evaluate the employee based on how well he compared to an established standard of traits/behaviors such as quantity and quality of work, job knowledge, cooperation, loyalty, dependability, attendance, honesty, integrity, attitudes, and initiative. *(Source: Eddie Seal/Bloomberg News/Getty Images, Inc.)*

Exhibit 10-2

Sample Checklist Items for Appraising a Customer Service Representative

Checklists are completed by supervisors, but evaluated by HR staff. Items rated may have different weights.

	Yes	No
1. Are supervisor's orders usually followed?	___	___
2. Does the individual approach customers promptly?	___	___
3. Does the individual suggest additional merchandise to customers?	___	___
4. Does the individual keep busy when not serving a customer?	___	___
5. Does the individual lose his or her temper in public?	___	___
6. Does the individual volunteer to help other employees?	___	___

used to assess factors such as quantity and quality of work, job knowledge, cooperation, loyalty, dependability, attendance, honesty, integrity, attitudes, and initiative. However, this method is most valid when abstract traits such as loyalty or integrity are avoided, unless they can be defined in more specific behavioral terms.[25]

To use the graphic rating scale, the assessor goes down the list of factors and notes the point along the scale or continuum that best describes the employee. There are typically five to ten points on the continuum. The challenge in designing the rating scale is to ensure that factors evaluated and scale points are clearly understood and are unambiguous to the rater. Ambiguity can introduce bias.

Why are rating scales popular? Although they do not provide the depth of information that essays or critical incidents do, they are less time-consuming to develop and administer. They also provide a quantitative analysis useful for comparison purposes. Furthermore, in contrast to the checklist, more generalization of items makes it possible to compare individuals in diverse job categories.

Forced-Choice Appraisal Have you ever completed one of those tests that presumably gives you insights into what kind of career you should pursue? A question might be, for example, "Would you rather go to a party with a group of friends or attend a lecture by a well-known political figure?" If so, then you are familiar with the forced-choice format. The **forced-choice appraisal** is a type of checklist where the rater must choose between two or more statements. Each statement may be favorable or unfavorable. The appraiser's job is to identify which statement is most (or in some cases least) descriptive of the individual being evaluated. For instance, students evaluating their college instructor might have to choose between "(a) keeps up with the schedule identified in the syllabus,

forced-choice appraisal

A performance evaluation in which the rater must choose between two specific statements about an employee's work behavior.

Exhibit 10-3

Sample of Graphic Rating Scale Items and Format

Graphic rating scales provide a list of job skills and a continuum for the rater to evaluate the employee's performance on each skill. Graphic rating scales are relatively easy to complete and attempt to provide objective feedback.

Performance Factor	Performance Rating				
Quality of work is the accuracy, skill, and completeness of work.	☐ Consistently unsatisfactory	☐ Occasionally unsatisfactory	☐ Consistently satisfactory	☐ Sometimes superior	☐ Consistently superior
Quantity of work is the volume of work done in a normal workday.	☐ Consistently unsatisfactory	☐ Occasionally unsatisfactory	☐ Consistently satisfactory	☐ Sometimes superior	☐ Consistently superior
Job knowledge is information pertinent to the job that an individual should have for satisfactory job performance.	☐ Poorly informed about work duties	☐ Occasionally unsatisfactory	☐ Can answer most questions about the job	☐ Understands all phases of the job	☐ Has complete mastery of all phases of the job
Dependability is following directions and company policies without supervision.	☐ Requires constant supervision	☐ Requires occasional follow-up	☐ Usually can be counted on	☐ Requires little supervision	☐ Requires absolute minimum supervision

(b) lectures with confidence, (c) keeps interest and attention of class, (d) demonstrates how concepts are practically applied in today's organizations, or (e) allows students the opportunity to learn concepts on their own." All the preceding statements could be favorable, but we really don't know. As with the checklist method, to reduce bias, the right answers are unknown to the rater; someone in HRM scores the answers based on the answer key for the job being evaluated. This key should be validated so HRM is in a position to say that individuals with higher scores are better- performing employees.

The major advantage of the forced-choice method is that because the appraiser does not know the "right" answers, it reduces bias and distortion.[26] For example, the appraiser may like a certain employee and intentionally want to give him a favorable evaluation, but this becomes difficult if one is not sure of the preferred response. On the negative side, appraisers tend to dislike this method; many do not like being forced to make distinctions between similar-sounding statements. Raters also may become frustrated with a system in which they do not know what represents a good or poor answer. Consequently, they may try to second-guess the scoring key to align the formal appraisal with their intuitive appraisal.

Behaviorally Anchored Rating Scales An approach that has received considerable attention by academics in past years involves **behaviorally anchored rating scales (BARS)**. These scales combine major elements from the critical incident and graphic rating scale approaches. The appraiser rates the employees based on items along a continuum, but the points are examples of actual behavior on the given job rather than general descriptions or traits. The enthusiasm surrounding BARS grew from the belief that the use of specific behaviors, derived for each job, should produce relatively error-free and reliable ratings. Although this promise has not been fulfilled, it has been argued that this may be partly due to departures from careful methodology in developing the specific scales rather than to inadequacies in the concept. BARS forms are time-consuming to develop correctly.

Behaviorally anchored rating scales specify definite, observable, and measurable job behavior. Examples of job-related behavior and performance dimensions are generated by asking participants to give specific illustrations of effective and ineffective behavior regarding each performance dimension; these behavioral examples are then translated into appropriate performance dimensions. Those sorted into the dimension for which

behaviorally anchored rating scales (BARS)
A performance appraisal technique that generates critical incidents and develops behavioral dimensions of performance. The evaluator appraises behaviors rather than traits.

Behaviorally Anchored Rating Scale
Position: Employee Relations Specialist
Job Dimension: Ability to Absorb and Interpret Policies
This employee relations specialist:

9 ☐ Could be expected to serve as an information source concerning new and changed policies for others in the organization

8 ☐ Could be expected to be aware quickly of program changes and explain these to employees

7 ☐ Could be expected to reconcile conflicting policies and procedures correctly to meet HRM goals

6 ☐ Could be expected to recognize the need for additional information to gain a better understanding of policy changes

5 ☐ Could be expected to complete various HRM forms correctly after receiving instruction on them

4 ☐ Could be expected to require some help and practice in mastering new policies and procedures

3 ☐ Could be expected to know that there is always a problem, but go down many blind alleys before realizing they are wrong

2 ☐ Could be expected to incorrectly interpret guidelines, creating problems for line managers

1 ☐ Could be expected to be unable to learn new procedures even after repeated explanations

Exhibit 10-4
Sample BARS for an Employee Relations Specialist

This behaviorally anchored rating scale (BARS) evaluates how well an HR employee relations specialist can understand and interpret company policies by describing the levels of performance. Better performance earns higher point value.

Source: Reprinted from *Business Horizons* (August 1976), copyright 1976 by the Foundation for the School of Business at Indiana University. Used with permission.

they were generated are retained. The final group of behavior incidents is then numerically scaled to a level of performance each is perceived to represent. The identified incidents with high rater agreement on performance effectiveness are retained for use as anchors on the performance dimension. The results of these processes are behavioral descriptions such as anticipates, plans, executes, solves immediate problems; carries out orders; or handles emergency situations.

Exhibit 10-4 is an example of a BARS form for an employee relations specialist's scale.

BARS research indicates that, although it is far from perfect, it does tend to reduce rating errors. Possibly its major advantage stems from the specific feedback that it communicates.[27] The process of developing behavioral scales is valuable for clarifying to both the employee and the rater which behaviors represent good performance and which don't. Unfortunately, it, too, suffers from the distortions inherent in most rating methods.[28] These distortions will be discussed later in this chapter.

Relative Standards Methods

The second general category of appraisal methods compares individuals against other individuals. These methods are **relative standards** rather than absolute measuring devices. The most popular of the relative methods are group order ranking, individual ranking, and paired comparison.

relative standards
Evaluating an employee's performance by comparing the employee with other employees.

Group Order Ranking Group order ranking requires the evaluator to place employees into a particular classification, such as the "top 20 percent." This method, for instance, is often used in recommending students to graduate schools. Evaluators are asked to rank the student in the top 5 percent, the next 5 percent, the next 15 percent, and so forth. But when used by appraisers to evaluate employees, raters deal with all employees in their area. So, for example, if a rater has twenty employees, only four can be in the top fifth; and, of course, four also must be relegated to the bottom fifth.

The advantage of this group ordering is that it prevents raters from inflating their evaluations so everyone looks good or from forcing the evaluations so everyone is rated near the average—outcomes not unusual with the graphic rating scale. The main disadvantages surface, however, when the number of employees compared is small. At the extreme, if the evaluator is looking at only four employees, all may be excellent, yet the evaluator may be forced to rank them into top quarter, second quarter, third quarter, and low quarter. Theoretically, as the sample size increases, the validity of relative scores as an accurate measure increases, but occasionally the technique is implemented with a small group, utilizing assumptions that apply to large groups.

Another disadvantage, which plagues all relative measures, is the zero-sum game consideration. This means that any change must add up to zero. For example, if twelve employees in a department perform at different levels of effectiveness, by definition, three are in the top quarter, three are in the second quarter, and so forth. The sixth-best employee, for instance, would be in the second quartile. Ironically, if two of the workers in the third or fourth quartiles leave the department and are not replaced, then our sixth-best employee now falls into the third quarter. Because comparisons are relative, a mediocre employee may score highly only because he or she is the "best of the worst." In contrast, an excellent performer matched against "stiff" competition may be evaluated poorly, when in absolute terms his or her performance is outstanding.

individual ranking
Ranking employees' performance from highest to lowest.

Individual Ranking The **individual ranking** method requires the evaluator merely to list employees in order from highest to lowest. In this process, only one employee can be rated "best." If the evaluator must appraise thirty individuals, this method assumes that the difference between the first and second employee is the same as that between the twenty-first and the twenty-second. Even though some of these employees may be closely grouped, this method typically allows for no ties. In terms of advantages and disadvantages, the individual ranking method carries the same pluses and minuses as group-order ranking. For example, individual ranking may be more manageable in a department of six employees than in one where a supervisor must evaluate the nineteen employees who report to her.

CONTEMPORARY CONNECTION

Forced Rankings: Are They Working?

What if your human resource management professor was required to rank everyone in your class from the top performers to the bottom, and then fail the bottom 10 percent? Would that change your attitude toward the class? Would your performance improve? That's the basic philosophy of forced ranking performance appraisal systems.

Forced rankings are one of the most controversial trends in performance management systems in corporations. Companies such as General Electric, MetLife and Hewlett-Packard have used forced rankings to rank their employees from best to worst, and then use such rankings to determine pay levels as well as in other HRM decisions.

Why use this controversial rating strategy? The primary reason is that many executives became frustrated by managers who rated all their employees above average when in fact they weren't. In addition, these executives wanted to create a system that would increase the organization's competitiveness—one that would reward the very best performers and encourage poor performers to leave. So they turned to forced rankings—what has been called "rank and yank" by its critics. Financial giant American International Group (AIG) recently announced plans to introduce a compensations system based on employee ranking in response to criticism that financial firms tend to overpay employees.[29]

One of the better-known forced rankings systems was developed by General Electric. Its program is called the 20-70-10 plan. Under this system of evaluation, GE executives force managers to review all professional employees and identify their top 20 percent, middle 70 percent, and bottom 10 percent. GE then does everything possible to keep and reward the top performers, and fires all the bottom performers—the 10 percent. They do so to keep the company moving forward by continually raising the bar of successful performance.

Fans of forced rankings see such actions as continually improving an organization's effectiveness and a means of improving the organization's workforce. By doing so, the most deserving employees are rewarded most—both monetarily and with career advancement. They also see such systems as growing the best return on investment to shareholders.

Critics, on the other hand, argue that these programs are harsh and arbitrary and discourage cooperation and teamwork. It often pits one employee against another and leads to higher rates of turnover. Accordingly, morale suffers, and there is often a great distrust of the organization's leadership—which ultimately increases costs. Critics also say that these programs run counter to the belief held by many individuals that almost any worker is salvageable with proper guidance. Others have claimed that vague standards can result in discrimination. Capital One and Ford Motor Company settled class action suits by former employees who claimed that the forced rankings affected a disproportionate number of a particular sex, age group, or race. Research by Dr. Steve Scullen at Drake University has found that while the forced ranking system initially shows dramatic increases in performance, the performance benefits tend to decline over time. Microsoft chose to revamp their appraisal system, discontinuing the practice of requiring managers to make forced performance rankings.[30]

Consider this:

How would you feel about ranking the people who work for you and firing the bottom 10 percent? Is it an unethical practice? Would you be more motivated if you were one of the employees in the top 20 percent, receiving praise and a raise? Does most of the motivation come from fear or the need to excel?

Paired Comparison The **paired comparison** method selects one job trait, and then compares each employee in a group with the others. A score is obtained for each employee by simply counting the number of pairs in which the individual is superior at the job trait, ranking each individual in relationship to all others on a one-on-one basis as shown in Exhibit 10-5. If ten employees are evaluated, the first person is compared, one by one, with each of the other nine, and the number of times this person is preferred in any of the nine pairs is tabulated. Each of the remaining nine persons, in turn, is compared in the same way, and a ranking is formed by the greatest number of preferred "victories." This method ensures that each employee is compared against every other, but the method can become difficult when comparing large numbers of employees.

paired comparison
Ranking individuals' performance by counting the times any one individual is the preferred member when compared with all other employees.

Using Achieved Outcomes to Evaluate Employees

The third approach to appraisal makes use of achieved performance outcomes. Employees are evaluated on how well they accomplished a specific set of objectives determined as critical in the successful completion of their job. This approach may be referred to as

Exhibit 10-5
Ranking Employees by Paired Comparison

In the paired comparisons, five employees are being compared for their innovation and creativity on the job. The plus (+) means the employee being rated is better than the comparison employee. The minus (–) means the employee being rated is worse than the comparison employee. The employee receiving the most +s will be the highest ranked employee. In this chart, Admir is ranked highest with the most +s.

Job Skills Evaluated: Innovation and Creativity					
Employee being rated:					
Comparison with:	Admir	Laila	Carmen	Dante	Emilio
Admir		+	–	–	–
Betty	+		+	–	+
Carmen	+	–			
Dante	+	+	+		+
Emilio	+	–	–	–	

management by objectives (MBO)
A performance appraisal method that includes mutual objective setting and evaluation based on the attainment of the specific objectives.

goal setting but is more commonly referred to as **management by objectives (MBO)**.[31] Its appeal lies in its emphasis on converting overall objectives into specific objectives for organizational units and individual members.

MBO makes objectives operational by a process in which they cascade down through the organization. The organization's overall objectives are translated into specific objectives for each succeeding level in the organization—divisional, departmental, and individual.[32] Because lower-unit managers participate in setting their own goals, MBO works from the bottom up as well as from the top down. The result is a hierarchy that links objectives at one level to those at the next level. For the individual employee, MBO provides specific personal performance objectives. Each person, therefore, has an identified specific contribution to make to his or her unit's performance. If all the individuals achieve their goals, the unit will meet its goals. Subsequently, the organization's overall objectives will become a reality.

Common Elements in MBO Programs Four ingredients are common to MBO programs: specific goals, participative decision making, a specific time period, and performance feedback. Let's briefly look at each of these.

Specific Goals The objectives in MBO should be concise statements of expected accomplishments. It is not adequate, for example, merely to state a desire to cut costs, improve service, or increase quality.[33] Such desires need to be converted into tangible objectives that can be measured and evaluated—for instance, to cut departmental costs by 8 percent, to improve service by ensuring that all insurance claims are processed within seventy-two hours of receipt, or to increase quality by keeping returns to less than 0.05 percent of sales.

Participative Decision Making MBO objectives are not unilaterally set by the boss and assigned to employees, as is characteristic of traditional objective setting. Rather, MBO replaces imposed goals with participative goal setting. The manager and employee jointly choose the goals and agree on how they will be achieved.

Specific Time Period Each objective has a concise time in which it is to be completed, typically, three months, six months, or a year.

Performance Feedback The final ingredient in an MBO program is continuous feedback on performance and goals. Ideally, ongoing feedback allows individuals to monitor and correct their own actions. This is supplemented by periodic formal appraisal meetings in which superiors and subordinates review progress toward goals that lead to further feedback.

Does MBO Work? Assessing MBO effectiveness is a complex task. Let's review a growing body of literature on the relationship between goals and performance.[34] If factors such as a person's ability and acceptance of goals are held constant, more challenging goals lead to higher performance. Although individuals with difficult goals achieve them far less often than those who have easy goals, they nevertheless perform at a consistently higher level.

CONTEMPORARY CONNECTION

Facts on Performance Evaluations

Here are some interesting facts that put performance assessments in perspective:

- More than 90 percent of all U.S. organizations use some form of performance evaluations.[37]
- Almost three-fourths of all organizations evaluate nearly three-fourths of their employees each year.
- About half of all organizations evaluate employees more than once a year.

- About three in four employees see a direct link between their performance evaluations and their compensation—although compensation discussions are separated from performance reviews.
- Only one in five employees receives feedback from peers or customers in their performance evaluation process.

Moreover, studies consistently support the finding that specific, difficult goals, often referred to as "stretch goals," produce higher output than no goals or generalized goals such as "do your best." Feedback also favorably affects performance. Feedback lets a person know whether his or her effort is sufficient or needs to increase. It can induce a person to raise his or her goal level after attaining a previous goal and indicate ways to improve performance.

The results cited here are all consistent with MBO's emphasis on specific goals and feedback. MBO implies, rather than explicitly states, that goals must be perceived as feasible. Research on goal setting indicates that MBO is most effective if the goals are difficult enough to require some stretching.

A major assumption of MBO performance systems is that employees will be more committed to higher performance standards if the employee participates in the setting of the performance standards to be evaluated. The partnership of manager and employee in setting clear goals at the start of the evaluation period is what sets the MBO process apart from other evaluation methods.[35] Studies of actual MBO programs confirm that MBO effectively increases employee performance and organizational productivity. One of the more critical components of this effectiveness is top management commitment to the MBO process. When top managers had a high commitment to MBO and were personally involved in its implementation, productivity gains were higher than if this commitment was lacking.[36]

Factors That Can Distort Appraisals

The performance appraisal process and techniques that we have suggested present systems in which the evaluator is free from personal biases, prejudices, and idiosyncrasies. This is defended on the basis that objectivity minimizes potential arbitrary and dysfunctional behavior by the evaluator, which may adversely affect achievement of organizational goals. Thus, our goal should be to use direct performance criteria where possible.

It would be naïve to assume, however, that all evaluators impartially interpret and standardize the criteria on which their employees will be appraised. This is particularly true of jobs for which developing performance standards can be difficult—if not impossible. These would include, but are certainly not limited to, such jobs as researcher, teacher, engineer, and consultant. In the place of such standards, we can expect appraisers to use nonperformance or subjective criteria against which to evaluate individuals.[38]

A completely error-free performance appraisal is only an ideal HRM professionals can aim for. In reality, most appraisals fall short, often through one or more actions that can significantly impede objective evaluation. We've briefly described them in Exhibit 10-6.

Exhibit 10-6
Factors That Distort Appraisals

The appraisal process can be distorted by many factors, leaving the resulting appraisal meaningless. Evaluators need to be aware of the factors that can cause problems with the process and take care to eliminate their influence.

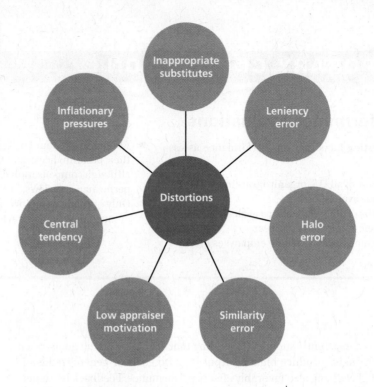

Leniency Error

Every evaluator has his or her own value system that acts as a standard against which appraisals are made. Relative to the true or actual performance an individual exhibits, some evaluators mark high, while others mark low. The former is referred to as positive **leniency error**, and the latter as negative leniency error. When evaluators are positively lenient in their appraisal, an individual's performance becomes overstated. In doing so, the performance is rated higher than it actually should be. Similarly, a negative leniency error understates performance, giving the individual a lower appraisal.

leniency error
Performance appraisal distortion caused by evaluating employees against one's own value system.

If all individuals in an organization were appraised by the same person, there would be no problem. Any error factor would be applied equally to everyone.[39] The difficulty arises when we have different raters with different leniency errors. For example, assume a situation where Jones and Smith are performing the same job for different supervisors with absolutely identical job performance. If Jones's supervisor tends to err toward positive leniency while Smith's supervisor errs toward negative leniency, we might be confronted with two dramatically different evaluations. Organizations have attempted to reduce lenience and other errors with supervisor training called "calibration" meetings. In these meetings, supervisors are coached in ways to be more consistent in rating employees. For example, if a five-point rating scale is used, supervisors discuss what employee behaviors would earn a rating of "1" on up to a rating of "5."[40]

Halo Error

halo error
The tendency to let our assessment of an individual on one trait influence our evaluation of that person on other specific traits.

The **halo error** or effect occurs when one is rated either extremely high or extremely low on all factors based on a rating of one or two factors. For example, if an employee tends to be conscientious and dependable, we might become biased toward that individual to the extent that we will rate him or her positively on many desirable attributes. Managers may also tend to give higher ratings to employees that they themselves have hired over those hired by other managers.[41]

People who design teaching appraisal forms for college students to fill out in evaluating instructor effectiveness each semester must confront the halo effect. Students tend to rate a faculty member as outstanding on all criteria when they are particularly appreciative of a few things he or she does in the classroom. Similarly, a few bad habits—showing up late for lectures, being slow in returning papers, or assigning an extremely demanding reading requirement—might produce negative ratings across the board.

One method frequently used to deal with the halo error is "reverse wording" evaluation questions so that a favorable answer for, say, question 17 might be 5 on a scale of 1 through 5, and a favorable answer for question 18 might be 1 on a scale of 1 through 5. Structuring questions in this way seeks to reduce the halo error by requiring the evaluator to consider each question independently. Another method, where more than one person is evaluated, is to have the evaluator appraise all ratees on each performance standard before going on to the next performance standard.

Similarity Error

When evaluators rate other people in the same way that the evaluators perceive themselves, they make a **similarity error**. That is, they project self-perceptions onto others. For example, the evaluator who perceives himself or herself as aggressive may evaluate others by looking for aggressiveness. Those who demonstrate this characteristic tend to benefit, and others who lack it may be penalized.

similarity error
Evaluating employees based on the way an evaluator perceives himself or herself.

Low Appraiser Motivation

If the evaluator knows that a poor appraisal could significantly hurt the employee's future—particularly opportunities for promotion or a salary increase—the evaluator may be reluctant to give a realistic appraisal. Evidence indicates that it is more difficult to obtain accurate appraisals when important rewards depend on the results.

Central Tendency

It is possible that regardless of who the appraiser evaluates and what traits are used, the pattern of evaluation remains the same. Sometimes the evaluator's ability to appraise objectively and accurately has been impeded by a failure to use the extremes of the scale. When this happens, we call the action **central tendency**. Central tendency occurs when a rater refuses to use the two extremes (for instance, outstanding and unacceptable, respectively). Raters prone to the central tendency error continually rate all employees as average. For example, if a supervisor rates all employees as 3 on a scale of 1 to 5, no differentiation among the employees exists. Failure to rate deserving employees as 5 or as 1, as the case warrants it, will only create problems, especially if this information is used for pay increases.

central tendency
The tendency of a rater to give average ratings.

Inflationary Pressures

A middle manager in a large Minnesota-based company could not understand why he had been passed over for promotion. He had seen his file and knew that his average rating by his supervisor was 88. Given his knowledge that the appraisal system defined outstanding performance at 90 or above, good as 80 or above, average as 70 or above, and inadequate performance as anything below 70, he was at a loss to understand why he had not been promoted. The manager's confusion was only somewhat resolved when he found out that the "average" rating for middle managers in his organization was 92. This example addresses a major potential problem in appraisals: inflationary pressures. This, in effect, is a specific case of low differentiation within the upper range of the rating choices.

Inflationary pressures have always existed but appear to have increased as a problem over the past three decades. As "equality" values have grown in importance in our society, as well as fear of retribution from disgruntled employees who fail to achieve excellent appraisals, evaluation has tended to be less rigorous, and negative repercussions from the evaluation have been reduced by generally inflating or upgrading appraisals. However, inflating these evaluations has put many organizations in a difficult position when having to defend their personnel action in the case of discharging an employee.

How would you rate the coaching effectiveness of Duke University Basketball Coach Mike Krzyzewski? If you evaluate him based on leading his teams to four NCAA championships and having the most wins in NCAA Division 1 basketball history, you might come to a positive conclusion.
(Source: Anthony J. Causi/Icon SMI/NewsCom)

Inappropriate Substitutes for Performance

A job with an absolutely clear definition of performance and foolproof measures for accurately assessing a worker's performance is rare. It is hard to find consensus on what is "a good job," and it is even more difficult to produce agreement on what criteria determine performance.[42] Criteria for a salesperson are affected by factors such as economic conditions and actions of competitors—factors outside the salesperson's control. As a result, the appraisal frequently uses substitutes for performance, criteria that are supposed to closely approximate performance and act in its place. Many of these substitutes are well chosen and give a good approximation of actual performance. However, the substitutes chosen are not always appropriate. It is not unusual, for example, to find organizations using criteria such as effort, enthusiasm, neatness, positive attitudes, conscientiousness, promptness, and congeniality as substitutes for performance. In some jobs, one or more of these criteria are part of performance. Obviously, enthusiasm does enhance teacher effectiveness; you are more likely to listen to and be motivated by an enthusiastic teacher than by one who is not; increased attentiveness and motivation typically lead to increased learning. But enthusiasm may in no way be relevant to effective performance for many accountants, firefighters, or copy editors. An appropriate substitute for performance in one job may be totally inappropriate in another.

Attribution Theory

attribution theory

A theory of performance evaluation based on the perception of who is in control of an employee's performance.

In a concept in management literature called **attribution theory**, employee evaluations are directly affected by a "supervisor's perceptions of who is believed to be in control of the employee's performance—the employer or the manager."[43] Attribution theory attempts to differentiate between elements the employee controls (internal) versus those the employee cannot control (external). Most people tend to believe that personal success has been earned by internal controls (hard work, perseverance, intelligence) and personal failures are due to external factors (difficult coworkers, out of date equipment, bad luck). The reverse tends to be true when viewing others. Their personal success is more likely due to external factors (good training, excellent supervision) and failures are likely caused by internal factors (laziness, procrastination, lack of ability). For example, if an employee fails to finish a project he has had six months to complete, a supervisor may view this negatively if he or she believes that the employee did not manage either the project or his time well (internal control). Conversely, if the project is delayed because top management requested a change in priorities, an understanding supervisor may see the incomplete project in more positive terms (external control).

One research study found support for two key generalizations regarding attribution:[44]

- When appraisers attribute an employee's poor performance to internal control, the judgment is harsher than when the same poor performance is attributed to external factors.
- When an employee performs satisfactorily, appraisers will evaluate the employee more favorably if the performance is attributed to the employee's own efforts than if the performance is attributed to outside forces.

Attribution theory is interesting and sheds new light on rater effects on performance evaluations, but it requires continued study. It does provide much insight on why unbiased performance evaluations are important. An extension of attribution theory relates to impression management, which takes into account how the employee influences the relationship with his or her supervisor. For example, when an employee positively impresses his or her supervisor, there is a strong likelihood that the individual's performance rating will be higher.

Creating More Effective Performance Management Systems

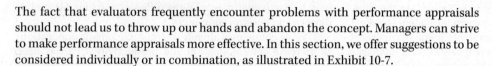

The fact that evaluators frequently encounter problems with performance appraisals should not lead us to throw up our hands and abandon the concept. Managers can strive to make performance appraisals more effective. In this section, we offer suggestions to be considered individually or in combination, as illustrated in Exhibit 10-7.

Use Behavior-Based Measures

As we have pointed out, the evidence favors behavior-based measures over those developed around traits. Many traits often related to good performance may, in fact, have little or no performance relationship. Traits such as loyalty, initiative, courage, reliability, and self-expression are intuitively desirable in employees, but are individuals who rate high on those traits higher performers than those who rate low? Of course, we can't definitively answer this question. We know employees sometimes rate high on these characteristics and are poor performers. Yet we can find others who are excellent performers but score poorly on traits such as these. Our conclusion is that traits like loyalty and initiative may be prized by appraisers, but no evidence supports the notion that certain traits will be adequate synonyms for performance in a large cross-section of jobs.

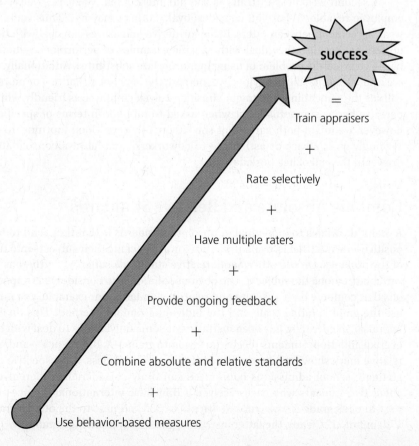

Exhibit 10-7
Toward a More Effective Performance Management System

A successful performance management system requires attention to many important factors.

CONTEMPORARY CONNECTION

The "Anywhere" Performance Appraisal

The place: A restaurant near you
The time: Someday soon
The situation: A sales manager and sales representative have been discussing the sales representative's annual performance review. They pull out their smart phones and access the company's Web-based performance management system to take a look at the appraisal form and comments made by the sales manager. Since the review went very well, the sales manager references the talent management software package and explains to the sales person that his promotion to a sales management position has been approved. As dessert arrives, the sales manager accesses the company's recruiting and staffing software on her smart phone and the two discuss which of the applicants recently recruited via Facebook should be interviewed to replace the sales rep. Last, they submit their expense reports on their phones with a click, and they're on their way.

Some of these functions already exist in reality, some are in development, but all will be tools that managers will likely use in the future to perform most aspects of human resource planning, recruitment, orientation, training, and appraisal. Smart phones like the Apple iPhone, Android, and BlackBerry have

the capability to run HR applications, and several companies are developing new HR related applications that work on mobile devices. It isn't easy. Screens are small, there's lots of data to deliver, security is a concern, and making applications easy to use sometimes requires different versions for mobile devices and desktop computers.

Many companies already use multiple mobile applications to increase communication and productivity. UPS has been using PDAs (Personal Digital Assistants) to evaluate drivers for several years. The PDAs allow managers to ride along with drivers and evaluate their performance in real time as they complete their deliveries. Evaluations are more accurate when the manager doesn't have to make notes that must be written up when they return to the office.[45]

Employers are recognizing that Gen Y workers want the same access to technology at work that they have in their personal life, and take a dim view of employers who insist on using technology that was developed before they were born. One software company has found that the biggest barrier to acceptance is HR executives who rose through the organization in the early days of cell phones and need a little convincing.[46]

A second weakness in traits is the judgment itself. What is loyalty? When is an employee reliable? What you consider loyalty, others may not. Thus traits suffer from weak agreement between raters. Behavior-derived measures can deal with both of these objections. Because they deal with specific examples of performance—both good and bad—we avoid the problem of using inappropriate substitutes. Additionally, because we are evaluating specific behaviors, we increase the likelihood that two or more evaluators will see the same thing. You might consider a given employee as friendly, while we might perceive her as standoffish. But when asked to rate her in terms of specific behaviors, however, we might both agree that she "frequently says 'Good morning' to customers," "willingly gives advice or assistance to coworkers," and "always consolidates her cash drawer at the end of her work day."

Combine Absolute and Relative Standards

A major drawback to individual or absolute standards is that they tend to be biased by positive leniency; that is, evaluators lean toward packing their subjects into the high part of the rankings. On the other hand, relative standards suffer when there is little actual variability among the subjects. The obvious solution is to consider using appraisal methods that combine both absolute and relative standards. For example, you might want to use the graphic rating scale and the individual ranking method. This dual method of appraisal, incidentally, has been instituted at some universities to deal with the problem of grade inflation. Students receive an absolute grade—A, B, C, D, or F—and next to it is a relative mark showing how this student ranked in the class. A prospective employer or graduate school admissions committee can draw considerably different conclusions about two students who each received a B in their international finance course when next to one's grade it says "ranked 4th out of 33," and next to the other's grade, "ranked 17th out of 21." Clearly, the latter instructor gave many more high grades.

Provide Ongoing Feedback

Several years back, a nationwide motel chain advertised, "The best surprise is no surprise." This phrase clearly applies to performance appraisals. Employees like to know how they are doing. The annual review, in which the appraiser shares the employees' evaluations with them, can become a problem, if only because appraisers put them off. This is more likely if the appraisal is negative, but the annual review is additionally troublesome if the supervisor "saves up" performance-related information and unloads it during the appraisal review. This creates an extremely trying experience for both evaluator and employee. In such instances, the supervisor may attempt to avoid uncomfortable issues that the employee will likely deny or rationalize.

The solution lies in the appraiser frequently discussing with the employee both expectations and disappointments. Providing the employee with repeated opportunities to discuss performance before any reward or punishment consequences occur will eliminate surprises at the formal annual review. Ongoing feedback should keep the formal sitting-down step from being particularly traumatic for either party. Additionally, ongoing feedback is the critical element in an MBO system that actually works.

Use Multiple Raters

As the number of raters increases, the probability of attaining more accurate information increases.[47] If rater error follows a normal curve, an increase in the number of raters will find the majority clustering about the middle. If a person has had ten supervisors, nine of whom rated him or her excellent and one poor, then we must investigate what went into that one poor rating. Maybe this rater identified an area of weakness needing training or an area to be avoided in future job assignments.[48] Therefore, by moving employees about within the organization to add evaluations, we increase the probability of achieving more valid and reliable evaluations—as well as helping support needed changes. Of course, we assume that the process functions properly and bias-free![49] And let's not forget about the self-rating. Giving employees the opportunity to evaluate themselves and using that information as part of the evaluation process has been shown to increase employee satisfactions.[50]

Use Peer Evaluations Have you ever wondered why a professor asks you to evaluate one another's contributions to a group or team project? The reasoning behind this action is that the professor cannot tell what every member did on the project, only the overall product quality. And at times, that may not be fair to everyone—especially if someone left most of the work up to the remaining group members.

Similarly, supervisors find it difficult to evaluate their employees' performance because they are not observing them every moment of the work day. Unfortunately, without this information, they may not be making an accurate assessment. And if their goal for the performance evaluation is to identify deficient areas and provide constructive feedback to their employees, they do these workers a disservice by not having sufficient data. One of the better means of gathering information is through peer evaluations. **Peer evaluations** are conducted by the employees' coworkers—people explicitly familiar with the behaviors involved in their jobs.

peer evaluation
A performance assessment in which coworkers provide input into the employee's performance.

The main advantages of peer evaluation are (1) the tendency for coworkers to offer more constructive insight to each other so that, as a unit, each will improve; and (2) recommendations tend to be more specific regarding job behaviors. Without specificity, constructive measures may be hard to obtain. But caution is in order because these systems, if not handled properly, could lead to increases in halo effects, leniency errors, and fear among employees. Thus, along with training supervisors to properly appraise employee performance, so too must management train peers to evaluate one another.

A slight deviation from peer assessments is a process called the **upward appraisal**, or the reverse review. Used in companies such as IBM, Ben and Jerry's, and the FAA, upward appraisals permit employees to offer frank and constructive feedback to their supervisors on such areas as leadership and communication skills.

upward appraisal
Employees provide frank and constructive feedback to their supervisors.

TIPS FOR SUCCESS

Team Performance Appraisals

Performance evaluation concepts have been developed almost exclusively with individual employees in mind. This reflects the historic belief that individuals are the core building block on which organizations are built.[58] But as we've witnessed, more contemporary organizations are restructuring themselves around teams. How should organizations using teams evaluate performance? Four suggestions have been offered for designing an effective system that supports and improves team performance.[59]

1. Tie team results to organization goals. It's important to find measures that apply to important goals the team should accomplish.
2. Begin with the team's customers and its work process to satisfy customers' needs. The final product the customer receives can be evaluated in terms of the customer's requirements. Transactions between teams can be evaluated based on delivery and quality. And the process steps can be evaluated based on waste and cycle time.
3. Measure both team and individual performance. Define the roles of each team member in terms of accomplishments that support the team's work process. Then assess each member's contributions and the team's overall performance.
4. Train the team to create its own measures. Having the team define its objectives and those of each member ensures everyone understands their role on the team and helps the team develop into a more cohesive unit.

Things to think about:

What concerns would you have about being part of a team evaluation? Should individual performance be measured too?

360-degree appraisals
Performance evaluations in which supervisors, peers, employees, customers, and the like evaluate the individual.

360-Degree Appraisals An appraisal device that seeks performance feedback from such sources as the person being rated, bosses, peers, team members, customers, and suppliers has become popular in organizations.[51] It's called the **360-degree appraisal**.[52] It's being used in approximately 90 percent of the Fortune 1,000 firms, which include Otis Elevator, DuPont, Nabisco, Pfizer, Exxon Mobil, Cook Children's Health Care System, General Electric, UPS, and Nokia.[53] This type of appraisal has become quite popular as downsizing has given supervisors greater responsibility and more employees who report directly to them. This makes it increasingly difficult for supervisors to have extensive job knowledge of each of their employees. The growth of project teams and employee involvement in today's companies places responsibility for evaluation at points at which people are better able to make an accurate assessment.[54]

The 360-degree feedback process also has some positive benefits for development concerns.[55] Many managers simply do not know how their employees view them and their work. For instance, the corporate comptroller for University Health Network in Toronto, Canada, was surprised to learn that the financial control system he strengthened over the past year actually seemed too bureaucratic to one of his peers. The feedback allowed the comptroller and peer to discuss the matter, resolve any tension between them, and enhance the internal control system now in place.[56]

Research studies into the effectiveness of 360-degree performance appraisals are generally reporting positive results from more accurate feedback, empowering employees, reducing subjective factors in the evaluation process, and developing leadership in an organization. But 360-degree systems are not without problems if used improperly.[57] They are difficult to develop and complex to analyze. Raters can "game the system" by artificially inflating or penalizing coworkers to help their own ratings. Anonymity of raters and rater training is necessary.

Rate Selectively

Appraisers should rate only in those areas in which they have job knowledge. If raters make evaluations on only dimensions they are in a good position to rate, the inter-rater agreement is increased and the evaluation is a more valid process. This approach also recognizes that different organizational levels often have different perspectives on the

www.dilbert.com   scottadams@aol.com

5-31-07   © 2007 Scott Adams, Inc./Dist. by UFS, Inc.

Exhibit 10-8
Ineffective Appraisals

Too often, managers take shortcuts when explaining the performance appraisal process and the actual evaluation.
(Source: © 2007 Scott Adams, Inc./Distributed by United Feature Syndicate, Inc.)

jobs and people being rated, and observe them in different settings. It works best if appraisers are as close as possible to the organizational level of the individual evaluated. The more levels separating the evaluator and employee, the less opportunity the evaluator has to observe the individual's work behavior and, not surprisingly, the greater the possibility for inaccuracies.

The specific application of these concepts makes immediate supervisors or coworkers the major input into the appraisal and lets them evaluate factors they are best qualified to judge. For example, when professors evaluate secretaries within a university, they often use such criteria as judgment, technical competence, and conscientiousness, whereas peers (other secretaries) evaluate, for example, job knowledge, organization, cooperation with coworkers, and responsibility.[60] Such an approach appears both logical and more reliable, because people appraise only those dimensions they are in a good position to judge.

Train Appraisers

If you cannot find good raters, the alternative is to develop good raters. Evidence indicates that training appraisers can make them more accurate raters.[61] Common errors such as halo and leniency can be minimized or eliminated when supervisors can practice observing and rating behaviors in workshops. "Calibration" workshops demonstrate techniques for eliminating bias and help raters learn how to understand performance standards better. Why should management bother to train these individuals? Because as shown in Exhibit 10-8, a poor appraisal is worse than no appraisal at all; they can demoralize employees, decrease productivity, and create a legal liability for the company.[62]

The Performance Appraisal Meeting

All the time spent linking goals to jobs, developing assessment criteria, creating forms, observing employees, and completing the appraisal can be sabotaged if the appraisal is presented poorly to the employee. Too often employees are handed an appraisal in a sealed envelope and told to sign it and return it soon without a face-to-face discussion, or the appraisal meeting is rushed with no real opportunity for constructive feedback. There are a number of steps employees can take to prepare for those important meetings.

Managers should prepare for, and schedule the appraisal in advance. This includes reviewing employee job descriptions, period goals that may have been set, and any performance data on the employees. It is important to note any comments or suggestions on last year's appraisal. The employee will most certainly remember them and expect their manager to comment on any efforts to improve any deficiency mentioned

Performance appraisal meetings are a very important part of the appraisal process, requiring preparation and planning. *(Source: Masterfile)*

The focus of the discussion should be on work behaviors, not on the employee.

the year prior. The appraisal should be scheduled well in advance to give employees the opportunity to prepare their own data for the meeting.

Explaining the purpose of the meeting in advance creates a supportive environment and puts employees at ease. Performance appraisals conjure up several emotions, most especially anxiety. Managers should make every effort to keep employees comfortable during the meeting, so that they are receptive to constructive feedback. Nonverbal communication should not be threatening.

By describing the purpose of the appraisal to employees, they will know precisely how the appraisal will be used. Will it have implications for pay increases, or other personnel decisions? If so, managers must make sure employees understand exactly how the appraisal process works and its consequences.

It is important to involve the employee in the appraisal discussion, including a self-evaluation. Performance appraisals should not be a one-way communication event. Although supervisors may believe they have to talk more in the meeting, that needn't be the case. Instead, employees should have ample opportunities to discuss their performance, raise questions about the appraisal, and add their own data/perceptions about their work.[63] One means of ensuring two-way communication is to have employees conduct a self-evaluation prior to the meeting. Managers should actively listen to their assessment. This involvement helps to create an environment of participation.

The focus of the discussion should be on work behaviors, not on the employee. One way of creating emotional difficulties is to verbally attack the employee. Therefore, the evaluator should narrow the discussion to the behaviors observed. Telling an employee, for instance, that his report stinks does not point out the specific problem with his performance. Indicating that he didn't devote enough time to proofreading the report describes the behavior that is problematic.

The evaluation should be supported with examples. Specific performance behaviors help clarify to employees the issues raised. Rather than saying something wasn't good (subjective evaluation), the evaluator should be as specific as possible in the explanations. So, for the employee who failed to proof the work, describing that the report had five grammatical mistakes in the first two pages alone would be a specific example.

Both positive and negative feedback should be given. Performance appraisals needn't be completely negative. Despite the perception that this process focuses on the negative, it should also be used to compliment and recognize good work. Positive, as well as negative, feedback helps employees gain a better understanding of their performance. For example, although the report was not up to the quality expected, the employee did do the work and completed the report in a timely fashion. That behavior deserves some positive reinforcement.

Evaluators should ensure that employees understand what was discussed in the appraisal. At the end of the appraisal, especially where some improvement is warranted, the manager should ask the employee to summarize what was discussed in the meeting. This will help to ensure that the manager has gotten the information across and the employee understands the appraisal and the reason for the evaluation.

A development plan should be generated. Most of the performance appraisal revolves around feedback and documentation, but it needs another component. Where development efforts are encouraged, a plan should be developed to describe what is to be done, when it should be completed, and what the supervisor will commit to aid in the improvement/enhancement effort.

International Performance Appraisal

As more organizations find themselves expanding into global markets and operations, they must take a look at how to evaluate the performance of workers in other countries and the expatriate managers or workers sent to work in other countries. Evaluating employee performance in international environments is more complicated than applying the performance management practices of the organization in the host country. Organizations are increasingly applying the Western practices that tie performance management to organizational strategy and strategic HRM, but cultural differences between the parent country and the host country must be considered. Cultural differences between the United States and England are not great, and practices may not need much adaption, but cultural differences between the United States and China, for example, are wider by comparison and changes must be made in the evaluation process.

Cultural values such as the degree to which the culture emphasizes collectivism over individualism, harmony over conflict, saving "face," and how the power distance between manager and worker is viewed, must be considered when developing a performance appraisal process. Employees in countries with "collectivist" cultures (Japan, China, Vietnam) that value the group more strongly than the individual will probably not react well to performance appraisal systems that evaluate the individual, raising suspicion and mistrust within the group. Evaluation of the work group or division may be a better choice. For example, if an individual in a collectivist culture makes a decision that benefits the group goals over personal goals, he may expect to be recognized for the decision rather than having his lack of personal achievement mentioned in an appraisal. Employees in countries with "individualist" cultures (Australia, France, Italy) will react much better to individual evaluations, but may not see much direct connection to a group performance appraisal.

When developing a system for appraisal of employees in international units, HRM has three basic choices: export the performance management system of the home country, develop unique performance management systems so each foreign unit has a unique cultural fit, or integrate the home country system with local culture to create a "hybrid" system. When deciding how to adapt the performance management system, HRM needs to balance integrating the organizational strategic mission and coordination of workforce alignment, organizational development, and employee development with sensitivity to building relationships in the local cultural context.[64]

Who Performs the Evaluation?

Companies must also consider who will be responsible for the process: the host-country management or the parent-country management. Although local managers would generally be considered a more accurate gauge, they typically evaluate expatriates from their own cultural perspectives and expectations, which may not reflect those of the parent country. For example, a participatory style of management is acceptable in some countries, and in others hierarchical values make it a disgrace to ask employees for ideas. Criteria evaluating customer service that includes smiling or maintaining eye contact may not be appropriate in cultures that may view sustained eye contact and smiling as strange or inappropriate. The way a performance appraisal form is constructed may also need to be adjusted. Research indicates that managers from Asian cultures are more likely to use midpoints in rating scales, whereas Americans are more likely to use either extreme on the scale.[65] Confusion may arise if forms used in the home

Are the performance evaluations conducted on Home Depot employees in Mexico different from those conducted on employees in the United States? Logic tells us that evaluations, to be effective, must be adapted to the country in which employees operate. *(Source: Tim Boyle/Getty Images)*

TIPS FOR SUCCESS

Performance Metrics in China

As you read through the discussion of performance appraisal materials in this chapter, you might be wondering if the methods and means of appraising employees in North America are similar to those practiced around the globe. There are similarities among all developed nations, but there are also some dramatic differences. To give you some perspective of this difference, let's look at how U.S. executives and Chinese executives are evaluated. Although the process may be similar, what's different is what is measured.

What do these differences tell us? They indicate what's important to be successful—and if a North American executive is sent to China (or vice versa), how that individual is measured will be different. Accordingly, the expatriate must understand the culture in which he or she will work and adjust work attributes accordingly. For instance, in the United States an executive can be creative and think outside the box for a solution. That same behavior in China is not rewarded, as conformance and compliance with the rules is the expectation.[66]

U.S. Executive Evaluation Focus	Chinese Executive Evaluation Focus
Ability to do the job	Industriousness and determination
Technical ability	
Management skills	Diligence
Cultural empathy	Positive attitude
Adaptability and flexibility	Compliance with rules
Creativity	

country are not adequately adapted to the language and cultural sensitivities of the host country. Also, home-office management may be so remote that it may not be fully informed about what is going on in an overseas office.

Home-office managements often measure performance by quantitative measures, such as profits, market shares, or gross sales. However, "simple" numbers are often quite complex in their calculations, and data are not always comparable. For example, local import tariffs can distort pricing schedules, which alter gross sales figures, a statistic often used when evaluating performance. Other performance measures may also be distorted. For example, factory productivity levels in Mexico may be below those of similar plants in the United States, but American-owned plant productivity in Mexico may be above that of similar Mexican-owned plants, making comparison difficult.

Summary

(This summary relates to the Learning Outcomes identified on page 242.) After having read this chapter, you can:

1. **Identify the three purposes of performance management systems and who they serve.** The three purposes of performance management systems are feedback, development, and documentation. They are designed to support employees, appraisers, and organizations.
2. **Explain the six steps in the appraisal process.** The six-step appraisal process is to (1) establish performance standards with employees, (2) set measurable goals (manager and employee), (3) measure actual performance, (4) compare actual performance with standards, (5) discuss the appraisal with the employee, and (6) if necessary, initiate corrective action.
3. **Discuss absolute standards in performance management systems.** Absolute standards refer to a method in performance management systems whereby employees are measured against company-set performance requirements. Absolute standard evaluation methods involve the essay appraisal, the critical incident approach, the checklist rating, the graphic rating scale, the forced-choice inventory, and the behaviorally anchored rating scale (BARS).

4. **Describe relative standards in performance management systems.** Relative standards refer to a method in performance management systems whereby an employee's performance is compared with that of other employees. Relative standard evaluation methods include group-order ranking, individual ranking, and paired comparisons.

5. **Discuss how MBO can be an appraisal method.** MBO becomes an appraisal method by establishing a specific set of objectives for an employee to achieve and reviewing performance based on how well those objectives have been met.

6. **Explain why performance appraisals might be distorted.** Performance appraisal might be distorted for several reasons, including leniency error, halo error, similarity error, central tendency, low appraiser motivation, inflationary pressures, and inappropriate substitutes for performance.

7. **Identify ways to make performance management systems more effective.** More effective appraisals can be achieved with behavior-based measures, combined absolute and relative ratings, ongoing feedback, multiple raters, selective rating, trained appraisers, peer assessment, and rewards to accurate appraisers.

8. **Describe the term 360-degree appraisal.** In 360-degree performance appraisals, evaluations are made by the employee, supervisors, co-workers, team members, customers, suppliers, and the like. In doing so, a complete picture of an employee's performance can be assessed.

9. **Explain the criteria for a successful performance appraisal meeting.** Performance appraisal meetings require manager preparation, a supportive environment, clear purpose, employee involvement, focus on work behaviors, specific work examples, positive and negative feedback, employee understanding, and an employee development plan.

10. **Discuss how performance appraisals may differ in a global environment.** Performance management systems used away from the home country may differ in who performs the evaluation and the format used. Cultural differences may dictate that changes in the U.S. performance management system are needed.

Demonstrating Comprehension

QUESTIONS FOR REVIEW

1. List three purposes for performance appraisals and explain who benefits from them.
2. Describe the appraisal process. How should it work?
3. Contrast the advantages and disadvantages of (1) absolute standards and (2) relative standards.
4. What is BARS? Why might BARS be better than trait-oriented measures?
5. Describe MBO, its advantages and disadvantages.
6. What are some major factors that distort performance appraisals?
7. How should performance appraisals change when teams, rather than individuals, are evaluated?
8. What is a 360-degree feedback process? How valid do you believe it to be?
9. Identify ways to make performance evaluations more effective. Do you believe one of your suggestions is of higher priority than the others? Explain.
10. How does the global nature of business affect performance management systems?

Key Terms

360-degree appraisals	critical incident appraisal	management by objectives (MBO)
absolute standards	documentation	paired comparison
attribution theory	forced-choice appraisal	peer evaluation
behaviorally anchored rating scales (BARS)	graphic rating scale	relative standards
	halo error	similarity error
central tendency	individual ranking	upward appraisal
checklist appraisal	leniency error	

HRM Workshop

Linking Concepts to Practice   DISCUSSION QUESTIONS

1. "Performance appraisal should be multifaceted. Supervisors should evaluate their employees, and employees should be able to evaluate their supervisors. And customers should evaluate them all." Do you agree or disagree with this statement? Discuss.
2. "The higher the position an employee occupies in an organization, the easier it is to appraise his or her performance objectively." Do you agree or disagree with this statement? Why?
3. "Using an invalid performance evaluation instrument is a waste of time." Do you agree or disagree with this statement? Discuss.
4. "Without a supportive culture in an organization, peer evaluations are subject to too many distortions. Accordingly, they should not be widely used." Do you agree or disagree? Defend your position.
5. "Customer feedback needs to be part of every employee's evaluation when that employee has customer contact." Do you agree or disagree? Explain your position.

Making a Difference   SERVICE LEARNING PROJECTS

The heart of performance management is feedback. Many community organizations can use help with communication and feedback.

- Volunteer with your local United Way campaign in their efforts to communicate their services and funding needs.
- Assist local non-profit organizations in setting up websites and responding to e-mails.
- Help a community organization survey volunteers for their feedback following an event such as a fundraising walk, run

or dinner, by preparing and mailing surveys or sending e-mails. Compile and present the results of the surveys.

As you put your service learning experience together, keep a journal of your activities, the time you spend, contact information for people you work with, and your thoughts about the process. When you're finished, make a presentation to your class about the experience and what you learned. What concepts from Chapter 10 were you able to apply?

Developing Diagnostic and Analytical Skills

Case Application 10:   GROWING PAINS AT MODERN OFFICE SUPPLY

"Sorry I'm late," sighs Fatima as she flops into a chair next to you at a local coffee shop. "Something came up at work. Lately, there's always something going wrong." Fatima is part of your study group for the PHR certification exam that meets at the coffee shop once a week and she's having trouble making the weekly meetings on time. She goes on to explain that her job in HR at Modern Office Supply has become one discipline problem after another and she doesn't know how much longer she can stand the negativity and tension.

Modern Office Supply has 200 employees in two locations in Kansas City, selling office furniture and supplies from an original "Warehouse Showroom," and a second retail-only location that opened three years ago. Fatima joined the company two years ago after a college internship. She works with another HR manager who has been with the company since it started 15 years ago. Fatima explained to the study group that discipline and morale has been going downhill as long as she's been there. Employees are complaining that the family atmosphere: is disappearing and they are starting to feel "disconnected." She explains that the company picnic last week was a disaster, with most of the warehouse staff showing up late after having their own pre-party. "I didn't tell Ben, the senior HR manager, but I think they may have even met with a union organizer," says Fatima wearily.

When your study group pressed Fatima for more information she shared the following:

- Ben has asked Fatima to make sure that performance appraisals are all up-to-date. She has found that only 60 percent of the appraisals are current. She has met with indifference or resistance from the managers who are behind in completing appraisals.
- There is only one appraisal form for all non-exempt hourly workers. Ben created the form several years ago so it would be fast and easy for supervisors to complete without much training. Employees are rated either 1 (Unsatisfactory), 2 (Improvement Needed), 3 (Satisfactory), 4 (Very Good), or 5 (Outstanding) on the following work traits:
- Adaptability
- Appearance
- Communication
- Decision making
- Dependability
- Interpersonal effectiveness
- Quality of work
- Quantity of work
- Teamwork

Each trait has room for a supervisor comment. Space is left at the end for the supervisor to make comments and suggestions and for the employee to write a comment.

- Supervisors complete the form quickly and often write "good job" or "can do better" in the space for comments. Ditto marks are often used in the comment space rather than repeating written comments. Completed forms are frequently sealed in an envelope and given to employees with instructions to read them over and return them to HR with comments and a signature. A few employees report that they haven't received appraisals in years, although their files contain unsigned copies of the forms.
- Ben is sure that he's trained the supervisors on how to complete the forms, but there hasn't been any training that Fatima has been aware of since she started with the company.

- Complaints from customers and co-workers about rude behavior and late deliveries prompted Fatima to meet with delivery driver Gale today about improving his performance. Gale felt he was being singled out as a minority and added, "I'm no worse than any other driver here!" He produced a copy of his last appraisal form with 4 (Very Good) marked in every category except for 3 (Satisfactory) for Quality of Work and Quantity of Work. Fatima took quick look at the appraisals for four other drivers, including the ones that complained about Gale, and found similar ratings in most categories except 4 (Very Good) for Quality of Work and Quantity of Work. Fatima completed a written warning and made a note to speak to Gale's supervisor.
- Rosa, a new customer service representative, came to Fatima in tears because she thinks her manager hates her. Her performance appraisal was a mix of 2 (Improvement Needed), 3 (Satisfactory),

Modern Office Supply
Performance Appraisal Form

1 Poor Performance
2 Needs Improvement
3 Average Performance
4 Above Average Performance
5 Excellent Performance

Job Skills:	*Performance Level:*					
Adaptability	1	2	3	4	5	Comments
Appearance	1	2	3	4	5	Comments
Communication	1	2	3	4	5	Comments
Decision making	1	2	3	4	5	Comments
Dependability	1	2	3	4	5	Comments
Interpersonal effectiveness	1	2	3	4	5	Comments
Quality of work	1	2	3	4	5	Comments
Quantity of work	1	2	3	4	5	Comments
Teamwork	1	2	3	4	5	Comments

Supervisor Comments:

Supervisor Signature _____ Date _____

Employee Comments:

Employee Signature _____ Date _____

Human Resource Manager _____ Date _____

and one 4 (Very Good) rating for Adaptability. Rosa's supervisor, Kelly, was surprised when Fatima questioned her about the appraisal. "It's a tough job," she said. "Rosa's only been here a year and she still has a lot to learn. I can't honestly say that she's 'Very Good' yet. I only have a couple of reps that actually deserve an 'Outstanding' rating."

■ Evaluations at the retail location seem to be slightly higher and as a result, salaries of the retail location employees have grown slightly higher than at the original warehouse showroom over the last three years causing tension between the two groups of employees.

■ All managers are evaluated annually by Hector, Modern Office's owner and founder. He uses an MBO process that includes meeting with each manager to assess the prior year's performance and jointly set goals for the next year. Hector loves the personal contact with the management staff, but growth and expansion in the last three years has left Hector with more managers, less time for their assessment meetings and little discussion about personal performance the rest of the year. Hector doesn't seem to review the prior year's goals before the meetings anymore, so managers are beginning to set easily achievable goals, knowing that Hector is getting out of touch and that the meeting doesn't have any consequences.

Fatima adds, "Ben set up the performance management system years ago when the company was about half the size it is now. It worked when Ben and Hector knew everyone, but we've really outgrown it and it shows. We can't afford a modern web-based system right now, but something has to be done. All I do anymore is listen to complaints and file disciplinary warnings. Ben won't fire anyone who deserves it because the appraisals aren't current and he's afraid they'll sue or claim discrimination. I'm starting to hate my job."

Your PHR study group agrees that the issues at Modern Office would be improved by applying some of the concepts you're reviewing for the certification exam. Fatima agrees and asks you to help her create a proposal to improve the performance management process at Modern Office.

Questions:

1. What is missing in the performance management process? In what ways would improving the performance management process help improve discipline and morale at Modern Office Supply?
2. How can ineffective performance management programs leave employers vulnerable for claims of discrimination?
3. How does the form used for hourly employees contribute to errors and distortions in the appraisal process? How would you revise the form reduce them? Explain other steps that need to be taken to further reduce distortions in the process.
4. What type of form would you recommend that would be more effective for the hourly employees? Construct an appropriate form for the delivery driver position.
5. How can the appraisal process for the managers be improved?

Working with a Team   BEHAVIORALLY ANCHORED RATING SCALES

After reviewing the process for developing a BARS (behaviorally anchored rating scale), you and your team will develop a BARS performance appraisal form to evaluate a college professor. The form will rate at least four different performance dimensions of your choice (for example, you might rate the professor's use of technology) and at least five different levels of behavioral incidents (ranking of level of performance). Present your form to the class, explaining your choice of criteria and the behaviors used in your ratings. Rating your human resource management professor is optional.

Working with a Team   THE 360-DEGREE PERFORMANCE APPRAISAL

Supervisors have not adapted as well as desired by management to a change in the appraisal system. As human resource management students, you and your class team have been asked to conduct a thirty-minute presentation for ten to fifteen supervisors at the next supervisors' meeting. Develop a presentation about the purposes of the performance management systems, who benefits, and the six basic steps; clarify the difference between relative and absolute standards, with possible distortions; and introduce the 360-degree feedback system.

Learning an HRM Skill   WRITING APPRAISAL COMMENTS

About the skill: Whether writing comments for an employee appraisal, a self-appraisal, or the 360-degree appraisal of a manager or coworker, most people struggle with what to say and how to say it. This is particularly true when the comment needs to address a problem. Complicating the issue is the fact that written comments are frequently what the employee remembers most about the appraisal form.

At Synygy, Inc., a company based in Chester, Pennsylvania, that provides sales performance management (SPM) solutions, coworker feedback is an integral part of a quarterly performance management process that encourages open communication and growth. Synygy helps its employees constructively enter feedback into an online system by educating them on the characteristics of effective coworker comments and providing specific examples. Consider these suggestions when sitting down to write comments on the next appraisal form you need to complete.

■ Make sure the comments you make support the scores or ratings on the appraisal form.
■ Don't make accusatory or hurtful personal comments. Comments should address specific behaviors, not personalities or motives.

- Point out positive as well as problematic behaviors. The purpose is to provide feedback on what a person does well and encourage continuing those behaviors as well as pointing out things that need improvement and making suggestions on how to improve.
- Be as specific as possible; *avoid generalities.* Try to give examples of behaviors you are criticizing. A person who receives a vague comment may have no idea what they are doing that is causing your perception. That means they certainly won't know what to do to change their behavior.
- When pointing out a problem, try to suggest a possible solution.
- When commenting on someone's progress in correcting a problematic behavior, recognize intermediate steps in improvement (many behaviors take time to improve).
- Be aware of the overall tone of your comments. Again, be as factual as possible. Don't convey blame. Think about how the person receiving your comments will feel when they read them.
- To the extent possible, your comments should summarize issues that you've already discussed with the person during the past quarter. Don't make comments "out of the blue." *This is especially true for mentors.*

Examples of Effective Comments

- You are driven and motivated in your work. You are very clear about what you own within the department. It would benefit the entire department if you paid more attention to the delivery and tone of some of your comments. Assigning a duty or responsibility sometimes comes across as a harsh directive instead of a transition of duties or responsibilities.
- When offering feedback after being presented with a new idea, it would be helpful if you recognized the possibility of a new process before immediately negating the idea. For example, when it was suggested that we rebuild the field templates for ProjX, you immediately resisted because of the time involved in implementation without considering the benefits of the change.
- You are a great asset to the team. You are very professional and focused on your work. Despite the difficult deadlines for the ProjX implementation, you maintained a positive attitude. You respond to problems without getting angry or frustrated. You often stay late to finish your work and are very conscientious of timelines and resources. Your most outstanding "value" from what I have seen is your attitude toward continuous improvement.
- You seem to have lost your focus, which is essential to being successful on ProjX. This is evident in that you have signed your initials to checklist items without fully performing the checks for the project, which resulted in poor quality and an excessive amount of client questions.

- You seem to take constructive criticism as a personal attack, rather than assistance from people who are trying to help. Your attitude over the past quarter, though it has improved somewhat recently, has been harmful to your relationship with your coworkers and your work quality because people on your team do not feel comfortable communicating with you. You have the ability to do your job extremely well, but haven't taken the initiative to do so.
- You have worked very hard to improve your technical skills by increasing your work with the ProjX field and verification templates and the data model documentation. You continuously work on improving your relationship with the client and your coworkers, and you try very hard to resolve inter-office problems quietly and maturely.
- My only criticism is that you tend to just ask for solutions to problems without completely understanding what the problem is—for example, the rounding problem on the field template from last week. Upon understanding the issue, you usually can arrive at the solution.
- You clearly have the desire to run projects but you have to be willing to put in the time on the details and learn how to be more thorough before you will have the ability to do so. Areas to improve: attention to detail, ability to communicate plan concepts and system specifics quickly and clearly, timeliness.
- You do what is necessary to make the client happy and are willing to put in extra time if things are behind. You have an excellent knowledge of the software tools and understand how your projects work. You could focus more on training your coworkers, which would benefit them and ease your burden. You have a lot to offer, don't keep it to yourself. Good client management skills and client focus. You are a lot of fun to work with.
- Your job skills and initiative are very good. You are always willing to help others solve problems even if it inconveniences you. You are very willing to work above and beyond the call of duty.
- One thing to possibly improve is your skills in managing others and in training others in your group about their projects. You have an intimate knowledge of your projects because you designed them, but sometimes you take for granted that others on the team may have more knowledge than they actually possess.
- Sometimes when fixing a problem, you do not readily explain how you are fixing it because you often work quickly. This is fine for solving problems, but if you explained the issues a little more clearly, it could be of great service to your team members.

Source: Synygy, Inc. Employee Handbook © 1995–2009.

Enhancing Your Communication Skills

1. Develop a two- to three-page paper describing the relationship between job analysis and performance evaluations. Cite specific examples where appropriate.
2. Research innovations in software used in the performance appraisal process. Select and report on at least three of these software packages in a two- to three-page paper. Explain the software features and benefits to HR managers.
3. Much has been written about how managers dread the appraisal process. Research some reasons that managers give for their dislike of appraising performance and suggest ways to improve the process so they aren't so afraid of it. Present your findings with three to five presentations slides.

(Source: Mlenny Photography/iStockphoto)

LEARNING OUTCOMES

After reading this chapter, you will be able to

1. Explain the various classifications of rewards.

2. Discuss why we call some rewards membership based.

3. Define the goal of compensation administration.

4. Discuss job evaluation and its three basic approaches.

5. Explain the evolution of the final wage structure.

6. Describe competency-based compensation programs.

7. Discuss why executives' salaries are significantly higher than those of other employees.

8. Describe the balance-sheet approach to international compensation.

Establishing Rewards and Pay Plans

11

As you're scrolling through the summer internship listings on your college's career planning website, the top employer in your area has your dream job listed. It couldn't be more perfect. The qualifications match yours exactly, it starts this summer, and they have a reputation of hiring the best interns upon graduation. You're polishing up your résumé in your head as you scroll to the bottom of the screen and see it—the word that makes you break out in a cold sweat—unpaid.

Don't they know you have to pay tuition to even have the internship count toward graduation?

This dilemma may be more common than you think, as unpaid internships are on the rise.[1] The economy has left some organizations financially unable to pay interns, while other organizations, such as advertising, sports marketing, the film industry, and even human resources, are in such high demand that there are many interns willing to work for free. According to the College Employment Research Institute, 75 percent of the 10 million U.S. college students will work as interns before graduating, and between 30 and 50 percent of those will not receive any pay.[2]

Part of the appeal is the perception that an unpaid internship is seen as more valuable to prospective employers, leaving students who cannot afford to work for 10 weeks without any pay at a disadvantage. If you're in one of the 50 to 60 percent of college programs that require internships,[3] the added burden of tuition makes the choice even harder.

Are unpaid internships legal? Yes and no. The Fair Labor Standards Act (FLSA) doesn't actually recognize internships, but allows "trainees" to be exempt from the minimum wage if these six factors are met:[4]

To be unpaid, an internship must:

Be similar to training that would be given in an educational environment.

Be for the benefit of the intern.

Not displace regular employees, and be conducted under close supervision of existing staff.

Not provide any immediate advantage from the activities of the intern for the employer. In fact, on occasion its operations may actually be impeded.

Not necessarily entitle the intern to a job at the conclusion of the internship.

Be clear to the employee and the intern that the internship position is not entitled to wages.[5]

According to Nancy Leppink, acting director of the Department of Labor's Wage and Hour Division, "If you're a for-profit employer or you want to pursue an internship with a for-profit employer, there aren't going to be many circumstances where you can have an internship and not be paid and still be in compliance with the law."[6] Non-profit groups like charities have less strict rules because people are allowed to do volunteer work for non-profits.

Abuses of the FLSA rules are common. Companies claim interns are getting valuable training, yet are assigned unskilled tasks such as shipping, shredding, photocopying, filing, answering e-mail, and for one health-conscious employer, wiping door knobs to prevent swine flu. Employers get away with it because interns rarely complain, knowing it will hurt recommendations and chances for a full-time job. Abuses have drawn the interest of officials in Oregon, California, and New York, who have begun to investigate and fine employers for labor law violations.

Don't get too discouraged. Many great companies do pay interns. In fact, of *BusinessWeek's* list of 50 Best Internships, all but two are paid, with the top employers in accounting and finance offering wages as high as $28 an hour.

Looking Ahead

What would you do if your dream internship was unpaid and you suspect it is in violation of FLSA rules?

Introduction

"What's in it for me?" Nearly every individual consciously or unconsciously asks this question before engaging in any behavior. Our knowledge of motivation and people's behavior at work tells us that people do what they do to satisfy needs. Before they do anything, they look for a payoff or reward.

The most obvious reward employees receive from work is pay. However, rewards also include promotions, desirable work assignments, and a host of other less obvious payoffs—a smile, peer acceptance, work freedom, or a kind word of recognition. We'll spend the majority of this chapter addressing pay as a reward as well as how organizations establish compensation programs.

Among the several ways to classify rewards, we have selected three of the most typical dichotomies: intrinsic versus extrinsic rewards, financial versus nonfinancial rewards, and performance-based versus membership-based rewards. As you will see, these categories are far from mutually exclusive, yet all share one common thread—they assist in maintaining employee commitment.

Intrinsic versus Extrinsic Rewards

intrinsic rewards
Satisfactions derived from the job itself, such as pride in one's work, a feeling of accomplishment, or being part of a team.

job enrichment
Enhancing jobs by giving employees more opportunity to plan and control their work.

extrinsic rewards
Benefits provided by the employer, usually money, promotion, or benefits.

Intrinsic rewards are the personal satisfactions one derives from doing the job. These are self-initiated rewards: pride in one's work, a sense of accomplishment, or enjoying being part of a work team.[7] **Job enrichment**, for instance, can offer employees intrinsic rewards by making work seem more meaningful. **Extrinsic rewards**, in contrast, include money, promotions, and benefits. They are external to the job and come from an outside source, mainly management.[8] Consequently, if an employee experiences a sense of achievement or personal growth from a job, we would label such rewards as intrinsic. If the employee receives a salary increase or a write-up in the company magazine, website, or blog, we would label these rewards as extrinsic. The general structure of rewards is summarized in Exhibit 11-1.

ETHICAL ISSUES IN HRM

Salary Negotiation and Discrimination

After months of recruiting for several hard-to-fill positions in your company, you're pleased to have found a few excellent candidates. When you extend your offer to the first candidate, the young man aggressively negotiates for a starting salary and benefits substantially above your starting offer. He backs up his demand by citing offers from his present employer and competing firms. You refer the issue to your VP for Human Resources who thought the young man interviewed extremely well and caves in to his demand for a generous starting salary package.

Next, you offer positions to equally qualified women and minority candidates who accept your initial salary offer graciously without any negotiation. How vulnerable are you to charges of pay discrimination? What will you do if the employees with less valuable starting packages find out about their coworker's enviable salary?

"There is nothing per se unlawful about a recruiter setting a salary based on the negotiating leverage of a candidate," says Richard Tuschman, member of the labor and employment and litigation practices at Epstein Becker & Green in Miami. "If a male candidate is able to bargain for a higher starting salary, it

may be permissible to yield to that, but the employer must ensure that the negotiations are done consistently with all candidates."[9] For example, if HR allows the male candidate to use other job offers and current employer salary in negations, the same information must be allowed for all candidates. HR cannot tell future candidates that the salary is not negotiable.

Employers also cannot consider qualifications that are above the requirements for the position. For example, if the position requires two years of work experience, the employer may not consider a higher level of education such as a bachelor's degree that is not required for the position when considering salary. And relying solely on an applicant's prior salary also presents problems because it may be evidence of past discrimination.

Ethical Questions:

Back to the sticky issue of what to say to the employees with lower starting salaries if they find out what their coworkers are earning. What would you do? How can you justify your actions? Should you offer them the same salaries? Can you forbid employees from discussing salaries?

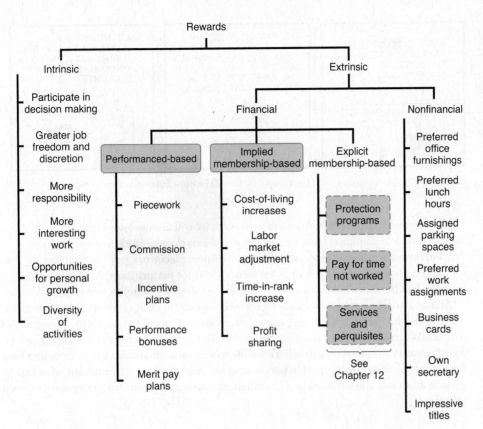

Exhibit 11-1
Structure of Rewards

Intrinsic rewards are the personal rewards or "warm fuzzy feelings" one gets from performing a job. Extrinsic rewards are financial and nonfinancial rewards such as money, promotions, and benefits. Notice that intrinsic rewards correlate well with the upper level needs and extrinsic rewards correlate well with the lower level needs. Do you see any correlation to other motivation theories?

Financial versus Nonfinancial Rewards

Rewards may or may not enhance the employee's financial well-being. Those that do, do so directly—through wages, bonuses, or profit sharing—or indirectly, through employer-subsidized benefits such as retirement plans, paid vacations, paid sick leaves, and purchase discounts.

Nonfinancial rewards present a variety of desirable extras for employees and organizations. These do not directly increase the employee's financial position, but make life on the job more pleasant. We will identify a few popular and innovative examples, but creation of these rewards is limited only by HRM's ingenuity and ability to use them to motivate desirable behavior.

The saying, "One person's food is another person's poison," applies to the entire subject of rewards, but specifically to nonfinancial rewards. What one employee views as "something I've always wanted," another might find relatively useless. Therefore, HRM must take great care in providing the right nonfinancial reward for each person. With proper selection, organizational benefits should produce significant increases in employee engagement and productivity.

If an employee is status conscious, a fancy office with a large desk, or signed artwork may be just what stimulates her toward top performance. Other status-oriented employees may value an impressive job title, access to the latest technology, their own administrative assistant, or a well-located parking space with their name clearly painted underneath the "Reserved" sign. Other employees may value opportunities to dress casually while at work or even work in part at home. Such incentives are within the organization's discretion and, carefully used, may enhance performance, as shown in Exhibit 11-2.

Performance-Based versus Membership-Based Rewards

Organizations allocate rewards based on either performance or membership criteria. HR representatives in many organizations will vigorously argue that their system rewards performance, but you should recognize that this isn't always the case. Few organizations actually

Exhibit 11-2
The "Slight Promotion"

Extrinsic rewards include impressive titles and preferred office furnishings, but the value of those rewards may vary depending on the employee. Not everyone is as easy to please as Asok in the Dilbert comic strip.

Source: © 2005 Scott Adams, Inc./ Distributed by United Feature Syndicate, Inc.

reward employees based on performance—a point we will discuss later in this chapter. Without question, the dominant basis for reward allocations in organizations is membership.

performance-based rewards
Rewards exemplified by the use of commissions, piecework pay plans, incentive systems, group bonuses, or other forms of merit pay.

Performance-based rewards use commissions, piecework pay plans, incentive systems, group bonuses, merit pay, or other forms of pay for performance. Membership-based rewards, yon the other hand, include cost-of-living increases, benefits, and salary increases attributable to labor-market conditions, seniority or time in rank, credentials (such as a college degree or a graduate diploma), a specialized skill, or future potential (for example, the recent MBA graduate from a prestigious university). The key point here is that membership-based rewards are generally extended regardless of an individual's, group's, or organization's performance. In any case, performance may be only a minor determinant of rewards, despite academic theories holding that high motivation depends on performance-based rewards.

Compensation Administration

Why do regional managers at Bank of America in Dallas, Texas, earn more than the bank associates? Intuitively, you might say that the regional managers are more skilled and have greater job responsibility, so they should earn more. But how about regional managers who specialize in commercial accounts? Should they make more or less than regional managers who supervise several branch operations? The answers to questions such as these lie in job evaluation.

Job evaluation is the process whereby an organization systematically establishes its compensation program. In this process, jobs are compared to determine each job's appropriate worth within the organization. In this section, we discuss the broader topic of compensation, narrow our discussion to job evaluation methods, and conclude with a review of an increasingly controversial topic—executive compensation.

Employees exchange work for rewards. Probably the most important reward, and the most obvious, is money. But not all employees earn the same amount of money. Why? The search for this answer moves us directly into the topic of compensation administration.

compensation administration
The process of managing a company's compensation program.

The goal of **compensation administration** is to design a cost-effective pay structure that will attract, motivate, and retain competent employees.[10] The structure should also appear fair to employees. Fairness is a term that frequently arises in the administration of an organization's compensation program.

Organizations generally seek to pay the least possible to minimize costs, so fairness means a wage or salary that is adequate for the demands and requirements of the job. Of course, fairness is a two-way street. Employees, too, want fair compensation. As we pointed out in our earlier discussion of motivation, if employees perceive an imbalance in their efforts–rewards ratio to some comparative standard, they will act to correct the inequity. Thus, both employers and employees pursue fairness.

Government Influence on Compensation Administration

In Chapter 3, we described how government policies shape and influence HRM. Some HR functions are more heavily influenced than others. For example, collective bargaining and the employee selection process are heavily constrained by government rules and regulations; employment planning and orientation are less so.

Compensation administration is also highly regulated. Government policies set minimum wages and benefits that employers must meet, and these policies provide protection for certain groups (see Exhibit 11-3). The laws and regulations we will discuss are highlights only, chosen to help make you aware that government constraints reduce

ETHICAL ISSUES IN HRM

The Secret Paycheck

What keeps you from comparing your paycheck with your coworkers? Is there a policy at work that prevents you from discussing how much you earn? Do you think you already know what they make? Turns out neither of these are very good reasons for keeping pay a secret.

Pay is frequently the subject of curiosity and gossip. In American culture, it's considered impolite and inappropriate to disclose one's own salary, but we still speculate about what our coworkers earn. Those of us who think we know how much our bosses and coworkers earn are probably wrong. Research shows that we tend to overestimate the pay of others. Websites like Glassdoor allow employees to share information about their employer, jobs, and salaries, anonymously skirting the pay secrecy policies for coworkers and job seekers.

Pay secrecy policies that forbid employees from discussing salaries are not uncommon, although they are mostly unenforceable. The National Labor Relations Act has protected the rights of most non-supervisory employees and employees engaged in collective bargaining to discuss wages since 1965.[11] So why do companies still have policies prohibiting discussing salaries? Some are concerned that it might lead to morale problems or jealousy over the higher salary of a coworker. It could also cause problems if a competitor found out and was able to mount a "hiring attack" to lure away the top producers.

Arguments against pay secrecy policies are mounting, however. One proponent of eliminating pay secrecy is Ed Lawler, a professor at the University of Southern California. He argues that if people challenge a pay system, it may be because they are right in doing so. "Maybe you really are doing a bad job and getting that feedback directly—and based on valid data—is a good thing because it can stimulate you to improve."[12] Another concern is that pay secrecy may be masking pay discrimination. Pay secrecy rules make it difficult to determine coworker salaries for comparison if you feel that you are earning less than others in your same position and may be the victim of discrimination.

Timely information is important, too. The Lilly Ledbetter Fair Pay Act was passed to allow employees more time to discover pay discrepancies that may be discriminatory.[13] Lilly Ledbetter was a Goodyear employee who filed a pay discrimination suit against her employer after being anonymously informed that male coworkers had been paid significantly more than she was for the same work for many years. Her case went all the way

(Source: Zorani/iStockphoto)

to the Supreme Court, which determined that her complaint was made too long after the discriminatory pay decision was made. There is concern that the practice of pay secrecy may be intended to make discovery of discriminatory practices so difficult that an employee will miss the 180 day deadline.

Ethical Questions:

Do you want to know how much money your coworkers earn? How eager are you to tell them how much you earn? Is pay secrecy a valid management tool to prevent jealousy and morale problems, or is it an unfair practice that hides discrimination and ineffective compensation policies?

EMPLOYEE RIGHTS
UNDER THE FAIR LABOR STANDARDS ACT
THE UNITED STATES DEPARTMENT OF LABOR WAGE AND HOUR DIVISION

FEDERAL MINIMUM WAGE
$7.25 PER HOUR
BEGINNING JULY 24, 2009

OVERTIME PAY

At least 1½ times your regular rate of pay for all hours worked over 40 in a workweek.

CHILD LABOR

An employee must be at least **16** years old to work in most non-farm jobs and at least **18** to work in non-farm jobs declared hazardous by the Secretary of Labor.

Youths **14** and **15** years old may work outside school hours in various non-manufacturing, non-mining, non-hazardous jobs under the following conditions:

No more than
- **3** hours on a school day or **18** hours in a school week;
- **8** hours on a non-school day or **40** hours in a non-school week.

Also, work may not begin before **7 a.m.** or end after **7 p.m.**, except from June 1 through Labor Day, when evening hours are extended to **9 p.m.** Different rules apply in agricultural employment.

TIP CREDIT

Employers of "tipped employees" must pay a cash wage of at least $2.13 per hour if they claim a tip credit against their minimum wage obligation. If an employee's tips combined with the employer's cash wage of at least $2.13 per hour do not equal the minimum hourly wage, the employer must make up the difference. Certain other conditions must also be met.

ENFORCEMENT

The Department of Labor may recover back wages either administratively or through court action, for the employees that have been underpaid in violation of the law. Violations may result in civil or criminal action.

Employers may be assessed civil money penalties of up to $1,100 for each willful or repeated violation of the minimum wage or overtime pay provisions of the law and up to $11,000 for each employee who is the subject of a violation of the Act's child labor provisions. In addition, a civil money penalty of up to $50,000 may be assessed for each child labor violation that causes the death or serious injury of any minor employee, and such assessments may be doubled, up to $100,000, when the violations are determined to be willful or repeated. The law also prohibits discriminating against or discharging workers who file a complaint or participate in any proceeding under the Act.

ADDITIONAL INFORMATION

- Certain occupations and establishments are exempt from the minimum wage and/or overtime pay provisions.
- Special provisions apply to workers in American Samoa and the Commonwealth of the Northern Mariana Islands.
- Some state laws provide greater employee protections; employers must comply with both.
- The law requires employers to display this poster where employees can readily see it.
- Employees under 20 years of age may be paid $4.25 per hour during their first 90 consecutive calendar days of employment with an employer.
- Certain full-time students, student learners, apprentices, and workers with disabilities may be paid less than the minimum wage under special certificates issued by the Department of Labor.

For additional information:
1-866-4-USWAGE
(1-866-487-9243)   TTY: 1-877-889-5627
WHD U.S. Wage and Hour Division
WWW.WAGEHOUR.DOL.GOV

U.S. Department of Labor | Wage and Hour Division

WHD Publication 1088 (Revised July 2009)

Exhibit 11-3
Federal Minimum Wage

Employers are required to display an approved poster informing employees of the legal minimum wage. The U.S. Department of Labor provides posters available for download at www.dol.gov. Individual states may enact minimum wage laws that are higher than the federal minimum, but not lower. http://www.dol.gov/whd/regs/ compliance/posters/minwage.pdf

HRM's discretion on compensation decisions. An abundance of laws and regulations define the general parameters within which managers decide what fair compensation is. Let's look at some of these.

Fair Labor Standards Act Starbucks and Walmart are among the many employers that have been found to have violated laws regulating pay. Starbucks had been distributing tip money to supervisors in addition to the baristas (coffee-making employees) who earned the tips. The supervisors could not be in the "tip pool" because their positions allowed them to hire, fire, supervise, and direct other workers. Starbucks was ordered to repay over $100 million to the baristas who had their tips diverted to managers.[14] Walmart agreed to pay over $700 million to settle lawsuits nationwide that alleged employees were routinely underpaid. Among the alleged practices at Walmart were not allowing employees to take rest and meal breaks in violation of state laws, and discouraging employees from submitting overtime hours in violation of federal laws.[15] Walmart and Starbucks are hardly alone. The U.S. Department of Labor estimates that seven in ten U.S. employers are violating wage and hour regulations. These costly errors are part of a trend that has caused the yearly number of wage complaints filed with the Department of Labor to double in the last ten years.[16] How can an employer prevent being part of the 70 percent of employers that run into trouble? It's simple—know the law!

The **Fair Labor Standards Act (FLSA)** sets federal requirements for minimum wages, overtime pay, record keeping, and child labor restrictions. Nearly all organizations are covered by the FLSA, but not all employees are covered. The act identifies two primary

> **Fair Labor Standards Act (FLSA)**
> Passed in 1938, this act established laws outlining minimum wage, overtime pay, and maximum hour requirements for most U.S. workers.

CONTEMPORARY CONNECTION

The Minimum Wage Debate

An estimated 4.5 million workers, or approximately 4 percent of the U.S. workforce, received an increase in their wages when the minimum wage climbed to $7.25 in 2009. Minimum wage laws are controversial. Strong arguments are made on either side of the argument as to whether an increase in the minimum wage helps or hurts workers. Let's look at both sides of the debate.

Proponents argue that wages tend to lag behind the cost of living, and an increase in wages helps to reverse a decline in real wages for low-wage workers. Before the most recent increase, the minimum wage had not been adjusted in nearly ten years. Young people and women seem to be the most affected. Half of those in minimum wage jobs are under the age of twenty-five and nearly 75 percent are employed in jobs in the service industry. About 3 percent of women who earn hourly wages reported earning wages at or less than the federal minimum compared to about 1 percent of men.

In the United States, the threshold poverty level for a family of two is $14,710. Someone who earns minimum wage will earn approximately $15,080 (40 hours × 52 weeks × $7.25), so a family of two with one wage earner is barely above the poverty level. The average minimum wage worker is responsible for over half (54 percent) of household income, and over half of the 4.4 million minimum wage workers belong to families that have household incomes under $35,000 a year. Opponents of increasing the minimum wage cite the problems of increasing costs to employers.

They note that in a globally competitive marketplace, every cent added to the cost of doing business drives up the overall costs to the organization—and ultimately erodes competitive opportunities. Increased wage requirements may also result in less demand for workers, ultimately hurting the hourly workers the hike in wages was designed to help.

Although the U.S. minimum wage rate is not the highest among industrialized nations, it is significantly higher than many countries that compete with the United States for goods and services. In addition, states and even cities have the right to increase the minimum wage in their locations based on market demands. Furthermore, many opponents of the increase cite that the issue is not about wages but about education. There is a direct correlation between one's education level and one's wages. A better-educated, higher skilled worker is more valuable to organizations, and thus market mechanisms increase what an organization is willing to pay for that individual's service.

Consider this:

What's your opinion as to whether the federal minimum wage rate should continue to be increased? Is the starting wage in your area above minimum wage for workers that are most likely to earn minimum wage such as the young, part-time, or unskilled worker? Clearly there are no easy solutions to this debate.[18]

exempt employees
Employees in positions that are exempt from most employee protection outlined in the Fair Labor Standards Act, especially overtime pay.

nonexempt employees
Employees who are covered by the Fair Labor Standards Act, including overtime pay and minimum wage provisions.

categories of employees: exempt and nonexempt. **Exempt employees** would include, for instance, those in professional and managerial jobs. Under the act, jobs categorized as exempt are not required to meet FLSA standards, especially in the area of overtime pay. Workers earning less than $23,660 per year or $455 per week are guaranteed overtime protection.[17]

On the other hand, **nonexempt employees** receive certain protections under the FLSA. Specifically, employees in these jobs are eligible for premium pay—typically time-and-a-half—when they work more than forty hours in a week. Moreover, these jobs must be paid at least the minimum wage, which was set at $7.25 in 2009. Some states and cities require wages higher than the federal minimum. In certain circumstances, employees may be paid less than the minimum. For example, if an employee earns tips, employers may pay a direct wage of $2.13 and consider those tips part of employees' wages. Employers may claim a "tip credit" for the remaining amount, but if the tip credit and the direct wage are less than the minimum wage, the employer must make up the difference.

Both federal and state governments have also enacted laws requiring firms that contract with the government to pay prevailing wage rates. In the federal sector, the secretary of labor must review industry rates in the specific locality to set a prevailing rate, which becomes the contract minimum prescribed under the Walsh-Healy Act. Under this act, government contractors must also pay time-and-a-half for all work in excess of eight hours a day or forty hours a week.

The Civil Rights and Equal Pay Acts   The Civil Rights and the Equal Pay Acts, among other laws, protect employees from discrimination. Just as it is illegal to discriminate in hiring, organizations cannot discriminate in pay on the basis of race, color, creed, age, or sex.

Equal Pay Act of 1963
This act requires equal pay for equal work.

The **Equal Pay Act of 1963** mandates that organizations compensate men and women doing the same job in the organization with the same rate of pay.[19] The Equal Pay Act was designed to lessen the pay gap between male and female pay rates. Despite progress, women in general still earn roughly 78 percent of what their male counterparts earn.[20] Some of this difference is attributable to perceived male-versus female-dominated occupations, but the Equal Pay Act requires employers to eliminate pay differences for the same job. Salaries should be established based on skill, responsibility, effort, and working conditions. For example, if an organization is hiring customer service representatives, new employees must be paid the same initial salary, regardless of gender, because the attributes for the job are the same. It is important to note that the Equal Pay Act typically affects only initial job salaries. If two workers, one male and one female, perform at different levels during the course of the year, and if performance is rewarded, the act allows that in the next period their pay may be different.

Job Evaluation and the Pay Structure

The essence of compensation administration is job evaluation and the establishment of a pay structure. Let's now turn our attention to job evaluation topics and practices.

Job Evaluation

In Chapter 5, we introduced job analysis as the process of describing job duties, authority relationships, skills required, conditions of work, and additional relevant information. We stated that job analysis data could help develop job descriptions and specifications, as well as job evaluations. By job evaluation, we mean using job analysis information to systematically determine the value of each job in relation to all jobs within the organization. In short, a job evaluation seeks to rank all jobs in the organization in a hierarchy that reflects the relative worth of each. It's important to note that this is a ranking of jobs, not people. Job evaluation assumes normal job performance by a typical worker. So, in effect, the process ignores individual abilities or performance.

The ranking that results from job evaluation is not an end in itself. It should be used to determine the organization's pay structure. Note that we say should; in practice, this is not always the case. External labor market conditions, collective bargaining, and individual skill differences may require a compromise between the job evaluation ranking and the actual pay structure. Yet even when such compromises are necessary, job evaluation can provide an objective standard from which modifications can be made.

Isolating Job Evaluation Criteria

The heart of job evaluation is determining appropriate criteria to arrive at the ranking.[21] It is easy to say that jobs are valued and ranked by their relative job worth, but ambiguity increases when we attempt to state what places one job higher than another in the job structure hierarchy. Most job-evaluation plans use responsibility, skill, effort, and working conditions as major criteria, but each of these, in turn, can be broken down into more specific terms. Skill, for example, is "an observable competence to perform a learned psychomotor act (like keyboarding)."[22] But other criteria can and have been used: supervisory controls, complexity, personal contacts, and the physical demands needed.[23]

You should not expect the criteria to be constant across jobs. Because jobs differ, it is traditional to separate them into common groups. For example, production, clerical, sales, professional, and managerial jobs may be evaluated separately. Treating like groups similarly allows for more valid rankings within categories, but doesn't necessarily establish the importance of criteria between job categories. Separation by groups may permit HR to say the position of software developer requires more mental effort than that of shipping supervisor, and subsequently receives a higher ranking, but it does not readily resolve whether greater mental effort is necessary for software designers or customer service managers.

Job Evaluation Methods

Three basic methods of job evaluation are currently in use: ordering, classification, and point methods.[24] Let's review each of these.

Ordering Method The **ordering method** (or ranking method) requires a committee—typically composed of both management and employee representatives—to arrange jobs in a simple rank order, from highest to lowest. No attempt is made to break down the jobs by specific weighted criteria. The committee members merely compare two jobs and judge which one is more important or more difficult to perform. Then they compare another job with the first two, and so on until all the jobs have been evaluated and ranked.

The most obvious limitation to the ordering method is its sheer unmanageability with numerous jobs. Imagine the difficulty of correctly ranking hundreds or thousands of jobs in an organization. Other drawbacks to consider are the method's subjectivity—no definite or consistent standards by which to justify the rankings—and the fact that because jobs are ranked in order, we cannot know the distance between rankings.

Classification Method The **classification method** was made popular by the U.S. Civil Service Commission, now the Office of Personnel Management (OPM). The OPM requires that classification grades be established and published in what they call their general schedules. These classifications are created by identifying some common denominator—skills, knowledge, responsibilities—to create distinct classes or grades of jobs. Examples might include shop jobs, clerical jobs, and sales jobs, depending, of course, on the type of jobs the organization requires.

Once the classifications are established, they are ranked in an overall order of importance according to the criteria chosen, and each job is placed in its appropriate classification. This latter action generally requires comparing each position's job description against the classification description and benchmarked jobs. At the OPM, for example, evaluators have classified

ordering method
Ranking job worth from highest to lowest.

classification method
Evaluating jobs based on predetermined job grades.

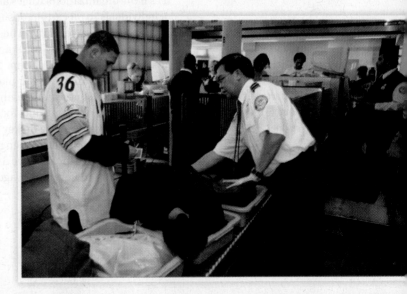

How much should we pay for security? That question may be difficult to answer, but the federal government's classification system tells us that this transportation security screener is paid a minimum salary between $28,600 and $48,200, depending on work location.
(Source: © AP/Wide World Photos)

both a statistician at the Department of Energy and a chemical engineer at the Environmental Protection Agency as positions at the GS-7 grade, and an electrician at the Department of the Army and an industrial equipment mechanic at the Military District of Washington as positions at the GS-10 grade.[25]

The classification method shares most of the disadvantages of the ordering approach, plus the difficulty of writing classification descriptions, judging which jobs go where, and dealing with jobs that appear to fall into more than one classification. On the plus side, the classification method has proven itself successful and viable in classifying millions of kinds and levels of civil service jobs.

point method
Breaking down jobs based on identifiable criteria and the degree to which these criteria exist on the job.

Point Method HR develops a **point method** by breaking jobs down into categories such as education, skill, effort, responsibility and working conditions. Points are assigned to each category based on the importance of the criteria to successful performance of the job. Points may be weighted more heavily if increased education, skill or experience are required for the position. Pay grades or ranges are assigned to jobs based on the total number of points.

The point method offers the greatest stability of the four approaches presented. Jobs may change over time, but the rating scales established under the point method stay intact. Additionally, the methodology underlying the approach contributes to a minimum of rating error. On the other hand, the point method is complex and therefore costly and time-consuming to develop. The key criteria must be carefully and clearly identified, degrees of factors must be agreed on in terms all raters recognize, the weight of each criterion must be established, and point values must be assigned to degrees. Although it is expensive and time-consuming to both implement and maintain, the point method appears to be the most widely used method. Furthermore, this method can effectively address the comparable worth issue (see Chapter 3).

Establishing the Pay Structure

Once the job evaluation is complete, the data generated become the nucleus of the organization's pay structure. This means establishing pay rates or ranges compatible with the ranks, classifications, or points arrived at through job evaluation.

Any of the three job evaluation methods can provide the necessary input for developing the organization's overall pay structure. Each has its strengths and weaknesses, but because of its wide use, we will use the point method to show how point totals are combined with compensation survey data to form wage curves.

compensation surveys
Used to gather factual data on pay practices among firms and companies within specific communities.

Compensation Surveys Many organizations use surveys to gather factual information on pay practices within specific communities and among firms in their industry. They use this information for comparison purposes. It can tell compensation committees if the organization's wages are in line with those of other employers and, in shortages of individuals to fill certain positions, may help set wage levels. Where does an organization find wage salary data? The U.S. Department of Labor, through its Bureau of Labor Statistics, regularly publishes a vast amount of wage data broken down by geographic area, industry, and occupation. Many industry and employee associations also conduct **compensation surveys** and make their results available. Organizations also can conduct their own surveys, and many large ones do.

It would not be unusual, for instance, for the HRM director at Microsoft in Seattle to regularly share wage data on key positions. This person might identify jobs such as maintenance engineer, electrical engineer, computer programmer, or administrative assistant, and share comprehensive descriptions of these jobs with other firms in the industry. In addition to the average wage level for a specific job, other information frequently

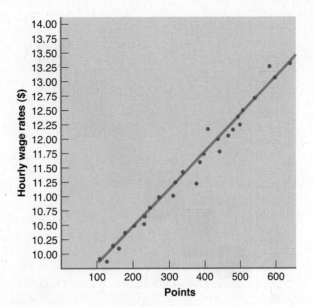

Exhibit 11-4
A Wage Curve

Wage curves like this one plot a position's value in points against the wages paid for each of those positions. Jobs that do not fall within an accepted range may be "red circled."

reviewed includes entry-level and maximum wage rates, shift differentials, overtime pay practices, vacation and holiday allowances, the number of pay periods, and the length of the normal work day and work week.

Wage Curves After the compensation committee arrives at point totals from job evaluation and obtains survey data on what comparable organizations are paying for similar jobs, a wage curve can be fitted to the data. An example of a wage curve is shown in Exhibit 11-4. This example assumes use of the point method and plots point totals and wage data. A separate wage curve can be constructed based on survey data and compared for discrepancies.

A completed wage curve tells the compensation committee the average relationship between points of established pay grades and wage base rates. Furthermore, it can identify jobs whose pay is out of the trend line. When a job's pay rate is too high, it may be identified as a "red circle" rate. This means that the pay level is frozen or below-average increases are granted until the structure adjusts upward to put the circled rate within the normal range. Of course, a wage rate may be out of line but not red circled. The need to attract or keep individuals with specific skills may require a wage rate outside the normal range, although continuing to attract these individuals may ultimately upset the internal consistencies supposedly inherent in the wage structure. A wage rate may also be too low. Such undervalued jobs carry a "green circle" rate, and the company may attempt to grant these jobs above-average pay increases or salary adjustments.

The Wage Structure It is only a short step from plotting a wage curve to developing the organization's **wage structure**. Jobs similar in terms of classes, grades, or points are grouped together. For instance, pay grade 1 may cover the range from 0 to 150 points, pay grade 2 from 151 to 300 points, and so on. As shown in Exhibit 11-5, the result is a logical hierarchy of wages. The more important jobs are paid more; and as individuals assume jobs of greater importance, they rise within the wage hierarchy. Jobs may also be paid in accordance with knowledge- or competency-based pay.

Notice that each pay grade has a range and that the ranges overlap. Typically, organizations design their wage structures with ranges in each grade to reflect different tenure in positions, as well as levels of performance. Additionally, although most organizations create a degree of overlap between grades, employees who reach the top of their grade can increase their pay only by moving to a higher grade. However, wage structures are adjusted every several years (if not every year), so that employees who top out in their pay grade aren't maxed out forever.

wage structure
A pay scale showing ranges of pay within each grade.

Exhibit 11-5
A Sample Wage Structure

Jobs with similar classes, grades, or points are grouped together to create an organization's wage structure. Grades overlap each other, encouraging employees reaching the top of one pay grade to move to a higher grade.

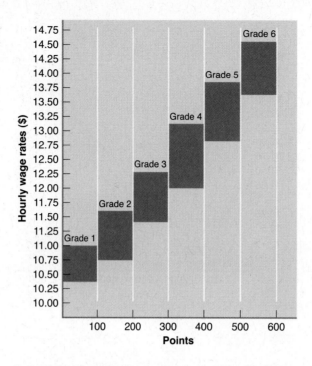

External Factors

When determining the wage structure, HR must also consider external factors like geographic differences in wages and labor supply. Consideration must also be given to how the organization will react to the wage structures of competing organizations.

Geographic Differences Cost of labor is a function of supply and demand, among many other factors. When local supply of labor falls short of demand, wages will increase. Conversely if the local labor supply exceeds demand, wages will decrease. This can cause wage fluctuations in some geographic areas or cities, depending on how far workers are willing to travel for a job. Many states provide salary information organized by county or city for employers to use. For example, a company that runs long-term health care facilities may pay minimum wage for certified nursing assistants in an area with few employers, yet need to pay substantially more than minimum wage in a city where there are many employers competing for people with those skills.

Labor Supply When unemployment rates are low, employers must work harder to attract qualified workers. This often includes raising wages to tempt workers to leave their current employment and apply. When unemployment rates are high, wages tend to be depressed because employers have a plentiful supply of applicants. Employers may also encounter situations where there is an oversupply of workers with one set of skills, such as framing carpenters, but a shortage of workers with another set of skills, such as welders. This would require a higher starting salary to attract workers with the correct skills.

Competition Just as an organization must consider competition when setting prices for goods and services, they must consider the influence of competition on wages. When setting a policy on how to react to competition wages, HR professionals have three choices:[26]

- *Match* the competition by paying the market or going rate for labor. This ensures that the pay remains competitive, allowing employers to manage labor costs while still being able to attract qualified workers.
- *Lead* the competition by paying higher wages than competing employers. This may seem like an expensive proposition, but many organizations feel that by "leading" the market, they will be able to attract better qualified employees, leading to lower training costs, better productivity, and lower turnover.
- *Lag* the market by paying slightly less than the prevailing levels in the marketplace. This will lower labor costs, but will make it more difficult to attract and maintain qualified workers. Training and turnover costs will often offset any gains made by paying lower wages.[27]

Cost of Living Inflation raises the price of consumer goods and reduces the buying power of wages in real terms. The Consumer Price Index (CPI) is compiled by the U.S. Department of Labor's Bureau of Labor Statistics and reports monthly on the prices consumers pay for a representative basket of goods and services.[28] As the CPI increases, wages must also increase to allow workers to maintain their standard of living. The cost of living also varies according to location, prompting some large cities such as San Francisco to set their own minimum wage that is higher than the federal or even state minimum wage.

Collective Bargaining The major function of most unions or collective bargaining units is to negotiate for the wages of its members. We will discuss this in more detail in Chapter 14, "Understanding Labor Relations and Collective Bargaining."

Communicating with Employees No matter how the wage structure is developed, employees must know how the system is derived. If an organization neglects to inform its employees and fails to communicate how the process works, it will only lead to problems later. In fact, many reports note that how the pay plan is communicated is just as important as what is communicated.[29] Accordingly, organizations that want the most from their compensation system will find communicating the process to employees a major leap toward achieving compensation goals.[30]

Special Cases of Compensation

As organizations rapidly change in this dynamic world, so, too, do compensation programs. Most notably, organizations are finding that they can no longer increase wage rates by a certain percentage each year (cost-of-living raise) without some comparable increase in performance. Subsequently, more organizations are moving to varied themes of pay for performance. These may include incentive compensation plans, and competency- and team-based compensation. Let's take a closer look at each of these.

Incentive Compensation Plans

In addition to the basic wage structure, organizations sincerely committed to developing a compensation system designed around performance should consider incentive pay. Typically given in addition to—rather than in place of—the basic wage, incentive plans can add a dimension to the wage structure we have previously described.[31] Incentives can be paid based on individual, group, or organization-wide performance—a pay-for-performance concept.

Individual Incentives **Individual incentive plans** pay off for individual performances.[32] Popular approaches include merit pay, piecework plans, time-savings bonuses, commissions, and stock options. One popular and almost universally used incentive system is **merit pay**. Under a merit pay plan, employees who receive merit increases have a sum of money added to their base salary. Somewhat similar to a cost-of-living raise, merit pay differs in that the percentage of increase to the base wage rate is attributable solely to performance. Those who perform better generally receive more merit pay.

> **individual incentive plans**
> Motivation systems based on individual work performance.
>
> **merit pay**
> An increase in pay, usually determined annually.

Although the merit pay plan is the most widely used, the best-known incentive is undoubtedly piecework. Under a straight piecework plan, the employee is typically guaranteed a minimal hourly rate for meeting some pre-established standard output. When output exceeds this standard, the employee earns so much for each piece produced. Differential piece-rate plans establish two rates—one up to standard, and another when the employee exceeds the standard. The latter rate, of course, is higher to encourage the employee to beat the standard. Individual incentives can be based on time saved as well as output generated. The employee can expect a minimal guaranteed hourly rate, but in this case, the bonus is achieved for doing a standard hour's work in less than sixty minutes. Employees who produce an hour's work in fifty minutes obtain a bonus percentage (say, 50 percent) of the labor saved.

Salespeople frequently work on commission. Added to a lower base wage, they earn a percentage of the sales price. On toys, for instance, it may be a hefty 25 or 30 percent. On sales of multimillion-dollar aircraft or city sewer systems, commissions are frequently 1 percent or less.

Individuals in construction trades are sometimes paid on a piecework basis. The more they install in a day, the more they earn. Accordingly, their pay is up to them. *(Source: Steve Cole/iStockphoto)*

Individual incentives work best with clear performance objectives and independent tasks.[33] Otherwise, individual incentives can create dysfunctional competition or encourage workers to cut corners. Coworkers can become the enemy, individuals can create inflated perceptions of their own work while deflating the work of others, and the work environment may become characterized by reduced interaction and communications between employees. And cutting corners may compromise quality and safety.

A potentially negative effect of incentive for performance is that you may "get what you pay for." When incentives are tied to specific goals (only part of the total outcomes expected from a job), people may avoid performing unmeasured, and thus not rewarded, activities in favor of measured, rewarded ones. For example, if your school sponsored a lecture by an internationally recognized speaker, and your instructor decided to take your class, would you go? Your response might be contingent on whether the lecture was a requirement, the content might be on an exam, and attendance would be taken. If it was just for your information, attending might not be as high a priority. Thus despite the fact that they may have negative consequences, such as leaving other activities neglected, individual incentives are widely used.

Merit pay, too, has been used as a substitute for cost-of-living raises. Similar to a cost-of-living raise, merit monies accrue permanently to the base salary and become the new base from which to calculate future percentage increases. The problem with merit pay or a cost-of-living system, then, is that pay increases may become expected. But what if the company has a bad year, or employees fail to produce to expectations? Under these traditional systems, workers still expect wage increases. Theoretically, they should give some of their salary back!

Some occupations have been slow to develop merit pay plans, often because standards are difficult to establish or evaluate. Teaching at a college is a good example. Consider the different types of teaching styles you've observed, the different degrees of difficulty in subject matter, and various levels of dedication to students, and you get an idea of how hard merit plans can be to establish.

group incentive
Motivational plan provided to a group of employees based on their collective work.

Group Incentives   Each individual incentive option we describe can also work for groups. That is, two or more employees can be paid for their combined performance. **Group incentives** make the most sense when employees' tasks are interdependent and thus require cooperation.

organization-wide incentive
A motivation system that rewards all facility members based on how well the entire group performed.

Organization-Wide Incentives   **Organization-wide incentives** aim to direct the efforts of all employees toward achieving overall organizational effectiveness. This type of incentive produces rewards for all employees based on organization-wide cost reduction or profit sharing. Lincoln Electric, a 115-year-old company based in Ohio that manufactures arc welding equipment and supplies, has had a year-end bonus system for decades. Over the years, the Lincoln Electric plan has paid off handsomely when employees beat previous years' performance standards. Bonuses over the last ten years have averaged 40 percent of the employee's annual earnings.[34]

Scanlon Plan
An organization-wide incentive program focusing on cooperation between management and employees through sharing problems, goals, and ideas.

One of the best-known organization-wide incentive systems is the **Scanlon Plan**.[35] It seeks cooperation between management and employees through sharing problems, goals, and ideas. (It is interesting to note that many quality circle programs instituted in the 1980s were a direct outgrowth of the Scanlon Plan.) Under Scanlon, each department in the organization has a committee composed of supervisor and employee representatives. Suggestions for labor-saving improvements are funneled to the committee. If accepted, cost savings and productivity gains are shared by all employees, not just the individual who made the suggestion. Typically, about 80 percent of the suggestions prove practical and are adopted.

IMPROSHARE
An incentive plan that uses a specific mathematical formula for determining employee bonuses.

Another incentive plan called **IMPROSHARE**, a contraction of Improving Productivity through Sharing, uses a mathematical formula to determine employees' bonuses.[36] For example, if workers save labor costs in producing a product, a predetermined portion of the labor savings goes to the employee. Profit-sharing plans, or gain sharing plans, are also organization-wide incentives. They allow employees to share in the firm's success by distributing part of the company's profits back to the workers. For instance, at Chamberlin Rubber in Rochester, New York, employees receive 75 percent of company profits. Company President Bill Lanigan implemented the profit-sharing plan after a year of tough losses, and found immediate and impressive results. Profitability returned, employees felt more accountable, and quickly assisted in making quality improvements. Managers' jobs became more manageable as the employees became more engaged. Turnover has nearly disappeared and over $800,000 is paid annually in bonuses. Lanigan says, "Hiring and firing are very expensive. We've virtually eliminated that, because people don't want to leave."[37]

All organization-wide incentives suffer however, from a *dilution effect*. It is hard for employees to see how their efforts affect organization's overall performance. These plans also tend to distribute payoffs at wide intervals; a bonus paid in March 2014 for your efforts in 2013 loses a lot of its reinforcement capabilities. Finally, we should not overlook what happens when organization-wide incentives become both large and recurrent. When this happens, employees often begin to anticipate and expect the bonus. Employees may adjust their spending patterns as if the bonus was a certainty, and the bonus may lose some of its motivating properties. When that happens, it can be perceived as a membership-based reward.

In the holiday movie classic, "National Lampoon's Christmas Vacation," Clark Griswold looses his cool when the Christmas bonus he was counting on to put a swimming pool in the backyard is replaced with a one year membership to the Jelly of the Month Club.
(Source: Warner Bros./Photofest)

Paying for Performance

Pay-for-performance programs compensate employees based on a performance measure. Piecework plans, gain sharing, wage incentive plans, profit sharing, and lump sum bonuses are examples of pay-for-performance programs.[38] These forms of pay differ from more traditional compensation plans in that instead of paying an employee for time on the job, pay is adjusted to reflect performance measures that might include individual productivity, team or work group productivity, departmental productivity, or the overall organization's profits for a given period.[39]

Performance-based compensation is probably most compatible with demonstrating to employees a strong relationship between their performance and the rewards they receive.[40] Rewards allocated solely on nonperformance factors—seniority, job title, or across-the-board cost-of-living raises—may encourage employees to reduce their efforts.

Pay-for-performance programs are gaining in popularity in organizations. One survey found that almost 90 percent were practicing some form of pay-for-performance for salaried employees.[41] Skyline Construction in San Francisco offered employees the chance to take lower salaries in exchange for potentially higher bonuses based on performance. Company president, David Hayes, was astonished when 75 percent of the employees requested the lowest salary combination with the highest percentage bonus. After two years, their sales had nearly doubled from $36 million to $71 million, with a corresponding drop in costs as a percentage of sales.[42] This clearly illustrates the benefits of both motivation and cost control.

From a motivation perspective, conditioning some or all of a worker's pay on performance measures focuses his or her attention and effort on that measure, then reinforces continued effort with rewards. However, if the employee's, team's, or organization's performance declines, so does the reward, thus encouraging strong efforts and motivation. On the cost-savings side, performance-based bonuses and other incentive rewards avoid the fixed expense of permanent—and often annual—salary increases. Bonuses typically do not accrue to base salary; the amount is not compounded in future years, thus saving the company money.

A recent extension of the pay-for-performance concept, **competency-based compensation**, is used in such industries as diverse as healthcare and energy production. A competency-based compensation program pays and rewards employees on their skills,

pay-for-performance programs Rewarding employees based on their job performance.

competency-based compensation Organizational pay system that rewards skills, knowledge, and behaviors.

Exhibit 11-6
Sample Pay Bands

The pay bands illustrated here include a minimum, midpoint, and maximum for each salary band.

HUMAN RESOURCES

SC Budget and Control Board

State of South Carolina Pay Bands

Home Page

jobs.sc.gov

Hot Topics

Career Opportunities

Employee Services

Employer Services

Training & Development

How to Contact Us

OHR Webmail

Other Agencies

State Employees Weather Alert

Band – Minimum – Midpoint – Maximum
01 – $15,080 – $20,696 – $26,312
02 – $17,310 – $24,668 – $32,027
03 – $21,063 – $30,019 – $38,975
04 – $25,627 – $36,520 – $47,413
05 – $31,182 – $44,438 – $57,695
06 – $37,945 – $54,074 – $70,204
07 – $46,169 – $65,793 – $85,417
08 – $56,176 – $80,055 – $103,934
09 – $68,350 – $97,404 – $126,458
10 – $83,165 – $118,514 – $153,964

Effective July 1, 2012

Source: South Carolina Budget and Control Board, Office of Human Resources, http://www.ohr.sc.gov/OHR/employer/OHR-paybands.phtm.

knowledge, or behaviors.[43] These competencies may include such behaviors and skills as leadership, problem solving, decision making, or strategic planning. Pay levels reflect the degree of competency. Pay increases in a competency-based system reward growth in personal competencies as well as contributions to the overall organization.[44] Accordingly, an employee's rewards directly reflect his or her ability to contribute to achievement of the organization's goals and objectives.

This is, in essence, a pay scheme based on employees' specific competencies. These may include knowledge of the business and its core values, skills to fulfill these core requirements, and demonstrated employee behaviors. In competency-based pay plans, these preset levels are called **broad-banding**.[45] Among the banding programs documented, some have as few as four bands with no salary ranges, and others more than ten bands and several salary ranges. For example, Exhibit 11-6 shows a ten-band compensation program for state employees in South Carolina. Broad-banding also can help develop wage structures on factors other than skills.

broad-banding

Paying employees at preset levels based on their level of competency.

Those who possess competencies within a certain range will be grouped together in a pay category. Pay increases, then, recognize growth in personal competencies, as well as the contribution one makes to the organization. Accordingly, career and pay advancement may not be tied specifically to a promotion, but rather to how much more one can contribute to the organization's goals and objectives.

You may be thinking that this seems similar to our previous discussion of the point method of job evaluation. However, the point method looked specifically at the job and its worth to the company. Competency-based pay plans assess these points based on the value the employee adds in assisting the organization to achieving its goals. As more organizations move toward competency-based pay plans, HRM will play a critical role. Just as we discussed in Chapter 5 regarding employment planning, once the direction of the organization is established, attracting, developing, motivating, and retaining competent individuals become essential. This will continue to have implications for recruiting, training and development, career development, and performance appraisals, as well as pay and reward systems. Not only will HRM ensure that it has the right people at the right place, but it will have assembled a competent team of employees who add significant value to the organization.

Team-Based Compensation

You've just been handed the course syllabus for a business policy course you're taking this semester, and you quickly glance at how the final grade will be calculated: two tests—a midterm and a final—and a class project. Intrigued, you read more about the class project. You and four other classmates must thoroughly analyze a company's operations. You will make recommendations about the company's financial picture, human resources, product lines, competitive advantage, and strategic direction. The group must turn in a report of no less than fifty pages, double-spaced, and make a thirty-minute class presentation about your suggested turnaround. The report and presentation account for 75 percent of the course grade, and each team member will receive the same project grade. Do you think it's fair? Is there too much riding on the efforts of others? What happens if one of your teammates isn't any help or has personal issues that result in dropping the class after the project has started? Are you held accountable for his effort? Welcome to the world of team-based compensation.

Today's dynamic organizations place much more emphasis on involving employees in most relevant aspects of the job. When organizations group employees into teams and empower them to meet goals, teams reap the benefits of their productive effort. That is, **team-based compensation** plans are tied to team-based performance.[46]

Under a team-based compensation plan, team members who work on achieving—and in many cases, exceeding—established goals often share equally in the rewards (although, in the truest sense, teams allocate their own rewards). Providing for fair treatment of each team member encourages group cohesiveness.[47] Yet this does not occur overnight. Rather, it requires several key components. For instance, effective teams have a clear purpose and goals. They understand what is expected of them and that their effort is worthwhile.[48] Teams also need the necessary resources to complete their tasks. Because their livelihood may rest on accomplishing their goals, a lack of necessary resources may doom a team effort before it begins. Finally, mutual trust among the team members is critical. They must respect each other, effectively communicate with one another, and treat each member fairly and equitably. Failure here may create serious obstacles that defeat the sense of purpose group cohesiveness can foster.

team-based compensation
Pay based on how well the team performed.

Executive Compensation Programs

Executive compensation has become one of HR's most controversial issues. Although CEO pay declined somewhat during the recession, it's estimated that as early as 2010, nearly three-quarters of CEOs received raises that put their compensation back to pre-recession levels.[49] Executive pay has risen from about twenty-four times the salary of an average worker in 1965 to over 300 times the pay of the average worker in 2011.[50] Exhibit 11-7 gives an indication of the total compensation package of a typical U.S. CEO.

Pay is only part of the story. Executives frequently operate under bonus and stock option plans that can dramatically increase their total compensation. A senior executive at Occidental Petroleum Viacom, Oracle, DirectTV, Comcast, Walt Disney, or Time Warner can, in a good year, earn total compensation packages upwards of $50 million.[51] We want to briefly look at how such compensations come about and why. Executives also receive perquisites (called perks) or special benefits that others do not. What are these, and how do they impact executive motivation?

Age	57
Years as CEO	8
Years with company	19
Salary	$1.1 million
Annual bonus	$2.2 million
Value realized on exercised options	$2.7 million
Value realized on vested stock awards	$22.5 million
Total 1-year compensation	$9.0 million

Exhibit 11-7
Average U.S. CEO Compensation

Salary is only the beginning of the total compensation package for top executives. Bonuses and stock options add considerable value to the package.

Source: www.nytimes.com accessed November 12, 2011.

Salaries of Top Managers

It is well known that executives in the private sector receive considerably higher compensation than their counterparts in the public sector. Mid-level executives regularly earn base salaries of $150,000 to $225,000; the CEO of a billion-dollar corporation can expect a total compensation package in excess of $25 million, and base salaries of $1 million or more are not unusual among senior management of Fortune 100 firms. In 2010, for instance, the average compensation for executives in U.S. corporations was above $9 million.[52] Management superstars, like top athletes in professional sports, are wooed with signing bonuses, interest-free loans, performance incentive packages, and guaranteed contracts. Of course, as in the case of athletes, some controversy surrounds the large dollar amounts paid to these executives (see Ethical Issues in HRM).[53]

Supplemental Financial Compensation

Most of the CEO compensation packages we've discussed so far include their total compensation—base salary plus bonuses and stock options. Bonuses and stock options dramatically increase the total compensation that executives receive. Much of this additional compensation is obtained through a deferred bonus—that is, the executive's bonus is computed on the basis of a formula, usually taking into account increases in sales and profits. This bonus, although earned in the current period, may be distributed over several future periods. Therefore, it is not unusual for an executive to earn a $1 million bonus but have it paid out at $50,000 a year for twenty years. The major purpose of such deferred compensation is to increase the cost to the executive of leaving the organization.

ETHICAL ISSUES IN HRM

Are U.S. Executives Overpaid?

Are organizations paying U.S. executives too much? Is an average salary in excess of $120 million justifiable? In any debate, there are two sides to the issue. Support for paying this amount points to the fact that these executives have tremendous organizational responsibilities. They not only have to manage the organization in today's challenging environment, they must keep it moving into the future. Their jobs are not 9-to-5, but often ten to fourteen hours a day, six to seven days a week. If jobs are evaluated on the basis of skills, knowledge, abilities, and responsibilities, executives should be highly paid.[54]

Furthermore, there is the issue of motivation and retention.[55] If you want these individuals to succeed and stay with the company, you must provide a compensation package that motivates them to do so. Incentives based on various measures also provide the impetus for them to excel.[56] Finally, executive salary is a function of supply and demand. Boards are willing to pay lucrative compensation packages to CEOs who possess such scarce skills and talent that enable them to provide returns to stockholders.[57]

On the other hand, most of the research done on executive salaries questions the linkage of compensation to performance.[58] Even when profits are down, many executives are paid handsomely. In fact, American company executives are some of the highest-paid in the world. Additionally, when performance problems lead to dismissal, some executives are paid phenomenal severance packages. For example, in the year prior to the collapse of their organizations, the CEOs of Lehman Bros., Merrill Lynch, and Bear Stearns all made over $40 million. These CEOs were in charge of the most troubled financial firms in the country and still took home huge salaries plus golden parachutes that provided a financial cushion to take the sting out of unemployment.[59]

U.S. executives make two to five times the salaries of their foreign counterparts—even though some executives in Japanese-based organizations perform better. In 2010, the average CEO earned a 12 percent increase in total pay while the average worker's increase was 3 percent,[60] and U.S. CEOs made 400 times as much as the average employee.

In 2011, Occupy Wall Street started in Liberty Square in Manhattan's Financial District as a citizen's protest over the lopsided power balance between major banks, multinational corporations, and the richest 1 percent of people, including overpaid CEOs. The movement spread across the U.S. and to other countries as people started to identify with the "other 99 percent."

Ethical Questions

Do you believe that U.S. executives are overpaid? What's your opinion? Would performance suffer if compensation of U.S. executives is brought more in line with salaries paid to foreign counterparts?

In almost all cases, executives who voluntarily terminate their employment must forfeit their deferred bonuses. One of the main reasons why there are so few voluntary resignations among the ranks of senior management is that these executives would lose hundreds of thousands of dollars in deferred income.

Interestingly, another form of bonus, the hiring bonus, has arisen in the past decade, purposely designed to help senior executives defray the loss of deferred income. It is now becoming increasingly popular to pay senior executives a hiring bonus to sweeten the incentive for them to leave their current employer and forfeit their deferred bonuses and pension rights. These bonuses often do provide deferred income to compensate for loss of pension rights.

Stock options also have been a common incentive offered to executives. They generally allow executives to purchase, at some time in the future, a specific amount of the company's stock at a fixed price. Under the assumption that good management will increase the company's profitability and therefore the price of the stock, stock options are viewed as performance-based incentives. It should be pointed out, however, that the use of stock options is heavily influenced by the current status of the tax laws. In recent years, tax reform legislation has taken away some of the tax benefits that could accrue through the issuance of stock options. The success, however, of these changes to curb CEO compensation is limited at best. Deferred pay and supplemental retirement plans appear to be vehicles that skirt around the legalities of tax regulations.[61]

How much is an executive worth? At Oracle, it's a lot. In 2011, founder and CEO, Larry Ellison, received more than $71 million in total compensation including bonuses and stock options. *(Source: Reuters/Jean-Paul Pellisier/Landov)*

Supplemental Nonfinancial Compensation: Perquisites

Executives are frequently offered a variety of perquisites not offered to other employees. The logic of offering these **perquisites**, or perks, from the organization's perspective, is to attract and keep good managers and motivate them to work hard in the organization's interest. In addition to the standard benefits offered to all employees (see Chapter 12), some benefits are reserved for privileged executives. Popular perks include the payment of life insurance premiums, club memberships, company automobiles, liberal expense accounts, supplemental disability insurance, supplemental retirement accounts, postretirement consulting contracts, and personal financial, tax, and legal counseling. Some also may be given mortgage assistance.

A benefit for top executives is the **golden parachute**. The golden parachute was originally designed by top executives as a means of protecting themselves if a merger or hostile takeover occurred. These parachutes typically provide either a severance salary to the departing executive or a guaranteed position in the newly created (merged) operation. The idea was to provide an incentive for the executive to stay with the company and fight the hostile takeover—rather than leave the organization. In recent years, they have become a common part of executive contracts, providing several years' salary and allowing sales of stock options earlier than normally allowed in the event the executive leaves his position for any reason, including being fired for poor performance. This expense has drawn sharp criticism as displaced executives at Motorola, IBM, Hewlett-Packard, and Yahoo have received severance packages from $10 million to as high as $67 million.[62,63]

perquisites
Attractive benefits, over and above a regular salary, granted to executives, also known as "perks."

golden parachute
A financial protection plan for executives in case they are severed from the organization.

International Compensation

Probably one of the most complex functions of international HRM is the design and implementation of an equitable international compensation program.[64] The first step in designing an international compensation package is to determine if one policy will apply to all employees or if *parent-country nationals* (PCNs), *host-country nationals* (HCNs), and *third-country nationals* (TCNs) will be treated differently. Currently, American PCNs and HCNs are commonly treated separately, often also differentiating among types of expatriate assignments (temporary or permanent transfer) or employee status (executive, professional, or technical). It is also necessary to thoroughly understand the statutory requirements of each country to ensure compliance with local laws. International compensation packages in the United States generally use the balance-sheet approach, which considers four factors: base pay, differentials, incentives, and assistance programs.

Base Pay

Ideally, this equals the pay of employees in comparable jobs at home, but the range of pay scales in most countries is far narrower than in the United States. Thus, whereas a middle manager in a U.S. factory might earn $75,000 a year, the same manager in Germany might earn the equivalent of $110,000. However, the U.S. higher-level executive might earn $500,000 and her counterpart in Germany only the equivalent of $150,000. How can human resource managers satisfy the middle manager who earns a third less than the counterpart where he works, while also satisfying the German executive who earns less than her U.S. counterpart?

In addition to fairness among overseas employees, foreign currencies and laws must be considered. Should expatriates be paid in U.S. dollars or the local currency—or a combination of the two? How does the organization deal with changes in currency values? Do restrictions apply to either bringing in or taking out dollars or the local currency? If so, how are savings handled? Should salary increases follow the same standards as those established for domestic employees or local standards? Does the expatriate pay U.S. or foreign income taxes?

Taxation is a major factor in calculating equitable base pay rates. Where substantial differences exist in tax rates—for instance in Sweden, where income taxes are about 50 percent of salary—will the base pay be adjusted for the actual loss of net income? The U.S. State Department has negotiated agreements with every country to determine where income will be taxed, but the protection of income from foreign tax rates creates new administrative requirements for the organization. Almost all multinational corporations have some tax protection plan so that the expatriate pays no more taxes than if she were in her home country.

Differentials

The cost of living fluctuates around the world, and the value of the dollar to foreign currencies affects prices. For example, if a gallon of regular unleaded gasoline (in USD) in the United States were $3.55; in England it might be equivalent to $8.04; and in Hong Kong, $7.76. Differentials offset the higher costs of overseas goods, services, and housing. The State Department, which has employees in almost every country in the world, publishes a regularly updated comparison of global costs of living used by most multinational corporations for providing differentials to maintain the standards of living the expatriate would enjoy if he or she were home.[65]

If you've just been sent to Bonn, Germany, by your company, your compensation will need adjustment. In the United States, you've been paying around $4 a gallon for gas, but in Germany, it's about 1.49 euros per liter, or about $7.75 a gallon in U.S. dollars. That difference can change a personal budget quickly.
(Source: Adam Berry/Getty Images,Inc.)

Occasionally overseas assignments may be in a country with difficult living conditions such as an emerging market with an isolated location, political instability, high crime rate, limited access to good housing, schools, and healthcare. In this case, the expatriate employee may be offered a "hardship differential" as compensation for the added inconvenience and expense of living in difficult conditions. Examples of countries that are considered "hardship" destinations include Nigeria, India, and China.[66] Hardship differentials may be on the decline as conditions in developing countries improve worldwide, and 80 percent of young graduates indicate a preference for an expatriate position, sensing great career opportunities.[67]

CONTEMPORARY CONNECTION

Compensation in a Global Environment

Although similarities do exist, there are major differences between compensation practices in developed countries. Below is a comparison of minimum wage rates for the United States and several other countries

Country	Minimum Wage Rate Country as Annual Salary
Germany	No minimum wage
Sweden	No minimum wage
Singapore	No minimum wage
Vietnam	$1,255
Russia	$1,980
El Salvador	$2,187 but varies by industry
Japan	$11,254 but varies by state
United States	$15,080
France	$17,701
Australia	$29,640
United Kingdom	$22,597

Source: International Monetary Fund, "World Economic Outlook Database," at www.imf.org.

Incentives

Not all employees are willing to leave family, friends, and the comfort of home support systems for long periods of time. Thus, mobility inducements to go on foreign assignments are regularly offered. These may include monetary payments or services, such as housing, a car, chauffeur, and other incentives. But companies must decide how a hardship premium should be paid. As a percent of salary? In a lump-sum payment? In home or foreign currency? If foreign housing is provided, what happens to the vacant home back in the United States or to the family housing situation when they eventually return? Incentives require careful planning before, during, and after the overseas assignment.[68]

Assistance Programs

As with any relocation, the overseas transfer requires many expenditures for the employee's family. Some assistance programs commonly offered by multinational corporations include household goods shipping and storage; purchase of major appliances; legal clearance for pets and their shipment; home sale/rental protection; automobile protection; temporary living expenses; travel, including prerelocation visits and annual home leaves; special/emergency return leaves; education allowances for children; club memberships (for corporate entertaining); and security (including electronic systems and bodyguards), if necessary.

Clearly, the design of a compensation system for employees serving overseas is complex and requires enormous administrative expertise, particularly when an organization has expatriates posted in many different countries.

Summary

(This summary relates to the Learning Outcomes identified on page 274.) After having read this chapter, you can:

1. **Explain the various classifications of rewards.** Rewards can be classified as (1) intrinsic or extrinsic, (2) financial or nonfinancial, or (3) performance-based or membership-based.

2. **Discuss why some rewards are considered membership-based.** Some rewards are membership-based because one receives them for belonging to the organization. Employee benefits are an example of membership-based rewards, in that every employee receives them regardless of performance levels.

3. **Define the goal of compensation administration.** Compensation administration seeks to design a cost-effective pay structure that will not only attract, motivate, and retain competent employees, but also seem fair to them.

4. **Discuss job evaluation and its three basic approaches.** A job evaluation systematically determines the value of each job in relation to all jobs within the organization. The three basic approaches to job evaluation are (1) the ordering method, (2) the classification method, and (3) the point method.

5. **Explain the evolution of the final wage structure.** The final wage structure evolves from job evaluation input, compensation survey data, and the creation of wage grades.

6. **Describe competency-based compensation programs.** Competency-based compensation views employees as a competitive advantage in the organization. Compensation systems are established in terms of employee knowledge, skills, and demonstrated behaviors. Possession of these three factors is evaluated and compensated according to a broad-banded salary range established by the organization.

7. **Discuss why executives receive significantly higher salaries than other employees in an organization.** Executive compensation is higher than that of rank-and-file personnel and also includes other financial and nonfinancial benefits not otherwise available to operative employees. This is done to attract and retain executives and motivate them to higher performance levels.

8. **Identify the balance-sheet approach to international compensation.** The balance-sheet approach to international compensation takes into account base pay, differentials, incentives, and assistance programs.

Demonstrating Comprehension

QUESTIONS FOR REVIEW

1. Contrast intrinsic and extrinsic rewards.
2. How do financial and nonfinancial rewards differ?
3. What is a membership-based reward? How does it differ from a performance-based reward?
4. What is compensation administration? What does it entail?
5. How do governmental influences affect compensation administration?
6. What is job evaluation? Discuss the three basic methods of job evaluation.
7. What are the advantages and disadvantages of (a) individual incentives, (b) group incentives, and (c) organization-wide incentives?
8. What is broad-banding and how does it work?

Key Terms

broad-banding	golden parachute	organization-wide incentive
classification method	group incentive	pay-for-performance programs
compensation administration	IMPROSHARE	performance-based rewards
compensation surveys	individual incentive plans	perquisites
competency-based compensation	intrinsic rewards	point method
Equal Pay Act of 1963	job enrichment	Scanlon Plan
exempt employee	merit pay	team-based compensation
extrinsic rewards	nonexempt employee	wage structure
Fair Labor Standards Act (FLSA)	ordering method	

HRM Workshop

Linking Concepts to Practice   DISCUSSION QUESTIONS

1. Would you rather work for an organization where everyone knows what others are earning or an organization where this information is kept secret? Why?
2. "Subjectivity can be successfully removed from the compensation administration process." Build an argument for and against this statement.
3. Team compensation allows some individuals to work harder than others, yet receive the same pay. Do you agree or disagree? Defend your position.

4. "U.S. executives earn every dollar of their pay. People who complain about these people earning millions are just envious that they are not being paid at that level." Build an argument for and against this statement.

Making A Difference   SERVICE LEARNING PROJECTS

Many of the rewards of community service and volunteering are intrinsic. Let's hand out a few extrinsic rewards too.

- Create a "Volunteer Appreciation Event" for a local organization, your college or the United Way.
- Assist your college in developing student activities for the Martin Luther King Day of Service. If your college doesn't participate in the Martin Luther King Day of Service, contact student government or the student activities office to develop an activity.

As you put your service learning experience together, keep a journal of your activities, the time you spend, contact information for people you work with, and your thoughts about the process. When you're finished, make a presentation to your class about the experience and what you learned. What concepts from Chapter 11 were you able to apply?

Developing Diagnostic and Analytical Skills

Case Application 11: WHAT IS FAIR AT EXACTITUDE MANUFACTURING?

Shannon McLaughlin has been the HR Vice President at Exactitude Manufacturing, a firm that manufactures engine parts for aircraft engines and power generation equipment in four factories in Kansas, Missouri, Texas, and New York, for three years. Much of that time has been spent developing a new system that aligns HR strategy with Exactitude's organizational emphasis on high quality manufacturing. New demands for higher productivity and product quality call for increased training and integration of more complex technology in the manufacturing process. The new system realigns wages for production employees, assemblers, inspectors, trainers, and machinists into five tiers in place of the previous system that had six pay grades.

Tier	Positions	Salary
1	Production 1 Assembler 1	Base wage
2	Inspector 1	Base wage +.25/hour
3	Assembler 2	Base wage +.50/hour
4	Inspector 2 Production 2 Trainer	Base Wage +.75/hour
5	Machinists	Skilled trade wage

The new tier system is based on skills, training, and responsibility.

- **Tier 1** Production and Assembler 1 workers receive a base wage. These positions are entry level and require little training. Minimal skill levels are necessary.
- **Tier 2** Inspector 1 workers receive $.25 per hour over base pay. They inspect work done by Production 1 and Assembler 1 for accuracy and quality of work. The Inspector position requires continuous training to meet quality standards.
- **Tier 3** Assembler 2 workers receive $.50 over base pay. They are responsible for running essential equipment. The position requires ongoing training and continuous improvement.
- **Tier 4** This tier includes Inspector 2, Production 2 and Trainers who receive $.75 over base pay. These positions require skill in running precision equipment, training new employees, and/or performing inspections in high volume/critical areas that have little or no tolerance for error. These positions require extensive training and a high skill level.
- **Tier 5** This tier is limited to Machinists who are placed in a skilled trade category that reflects their higher skill level, additional education, and training. New machinists start at a base wage set

for skilled trade with adjustments for geographic differences in pay and competition for qualified workers. Wage increases are received at 6 months, 1 year, and 2 years on the job.

The new system emphasizes employee development and training to increase skills and ability. A "job bid" system was established to allow employees to bid on existing open jobs or new jobs created due to increased production throughout the facility. Employees who have completed training and are qualified to perform the work listed in the job description are allowed to bid on a job in a higher tier up to three times a year if positions are available. Jobs are awarded to qualified employees based on training, education, and skill level. Geographical differences were only taken into account for hourly employees when determining yearly cost-of-living raises.

The new program was implemented six months ago. Employees initially greeted the idea with skepticism and concern, but with little real opposition. In the last three months, however, an increasing number of production workers have shown strong opposition ranging from resentment to anger to work slow-downs. Shannon expected some resistance, but the increased opposition was worrisome. She gathered the HR staff from all four locations to assess the implementation of the new compensation system. She greeted the HR staff by saying, "We knew that the new compensation system would need to be adjusted as it was implemented, and we will take a close look at the concerns you've gathered from our employees." Shannon went on to say, "We've been careful to design a compensation system that supports our strategy. The foundation of the system is good and I'm confident that we can address the implementation problems with minor adjustments and better communication."

As the meeting progressed, the HR staff and presented a list of employee and management concerns:

- Production workers with less seniority and experience are unhappy with the new pay grades. They feel that it takes longer to move to a higher tier position due to the increased training requirements.

- More senior employees feel that the system doesn't respect their longevity, loyalty, and experience. They are frustrated that younger employees qualify for higher tier positions because of their training in newer technology. They feel that seniority should be a stronger factor in considering promotions.

- Starting salaries for machinists at comparable positions in different Exactitude locations vary widely due to adjustments for external factors such as the local labor market and cost of living. For example, a plant near St. Louis competes for qualified machinists with a much larger industrial manufacturer located within a few miles, driving starting hourly wages up to $24 per hour. At a similar facility in rural Kansas, machinists start at $18 per hour. Production employees who start at the lower wages resent the differences.

- Employee development and training activities necessary to bid for higher tier positions will begin in three months. Senior production workers eager for a show of status and increased income are concerned that the delay in rolling out the training is another show of disrespect for their commitment and value to the organization.

Questions:

1. What external factors would be relevant for Exactitude to consider when establishing wages in the different manufacturing locations? What resources are available to determine the necessary adjustments?
2. How does Exactitude utilize intrinsic and extrinsic rewards to improve employee satisfaction and performance?
3. How will the new compensation plan help align compensation with Exactitude's strategic emphasis on quality and productivity?
4. What would you suggest that HR do to address the employee concerns?
5. Which Job Evaluation Method seems to best describe the job tier system at Exactitude?

Working with a Team UNDERSTANDING INCENTIVE PLANS

As a team, schedule a fifteen-minute interview with a compensation specialist in the human resources department of your employer, college, university, hospital, or other organization to ask the following questions. Summarize your results in a one to two page report for your team to present to your class in a five-minute presentation. You may also want to develop a comparison chart based on your team's results.

1. Could you share a brief job description of a compensation specialist?

2. Do you participate in wage surveys? Can you provide results of a recent survey or samples of types of questions asked?
3. What factors do you consider in developing compensation surveys?
4. What types of plans, if any, does your organization use to provide incentive to employees? How is each plan implemented, and how successful has it been?

Learning an HRM Skill PAY-FOR-PERFORMANCE GOAL SETTING

About the skill: Employees should have a clear understanding of what they're attempting to accomplish. Furthermore, as a supervisor, you must see that this task is achieved by helping your employees set work goals. This appears to be common sense, but it doesn't always happen. Setting pay-for-performance objectives is a skill

that every manager needs to perfect. You can better facilitate this process by following these guidelines:

1. ***Identify an employee's key job tasks.*** Goal setting begins by defining what you want your employees to accomplish. The best source for this information is each employee's job description.

2. ***Establish specific and challenging goals for each key task.*** Identify the level of performance expected of each employee. Specify a target for employees to hit. Specify deadlines for each goal to reduce ambiguity, but do not set them arbitrarily. Make them realistic given the tasks to be completed.

3. ***Allow employees to actively participate.*** Employees who participate in goal setting are more likely to accept the goals. However, it must be sincere participation. That is, employees must perceive that you truly seek their input and are not just going through the motions.

4. ***Set priorities.*** When you give someone more than one goal, be sure to rank the goals in order of importance. Setting priorities encourages employees to take action and expend effort on each goal in proportion to its importance. Rate goals for difficulty and importance, not to encourage people to choose easy goals, but so that individuals can receive credit for trying difficult goals, even if they don't fully achieve them.

5. ***Build in feedback mechanisms to assess goal progress.*** Feedback lets employees know whether their level of effort is sufficient to attain the goal. Feedback should be both self- and supervisor-generated. In either case, feedback should be frequent and recurring.

6. ***Link rewards to goal attainment.*** It's natural for employees to ask, "What's in it for me?" Linking rewards to achieving goals will help answer that question.

Enhancing Your Communication Skills

1. Develop a pay-for-performance system for professors at your college or university. Explain how you would evaluate and reward performance.

2. Develop a two- to three-page paper on the advantages and disadvantages of competency-based compensation programs. Use specific examples where appropriate.

3. Research current figures on executive compensation. Present the major arguments for the necessity of their high salaries and the major arguments that salaries are too high with a minimum of six presentation slides, ending with your conclusion supporting one side of the argument or the other.

4. Working on a team project in class is somewhat similar to working on a team in an organization. Assume your professor gave you the opportunity to develop a "team" reward (grading) procedure for your class project. Indicate what that grading procedure would look like and how you would implement it to maximize the benefits to (a) your learning and (b) your reward.

(Source: Photo courtesy AnnMarie Morse, www.michelleslaw.com)

LEARNING OUTCOMES

After reading this chapter, you will be able to

1. Discuss why employers offer benefits to their employees.

2. Contrast Social Security, unemployment compensation, and workers' compensation benefits.

3. Identify and describe the major types of health insurance options.

4. Discuss the important implications of the Employee Retirement Income Security Act.

5. Outline and describe major types of retirement programs organizations offer.

6. Explain the reason companies offer vacation benefits to their employees.

7. Describe the purpose of disability insurance programs.

8. List the various types of flexible benefit option programs.

Employee Benefits

12

Michelle Morse was junior at Plymouth State College in New Hampshire when she was diagnosed with colon cancer. Knowing that cancer treatments would make it difficult for her to take a full load of classes, her doctors recommended that she take a medical leave of absence from college until she was well enough to return. Michelle and her family were shocked to learn that she could only be covered under her family's health plan if she was a full-time student. Her mother could continue her coverage, but she would have to pay an additional $550 each month, bringing the family's monthly premium to $1,100.[1]

Knowing that the family could not afford the additional expense, Michelle and her family met with university administration to develop a plan to enable Michelle to maintain her full-time student status while undergoing cancer treatment. Throughout her treatment, Michelle and her mother lobbied the New Hampshire legislature to pass a bill requiring health insurance companies to continue coverage for college students who were required to take leaves of absence due to medical reasons.

Michelle graduated from college, but lost her battle with cancer at age twenty-two in November of 2005. The New Hampshire legislature passed a law in June of 2006 that allows college students to take up to twelve months of medical leave without losing health insurance coverage.[2]

In 2008, President Bush signed Michelle's Law, named in her honor, requiring health plans to continue coverage for up to a year for dependent children at post secondary educational institutions who must take leave for medical reasons. In 2010, the Patient Protection and Affordable Care Act was signed into law by President Obama, requiring private insurers that offer dependent coverage to allow young adults up to age 26 to remain on their parent's insurance plan without any additional requirements such as full-time student status. A few states extend coverage past that age.

Since the Affordable Care Act went into effect, the share of 18–25 year olds without insurance coverage has dropped from 28 percent to under 25 percent.[3] Even though there have been significant gains, young adults remain less likely to be insured than any other age group.[4] Many are in low wage jobs that do not offer coverage, or they pass on coverage in order to get a little extra pay. Although many in this age group claim they are young, healthy, and do not need insurance, one in six will develop a chronic illness during this time and may have trouble paying medical bills. In fact, the most common reasons students take leave from college are mental disorders; major illnesses such as cancer, diabetes, or asthma; drug and alcohol-related problems; or a serious traumatic injury.

Michelle's Law clearly got the ball rolling to protect young adults who need insurance coverage. Although the changes came too late for Michelle and her family, the law means that many will not have to make such difficult choices. Michelle's mother, AnnMarie Morse, explains, "Some people have asked me if it would have made a difference if Michelle got to take a leave of absence, and my response is 'we will never know.' I know Michelle never wanted anyone to have to face the same choice she did, which was to remain in school full-time to keep the insurance or leave school to treat a serious illness or injury and lose your insurance when you need it the most."[5]

Looking Ahead

Even before "Michelle's Law" and the Affordable Care Act, some employers provided extended insurance for family members. What motivated these employers to provide the added benefits?

Introduction

employee benefits
Membership-based, nonfinancial
rewards offered to attract and keep
employees.

When an organization designs its overall compensation program, a critical area of concern is what benefits to provide. Today's workers expect more than just an hourly wage or a salary; they want additional considerations that will enrich their lives. These considerations in an employment setting are called **employee benefits**.

Employee benefits have grown in importance and variety over the past several decades. Employers realize that benefits attract qualified applicants, affect whether applicants accept their employment offers or, once employed, determine if they stay with the organization. Benefits, therefore, are necessary components of an effectively functioning compensation program. Nearly two-thirds of workers indicate that their benefits are an important reason as to why they stay with their current employer and are satisfied with their jobs.[6] Benefits offer important financial advantages and security that would be difficult or prohibitively expensive for employees to acquire on their own. For example, it's possible for employees to purchase medical or life insurance on their own, but the group plans offered through an employer provide substantial price advantages. Employer-provided group plans can also offer waivers of medical examinations for insurance; guarantee issuance of policies, regardless of preexisting medical conditions; and portability of the policy if the employee leaves the employer.

The irony, however, is that although benefits must be offered to attract and retain good workers, benefits as a whole do not directly affect a worker's performance.[7] Benefits are generally membership-based, offered to employees regardless of their performance levels. This does not seem to be a logical business practice, but evidence indicates that inadequate benefits and services for employees may contribute to employee dissatisfaction and increased absenteeism and turnover.[8] Accordingly, the tremendously negative effect of failing to provide adequate benefits prompts organizations to spend tens of billions of dollars annually to ensure valuable benefits for each worker.

Federal legislation, labor unions, and the changing workforce have all led to growth in benefit offerings. Today's organizational benefits are more widespread, creative, and clearly more abundant. As indicated in Exhibit 12-1, employee benefits are designed to ensure value for each worker.

Costs of Providing Employee Benefits

Because the cost of employing workers includes both direct compensation and corresponding benefits and services, the growth in both benefits and services has resulted in dramatic increases in labor costs to organizations. How large are those costs? The Employee Benefit Research Institute estimates that U.S. employers spend over $1.4 *trillion* dollars each year on employee benefits. The Bureau of Labor statistics reports that in 2011, benefit costs for employers averaged $9.21 per hour worked and accounted for over 30 percent of total compensation, as illustrated in Exhibit 12-2.[9] This creates a challenge for employers as they attempt to control costs.

Employers have also found that benefits present attractive areas of negotiation when large wage and salary increases are infeasible. For example, if employees were to purchase life insurance on their own, they would have to pay for it with net dollars—that is, with what they have left after paying taxes. If the organization pays for it, the benefit is nontaxable (premiums paid on insurance up to $50,000) for each employee.[10]

Contemporary Benefits Offerings The number and types of benefits offered have increased dramatically, as have their costs. What has triggered the sweeping changes in benefits offerings that will carry us into the future? The answer to that question lies in part in the demographic composition of the workforce. Benefits offered to employees reflect many trends in our labor force. Dual-career couples, singles, singles with children, and individuals caring for their parents (elder care) must be considered. Equally important is the topic of benefit coverage for a worker's significant other: *domestic partner benefits*. Domestic partner benefits typically include medical, dental, or vision coverage for an

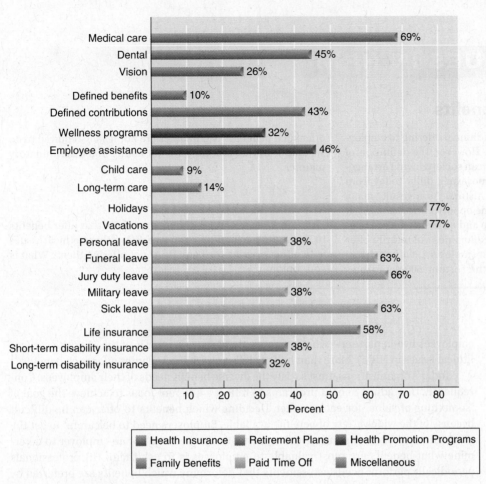

Exhibit 12-1
Private Employer Benefits
(Percent of Employees With
Access)

Employers offer a wide variety of
employee benefits, but as you
can see here, the package of
benefits they offer varies widely.

Source: U.S. Department of Labor, U.S. Bureau of Labor Statistics, "National Compensation Survey:
Employee Benefits in Private Industry in the United States," March 2011.

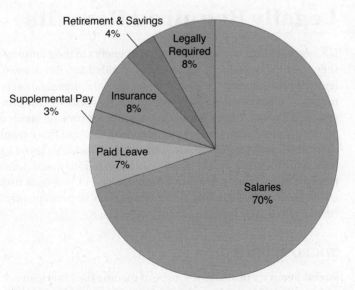

Exhibit 12-2
Total Compensation:
Where Does the Money Go?

Salaries paid to employees are
only about 70 percent of
compensation costs. The other
30 percent is the cost of required
and voluntary benefits.

Source: U.S. Department of Labor, U.S. Bureau of Labor Statistics,
"National Compensation Survey: Employee Benefits in Private Industry
in the United States," March 2011.

ETHICAL ISSUES IN HRM

Domestic Partner Benefits

Health insurance benefits are a traditional offering to employees and their immediate families. However, the definition of family has been changing in American society. Living arrangements, either heterosexual or homosexual, differ today from those in any other time in our history. As a result, many employees are demanding the same opportunities as married counterparts for medical coverage and other benefits for significant others. Although many companies voluntarily offer **domestic partner benefits** to their employees, it is just that— voluntary. Currently, over half of the Fortune 500 companies

offer such benefits.[12] Companies are not legally required to do so, and if they do not, they are not acting in a discriminatory manner.

Ethical questions:

What are the advantages for organizations that offer benefits to domestic partners of employees? Are there ethical issues with either offering the benefits or not offering them? What is your opinion?

---

domestic partner benefits
Benefits offered to an employee's live-in partner.

employee's live-in partner—whether or not that live-in partner is of the opposite sex (see Ethical Issues in HRM). More than half of all Fortune 500 companies offer such benefits.[11]

Today's organizations must satisfy the diverse benefit needs of their employees. Consequently, they adjust benefit programs to reflect a different focus to achieve the goal of "something of value" for each worker. Deciding which benefits to offer can be difficult because of the wide variety of benefits available. Employers need to be careful to get the most value out of every penny spent on benefits. The best way for an employer to determine what benefits are most valuable to employees is to ask them. HR professionals periodically perform needs assessments that determine which benefits are preferred by their employees. Employees appreciate the opportunity to have input into their benefit package.

Putting together a benefits package involves two issues: (1) what benefits must be offered by law and (2) what benefits and services will make the organization attractive to applicants and current workers. First, we'll explore legally required benefits.

Legally Required Benefits

legally required benefits
Employee benefits mandated by law.

U.S. organizations must provide certain benefits to their employees regardless of whether they want to or not, and they must be provided in a nondiscriminatory manner. With a few exceptions, hiring any employee requires the organization to pay Social Security premiums,[13] unemployment compensation, and workers' compensation. Additionally, any organization with fifty or more employees must provide family and medical leave. Companies either pay premiums associated with many of these **legally required benefits** or share costs with employees (as in the case of Social Security) to provide each employee with some basic level of financial protection at retirement, termination, or as a result of injury. These benefits provide a broad range of personal financial security when an employee is unable to work, either temporarily or permanently. It's important to understand each of these four important programs.

Social Security

Social Security
Retirement, disability, and survivor benefits paid by the government to the aged, former members of the labor force, the disabled, or their survivors.

Social Security provides a source of income for American retirees, disabled workers, and surviving dependents of workers who have died. Social Security also provides some health insurance coverage through the federal Medicare program. In 2010, Social Security paid out $740 billion to more than 57 million eligible workers in the United States.[14]

Social Security insurance is financed by employee contributions matched by the employer, and computed as a percentage of the employee's earnings. In 2011, for instance, the rate was 10.4 percent (4.2 percent for employees and 6.2 percent levied on the employer) of the worker's earnings up to $106,800. Additionally, 2.9 percent is assessed for Medicare on all earned income. Similar to Social Security, employer and employee split this assessment, paying 1.45 percent each in payroll taxes. There are no maximum earnings for the Medicare portion of Social Security.

Workers must earn forty credits to be eligible for Social Security retirement benefits. Workers can earn credits for each $1,130 they earn, with a maximum of four credits earned in a year.[15] Prior to 1983, employees became eligible for full benefits at age sixty-five. With revisions to Social Security laws, those born in 1960 and later must wait until age sixty-seven before receiving full retirement benefits.[16]

Keep in mind, however, that Social Security is not intended to be employees' sole source of retirement income. Social Security benefits vary, based on the previous year's inflation, additional earnings, and recipient age. For 2012, the maximum monthly Social Security retirement check for a worker retiring at age sixty-six was $2,513. Given longer life expectancies and a desire to maintain their current standards of living, workers today are expected to supplement Social Security with their own retirement plans. This is true whether or not Social Security will still be around in the year 2041.

Unemployment Compensation

Unemployment compensation laws provide benefits to employees who meet the following conditions: they are without a job, have worked a minimum number of weeks, have applied to their state employment agency for unemployment compensation, have registered for available work, and are willing and able to accept any suitable employment offered them through their state unemployment compensation commission. Unemployment compensation is designed to provide an income to individuals who have lost a job through no fault of their own (for example, layoffs or plant closing). Being fired from a job, however, may result in a loss of unemployment compensation rights.

Funds for paying unemployment compensation come from combined federal and state taxes imposed on the taxable wage base of the employer. At the federal level, the unemployment tax (called FUTA) is 6.0 percent on the first $7,000 of earnings of employees. States that meet federal guidelines are given a 5.4 percent credit, thus reducing the federal unemployment tax to 0.08 percent, or $42 per employee.[20]

State unemployment compensation tax is often a function of a company's unemployment experience; that is, the more an organization lays off employees, the higher its rate. Rates for employers range, for example, from 0.03 to 10.3 percent of state-established wage bases.[21] Eligible unemployed workers receive an amount that varies from state to state but is determined by the worker's previous wage rate and the length of previous employment. Compensation is provided for only a limited period—typically, the base is twenty-six weeks but may be extended by the state another twenty-six weeks during times when unemployment runs high.[22] Long periods of high unemployment can deplete state jobless funds to the point that they run out of money, as several states have experienced recently. In that case, the states may borrow from the federal government's unemployment trust fund.

How does this couple manage their retirement? Years ago, some believed that Social Security was the answer. But with life expectancy increasing and the looming insolvency of the Social Security trust fund, that's not the case anymore. In fact, Social Security was never meant to be a sole source of retirement funds. Rather, it was supposed to provide additional income for retirees, disabled workers, and surviving dependents of workers who have died. *(Source: Christopher Bissell/ Stone/Getty Images, Inc.)*

unemployment compensation Employee insurance that provides some income continuation in the event an employee is laid off.

CONTEMPORARY CONNECTION

Look Out for the Silver Tsunami

The U.S. is bracing for the Silver Tsunami, but this tidal wave won't wreak havoc on our coastlines. This tsunami is heading directly for our Social Security system, and if precautions are not taken soon, it could possibly wipe it out by 2041.[17]

The first ripple of the Silver Tsunami arrived in February of 2008 when a retired seventh-grade teacher named Kathleen Casey-Kirschling received her first Social Security check. Casey-Kirschling was born one second after midnight on January 1, 1946, and became the nation's first "baby boomer," the nickname given to the large part of the U.S. population born in the years following World War II.

It is estimated that for the next twenty years, 10,000 Americans each day will become eligible for Social Security.[18] The Social Security Administration estimates that trust fund reserves are sufficient to pay full benefits through 2033. After that benefits will need to be paid from tax income and might only pay three-quarters of the scheduled benefits through 2085.[19] Lawmakers have discussed several ways to fix the problem, but the tough measures necessary for any permanent solution haven't received much bipartisan support in Congress.

Casey-Kirschling is confident that Congress will eventually take responsibility to fix the problem. "I do think they will come up a solution," she said. Millions of Americans following her into retirement hope she's right.

(Source: ©Sam Woolfe/AP/Wide World Photos)

Consider this:

How do you think the problem should be fixed? Does HR have a responsibility to help employees plan for retirement? What can HR do to help?

Unemployment compensation and parallel programs for railroad, federal government, and military employees cover more than 75 percent of the workforce. Major groups excluded include self-employed workers, employees of organizations employing fewer than four individuals, household domestics, farm employees, and state and local government employees. As past recessions have demonstrated, unemployment compensation provides stable spending power throughout the nation. In contrast to the early 1930s, when millions of workers lost their jobs and had no compensatory income, unemployment compensation provides a floor that allows individuals to continue looking for work while receiving assistance through the transitory period from one job to the next.

Workers' Compensation

workers' compensation
Employee insurance that provides income continuation if a worker is injured on the job.

Every state currently has some type of **workers' compensation** to compensate employees (or their families) for death or permanent or total disability resulting from job-related endeavors, regardless of fault. Federal employees and others working outside the U.S. border are covered by separate legislation. Workers' compensation exists to protect employees' salaries and to attribute the cost for occupational accidents and rehabilitation to the employing organization. This accountability factor considers workers' compensation costs as part of labor expenses incurred in meeting the organization's objectives.

Workers' compensation benefits are based on fixed schedules of minimum and maximum payments. Comprehensive disability payments are computed by considering the employee's current earnings, future earnings, and financial responsibilities.

The entire cost of workers' compensation is borne by the organization. Its rates are set based on the actual history of company accidents, the type of industry and business

REAL HR ENCOUNTERS

Abusing Worker's Compensation

Occasionally employees find creative ways to use benefits they are not entitled to. HR professionals are often required to "play detective" and investigate Worker's Compensation claims when they don't appear to be legitimate. The following employees didn't do a very good job of covering up their false claims:

- The employee was asked to work overtime on a Saturday. He called the supervisor on Saturday morning and said that he hurt his back on Friday and wasn't able to work. The sympathetic supervisor asked the employee to report to the work site to complete the worker's compensation claim paperwork so the employer could schedule an appointment with a designated physician for necessary medical treatment. Upon arrival at the work site, the employer observed him get out of his pickup truck, lift a wheel chair out of the

back of the truck and wheel himself in to the building. He completed the paperwork for worker's compensation and was asked to remain at work until his medical appointment. He reported that he didn't want to because he had taken an old prescription for the pain, which was a violation of the company drug/alcohol policy. Following the meeting, he wheeled himself out of the building, lifted the wheelchair into the pickup truck and drove away.

- Another employee with a back injury reported that the pain increased every Wednesday and Friday, preventing him from completing his job duties. He requested permission to leave work at approximately the same time on those days. The employer's research found that on the days the employee left work early, he reported promptly to his second job as a bartender.

operation, and the likelihood of accidents occurring. The organization, then, protects itself by covering its risks through insurance. Some states provide an insurance system, voluntary or required, for handling workers' compensation. Some organizations may also cover their workers' compensation risks by purchasing insurance from private insurance companies. Finally, some states allow employers to self-insure. Self-insuring—usually limited to large organizations—requires the employer to maintain a fund from which benefits can be paid.

Most workers' compensation laws stipulate that the injured employee will be compensated by either monetary allocation or payment of medical expenses, or a combination of both. Almost all workers' compensation insurance programs, whether publicly or privately controlled, provide incentives for employers to maintain good safety records. Insurance rates are computed based on the organization's accident experience; hence employers are motivated to keep accident rates low.

Family and Medical Leave Act

The last legally required benefit facing organizations with fifty or more employees is the Family and Medical Leave Act of 1993. Recall from our discussion in Chapter 3 that the FMLA was passed to provide employees the opportunity to take up to twelve weeks of unpaid leave each year for family or medical reasons.

Voluntary Benefits

The voluntary benefits offered by an organization are limited only by management's creativity and budget.[23] Exhibit 12-1 (see page 303) illustrates the many different benefits offered—almost all of which carry significant costs to the employer. Exhibit 12-3 illustrates the number of employers offering benefits. Some of the most common and critical ones are health insurance, retirement plans, time off from work, and disability and life insurance benefits. Organizations work hard to put together a package of voluntary benefits that will attract, motivate, and retain the most qualified employees. Exhibit 12-4 illustrates a very competitive package of voluntary benefits similar to packages found at larger telecommunications companies.

Exhibit 12-3
How Many Employers Offer Health Benefits?

The percentage of employers offering health benefits to employees has remained steady in recent years.[26]

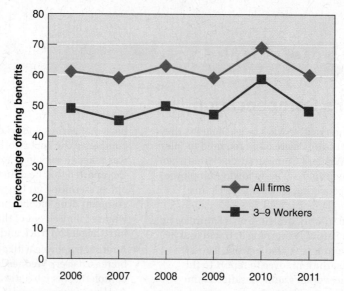

Source: Kaiser/HRET Survey of Employer-Sponsored Health Benefits, 1999–2011. This information was reprinted with permission from the Henry J. Kaiser Family Foundation. The Kaiser Family Foundation is a nonprofit private operating foundation, based in Menlo Park, California, dedicated to producing and communicating the best possible analysis and information on health issues.

Exhibit 12-4
Benefits Overview

This table outlines benefits that are common at large communications companies. Which do you find most attractive?

Benefits	Date Eligible	Minimum Weekly Hours for Eligibility
Health Benefits	After one month of employment with minimum weekly hours	30 hours
• Medical		
• Prescription Medications		
• Dental		
• Vision		
• Orthodonture		
Life Insurance	After one month of employment with minimum weekly hours	30 hours
• Employee		
• Dependent		
• AD&D		
Domestic Partner Benefits	After one month of employment with minimum weekly hours	30 hours
Disability Protection	After 6 months of employment	30 hours
• Short-Term Disability		
• Long-Term Disability		
Optional Benefits	After one month of employment	30 hours
• Pre-paid Legal Services		
• Long-Term Care Insurance		
• Car and Homeowners Insurance		
• Pet Health Insurance		
Financial Planning	Upon employment	None
• 401k Plan		
• Employee Stock Purchase Plan		30 hours

Exhibit 12-4
(Continued)

Benefits	Date Eligible	Minimum Weekly Hours for Eligibility
More Benefits		
• Paid Time Off	Upon employment	30 hours
• Employee Assistance Program		
• Travel Insurance		
• Charitable Contribution Matching		
• Adoption Assistance		
• Relocation Assistance		
• Employee Discounts		
• Employee Wellness Center		
• Personal Training		
• Tuition Reimbursement		

Health Insurance

We all have healthcare needs, and most organizations today offer some health insurance coverage to their employees. This coverage has become one of the most important benefits for employees because of the tremendous increases in the cost of healthcare. Let's look at some facts and figures on the increasing costs of healthcare insurance to employers and employees:[24]

- The average annual premiums for employer-sponsored health insurance are $5,429 for single coverage and $15,073 for family coverage.
- Health insurance premiums increased 140 percent from 2001 to 2011.
- Average employer healthcare costs were $9.21 per hour in 2011, which was 30.9 percent of average total compensation per employee.[25]
- Healthcare costs are growing faster than wages.

These costs are expected to continue to rise. As a result, many organizations have been looking at a variety of cost-cutting measures, including:

- Raising deductibles or percentage of premiums that employees pay.
- Implementing or strengthening "wellness" programs.
- Adding stronger financial incentives for participation in wellness programs, such as lower premiums for employees.
- Availability of prescription drug mail-order with smaller co-pays or mandatory generic prescriptions.
- Adding a smoker surcharge.
- Availability of Employee Assistance Programs.
- Onsite clinics.[27]

Although insurance costs are difficult to contain, employers see it as an important advantage and work hard to provide affordable benefits. In addition to its role in attracting and maintaining a qualified workforce, a major purpose of health insurance is to protect the employee and his or her immediate family from the catastrophes of a major illness and to minimize their out-of-pocket expenses for medical care. Without health insurance, almost any family's finances face depletion if a major illness occurs.

Any type of health insurance offered to employees generally provides coverage that can be extended beyond the employee to include a spouse, domestic partner, and dependents. Healthcare coverage generally focuses on hospital and physician care. It also typically covers major medical expenses such as prescriptions, medical supplies, and equipment necessary for treatment and recovery. Specific coverage will vary based on the organization's chosen healthcare plan. Generally, five types appear more frequently than others: traditional healthcare coverage, health maintenance organizations (HMOs), preferred provider organizations (PPOs), point-of-service (POS), and "consumer-driven health plans" (CDHP), also called "high deductible health plans" (HDHP). All five are designed to provide protection for employees, but each does so in a different way. Let's look at each of these various types of plans.

Traditional Health Insurance Traditional insurance offers coverage for health services provided by any healthcare provider. It usually includes three categories of coverage:

- Hospitalization: pays for hospital stays with limits, usually 120 days
- Medical/Surgical: pays for services of doctors, procedures, nursing care, drugs, and hospital services such as anesthesia, tests, lab work, etc.
- Major Medical: pays for major illnesses and their associated expenses such as oxygen, home care, and extended hospital stays over 120 days

Traditional insurance is available through providers such as Aetna, Blue Cross and Blue Shield, Cigna, and United HealthCare. Traditional insurance has become quite expensive, and now is less than 1 percent of employer provided coverage. Many employers are turning to newer types of healthcare plans to manage rising costs.

health maintenance organization Provide comprehensive health services for a flat fee.

Health Maintenance Organizations **Health Maintenance Organizations (HMOs)** strive to provide quality healthcare at a lower cost for their members. An employee belonging to an HMO chooses a primary care physician who has a contract with the HMO and is considered "in-network." The HMO pays for all services the primary care physician provides and the employee usually pays a small co-pay.

The major disadvantage, however, is that HMOs provide full coverage only if clients receive services from selected providers. Furthermore, being seen outside of the HMO for other services requires either permission from the primary care physician or greater out-of-pocket expense. Accordingly, an HMO arrangement significantly limits freedom of healthcare choice. The limitations have been one of the greatest concerns expressed regarding HMOs. However, for many, the cost savings far outweigh the imposed restrictions.

preferred provider organizations (PPOs) Organization that requires using specific physicians and healthcare facilities to contain the rising costs of healthcare.

Preferred Provider Organizations **Preferred Provider Organizations (PPOs)** have a large network of doctors, hospitals, and other related medical service facilities to provide services at a reduced cost. In return for accepting this lower cost, the employer or the insurer promises to encourage employees to use their services.

A PPO can provide much of the same services that an HMO provides, and an individual need not use a specific facility—such as a designated hospital. So long as a physician or the medical facility is participating in the health network, the services are covered. The employee who uses a participating physician typically incurs a fixed out-of-pocket expense (defined by the agreement). In those cases, the PPO takes the form of traditional health insurance. However, if an employee decides to go elsewhere for services, the service fee is reimbursed according to specific guidelines. PPOs attempt to combine the best of both HMOs and traditional insurance.

point-of-service (POS) Healthcare plan that includes primary care physicians but allows greater flexibility for using services out of the network.

Point-of-Service **Point-of-Service (POS)** plans require that primary care physicians provide most health services and make referrals like HMOs. Those referrals can be out-of-network, but the employee must pay the service provider and seek partial reimbursement. These plans include elements of HMO and PPO plans, but tend to be less expensive for the employer.

consumer driven health plan (CDHP) Combines a health plan with a high deductible with a health savings account that the insured uses to pay for deductibles and medical care.

Consumer Driven Health Plan **Consumer Driven Health Plans (CDHP)** are relatively new and are gaining popularity (see Exhibits 12.5 and 12.6) because they are inexpensive for the employer and offer the greatest flexibility for the employee. They include three parts:

- An employer-provided health plan that has a high deductible, possibly as high as $5,000 per year.
- A health savings account (HSA) with tax advantages to which the employee or the employer contribute.
- Decision support and counseling to assist employees to make informed healthcare services decisions.

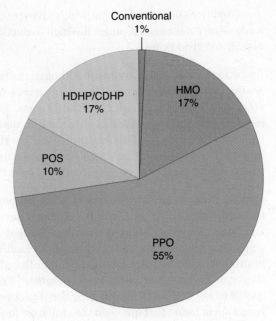

Exhibit 12-5
What Types of Health Plans Do Employers Offer?

The number of employers who offer conventional health plans has declined from 73 percent in 1988 to under 1 percent in 2011. PPO plans have seen the biggest increases, but HDHP/CDHP plans are rapidly gaining in popularity.[28]

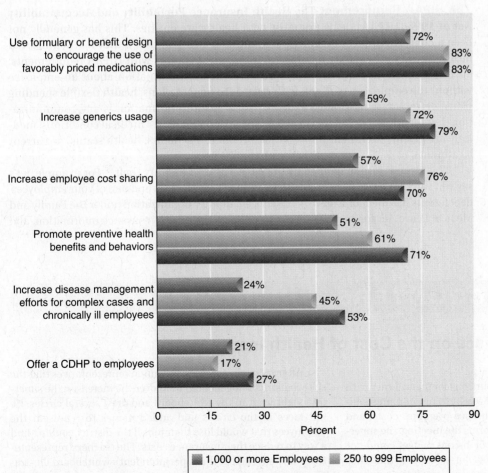

Exhibit 12-6
How Do Employers Reduce the High Cost of Healthcare Coverage?

Employers of all sizes attempt to reduce the high cost of providing health insurance by promoting use of generic medications, healthy lifestyles, and sharing the cost of coverage with employees.[29]

Source: "Top Strategies to Control Healthcare Costs" (Will Plans Abandon $1.4B in Annual CDHP Profits? Forrester Research, Inc., February 2007.)

Employees use money in the health savings account to pay for deductibles and other medical care not covered under the high deductible health plan, such as prescriptions, dental, and vision care.

Employer-Operated Coverage Although the types of insurance programs mentioned are the most popular means of health insurance today, many companies are looking for other options to contain rising healthcare costs. To this end, some companies have begun reviewing the concept of self-insuring and in many of these instances, using the assistance of a third-party administrator (TPA).[30] In this case, the employer typically establishes a trust fund to pay for the health benefits used.[31] For the most part, this employer trust fund has received favorable treatment from the IRS.

Consolidated Omnibus Budget Reconciliation Act (COBRA)
Provides for continued employee benefits up to three years after an employee leaves a job.

Health Insurance Continuation What happens to an employee's health insurance coverage if that employee leaves the organization or is laid off? The answer to that question lies in the **Consolidated Omnibus Budget Reconciliation Act (COBRA)**. When employees resign or are laid off through no fault of their own, they may continue their health insurance benefits for eighteen months, although under certain conditions, the time may be extended to thirty-six months.[32] Employers must notify employees who qualify to use COBRA to extend their benefits coverage within thirty days of the layoff or reduction in hours that qualified the employee for COBRA benefits.[33]

The cost of COBRA is paid solely by the employee. The employer may also charge the employee a small administrative fee for this service. However, COBRA requires employers to offer this benefit through the company's current group health insurance plan, which is at a rate that is typically lower than if the individual had to purchase the insurance himself or herself.[34]

Health Insurance Portability and Accountability Act of 1996 (HIPAA)
Ensures confidentiality of employee health information.

The HIPAA Requirement The **Health Insurance Portability and Accountability Act of 1996 (HIPAA)** deals primarily with healthcare entities. This has generally not been a concern for most organizations, but many learned that if they had self-insured health insurance benefit programs, they, too, must comply with HIPAA requirements. Such organizations cannot release protected health information about an employee without the employee's consent, with regards to benefit plans, health flexible spending plans, or employee assistance plans. Personal health information is any communication that identifies and relates to an employee or dependents' medical conditions, medical care given, enrollment information, premium payments, health status, or current treatments.

This issue is also magnified by the concerns over identity theft.[35] For example, let's say you work for a self-insured health insurance organization and one of your employees' dependents has filed for a leave of absence in another organization under the Family and Medical Leave Act for an illness. Your form holds the health insurance information, and

REAL HR ENCOUNTERS

Whiteboard Puts a Face on the Cost of Health Insurance

Kathy Mabe, HR Professional
As a representative of a health insurance company, I met with school district administrators and teacher's union representatives about increasing health insurance premium costs, and what they could do about them. During the meeting, the superintendent explained that the school district budget could not absorb the increased cost. He went on to explain that they would be forced to reduce coverage or cut jobs if the teachers' union didn't agree to increase the deductable and co-insurance teachers would need to pay in order to keep the same coverage.

After failing to convince the union representatives that the school district budget could not cover the increases, the superintendent went to the whiteboard and drew several circles. He put faces in the circles and added names to represent the employees that would lose their jobs if the district couldn't find a way to reduce their insurance costs. The teachers' representatives were shocked at the superintendent's whiteboard illustration, but it apparently made an impression. In the end, the teachers' union agreed to make changes, and the employees depicted in the whiteboard kept their jobs.

the dependent's organization asks you to verify the medical claim. Without written consent of the employee, you cannot release such information. In doing so, you may incur substantial penalties—upward of $100 per day, per violation, up to a maximum of $25,000 annually. Interestingly, a facility that does drug testing for an organization cannot release drug test results to employers without written consent of the person being tested. As a result of HIPAA, organizations need to ensure that they have the proper consent forms in place and signed by the employees before such information is gathered.

Patient Protection and Affordable Care Act The **Patient Protection and Affordable Care Act** was passed by Congress in 2010, significantly changing the responsibilities of consumers, employers, and insurance companies. The act reforms the healthcare insurance system in the U.S. by expanding the availability and regulation of health insurance coverage and making significant changes to how health insurance coverage is provided and paid for. Some of the changes include:

- **Individual responsibility** for purchasing minimum insurance coverage. Beginning in 2014, individuals who do not purchase coverage must pay a fine.
- **States are required to create Health Insurance Exchanges** where individuals and small employers can purchase insurance.
- **Employer responsibility is expanded**. Although they are not required to provide employee insurance coverage, employers with over fifty full-time employees who do not provide coverage are required to pay a penalty. Penalties also apply to employers who provide plans that are either too expensive for employees to afford, or provide very little coverage. Employers with more than 200 employees are required to enroll all employees, unless an employee wants to opt out. Employers must report the value of employee health insurance benefits on W-2 forms. Wellness and prevention discounts may be offered to employees who participate in wellness programs beginning in 2014. Free Choice vouchers must be offered to employees who want to purchase their own coverage through the Health Insurance Exchanges.
- **Insurance companies are required to expand coverage**. They must eliminate lifetime limits, end restrictions on pre-existing conditions, restrict annual limits, and provide coverage for employee's children up to age twenty-six.

Other provisions include caps to Healthcare Spending Accounts, taxes on expensive insurance plans, creation of long-term care coverage purchased through the workplace, and protections for nursing mothers up to a year after the birth of a child that include breaks to express milk in a private location.

A Supreme Court decision in 2012 left the act largely intact but challenges and changes to the act are expected before all provisions are implemented.[36]

> **Patient Protection and Affordable Care Act**
> Reforms the healthcare insurance system in the U.S. by expanding the availability and regulation of health insurance coverage and making significant changes to how health insurance coverage is provided and paid for.

Retirement Benefits

Retirement plans can be a way to attract qualified employees of all ages. They can increase retention, productivity, and employee satisfaction. The plans currently offered are evolving, however, to reflect the financial realities of an unpredictable economy and the needs and wants of both employers and employees. Most recognize the limitations of the Social Security system and are developing plans that do not rely on Social Security to sustain the lifestyle most people have grown accustomed to in their working years. Social Security payments must be just one component of a properly designed retirement system. The other components are employer retirement plans and savings employees have amassed over the years. Retirement plans are highly regulated by the **Employee Retirement Income Security Act (ERISA)** of 1974. Let's take a brief look at ERISA before we discuss the different retirement programs.

ERISA was passed in response to public outcry over the failure of underfunded pension plans that left retirees with meager benefits and vesting requirements that made it

> **Employee Retirement Income Security Act (ERISA)**
> Law passed in 1974 designed to protect employee retirement benefits.

very difficult for employees to earn the right to pensions they believed were guaranteed. Pension plans almost always require a minimum tenure with the organization before the individual has a guaranteed right to pension benefits, regardless of whether they remain with the company. These permanent benefits—or the guarantee of a pension when one retires or leaves the organization—are called vesting rights. In years past, employees needed extensive tenure in an organization before they were entitled to their retirement benefits—if they were entitled at all. This meant, for instance, that a sixty-year-old employee with twenty-three years of service who left the company—for whatever reason—could possibly have no right to a pension benefit. ERISA was enacted to prevent such abuses.

> Vesting rights guarantee an employee's right to a pension benefit.

vesting rights
The permanent right to pension benefits.

ERISA requires employers who decide to provide a pension or profit-sharing plan to design their retirement program under specific rules. Typically, each plan must convey to employees any information relevant to their retirement. **Vesting rights** in organizations now typically come after six years of service, and pension programs must be available to all employees over age twenty-one.[37] Employees with fewer than six years of service may receive a prorated portion of their retirement benefit. This shorter vesting period, which came into effect with the 1986 Tax Reform Act, is crucial for employees, especially when one considers that the length of service in companies today is becoming shorter. With this shorter vesting period, employees who leave companies after six years generally can carry their retirement rights with them. That is, ERISA makes pension rights portable.[38]

Pension Benefit Guaranty Corporation (PBGC)
The organization that lays claim to corporate assets to pay or fund inadequate pension programs.

Guidelines for the termination of a pension program were also created by ERISA. Should an employer voluntarily terminate a pension program, the **Pension Benefit Guaranty Corporation (PBGC)** must be notified. Similarly, the act permits the PBGC, under certain conditions (such as inadequate pension funding), to lay claim on corporate assets—up to 30 percent of net worth—to pay benefits promised to employees. Additionally, when a pension plan is terminated, the PBGC requires the employer to

ETHICAL ISSUES IN HRM

Airline Pensions Crash and Burn

When United Airlines could no longer fund its pension plans, it turned them over to the Pension Benefit Guaranty Corporation (PBGC), and became the largest pension plan failure in history, owing over $9 billion to the pension.

So far, the PBGC manages the pensions of over 4,200 companies that failed to adequately fund their defined benefit pension plans, including several airlines such as Delta, Eastern, TWA, and US Airways.[41] These airline employees will continue to receive pensions, but under PBGC guidelines, pensions are limited to a maximum of $54,000 a year. In many cases, this is half of the annual benefit airline employees were expecting under the airline's defined benefit pension plan. Many employees will make substantially less, particularly if they retire before they reach age sixty-five.[42]

How did this happen? Deregulation, competitive pressures, and the economy have all led to serious financial problems for the large airline carriers. As the amount of money the companies owed to retirees and potential retirees increased, airline income decreased and the retirement funds

earnings decreased, leaving the pension plan underfunded. After the PBGC takes over the underfunded pension plan, it works out a plan to pay the retirement obligations with pension plan assets, but if they aren't enough, taxpayers make up the difference.

Bad news for the retirees can also mean good news for the company, however. Without the financial burden of the retirement fund liabilities, the company can emerge with lower operating costs and become more financially stable and competitive. United and Delta restructured following their bankruptcy and continued to fly. Essentially, this means that broken promises to employees and retirees who were counting on their retirement pension income could potentially save jobs.

Ethical Questions:
Should retirees be insulated from the financial problems of their former employers, or should they share in the financial consequences as the current employees do?

notify workers and retirees of any financial institution that will handle future retirement programs for the organization.[39]

Another key aspect of ERISA is its requirement for a company to include a **summary plan description (SPD).** Summary plan descriptions are designed to inform employees about company benefits in terms the "average" employee can understand.[40] This means that employers must inform employees of the details of their retirement plans, including such items as eligibility requirements and employee rights under ERISA. Finally, it's important to note another law that has had a significant effect on ERISA, the 1984 Retirement Equity Act. This act decreased plan participation from age twenty-five to twenty-one, but its main effect was to deal with gender issues in retirement programs. Specifically, women who left the workforce during childbearing years often found themselves penalized in terms of their retirement years of service if their ten years of employment were not consecutive. Years of service need not be consecutive under the new requirements. The Retirement Equity Act also requires plan participants to provide written approval from a spouse who is a prospective survivor before the participant can waive survivor benefits for the surviving spouse.

Defined Benefit Plans

This plan specifies the dollar amount benefit workers will receive at retirement. The amount typically revolves around some fixed monthly income for life or a variation of a lump-sum cash distribution. The amount and type of the benefit are set, and the company and possibly the employee contribute the set amount each year into a trust fund. The amount contributed each year is calculated on an actuarial basis—considering variables such as length of service, how long plan participants are expected to live, their life-time earnings, and how much return the trust portfolio will receive (for example, 5 percent or 10 percent annually). The pension pay-out formulas used to determine retirement benefits vary widely.

Defined benefit plans have become scarce in private industry, but remain common for state and local governments or industries that are highly unionized.

Defined Contribution Plans

Defined contribution plans differ from defined benefit plans in at least one important area: no specific dollar benefits are fixed. That is, under a defined contribution plan, each employee has an individual account, to which both the employee and the employer may make contributions.[43] The plan establishes rules for contributions. For example, a company's defined contribution pension plan could allow employees to select both a money purchase plan (described next) and a profit-sharing plan in which the company matches up to 6 percent of salary. In a defined contribution plan, the money is invested and projections are offered as to probable retirement income levels. However, the company is not bound by these projections, and accordingly avoids unfunded pension liability problems. This has made defined contribution plans a popular trend in new qualified retirement planning. Additionally, variations in plan administration frequently allow the employee some selection in the investment choices. For instance, an employee may

This employee, and thousands like her, works hard for many years and dreams that one day she will retire. ERISA was enacted—with its enforcement arm, the Pension Benefit Guaranty Corporation—to ensure that retirement funds will in fact be there when retirement comes. *(Source: Ryan McVay/ Stone/Getty Images, Inc.)*

summary plan description (SPD)
An ERISA requirement of explaining to employees their pension program and rights.

defined benefit plan
A retirement program that pays retiring employees a fixed retirement income based on average earnings over a period of time.

defined contribution plan
No specific benefit payout is promised because the value of the retirement account depends on the growth of contributions of employee and employer.

Although matching an employee's contributions to a 401k retirement account is a popular way for employers to help employees prepare for retirement, difficult economic conditions may require an employer to cut or eliminate those contributions. FedEx, along with UPS, 7-Eleven, Macy's, Sprint, and many others have occasionally reduced or temporarily halted their 401k match when met with financial challenges. *(Source: Dennis MacDonald/Alamy Limited)*

individual retirement accounts
A type of defined contribution plan with employer contributions.

select bonds for security, common stocks for appreciation, an inflation hedge, or some type of money market fund.

Money Purchase Pension Plans Money purchase pension plans are one type of defined contribution plan. Under this arrangement, the organization commits to deposit annually a fixed amount of money or a percentage of the employee's pay into a fund. [44] IRS regulations, however, permit a maximum 25 percent of a worker's pay. Money purchase plans have no fixed specific retirement dollar benefits as under a defined benefit plan. Companies do make projections of probable retirement income based on various interest rates, although the company is not bound to the projection.

Profit-Sharing Plans Profit-sharing pension plans are yet another variation of defined contribution plans. Under such a plan, the company contributes to a trust fund account an optional percentage of each worker's pay (maximum allowed by law is 25 percent). This, of course, is guided by profit level, although it isn't even necessary for the employer to make a profit to make contributions. The operative word in profit-sharing plans is optional. The company is not bound by law to make contributions every year. It should be noted, however, that although employers are not bound by law, the majority of employers feel a moral obligation to make a contribution. Often they will keep to a schedule, even when profits are slim or nonexistent. [45]

Individual Retirement Accounts Individual retirement accounts have gone through many changes. Two types now exist to assist small business owners and self-employed people.

- Simplified employee pension plan IRA (SEP IRA) allows small business owners to contribute up to 25 percent of an employee's compensation into an individual retirement account. The plan is easy to create and has tax savings to the employer, but contributions can only be made by the employer.
- Savings incentive match plan for employees IRA (SIMPLE IRA) allows employers that have no retirement plan and one hundred or fewer employees to contribute to an IRA. Employees can contribute to a SIMPLE IRA, as long as the employer matches the employee contribution up to $11,500. [46]

401(k)s The Tax Equity and Fiscal Responsibility Act (TEFRA) established capital accumulation programs, more commonly known as 401(k)s or thrift-savings plans. A 401(k) program is named after the IRS tax code section that created it. These programs permit workers to set aside a certain amount of their income on a tax-deferred basis through their employer. Many companies match employee contributions up to a maximum percentage. The most common match is 50 cents for each dollar of employee contribution up to the first 6 percent of pay. [48] Company matches may be suspended during difficult financial conditions, but many resume matching employee contributions when their economic outlook improves. Contributions are not taxed as income until the employee withdraws them.

A twist on the 401k allows employees to pay taxes on their contribution when they are earned and contributed to the 401k. The money is allowed to grow until retirement, and the increases earned are not taxable when the retiree withdraws the income. These are called Roth Contributions, and basically allow the employees to prepay the taxes on retirement income.

Many organizations have developed 401(k) programs as replacements to their Defined Benefit pension programs. Both employers and employees have found advantages to offering capital accumulation plans. The cost of providing retirement income for employees is lower, and employees can supplement their retirement program and often participate in investments. Employees are offered the ease of contributing to their 401(k) through payroll deductions.

Paid Time Off

Various benefits provide pay for time off from work. The most popular of these are vacation and holiday leave and disability insurance, which includes sick leave and short- and long-term disability programs. Although we'll present these as separate items, some organizations lump all paid time off into a single bank of time called paid time off (PTO), as shown in Exhibit 12-7. As the time is used, it is charged to one's account whether it is used for vacation or sick leave.

Vacation and Holiday Leave

After employees have been with an organization for a specified period of time, they usually become eligible for a paid vacation. Common practice is to relate the length of vacation to the length of tenure and job classification in the organization. For example, after six months' service with an organization, an employee may be eligible for one week's vacation; after a year, two weeks; after five years, three weeks; and after ten or more years, four weeks.[50] It is interesting to note that U.S. workers have shorter vacation periods than many industrialized nations. For example, U.S. workers have, on average, fifteen days of vacation each year; employees in Sweden, Denmark, Austria, and Spain average thirty or more days of vacation each year; and in Japan, it's twenty-five days.[51] Another interesting statistic was revealed by a 2011 survey that found that as many as 70 percent of American workers didn't take all of their vacation time. Reasons included anxiety over job security, heavy workloads resulting from minimal staffing, and cultures that value devotion to the job over personal life. Employers may not

Employee Status	Years of Service	PTO Days	Accrued Per 2 Week Pay Period
Non-Exempt	Up to 3	28	8.62
	3 to 10	33	10.15
	10 and over	35	10.77
Exempt	Up to 3	33	10.15
	3 to 10	35	10.77
	10 and over	38	11.69

Exhibit 12-7
Sample Paid Time Off (PTO) Policy[49]

PTO combines holiday, vacation, and sick leave into one account managed by employees. PTO is accrued according to the amount of time employees worked and the employees' position, as shown in this table, similar to PTO programs in large medical centers.

Employees working less than 40 hours per week but more than 20 hours per week will earn PTO on a prorated basis. Staff working less than 20 hours per week are not eligible for PTO. Employees may sell back PTO or donate PTO according to the guidelines in the Benefits Handbook.
Employees will be allowed bereavement and jury duty according to the guidelines in the Benefits Handbook.

Exhibit 12-8
Paid Vacation Mandated in
Selected Countries

Most developed countries require
employers to offer some paid
vacation every year.[56]

Country	Paid Vacation Mandated
Australia	4 weeks
China	None required
Germany	24 days
India	12 days
Japan	10 days
Mexico	6 days
Norway	25 days
United States	None required

benefit much from the increased number of days spent on the job. Right Management, sponsors of the survey, warn that vacation time is fundamental to a healthy, productive work force.[52]

The rationale behind paid vacation is to provide a break in which employees can refresh themselves. This rationale is important but sometimes overlooked. For example, companies that allow employees to accrue vacation time and sell back to the company any unused vacation days lose sight of the regenerative "battery charging" intent. The cost may be the same to the employer (depending on how long vacation time can be accrued), but employees who do not take a break ultimately may be adversely affected, which can ultimately affect productivity. Moreover, many employees simply cannot completely leave the office behind. Nearly 25 percent of all employees check in with their office daily while on vacation.[53]

Holiday pay is paid time off to observe some special event—federally mandated holidays (such as New Year's Day, Presidents' Day, Martin Luther King Jr.'s Birthday, Memorial Day, Labor Day, Thanksgiving, or Christmas), company-provided holidays (such as Christmas Eve and New Year's Eve), or personal days (days employees can take off for any reason). In the United States, employees average ten paid holidays per year.[54] Most other countries are similar, with averages of eight paid holidays in the United Kingdom, twelve in Italy, and fourteen in Spain and Portugal.[55]

Disability Insurance Programs

Employees today recognize that salary continuation for injuries and major illnesses is almost more important than life insurance. Most employees face a greater probability of a disabling injury that requires an absence from work of more than ninety days than dying before retirement. Programs to address this area of need can be broken down into two broad categories: short-term and long-term disability programs.[57] Almost all employers offer some type of short-term disability plan. Categories under this heading include the company sick-leave policy, short-term disability programs,[58] state disability laws, and workers' compensation. Each helps replace income in the event of an injury or a short-term illness.[59] For many, this short-term period is defined as six months or less.

Sick Leave One of the most popular types of short-term disability programs is a company's sick-leave plan. Sick leave is allocated at a specific number of days a year.[60] In some organizations, the number of sick days allowed to employees may be expanded relative to years of service with the organization. Each year of employment may entitle the worker to two additional days of sick leave. Regardless of whether sick leave is used, it continues to accumulate (usually up to some maximum number of days). Employees who have been with the company the longest accumulate the most sick-leave credit.

Sick-leave abuse has often been a problem for organizations.[61] The belief, too, that one should amass sick leave for use later in life is quickly diminishing. That belief may have been popular when workers tended to join an organization early in their career and retire from that company, but today's mobility renders long-term focus largely meaningless. This is especially alarming when we consider that sick days are not usually transferable to another organization. Thus, the "use them or lose them" concept may only hinder productivity. Recent attempts to combat this potential for sick-leave abuse include financial incentives to individuals who do not fully use their sick leave for the year. Organizations may reward attendance with "well pay." Well pay provides a monetary inducement for workers not to use all of their sick leave, perhaps by buying back unused sick leave, lumping sick-leave days into years of service in calculating retirement benefits, or even having special drawings for those who qualify. Some companies allow workers to donate sick leave to coworkers who have serious illnesses and have exhausted their sick leave.[62] Such incentives intend to serve as a bonus and encourage judicious use of sick time.

Short-Term Disability Plans Employers may provide employees with a short term disability plan that provides a percentage of the employee's income (usually around 70 percent) if the employee must be absent from work due to an illness or injury and has already used all or a predetermined number of sick leave days. These plans usually provide coverage up to six months.

Long-Term Disability Plans When health insurance coverage for prevention fails to prevent major illness, and extended time off work is insufficient for recuperation, employees may need a long-term disability benefits program. Similar to short-term disability, long-term disability programs provide replacement income for an employee who cannot return to work and whose short-term coverage has expired. Long-term disability usually becomes effective after six months. Temporary or permanent long-term disability coverage is in effect in almost all companies.

The benefits paid to employees are customarily set between 50 and 67 percent, with 60 percent salary replacement the most common. Plans may provide coverage for two to five years, but may continue until retirement age. The employee may be required to provide proof of further disability after the two to five year limit. Plan providers may work with the employee to assist him or her to gain employment in the original occupation, or train him or her in another profession.

ETHICAL ISSUES IN HRM

Making Sick Leave a Required Benefit?

Sick leave may be leaving the category of "voluntary benefits" and moving to the "required benefits" category, depending on where you live. Philadelphia is the latest city to require sick leave for employees, joining San Francisco, Milwaukee, Wisconsin, and Washington, D.C., as cities that have passed local requirements that employers provide paid sick leave to employees. This trend has led to proposals requiring sick leave in twelve states. Legislation has been introduced in Congress supporting a federal requirement for paid sick leave throughout the country.

The Milwaukee ordinance requires that employers within the city that employ ten or more workers provide a minimum of one hour of paid sick leave for every thirty hours worked up to seventy-two hours per year. Employers with fewer than ten employees are only required to provide up to forty hours per year.

According to the Bureau of Labor Statistics, 43 percent of workers in private industry, or 50 million employees, do not get any paid sick leave. Supporters of the initiatives claim that mandatory paid sick leave would save money for employers because sick employees would stay home rather than come to work and spread illness, reducing productivity. Most other industrialized countries require some paid sick leave. Opponents include business groups that point out that nothing is free. Cuts would be made in other areas such as pay, or benefits such as healthcare and vacations.

Ethical Questions:

Should paid sick leave become a legal requirement? Do the benefits outweigh the costs? Where do you stand?

CONTEMPORARY CONNECTION

Leaving It Up to You: Paid Time Off Leave (PTO)

Diane's employer allowed her a relatively generous fifteen sick days each year. She was even allowed to accumulate them up to a total of ninety days. That didn't take too long because Diane very rarely called in sick. But when her daughter's medical condition required that they travel out of state for major surgery, she was told that only two days would qualify for paid leave because it was a family member who was ill, not Diane. Many years later, Diane is still annoyed with the policy she sees as unethical. "Parents learn to lie to their employers" explained Diane, "conscientious employees don't really want to miss work, so they go to work sick and only call in when their kids are sick."

Some companies have solved this problem by doing away with labels such as "sick leave" and "vacation" and replaced them with a bank of time called "Paid Time Off, " or PTO. A recent survey by the International Foundation of Employee Benefit Plans estimates that 30 percent of U.S. corporations offer a PTO bank.[63] PTO is accrued either annually or monthly, much like other types of leave. The employee uses the days in the PTO bank for vacation, sick leave, or personal days with no explanation necessary to the employer. Officially, the employer doesn't care why the employee is gone, although they may still ask for recordkeeping purposes. Employees like Diane wouldn't be tempted to be dishonest when requesting leave for a reason that might not otherwise be covered. This seems like a win-win for all, but as with any policy, there are pros and cons:

Pro: Employees like the idea of PTO, and it assists with recruiting and retention. Healthy employees can take unused time off for extra vacation days. Employees feel that they are being more honest with employers about the reasons they are not at work. Employees appreciate the flexibility and trust that employers offer with PTO policies. Unexpected absences are reduced as employees schedule a PTO day in advance rather than call in sick when missing work for a personal reason. PTO offers privacy to employees who may not want to explain that they are missing work for medical tests and doctor's appointments.

Con: Abuses may occur. Since the employer officially doesn't care why the employee is gone, employees may miss work for reasons they would not have missed work for under a traditional leave plan. Employees may use more leave under a PTO plan. Employees may think of all PTO time as "vacation" time, so if they are sick, they come to work anyway, spreading illnesses to their coworkers.

Abuses can be reduced if the culture of the company encourages trust and empowerment and employees are evaluated by results. Clear guidelines for using the PTO system, employee education, and encouraging sick employees to go home will also help make the system work properly.

Consider this:
Would you use your paid leave time differently if you were able to take PTO time rather than sick time? Do leave policies encourage workers to come to work sick? Have you seen a similar situation with classes that have attendance policies?

Survivor Benefits

Many companies offer life insurance as a benefit to provide protection to the families of employees. Life insurance programs are one of the more popular employee benefits.

Group Term Life Insurance

Life insurance is one of the most common and most popular voluntary benefits. Many employers offer a small amount of group term life insurance to full-time employees. This coverage is frequently equal to the employee's annual salary, but a survey by *Workforce Management* found that 75 percent of employers offer supplemental life insurance that allows the employee to increase the amount of coverage for an additional fee paid by the employee. The additional coverage may be two to five times the employee's salary or original coverage, and may not require a medical examination. Many employers also offer opportunities for employees to purchase life insurance for a spouse and dependents at group rates. The additional fee is usually substantially less than the employee would have to pay if the insurance was purchased individually from another provider. Employees rate the opportunity to purchase supplemental insurance as a very desirable benefit, making it valuable to the employer for recruitment, retention, and employee satisfaction.[64]

Travel Insurance

Travel insurance policies cover employees' lives in the event of death while traveling on company time. A typical policy would pay five times the employee's salary up to $1 million. Depending on any unique policy provisions, the insurance typically will be paid as long as an employee is conducting business-related activities when the death occurs. An employee who normally commutes to work would not be covered under an employer-paid travel insurance benefit if an accident happened on the way. Employers that require extensive international travel may also provide air ambulance service to return ill or injured employees back to the United States.

Employee Services and Family-Friendly Benefits

Employees may receive these services at no cost or at a cost shared with the organization. Services may include such benefits as sponsored social and recreational events, employee assistance programs, credit unions, housing, tuition reimbursement, gym memberships, paid jury duty time, uniforms, military pay, company-paid transportation and parking, free food, childcare services or referrals, and even repair services for bicycles, cars, and appliances. Companies can be as creative as they like in putting together their benefits program—many offer onsite fitness centers, and some have even added free massages and haircuts for their employees! The crucial point is to provide a package containing benefits in which employees have expressed some interest and perceive some value. Employees appreciate efforts to help them balance their career and personal life. For example, working parents at Best Buy's Richfield, Minnesota, headquarters love the onsite day care, and an onsite doctor and pharmacy really help provide work-life balance. A growing number of employers are even allowing new parents to bring infants to work until they reach crawling stage.

> A key component of any benefit package is offering employees something in which they have an interest and that they value.

An Integrative Perspective on Employee Benefits

When an employer considers offering benefits to employees, one of the main considerations is to keep costs down. Traditionally, employers attempted to do this by providing a package of benefits to their employees—whether employees wanted or needed any particular benefit, or used it at all. Rising costs and a desire to let employees choose what they want, has led employers to search for alternative measures of benefits administration. The leading alternative to address this concern was the implementation of flexible benefits. Although flexible benefits offer greater choices to employees (and might have a motivational effect), we must understand that they are provided mainly to contain benefit costs. The term **flexible benefits** refers to a system whereby employees are presented with a menu of benefits and asked to select, within monetary limits imposed, the employee benefits they desire.[65] Today, almost all major corporations in the United States offer flexible benefits. Three plans are popular: flexible spending accounts, modular plans, and core-plus options.

flexible benefits
A benefits program in which employees pick benefits that most meet their needs.

Flexible Spending Accounts

Flexible spending accounts, approved and operated under Section 125 of the Internal Revenue Code (IRC), are special types of flexible benefits that permit employees to

flexible spending accounts
Allow employees to set aside money before payroll taxes to pay for healthcare or dependent care.

set aside money to pay for medical expenses not covered by insurances.[66] For example, Abbott Laboratories employees can set aside up to $5,000 per year for reimbursement for eligible out-of-pocket healthcare expenses (such as co-payments for office visits, prescription drugs, some over-the-counter drugs, contact lenses, eyeglasses, orthodontia, and hearing aids) through the Healthcare Flexible Spending Account. Abbott employees may also contribute up to $5,000 to a dependent care flexible spending account, which can be used to reimburse child care or elder care for eligible dependents.[67]

By placing a specified amount into a spending account, the employee can pay for these services with monies not included in W-2 income, which can result in lower federal, state, and Social Security tax rates and increase individual spending income. Such accounts also provide Social Security tax savings for the employer. We've presented an example of how using a flexible spending account can result in more take-home pay for an employee (see Exhibit 12-9). Ironically, although the benefits of flexible spending accounts are clear, it is estimated that fewer than 18 percent of all employees actually use them.[68]

Despite tax benefits for employees, workers must understand that flexible spending accounts are heavily regulated. Each account established must operate independently. For instance, money set aside for dependent-care expenses can be used only for that purpose. One cannot decide later to seek reimbursement from one account to pay for services where no account was established or to pay for services from another account because all monies in the designated account have been withdrawn. Additionally, money deposited into these accounts must be spent during the period or forfeited. Unused monies do not revert back to the employee as cash, but typically revert back to the company. This point must be clearly communicated to employees to avoid misconception of the plan requirements. The "use it or lose it" nature of the flexible spending account may account for the low participation rates.

Exhibit 12-9
An Example of Take-Home Pay (With and Without a Flexible Spending Account).

	Without Flexible Account	With Flexible Account
Gross Monthly Pay	$2,500	$2,500
Retirement Deduction	150	150
Pretax Payroll Deduction	0	600*
Administrative Fee	0	5
Taxable Gross Income	$2,350	$1,750
Payroll Taxes	530	315
Amount of Paycheck	$1,819	$1,435
After-Tax Expense	600*	0
Spendable Monthly Pay	$1,219	$1,435
Additional Monthly Income with Flexible Spending Account		$216

*Assumes an employee is depositing monies monthly in a flexible spending account in the following way:

Health insurance deduction	$150
Dental insurance deduction	$20
Dependent care deduction	$400
Medical expenses deduction	$30

Source: Based on a similar example presented in South Carolina Budget and Control Board, 2006 Money Plus (2005), p. 7. Some numbers have been rounded to simplify exhibit.

Modular Plans

The modular plan of flexible benefits is a system whereby employees choose a predesigned package of benefits. As opposed to selecting cafeteria style, modular plans contain a prearranged package of benefits that are designed to meet particular needs of groups of employees. For example, suppose a company offers its employees two separate modules. Module 1 benefits consist of a life insurance policy at two times annual earnings and HMO healthcare insurance (no dental or vision coverage); this policy is provided to all employees at no cost to them. Module 2 benefits consist of a life insurance policy of two times annual earnings, traditional health insurance, and dental and vision coverage. This plan, however, requires a biweekly pretax payroll deduction of $57. Choice does exist, but it is limited to selecting either of the packages in its entirety.

Core-Plus Options Plans

A core-plus options flexible benefits plan exhibits more of a menu selection than the two programs just mentioned. Under this arrangement, employees typically receive coverage of core areas—usually medical coverage, life insurance at one time annual earnings, minimal disability insurance, a 401(k) program, and standard time off from work with pay.[69] These minimum benefits give employees basic coverage from which they can build more extensive packages, and the core-plus option helps keep benefit costs relatively stable. Under the core-plus plan, employees select other benefits that may range from more extensive coverage of the core plan to spending accounts. Employees generally receive credits to purchase their additional benefits, calculated according to an employee's tenure in the company, salary, and position held. As a rule of thumb, in first-time installations, the credits given equal the amount needed to purchase the identical plan in force before flexible benefits arrived; that is, no employee should be worse off. If the employee decides to select exactly what was previously offered, he or she may purchase such benefits with no added out-of-pocket expenses (co-payments). Payments would now be made before taxes.

Benefits in a Global Environment

Benefits packages offered in other countries are often tailored specifically to the countries unique culture, government regulations, and competition for the best employees. HR must develop a benefits strategy that responds to the different combinations of benefits provided by the government, benefits the government requires the employer to provide, and additional benefits employers provide to be competitive. Figure 12-10 illustrates common benefits strategies in a few selected countries.

Popular categories of employee benefits vary widely when applied to a global workforce.

- **Leaves** provide some of the biggest differences in benefits that governments require employers to offer. On the low end, China and U.S. federal laws do not require employers to offer any paid vacation or leave time. U.S. employers typically voluntarily offer 10 to 15 days of leave annually. Most developed countries require a few days to several weeks of vacation time each year. Additionally, approximately two thirds of all countries require paid maternity leaves of 4 to 12 months.[71]
- **Healthcare** is a government provided benefit in many countries, making it unnecessary for employers to provide them. Employers may find that healthcare services in some countries are very basic and employers often offer supplemental health insurance.
- **Pension Plans** similar to defined benefit plans or Social Security are provided by many governments, and employers are not required to provide additional

Exhibit 12-10
Examples of Benefits Offered in Selected Countries

Employers must consider each country's combination of government provided benefits, benefits that employers are required to provide, and benefits that are offered voluntarily to match competition and provide motivation.

Country	Government-mandated benefits	Government-provided benefits	Culturally attractive/ motivational benefits
Canada	Vacation days Holidays Time off for child care, elder care, and hardship	Universal healthcare Unemployment insurance Prescription drugs Eye care Dental care Workers' compensation Maternity/paternity leave Employment standards	Vacation Maternity/paternity leave Business travel Work/life balance initiatives Extra health benefits
China	Pension insurance Medical insurance Unemployment insurance Maternity insurance Housing fund Paid annual leave Medical treatment period (for non-occupational injuries and illnesses)	Pension Medical insurance Occupational injury benefits Unemployment benefits Maternity benefits Housing fund	Supplemental medical benefits Dependent medical benefits Company outings/travel
Germany	Social security Health insurance Parental leave Protection of working mothers Minimum wage, in some industries Health insurance Long-term-care insurance Six weeks' sick pay	Social security Health insurance Long-term-care insurance Unemployment insurance Occupational accident insurance Federal child-raising allowance Federal parental benefit	Company car Company pension Sabbatical Additional days off for special reasons Company-sponsored day care Free lunch Preventive medical services

Title above table: Global Benefits Around the World[70]

Source: Excerpted from "Global Benefits Around the World," a web extra to "Learn the Landscape" by David Tobenkin in *HR Magazine*, May 2011. Copyright 2011, Society for Human Resource Management, Alexandria, VA. Used with permission. All rights reserved.

retirement benefits. In countries with no established pension plans, employers may offer their own defined contribution benefit plan.

- **Other Benefits** may be provided to stay competitive or to provide tax relief for workers. For example, an employer may provide transportation or housing rather than salary to reduce income taxes the employee would owe. Other benefits may include travel, education benefits including English classes, and cafeteria benefit plans for executives who want to tailor their benefit packages.[72]

Summary

(This summary relates to the Learning Outcomes identified on page 300). After having read this chapter, you can:

1. **Discuss why employers offer benefits to their employees.** Employers offer benefits to employees to attract and retain them. Benefits are expected by today's workers, and must provide meaning and value to the employees.

2. **Contrast Social Security, unemployment compensation, and workers' compensation benefits.** Social Security is an insurance program funded by current employees to provide (1) a minimum level of retirement income, (2) disability income, and (3) survivor benefits. Unemployment compensation provides income continuation to employees who lose a job through no fault of their own. Unemployment compensation typically lasts for twenty-six weeks. Workers' compensation provides income continuation for employees who are hurt or disabled on the job. Workers' compensation also covers work-related deaths or permanent disabilities. All three are legally required benefits.

3. **Identify and describe the major types of health insurance options.** The major types of health insurance benefits offered to employees are traditional, health maintenance organizations, preferred provider organizations, point of service, and consumer driven health plans. Traditional plans allow the employee to use any healthcare provider and the insurance company will reimburse the expense. HMOs and PPOs are designed to provide a fixed out-of-pocket alternative to healthcare coverage and negotiate for reduced rates for plan members. Point of Service plans are similar to HMOs and PPOs, but allow plan members more flexibility for healthcare outside the network. Consumer driven health plans include insurance with a high deductible, and a savings account that the insured uses for deductibles and out-of-pocket expenses.

4. **Discuss the important implications of the Employee Retirement Income Security Act.** The Employment Retirement Income Security Act (ERISA) has had a significant effect on retirement programs. Its primary emphasis is to ensure that employees have a vested right to their retirement monies, that appropriate guidelines are followed in the event of a retirement plan termination, and that employees understand their benefits through the summary plan description.

5. **Outline and describe major types of retirement programs offered by organizations.** The most popular types of retirement benefits offered today are Social Security, defined benefit pension plans, and defined contribution plans including money purchase pension plans, profit-sharing plans, individual retirement accounts, and 401(k)s.

6. **Explain the reason companies offer their employees vacation benefits.** The primary reason for a company to provide a vacation benefit is to allow employees a break from work in which they can refresh and reenergize themselves.

7. **Describe the purpose of disability insurance programs.** Disability benefit programs ensure income replacement for employees when a temporary or permanent disability arises from an injury or extended illness (typically originating off the job).

8. **List the various types of flexible benefit option programs.** Flexible benefits programs come in a variety of packages. The most popular versions existing today are flexible spending accounts, modular plans, and core-plus options.

Demonstrating Comprehension

QUESTIONS FOR REVIEW

1. Describe why companies provide benefits to their employees. What effect do companies expect benefits will have on employee work behaviors?
2. How does ERISA provide protection for a worker's retirement?
3. Identify and describe four legally required benefits.
4. Describe why an employee might select a PPO health insurance benefit over an HMO.

5. Describe the difference between a defined benefit pension plan and a defined contribution pension plan.
6. Describe the inherent potential for abuse in offering a sick-leave benefit.
7. Describe three types of flexible benefits programs.

Key Terms

Consolidated Omnibus Budget Reconciliation Act (COBRA)	flexible benefits	Pension Benefit Guaranty Corporation (PBGC)
consumer-driven health plan (CDHP)	flexible spending accounts	point-of-service plans (POS)
defined benefit plan	Health Insurance Portability and Accountability Act of 1996 (HIPAA)	preferred provider organization (PPO)
defined contribution plan	health maintenance organization (HMO)	Social Security
domestic partner benefits		summary plan description
employee benefits	individual retirement account (IRA)	unemployment compensation
Employee Retirement Income Security Act (ERISA)	legally required benefits	vesting rights
		workers' compensation

HRM Workshop

Linking Concepts to Practice DISCUSSION QUESTIONS

1. "Social Security should serve as a foundation for employee retirement programs. Therefore, Congress should explore more extensive revisions to the program to ensure that the next generation of retirees will receive the benefit." Do you agree or disagree with this statement? Explain your response.
2. "Social Security disability and survivor benefits should be the sole responsibility of each employee. A company simply cannot be responsible for the financial welfare of its employees. Additionally, legally required benefits provide some level

of worker protection. Therefore, a major means of containing benefit costs should be elimination of disability and survivor benefits." Do you agree or disagree? Explain your response.
3. "Flexible benefits programs are employer inducements to reduce benefits costs. The average employee has neither the ability nor information to make such important choices. Employees should suspect such programs." Do you agree or disagree? Explain your response.

Making A Difference SERVICE LEARNING PROJECTS

Employee healthcare is a highly valued benefit. Many healthcare provider organizations are in need of volunteers.

■ Register as a volunteer for your local hospital or medical center, hospice or free clinic.

■ Contact a nearby organization that helps families dealing with serious illnesses such as the Ronald McDonald House or Target House. Offer assistance with meals, cleaning, or babysitting.
■ Contact your local office of the American Red Cross about volunteer opportunities.

■ Search www.healthcarevolunteer.com or another non-profit organization that helps match volunteers with healthcare organizations that need volunteers.

As you put your service learning experience together, keep a journal of your activities, the time you spend, contact information for people you work with, and your thoughts about the process. When you're finished, make a presentation to your class about the experience and what you learned. What concepts from Chapter 12 were you able to apply?

Developing Diagnostic and Analytical Skills

Case Application 12: PERKS AND PROFITS

Imagine working in an organization where employee morale is low, turnover is high, and the costs of hiring are astronomical. If that were the case, you'd imagine the employer would go to great lengths to find, attract, and retain quality employees. Couple this goal with the reality of the economic picture—you simply cannot afford to provide expensive benefits for employees who may leave you for a different employer offering an extra $1,000 in salary or benefits. Knowing that 41 percent of all employees have no loyalty to their employers and will move on if a better offer comes adds to the dilemma.

These issues clearly are a concern for organizations like Genentech or Zappos. But they don't fret over them. That's because they have found that treating employees with respect, and giving them such things as bonuses, rewards for longevity, onsite child care, lunches, and sending employees home with prepared dinners really works.

Genentech is a California company that "develops and produces drugs that cure diseases," according to the company website.[73] The company celebrated its thirteenth year on *Fortune's* "Best Places to Work" list in 2011, also receiving "Best Places to Work" honors from *Working Mother*, *LGBT Equality*, and *Computerworld*. The reasons for this recognition are the important work that they do and the strong company culture that values equality and communication. Any discussion of how great it is to work at Genentech always circles back to the benefits that show a real respect for employees. In addition to traditional benefits like retirement and healthcare, they provide family-friendly perks such as unlimited sick leave, personal concierge service, flexible work scheduling, childcare, nursing mother's rooms, onsite nurses, adoption assistance, and company sponsored family events. The list of innovative benefits goes on to include unusual benefits like pet insurance, free snacks, and paid six week sabbaticals every six years![74] Zappos, the online shoe retailer, offers perks that match their fun-loving culture like pajama parties, nap rooms, regular happy hours, and a full-time life coach.[75]

Have these benefits worked for Genentech and Zappos? If you translate longevity to morale and loyalty, you'd say they have. Both boast low turnover rates and high employee ratings for workplace satisfaction.

Questions:

1. Describe the importance of employee benefits as a strategic component of fulfilling the goals of HRM at Genentech and Zappos.
2. Explain how Genentech and Zappos use employee benefits as a motivating tool.
3. Do you believe the incentive benefits such as those offered at Genentech and Zappos can be used in other organizations? Why or why not?

Working with a Team   BENEFIT SELECTIONS

Using Exhibit 12-11, determine the mix of benefits that would best fit your needs. After choosing your benefits, form teams of three to five members and answer the following questions.

1. Explain the reasons for the choices you made. What compelled you to make those specific benefit choices?
2. Compare the benefits you have chosen with those chosen by members of your team. What similarities exist? Differences?
3. Five years from now, would you choose different benefits from those you selected today? Why or why not?

Exhibit 12-11
Sample Flexible Benefit
Selection Sheet[a]

Name Chris Reynolds			**Years of Service:**	3
Annual Earnings: $38,000			**Credits to Spend**[b]	6330
Healthcare:[c]			**Vacation:**[d]	
HMO	Core		1 week	Core
PPO	3280		2 weeks	730
			3 weeks	1460
Life Insurance:[e]			4 weeks	2190
1 x AE	Core		**Paid Holidays:**[f]	
2 x AE	273		7 days	Core
3 x AE	546			
4 x AE	819		**Personal Days:**[g]	
			1 day	Core
Disability Insurance:			2 days	146
50% AE	Core		3 days	292
55% AE	240			
60% AE	480		**Retirement [401(k)]:**	
65% AE	720		2% match	Core
			3% match	760
Dental Coverage:			4% match	1520
Dental HMO	Core		5% match	2280
Dental PPO	240		6% match	3040

[a]All cost figures represent single employee coverage only, where applicable. For additional family coverages for health insurance, see footnote 3.
[b]All flexible credits are based on 37 percent of annual salary (AE). Flexible spending credits are those credits available to you to spend on benefits. Credits available for spending is the difference between total flexible credits and costs associated with core coverage. Any amount spent beyond "credits" will be deducted evenly over your 26 biweekly paychecks.
[c]Healthcare coverage is based on $283.33 per month for employee coverage only. Add $165 for employee plus one, and $228 for employee plus two or more per month for either coverage.
[d]Vacation costs are calculated at 1/52 of annual earnings.
[e]Life insurance is calculated at $.072 per $1,000 of life insurance.
[f]Based on 2,080 hours worked annually and a cost per hour rate.
[g]Based on 2,080 hours worked annually and a cost per hour rate.

Learning An HRM Skill   CALCULATING A LONG-TERM DISABILITY PAYMENT

About the skill: Much of the work of a benefits specialist revolves around mathematics and finance calculations.[76] Specific skills are hard to find. However, it is clear that any benefits specialist needs excellent computer skills, especially in spreadsheet applications. To this end, here's a scenario that a benefits specialist may face that lends itself to the use of a spreadsheet application. To practice this skill, place the following information and calculations on a spreadsheet.

Suppose an employee makes $36,000 per year ($3,000 per month). Your organization offers employees a long-term disability (LTD) insurance benefit at 65 percent of earnings, with a monthly cap at $4,000. The company's LTD is also integrated with Social Security disability payments (SSDI) such that no more than 70 percent of salary is covered. The employee has a verifiable illness, is unable to work in any occupation, and has been covered under the company's short-term disability plan for the past six months (the required time before long-term disability starts). To determine this employee's long-term disability payment, you need to know the amount of SSDI monthly payment. Your research reveals that this

employee is entitled to $8,400 in SSDI payments a year ($700 a month). You now have enough data to complete this employee's LTD. After the calculations have been made, you see that this employee, given his circumstances, is eligible for a payment of $500 from SSDI and $900 from the LTD policy. Even though the LTD limit of 65 percent of the employee's salary would be $1,300, the total of LTD integrated with SSDI may not exceed $1,400 (70 percent of monthly salary). Here are the calculations:

- 65 percent of annual earnings/month $1,950 ($3,000 × .65)
- 70 percent of monthly income for integration with Social Security $2,100 ($3,000 × .70)
- SSDI benefit $8,400/12 = $700/month = $700 (given)
- Proposed total monthly payment without Social Security integration $2,650 ($1,950 + $700)
- Proposed total monthly payment with Social Security integration = $2,100 (maximum)
- Overage $550 ($2,650 − $2,100)
- Actual LTD payment $1,400 ($1,950 − $550)(LTD overage)

Enhancing Your Communication Skills

1. Search YouTube for a short video related to an employee benefits topic in Chapter 12. Develop a 5–10 minute presentation to your class explaining how the video relates to employee benefits.

2. Survey local employers for the types of benefits they offer. Divide them into categories of small employers with up to 100 employees, medium employers with up to 500 employees, and large employers with over 500 employers. Develop a presentation with visual aids to explain your conclusions and any trends you determine.

3. Survey the perks offered by employers to:

   - your college president
   - a local manufacturer
   - a local financial institution
   - other large employer

   Prepare a two to three page paper comparing the perks offered in your community to those in other areas of the country.

4. Discuss the pros and cons of offering benefits for the sake of being competitive and innovative in a two to three page paper with two sources. In your discussion, address whether you believe it's possible for benefits to become fads.

5. One controversy surrounding benefits administration today is offering domestic partner benefits. Develop a presentation with 3–5 presentation slides arguing (1) why domestic benefits should be offered to organizational members, and (2) why they shouldn't. End the presentation with your support of one side or the other.

(Source: Darcy Padilla/The New York Times/Redux Pictures)

LEARNING OUTCOMES

After reading this chapter, you will be able to

1. Discuss the organizational effect of the Occupational Safety and Health Act.

2. List the Occupational Safety and Health Administration's (OSHA) enforcement priorities.

3. Explain what punitive actions OSHA can impose on an organization.

4. Describe what companies must do to comply with OSHA record-keeping requirements.

5. Identify ways that OSHA assists employers in creating a safer workplace.

6. Describe most commonly cited OSHA safety violations.

7. Explain what companies can do to prevent workplace violence.

8. Define stress and the causes of burnout.

9. Explain how an organization can create a healthy work site.

10. Describe the purposes of employee assistance and wellness programs.

Ensuring a Safe and Healthy Work Environment

They are teams of skilled professional athletes and have an abundance of strength, agility, and stamina. They brighten our day when they come through for us. We brag of their performance and wait anxiously for their next appearance. They proudly wear the uniforms of brown, purple and orange, or the good old red, white, and blue. We are referring of course to the delivery drivers for UPS, FedEx, and the U.S. Postal Service.

Is it a stretch to call them athletes? *Webster's Dictionary* defines an athlete as "A person who is trained or skilled in exercises, sports, or games requiring physical strength, agility, or stamina." That certainly seems to apply to the drivers of UPS, FedEx, and the U.S. Postal Service. How about other professions? Would the strength, flexibility, and concentration it takes to be a firefighter, paramedic, or baggage handler qualify them as athletes, too? How about workers at Boeing who bend, twist, and crawl through small sections of an aircraft, lifting and carrying heavy equipment all day? Would the definition extend that far?

Many of us underestimate the amount of physical exertion and activity in our jobs. The U.S. Department of Labor data indicates that sprains and strains are the leading type of illness or injury in every major industry sector, accounting for 40 percent of all injuries.[1] Most are caused by falls or overexertion. Sounds pretty similar to athletic injuries, doesn't it?

Volkswagen has taken the comparison seriously and requires all production workers at a new plant in Tennessee to participate in a fitness program for "industrial athletes." Volkswagen spokesman Scott Wilson said the training is "focused on getting each and every one of us,

no matter what our job is at the plant, prepared to show up and perform at the highest level of professional excellence."[2] The daily two-hour workout sessions are linked to movements employees will use at work and include stretching, cardiovascular strength, endurance, grip, and how much employees can push and pull.[3]

UPS has similar goals. When considering that the average UPS driver lifts over 1 million pounds annually while climbing in and out of trucks, handling an average of 350 packages daily, they turned to fitness professionals to try to prevent and control injuries efficiently and control costs related to injuries on the job. Measures implemented include a warm-up "Three-Minute-Drill," training in hydration, nutrition, strength, core training, conditioning, and body mechanics. One UPS region saw dramatic improvements including an 85 percent reduction in injuries and a 60 percent decrease in worker's compensation costs.

Many companies are recognizing the similarities between the strength, skill, and stamina needed on the job and in athletics. The U.S. Postal Service, FedEx, and Coca-Cola have also created programs to support the industrial athlete by hiring athletic trainers, creating conditioning and stretching programs, developing exercise routines, and providing advice on nutrition to help them keep in the game.

Looking Ahead

How would you feel about being required to join an exercise or fitness program for your job? Would an exercise program be appropriate for less strenuous positions such as an office worker or retail salesperson?

Introduction

Organization officials have a legal and moral responsibility to ensure that the workplace is free from unnecessary hazards. Conditions surrounding the workplace must be safe for employees' physical and mental health. Of course, accidents can and do occur, and the severity of them may astound you. Approximately 4,500 work-related deaths and approximately 3.1 million injuries and illnesses are reported each year in the United States.[4] The Occupational Safety and Health Administration (OSHA) tracks and reports the causes of accidents and injuries in the United States every year. Can you guess the most common cause of occupational injury in the United States? Read on and you'll learn! OSHA also provides many services to help employers keep the workplace safe. Many companies find that money spent on creating a safe and healthy work environment creates savings of lost work time, worker's compensation claims, and insurance premiums, and increases productivity.

The Occupational Safety and Health Act

The passage of the Occupational Safety and Health Act (OSH Act) dramatically changed HRM's role in ensuring that physical working conditions meet adequate standards (Exhibit 13-1). As the Civil Rights Act altered organizational commitment to affirmative action, the OSH Act has altered organizational health and safety programs. The impact of the OSH Act on the workplace has been profound. Since the act became law in 1970, annual workplace fatalities have fallen from 14,000 to under 5,000.

OSH Act legislation established comprehensive and specific health standards, authorized inspections to ensure the standards are met, empowered the Occupational Safety and Health Administration (OSHA) to police organizations' compliance, and required employers to keep records of illness and injuries and calculate accident ratios. The act applies to almost every U.S. business engaged in interstate commerce.

Those organizations not meeting the interstate commerce criteria of the OSH Act are generally covered by state occupational safety and health laws. The Occupational Safety and Health Administration (OSHA) provides industry safety standards for four major categories of employers: general industry, construction, agriculture, and maritime. In addition to the standards provided for these specific industries, a **General Duty Clause** covers any potentially dangerous or unhealthy workplace conditions that aren't covered by specific industry regulation. This allows OSHA flexibility in regulating any workplace activity, and making sure that the safety and health of employees is protected. For example, ergonomic injuries or musculoskeletal disorders (MSDs) affecting workers as a result of their jobs are covered under the General Duty Clause. This is a broad category and it isn't easy to define all of the types of musculoskeletal injuries that can occur as a result of everyday work situations. Employers are responsible for knowing standards and ensuring compliance while OSHA develops training and education programs to help employers understand the regulations and stay in compliance.

General Duty Clause
Covers any potentially dangerous or unhealthy workplace condition that isn't covered by specific OSHA industry regulation.

OSHA Inspection Priorities

Enforcement of OSHA standards varies depending on the nature of the event and the organization. Typically, OSHA enforces the standards based on a six-item priority listing.[6] These are, in descending priority: imminent danger; serious accidents resulting in death or hospitalization of three or more employees; a current employee complaint; inspections of target industries with a high injury ratio; and random inspections.

imminent danger
A condition where an accident is about to occur.

1. **Imminent danger** refers to a condition in which an accident is about to occur. Although this is given top priority and acts as a preventive measure, imminent danger situations are hard to define. Generally imminent danger is considered to be a situation where the risk of grave injury or death is so likely that it could happen

Exhibit 13-1
OSHA Protection
OSHA provides legally required posters like this one for free download at www.osha.gov.

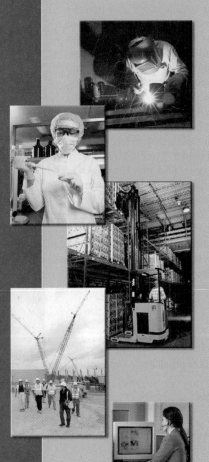

Job Safety and Health
It's the law!

OSHA®
Occupational Safety
and Health Administration
U.S. Department of Labor

EMPLOYEES:
- You have the right to notify your employer or OSHA about workplace hazards. You may ask OSHA to keep your name confidential.

- You have the right to request an OSHA inspection if you believe that there are unsafe and unhealthful conditions in your workplace. You or your representative may participate in that inspection.

- You can file a complaint with OSHA within 30 days of retaliation or discrimination by your employer for making safety and health complaints or for exercising your rights under the *OSH Act*.

- You have the right to see OSHA citations issued to your employer. Your employer must post the citations at or near the place of the alleged violations.

- Your employer must correct workplace hazards by the date indicated on the citation and must certify that these hazards have been reduced or eliminated.

- You have the right to copies of your medical records and records of your exposures to toxic and harmful substances or conditions.

- Your employer must post this notice in your workplace.

- You must comply with all occupational safety and health standards issued under the *OSH Act* that apply to your own actions and conduct on the job.

EMPLOYERS:
- You must furnish your employees a place of employment free from recognized hazards.

- You must comply with the occupational safety and health standards issued under the *OSH Act*.

This free poster available from OSHA –
The Best Resource for Safety and Health

Free assistance in identifying and correcting hazards or complying with standards is available to employers, without citation or penalty, through OSHA-supported consultation programs in each state.

1-800-321-OSHA (6742)
www.osha.gov

OSHA 3165-12-06R

ETHICAL ISSUES IN HRM

Legacy of a Tragedy

On a Saturday afternoon in March of 1911, 146 young women died when a fire swept through the Triangle Shirtwaist factory in New York City. The fire spread quickly, fed by scraps of fabric, tissue patterns, and paper boxes that littered the floor of their ninth floor workplace.

Fire exits had been locked by the owner who claimed that workers used them to steal fabric and garments. Fire escapes collapsed under the weight of the women trying to flee the building, many plunging to their death, nine stories below. Elevator cables snapped under the strain with many workers trapped inside. Fire hoses in the building were rotted and useless. Firefighters found their ladders were several stories too short and water from their hoses could not reach the flames. Onlookers were horrified to see women jumping to their deaths on the Manhattan sidewalks rather than be burned alive.

The factory owners were found not guilty of any criminal charges from their negligence and paid $75 per life lost during the fire. Public outcry over the tragedy and perceived lack of justice that followed was a catalyst for change. "It started making employers aware of their responsibility to their workforce," says Darryl Hill, current President of the American Society of Safety Engineers, an organization that was formed a few months after the tragedy. "Employers today understand that no employee should have to sacrifice their life or their health in the course of employment," says Hill. Some of the things we see in the workplace today in response to the tragedy 100 years ago include:

- Automatic sprinklers
- Unlocked exit doors that swing outward
- Push bars on exterior doors to allow quick exit
- Fire drills
- Increased power for Fire Marshals
- Worker Compensation

Many feel that we still have a long way to go to assure worker safety. In fact, the U.S. Department of Labor estimates that 98 percent of garment factories in Los Angeles alone have health and safety problems serious enough to lead to severe injuries or death.[5]

Ethical Questions:

In the absence of laws that demand safer working conditions, can the actions of employers such as locking the exits, inadequate fire escapes and elevators, or failing to have working fire hoses be considered unethical? Are there additional actions beyond those required by law that employers should take to protect workers in today's workplace?

(Source: UPI/Cornell University/Landov LLC)

before OSHA has a chance to investigate. According to OSHA, this includes examples such as "unstable trench or exposed electrical wire that could cause a serious or fatal accident immediately under present conditions. It also may be a health hazard such as toxic substances or dangerous fumes, dusts, or gases that could cause death or irreversible physical harm, shorten life, or reduce physical or mental performance."[7]

2. **Fatalities and catastrophes** include recent incidents resulting in a death or hospitalization of three or more employees. An organization must report these serious incidents to the OSHA field office within eight hours of occurrence. This permits the investigators to review the scene and try to determine the cause of the accident. For example, heart attacks that occur during the work day should be reported so that OSHA can investigate if they are caused by the work or work environment.

3. **Employee Complaints** If an employee sees a violation of OSHA standards, that employee has the right to call OSHA and request an investigation. The worker may

even refuse to work on the job in question until OSHA has investigated the complaint. This is especially true when a union is involved. For instance, some union contracts permit workers to legally refuse to work if they believe they are in significant danger. Accordingly, they may stay off the job with pay until OSHA arrives and either finds the complaint invalid or cites the company and mandates compliance.[8]

4. **Referrals** from other federal, state or local agencies, individuals, or news media.

5. **Follow-ups** on organizations that have previously been cited to make sure corrective action has been taken.

6. **Planned or Programmed Investigations** OSHA has limited resources, and its budget has been significantly cut in the past. In order to have the largest effect, OSHA began to partner with state health and safety agencies and together direct their attention to those industries with the highest injury rates—industries such as chemical processing, roofing and sheeting metal, meat processing, lumber and wood products, transportation, and warehousing.

The final OSHA priority is *random inspection.* Originally, OSHA inspectors were authorized to enter any work area premises, without notice, to ensure that the workplace was in compliance. In 1978, however, the Supreme Court ruled in **Marshall v. Barlow's, Inc.**[9] that employers are not required to let OSHA inspectors enter the premises unless the inspectors have search warrants. This decision does not destroy OSHA's ability to conduct inspections, but forces inspectors to justify their choice of inspection sites more rigorously. That is, rather than trying to oversee health and safety standards in all of their jurisdictions, OSHA inspectors often find it easier to justify their actions and obtain search warrants if they appear to be pursuing specific problem areas.

Marshall v. Barlow's, Inc.
Supreme Court case that stated an employer could refuse an OSHA inspection unless OSHA had a search warrant to enter the premises.

Attorneys who deal with OSHA suggest that companies cooperate rather than adopt a confrontational stance. Only a small percentage of companies require OSHA inspectors to obtain a warrant. OSHA inspectors are not supposed to be influenced by the warrant requirement when inspecting a business, but it may raise questions. Cooperation focuses on permitting the inspection but only after reaching consensus on the inspection process. That's not to say, however, that the company may keep inspectors from finding violations. If they are found, inspectors can take the necessary action. Finally, attorneys recommend that any information regarding the company's safety program be discussed with the OSHA inspector, emphasizing how the program is communicated to employees and how it is enforced.

Should an employer believe that the fine levied is unjust or too harsh, the law permits the employer to file an appeal. This appeal is reviewed by the Occupational Safety and Health Review Commission, an independent safety and health board. Although this commission's decisions are generally final, employers may still appeal commission decisions through the federal courts.

> Companies should cooperate with OSHA inspections rather than adopt confrontational stance.

OSHA Record Keeping Requirements

Under the OSH Act, employers in industries where a high percentage of accidents and injuries occur must maintain safety and health records. Some organizations such as universities and retail establishments are exempt from record keeping because of the low incidence of injury. It's important to note, however, that organizations exempt from record-keeping requirements must still comply with the law itself; their only exception is the reduction of time spent on maintaining safety records. The basis of record keeping for the OSH Act is the completion of OSHA Form 300 (see Exhibit 13-2). Employers are required to keep these safety records on file for five years. If an organization has multiple sites, a 300 form must be maintained for each site. Exempt organizations may be notified to keep the 300 form and participate in the Survey of Occupational Injuries and Illnesses for a specific year.

What types of accidents or illnesses must be reported to comply with OSHA record-keeping requirements? According to the act, any work-related illness (no matter how insignificant it may appear) must be reported on Form 300. Injuries, on the other hand, are reported only when they require medical treatment (besides first aid) or involve loss of consciousness, restriction of work or motion, or transfer to another job.

Exhibit 13-2
OSHA Form 300

The OSHA Form 300 is a tool for recording and reporting any injuries or illnesses in the workplace.

OSHA's Form 300 (Rev. 01/2004)

Log of Work-Related Injuries and Illnesses

You must record information about every work-related death and about every work-related injury or illness that involves loss of consciousness, restricted work activity or job transfer, days away from work, or medical treatment beyond first aid. You must also record significant work-related injuries and illnesses that are diagnosed by a physician or licensed health care professional. You must also record work-related injuries and illnesses that meet any of the specific recording criteria listed in 29 CFR Part 1904.8 through 1904.12. Feel free to use two lines for a single case if you need to. You must complete an Injury and Illness Incident Report (OSHA Form 301) or equivalent form for each injury or illness recorded on this form. If you're not sure whether a case is recordable, call your local OSHA office for help.

Year 20___

U.S. Department of Labor
Occupational Safety and Health Administration

Form approved OMB no. 1218-0176

Attention: This form contains information relating to employee health and must be used in a manner that protects the confidentiality of employees to the extent possible while the information is being used for occupational safety and health purposes.

Establishment name _____

City _____   State _____

Identify the person			Describe the case			Classify the case							Check the injury column or choose one type of illness:					
(A) Case no.	(B) Employee's name	(C) Job title *(e.g., Welder)*	(D) Date of injury or onset of illness	(E) Where the event occurred *(e.g., Loading dock north end)*	(F) Describe injury or illness, parts of body affected, and object/substance that directly injured or made person ill *(e.g., Second degree burns on right forearm from acetylene torch)*						Enter the number of days the injured or ill worker was:								

CHECK ONLY ONE box for each case based on the most serious outcome for that case:

	Death (G)	Days away from work (H)	Remained at Work		Away from work (K)	On job transfer or restriction (L)	(M)					
			Job transfer or restriction (I)	Other recordable cases (J)			Injury (1)	Skin disorder (2)	Respiratory condition (3)	Poisoning (4)	Hearing loss (5)	All other illnesses (6)

(rows, each with month/day date field and blank lines, followed by checkbox columns G, H, I, J; ___days (K); ___days (L); injury/illness checkboxes 1–6)

month/day   ___ days   ___ days

month/day   ___ days   ___ days

month/day   ___ days   ___ days

month/day   ___ days   ___ days

month/day   ___ days   ___ days

month/day   ___ days   ___ days

month/day   ___ days   ___ days

month/day   ___ days   ___ days

month/day   ___ days   ___ days

month/day   ___ days   ___ days

month/day   ___ days   ___ days

month/day   ___ days   ___ days

month/day   ___ days   ___ days

Page totals ▶

Be sure to transfer these totals to the Summary page (Form 300A) before you post it.

| | Injury (1) | Skin disorder (2) | Respiratory condition (3) | Poisoning (4) | Hearing loss (5) | All other illnesses (6) |

Page ___ of ___

Public reporting burden for this collection of information is estimated to average 14 minutes per response, including time to review the instructions, search and gather the data needed, and complete and review the collection of information. Persons are not required to respond to the collection of information unless it displays a currently valid OMB control number. If you have any comments about these estimates or any other aspects of this data collection, contact: US Department of Labor, OSHA Office of Statistical Analysis, Room N-3644, 200 Constitution Avenue, NW, Washington, DC 20210. Do not send the completed forms to this office.

Exhibit 13-2
Continued

OSHA's Form 300A (Rev. 01/2004)

Summary of Work-Related Injuries and Illnesses

U.S. Department of Labor
Occupational Safety and Health Administration

Year 20___

Form approved OMB no. 1218-0176

All establishments covered by Part 1904 must complete this Summary page, even if no work-related injuries or illnesses occurred during the year. Remember to review the Log to verify that the entries are complete and accurate before completing this summary.

Using the Log, count the individual entries you made for each category. Then write the totals below, making sure you've added the entries from every page of the Log. If you had no cases, write "0."

Employees, former employees, and their representatives have the right to review the OSHA Form 300 in its entirety. They also have limited access to the OSHA Form 301 or its equivalent. See 29 CFR Part 1904.35, in OSHA's recordkeeping rule, for further details on the access provisions for these forms.

Number of Cases

Total number of deaths

(G) _____

Total number of cases with days away from work

(H) _____

Total number of cases with job transfer or restriction

(I) _____

Total number of other recordable cases

(J) _____

Number of Days

Total number of days away from work

(K) _____

Total number of days of job transfer or restriction

(L) _____

Injury and Illness Types

Total number of . . .
(M)

(1) Injuries _____
(2) Skin disorders _____
(3) Respiratory conditions _____

(4) Poisonings _____
(5) Hearing loss _____
(6) All other illnesses _____

Establishment information

Your establishment name _____

Street _____

City _____ State _____ ZIP _____

Industry description (e.g., Manufacture of motor truck trailers)
_____

Standard Industrial Classification (SIC), if known (e.g., 3715)
_ _ _ _

OR

North American Industrial Classification (NAICS), if known (e.g., 336212)
_ _ _ _ _ _

Employment information (If you don't have these figures, see the Worksheet on the back of this page to estimate.)

Annual average number of employees _____

Total hours worked by all employees last year _____

Sign here

Knowingly falsifying this document may result in a fine.

I certify that I have examined this document and that to the best of my knowledge the entries are true, accurate, and complete.

_____   _____
Company executive   Title

(____) _____   _____
Phone   Date

Post this Summary page from February 1 to April 30 of the year following the year covered by the form.

Public reporting burden for this collection of information is estimated to average 50 minutes per response, including time to review the instructions, search and gather the data needed, and complete and review the collection of information. Persons are not required to respond to the collection of information unless it displays a currently valid OMB control number. If you have any comments about these estimates or any other aspects of this data collection, contact: US Department of Labor, OSHA Office of Statistical Analysis, Room N-3644, 200 Constitution Avenue, NW, Washington, DC 20210. Do not send the completed forms to this office.

TIPS FOR SUCCESS

When OSHA Comes to Call

Even the most cautious and conscientious employer occasionally has an employee concern or injury that results in a complaint to OSHA. It isn't the end of the world, and the employer won't be invaded by an army of uncooperative OSHA Officers. There is a clearly outlined procedure that starts even before OSHA inspectors appear. Here's an abbreviated explanation:

Inspection Process

Before your inspection, the OSHA compliance officer becomes familiar with as many relevant facts as possible about the workplace, taking into account such things as the history of the establishment, the nature of the business, and the particular standards that are likely to apply.

Inspector's Credentials

An inspection begins when the OSHA compliance officer arrives at the establishment. He or she displays official credentials and asks to meet an appropriate employer representative.

Opening Conference

The official will initiate an opening conference and explain why the establishment was selected. The compliance officer then explains the purpose of the visit, the scope of the inspection, and the standards that apply. The employer will be given a copy of any employee complaint that may be involved. If the employee has requested anonymity, his or her name will not be revealed. The employer is asked to select an employer representative to accompany the compliance officer during the inspection. An authorized employee representative may also participate.

Inspection Tour

The compliance officer and accompanying representatives proceed through the establishment, inspecting work areas for compliance with OSHA standards. The compliance officer decides where to go and how long to stay. During the tour, the compli-

ance officer may talk to employees, take photos, and take readings of things like decibel levels and air quality.

The compliance officer will inspect records of deaths, injuries, and illnesses, which the employer is required to keep. He or she will check to see that a copy of the illness and injury totals from OSHA forms have been posted and that the OSHA workplace poster (OSHA 2203) is prominently displayed. Where records of employee exposure to toxic substances and harmful physical agents have been required, they also are examined.

The general health and safety of the workplace will also be evaluated as related to specific OSHA standards, or to recognized hazards cited under the General Duty Clause. Depending on the type of industry and the operations involved, these may include: emergency action plan, fire prevention plan, emergency response plan, lockout/tagout program, respirator program, confined space entry program, hazard communication program, etc.

During the course of the inspection, the Compliance Officer will point out to the employer any unsafe or unhealthful working conditions observed. At the same time, he or she will discuss possible corrective action if the employer so desires. An inspection tour may cover part or all of an establishment, even if the inspection resulted from a specific complaint, fatality, or catastrophe.

Closing Conference

After the inspection tour, a closing conference is held between the compliance officer and the employer or the employer representative. The compliance officer will cover all unsafe or unhealthful conditions observed on the inspection and indicate all apparent violations for which a citation may be issued or recommended. The employer is told of appeal rights. The compliance officer does not indicate any proposed penalties. Only the OSHA area director has that authority, and only after having received a full report.[10]

To help employers decide whether an incident should be recorded, OSHA offers a schematic diagram for organizations to follow (see Exhibit 13-3). Using this decision tree, organizational members can decide if, in fact, an event should be recorded. If so, the employer is responsible for recording it under one of three areas on OSHA's Form 300: death; days away from work or remained at work; job transfer or restriction; other recordable cases. It's also necessary to indicate the injury or illness (see Exhibit 13-2). Part of this information is then used to determine an organization's incidence rate. An incidence rate reflects the "number of injuries, illnesses, or (lost) workdays related to a common exposure base rate of 100 full-time workers." OSHA uses this rate to determine which industries and organizations are more susceptible to injury. Let's look at the incidence rate formula and use it in an example.

To determine the incidence rate, the formula $(N/EH) \times 200{,}000$ is used, where

- N is the number of injuries and/or illnesses or lost workdays.
- EH is the total hours worked by all employees during the year.
- 200,000 is the base hour rate equivalent (100 workers $\times$ 40 hours per week $\times$ 50 weeks per year).

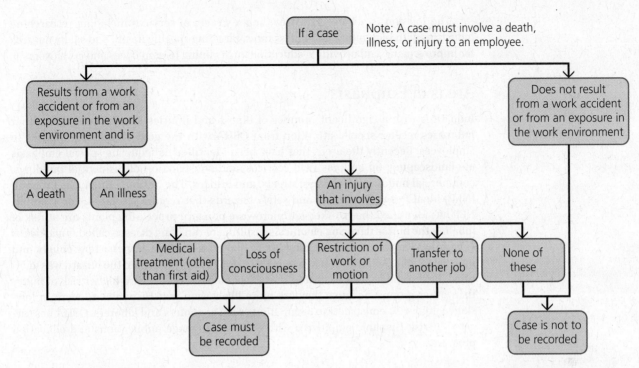

Exhibit 13-3
Determining Recordability of
a Case Under OSHA

This flow chart shows the
decision process used to answer
the question: "Does this illness or
injury need to be recorded?"

incidence rate
Number of injuries, illnesses, or
lost workdays as it relates to a
common base of full-time
employees.

In using the formula and calculating an organization's accident rate, assume we have an organization with 1,800 employees that experienced 195 reported accidents over the past year. We would calculate the **incidence rate** as follows: (195/3,600,000) × 200,000.[11] The incidence rate, then, is 10.8. The significance of 10.8 depends on several factors. If the organization is in the meatpacking plant industry, where the industry average incidence rate is 14.9, the company is doing well. If, however, they are in the amusement and recreation services industry, where the industry incidence rate is 2.2, 10.8 indicates a major concern.[12]

OSHA Punitive Actions

An OSHA inspector has the right to levy a fine against an organization for noncompliance. Levying the fine is more complicated than described here. An organization that fails to bring a red-flagged item into compliance can be assessed a severe penalty. As originally passed in 1970, the maximum penalty was $10,000 per occurrence per day. However, with the Omnibus Budget Reconciliation Act of 1990, that $10,000 penalty can increase to $70,000 if the violation is severe, willful, and repetitive.[13] The agency has increased inspections and has been viewed as taking a tougher stance on workplace health and safety issues. Certain companies have seen what that focus can mean. In 2010, for example, OSHA conducted nearly 41,000 inspections and issued more than 96,000 violations.[14] Fines are not levied for safety violations alone. A company that fails to keep its OSH Act records properly can be subjected to stiff penalties. If an employee death occurs on the job, executives in the company may be criminally liable.

OSHA: A Resource for Employers

Although inspection, regulation enforcement, record keeping, and processes for violations are major areas of emphasis for OSHA, the organization provides many other services to workers and employers. OSHA's mission statement is:

> OSHA's role is to promote the safety and health of America's working men and women by setting and enforcing standards; providing training, outreach, and education; establishing partnerships; and encouraging continual process improvement in workplace safety and health.

The mission is achieved by providing a variety of services including researching industries with high injury and illness rates, targeting specific health and safety hazards for improvement, and providing education and training to employees and employers.

Areas of Emphasis

Industries with a significant number of illness and injuries as compared with other industries receive special attention from OSHA with the goal of reducing injuries to employees. Recently the areas that have been identified as requiring special emphasis are landscaping; oil and gas field services; and construction of residential buildings, commercial buildings, highways, streets, and bridges. The National Emphasis Program (NEP) identifies major health and safety hazards that require attention. For example, NEP has identified that workers at microwave popcorn processing plants are at risk of inhaling the butter flavoring chemicals resulting in rare lung disease called *bronchiolitis obliterans.* Symptoms include progressive shortness of breath, persistent cough, and unusual fatigue. Action was taken quickly to protect workers when the hazard was identified. Research has also indicated that Hispanic workers are at a higher risk of injury than other groups, because they are more likely than non-Hispanics to work in low-skilled, high-risk construction occupations such as roofers and laborers. OSHA has targeted at-risk Hispanic employees with Spanish language publications and education programs.

Education and Training

OSHA's extensive website provides an enormous amount of practical, easy to read and understand information for employees and employers. Regulations are clearly defined and compliance and inspection procedures are explained in simple terms. Education and training are a major emphasis of the OSHA website, and include downloadable forms, templates for forms such as Materials Safety Data Sheets, handbooks for small business, e-mail newsletters, training program information, and interactive online training called "eTools" that covers dozens of occupational safety and health topics. The OSHA site is available in English and Spanish.

While employers provide all the safety equipment required, sometimes accidents happen. In many cases, the cause is human error. As these window washers know, there's little margin of error before an accident happens. *(Source: ©AP/Wide World Photos)*

Assisting Employers in Developing a Safer Workplace

OSHA has made it a priority to work with small businesses in making the regulatory environment a little less intimidating. The language of the OSHA standards is now easier to understand, unnecessary rules have been eliminated, along with thousands of pages of regulations. An effort to reach out to small and entrepreneurial businesses and provide assistance and education includes the development of a four-part program to assist employers in developing a safer workplace. The four-part program includes the following.[15]

Management Commitment and Employee Involvement A first step toward safety is a strong management commitment to providing a safe and healthy workplace. Convincing employers to commit the time, effort, and expense necessary to protect employees should be easy considering the cost saving benefits, including:

- Healthier employees
- Lower worker's compensation costs
- Reduced medical expenses
- Better quality products

- Increased productivity
- Increased morale
- Better labor/management relations

Once management has chosen to lead the way with a strong commitment to safety, it must be demonstrated with clear policies and action. Employee involvement must be developed by including them in identifying safety and health problems. Employee insight and perspective is a valuable resource and their cooperation is necessary. Their safety and goodwill is important to business success. How can a company get them involved? Employers can:[16]

- Develop and post a company worker safety policy near the required OSHA workplace poster (see Exhibit 13-1).
- Hold regular meetings on safety and health with employees.
- Require all management to follow the same safety standards as employees, including wearing hard hats, safety glasses, and footwear.
- Create and post written safety responsibilities for line managers, supervisors, and employees.
- Allow adequate time and resources to determine hazards and correct them.
- Regularly review and evaluate safety initiatives with employees.
- Provide safety incentives including awards, prizes, or cash for workers or work units with excellent safety records.
- Establish safety committees and identify safety representatives representing all levels of employees.

Worksite Analysis Employers hold responsibility for understanding what is necessary to keep workers safe from harm. Employers who lack expertise in determining all possible hazards and relevant standards should consider asking their state or regional OSHA programs for a free and confidential visit. Private safety consultants also offer similar services for a fee.

Self-inspections by managers and employees can provide valuable insight into potential and existing problems and how to prevent them. Employees should be encouraged to report concerns honestly and promptly without fear of reprisals. Records of previous injuries and illness may indicate patterns that help prevent future problems.

Hazard Prevention and Control Worksite analysis may uncover hazards that must be eliminated or controlled. OSHA state offices may provide valuable advice on how to do this, but there are many things employers can do themselves too. For example, once safe work procedures are established, they can provide adequate training so all employees can understand and demonstrate the safe procedures. A company can also make compliance with the procedures more than voluntary. Employees may consider safety equipment or protective clothing to be bulky, hot, or uncomfortable and may need some encouragement to use it. Refusal to use protective clothing or equipment must be taken seriously. The company disciplinary policy should be used by providing warnings and appropriate consequences to employees who do not comply with safety policies. If personal protective equipment (PPE) is necessary, employers need to make sure employees know why it is necessary, when to use it, and how to maintain it. It is important to remember that if safety equipment such as goggles is required, the employer must pay for it.[20]

Companies must maintain equipment regularly to prevent breakdowns and hazardous situations. There needs to be a plan for fires and any natural disasters that an area is likely to experience and drills should be conducted so employees know how to respond quickly. All hazardous materials should be labeled and employees must have access to **material safety data sheets (MSDS)**. Finally, employers should consider

material safety data sheet (MSDS) Employers with hazardous chemicals in the workplace are required to label them clearly and provide material safety data sheets (MSDS). Complete MSDS forms are usually made available by the manufacturer of the chemical product.

(Source: Marko Misic/iStockphoto)

CONTEMPORARY CONNECTION

OSHA's Top Ten Violations

Every year, OSHA complies and reports statistics on the most common workplace safety violations.[17] This list explains the top ten most cited violations for 2011:[18]

1. *Fall protection* OSHA provides employers with standards indicating where fall protection is required for employees working over four feet off the ground in general industry; six feet in construction. The standards include what type of fall protection must be used in given situations. The majority of falls are from ladders and roofs and they are the leading cause of death on the job.

2. *Scaffolding* Employers must protect employees from falls and falling objects when they are using scaffolding more than ten feet off the ground; 72 percent of workers injured in scaffold accidents attributed the accident to either the planking shifting or falling, the employee falling, or being struck by a falling object. Forty-four people were killed in 2010 from scaffold accidents.

3. *Hazard communication* Employers are required to inform employees of the hazards of all chemicals in the workplace. Hazardous chemicals must be labeled and employees must be trained how to handle them. Material safety data sheets (MSDS) that explain the chemicals must be available to all employees.

4. *Respiratory protection* OSHA estimates that five million workers are required to wear respirators in over one million workplaces in the United States. Respirators protect against harmful dust, fog, smoke, gas, vapors, sprays, and environments where oxygen may be insufficient. This prevents cancer, lung disease, and even death.

5. *Control of hazardous energy, lockout/tagout* OSHA standards require that power for equipment and machinery be cut during maintenance and servicing. This prevents situations where an employee servicing the equipment may be injured because another worker turns the power back on by mistake. OSHA estimates

that lockout/tagout (LOTO) procedures protect approximately 3 million workers who work with machinery or equipment.

6. *Electrical wiring* Electricity is a common workplace hazard. Standards protect electricians and construction workers who come into direct contact with electricity as well as workers who come into indirect contact with electricity. That includes nearly everyone.

7. *Powered industrial trucks (PIT)* Powered equipment such as forklifts, motorized hand trucks, and pallet jacks are covered by OSHA standards. Standards cover design, maintenance, operation, and training procedures. Every year, employees are injured because of unsafe operation of powered industrial trucks when they are accidentally driven off loading docks or strike an employee. Property damage is also common.

8. *Ladders* Falls from ladders and scaffolding combined are the biggest cause of occupational injury in the United States. In recent years, deaths from falls have varied from 160 to 809. Employers are required to protect workers who work over dangerous equipment or machinery, regardless of the distance.

9. *Electrical systems* This standard covers requirements for the way electrical systems in the workplace are designed. Workers should be protected from poorly designed electrical systems and workplace electrical hazards. According to the **National Institute for Occupational Safety and Health (NIOSH)**, electrocution is the third leading cause of work-related injury death among 16–17-year-olds. Examples of hazards include coming into contact with power lines while working on roofs, using ladders, operating vehicles with telescoping equipment, and tree trimming.[19]

10. *Machine guarding* Moving machine parts must be covered or protected to prevent injuries like crushed fingers or hands, burns, eye injuries, or accidental amputations.

asking a local doctor or nurse to provide assistance in developing a plan for handling first aid or medical emergencies. Organizations should ask for employees to volunteer as first responders and provide the necessary training if medical assistance isn't quickly accessible.

National Institute for Occupational Safety and Health (NIOSH)
The government agency that researches and sets OSHA standards.

Training for Employees, Supervisors, and Managers Owners and managers need to be sure that employees understand possible workplace hazards and are trained in how to handle them. OSHA state consultants or private safety consultants will be able to recommend and provide relevant training for every business. An employer should attempt to make training memorable by making it interesting and interactive. And they shouldn't forget to provide training to new employees, or employees who are moving to new jobs. Finally, companies need to utilize the OSHA website for information about additional training programs.

Contemporary Health and Safety Issues

Safety is everyone's responsibility and should be part of the organization's culture. Top management must show its commitment to safety by providing resources to purchase safety devices and maintaining equipment. Furthermore, safety should become part of every employee's performance goals. As we mentioned in Chapter 10 on performance evaluations, if something isn't included, there's a tendency to diminish its importance. Employers must always be aware of trends and developments that may produce concerns for the health and safety of employees. Let's examine several topics of current concern to employers.

Workplace Violence

Recent episodes of violence in the workplace, on college campuses, and at schools have made us painfully aware that we cannot take safety for granted. No organization is immune, and the problem appears to be growing.[21] An employee leaves the company's sensitivity training seminar and kills several of his coworkers; an upset purchasing manager stabs his boss because they disagreed over how paperwork was to be completed; a disgruntled significant other enters the workplace and shoots his mate; an employee becomes violent over having his wages garnished—incidents like these make the headlines. Workers in late-night retail establishments and health-care employees are also at a high risk of violence from customers and patients.[22] Consider the following statistics: every year over 500 employees are murdered, and more than 500,000 are victims of violent crimes at work or on duty.[23] Although the rate of workplace violence has been declining since 1993, workers are more likely to be a victim of a violent crime at work than when not at work. In the U.S., full-time workers have a one in four chance of being attacked, threatened, or harassed at work each year.[24] Bartenders, law enforcement officers, and security guards have the highest rates of violence, but it occurs in every industry.

According to OSHA, employees at increased risk of violence are workers who exchange money with the public, make deliveries, work alone or in small groups, work late night or early morning hours, or work in community settings where extensive contact with the public is necessary. This would include health care and social service workers, probation officers, gas and utility employees, phone and cable installers, retail workers, letter carriers, and taxi drivers, to name a few.[25] The issue for employers is how to prevent on-the-job violence and reduce liability should an unfortunate event occur.[26] Because the circumstances of each incident are different, a specific plan of action for companies is difficult to detail. However, we have several suggestions. First, the organization must develop a plan to deal with the issue. This may mean reviewing all corporate policies to ensure that they do not adversely affect employees. In fact, the many cases where violent individuals caused mayhem in an office setting but didn't commit suicide have had one common factor: these employees were treated with neither respect nor dignity.[27] They were laid off without any warning, or they perceived they were being treated too harshly in the discipline process. Sound HRM practices can help to ensure respect and dignity for employees even in the most difficult issues such as terminations. All crisis and emergency plans should be developed with local authorities and reviewed annually.

Organizations must also train their supervisory personnel to identify troubled employees before problems escalate to violence.[28] Employee assistance programs (EAPs) can be designed specifically to help these individuals. Rarely does an individual go from being happy to committing some act of violence overnight. Furthermore, if supervisors are better able to spot the types of demonstrated behaviors that may lead to violence, they can remove those who cannot be helped through an employee assistance program before others are harmed.[29]

> More than 500 employees are murdered and more than 500,000 employees are assaulted on the job each year.

Organizations should also implement stronger security mechanisms.[30] For example, many women killed at work following a domestic dispute die at the hands of someone who didn't belong on company premises. These individuals, as well as weapons—must be kept from entering the facilities altogether.[31]

Sadly, no matter how careful the organization, or what attempts at prevention, workplace violence will occur.[32] In those cases, the organization must be prepared to handle the situation and offer whatever assistance it can to deal with the aftermath.[33]

Indoor Air Quality

Unhealthy work environments are a concern to everyone. If workers cannot function properly at their jobs because of constant headaches, watering eyes, breathing difficulties, or fear of exposure to materials that may cause long-term health problems, productivity will decrease. Work environments that may contain airborne contaminants from office machines, cleaning products, construction activities, carpets and furnishings, perfumes, water-damaged building materials, latex products, air fresheners, microbial growth (fungal, mold and bacterial), insects, and outdoor pollutants are sometimes referred to as **sick buildings**. Other factors such as indoor temperatures, relative humidity, and ventilation levels can also affect how individuals respond to the indoor environment.[34]

sick building
An unhealthy work environment.

Consequently, creating a healthy work environment is not only the right thing to do, it also benefits the employer. Links between extended exposure to asbestos and lung cancer have prompted various federal agencies such as the EPA to require companies to remove asbestos altogether or at least seal it so that it cannot escape into the air. But asbestos is not the only culprit. Germs, fungi, mold, and a variety of synthetic pollutants cause problems, too.[35] Although specific problems and their elimination go beyond the scope of this text, some suggestions for keeping the workplace healthy include:[36]

- Make sure workers have enough fresh air. The cost of providing it is minimal compared with the expense.
- Avoid suspect building materials and furnishings. As a general rule, if it stinks before installation, it will emit an odor afterward. Substitute tacks for smelly carpet glue or natural wood for chemically treated plywood.
- Test new buildings for toxins before occupancy. Failure to do so may lead to health problems. Most consultants say that letting a new building temporarily sit vacant allows the worst fumes to dissipate.
- Provide a smoke-free environment.
- Keep air ducts clean and dry. Water in air ducts is a fertile breeding ground for molds and fungi. Servicing the air ducts periodically can help eliminate growths before they cause harm.
- Pay attention to workers' complaints. Dates and particulars should be recorded by a designated employee. Because employees often are closest to the problems, they are a valuable source of information.

The Smoke-Free Environment

While smoking in public is not banned nationwide, most states have some type of ban on smoking in public in place. The dangers and health problems associated with smoking have been well documented, and they translate into a variety of increased costs for employers and employees. Smokers have significantly higher absentee, injury, accident, and disciplinary rates than nonsmoking employees. Smokers are also more likely to be admitted to a hospital and have longer hospital stays, which increases costs of employer provided healthcare coverage. These costs to employers have been estimated at over $3,000 per smoking employee.[37] A few states provide exceptions for restaurants, bars, and casinos creating concern that hospitality workers in those states are exposed to increased health risks from second hand smoke.[38]

Hospitals, insurance companies, and medical businesses are among the growing number of employers who are not only banning smoking during work hours, but are implementing policies that prevent employees from smoking at all. Federal law does not protect smokers from employment discrimination, but several states have laws that prohibit employers from making employment related decisions based on whether an employee or potential employee is a smoker. Implementation of these policies takes time and may involve incentives such as health tests and screening, smoking cessation classes, assistance from Employee Assistance Programs (EAP), competitions, prizes, fitness center memberships and financial incentives such as reduction in insurance premiums for quitting or increases for failure to quit.[39]

Repetitive Stress Injuries

Whenever workers are subjected to a continuous motion like keyboarding, without proper workstation design (seat and keyboard height adjustments), they run the risk of developing **repetitive stress injuries,** or **musculoskeletal disorders (MSDs)**. These disorders, which account for nearly 40 percent of annual workplace illnesses include headaches, swollen feet, back pain, or nerve damage, cost U.S. companies several billion dollars annually, and account for one-third of all workers' compensation claims.[40] The most frequent site of this disorder is in the wrist, called **carpal tunnel syndrome**.

repetitive stress injuries
Injuries sustained by continuous and repetitive movements of the hand.

musculoskeletal disorders (MSDs)
Continuous-motion disorders caused by repetitive stress injuries.

carpal tunnel syndrome
A repetitive-motion disorder affecting the wrist.

CURRENT CONNECTION

Faith in the Slaughterhouse

Employees at Tyson Foods Pork Processing plant in Perry, Iowa have a friend in Reverend Erasmo Velez. Velez, a Presbyterian minister, is employed by Tyson to provide pastoral care, counseling, and be a good listener to all 1,100 Tyson employees, regardless of religious affiliation. Velez is among a rising number of "Workplace Chaplains" at businesses ranging from a Coca-Cola bottling plant to a Cadillac dealership. Tyson employs chaplains in seven Iowa plants and eighty-one facilities nationally.

There are at least 2,400 chaplains in companies throughout the United States, according to Marketplace Chaplains, an organization that supplies chaplains to businesses that are not large enough to hire one themselves.[47] Velez tries to visit all departments at the huge processing plant regularly, becoming a familiar presence to employees who might not need his guidance and comfort today, but may tomorrow. Issues of concern might include drug and alcohol abuse or family problems such as a worker who was distracted and upset because she was estranged from her grandson. Velez visits workers in the hospital, officiates at weddings and funerals, and discusses everyday life with the workers. "It's nice to have them around," states one employee, who goes on to say, "It's nice to

have the spiritual help if people have a problem and need to talk about it."

Brian Jackson, a supervisor, feels that the chaplains are a good complement to the supervisor employee relationship. "When it's a little too personal for us, they can help team members with their personal problems." Conversations are confidential, but the chaplains must go to the company if an employee threatens violence, reports discrimination or harassment, or works without proper documentation. The chaplains avoid discussing issues that are covered by union contracts.

Benefits of the workplace chaplain program include a reduction of turnover in high-stress jobs such as the pork processing plant in Perry. Other companies have found that the presence of a chaplaincy program assists in recruiting.[48]

Consider this:
Should HR or management attempt to provide the services that the chaplains provide? How would the chaplain services help with recruiting? What other benefits might the employer see from providing chaplain services?

It affects more than 40,000 U.S. workers and costs companies more than $60 million annually in health-care claims.[41] Given the magnitude of problems associated with MSDs, OSHA issued standards in late 2000 to combat this workplace problem that saved nearly $10 billion from reduced work-related injuries.[42]

One chief means of reducing the potential effects of cumulative trauma disorders for an organization, however, is through the voluntary use of ergonomics.[43] Ergonomics involves fitting the work environment to the individual. Reality tells us that every employee is different in shape, size, height, and so forth. Expecting each worker to adjust to standard office furnishings is just not practical. Instead, recognizing and acting on these differences, ergonomics looks at customizing the work environment until it is not only conducive to productive work but keeps the employee healthy.[44]

When we speak of ergonomics, we are primarily addressing two main areas: the office environment and office furniture.[45] Organizations are reviewing office settings, the work environment, and space utilization in an effort to provide more productive atmospheres. This means that new furniture purchased is designed to reduce back strain and fatigue. Properly designed and fitted office equipment can also help reduce repetitive stress injuries.[46] Furthermore, companies are using colors, rather than traditional white walls, and experimenting with lighting brightness as a means of lessening employee exposure to harmful eyestrain associated with computer monitors.

Stress

stress

A dynamic condition in which an individual confronts an opportunity, constraint, or demand related to a desire and perceives the outcome both uncertain and important.

Stress is a dynamic condition in which an individual confronts an opportunity, constraint, or demand related to what he or she desires, and for which the outcome is perceived as both uncertain and important. Stress can manifest itself in both positive and negative ways. Stress is said to be positive when the situation offers an opportunity for one to gain something; for example, the psyching up an athlete goes through can be stressful but can lead to maximum performance. When constraints or demands are placed on us, however, stress can become negative.[49] Let us explore these two features—constraints and demands.

Constraints are barriers that keep us from doing what we desire. Purchasing a new car may be your desire, but if you cannot afford it, you are constrained from purchasing it. Accordingly, constraints take control of a situation out of your hands. If you cannot afford the car, you cannot buy it. Demands, on the other hand, may cause you to give up something you desire. If you wish to go to a movie with friends on Tuesday night but have a major examination Wednesday, the examination may take precedence. Thus, demands preoccupy your time and force you to shift priorities.

Constraints and demands can lead to potential stress. When coupled with uncertainty about the outcome and its importance, potential stress becomes actual stress. Regardless of the situation, if you remove uncertainty or importance, you remove stress. For instance, you may have been constrained from purchasing the car because of your budget, but if you just won one in a radio-sponsored contest, the uncertainty element is significantly reduced. Furthermore, if you are auditing a class for no grade, the importance of the major examination is essentially nil. Constraints or demands that affect an important event and leave the outcome unknown add pressure—pressure resulting in stress.

It is important to recognize that both good and bad personal factors may cause stress. Of course, when you consider the restructuring and other changes occurring in U.S. organizations, it is little wonder that stress is so rampant in today's companies. According to the Society of Human Resource Management (SHRM) common workplace stressors include:[50]

- Lack of control
- Time/deadline pressure

- Poor relationships
- Excessive travel
- Lack of consultation/communication
- Work overload
- Understaffing
- Organizational change
- Threat of layoff

Stress can lead to decreased productivity, poor work quality, apathy, illness, and increased absenteeism[51] Stressed-out workers adversely affect the work of coworkers and supervisors may provide poor customer service.

As an extreme example of workplace stress, in Japan there is a concept called **karoshi,** which refers to death from overworking—employees who die after working more than 3,000 hours the previous year—18-plus hours each day with nearly every minute scheduled out in specific detail. One in six Japanese employees works more than 3,100 hours annually. Upward of 10,000 individuals die each year from heart attack or stroke, and karoshi is listed as their cause of death.[52]

karoshi
A Japanese term meaning death from overworking.

In Japan, upward of 10,000 individuals die annually from being overworked.

stressor
Something that causes stress in an individual.

Common Causes of Stress

Stress can be caused by factors called **stressors.** Causes of stress can be grouped into two major categories: organizational and personal, as shown in Exhibit 13-4.[53] Both directly affect employees and, ultimately, their jobs.

There is no shortage of stressors within any organization.[54] Pressures to avoid errors or complete tasks in a limited time, a demanding supervisor, and unpleasant coworkers are a few examples. Below, we organize stressors into five categories: task, role, and interpersonal demands; organization structure; and organizational leadership.

Task demands relate to an employee's job. They include the design of the person's job (autonomy, task variety, degree of automation), working conditions, and the physical work layout. Work quotas can put pressure on employees when their outcomes are perceived as excessive.[55] The more interdependence between an employee's tasks and the tasks of others, the more potential stress is present. Autonomy, on the other hand, tends to lessen stress. Jobs where temperatures, noise, or other working conditions are

Personal stress
Personality type
Family matters
Financial problems

+ **→**

Employee stress

Organizational stress
Role ambiguity
Role conflict
Role overload
Technology
Layoffs
Restructuring

Exhibit 13-4
Major Stressors

Sources of stress in an employee's life come from the organization and from personal life. Stress from each source tends to affect performance in the other.

Having a really aggravating day? It appears this employee is, too. After significant staffing cutbacks in the organization, she now does the work once handled by three workers. She still has a job, but the job is often overwhelming, causing stress. *(Source: Sean Locke/iStockphoto)*

dangerous or undesirable can increase anxiety. So, too, can working in an overcrowded room or in a visible location where interruptions are constant.

Role demands relate to pressures placed on an employee as a function of the particular role he or she plays in the organization. **Role conflicts** create expectations that may be hard to reconcile or satisfy. **Role overload** is experienced when the employee is expected to do more than time permits. **Role ambiguity** is created when role expectations are unclear and the employee is unsure what to do.

Interpersonal demands are pressures created by other employees. Lack of social support from colleagues and poor interpersonal relationships can cause considerable stress, especially among employees with a high social need.

Organization structure can increase stress. Excessive rules and an employee's lack of opportunity to participate in decisions that affect him or her are examples of structural variables that might be potential sources of stress.

Organizational leadership represents the supervisory style of the organization's company officials. Some managers create a culture characterized by tension, fear, and anxiety. They establish unrealistic pressures to perform in the short run, impose excessively tight controls, and routinely fire employees who don't measure up. The effects of this style of leadership flow down through the organization to all employees.

Personal factors that can create stress include family issues, personal economic problems, and inherent personality characteristics. Because employees bring their personal problems to work with them, a manager must first understand these personal factors in order to fully understand employee stress. Evidence also indicates that employee personality affects susceptibility to stress. The most commonly used descriptions of these personality traits is called Type A–Type B dichotomy.

Type A behavior is characterized by a chronic sense of time urgency, excessive competitive drive, and difficulty accepting and enjoying leisure time. The opposite of Type A is **Type B behavior**. Type Bs rarely suffer from time urgency or impatience. Until quite recently, it was believed that Type As were more likely to experience stress on and off the job. A closer analysis of the evidence, however, has produced new conclusions.

It has been found that only the hostility and anger associated with Type A behavior is actually associated with the negative effects of stress. And Type Bs are just as susceptible to these same anxiety-producing elements. Managers must recognize that Type A employees are more likely to show symptoms of stress even if organizational and personal stressors are low.

role conflicts
Expectations that are difficult to reconcile or achieve.

role overload
When an employee is expected to do more than time permits.

role ambiguity
When an employee is not sure what work to do.

type A behavior
Personality type characterized by chronic urgency and excessive competitive drive.

Symptoms of Stress

What signs indicate that an employee's stress level might be too high? Stress reveals itself in three general ways: physiological, psychological, and behavioral symptoms.

Most early interest in stress focused on health-related, or physiological concerns. This was attributed to the realization that high stress levels result in changes in metabolism, increased heart and breathing rates, increased blood pressure, headaches, and increased risk of heart attacks. Because detecting many of these requires medical training, their immediate and direct relevance to managers is negligible.

Of greater importance to managers are psychological and behavioral symptoms of stress; those that can be witnessed in the person. The psychological symptoms appear as increased tension and anxiety, boredom, and procrastination, which can all lead to productivity decreases. So, too, can behaviorally related symptoms such as changes in eating habits, increased smoking or substance consumption, rapid speech, or sleep disorders.

CONTEMPORARY CONNECTION

Is "Cyberloafing" Really a Good Thing?

The subject line on an e-mail from a colleague states, "You have to see this!" When you click on the link within the e-mail, you're rewarded with a video of a cat playing the piano. After watching the video you decide to check Facebook for the latest updates before getting back to work.

Does this scenario sound familiar? It's called cyberloafing and depending on who you ask, it's either an expensive waste of employee time or a break in routine that fosters productivity and creativity.

Cyberloafing refers to the act of employees using their organization's Internet access during work hours to surf non–job-related Web sites and to send or receive personal emails. The evidence indicates that cyberloafing is consuming a lot of time among workers who have Internet access. Research suggests that American employees with Internet access spend up to 24 percent of the workday visiting sites unrelated to their job.

If the work itself isn't interesting or creates excessive stress, employees are likely to be motivated to do something else. However, a study entitled "Impact of Cyberloafing on Psychological Engagement" has found that cyberloafing can actually have a beneficial effect on employee concentration, productivity, and creativity. The study compares a few minutes of web surfing to a snack break or a few minutes spent chatting with coworkers.

Workers involved in the study were more productive and focused when allowed short breaks to surf the Internet than coworkers who were not allowed Internet access during breaks.

Not all web surfing is appropriate or beneficial. Employers need to make clear Internet usage policies that define which online activities are appropriate (playing games, checking e-mail, and Facebook) versus those that are not allowed (online porn and gambling).

Employers should strive to make jobs more interesting to employees, provide formal breaks to overcome monotony, and establish clear guidelines so employees know what online behaviors are expected. Many employers are also installing Web monitoring software that blocks illegal and illicit websites. Other benefits of monitoring software include controlling activities such as streaming video that consume company bandwidth and slow down computers for employees that are actually working; keeping tabs on the employees that are wasting excessive time online; and reducing exposure to viruses and malware that lurk on questionable Internet sites.[56]

Consider this:

Is cyberloafing beneficial to your personal situation when you're working or studying?

Reducing Stress

Reducing stress presents a dilemma for managers.[57] Some stress in organizations is absolutely necessary; without it, workers lack drive and incentive. Accordingly, whenever we consider stress reduction, we want to reduce its dysfunctional aspects.

One of the first means of reducing stress is to make sure that employees are properly matched to their jobs—and that they understand the extent of their "authority." Furthermore, letting employees know precisely what is expected of them reduces role conflict and ambiguity. Redesigning jobs can also help ease work overload-related stressors. Employees need input in what affects them: involvement and participation have been found to lessen stress.

Employers must recognize that no matter what they do to eliminate organizational stressors, some employees will still stress out. Employers have little or no control over personal factors. They also face an ethical issue when personal factors cause stress. That is, just how far can one intrude on an employee's personal life? To help deal with this issue, many companies have started employee assistance and wellness programs.[58]

These employer-offered programs are designed to assist employees in financial planning, legal matters, health, fitness, stress, and similar areas where employees are having difficulties.

type B behavior
Personality type characterized by lack of either time urgency or impatience.

A Special Case of Stress: Burnout

Worker **burnout** is costing U.S. industry billions of dollars. Burnout is a multifaceted phenomenon, the byproduct of both personal and organizational variables. It can be defined as a function of three concerns: "chronic emotional stress with (a) emotional

burnout
Chronic and long-term stress.

Organization Characteristics	Perceptions of Organization	Perceptions of Role	Individual Characteristics	Outcomes
Caseload	Leadership	Autonomy	Family/friends	Satisfaction
Formalization	Communication	Job involvement	Support	Turnover
Turnover rate	Staff support	Being supervised	Sex	
Staff size	Peers	Work pressure	Age	
	Clarity	Feedback	Tenure	
	Rules and procedures	Accomplishment	Ego level	
	Innovation	Meaningfulness		
	Administrative support			

Exhibit 13-5
Variables Found to Be Significantly Related to Burnout[61]

Burnout can come from a variety of job and personal issues. HRM professionals need to identify the symptoms and causes of burnout.

and/or physical exhaustion, (b) lowered job productivity, and (c) dehumanizing of jobs."[59] Note that none of the three concerns includes long-term boredom. Boredom, often referred to as burnout, is not the same.

Causes and Symptoms of Burnout The factors contributing to burnout can be identified as follows: organization characteristics, perceptions of the organization, perceptions of role, individual characteristics, and outcomes.[60] Exhibit 13-5 summarizes these variables. Although they can lead to burnout, their presence does not guarantee that burnout will occur. Much of that outcome is contingent on the individual's capability to work under and handle stress. Because of this contingency, stressful conditions result in a two-phased outcome: the first level is the stress itself and the second level is the problems that arise from its manifestation.

Reducing Burnout Recognizing that stress is a fact of life and must be properly channeled, effective organizations establish procedures for reducing these stress levels before workers burn out. Although no clear-cut remedies are available, four techniques are proposed:[62]

1. *Identification* Analyze the incidence, prevalence, and characteristics of burnout in individuals, work groups, subunits, or organizations.

2. *Prevention* Attempt to prevent the burnout process before it begins.

3. *Mediation* Develop procedures for slowing, halting, or reversing the burnout process.

4. *Remediation* Aid or redirect individuals who are already burned out or are rapidly approaching the end stages of this process.

The key point is to first make accurate identification, and then tailor a program to meet that need. The costs associated with burnout lead many companies to implement a full array of programs—including Employee Assistance Programs (EAPs)—to help alleviate the problem. Many of these programs are designed to do two tasks: increase productivity and make the job more pleasant for the worker.

Employee Assistance Programs

employee assistance programs (EAPs)
Specific programs designed to help employees with personal problems.

No matter what kind of organization or industry one works in, employees will occasionally have personal problems. Whether the problem relates to job stress or to legal, marital, financial, or health issues, one commonality exists: if an employee experiences a personal problem, sooner or later it will manifest itself at the workplace in terms of lowered productivity, increased absenteeism, or turnover (behavioral symptoms of stress). To help employees deal with these personal problems, more companies are implementing **employee assistance programs (EAPs).**

A Brief History of EAPs

So far, we have discussed the various aspects of HRM designed to create an environment where an employee can be productive. We emphasized finding the right employees to fit the jobs, training them to do the job, and then giving them a variety of opportunities to excel. All of this takes considerable time and money. Employees need time to become fully productive—a process that requires the company to invest in its people. As with any investment, the company expects an adequate return. Now, how does this relate to EAPs?

Contemporary employee assistance programs (EAPs) are extensions of programs that had their start in U.S. companies in the 1940s.[63] Companies such as DuPont, Standard Oil, and Kodak recognized that some employees were experiencing problems with alcohol. Formal programs were implemented on the company's site to educate these workers about the dangers of alcohol and help them overcome their addiction. The rationale for these programs, which still holds today, is returning a productive employee to the job as swiftly as possible. For example, suppose Robert has been with your company for years. Robert was always a solid performer, but lately you notice his performance declining. The quality of his work is diminishing; he has been late three times in the past five weeks, and rumor has it that Robert has a problem with alcohol. You have every right to discipline Robert according to the organization's discipline process, but discipline alone is unlikely to help, and after a time, you may end up firing him. You'll lose a once-good performer and must fill the position with another—a process that may take eighteen months to finally achieve Robert's productivity level. Instead of firing him, you decide to refer Robert to the organization's EAP. This confidential program works with Robert to determine the cause(s) of his problems and seeks to help him overcome them. He meets frequently at first with the EAP counselor, and after a short period of time, Robert is back on the job—with performance improving.[64] After four months, he is performing at the level prior to when the problem got out of hand. You have a fully productive employee back in four months, as opposed to possibly eighteen months, had you fired and replaced Robert.

> Studies suggest that companies save at least $5 for every dollar spent on EAPs.

EAPs Today

Following their early focus on alcoholic employees, EAPs have ventured into new areas such as smoking cessation programs, adoption counseling, legal assistance, death of a loved one, and child–parent relations.[65] However, one of the most notable areas is the use of EAPs to help control rising health insurance premiums, especially in mental health and substance abuse services.[66]

Organizations do see returns on these investments. U.S. companies spend almost $1 billion each year on EAP programs. Studies suggest that most companies save from $5 to $16 for every EAP dollar spent.[67] That, for most organizations, is a significant return on investment!

No matter how beneficial EAPs may be to an organization, one aspect cannot be taken for granted: employee participation. Employees must see EAPs as worthwhile, and designed to help them deal with personal problems.[68] To accept EAPs, employees need to know about the program and understand its confidential nature.[69] Accordingly, they need extensive information regarding how the EAP works, how they can use its services, and its guaranteed confidentiality. Furthermore, supervisors must be properly trained to recognize changes in employee behaviors and to refer them to the EAP in a confidential manner.[70]

Wellness Programs/Disease Management

Many organizations have implemented **wellness programs**. These programs are varied and may focus on smoking cessation, weight control, stress management, physical fitness, nutrition education, early diagnosis of health problems, prevention and education about life-style related illnesses, violence protection, work-team problem intervention, and other issues.[71] Wellness programs can help cut employer health costs and lower

wellness programs
Organizational programs designed to keep employees healthy.

ETHICAL ISSUES IN HRM

Smokers and the Obese Need Not Apply

Almost every organization in the United States recognizes that it's imperative to have healthy employees. Given the significant cost increases in health insurance coverage for employees (see Chapter 12), employers have looked at a number of ways to reduce these ever-increasing financial burdens. Many have implemented wellness/disease-management programs designed to assist employees in maintaining a healthy life.

Programs such as exercise, diet, blood pressure control, and smoking cessation can be found in nearly all organizations that offer such assistance to employees. But some other organizations are viewing this a bit differently. Rather than assist employees in preventing such difficulties, they are simply deciding to not hire smokers and individuals who are obese because of the increased risk of health issues. As long as obesity is not attributable to a disability (which would be a potential EEO violation), the organization has every right to do so. Only some states protect the rights of smokers in regard to employment and smokers may be charged higher insurance premiums in any state.

Statistics show that the smokers and the obese have greater health problems, which increase the cost of health insurance to the organization. And these costs are not just for health insurance premiums but may also include increases in an organization's life and disability insurance, as well as work-ers' compensation. Whirlpool Corp. suspended thirty-nine smokers for claiming on their benefits enrollment form that they were nonsmokers to avoid a $500 annual tobacco-use surcharge on their health insurance premium. Scott's Miracle Gro prohibits smoking by employees and fires those who fail random tests for nicotine.

Discrimination against the obese is much more subtle than the policies against smokers. Research at the University of Hawaii has found that in the absence of policies against hiring the obese, overweight people are discriminated against in the hiring process because employers are concerned about insurance costs and future health conditions as well as the perception that they may have physical limitations that would limit their ability to do their job.[74] Research seems to indicate that the perceptions may be true. Obesity is costing U.S. corporations more than $13 billion annually and results in more than 50 million lost productive days at work. The obese spend approximately 90 million days in the hospital each year. As such, refusing to hire them is viewed as a cost-cutting matter.[75]

Ethical questions:

What's your feeling on this issue? Should employers be allowed to "discriminate" against smokers and the obese? Why or why not?

---

absenteeism and turnover by preventing health-related problems.[72] Healthcare products company, Johnson and Johnson, reported that their employee healthcare costs dropped from $13 million to $4.5 million after they created a wellness program that included screening for high cholesterol, high blood pressure, diabetes, cancer cardiovascular disease, and other conditions. The program also included seminars on stress management and other health issues.[73]

It is interesting to note that similar to EAPs, wellness programs work only when employees see value in them. This requires top management support—resources and personal use of the programs—or the wrong message may be sent to employees. Second, wellness programs need to serve the family as well as the employees themselves. This not only provides an atmosphere where families can get healthy together, it also reduces possible medical costs for dependents. And finally comes the issue of employee input. Even the best programs, if designed without considering employees' needs, may fail. Organizations need to invite participation by asking employees what they'd use if available. Although many organization members know that exercise is beneficial, few companies initially addressed how to involve employees. But after finding out that employees would like on-site workout facilities or exercise classes, many organizations began appropriate program development.

As wellness programs continue to expand in corporate America, top management support is still intermittent but increasing. Why? Because in finding out how to involve senior executives it was discovered that they, too, wanted a place to go for exercise. Many of these executives receive membership in health clubs as perks. Whether executives or support staff participate in wellness programs or EAPs, U.S. organizations appear to be continuing their efforts to support a healthy work environment. The companies reap a good return on their investments, and programs such as EAP and wellness have proven to be win–win opportunities for all involved.[76]

Anyone who travels outside the United States should visit the U.S. State Department's Travel and Living Abroad website. This site provides such valuable information as "Emergencies and Warnings, Living Abroad," and other helpful links that can assist in preparing for foreign travel. *(Source: Image from http://www. state.gov/travel/)*

International Safety and Health

It is important to know the safety and health environments of each country in which an organization operates. Generally, corporations in Western Europe, Canada, Japan, and the United States put great emphasis on the health and welfare of their employees. However, most businesses in less-developed countries have limited resources and thus cannot establish awareness or protection programs.

Most countries have laws and regulatory agencies that protect workers from hazardous work environments. It is important for American firms to learn the often complex regulations that exist, as well as cultural expectations of the local labor force. Manufacturers, in particular, where a myriad of potentially hazardous situations exist, must design and establish facilities that meet the expectations of the local employees, not necessarily those of Americans.

International Health Issues

Corporations preparing to send executives on overseas assignments should have a few basic health-related items on every checklist:

- *Up-to-date vaccinations* against infectious diseases such as cholera, typhoid, and smallpox. Each country has its own vaccination requirements for entry. In addition, the U.S. Department of State Traveler Advisories hotline provides alerts to specific problems with diseases or regions within a country. The Center for Disease Control (CDC) website also contains vaccination information for destinations worldwide.
- *A general first-aid kit* This should include all over-the-counter medications such as aspirin and cold and cough remedies that the employee or family members would usually take at home, but that might not be available at the overseas drugstore. In addition, any prescription drugs should be packed in twice the quantity expected to be used, and should never be packed entirely in checked luggage in case it gets lost. It also is advisable to know the generic name—not the U.S. trade name—of any pharmaceutical. Finally, special items such as disinfectant solutions to treat fresh fruit or vegetables and water-purifying tablets should be included as the sanitation system of the host country warrants.
- *Emergency plans* Employees should contact their health insurance provider for procedures and coverage if they become injured or ill while traveling. Contact

information for the U.S. embassy or consulate and any contact information an employee's health insurance provider may require should be gathered ahead of time. Additional travel insurance that will provide emergency transportation back to the United States if desired should be purchased. On arrival at the foreign destination, employees should check out the local medical and dental facilities and what care can be expected in the host country. This might include evacuation of a sick or injured employee or family member to another city or even another country. For example, expatriates in China often prefer to go to Hong Kong even for regular medical checkups. It is always wise to take along copies of all family members' medical and dental records.

International Safety Issues

Safety for the employee has become increasingly an issue of security, both while traveling and after arrival. Again, the U.S. State Department provides travel alerts and cautions on its web page.

Safety precautions, however, begin before the overseas journey. The goal is to blend into the crowd as much as possible. Many corporations offer the following advice for traveling executives: blending in includes wearing low-key, appropriate clothing, not carrying expensive luggage, avoiding luggage tags with titles such as "vice president," and, if possible, traveling in small groups. On arrival at the airport, it is advisable to check in at the airline's ticket counter immediately and go through security checkpoints to wait in the less public gate area.

Once the expatriate family has landed, the goal remains to blend in. These individuals must acquire some local "savvy" as quickly as possible; in addition to learning the language, they also must adapt to local customs and try to dress in the same style as the local people.

Foremost on many individuals' minds when they go abroad is security. Organizations that have executives in dangerous areas of the world often provide electronic security systems for home and office, as well as bodyguards or armed chauffeurs, but individual alertness is the key factor. Kidnappers often seek potential targets who are valuable to either a government or corporation, with lots of family money or a wealthy sponsor, and they look for an easy opportunity to plan and execute the kidnapping. This last criterion makes it important to avoid set routines for local travel and other behaviors. The employee should take different routes between home and office, and the children should vary their paths to school. The family food shopping should be done at varying times each day or in different markets, if possible. These and other precautions, as well as a constant awareness of one's surroundings, are important for every family member.

Summary

(This summary relates to the Learning Outcomes identified on page 330.) After having read this chapter you can:

1. **Discuss the organizational effect of the Occupational Safety and Health Act.** The Occupational Safety and Health Act (OSH Act) outlines comprehensive and specific safety and health standards.

2. **List Occupational Safety and Health Administration (OSHA) enforcement priorities.** OSHA has an established five-step priority enforcement process consisting of imminent danger, serious accidents, employee complaints, inspection of targeted industries, and random inspections.

3. **Explain what punitive actions OSHA can impose on an organization.** OSHA can fine an organization up to a maximum penalty of $70,000 if the violation is severe, willful, and repetitive. For violations not meeting those criteria, the maximum fine is $7,000. OSHA may, at its discretion, seek criminal or civil charges against an organization's management if they willfully violate health and safety regulations.

4. **Describe what companies must do to comply with OSHA record-keeping requirements.** Companies in selected industries must complete OSHA Form 300 to record job-related accidents, injuries, and illnesses. This information is used to calculate the organization's incidence rate.

5. **Identify ways that OSHA assists employers in creating a safer workplace.** OSHA helps employers through education, training programs, and developing a four-part program for businesses that includes: developing management commitment and employee involvement, worksite analysis to identify problems, hazard prevention and control, and training for employees, supervisors, and managers.

6. **Describe the most cited OSHA safety violations.** The ten most cited safety violations include: scaffolding, fall protection, hazard communication, control of hazardous energy, respiratory protection, electrical wiring, powered industrial trucks, ladders, machine guarding, and electrical systems.

7. **Explain what companies can do to prevent workplace violence.** A company can help prevent workplace violence by ensuring that its policies are not adversely affecting employees, by developing a plan to deal with the issue, and by training its managers in identifying troubled employees.

8. **Define stress and the causes of burnout.** Stress is a dynamic condition in which an individual is confronted with an opportunity, constraint, or demand for which the outcome appears important and uncertain. Burnout is caused by a combination of emotional and/or physical exhaustion, lower job productivity, or dehumanizing jobs.

9. **Explain how an organization can create a healthy work site.** Creating a healthy work site involves removing any harmful substance, such as asbestos, germs, mold, fungi, cigarette smoke, and so forth, thus limiting employee exposure.

10. **Describe the purposes of employee assistance and wellness programs.** Employee assistance and wellness programs offer employees a variety of services to support mental and physical health, which in turn helps contain organization health-care costs.

Demonstrating Comprehension

QUESTIONS FOR REVIEW

1. What are the objectives of the Occupational Safety and Health Act?
2. Describe the priorities of OSHA investigations.
3. Identify three methods of preventing accidents.
4. How are incidence rates calculated? What do the results indicate?
5. What is stress? How can it be positive?
6. Differentiate between physiological, psychological, and behavioral stress symptoms.
7. What can organizations do to help prevent workplace violence?
8. Describe how EAPs and wellness programs help an organization control rising medical costs.
9. What must an organization do differently with respect to health and safety when operating in another country?

Key Terms

burnout
carpal tunnel syndrome
employee assistance programs (EAPs)
General Duty Clause
imminent danger
incidence rate
karoshi
Marshall v. Barlow's, Inc.

material safety data sheet (MSDS)
musculoskeletal disorders (MSDs)
National Institute for Occupational
   Safety and Health (NIOSH)
repetitive stress injuries
role ambiguity
role conflicts
role overload

sick building
stress
stressor
Type A behavior
Type B behavior
wellness program

HRM Workshop

Linking Concepts to Practice   DISCUSSION QUESTIONS

1. "Safety and health practices are good business decisions." Build an argument supporting this statement.
2. "OSHA inspections can become a cat-and-mouse maneuvering activity for organizations. This doesn't serve the interest of the organization, the employees, or OSHA." Do you agree or disagree? Explain your response.
3. "Employers should be concerned with helping employees cope with both job-related stress and off-the-job stress." Do you agree or disagree? Discuss.
4. "Supervisors should know which employees are having troubles and may ultimately cause harm to other employees.

When they identify such an individual, they should take some action to ensure that the employee receives assistance before a disaster strikes." Build an argument supporting this statement and one that does not.
5. Some medical experts believe that regular daily exercise results in better health, improved conditioning, and greater tolerance of stressful situations. What would you think about being employed by a company that required you to work out daily on company time? Do you think this would help or hurt the company's recruiting ability? Explain your position.

Making A Difference   SERVICE LEARNING PROJECTS

Safety and health are often taken for granted until they are gone. Look for ways to help people in need.

- Contact your local chapter of the Red Cross about ways you can help with their local activities or with disaster relief. You may be able to make and serve meals for local homeless or put "comfort kits" together for people who have experienced recent disasters.

- If you're a little handy, contact a local organization such as Rebuilding Together that assists the elderly or disabled with

winterizing their homes or projects that make their homes safer by installing hand rails on stairs or window locks.

As you put your service learning experience together, keep a journal of your activities, the time you spend, contact information for people you work with, and your thoughts about the process. When you're finished, make a presentation to your class about the experience and what you learned. What concepts from Chapter 13 were you able to apply?

Developing Diagnostic and Analytical Skills

Case Application 13: PROTECTION OSHA-STYLE

Some employers cringe at the thought of OSHA regulations and inspections. These organizations often feel that the regulations are costly to follow, require them to implement practices or procedures that are not needed, and are just plain restrictive. OSHA, on the other hand, sees this differently. If by their actions they can prevent workplace injury or death, then OSHA inspectors feel these inconveniences are worth it. Consider the following:[77]

- OSHA compliance officers from the El Paso, Texas, District Office made two employees who were working eighty feet above ground stop working until a fall protection system was installed. The workers and the company complied with the request.
- A construction worker at National Riggers and Erectors is glad such fall protection systems exist. Working in Green Bay, Wisconsin, on the renovation to the Green Bay Packers' football stadium, this worker slipped off a beam while working some six stories above the ground. Through the use of his fall protection gear, he was rescued unharmed and was able to return to work. Not sixty days later, this same system protected a second fall victim at the stadium. Both of these workers undoubtedly would have died from the fall without such protection.
- Two window washers were left dangling high above the ground after their scaffolding broke. Again their safety equipment

prevented them from a certain death—dangling them high above the ground while they awaited rescue.
- Several workers were ordered off a deteriorating floor at a demolition site in Chicago. The inspector noticed the flooring was not stable while workers worked to dismantle part of the floor overhead. Within hours of having the workers removed, the overhead floor caved in—right at the spot where the workers previously stood.
- An OSHA inspector ordered a worker out of a trench that had no shoring or protection from the side walls caving in. Barely thirty seconds after the worker left the trench, it collapsed. Had this worker not followed the inspector's order to get out, he surely would have been seriously injured or killed.

Such stories—some successful and others tragic—occur every day. Unfortunately, headlines are not typically made unless there is a disaster. For OSHA, the success stories are what employee safety is all about—preventing the death or serious injury of all employees!

Questions:

1. What roles do OSHA inspections play in preserving safe and healthy work environments? Discuss.
2. "OSHA shouldn't have to inspect every worksite. Employers should act as their own safety inspectors and take action that

is warranted." Build an argument supporting this statement, and one opposing this statement.

3. Had any of the five events listed above led to serious injury or death, do you believe the employer was liable? Why or why not? If you believe the employer is liable, do you believe any of these could be construed as willful and severe? Defend your position.

Working with a Team   HEALTH AND SAFETY

Your team may wish to role-play this case for the class and then discuss what the supervisor in the scenario should do and how he should respond.

Joaquin has been a machinist for Linco Tool and Die, a manufacturer of engine parts for large motors, for sixteen years. Lately, more of Joaquin parts have been rejected for errors; he seems preoccupied with outside matters—leaving early, asking to take off days beyond sick days allowed. He has missed three work days in two weeks, and Jonas, his supervisor, wondered if he smelled alcohol on his breath after lunch yesterday. Jonas hasn't said anything yet; he doesn't want to invade Joaquin's privacy. He thinks Joaquin, who in the past has been cooperative, positive, highly productive, and rarely sick or absent, may just be going through a tough time. Besides, the past month has been difficult because a major shipment required overtime and all machinists have been asked to work eighty to ninety-five hours a week until the shipment is complete.

At lunch, Jonas overhears an argument between Joaquin and a coworker, Elizabeth, each blaming the other for a part being rejected by quality assurance. Joaquin tells Elizabeth to "stay out of his way and his area," and that "the next time they'll settle it outside," poking her in the chest with his finger. Joaquin then slams a $1,250 gauge down on the floor, shouts profanities, and adds, "I don't care if the part falls off or if this place burns to the ground, anymore; I've about had all I can take of you and this place! You know my wife left me for my best friend last week, left me with a two-year-old to raise by myself, and my other kid got expelled for possession. It just doesn't much matter to me what you think, so I'd leave me alone if I were you!" Jonas heads for the human resource office, unsure of how to proceed.

Here are some questions to guide you:

1. What should Jonas do?
2. What advice would you, as the human resource manager, give Jonas?
3. How should Jonas respond to the immediate situation?
4. How can you apply the assessment questions regarding violence to help Jonas and other supervisors handle future situations more effectively?

Learning an HRM Skill   DEVELOPING SAFETY SKILLS

About the skill: Here are several steps we recommend for developing an organization's safety and health program. Whether or not such programs are chiefly the responsibility of one individual, every supervisor must work to ensure that the work environment is safe for all employees.

1. *Involve management and employees in developing a safety and health plan.* If neither group can see the usefulness and the benefit of such a plan, even the best plan will fail.

2. *Hold someone accountable for implementing the plan.* Plans do not work by themselves. They need someone to champion the cause. This person must have the resources to put the plan in place and also must be accountable for what it's intended to accomplish.

3. *Determine the safety and health requirements for your work site.* Just as each individual is different, so is each workplace. Understanding the specific needs of the facility will aid in determining what safety and health requirement will be necessary.

4. *Assess workplace hazards in the facility. Identify potential health and safety problems on the job.* Understanding what exists helps you determine preventive measures.

5. *Correct hazards that exist.* Fix or eliminate hazards identified in the investigation. This may mean decreasing the effect of the hazard or controlling it through other means (for example, protective clothing).

6. *Train employees in safety and health techniques.* Make safety and health training mandatory for all employees. Employees should be instructed in how to do their jobs in the safest manner and understand that any protective equipment provided must be used.

7. *Develop the employee mindset that the organization is to be kept hazard-free.* Often employees are the first to witness problems. Establish a means for them to report their findings, including having emergency procedures in place, if necessary. Ensuring that preventive maintenance of equipment follows a recommended schedule can also prevent breakdown of equipment from becoming a hazard.

8. *Continuously update and refine the safety and health program.* Once the program has been implemented, it must continuously be evaluated and necessary changes made. Documenting program progress is necessary for this analysis.

Enhancing Your Communication Skills

1. Visit OSHA's website (www.osha.gov). Locate a news release on an OSHA activity. Provide a two- to three-page summary of the news release, focusing on what OSHA is intending to do, the effect on workers, and the effect on employers.

2. Develop a two- to three-page argument on why sick buildings should be "cured" immediately. Support your position with appropriate documentation.

3. Search YouTube at www.youtube.com for a 2–5 minute video about employee assistance programs and the services provided. Prepare a presentation to your class including the content of the video.

4. Research contemporary employee health and safety issues such as: lack of sleep, bullying in the workplace, workplace spirituality, or another topic of personal interest. Present your research to your class with a 10–15 minute multimedia presentation.

(Source: Barbara Rodriguez/©AP/Wide World Photos)

LEARNING OUTCOMES

After reading this chapter, you will be able to

1. Define the term *union*.

2. Discuss what effect the Wagner and the Taft-Hartley Acts had on labor-management relations.

3. Identify the significance of Executive Orders 10988 and 11491 and the Civil Service Reform Act of 1978.

4. Describe the union-organizing process.

5. Describe the components of collective bargaining.

6. Identify the steps in the collective-bargaining process.

7. Explain the various types of union security arrangements.

8. Describe the role of a grievance procedure in collective bargaining.

9. Identify the various impasse-resolution techniques.

10. Discuss how sunshine laws affect public-sector collective bargaining.

Understanding Labor Relations and Collective Bargaining

14

Support for unionized labor has been divided by political party lines for decades with pro-labor, pro-regulation Democrats more likely to agree with union initiatives, while pro-business, anti-regulation Republicans less likely to support unions and their goals.

This was clear in Wisconsin when Republican Governor Scott Walker went to war with public employee unions in an effort to reduce rights to collective bargaining. Negotiations grew tense as hundreds of protesters filled the Wisconsin capitol building and fourteen Democratic legislators fled the state and went into hiding in an effort to stall the process and prevent the legislation from passing.

Republican legislators eventually found a way to pass the legislation in the Democrats' absence, but protests by students and other citizens continued for months.

Much of the recent criticism of unions has been leveled at public-sector unions who represent federal, state and city and university and public school employees, including teachers. During the recession, public-sector unions were the focus of criticism by many who hold them partly responsible for state and city budget problems.

Others have criticized the relatively generous benefits packages received by many public employees compared with private sector employees. Many private-sector employees have seen reductions in benefits or been required to contribute more toward the cost of benefits. This has led to calls for reduction in public-sector salaries, benefits or restricting collective bargaining rights.

Public-sector employees are one of organized labor's last areas of strength. Union membership has declined in every other area of employment, reducing their clout and visibility. Recent labor disputes in the NFL and NBA have been perceived as frivolous disputes between millionaires which has further reduced sympathy for unions and their goals. The message that unions fought for decades to guarantee the rights of all workers seems to be lost.

Of the 17 percent of American households that have at least one member who belongs to a union, the approval rate of organized labor is 78 percent, while only 48 percent of households with no union members approve.[1] Another poll by Pew Research Center found that although unions struggle for approval, a majority of Americans feel that they are responsible for higher salaries and fairer work rules for everyone.[2]

Although popularity is decreasing, 61 percent of Americans oppose legislation that eliminates collective bargaining rights for public unions. We may not totally agree with unions, but we don't want them to disappear either.

Looking Ahead

What do you think about unions and their goals? How do your personal politics or past experiences influence your position? Does the good they do outweigh the inconvenience of conflicts that may arise?

Introduction

union

Organization of workers, acting collectively, seeking to protect and promote their mutual interests through collective bargaining.

A **union** is an organization of workers, acting collectively, seeking to promote and protect its mutual interests through collective bargaining. However, before we can examine the activities surrounding the collective bargaining process, it is important to understand the laws that govern the labor-management relationship, what unions are, and how employees unionize. Although just under 12 percent[3] of the private sector workforce is unionized, the successes and failures of organized labor's activities affect most segments of the workforce in two important ways.[4] First, major industries in the United States—such as automobile manufacturing, communications, construction, as well as all branches of transportation—are unionized, and so unions have a major effect on important sectors of the economy (see Exhibit 14-1). Second, gains made by unions often spill over into other, nonunionized sectors of the economy.[5] So, the wages, hours, and working conditions of nonunion employees at a Linden, New Jersey, lumberyard may be affected by collective bargaining between the United Auto Workers and General Motors at one of the latter's North American assembly plants.

For many managers, HRM practices in a unionized organization consist chiefly of following procedures and policies laid out in the labor contract. This labor contract, agreed to by both management and the labor union, stipulates, in part, the wage rate, hours of work, and terms and conditions of employment for those covered by the negotiated agreement. Decisions about how to select and compensate employees, employee benefits offered, procedures for overtime, and so forth are no longer the sole decision of management for jobs that fall under the unions' jurisdiction. Such decisions are generally made when the labor contract is negotiated.

The concept of labor relations and the collective-bargaining process may have different meanings to different individuals depending on their experience, background, and so on. We can examine these areas by understanding both the laws that underpin labor-management relationships and why people join unions.

Exhibit 14-1

Union Membership by Industry Classification (Selected)[6]

The percentage of employees represented by a union varies by industry, as this chart indicates. Government and transportation workers tend to be the most likely to belong to a union.

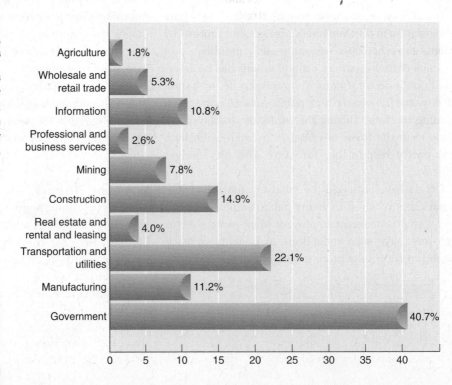

Why Employees Join Unions

Individuals join unions for reasons as diverse as the people themselves. Just what are they seeking to gain when they join a union? The answer to this question varies—perhaps it is a family history of union membership[7] or an attractive union contract—but the following captures the most common reasons.

Higher Wages and Benefits

The power and strength of numbers sometimes help unions obtain higher wages and benefit packages for their members than employees can negotiate individually. One or two employees walking off the job over a wage dispute is unlikely to significantly affect most businesses, but hundreds of workers going out on strike can temporarily disrupt or even close down a company. Additionally, professional bargainers employed by the union may negotiate more skillfully than any individual could on his or her own behalf. The AFL-CIO, a federation of over fifty labor unions, estimates that employees in unions earn 30 percent more than workers in comparable jobs who do not belong to unions. Union members are also 50 percent more likely to have health insurance benefits or paid personal leave and nearly 300 percent more likely to have a defined-benefit pension plan.[8]

Greater Job Security

Unions provide their members with a sense of independence from management's power to arbitrarily hire, promote, or fire. The collective-bargaining contract will stipulate rules that apply to all members, thus providing fairer and more uniform treatment.

Influence Over Work Rules

Where a union exists, workers can help determine the conditions under which they work and have an effective channel through which they can protest conditions they believe are unfair. Therefore, a union not only represents the worker but also provides rules that define channels in which worker complaints and concerns can be registered. Grievance procedures and rights to third-party arbitration of disputes are examples of practices typically defined and regulated as a result of union efforts.

Compulsory Membership

Many labor agreements contain statements commonly referred to as **union security arrangements**. When one considers the importance of security arrangements to unions—importance related to numbers and guaranteed income—it is no wonder that such emphasis is placed on achieving a union security arrangement that best suits their goals. Such arrangements range from compulsory union membership to giving employees the freedom in choosing to join the union.[9] The various types of union security arrangements—the union shop, the agency shop, and the right-to-work shop, as well as some special provisions under the realm of union security arrangements are explained below.

union security arrangements
Labor contract provisions designed to attract and retain dues-paying union members.

The most powerful relationship legally available to a union is a **union shop**. This arrangement stipulates that employers, while free to hire whomever they choose, may retain only union members. That is, all employees hired into positions covered under the terms of a collective-bargaining agreement must, after a specified probationary period of typically thirty to sixty days, join the union or forfeit their jobs.[10]

union shop
Any nonunion workers must become dues-paying members within a prescribed period of time.

Right to work laws exist in twenty-two states prohibiting agreements that require employees to join a union as a condition of employment (see Exhibit 14-2). Employees in right to work states are guaranteed the right to decide for themselves whether they want

right to work laws
Prohibit union membership as a condition of employment.

Right to work state

Forced-unionism state

Exhibit 14-2
States with Right to Work Laws

This map illustrates the twenty-two states with right to work laws that guarantee employees the right to choose whether to join a union or not. (*Source:* National Right to Work Committee, http://www.nrtwc.org.)

agency shop
A union security arrangement whereby employees must pay union dues to the certified bargaining unit even if they choose not to join the union.

open shop
Employees are free to join the union or not, and those who decline need not pay union dues.

maintenance of membership
Requires an individual who chooses to join a union to remain in the union for the duration of the existing contract.

dues check-off
Employer withholding of union dues from union members' paychecks.

to support the union financially. These states are often targets of unions who would like to see the laws changed to provide a more supportive environment for unions. The National Right to Work Committee provides support for those who oppose compulsory union membership.

An agreement that requires nonunion employees to pay the union a sum of money equal to union fees and dues as a condition of continuing employment is referred to as an **agency shop**. This arrangement was designed as a compromise between the union's desire to eliminate the "free rider" and management's desire to make union membership voluntary. In such a case, if for whatever reason workers decide not to join the union (for example religious beliefs and values), they still must pay dues. Because workers will receive benefits negotiated by the union, they must pay their fair share. However, a 1988 Supreme Court ruling upheld nonunion members' claims that although in an agency shop they are forced to pay union dues, those monies must be specifically used for collective-bargaining purposes only—not for political lobbying.

The least desirable form of union security from a union perspective is the **open shop,** in which joining a union is totally voluntary. Those who do not join are not required to pay union dues or any associated fees. Workers who do join, typically have a **maintenance-of-membership** clause in the existing contract that dictates certain provisions. Specifically, a maintenance-of-membership agreement states that employees who join the union are compelled to remain in the union for the duration of the existing contract. When the contract expires, most such agreements provide an escape clause—a short interval of time, usually ten days to two weeks—in which employees may choose to withdraw their membership from the union without penalty.

A provision that often exists in union security arrangements is a **dues check-off,** which occurs when the employer withholds union dues from members' paychecks. Similar to other pay withholdings, the employer collects the dues money and sends it to the union. Employers provide this service, and the union permits them to do so for several reasons. Collecting dues takes time, so a dues check-off frees the union from collecting dues or setting up automatic withdrawals from members' checking accounts. Furthermore, recognizing that union dues are the primary source of union income, knowledge of how much money is in the union treasury can clue management into whether a union is financially strong enough to endure a strike. Employers wishing to weaken a union's finances have eliminated the dues check-off, forcing union representatives to collect dues themselves.

Dissatisfaction with Management

Employees who are leading the movement to certify unions in businesses like Walmart rally employees that are dissatisfied with the actions of managers. If employees are upset with company policies for benefits, promotions, the way their supervisor handles problems, or the discipline of a coworker, they are likely to seek help from a union. In fact, it is reasonable to believe that when employees vote to unionize, it's often a vote against management or their immediate supervisor rather than a vote in support of a particular union.[11]

Labor Legislation

The legal framework for labor-management relationships has played a crucial role in its development. Rather than present the detailed history and development of labor law, our discussion will focus on two important laws that have shaped much of the labor relations process. We'll then briefly summarize other laws that have helped shape labor-management activities.

The Wagner Act

The National Labor Relations Act of 1935, commonly referred to as the **Wagner Act**, is the basic bill of rights for unions. This law guarantees workers the right to organize and join unions, bargain collectively, strike, and pursue activities that support their objectives. In terms of labor relations, the Wagner Act specifically requires employers to bargain in good faith over mandatory bargaining issues—wages, hours, and terms and conditions of employment.

The Wagner Act is cited as shifting the balance of power to favor unions for the first time in U.S. labor history. This was achieved in part through the establishment of the **National Labor Relations Board (NLRB)**. This administrative body, consisting of five members appointed by the president of the United States, was given the responsibility for determining appropriate bargaining units, conducting elections to determine union representation, and preventing or correcting employer actions that can lead to unfair labor practice charges. The NLRB, however, has only remedial, and not punitive, powers.

Unfair labor practices are defined in Section 8 of the act and include any employer tactics that:

- Interfere with, restrain, or coerce employees in the exercise of rights to join unions and to bargain collectively
- Dominate or interfere with the formation or administration of any labor organization or discriminate against anyone because of union activity
- Discharge or otherwise discriminate against any employee because he or she filed or gave testimony under the act
- Refuse to bargain collectively with the representatives chosen by the employees

The Wagner Act provided the legal recognition of unions as legitimate interest groups in American society, but many employers opposed its purposes. Some employers, too, failed to live up to the requirements of its provisions. That's because

Wagner Act
Also known as the National Labor Relations Act of 1935, this act gave employees the right to form and join unions and to engage in collective bargaining.

National Labor Relations Board (NLRB)
Established to administer and interpret the Wagner Act, the NLRB has primary responsibility for conducting union representation elections.

employers recognized that the Wagner Act didn't protect them from unfair union labor practices such as holding "wildcat strikes," which involve striking against the employer even though a valid contract is in effect. The belief that the balance of power had swung too far to labor's side, and the public outcry stemming from post-World War II strikes, led to passage of the Taft-Hartley Act (Labor-Management Relations Act) in 1947.

The Taft-Hartley Act

Taft-Hartley Act
Amended the Wagner Act by addressing employers' concerns in terms of specifying unfair union labor practices.

The major purpose of the **Taft-Hartley Act** was to amend the Wagner Act by addressing employers' concerns in terms of specifying unfair union labor practices. Under Section 8(b), Taft-Hartley states that it is an unfair labor practice for unions to:

- Restrain or coerce employees in joining the union or coerce the employer in selecting bargaining or grievance representatives
- Discriminate against an employee to whom union membership has been denied or to cause an employer to discriminate against an employee
- Refuse to bargain collectively
- Engage in strikes and boycotts for purposes deemed illegal by the act
- Charge excessive or discriminatory fees or dues under union shop contracts
- Obtain compensation for services not performed or not to be performed

The Taft-Hartley Act also made closed shop arrangements illegal. Prior to passage of the act, the closed shop dominated labor contracts. In closed shops a union controlled the source of labor. Under this arrangement, an individual would join the union, be trained by the union, and was sent to work for an employer by the union. In essence, the union acted as the clearinghouse of employees. When an employer needed employees—for whatever duration—the employer would contact the union and request that these employees start work. When the job was completed, and the employer no longer needed the employees, they were sent back to the union. By declaring the closed shop illegal, Taft-Hartley began to shift the pendulum of power away from unions. Furthermore, in doing so, the act enabled states to enact laws that would further reduce compulsory union membership.

Taft-Hartley also included provisions that prohibited secondary boycotts and gave the president of the United States the power to issue an eighty-day cooling-off period when labor–management disputes affect national security. President Bush used this provision in 2002 during the International Longshore and Warehouse Union and the Pacific Maritime Association's labor dispute—the first time the injunction had been used in about twenty-five years.[12] A secondary boycott occurs when a union strikes against Employer A (a primary and legal strike) and then strikes and pickets against Employer B (an employer against which the union has no complaint) because of a relationship that exists between Employers A and B, such as Employer B handling goods made by Employer A. Taft-Hartley also set forth procedures for workers to decertify, or vote out, their union representatives.

Whereas the Wagner Act required only employers to bargain in good faith, Taft-Hartley imposed the same obligation on unions. Although the negotiation process is described later in this chapter, it is important to understand the term *bargaining in good faith*. This does not mean that the parties must reach agreement, but rather that they must come to the bargaining table ready, willing, and able to meet and deal, open to proposals made by the other party, and with the intent to reach a mutually acceptable agreement. Realizing that unions and employers might not reach agreement and that work stoppages might occur, Taft-Hartley also created the **Federal Mediation and Conciliation Service (FMCS)** as an independent agency separate from the Department of Labor. The mission of the FMCS is to send a trained representative to assist in negotiations. Both employer and union have the responsibility to notify the FMCS when other attempts to settle the dispute have failed or contract expiration is pending. An FMCS mediator is not empowered to force parties to reach an agreement, but he or she can use persuasion and other means of diplomacy to help them reach their own resolution of differences. Finally, a fact worth noting was the amendment in 1974 to extend coverage

Federal Mediation and Conciliation Service (FMCS)
A government agency that assists labor and management in settling disputes.

DIVERSITY TOPICS

Unions and EEO

Although much of the legal discussion so far in this section has focused specifically on labor legislation, it's important to recognize that many of the laws discussed in Chapter 3 apply to labor organizations as well. For instance, the Equal Pay Act of 1963 requires that wages agreed to during collective bargaining must not be differentiated on the basis of sex. In labor-relations settings, pay may differ only on the basis of skill, responsibility, accountability, seniority, or working conditions.

The Civil Rights Act of 1964 is as relevant to labor organizations as it is to management. Title VII of the act means that not only must unions discontinue any discriminatory practices; they must also actively recruit and give preference to minority group members. For example, if a labor union is located in a geographic area with a large minority population, the union must make an effort to recruit these individuals into the union's apprenticeship programs. This means that unions have to place advertisements where they will be easily found by minority applicants. Failure to take such affirmative

action steps may result in a union being found guilty of discrimination.

With regard to the Age Discrimination in Employment Act of 1967, unions cannot mandate retirement of any of their members. However, a union can stop contributing to a worker's pension after the individual reaches the age of seventy, just as a company can. Additionally, labor unions, in complying with the provisions of the Vocational Rehabilitation Act and the Americans with Disabilities Act, must take affirmative action measures to recruit, employ, and advance all qualified disabled individuals. This means that unions must make reasonable accommodations for people with disabilities, such as easy-access ramps for people needing wheelchairs, adaptive computer software for people with vision problems, and meal breaks or places for people with type 1 diabetes to a private area to test blood sugar levels, take insulin, or rest until blood sugars become normal. The same holds true for abiding by the provisions of the Family and Medical Leave Act.

to the healthcare industry. This healthcare amendment now affords Taft-Hartley coverage to for-profit and nonprofit hospitals, as well as special provisions for the healthcare industry, both profit and nonprofit, as to bargaining notice requirements and the right to picket or strike.[13]

Other Laws Affecting Labor-Management Relations

The Wagner and Taft-Hartley Acts are the most important laws influencing labor-management relationships in the United States, but other laws, too, are pertinent to our discussion (see Diversity Topics: Unions and EEO). Specifically, these are the Railway Labor Act; the Landrum-Griffin Act; Executive Orders 10988 and 11491; the Racketeer Influenced and Corrupt Organizations Act of 1970; and the Civil Service Reform Act of 1978. Let's briefly review the notable aspects of these laws.

The Railway Labor Act of 1926 The **Railway Labor Act** provided the initial impetus for widespread collective bargaining in the United States.[14] Although the act covers only the transportation industry, it was important because workers in these industries were guaranteed the right to organize, bargain collectively with employers, and establish dispute settlement procedures in the event that no agreement was reached at the bargaining table. This dispute settlement procedure allows congressional and presidential intercession in the event of an impasse.[15] The act makes it more difficult for transportation workers to organize and provides mandatory dispute resolution procedures to avoid strikes in all but the most major disputes when all attempts at mediation have been exhausted. The goal is to restrict strikes that may disrupt national rail and air travel. FedEx was originally founded as an airline, and as such is subject to regulation by the Railway Labor Act (RLA), which makes strikes by FedEx drivers much less likely than by drivers of their competitor UPS, which is regulated by the National Labor Relations Act. UPS has often protested that FedEx should be subject to the National Labor Relations Act, eliminating the competitive advantage FedEx holds because FedEx drivers may not strike.

Railway Labor Act
Provided the initial impetus to widespread collective bargaining.

Landrum-Griffin Act of 1959
Also known as the Labor and Management Reporting and Disclosure
Act, this legislation protected
union members from possible
wrongdoing on the part of their
unions. It required all unions to
disclose their financial statements.

Landrum-Griffin Act of 1959   The **Landrum-Griffin Act of 1959** (Labor Management Reporting and Disclosure Act) was passed to address the public outcry over misuse
of union funds and corruption in the labor movement. This act, like Taft-Hartley, was an
amendment to the Wagner Act.[16]

The purpose of the Landrum-Griffin Act is to monitor internal union activity by making officials and those affiliated with unions (for example, union members and trustees)
accountable for union funds, elections, and other business of the union. Much of this act
is part of an ongoing effort to prevent corrupt practices and to keep organized crime from
gaining control of the labor movement.[17] The act requires unions to file annual reports to
the Department of Labor regarding administrative matters such as their constitutions and
bylaws, administrative policies, elected officials, and finances. This information is available to the public. Furthermore, Landrum-Griffin allowed all members of a union to vote
regardless of race, sex, and national origin. This provision gave union members certain
rights that were unavailable to the general public until the passage of the Civil Rights Act
of 1964. Landrum-Griffin also required that all who voted on union matters would do so in
a secret ballot, especially when the vote concerned the election of union officers.

Executive Orders 10988 and 11491   Both of these executive orders deal specifically
with labor legislation in the federal sector.[18] In 1962, President Kennedy issued Executive
Order 10988, which permitted, for the first time, federal government employees the right
to join unions. The order required agency heads to bargain in good faith, defined unfair
labor practices, and specified the code of conduct to which labor organizations in the
public sector must adhere. Strikes, however, were prohibited.[19]

Although this executive order effectively granted organizing rights to federal employees, areas for improvement were identified, particularly the need for a centralized agency
to oversee federal labor relations activities. To address these deficiencies, President
Richard Nixon issued Executive Order 11491 in 1969. This executive order made federal
labor relations more like those in the private sector and standardized procedures among
federal agencies. The order gave the assistant secretary of labor the authority to determine appropriate bargaining units, oversee recognition procedures, rule on unfair labor
practices, and enforce standards of conduct on labor relations. It also established the
Federal Labor Relations Council (FLRC) to supervise implementation of Executive Order
11491 provisions, handle appeals from decisions of the assistant secretary of labor, and
rule on questionable issues.

Both of these executive orders were vital in promoting federal-sector unionization.
However, if a subsequent administration ever decided not to permit federal-sector unionization, a president would have had only to revoke a prior executive order. To eliminate
this possibility, and to remove federal-sector labor relations from direct control of a president, Congress passed the Civil Service Reform Act.

Racketeer Influenced and Corrupt
Organizations Act (RICO)
Law passed to eliminate any
influence on unions by members
of organized crime.

Racketeer Influenced and Corrupt Organizations Act (RICO) of 1970   The **Racketeer Influenced and Corrupt Organizations Act (RICO)** serves a vital purpose in labor
relations. RICO's primary emphasis with respect to labor unions is to eliminate any influence exerted on unions by members of organized crime.[20] It is a violation of RICO if "payments or loans are made to employee representatives, labor organizations, or officers and
employees of labor organizations,"[21] where such action occurs in the form of "bribery,
kickbacks, or extortion."[22] RICO has been used to oust a number of labor officials alleged
to have ties to organized crime.[23]

Civil Service Reform Act
Replaced Executive Order 11491 as
the basic law governing labor
relations for federal employees.

Civil Service Reform Act of 1978   Title VII of the **Civil Service Reform Act** established
the Federal Labor Relations Authority (FLRA) as an independent agency within the executive branch to carry out the major functions previously performed by the FLRC. The
FLRA was given the authority to decide, subject to external review by courts and administrative bodies,[24] union election and unfair labor practice disputes, and appeals from
arbitration awards, and to provide leadership in establishing policies and guidance. An
additional feature of this act is a broad-scope grievance procedure that can be limited
only by the negotiators. Under Executive Order 11491, binding arbitration had been
optional. The Civil Service Reform Act of 1978 contains many provisions similar to those
of the Wagner Act, with two important differences. First, in the private sector, the scope

of bargaining includes wages, benefits, and mandatory subjects of bargaining. In the federal sector, wages and benefits are not negotiable—they are set by Congress. Additionally, the Reform Act prohibits negotiations over union security arrangements.

Unionizing Employees

Employees are unionized after an extensive and sometimes lengthy process called the organizing campaign. Exhibit 14-3 contains a simple model of how the process typically flows in the private sector. Let's look at these elements.

Efforts to organize a group of employees may begin by employee representatives requesting a union to visit the employees' organization and solicit members. The union itself might initiate the membership drive, using methods as old as picket lines or as new as Facebook, Twitter, and YouTube to promote their benefits to workers. One of the important tasks at the beginning of this activity is determining which employees are eligible to vote on union representation. Supervisors are excluded from union membership, so employees must be classified before they are eligible to vote in the representation election. It isn't always simple to determine who is a supervisor. The NLRB has held that an employee may be a supervisor if they act in a supervisory role 10 to 15 percent of the time. For example, in the nursing industry, charge nurses have often been in limbo. Unions claim that these individuals represent patients, like other nurses, and thus should be part of the bargaining unit. Management, on the other hand, says they exercise independent decision making in guiding the actions of other nurses—actions typical of a supervisor. Thus, management considers them ineligible for the bargaining unit. Management may want to designate as many employees as possible with supervisory responsibilities to limit the number of potential union members.[25]

Regardless of who actually belongs in the voting population, as established by the NLRB, the union must secure signed **authorization cards** from at least 30 percent of the employees it wishes to represent. Employees who sign the cards indicate that they wish the particular union to be their representative in negotiating with the employer.

Although a minimum of 30 percent of the potential union members must sign the authorization card prior to an election, unions are seldom interested in bringing to vote situations in which they merely meet the NLRB minimum. After all, to become the certified bargaining unit, the union must be accepted by a majority of those eligible voting workers.[26] Acceptance in this case is determined by secret ballot. This election, held by the NLRB, is called a **representation certification (RC)** and can occur only once in twelve months. Thus, the more signatures on the authorization cards, the greater the chances the union will win certification to represent the workers.

Even when a sizable proportion of the workers sign authorization cards, the victory is by no means guaranteed. Management rarely is passive during the organization drive (see Tips for Success). Although laws govern what management can and cannot do, management in an organization may attempt to persuade potential members to vote no. Union organizers realize that such persuasion may work, and thus unions usually require a much higher percentage of authorization cards to increase their odds of obtaining a majority. When that majority vote is received, the NLRB certifies the union and recognizes it as the exclusive bargaining unit. Whether the individual in the certified bargaining union voted for or against the union, each worker is covered by the negotiated contract and must abide by its governance.

Once a union has been certified, is it there forever? Certainly not. On some occasions, union members may become so dissatisfied with the union's actions in representing them that they may attempt to turn to another union or have no union at all. In either case, the rank-and-file

authorization card
A card signed by prospective union members indicating that they are interested in having a union election held at their work site.

representation certification (RC)
The election process whereby employees vote in a union as their representative.

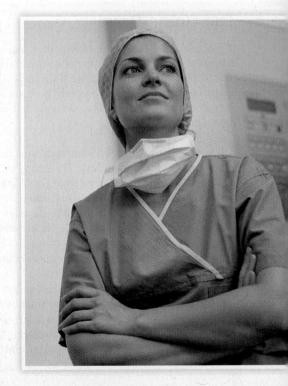

Should this charge nurse be considered part of the bargaining unit? That matter has been the subject of several NLRB and court cases. The unions believe so because the nurse administers patient care. Hospital management sees this individual as a supervisor and ineligible for inclusion to the certified bargaining unit.
(Source: Jochen Sand/Digital Vision/Getty Images, Inc.)

Exhibit 14-3
Union Organizing Process

Each of the steps in the process of organizing and certifying a union are clearly defined. Both the union and management must respect the rights of the other.

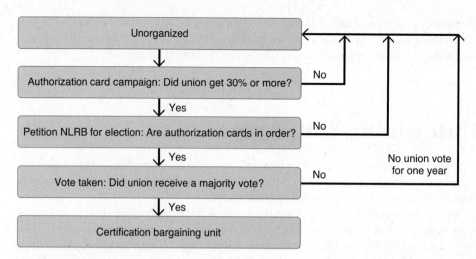

representation decertification (RD)

The election process whereby union members vote out their union as their representative.

members petition the NLRB to conduct a **representation decertification (RD)**. Once again, if a majority of the members vote the union out, it is gone. However, once the election has been held, no other action can occur for another twelve months. This grace period protects the employer from employees decertifying one union today and certifying another tomorrow.

Finally, and even more rare than an RD, is a representation decertification (RM) initiated by management. The guidelines for the RM are the same as for the RD, except that the employer leads the drive. Although RDs and RMs are ways of decertifying unions, it should be pointed out that most labor agreements bar the use of either form of decertification during the term of the contract.

Unions' organizing drives may or may not be successful, but when they do achieve their goal to become the exclusive bargaining agent, the next step is to negotiate the contract. In the next section, we'll look at the specific issues surrounding collective bargaining.

TIPS FOR SUCCESS

The Union Drive

What can management do when they learn that a union-organizing drive has begun in their organization? Labor laws permit them to defend themselves against the union campaign, but they must do so properly. Here are some guidelines for management as to what to do and what not to do during the organizing drive.[27]

- If your employees ask for your opinion on unionization, respond in a natural manner. For example, "I really have no position on the issue. Do what you think is best."
- You can prohibit union-organizing activities in your workplace during work hours only if they interfere with work operations. This may apply to the organization's e-mail activity, too.
- You can prohibit outside union organizers from distributing union information in the workplace.
- Employees have the right to distribute union information to other employees during breaks and lunch periods.
- Don't question employees publicly or privately about union-organizing activities—for example, "Are you planning to go to that union rally this weekend?" But if an

employee freely tells you about the activities, you may listen.

- Don't spy on employees' union activities, for example, by standing in the cafeteria to see who is distributing pro-union literature.
- Don't make any threats or promises related to the possibility of unionization. For example, "If this union effort succeeds, upper management is seriously thinking about closing down this plant, but if it's defeated, they may push through an immediate wage increase."
- Don't discriminate against any employee who is involved in the unionization effort.
- Be on the lookout for efforts by the union to coerce employees to join its ranks. This activity by unions is an unfair labor practice. If you see this occurring, report it to your boss or to human resources. In this case, your organization may also want to consider filing a complaint against the union with the NLRB.

Things to think about:

How would you feel if your employees were pursuing union representation? Would you be offended or resentful? Why?

Collective Bargaining

Collective bargaining typically refers to the negotiation, administration, and interpretation of a written agreement between two parties that covers a specific period of time. This agreement, or contract, lays out in specific terms the conditions of employment— that is, what is expected of employees and any limits to management's authority. In the following discussion, we take a somewhat larger perspective and also consider the organizing, certification, and preparation efforts that precede actual negotiation.

Most of us hear or read about collective bargaining only when a contract is about to expire or when negotiations break down, such as the NFL and NBA lockouts of 2011. Although large-scale strikes in the United States have been declining in number in recent years, strikes such as the Writer's Guild of America strike in 2007–2008 and the National Hockey League lockout of 2004–2005 remind us that bargaining between employers and unions can break down and cause disruptions. Collective-bargaining agreements cover about half of all state and local government employees and one-ninth of employees in the private sector. The wages, hours, and working conditions of these unionized employees are negotiated usually for two or three years at a time. Only when these contracts expire and management and the union cannot agree on a new contract do most of us become aware that collective bargaining is an important part of HRM.

collective bargaining
The negotiation, administration, and interpretation of a written agreement between two parties, at least one of which represents a group that is acting collectively, and that covers a specific period of time.

Objective and Scope of Collective Bargaining

The objective of collective bargaining is to agree on a contract acceptable to management, union representatives, and the union membership. What is covered in this contract? The final agreement will reflect the issues of the particular workplace and industry in which the contract is negotiated.[28] Although contracts can contain a variety of topics, four issues appear consistently throughout all labor contracts. Three of the four are mandatory bargaining issues, which means that management and the union must negotiate in good faith over these issues. These mandatory issues were defined by the Wagner Act as wages, hours, and terms and conditions of employment. The fourth issue covered in almost all labor contracts is the grievance procedure, which is designed to permit the adjudication of complaints. Before we progress further into collective bargaining, let's examine these four issues.

When unions and employers can't come to an agreement, either side may call a halt to work. Unions may go on strike or employers may prevent them from working with a lockout like the one that shortened the 2011 NBA season by six weeks. *(Source: Patrick McDermott/ Getty Images, Inc.)*

Collective Bargaining Participants

Collective bargaining was described as an activity that takes place between two parties. In this context, the two parties are labor and management. We will take a look at how these two parties are represented and the role government plays in the process.

Management's representation in collective bargaining talks tends to depend on the size of the organization. In a small firm, for instance, bargaining is probably done by the president. Few small firms have a specialist who deals only with HRM issues; the president of the company often handles this task. Larger organizations usually have an HRM department with full-time industrial relations experts. In such cases, we can expect management to be represented by the senior manager for industrial relations, corporate executives, and company lawyers—with support provided by legal and economic specialists in wage and salary administration, labor law, benefits, and so forth.

On the union side, we typically expect to see a bargaining team composed of an officer of the local union, local shop stewards, and some representation from the international/national union.[29] Again, as with management, representation is modified to reflect the size of the bargaining unit. If negotiations involve a contract that will cover 50,000 employees at company locations throughout the United States, the team will be dominated by international/national union officers (those most often with a broader perspective of the implication of a contract) with a strong supporting cast of economic and legal experts employed by the union. In a small firm or for local negotiations covering special issues at the plant level for a nationwide organization, bargaining representatives for the union might be the local officers and a few specially elected committee members.

Watching over these two sides is a third party—the government. In addition to providing the rules under which management and labor bargain, government provides a watchful eye on the two parties to ensure the rules are followed, and it stands ready to intervene if an agreement on acceptable terms cannot be reached, or if the impasse undermines the nation's well-being.

The Collective-Bargaining Process

Let's now consider the actual collective-bargaining process. Exhibit 14-4 contains a simple model of how the process typically flows in the private sector—which includes preparing to negotiate, actual negotiations, and administering the contract after it has been ratified.

Preparing to Negotiate Once a union has been certified as the bargaining unit, both union and management begin the ongoing activity of preparing for negotiations. We refer to this as an ongoing activity because ideally it should begin as soon as the previous contract is agreed upon or union certification is achieved. Realistically, it probably begins anywhere from six months to a year before the current contract expires. We can consider the preparation for negotiation as composed of three activities: fact gathering, goal setting, and strategy development.

Information is acquired from both internal and external sources. Internal data include grievance and accident records; employee performance reports; overtime figures; and reports on transfers, turnover, and absenteeism. External information should include statistics on the current economy, both at local and national levels; economic forecasts for the short and intermediate terms; copies of recently negotiated contracts by the union to determine what issues the union considers important; data on the communities in which the company operates—cost of living, changes in cost of living, terms of recently negotiated labor contracts, and statistics on the labor market; and industry labor statistics to see what terms other organizations, employing similar types of personnel, are negotiating.

With homework done, information in hand, and tentative goals established, both union and management must put together the most difficult part of the bargaining preparation activities, a strategy for negotiations. This includes assessing the other side's power and specific tactics.

Negotiating at the Bargaining Table Negotiation customarily begins with the union delivering to management a list of demands. By presenting many demands, the union creates significant room for trading in later stages of the negotiation; it also disguises the union's real position, leaving management to determine which demands are adamantly sought, which are moderately sought, and which the union is prepared to quickly abandon. A long list of demands, too, often fulfills the internal political needs of the union. By seeming to back numerous wishes of the union's members, union administrators appear to be satisfying the needs of the many factions within the membership.

Both union and management representatives may publicly accentuate their differences, but the real negotiations typically go on behind closed doors. Each party tries to assess the relative priorities of the other's demands, and each begins to combine proposals into viable packages. Next comes the attempt to make management's highest offer

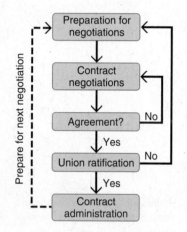

Exhibit 14-4
The Collective-Bargaining Process

This flowchart illustrates the steps in the collective-bargaining process.

approximate the lowest demands that the union is willing to accept. Hence, negotiation is a form of compromise. An oral agreement is eventually converted into a written contract, and negotiation concludes with the union representatives submitting the contract for ratification or approval from rank-and-file members. If the rank-and-file members vote down the contract, negotiations must resume.

Contract Administration   Once a contract is agreed on and ratified, it must be administered. Contract administration involves four stages: (1) providing the agreement information to all union members and managers; (2) implementing the contract; (3) interpreting the contract and grievance resolution; and (4) monitoring activities during the contract period.[30]

Providing agreement information to all concerned requires both parties ensures that changes in contract language are clearly explained. For example, the most obvious would be hourly rate changes; HRM must make sure its payroll system is adjusted to the new rates as set in the contract. Likewise, changes in work rules, hours, and such must be communicated. If both sides agree to something not in existence before, such as mandatory overtime, all must be informed of how it will work. Neither the union nor the company can simply hand a copy of the contract to each organization member and expect it to be understood. It will be necessary to hold meetings to explain the new terms of the agreement.

Implementing the contract ensures that all communicated changes take effect and that both sides comply with the contract terms. One concept to recognize during this phase is management rights. Typically, management is guaranteed the right to allocate organizational resources in the most efficient manner; to create reasonable rules; to hire, promote, transfer, and discharge employees; to determine work methods and assign work; to create, eliminate, and classify jobs; to lay off employees when necessary; to close or relocate facilities with a sixty-day notice; and to institute technological changes. Of course, good HRM practices suggest that whether the contract requires it or not, management would be wise to notify the union of major decisions that will influence its membership.

Interpreting the contract and grievance process is probably the most important element of contract administration. Almost all collective-bargaining agreements contain formal procedures for resolving grievances of contract interpretation and application. These contracts have provisions for resolving specific, formally initiated grievances by employees concerning dissatisfaction with job-related issues. It is necessary for the contract to spell out the procedures for handling contractual disputes.[31]

    Grievance procedures are typically designed to resolve grievances as quickly as possible and at the lowest level possible in the organization (see Exhibit 14-5).[32] The first step almost always has the employee attempting to resolve the grievance with his or her immediate supervisor. If it cannot be resolved at this stage, it is typically discussed with the union steward and the supervisor. Failure at this stage usually brings in the individuals from the organization's industrial relations department and the chief union steward. If the grievance still cannot be resolved, the complaint passes to the facility's manager, who typically discusses it with the union grievance committee. Unsuccessful efforts at this level give way to the organization's senior management and typically a representative from the national union. Finally, if those efforts are unsuccessful in resolving the grievance, the final step is for the complaint to go to arbitration—called grievance (rights) arbitration.

    In practice, we find that almost all collective-bargaining agreements provide for grievance (rights) arbitration as the final step to an impasse. Of course, in small organizations these five steps described tend to be condensed, possibly moving from discussing the grievance with the union steward to taking the grievance directly to the organization's senior executive or owner, and then to arbitration, if necessary.

Monitoring activities during the contract period is the final stage in the process of contract administration. Both the company and union will gather data on how the contract

grievance procedure
A complaint-resolving process contained in union contracts.

Exhibit 14-5
A Sample Grievance
Procedure

A typical grievance procedure
begins at Step 1 with an
informal meeting between the
employee and supervisor and
may include a union steward or
other local union representative.
The grievance may be settled at
any point, ending the process. If
the problem is not resolved, it
advances to the next step,
involving specialists in
grievance resolution from
management or the union.

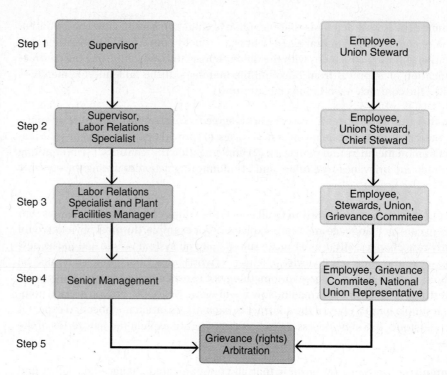

Step 1	Supervisor
Step 2	Supervisor, Labor Relations Specialist
Step 3	Labor Relations Specialist and Plant Facilities Manager
Step 4	Senior Management
Step 5	Grievance (rights) Arbitration

impacts the company and workers, such as the effect on productivity, employee turnover,
and the number of grievances and concerns. By monitoring activities covered by the contract, the company and union can assess the effectiveness of the current contract, recognize when problem areas or conflicts arose, and indicate what changes might need to be
made in subsequent negotiations.[33]

Failure to Reach Agreement

Although contract negotiations aim to achieve an agreement acceptable to all concerned parties, sometimes that goal is not achieved. Negotiations do break down,
and an impasse occurs. These events may be triggered by internal issues in the union,
the desire to strike against the company, the company's desire to lock out the union,
or its knowledge that striking workers can be replaced. Let's explore some of these
areas.

economic strike

An impasse that results from labor
and management's inability to
agree on the wages, hours, and
terms and conditions of a new
contract.

wildcat strike

An unauthorized and illegal strike
that occurs during the terms of an
existing contract.

Strikes versus Lockouts Negotiations have only two possible preliminary outcomes.
First, and obviously preferable, is agreement. The other, lacking any viable solution to the
parties' differences, is a strike or a lockout.

There are several types of strikes. The most relevant to contract negotiations is the
economic strike. An economic strike occurs when the two parties fail to reach a satisfactory agreement before the contract expires. When that deadline passes, the union
leadership will typically instruct its members not to work, and to leave their jobs.[34]
Although in today's legal climate, replacement workers can be hired, and no disciplinary
action can be taken against workers who participate in economic strike activities (see
Ethical Issues in HRM).

Another form of strike is the **wildcat strike**. A wildcat strike generally occurs when
workers walk off the job because of something management has done. For example, if a
union employee is disciplined for failure to call in sick according to provisions of the
contract, fellow union members may walk off the job to demonstrate their dissatisfaction with management action. It is important to note that these strikes happen while a
contract is in force—an agreement that usually prohibits such union activity. Consequently, wildcat strikers can be severely disciplined or terminated. In the past, the most

powerful weapon unions in the private sector had was the economic strike. By striking, the union was, in essence, withholding labor from the employer, thus causing the employer financial hardships. For instance, U.S. organizations lost nearly 300,000 work-days to strike activity in 2010. As dramatic as it sounds, it was the second lowest annual total days of work lost since 1947.[35]

Unions are finding that strikes are becoming a less effective bargaining tool for several reasons. Economic conditions may leave employers facing layoffs, making strikes unwise, and public perception of strikes has become less sympathetic in recent years. Organizations are also more inclined to replace striking workers. Although strike activity fell to a near record low in 2010, worker dissatisfaction with some management practices may increase strike activity at any time.

Managers may also use a **lockout** to try to end a disagreement with workers. A lockout, as the name implies, occurs when the organization denies unionized workers access to their jobs during an impasse. A lockout, in some cases, is the first step in management's hiring of replacement workers. In others, it's management's effort to protect their facilities and machinery and other employees at the work site. In either case, the strategy is the same. Each side attempts to apply economic pressure on its opponent to sway negotiations in its own direction. When negotiations reach a point that both parties are unwilling to negotiate any further, they are said to have reached an impasse. Impasse-resolution techniques are designed to help such situations.

> **lockout**
> A situation in labor-management negotiations whereby management prevents union members from returning to work.

Lockouts were once rare, but have been on the rise in recent years as unions have lost strength and employers become more firm in their negotiations. Recent lockouts have include the National Football League (NFL) referees, National Basketball Association (NBA) players, nurses in California, and over 1,300 workers at American Crystal Sugar.[36]

ETHICAL ISSUES IN HRM

The Striker Replacement Dilemma

Work stoppages can be used by either management or labor to try to gain an advantage when negotiations for wages and working conditions break down. For example, when labor shortages exist, or when inventories are in short supply, a union strike could have serious ramifications for the company. Likewise, when economic conditions create a surplus of labor and inventories are high, management has the upper hand and could easily lock out the union to achieve its negotiation goals.

In fact, both the Wagner and Taft-Hartley Acts saw to it that the playing field was as fair as possible by requiring both sides to negotiate in good faith and permitting impasses if they should be warranted. For decades, this scenario played itself out over and over again.

Timing of a contract's expiration proved critical for both sides. For example, a Midwest farm equipment manufacturer found that contract negotiations always broke down in November and resulted in a short strike that coincided with deer hunting season.

Hiring replacement workers became a tool to break unions after President Ronald Reagan fired striking air traffic controllers and hired their replacements. Other organizations including Firestone, Caterpillar, the National Football League, and John Deere realized that using replacement workers could be to their advantage. The union members either came back to work on management's terms or they lost their jobs—period. Undoubtedly, in any strike situation, management has the right to keep its doors open and to keep producing what it sells. That may mean using supervisory personnel in place of striking workers, or in some cases, bringing in replacements.

Ethical questions:

Does a law that permits replacement workers undermine the intent of national labor law? Does it create an unfair advantage for organizations that play hardball just to break the union? Should a striker-replacement bill (which would prevent permanent replacement workers from being hired) be passed? Should striking workers' jobs be protected while they exercise their rights under the Wagner Act? What's your opinion?

Economic strikes left 45,000 U.S. employees idle for nearly 300,000 workdays in 2010. In the United States and Canada, the trend is for fewer but longer strikes. Nurses striking in Pennsylvania and construction workers in Chicago accounted for nearly two-thirds of the lost workdays. (Source: © AP/Wide World Photos)

Impasse-Resolution Techniques When labor and management in the private sector cannot reach a satisfactory agreement, they may need the assistance of an objective third party. This assistance comes in the form of conciliation and mediation, fact-finding, or interest arbitration.

Conciliation and mediation are two closely related impasse-resolution techniques. Both are techniques whereby a neutral third party attempts to help labor and management resolve their differences. Under conciliation, however, the third party role is to keep negotiations going. In other words, this individual is a go-between—advocating a voluntary means through which both sides can continue negotiating. Mediation goes one step further. The mediator attempts to pull together the common ground that exists and make settlement recommendations for overcoming barriers between the two sides. A mediator's suggestions, however, are only advisory and not binding on either party.

Fact-finding is a technique whereby a neutral third party conducts a hearing to gather evidence from both labor and management. The fact-finder then renders a decision as to how he or she views an appropriate settlement. Similar to mediation, the fact-finder's recommendations are suggestions only—they, too, are not binding on either party.

The final impasse-resolution technique is called **interest arbitration**. Under interest arbitration, generally a panel of three individuals—one neutral and one each from the union and management—hears testimony from both sides. After the hearing, the panel renders a decision on how to settle the current contract negotiation dispute. If all three members of the panel are unanimous in their decision, that decision is binding on both parties.

Public-sector impasse-resolution techniques show notable differences. For instance, many states that do permit public-sector employee strikes require some form of arbitration. Decisions rendered through arbitration are binding on both parties. Arbitration takes two forms: package selection and issue-by-issue selection. Package selection (or final-offer arbitration) means that the arbitrator selects either the union or management proposal in its entirety. Issue-by-issue selection allows the arbitrator to select from union or management proposals for each issue being negotiated. For example, the arbitrator may select management's proposal for benefits, but select the union's proposal for another issue, such as wages.

Critical Issues for Unions Today

The declining percentage of unionized workforce throughout the past few decades raises several questions. Why has union membership declined? Can labor and management find a way to work together more harmoniously? Is public-sector unionization different from that in the private sector? And where are unions likely to focus their attention in the next decade? In this section, we'll look at these issues.

Union Membership: Where Have the Members Gone?

Unions began to witness significant union gains with the passage of the Wagner Act in 1935. In fact, by the early 1940s, union membership in the United States reached its pinnacle of approximately 36 percent of the workforce. Since that time, however, there's been a steady decline (see Exhibit 14-6). From their heyday of almost 36 percent in the early 1940s to 11.8 percent in 2012, unions don't appear to be the force they once were.[38] But don't count unions out. Stagnant worker wages, health insurance cutbacks, displeasure with cost-cutting measures and company policies are making union philosophies more attractive to

conciliation and mediation
Impasse resolution techniques using an impartial third party to help management and the union to resolve the conflict.

fact-finding
The technique whereby a neutral third party conducts a hearing to gather evidence and testimony from the parties regarding the differences between them.

interest arbitration
An impasse resolution technique used to settle contract negotiation disputes.

CONTEMPORARY CONNECTION

The Union Summer

Looking for a unique internship? How about applying to a union? Borrowing a page from many private sector organizations looking to find good talent, the AFL-CIO has a program called the Union Summer Program. The Union Summer Program is a five-week internship to help interested college students learn skills for union-organizing activities. It's proven to be a good training ground for individuals who may have an interest in working for a union, as well as a "sourcing" activity for unions to find qualified talent.

The Union Summer Program seeks to bring together individuals "committed to uniting workers, students, and community activists to bring about social justice through workplace and community organizing."[37] During the summer internship, these students work in a variety of activities that typically take place during an organizing campaign. For example, interns may interview potential union members to find out what they believe needs to be changed in their work setting. They may also assist the union and potential members with organizing picket lines, as well as educating community members on workers' rights issues. Since its inception, the program has had several thousand summer interns.

Consider this:
How would this experience enhance your HR qualifications? What skills might you learn?

employees. Unions are also changing some of their organizing tactics, and public sentiment might be changing to support and sympathize with union causes (see Contemporary Connection). Unions have recently been effective in recruiting members in the service sectors such as retail workers, hospitality workers, and public sector employees.[39]

Labor-Management Cooperation

Historically, the relationship between labor and management was built on conflict. The interests of labor and management were seen as basically at odds—each treating the other as the opposition. But times are changing. Management has become increasingly aware that successful efforts to increase productivity, improve quality, and lower costs require employee involvement and commitment. Similarly, some labor unions have recognized that they can help their members more by cooperating with management rather than fighting them.

Many U.S. labor laws were created in an era of mistrust and antagonism between labor and management, creating a barrier to both parties becoming cooperative

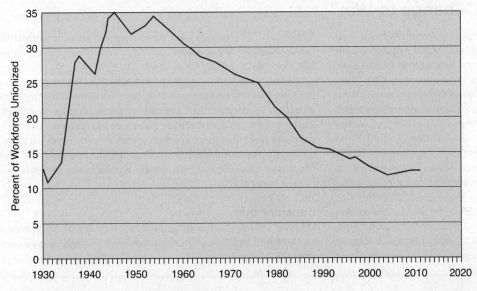

Exhibit 14-6
Trends in Union Membership
Union membership has been declining for several decades although the decline has slowed recently.

partners.[40] For example, the National Labor Relations Act was passed to encourage collective bargaining and to balance workers' power against that of management. That legislation also sought to eliminate the practice of firms setting up company unions for the sole purpose of undermining efforts of outside unions organizing their employees. The law prohibited employers from creating or supporting a "labor organization." The National Labor Relations Board has ruled that Electromation, a non-union manufacturing company, was participating in an unfair labor practice when it set up employee action committees. The NLRB determined that the committees were not actually set up to provide employee input into safety and health issues, but to "impose its own unilateral form of bargaining on employees" by discussing wages, hours, and working conditions. Electromation's actions were viewed as a means of thwarting a Teamsters Union organizing campaign that began in its Elkhart, Indiana, plant. Certain implications of the Electromation case and a broader NLRB interpretation in the Crown Cork and Seal case indicated that companies could have such programs as quality circle, quality of work life, and other employee involvement programs under federal labor laws.

Although this issue had been the subject of Congressional debate, the current legal environment doesn't prohibit employee-involvement programs in the United States. Rather, to comply with the law, management must give employee-involvement programs independence. That is, when such programs become dominated by management, they're likely to be interpreted as groups that perform some functions of labor unions but are controlled by management. Actions indicating that an employee-involvement program is not dominated by management might include choosing program members through secret-ballot elections, giving program members wide latitude in deciding what issues to deal with, permitting members to meet apart from management, and specifying that program members are not susceptible to dissolution by management whim. The key theme labor laws convey is that where employee-involvement programs are introduced, members must have the power to make decisions and act independently of management.

Public-Sector Unionization

Unionizing government employees, either in the federal sector or in state, county, and municipal jurisdictions, has proven lucrative for unions.[42] Significant gains have been

CONTEMPORARY CONNECTION

Union Split Creates "Change to Win"

Throughout the past several decades, the percent of the unionized workforce has continually declined. In 2005, disagreement over how to reach workers and form new unions boiled over, resulting in several member unions leaving the AFL-CIO. Their reason: they believed the AFL-CIO wasn't paying enough attention to the kind of workers that these unions represent. Currently, four unions (International Brotherhood of Teamsters, Service Employees International Union, United Farm Workers of America, and United Food and Commercials Workers International) are part of the breakaway union federation called "Change to Win," and are attempting to unionize more service-type employees. Change to Win unions feel they can reach out in a way that the AFL-CIO could not by organizing many of today's working poor working in service occupations. "The future of the unions is the $8 an hour home health care worker," according to David Gregory, professor of law at St. John's University. "The unions may have regained membership with lower-wage service workers, but they cannot regain the dues lost along with the higher-paid jobs."[41]

Service sector jobs may not pay as well as the manufacturing jobs that the unions have lost, but jobs in health care, construction, and education are not as easily shipped overseas. These new union members are also more likely to vote in political races than nonunion workers, possibly proving more influential in elections and pro-labor legislation such as the Employee Free Choice Act, which would make it easier for unions to organize.

Consider this:

Will the unions stage a comeback in a new form? Will service workers join the unions in numbers large enough to maintain union influence?

made in these sectors, as unions increased membership from 11 percent in 1970 to nearly 37 percent in 2011.[43] In fact, these white-collar unionized jobs account for nearly one-half of all union membership.[44] But labor relations in the government sector differ from their private-sector counterpart. For example, in the federal sector, wages are nonnegotiable and compulsory membership in unions is prohibited. At the state, county, and local levels, laws must be passed to grant employees in any jurisdiction the right to unionize— and more importantly, the right to strike. Yet probably the most notable difference lies in determining "who's the boss."

In a private company, management is the employer. This, however, is not the case in government sectors. Instead, a president, a governor, a mayor, a county executive, and so forth is responsible for the government's budget. These elected officials have fiduciary responsibilities to their citizenry. Who, then, "owns" the government? The people, of course. Accordingly, unionized employees in the public sector actually negotiate against themselves as taxpayers. And even if some agreement is reached, the negotiated contract cannot be binding, even though the union members support it, until some legislative body has approved it.

Finally, because these negotiations are a concern to the general public, citizens have the right to know what is going on. This is handled through *sunshine laws.*[45] These laws require parties in public-sector labor relations to make contract negotiations open to the public. Closed sessions are only allowed when either party reviews their position with the designated negotiation representative. Actual negotiation between parties is public. This freedom of information is based on the premise that the public-sector negotiations directly affect all taxpayers and thus should provide direct information regarding what is occurring. However, although information is important, sunshine laws have been questioned by labor-relations personnel. They contend that what the public may see or hear during open negotiations may ultimately differ from the final contract, and public members who do not understand what happens in negotiations may gain a false sense of negotiation outcomes. Sunshine laws differ in every state and are constantly evolving.

As the world of work continues to radically evolve, it is safe to assume that unions will target an even broader group of employees. The same issues that unions sold fifty years ago to interest people in the union cause including wages, benefits, job security, and a say in how employees are treated at work, are the same concerns of employees in the new millennium. Restructuring, consolidation, and layoffs in corporate America have forced affected workers to pay closer attention to what the unions promise. For the health-care professionals, for example, who voted to be represented by unions, this has resulted in job security and wages and benefits above their nonunion counterparts.[46] Hospitals and healthcare workers appear to be an area of emphasis for union organizing in the future.

Will unions survive? Only time will tell. But remember, the decline in union membership—especially in the traditional industries in the 1970s—was brought about in part by people achieving their middle-class status. As organizational changes threaten this social class rank, we have every reason to believe that workers will present a unified, mutual front to the employer. In some cases, that is best achieved through union activities. Union membership has stabilized at just under 12 percent in recent years. It's likely that losses in industrial union membership have been offset by the increases seen in membership in the health care and service worker sector.

International Labor Relations

When discussing labor relations in other countries, it's important to know that we're not making "apples to apples" comparisons. Labor relations practices, and the percent of the workforce unionized, differ in every country (see Exhibit 14-7). The number of reported union members is calculated in each country using different criteria and doesn't always include all labor groups, or it may include labor associations that do not actively promote labor issues. Also, a country with a high "union density" (percent of workers who are eligible to belong to a union who actually join) may actually have unions that are not very

Exhibit 14-7

Unionization Around the World[47,48,49]

China reports that 74 percent of workers eligible to belong to a union are union members. It helps to understand that the All-China Federation of Trade Unions (ACFTU) is a monopoly with 170 million members and is controlled by the Communist Party.

Country	Percent Unionized
China	74
Sweden	68
Belgium	52
Canada	27
United Kingdom	27
Germany	19
Australia	19
Japan	19
Spain	16
Mexico	15
United States	11
France	8

strong or are too close to government influence to effectively advocate for the worker members, such as unions in China.

The business approach to unionism, or emphasizing economic objectives, is uniquely American. In Europe, Latin America, and elsewhere, unions have often evolved out of a class struggle, resulting in labor as a political party. The basic difference in perspective sometimes makes it difficult for U.S. expatriates to understand how the labor-relations process works because even the same term may have different meanings. For example, in the United States, "collective bargaining" implies negotiations between a labor union and management. In Sweden and Germany, it refers to negotiations between the employers' organization and a trade union for the entire industry. Furthermore, arbitration in the United States usually refers to the settlement of individual contractual disputes, whereas in Australia arbitration is part of the contract bargaining process.

Not only does each country have a different history of unionism, each government has its own view of its role in the labor-relations process.[50] This role is often reflected in the types and nature of the regulations in force. The U.S. government generally takes a hands-off approach toward intervention in labor-management matters, but the Australian government, to which the labor movement has strong ties, is inclined to be more involved. Thus, not only must the multinational corporate industrial relations office be familiar with the separate laws of each country, it also must be familiar with the environment in which those statutes are implemented.

China's rise as an industrial power has facilitated a population shift to larger cities as demand for factory workers has increased. Union membership in China has climbed to over 200 million,[51] doubling membership since 2000.[52] The All China Federation of Trade Unions (ACFTC) is the only recognized union federation in China and operates much like the AFL-CIO, representing dozens of trade and industrial unions. ACFTC is the largest union federation in the world, with more members than the rest of the world's trade unions put together. ACFTC sponsors legislation supporting workers' rights and works to unionize foreign owned companies like Walmart, McDonald's, and Dell.

The role of the union in China is quite different from many Western unions. Rather than provide support for collective bargaining, the role of ACFTC is to be proactive in preventing labor disputes, and develop "harmonious industrial relations."[53] The ACFTU primarily acts to stabilize labor relations and as a liaison with the government to prevent work disruptions. Few workers file complaints with the union and many view the union as more sympathetic to the employer and government than the member workers. This distrust has led to increased worker strikes and formation of unofficial independent trade unions. In 2011, over 2,000 workers at a South Korean owned LG factory went on strike after year-end bonuses were cut. Year-end bonuses are typically equivalent to one month's salary of $221.[54] The number of strikes has doubled since 2006, creating a troubling trend that concerns the government and employers.

Understanding international labor relations is vital to an organization's strategic planning. Unions affect wage levels, which in turn affect competitiveness in both labor and product markets. Unions and labor laws may limit employment-level flexibility through security clauses that tightly control layoffs and terminations (or redundancies). This is especially true in such countries as England, France, Germany, Japan, and Australia, where various laws place severe restrictions on employers.

Differing Perspectives toward Labor Relations

If labor relations can affect the organization's strategic planning initiatives, it is necessary to consider the issue of headquarters' involvement in host-country international union relations. The organization must assess whether the labor-relations function should be controlled globally from the parent country, or whether it would be more advantageous for each host country to administer its own operation. There is no simple means of making this assessment; frequently, the decision reflects the relationship of the product market at home to that of the overseas product market. For instance, when domestic sales are larger than those overseas, the organization is more likely to regard the foreign office as an extension of the domestic operations. This is true for many U.S. multinational organizations because the home market is so vast. Thus, American firms have been more inclined to keep labor relations centrally located at corporate headquarters. Many European countries, by contrast, have small home markets with comparatively larger international operations; thus, they are more inclined to adapt to host-country standards and have the labor-relations function decentralized.

Another divergence among multinational companies in their labor relations is the national attitude toward unions. Generally, American multinational corporations view unions negatively at home and try to avoid workforce unionization. Europeans, on the other hand, have had greater experience with unions, are accustomed to a larger proportion of the workforce being unionized, and are more accepting of the unionization of their own workers. In Japan, as in other parts of Asia, unions are often closely identified with an organization.

The European Union

The European Union brings together a dozen or more individual labor relations systems. For both the member nations and other countries doing business in Europe, such as the United States and Japan, it is important to understand the dynamics of what will necessarily be a dramatically changing labor environment. Unions in Europe have encountered the same challenges as unions in the U.S. Factories have closed and production has moved to countries with lower wages. As a result, trade unions have seen declines in membership. Public sector unions remain strong in many countries.

Many European countries have been hit hard by a debt crisis caused by the recession, real estate market collapse, and years of borrowing money for expansion and generous benefits for public employees and citizens. As countries such as Greece, Ireland, Spain, Portugal, and Italy struggle to repay their debts, they have been forced to reduce spending and make cuts in benefits that workers and citizens expect. As a result, public employees in the U.K., Belgium, Spain, France, and other countries have gone on strike in protest. These strikes have stopped rail service, closed schools, ferries, airports, and hospitals as workers protest cutbacks in benefits and raising of retirement ages proposed to balance government budgets and repay debt.

Unions can be found in most industrialized nations in the world. Workers around the world have found it useful to collectively fight for better wages, benefits, and working conditions. *(Source: © AP/ Wide World Photos)*

Summary

(This summary relates to the Learning Outcomes identified on page 358.) After having read this chapter you can:

1. **Define the term *unions*.** A union is an organization of workers, acting collectively, seeking to promote and protect their mutual interests through collective bargaining.

2. **Discuss the effects of the Wagner and the Taft-Hartley Acts on labor-management relations.** The Wagner (National Labor Relations) Act of 1935 and the Taft-Hartley (Labor-Management Relations) Act of 1947 represent the most direct legislation affecting collective bargaining. The Wagner Act gave unions the freedom to exist and identified employer unfair labor practices. Taft-Hartley balanced the power between unions and management by identifying unfair union labor practices.

3. **Identify the significance of Executive Orders 10988 and 11491 and the Civil Service Reform Act of 1978.** Executive Orders 10988 and 11491 paved the way for labor relations to exist in the federal sector. Additionally, Executive Order 11491 made federal labor relations similar to its private-sector counterpart. The Civil Service Reform Act of 1978 removed federal-sector labor relations from under the jurisdiction of the president and established a forum for its continued operation.

4. **Describe the union-organizing process.** The union-organizing process officially begins with the completion of an authorization card. If the required percentage of potential union members shows their intent to vote on a union by signing the authorization card, the NLRB will hold an election. If 50 percent plus one of those voting votes for the union, then the union is certified to be the bargaining unit.

5. **Describe the components of collective bargaining.** Collective bargaining typically refers to the negotiation, administration, and interpretation of a written agreement between two parties that covers a specific period of time.

6. **Identify the steps in the collective-bargaining process.** The collective-bargaining process is comprised of the following steps: preparation for negotiations, negotiations, and contract administration.

7. **Explain the various types of union security arrangements.** The various union security arrangements are the closed shop (made illegal by the Taft-Hartley Act); the union shop, which requires compulsory union membership; the agency shop, which requires compulsory union dues; and the open shop, which enforces workers' freedom of choice to select union membership or not.

8. **Describe the role of a grievance procedure in collective bargaining.** The grievance procedure provides a formal mechanism in labor contracts for resolving issues over the interpretation and application of a contract.

9. **Identify the various impasse-resolution techniques.** The most popular impasse-resolution techniques include mediation (a neutral third party informally attempts to bring the parties to agreement); fact-finding (a neutral third party conducts a hearing to gather evidence from both sides); and interest arbitration (a panel of individuals hears testimony from both sides and renders a decision).

10. **Discuss how sunshine laws affect public-sector collective bargaining.** Sunshine laws require parties in the public sector to make their collective-bargaining negotiations open to the public.

Demonstrating Comprehension

QUESTIONS FOR REVIEW

1. What is a union and why do they exist?
2. What three pieces of legislation have been most important in defining the rights of management and unions?
3. What is the process for establishing a union as the legal collective-bargaining representative for employees?

4. Why is compulsory union membership so important to unions?
5. Where are unionizing efforts focused today?
6. What is collective bargaining? How widely is it practiced?
7. Describe the collective-bargaining process.
8. What is the objective of collective bargaining?
9. Why do a union's initial list of demands tend to be long and extravagant?

Key Terms

agency shop
authorization card
Civil Service Reform Act
collective bargaining
conciliation and mediation
dues check-off
economic strike
fact-finding
Federal Mediation and Conciliation
    Service (FMCS)

grievance procedure
interest arbitration
Landrum-Griffin Act of 1959
lockout
maintenance of membership
National Labor Relations Board
    (NLRB)
open shop
Racketeer Influenced and Corrupt
    Organizations Act (RICO)

Railway Labor Act
representation certification (RC)
representation decertification (RD)
right to work laws
Taft-Hartley Act
union
union security arrangements
union shop
Wagner Act
wildcat strike

HRM Workshop

Linking Concepts to Practice   DISCUSSION QUESTIONS

1. "All that is required for successful labor-management relations is common sense, sound business judgment, and good listening skills." Do you agree or disagree with this statement? Explain.
2. Given your career aspirations, might you join a union? Why or why not? Explain.
3. "An employer might not want to stifle a union-organizing effort. In fact, an employer might want to encourage his employees to join a union." Do you agree or disagree with this statement? Explain your position.
4. "If management treats employees well, pays them a fair wage, communicates with them, and ensures that they have a safe and healthy work environment, there is no need for a union." Do you agree or disagree with the statement? Explain your position.

Making A Difference   SERVICE LEARNING PROJECTS

Labor unions take many forms and they may even exist on your own campus. Take this opportunity to meet the members in person.

- Ask your college Human Resource department about contact information for union representatives of college employees. Contact those representatives about volunteer opportunities.
- Contact local trade unions about volunteer activities such as assisting with local Labor Day parades, picnics or other activities.
- Volunteer to assist the teacher associations at local K-12 school districts with their efforts.

As you put your service learning experience together, keep a journal of your activities, the time you spend, contact information for people you work with, and your thoughts about the process. When you're finished, make a presentation to your class about the experience and what you learned. What concepts from Chapter 14 were you able to apply?

Developing Diagnostic and Analytical Skills

Case Application 14: MANAGER'S CONCERNS SPIRAL AS VIDEO GOES VIRAL

Exactitude Manufacturing implemented a new compensation system a year ago and it hasn't been very well received by their employees. Pay grades were reduced from six to five, and pay was tied to skills, training and level of responsibility rather than seniority. As a result some of the most senior and highly skilled workers are already at the top of their pay grades. They haven't had a raise in a year and will only see slight pay increases for several years to come. They are understandably frustrated and have been complaining to co-workers, supervisors, human resource managers and anyone else who will listen.

The problem has been particularly difficult in the St. Louis Missouri facility. Several employees have posted their complaints on Twitter and their personal Facebook pages. To make matters even worse, a video has surfaced on YouTube featuring several Exactitude employees in a satirical music video that depicts Exactitude managers as clueless, inept and money hungry. Older workers are pictured sitting in trash cans portraying them as pushed aside because of their age. The video is gaining in popularity and a local TV station has featured it in a news segment that casts Exactitude in a negative light. Even more troubling is the recent appearance of radio and television ads on local stations that explain the benefits of union membership. The ads are probably directed at the disgruntled Exactitude employees.

HR Director Shannon McLaughlin was called to the facility to meet with nervous managers and supervisors. "What can we do?" asked Anthony, the plant manager. "What if we offer to go back to the old pay plan if they agree not to talk to union organizers? I think that would make them happy." Bert, a production supervisor, explained, "I'm pretty sure they made the video in the factory on their breaks, and sent it with their company e-mail accounts. Should we discipline them for that?"

Carla, another production supervisor, said, "I think there's an information meeting planned with the union. I know where it is. I can go there and see who is interested. If it's the older guys in the video we could offer them early retirement and that would take care of the problem."

Tyler, a manager at the facility, added, "Everyone shouldn't be so concerned. Acme Manufacturing had a union when I worked there and it wasn't bad at all. The management worked closely with the union on all sorts of issues and everyone got along really well. I was there five years and we never went on strike."

Quang, another manager, agreed. "I don't think it's going to be a big problem. There's a rumor that if a union is certified, Exactitude will shut this plant down and move production to one of the other three plants. That will probably scare enough people that the union will never get certified," he added.

Shannon interrupted the discussion. "You've brought up some really important issues, and I need your cooperation in clearing up some misconceptions before we do anything at all."

Questions:

1. Evaluate Anthony, Bert, Carla and Quang's concerns thoroughly. Which actions are problematic and why?
2. What are the steps employees need to take if they wish to certify a union to represent them?
3. Suggest ways that Exactitude could establish a situation similar to the one Tyler described if a union is certified.

Working with a Team   HANDLING A GRIEVANCE

Break into teams of three. This role-play requires one person to play the role of the HR director (Chris), another to play the role of the employee (Pat), and a third to play the role of the union steward (C.J.).

Each team member should read the following scenario and the excerpt from the union contract and then role-play a meeting in Chris's office. This role-play should take no more than 15 minutes.

Scenario The head of security for your company has recently been focusing attention on the removal of illegal substances from the company's workplace. One morning last week, a guard suspected the possession of a controlled substance by an employee, Pat. The guard noticed Pat placing a bag in a personal locker and subsequently searched the locker. The guard found a variety of pills, some of which he thought were nonprescription types. As Pat was leaving work for the day, the security guard stopped Pat with a request for Pat to empty the contents of the bag being carried. Pat was not told why the request was being made. Pat refused to honor the request and stormed out of the door, leaving the company's premises. Pat was terminated the next morning by the boss for refusing to obey the legitimate order of a building security guard. Feeling unable to address the issue satisfactorily

with Pat's supervisor, Pat and C.J. have set up this meeting with Chris.

Chris has just gone into a meeting with Pat and C.J. Chris wishes to enforce Pat's supervisor's decision to terminate Pat and justify the reason for it. C.J. and Pat, on the other hand, claim this action is a violation of the union contract.

Relevant Contract Language The following is excerpted from the labor agreement:

> An employee who fails to maintain proper standards of conduct at all times, or who violates any of the following rules, shall be subject to disciplinary action.
>
> Rule 4: Bringing illegal substances, firearms, or intoxicating liquors onto company premises, using or possessing these on company property, or reporting to work under the influence of a substance is strictly prohibited.
>
> Rule 11: Refusal to follow supervisory orders or acting in any way insubordinate to any company agent is strictly prohibited.

Role for Chris To handle this grievance, listen to the employee's complaint, investigate the facts as best you can, make your decision, and explain it clearly.

Learning an HRM Skill   NEGOTIATION SKILLS

About the skill: The essence of effective negotiation can be summarized in the following six recommendations.[55]

1. ***Research your opponent.*** Acquire as much information as you can about your opponent's interests and goals. What people must he or she appease? What is his or her strategy? This information will help you better understand your opponent's behavior, predict his or her responses to your offers, and frame solutions in terms of his or her interests.
2. ***Begin with a positive overture.*** Research shows that concessions tend to be reciprocated and lead to agreements. As a result, begin bargaining with a positive overture—perhaps a small concession—and then reciprocate your opponent's concessions.
3. ***Address problems, not personalities.*** Concentrate on the negotiation issues, not on the personal characteristics of your opponent. When negotiations become tough, avoid the tendency to attack your opponent. You disagree with your opponent's ideas or position, not him or her personally.

Separate the people from the problem and don't personalize differences.

4. ***Pay little attention to initial offers.*** Treat an initial offer as merely a point of departure. Everyone needs an initial position, and initial positions tend to be extreme and idealistic. Treat them as such.
5. ***Emphasize win-win solutions.*** If conditions are supportive, look for an integrative solution. Frame options in terms of your opponent's interests and look for solutions that allow your opponent, as well as you, to declare a victory.
6. ***Be open to accepting third-party assistance.*** When stalemates are reached, consider the use of a neutral third party—a mediator, an arbitrator, or a conciliator. Mediators can help parties come to an agreement, but they don't impose a settlement. Arbitrators hear both sides of the dispute then impose a solution. Conciliators are more informal and act as a communication conduit, passing information between the parties, interpreting messages, and clarifying misunderstandings.

Enhancing Your Communication Skills

1. Research the effect that an economic recession has on union membership, contract negotiations, and other aspects of belonging to and working with unions. Present your findings in a two- to three-page research paper or a 3–5 minute presentation with presentation slides. Cite all references.
2. Select a video online that either supports or discourages union membership. Check the facts presented in the video for accuracy. Present your findings to your class.
3. Research Right to Work laws nationally and in your state. Does support of these laws seem to be increasing or

decreasing? What has been their effect in your state on labor and on business? Present your findings in a 5–10 minute presentation with a minimum of four presentation slides.
4. Organize a union in your Human Resource Management class. Determine student concerns and demands, considering things you think need to change and things you do not want to change. Act as the union representative and prepare a written proposal to present to your professor.

CHAPTER 1
The Dynamic Environment of HRM

1. S. Ladika, "Global Turmoil Tests Ability to Protect Workers," *Workforce Management*, online at http://www.workforce.com/article/20110407/NEWS02/304079992# accessed May 13, 2011.

2. D. Tobenkin, "Unrest Adds Stress, Opportunities for HR Managers in Middle East, Africa," *HR Magazine*, online at http://www.shrm.org/hrdisciplines/global/articles/pages/unrestmideastafrica.aspx accessed May 13, 2011.

3. "Global 500," online at http://money.cnn.com/magazines/fortune/global500/2010/countries/China.html accessed May 10, 2011.

4. Excerpt from Robert W. Lane, C.E.O. John Deere, at Iowa State University, (April 24, 2005).

5. Ibid.

6. "Global 500," online at http://money.cnn.com/magazines/fortune/global500/2010/countries/China.html accessed May 10, 2011.

7. A multinational corporation has significant operations in two or more countries. A transnational corporation maintains significant operations in two or more countries simultaneously and gives each the decision-making authority to operate in the local country.

8. For a more comprehensive coverage of the cultural dimension, see Geert Hofstede, *Cultural Consequences: International Differences in Work-Related Values* (Beverly Hills: Sage Publications, 1980).

9. "Top 25 Innovations," online at http://www.cnn.com/2005/TECH/01/03/cnn25.top25.innovations/index.html accessed May 10, 2011.

10. T. L. Friedman, *The World Is Flat: A Brief History of the Twenty-first Century* (New York: Farrar, Straus and Giroux, 2005), pp. 9–11.

11. "Tomorrow's Jobs," U.S. Bureau of Labor Statistics, http://www.bls.gov/oco/oco2003.htm (December, 18, 2007).

12. J. Schermerhorn, *Management*, 9th ed. (Hoboken: John Wiley & Sons, Inc., 2008), p. 159.

13. American Management Association "2007 Electronic Monitoring & Surveillance Survey" online at http://press.amanet.org/press-releases/177/2007-electronic-monitoring-surveillance-survey/accessed May 13, 2011.

14. Society of Human Resource Management, "2007–2008 Workplace Trends List," online at http://www.shrm.org/Research/FutureWorkplaceTrends/Documents/2008WorkplaceTrendsList.pdf accessed May 13, 2011.

15. H. F. Gale Jr., T. R. Wojan, and J. C. Olmsted, "Skills, Flexible Manufacturing Technology, and Work Organization," *Industrial Relations*, (January 2002), pp. 48–79.

16. Based on "Chief Blogging Officer Title Catching on With Corporations," *Advertising Age*, (May 1, 2008); M. Scott, "Worker E-Mail and Blogging Use Seen as Growing Risk for Companies," *Financial Week* (July 20, 2007); D. Kirkpatrick and D. Roth, "Why There's No Escaping the Blog," *Fortune* (January 10, 2005), pp. 40–44; S. E. Needleman, "Blogging Becomes a Corporate Job: Digital Handshake?" *Wall Street Journal*, (May 31, 2005), p. B-1; J. Segal, "Beware Bashing Bloggers," *HR Magazine*, (June 2005), pp. 165–171; and K. Wingfield, "Blogging for Business," *Wall Street Journal*, (July 20, 2005), p. A-1.

17. O. C. Richard, "Racial Diversity, Business Strategy, and Firm Performance: A Resource-Based View," *Academy of Management Journal*, (April 2000), pp. 164–177; and M. Lien, "Workforce Diversity: Opportunities in the Melting Pot," *Occupational Outlook Quarterly*, (Summer 2004), pp. 28–37.

18. A. Pomeroy, "A Passion for Diversity," *HR Magazine*, (March 2008), pp. 48–49.

19. DiversityInc, "The DiversityInc Top 50 Companies for Diversity 2011," online at http://www.diversityincbestpractices.com/cgi-bin/cms/DI_Top50.cgi?mode=view&id=8301/accessed May 14, 2011.

20. C. Dugas, "Boomers wanting to work past retirement age find limited options," *USA Today*, (August 11, 2010) online at http://www.usatoday.com/money/economy/employment/2010-08-10-1Aworkinglonger10_CV_N.htm accessed May 31, 2011.

21. B. Leonard, "Not All Training Programs Have Felt the Full Squeeze of Corporate Belt-Tightening," *HR Magazine*, (April 2002), p. 25; R. Koonce, "Redefining Diversity," *Training and Development*, (December 2001), pp. 22–33; and T. Colling, "Institutional Theory and the Cross-Cultural Transfer of Employment Policy: The Case of Workforce Diversity in US Multinationals," *Journal of International Business Studies*, (May 2005), pp. 304–321.

22. See Society of Human Resource Management, "What Are Some Strategies for Recruiting and Retaining a Diverse Workforce?" *Workplace Diversity Initiative*, (September 29, 2000), pp. 1–3.

23. B. Benham, "Get Your Share," *Working Woman* (April 2001), pp. 54–58.

24. See, for instance, "Focus on the 100 Best–Top 10 2008," *Working Mother Magazine Online*, www.workingmother.com accessed May 24, 2009.

25. Economist Intelligence Unit Limited, "Global Firms in 2020: The Next Decade of Change for Organisations and Workers," *Economist*, 2010.

26. D. Kubal and J. Newman, "Work-Life Balance Becoming a Key Tool for Retention," *Workforce Management*, (May 7, 2008), online at http://www.workforce.com/article/20080507/Tools/305079992/work-life-balance-becoming-a-key-tool-for-retention accessed December 15, 2008.

27. See, for instance, L. Belkin, "From Dress-Down Friday to Dress-Down Life," *New York Times*, (June 22, 2003), p. 1; and E. Tahminicioglu, "By Telecommuting, the Disabled Get a Key to the Office, and a Job," *New York Times*, (July 20, 2003), p. 1.

28. See, for example, "U.S. Employers Polish Image to Woo a Demanding New Generation," *Manpower Argus*, (February 2000), p. 2.

29. L. L. Martins, K. B. Eddleston, and J. F. Veiga, "Moderators of the Relationship Between Work-Family Conflict and Career Satisfaction," *Academy of Management Journal*, (May 2002), pp. 399–409; and L. Carlson, "Work-Life Benefits Don't Guarantee Work-Life Balance: Having a Work-Life Benefits Program Isn't Enough: You Must Be Sure That Executives and Managers Are Walking the Talk," *Employee Benefits News*, (August 1, 2005), pp. 1–2.

30. Grant Thornton International Ltd. "Proportion of women in senior management falls to 2004 Levels," online at http://www.gti.org/pressroom accessed March 8, 2011.

31. L. Rubis, "What the World Needs Now: More Skilled Tradespeople," *HR Magazine*, HR Trendbook 2011.

32. K. J. Bartsch, "The employment projections for 2008–2018," Occupational Outlook Division, Office of Occupational Statistics and Employment Projections, Bureau of Labor Statistics, (November 2009).

33. Manpower, "World of Work Insight: Strategic Migration—A Short-Term Solution to the Skilled Trades Shortage," (August 2010).

34. T. Minton-Eversol, "U.S., Canadian Firms Look Past Borders," *HR Magazine*, (April 2008), p. 36.

35. M. Selva, "HSBC layoffs: 30,000 jobs to be cut in global overhaul," The Christian Science Monitor, (August 1, 2011), online at http://www.csmonitor.com/Business/Latest-News-Wires/2011/0801/HSBC-layoffs-30-000-jobs-to-be-cut-in-global-overhaul accessed September 11, 2011.

36. L. M. Gossett, "The Long-Term Impact of Short-Term Workers," *Management Communication Quarterly*, (August 2001), pp. 115–120.

37. For an interesting background perspective of contingent workers, see S. F. Befort, "Revisiting the Black Hole of Workplace Regulation: A Historical and Comparative Perspective of Contingent Work," *Berkeley Journal of Employment and Labor Law,* (Summer 2003), pp. 153–178.

38. A. Rassuli, "Evolution of the Professional Contingent Workforce," *Journal of Labor Research,* (Fall 2005), Vol. 26, Issue 4.

39. See, for instance, B. A. Lautsch, "Uncovering and Explaining Variance in the Features and Outcomes of Contingent Work," *Industrial and Labor Relations Review,* (October 2002), pp. 23–44.

40. See K. J. Bannan, "Breakaway (A Special Report)—Getting Help—Together: By Bundling Job-Recruiting Efforts, Small Firms Seek Attention—and Leverage," *Wall Street Journal,* (April 23, 2001), p. A-12.

41. D. Karwatka, "W. Edwards Deming and Modern Factory Quality Control," *Tech Directions,* (May 2008), Vol. 67, Issue 10.

42. See, for example, J. McElroy, "Six Lessons for Ford," *Ward's Auto World* (December 2001), p. 17.

43. "Continuous Improvement: Ten Essential Criteria," *Measuring Business Excellence,* (January 2002), p. 49.

44. K. B. Stone, "Kaizen Teams: Integrated HRD Practices for Successful Team Building"*Advances in Developing Human Resources,* (Feb. 2010), Vol. 12 Issue 1, pp. 61–77.

45. M. Budman, "Jim Champy Puts His 'X' on Reengineering," *Across the Board,* (March/April 2002), pp. 15–16.

46. D. J. Lynch, "Manufacturing losses weigh heavily on Ohio," *USA Today,* (March 3, 2008), pp. 1B–2B.

47. "Will More Offshoring Be a Result of Economic Uncertainties?," *HR Focus,* (June 2008), p. 21.

48. "Mergers and Acquisitions, Opportunities for Global Growth" *International Business Report,* 2011 Grant Thornton International online at http://www.internationalbusinessreport.com accessed September 14, 2012.

49. B. Tai and N. Lockwood, "Mergers and Acquisitions" *HR Magazine,* online at http://www.shrm.org/Research/Articles/Articles/Pages/Mergers_20and_20Acquisitions.aspx accessed May 26, 2009.

50. P. A. Cloninger, and T. T. Selvarajan. "Can Ethics Education Improve Ethical Judgment? An Empirical Study." *SAM Advanced Management Journal (07497075)* 75.4 (2010), pp. 4-49.

51. "Did Enron and SOX Change Ethical Behavior at U.S. Companies?," *HR Focus,* (February 2008), p. 22.

52. S. J. Hirschfeld, A Global Perspective on Investigating Employee Misconduct," *Workforce Management,* (July 23, 2009), online at http://www.workforce.com/article/20090723/NEWS02/307239988/a-global-perspective-on-investigating-employee-misconduct accessed May 31, 2011.

53. Ibid.

54. M. M. Clark, "Corporate Ethics Programs Make a Difference, But Not the Only Difference," *HR Magazine,* (July 2003), p. 36; and T. F. Shea, "Employees' Report Card on Supervisors' Ethics: No Improvement," *HR Magazine,* (April 2002), p. 29.

55. See also "Angels in the Boardroom," *BusinessWeek* (July 7, 2003), p. 12; and A. G. Peace, J. Weber, K. S. Hartzel, and J. Nightingale, "Ethical Issues in eBusiness: A Proposal for Creating the eBusiness Principles," *Business and Society Review* (Spring 2002), pp. 41–60.

56. M. Schoeff Jr., "U.S. Navy: Optimas Award Winner for General Excellence" *Workforce Management,* (December 14, 2009), online at http://www.workforce.com/article/20091211/NEWS02/312119978 accessed May 18, 2011.

57. D. Blottenberger, "All branches meet military recruiting goals," *Stars and Stripes,* (January 14, 2011), online at http://www.stripes.com/news/all-branches-meet-military-recruiting-goals-1.131869 May 19, 2011.

58. E. Slavin, "Sailors tapped for separation encouraged to convert to new job," *Stars and Stripes,* (May 11, 2011), online at http://www.stripes.com/news/sailors-tapped-for-separation-encouraged-to-convert-to-new-job-1.143298 accessed May 19, 2011.

59. U.S. Navy online at http://www.public.navy.mil/bupers-npc/support/Diversity/Pages/default2.aspx accessed May 19, 2011.

60. B. J. Asch, P. Heaton, and B. Savych, Institute, "Explaining Recent Army and Navy Minority Recruiting Trends" *Rand National Defense Research,* 2009, online at http://www.rand.org/pubs/monographs/MG861/ accessed May 19, 2011.

CHAPTER 2
Functions and Strategy

1. R. T. Ramos, "Home Depot Laying Off 1,000 Nationwide," *The Atlanta Journal-Constitution,* (January 26, 2010), online at http://www.ajc.com/news/business/home-depot-laying-off-1000-nationwide/nQb3m/ accessed May 20, 2011.

2. R. J. Grossman, "Remodeling HR at Home Depot," *HR Magazine* (November 2008), pp. 67–72.

3. T. Starner, "Restructuring HR," *Human Resource Executive,* online at http://www.hrexecutive.com accessed May 26, 2009.

4. "Home Depot restructuring Human Resources function, jobs could be cut."*International Herald Tribune,* (April 4, 2008) online at http://www.nytimes.com accessed April 5, 2008.

5. No specific date is identified regarding the "birth" of personnel departments, but the generally accepted inception of personnel was in the early 1900s in the BF Goodrich Company. Early personnel departments were often seen as performing relatively unimportant activities. In fact, the personnel department was often viewed as an "employee graveyard"—a place to send employees who were past their prime and couldn't do much damage.

6. C. H. Anderson, "Take Steps to Ensure HR Tactics Support Business Strategy," (May 30, 2008) online at http://www.shrm.org/hrdisciplines/orgempdev/articles/pages/hrtactics.aspx accessed September 14, 2012.

7. K. Gurchiek, "Staffing Issues Critical to Business Strategies, SHRM, (May 28, 2008), online at http://www.shrm.org/Publications/HRNews/Pages/StaffingIssuesCritical.aspx accessed May 30, 2008.

8. "Watson Wyatt Human Capital Index: Human Capital As a Lead Indicator of Shareholder Value," online at http://www.watsonwyatt.com/render.asp?catid=1&id=9047 accessed September 14, 2012.

9. See, for instance, N. W. Bryan, "HR by the Numbers," *Workforce,* (June 2000), pp. 94–104.

10. Boston Consulting Group "Creating People Advantage 2010: How Companies Can Adapt Their HR Practices for Volatile Times," (September 2010), online at http://www.shrm.org/Research/SurveyFindings/Documents/CreatingPeopleAdvantage2010.pdf accessed May 23, 2011.

11. P. J. Kiger, "Serious Progress in Strategic Workforce Planning," *Workforce Management,* (July 1, 2010), online at http://www.workforce.com/article/20100701/NEWS02/307019993/serious-progress-in-strategic-workforce-planning accessed May 23, 2011.

12. D. Schoeneman, "Can Google Come Out and Play?," *New York Times,* (December 31, 2006), online at http://www.nytimes.com/2006/12/31/fashion/31google.html?pagewanted=all&_moc.semityn.www accessed May 1, 2008.

13. See, for example, S. Bates, "Most Workers Only Moderately Engaged, Study Finds," *HR News,* (August 14, 2003), p. 1.

14. M. Royal and R. Masson, "Employee Engagement in Tough Times," *Workforce Management,* (May 2009) online at http://www.workforce.com/article/20090506/NEWS02/305069991 accessed May 31, 2011.

15. G. A. Stevens and J. Burley, "Piloting the Rocket of Radical-Innovation: Selecting the Right People for the Right Roles Dramatically Improves the Effectiveness of New Business Development," *Research Technology Management,* (March–April 2003), pp. 16–26.

16. J. Marquez, "The State of Compensation: Raising the Performance Bar," *Workforce Management,* (April 24, 2006), pp. 31–32.

17. See, for instance, S. Miller, "Employers Underestimate the Role of Benefits in Employee Loyalty," SHRM, (April 10, 2008), online at http://www.shrm.org/hrdisciplines/benefits/articles/pages/roleofbenefitsinloyalty.aspx accessed May 1, 2008.

18. N. C. Nelson, "Employee Retention Strategies for Small Businesses," SHRM White Paper, SHRM, (February 2008).

19. Information based on Society for Human Resource Management, "HR Basics 2000," (October 2000).

20. As we will show in Chapter 5, during a period of downsizing, the employment department may also handle layoffs.

21. It should be noted that compensation and benefits may be, in fact, two separate departments. However, for reading flow, we will consider the department as a combined, singular unit.

22. C. H. Anderson, "Take Steps to Ensure HR Tactics Support Business Strategy," SHRM, (May 2008), online at http://www.shrm.org/hrdisciplines/orgempdev/articles/pages/hrtactics.aspx accessed September 14, 2012.

23. M. Bruno, "Health Benefits Paramount for Workers When Choosing an Employer," *Financial Times*, (January 7, 2008).

24. See G. Roper, "Managing Employee Relations," *HR Magazine* (May 2005), pp. 101–104; and J. A. Segal, "Labor Pains for Union-Free Employers: Don't Be Caught Unaware of Nonunion Employees' Labor Law Rights," *HR Magazine*, (March 2004), pp. 113–118.

25. J. Finney, "Six secrets of top performers," *Communication World* 25.3 (2008): 23, *MasterFILE Premier*, EBSCO, online at http://www.ebscohost.com/public/masterfile-premier accessed May 25, 2011.

26. O. Protch, "abc's of supervisory communication," *Supervision* 69.10 (2008): 17, *MasterFILE Premier*, EBSCO, online at http://www.ebscohost.com/public/masterfile-premier accessed May 25, 2011.

27. D. K. Denton, "Creating a Self-Confident Workforce," *Journal for Quality & Participation* 33.3 (2010): 9, *MasterFILE Premier*, EBSCO, online at http://www.ebscohost.com/public/masterfile-premier accessed May 25, 2011.

28. "Employee Relations," *HR Magazine*, (February 2003), p. 127; and L. A. Weatherly, "HR Technology, Leveraging the Shift to Self-Service—It's Time to Go Strategic," online at www.shrm.org/research/quarterly/2005/0305RQuart_essay.asp, (March 2005) accessed March 15, 2005.

29. "HR Certification," Human Resource Certification Institute, online at www.hrci.org accessed September 14, 2012.

30. O. Protch, "abc's of Supervisory Communication," *Supervision* 69.10 (2008): 17, *MasterFILE Premier*, EBSCO, online at http://www.ebscohost.com/public/masterfile-premier accessed May 25, 2011.

31. "Human Resources," online at www.bls.gov accessed September 14, 2012.

32. L. Ryan, "The Sunny Side of Human Resources," *BusinessWeek*, (August 13, 2007), p. 15.

33. K. Gurchiek, "Survey: Key Skills Advance HR Career," *HR Magazine*, (April 2008), p. 38.

34. Ibid.

35. Watson Wyatt Worldwide, "Effective Recruiting Tied to Stronger Financial Performance," online at www.watsonwyatt.com/news/press.asp?id514959 (2005).

36. Ibid.

37. "HR Outsourcing Is Not All About the Money," *HR Magazine*, (April 2003), p. 14; and S. Bates, "Facing the Future," *HR Magazine*, (July 2002), p. 30.

38. T. Mallory, "May I Handle That for You?" *Inc.*, (March 2008), pp 40–42.

39. "IBM and American Airlines sign human resources services agreement," (March 2, 2007), online at http://www-03.ibm.com/press/us/en/pressrelease/21165.wss accessed September 14, 2012.

40. "A Watershed Year Predicted for HR Outsourcing," *HR Magazine;* (February 2006); S. Miller, "PEO Boom: Outsourcing for Small Firms Expected to Double by 2014," SHRM, (October 2007) online at http://www.shrm.org accessed May 30, 2008.

41. "Shared Services and Centers of Excellence SHRM Poll," SHRM, (August 6, 2010) online at http://www.shrm.org/Research/SurveyFindings/Articles/Pages/sharedservices.aspx accessed May 24, 2011.

42. W. Bliss, "Staffing the Human Resource Function," SHRM, (January 2011) online at http://www.shrm.org/templatestools/toolkits/pages/staffinghrfunction.aspx accessed May 24, 2011.

43. B. Leonard, "Organizations Benefit from Sharing HR Services," *HR Magazine*, (February 2000), p. 32.

44. M. R. Bryant, "Managing Human Resources in a Small Organization," SHRM, (December 30, 2010), online at http://www.shrm.org/templatestools/toolkits/pages/managinghumanresources.aspx accessed September 14, 2012.

45. T. Minton-Eversole, "Best Expatriate Assignments Require Much Thought, Even More Planning," SHRM Online Management Staffing (February 29, 2008) online at http://http://www.shrm.org/hrdisciplines/staffingmanagement/articles/pages/bestexpatriateassignments.aspx accessed September 14, 2012. May 25, 2011.

46. "Companies Juggle Cost Cutting With Maintaining Competitive Benefits for Overseas Assignments," Mercer International Assignments Survey 2010, online at http://cn.mercer.com/press-releases/1392525 accessed May 24, 2011

47. See, for instance, M. A. del Rio, "Expatriate Tax: Understanding the Spanish System," *Benefits and Compensation*, (July–August 2000), pp. 27–30.

48. Based on J. A. Segal, "The Joy of Uncooking," *HR Magazine*, (November 2002), online at http://www.shrm.org/Publications/hrmagazine/EditorialContent/Pages/1102segal.aspx accessed May 28, 2009.

49. Ibid.

50. "Bank of American Found in Violation of Sarbanes-Oxley Whistleblower Protection Provisions," U.S. Department of Labor, Occupational Safety & Health Administration, (September 14, 2011), online at http://www.osha.gov/pls/oshaweb/owadisp.show_document?p_table=NEWS_RELEASES&p_id=20667 accessed September 19, 2011.

51. C. Hirschman, "Someone to Listen: Ombuds Can Offer Employees a Confidential, Discrete Way to Handle Problems—But Setup and Communication Are Crucial to Making this Role Work Properly," *HR Magazine*, (January 2003), pp. 46–52.

52. "Frito Lay Mission Statement," online at http://www.pepsico.com accessed May 24, 2011.

53. A. Levenson, T. Faber, "Count on Productivity Gains," *HR Magazine*, (June 2009), p. 68-74.

54. Human Resource Certification Institute, See *PHR, SPHR, GPHR Handbook* (Alexandria: HRCI, Society for Human Resource Management, 2008).

CHAPTER 3
Equal Employment Opportunity

1. Compiled from C. M. Padalino, "Workplace Retaliation Lawsuits Don't have to Take an Eye for an Eye," *Workforce Management*, (April 29, 2011), online at http://www.workforce.com/article/20110429/NEWS02/304299993/workplace-retaliation-lawsuits-dont-have-to-take-an-eye-for-an-eye accessed June 14, 2011; R. Zeidner, "Consider Yourself a Retaliation Target," *HR Magazine*, (March 1, 2009), online at http://www.shrm.org/Publications/hrmagazine/EditorialContent/Pages/0309zeidner.aspx accessed June 14, 2011; "Retaliation," Equal Employment Opportunity, Commission, online at http://www.eeoc.gov/laws/types/retaliation.cfm accessed June 14, 2011.

2. Jackson Lewis Law Firm, "Charges of Job Discrimination against Employers Hit Record High in FY 2010 EEOC Reports," online at http://www.jacksonlewis.com accessed June 4, 2011.

3. "Your Rights Against Discrimination Based on Sexual Orientation" (July 2008), online at http://www.nolo.com/legal-encyclopedia/sexual-orientation-discrimination-rights-29541.html accessed June 4, 2011.

4. See, for instance, ReligiousTolerance.org, "Governments Which Have Recognized Same Sex Relationships" (2003), online at http://www.religioustolerance.org/hom_mar4.htm.

5. J. E. Whitney, "Religious and Ethnic Discrimination in the Workplace," Davis Brown Law Firm, Des Moines IA, 2011.

6. Equal Opportunity Employment Commission "Significant EEOC Race/Color Cases," online at http://www.eeoc.gov accessed June 6, 2011.

7. R. D. Alainiz, "Post 9/11 Religious Discrimination Claims Rise," online at http://www.achrnews.com accessed August 18, 2001.

8. "Religious Accommodation in the Workplace," Anti-Defamation League, online at http://www.adl.org/religious accessed June 6, 2011.

9. U.S. Bureau of Labor Statistics "Women at Work," (March 2011) online at http://www.bls.gov/spotlight/2011/women accessed June 7, 2011.

10. U.S. Equal Employment Opportunity Commission, "Charge Statistics FY1997 through FY2010," online at http://www1.eeoc.gov/eeoc/statistics/enforcement/charges.cfm?renderforprint=1 accessed June 7, 2011.

11. National Committee on Pay Equity, "Questions and Answers on Pay Equity," online at http://www.pay-equity.org/info accessed June 6, 2011.

12. L. Fitzpatrick, "Why Do Women Still Earn Less Than Men?," *Time*, (April 20, 2010), online at http://www.time.com/time/nation/article/0,8599, 1983185,00.html accessed June 6, 2011.

13. U.S. Bureau of Labor, Women's earnings and employment by industry, 2009," (February 16, 2011), online at http://www.bls.gov/opub/ted/2011/ted_20110216.htm accessed June 6, 2011.

14. C. Rampell, "The Gender Pay Gap by Industry," *New York Times*, online at http://economix.blogs.nytimes.com/2011/02/17/the-gender-pay-gap-by-industry/ accessed June 6, 2011.

15. The EEOA of 1972 amended Title VII in several ways, including expanding the definition of employer to include state and local government agencies and educational institutions, reducing the minimum number of employees in private sector-organizations from 25 to 15; and giving more power to the EEOC to file suit against alleged violators of Title VII.

16. Equal Employment Opportunity Commission, online at http://www.eeoc.gov, accessed June 8, 2011.

17. Compiled from U.S. Equal Employment Opportunity Commission, "EEOC Reports Job Bias Charges Hit Record High of Nearly 100,000 in Fiscal Year 2010," Press Release (January 1, 2011) online at http://www.eeoc.gov, and B. Leonard, "Rise in EEO Charges Impacts HR's Workload," (June 8, 2011) online at http://www.shrm.org accessed June 13, 2011.

18. ADEA is afforded to all individuals age 40 and older employed in organizations with 20 or more employees.

19. U.S. Equal Employment Opportunity Commission, "Age Discrimination," online at http://www.eeoc.gov accessed June 6, 2011.

20. U.S. Equal Employment Opportunity Commission, "Facts About Age Discrimination," online at http://www.eeoc.gov/facts/age.html accessed September 15, 2012.

21. U.S. Equal Employment Opportunity Commission, "Charge Statistics FY1997 through FY2010," online at http://www1.eeoc.gov/eeoc/statistics/enforcement/charges.cfm?renderforprint=1 accessed June 7, 2011.

22. "FAA Statement on Pilot Retirement Age," Federal Aviation Administration, (December 14, 2007), online at http://www.faa.gov/news/press_releases/news_story.cfm?newsId=10072 accessed September 14, 2012.

23. "Equal Pay Act of 1963," online at http://www.eeoc.gov/laws/statutes/epa.cfm accessed June 8, 2011.

24. "Ledbetter v. Goodyear Tire and Rubber Co.," U.S. Supreme Court online at http://www.supremecourt.gov/opinions/06pdf/05-1074.pdf accessed June 8, 2011.

25. Personal experience of Susan Verhulst, author.

26. U.S. Equal Employment Opportunity Commission, "Facts about pregnancy discrimination," online at http://www.eeoc.gov/facts/fs-preg.html accessed June 8, 2011.

27. J. E. Hall, M. T. Kobata and M. Denis, "Failure to Accommodate Pregnancy," *Workforce Management*, (June 2009), online at http://www.workforce.com/article/20090619/NEWS02/306199990 accessed June 8, 2011.

28. U.S. Equal Employment Opportunity Commission online at http://www.eeoc.gov accessed June 8, 2011.

29. H. J. Cain, "Disability Discrimination," Hopkins & Huebner PC, Des Moines IA, (September 14, 2009).

30. R. R. Hastings, "EEOC: Myths, Fears of Mental Disabilities a Barrier," SHRM, (March 17, 2011), online at http://www.shrm.org/hrdisciplines/Diversity/Articles/Pages/MythsFearsofMentalDisabilities.aspx accessed June 8, 2011.

31. "Consider Medical Aids When Determining Disability Status," *Workforce Management*, (July 1, 1999), online at http://www.workforce.com/apps/pbcs.dll/article?AID=/19990701/NEWS02/307019959 accessed September 14, 2012.

32. R. J. Grossman, "Countering a Weight Crisis," *HR Magazine*, (March 2004).

33. A. Smith "Expanded Leave Causes Complications," *HR Magazine*, (March 2008), p.28.

34. T. D. McCutchen, "Managing Family and Medical Leave," SHRM, (February 2011) online at http://www.shrm.org/templatestools/toolkits/pages/managingfamilyandmedicalleave.aspx acesssed February 28, 2011.

35. U.S. Department of Labor, "The Family and Medical Leave Act," online at http://www.dol.gov/whd/regs/compliance/1421.htm accessed June 9, 2011.

36. "Family and Medical Leave Act (FMLA) of 1993, Updated 3/2/09," SHRM, online at http://www.shrm.org/LegalIssues/FederalResources/FederalStatutesRegulationsandGuidanc/Pages/FamilyandMedicalLeaveActof1993.aspx accessed June 9, 2011.

37. U.S. Department of Labor, www.dol.gov/vets/ accessed September 14, 2012.

38. "Employment Situation of Veterans Summary," Bureau of Labor Statistics, online at http://www.bls.gov/cps accessed April 10, 2008.

39. "Employer Support of the Guard and Reserve," online at http://esgr.org/userra.asp?p5summary accessed June 23, 2008.

40. U.S. Department of Veterans Affairs, "VR & E Information for Employers," online at http://www.vba.gov accessed June 23, 2008.

41. EEOC, "EEOC Settles ADA Suit Against BNSF for Genetic Bias," (April 18, 2001), online at http://www.eeoc.gov/eeoc/newsroom/release/4-18-01.cfm accessed June 9, 2011.

42. U.S. Department of Labor, "Frequently asked questions regarding the Genetic Information Nondiscrimination Act," online at http://www.dol.gov accessed June 9, 2011.

43. U.S. Equal Employment Opportunity Commission, "Adoption of Questions and Answers To Clarify and Provide a Common Interpretation of the Uniform Guidelines on Employee Selection Procedures," online at http://www.eeoc.gov/policy/docs/qanda_clarify_procedures.html accessed June 9, 2011.

44. J. Harmon, "Identifying and Preventing Class Actions," *Workforce Management* (August 2004), online at http://www.workforce.com/section/03/article/23/81/53.html accessed September 27, 2012; and M. T. Johnson, "The Car Wreck You Can Stop," *Workforce Management*, (December 2003), pp. 18–20.

45. J. S. Dempsey, L. S. Forst, *An Introduction to Policing*, (New York: Cengage Learning, 2009), p. 202.

46. Connecticut v. Teal, U.S. Supreme Court, 102, Docket No. 2525 (1982).

47. We must note here that the 4/5ths rule, as established, does not recognize specific individuals' requirements; that is, a -minority could be any group. For example, when airlines hired only females as flight attendants, males were the minority.

48. McDonnell-Douglas Corp. v. Green, 411 U.S. 792, 80 (U.S. 1973).

49. McDonnell-Douglas Corp. v. Green, 411 U.S. 792, 80 (U.S. 1973).

50. R. Roosevelt Thomas Jr., "From Affirmative Action to Affirming Diversity," *Harvard Business Review*, (March–April 1990), p. 107.

51. S. Lau, A. Maingault and R. Dooley, "HR Solutions," *HR Magazine*, (January 2006).

52. J. B. Berman, "Defining the 'Essence of the Business': An Analysis of Title VII's Privacy Controls After Johnson Controls," *University of Chicago Law Review, (Summer 2000)*, p. 749.

53. Reasonable accommodation here is a difficult area not to support. If through the use of personal leave an individual can be accommodated, then no BFOQ exists. Also, the courts may view how an enterprise treats traditional Christian holidays in viewing reasonable accommodation. See T. I. Levy, "Religion in the Workplace," *Management Review*, (February 2000), pp. 38–40.

54. See, for example, K. C. Cash, G. R. Gray, and S. A. Rood, "A Framework for Accommodating Religion and Spirituality in the Workplace: Executive Commentary," *Academy of Management Executive*, (August 2000), pp. 124–134.

55. "FedEx Faces Lawsuit Citing Religious Bias Against an Ex-Driver," *Wall Street Journal*, (March 20, 2000), p. B-17.

56. C. J. Layton, "The Hiring Process, a Primer of Legal Dos and Don'ts," *Workforce Management*, (March 2008).

57. A disparate impact occurs when an HRM practice eliminates a group of individuals from job considerations. Disparate treatment exists when an HRM practice eliminates an individual from employment consideration.

58. Albemarle Paper Company v. Moody, 422 U.S. Supreme Court (U.S. 1975).

59. Wards Cove Packing Co., Inc., v. Atonio, U.S. Supreme Court, Docket No. 87-1387, June 5, 1989.

60. Bakke v. Regents of the University of California, 438 U.S. 265 (1978).

61. United Steelworkers of America v. Weber, 99 S. CT. 2721 (1979).

62. Firefighters Local 1784 v. Stotts, 467 Supreme Court, 561 (1984).

63. Wyant v. Jackson Board of Education, 106 Supreme Court, 842 (1986).

64. In EEOC v. Commercial Office Products, U.S. Supreme Court Docket No. 86-1696 (1988), the Court ruled that if a work-sharing arrangement exists between the EEOC and a state or local agency, the time limit increases to 300 days.

65. Adapted from the 1981 Guidebook to Fair Employment -Practices, pp. 123–161; unpublished manuscript by Stanley Mazaroff, Esquire, "A Management Guide to Responding to a Charge of Discrimination Filed with the EEOC" (Baltimore: Venable, Baetjer, and Howard, Attorneys-at-Law, 1994), p. 1. It should also be noted that the EEOC automatically refers all claims to the appropriate state agency. If, however, the state agency defers back to the EEOC, it will proceed with the case. See also Maria Greco Danaher, "EEOC Allowed to Pursue Discrimination Claim on Behalf of Pregnant Nurse," *HR News*, (October 2000), p. 6.

66. U.S. Equal Employment Opportunity Commission, "Charge Statistics: FY 1997 Through FY 2010," online at http://www.eeoc.gov/eeoc/statistics/enforcement/charges.cfm accessed June 9, 2011.

67. S. Sclafane "EEOC eyeing Bigger Targets, Industries," *National Underwriter*, (April 17, 2006), p. 10.

68. Under Section 503 of the Vocational Rehabilitation Act, those organizations that have a contract or subcontract in the amount of $2,500 must have affirmative action plans to hire the disabled. For the Vietnam Veterans Readjustment Act, the amount is $10,000.

69. "Validate Hiring Tests To Withstand EEO Scrutiny: DOL & EEOC Officials," *HR Focus*, (May 2008).

70. M. K. Zachary, "Sexual Harassment Procedures & Third Party Retaliation," *Supervision*, (March 2008), p. 23–26.

71. A. Joyce, "Lawsuits Shed new light on sexual harassment of teens," *Washington Post*, (December 2, 2004), p. A01.

72. U.S. Equal Employment Opportunity Commission Walmart Settles Employment Discrimination Claim By Two Who Are Deaf," online at http:// www.eeo.gov.

73. A. Joyce, "Lawsuits Shed new light on sexual harassment of teens," *Washington Post*, (December 2, 2004) p. A01.

74. U.S. Equal Employment Opportunity Commission, "Sexual-Harassment Charges: EOC & FEPAs Combined: FY 1997–FY 2010," online at www.eeoc.gov/stats/-harass.html accessed September 27, 2012.

75. U.S. Equal Opportunity Employment Commission, "Sexual Harassment Charges EEOC & FEPAs Combined: FY 1997-FY 2007," online at http://www.eeoc.gov/eeoc/statistics/enforcement/sexual_harassment.cfm accessed June 9, 2011.

76. "Federal Monitors Find Illinois Mitsubishi Unit Eradicating Harassment," *Wall Street Journal*, (September 7, 2000), p. A-8.

77. L. J. Munson, C. Hulin, and F. Drasgow, "Longitudinal Analysis of Dispositional Influences and Sexual Harassment: Effects on Job and Psychological Outcomes," *Personnel Psychology*, (Spring 2000), p. 21.

78. See also M. Rotundo, D. H. Nguyen, and P. R. Sackett, "A Meta-Analytic Review of Gender Differences in Perceptions of Sexual Harassment," *Journal of Applied Psychology* (October 2001), pp. 914–922.

79. Meritor Savings Bank v. Vinson, U.S. Supreme Court 106, Docket No. 2399 (1986).

80. R. D. Lee and P. S. Greenlaw, "Employer Liability for Employee Sexual Harassment: A Judicial Policy-Making Study," *Public Administration Review*, (March/April 2000), p. 127.

81. Ibid.

82. "DuPont Statement on Human Rights," DuPont online at http://www2.dupont.com/media/en-us/news-events/insights/human-rights.html accessed September 14, 2012.

83. It should be noted here that under Title VII and the Civil Rights Act of 1991, the maximum award under the federal act is $300,000. However, many cases are tried under state laws that permit unlimited punitive damages.

84. J. W. Janove, "Sexual Harassment and the Big Three Surprises," *HR Magazine*, (November 2001), pp. 123–130; and L. A. Baar and J. Baar, "Harassment Case Proceeds Despite Failure to Report," *HR Magazine*, (June 2005), p. 159.

85. In addition to the Ellerth case, a second Supreme Court ruling in 1998 (Faragher v. City of Boca Raton) reinforced similar-areas of employer liability in terms of sexual harassment charges. See, for example, J. W. Janove, "The Faragher/Ellerth Decision Tree," *HR Magazine*, (September 2003), pp. 149–155; W. L. Kosanovich, J. L. Rosenberg, and L. Swanson, "Preventing and Correcting Sexual Harassment: A Guide to the Ellerth/Faragher Affirmative Defense," *Employee Relations Law Journal*, (Summer 2002), pp. 79–99; and Milton Zall, "Workplace Harassment and Employer Liability," *Fleet Equipment*, (January 2000), p. B-1. See also, "Ruling Allows Defense in Harassment Cases," *HR Magazine*, (August 2004), p. 30.

86. A. Gross-Shaefer, R. Florsheim, and J. Pannetier, "The Swinging Pendulum: Moving from Sexual Harassment to Respectful Workplace Relationships," *Employee Relations Law Journal* (Fall 2003), pp. 50–70.

87. G. P. Panaro, "Investigation of Harassment Can Give Rise to Negligence Claim," *Fair Employment Practices Guidelines*, (June 2003), pp. 1–3.

88. R. Parloff, S. M. Kaufman, "The War Over Unconscious Bias," *Fortune*, (October 10, 2007), pp. 90–102.

89. Walmart Class, online at http://www.walmartclass.com/public_home.html accessed January 13, 2012.

90. See, for example, G. F. Dreher, "Breaking the Glass Ceiling: The Effect of Sex Ratios and Work-Life Programs on Female Leadership at the Top," *Human Relations*, (May 2003), pp. 541–563; and Cornell University School of Industrial and Labor Relations, Glass Ceiling Commission, "About the Glass Ceiling," *Glass Ceiling Commission* (2000), pp. 1–2.

91. Catalyst Foundation, "2007 Catalyst Census Finds Women Gained Ground as Board Committee Chairs," (December 10, 2007), online at http://www.catalyst.org, accessed September 27, 2012.

92. Grant Thornton International Ltd. "Proportion of women in senior mangement falls to 2004 levels," (March 8, 2011), online at http://www.grantthorntonibos.com accessed January 13, 2012.

93. "Federal Investigation into Coca-Cola Shifts to Pay-Bias Concerns," *Wall Street Journal*, (June 16, 2000), p. B-8.

94. J. Walsh, " Transgender Issue Plays Key Role in Anti-Bias Legislation," *Workforce Management*, (March 2011), online at http://www.workforce.com accessed June 9, 2011.

95. A. Smith, "HR Should Provide Training on Preventing Discrimination Based on Sexual Orientation," (May 24, 2011), online at http://www.shrm.org accessed June 9, 2011.

96. J. Moldover, "Employer's Dilemma: When Religious Expression and Gay Rights Cross," *New York Law Journal*, (October 31, 2007), online at http://www.law.com accessed June 9, 2011.

97. "Why do some employees react negatively to co-workers speaking other languages at work and how can HR help?," SHRM HR Knowledge Center, online at http://www.shrm.org accessed June 10, 2011.

98. D. D. Hatch, J. E. Hall, and M. T. Miklave, "New EEOC Guidance on National-Origin Discrimination," *Workforce*, (April 2003), p. 76.

99. See, for instance, U.S. Equal Employment Opportunity Commission, "EEOC Reaches Landmark 'English-Only' Settlement: Chicago Manufacturer to Pay Over $190,000 to Hispanic Workers," www.eeoc.gov/press/9-1-00.html,

(September 1, 2000), pp. 1–2; and Lisa Girion, "13 Phone Operators Win Record $709,284 in English-Only Suit," *Los Angeles Times,* (September 20, 2000), p. C-1.

100. U.S. Equal Employment Opportunity Commission, "Central Station Casino to Pay $1.5 Million in EEOC Settlement for National Origin Bias," U.S. online at http://www.eeoc.gov accessed August 17, 2009.

101. Council on Size and Weight Discrimination, "Statistics on Weight Discrimination: A Waste of Talent," online at http://www.cswd.org, accessed June 10, 2011.

102. J. Smerd, "Overweight Workers Face Bias in Hiring," *Workforce Management* (August 17, 2009), p. 26.

103. A. Smith, "Appearance Standards Challenged as Discriminatory," SHRM Online, (June 30, 2008), online at http://www.shrm.org accessed June 10, 2011.

104. S. Overman, "For some Chinese Job Hopefuls, Success Might Be in the Blood," SHRM Online, (January 1, 2008), online at http://www.shrm.org accessed June 10, 2011.

105. D. K. Srivastava, "Progress of Sexual Harassment Law in India, China and Hong Kong: Prognosis for Further Reform," *Harvard International Law Journal,* (August 11, 2010), volume 51.

106. B. Leonard, "Report: 10 Percent of Employees Report Harassment at Work," SHRM Online, (August 30, 2010), online at http://www.shrm.org accessed June 10, 2011.

107. S. Greenhouse, "Abercrombie and Fitch Bias Case is Settled," *New York Times,* (November 17, 2004).

108. F. Hansen, "Recruiting on the right side of the Law," *Workforce Management,* (May 2006), online at http://www.workforce.com accessed September 14, 2012.

109. This case is based on the U.S. Equal Employment Opportunity Commission, "Federal Express to Pay Over $3.2 Million to Female Truck Driver for Sex Discrimination, Retaliation," (February 25, 2004), online at http://www.eeoc.gov; and S. P. Duffy, "$3.2M Verdict Against FedEx for Sex Harassment," *New York Law Journal* (February 27, 2004), online at http://www.law.com/jsp/article.jsp?id51076428422471 accessed September 27, 2012.

110. 1-false; 2-true; 3-false; 4-true; 5-true; 6-true; 7-true; 8-true; 9-true; and 10-false.

CHAPTER **4**

Employee Rights and Discipline

1. K. Clark, "He could apply at Ghostbusters," *Des Moines Register.* Des Moines, Iowa: Nov 9, 2005. pg. A.1.

2. D. Gregorian, "Marijuana meatballs' cop loses bid to get his job back," *New York Post,* (February 4, 2010), online at http://www.nypost.com accessed July 9, 2011.

3. M. Slavit, "City Employees busted for taking beer from dump," KRCG 13, (April 15, 2010), online at http://www.connectmidmissouri.com accessed July 9, 2010.

4. Associated Press, "Walmart worker fired over semi-nude photo," *USA Today,* (January 7, 2005), online at http://www.usatoday.com accessed July 9, 2011.

5. D. K. Li, "UPS delivers message to fired guy: Stay out!," *New York Post,* November 17, 2010 online at http://www.nypost.com accessed July 9, 2011.

6. M. Morgenstein, "Worker at taxpayer-funded agency in Virginia plays hooky for 12 years," *CNN,* online at http://www.cnn.com accessed July 9, 2011.

7. U.S. Department of Health and Human Services, "The Privacy Act," online at http://www.hhs.gov accessed July 8, 2011.

8. "Personnel Records: Retention: Can we keep our personnel records on the computer of microfilm instead of paper?", SHRM, (November 12, 2005), online at http://www.shrm.org/TemplatesTools/hrqa/Pages/Canwekeepourpersonnelrecordsonthecomputeroronmicrofilminsteadofonpaper.aspx accessed June 15, 2011.

9. U.S. Department of Labor, "elaws," online at http://www.dol.gov/elaws accessed July 7, 2011.

10. U.S. Department of Labor, "Drug-Free Workplace Act of 1988 Requirements for Organizations," http://www.dol.gov/elaws/asp/drugfree/require.htm accessed July 7, 2011.

11. This act applies to all private-sector organizations except those organizations the Secretary of Labor deems too small (e.g., family-owned businesses). M. Heller, "Court Ruling that Employers' Integrity Test Violated ADA Could Open Door to Litigation," *Workforce Management* (September 2005), pp. 74–77.

12. However, when they are job related (required of someone who has fiduciary responsibilities in an organization), they may be used.

13. W. Ryberg, "Production area's last 100 workers say final goodbye to Maytag today," *Des Moines Register,* (November 30, 2007), p. 1, 2D.

14. Worker Adjustment and Retraining Notification Act, Public Law 100-379.

15. J. E. Hall, M. T. Kobata and M. Denis, "No WARN for Layoffs at Non-contiguous Facilities," *Workforce Management,* (November 2009), online at http://www.workforce.com/article/20091113/NEWS02/311139991# accessed July 6, 2011.

16. National Labor Relations Board (NLRB), online at http://www.nlrb.gov accessed January 17, 2012.

17. J. Deschenaux, J.D., "Employee Use of Social Media: Laws Fail to Keep Pace With Technology," SHRM, (March 16, 2011), online at http://www.shrm.org/legalissues/federalresources/pages/employeeuseofsocialmedia.aspx accessed July 12, 2011.

18. E. Frauenheim, "LinkedIn Referral Policies Could Raise Legal Rift," *Workforce Management,* (February 2011), online at http://www.workforce.com/article/20110217/NEWS02/302179991/linkedin-referral-policies-could-raise-legal-rift accessed July 12, 2011.

19. M. R. Bryant, "Managing Workplace Drug and Alcohol Testing," SHRM, (February 3, 2011), online at http://www.shrm.org/templatestools/toolkits/pages/drugandalcoholtesting.aspx accessed July 7, 2011.

20. R. Zeidner, "Putting Drug Screening to the Test," *HR Magazine,* (November 1, 2010), p. 25-30.

21. B. Leonard, "Poll: Majority Favors Drug Testing Appplicants," *HR Magazine,* (November 2011), p. 87.

22. Ibid.

23. "Drug Testing," American Civil Liberties Union, online at http://www.aclu.org/criminal-law-reform/drug-testing accessed January 16, 2012.

24. M. R. Bryant, "Managing Workplace Drug and Alcohol Testing," SHRM, (February 3, 2011), online at http://www.shrm.org/templatestools/toolkits/pages/drugandalcoholtesting.aspx accessed July 7, 2011.

25. B. Eisenberg and L. Johnson, "Being Honest About Being Dishonest," SHRM White Paper, (March 2001), online at http://www.shrm.org/hrresources/whitepapers_published/CMS_000397.asp.

26. See, for example, M. E. Paronto, D. M. Truxillo, T. N. Bauer, and M. C. Leo, "Drug Testing, Drug Treatment, and Marijuana Use: A Fairness Perspective," *Journal of Applied Psychology,* (December 2002), pp. 1159–1167; and H. J. Bernardin and D. K. Cooke, "Validity of an Honesty Test in Predicting Theft Among Convenience Store Employees," *Academy of Management Journal,* vol. 38, no. 5, (Fall 1993), pp. 1097–1108.

27. D. A. Keary, "The Skinny on Sarbanes-Oxley," SHRM, (May 16, 2003), online at http://www.shrm.org/hrnews_published/archives/CMS_004557.asp#P-4_0 accessed September 27, 2012.

28. A. Joyce, "Every Move You Make," *Washington Post,* (October 1, 2006), p. F1.

29. "Brain Food: Workplace Rights," *Management Today,* (August 4, 2003), p. 17.

30. C. H. Nelson Jr. and L. Tyson, "HR Undercover," *HR Magazine,* (October 2010), p. 107.

31. "Electronic Monitoring," *Society of Human Resource Management: Government Affairs,* (September 2000), pp. 1–3.

32. M. Saltzman, "Should You Monitor Employee E-Mail?," (October 2006) online at http://technology.inc.com/2006/10/01/should-you-monitor-employee-e-mail/ accessed September 14, 2012.

33. Z. A. Hummel, "Their BlackBerries—Your Problem," *Workforce Management*, (March 6, 2008), online at http://www.workforce.com/apps/pbcs.dll/article?AID=/20080306/NEWS02/303069991&template=print article accessed September 15, 2012.

34. A. Nancherla, "Surveillance Increases in Workplace," *T1D*, (May 2008), p. 12; and 2007 Electronic Monitoring & Surveillance Survey, American Management Association, online at http://press.amanet.org/press-releases/177/2007-electronic-monitoring-surveillance-survey/ accessed February 28, 2008.

35. M. France and D. K. Berman, "Big Brother Calling," *BusinessWeek*, (September 25, 2000), pp. 92–98.

36. M. A. Verespej, "Internet Surfing," *Industry Week*, (February 7, 2000), pp. 59–64; and L. M. Bernardi, "The Internet at Work: An Employment Danger Zone," *Canadian Manager*, (Summer 2000), pp. 17–18.

37. A. Joyce, "Every Move You Make," *Washington Post*, (October 1, 2006), p. F1.

38. Ibid.

39. M. Hamblen, "Privacy Concerns Dog IT Efforts to Implement RFID," *Computerworld*, (October 15, 2007), p. 26.

40. D. Marseller, "Employers' tracking of workers raises privacy concerns," *The Tennessean*, (January 16, 2012), online at http://www.wbir.com/rss/article/200805/2/Employers-tracking-of-workers-raises-privacy-concerns accessed January 16, 2012,

41. K. Tyler, "Sign in the Name of Love," *HR Magazine*, (February 2008), pp. 40–43.

42. Ibid.

43. *Payne v. Western and Atlantic Railroad Co.*, 812 Tenn. 507 (1884). See also C. Hirschman, "Off Duty, Out of Work," *HR Magazine*, (February 2003), pp. 51–52.

44. P. Falcone, "Fire My Assistant Now," *HR Magazine*, (May 2002), pp. 27–35; T. M. Shaughnessy, "How State Exceptions to Employment-at-Will Affect Wages," *Journal of Labor Research*, (Summer 2003), pp. 447–457; D. A. Ballam, "Employment-at-Will: The Impending Death of a Doctrine," *American Business Law Journal*, (Summer 2000), pp. 653–687; and R. M. Howie and L. A. Shapero, "Lifestyle Discrimination Statutes: A Dangerous Erosion of At-will Employment, a Passing Fad, or Both?" *Employee Relations Law Journal*, (Summer 2005), pp. 21–38.

45. Adapted from Carroll R. Daugherty, Enterprise Wire Co. 46 LA 359 (1966).

46. For a complete overview of this topic, see J. J. Moran, *Employment Law*, 2nd ed. (Upper Saddle River: Prentice Hall, 2002). See also M. Heller. "A Return to At-Will Employment," *Workforce*, (May 2001), p. 42.

47. *Toussaint v. Blue Cross and Blue Shield of Michigan*, 408 Michigan, 529, 292 N.W. 2d 880 (1980).

48. *Fortune v. National Cash Register*, 364 373 Massachusetts 91, 36 N.E. 2d 1251 (1977).

49. T. A. Felton, "Best Practices in Documenting Employee Discipline," *Workforce Management*, (January 2009), online at http://www.workforce.com/article/20090115/NEWS02/301159997/best-practices-in-documenting-employee-discipline accessed July 8, 2011.

50. W. Cottringer, "The ABC's of Employee Discipline," *Supervision*, (April 2003), pp. 5–8.

51. J. Schermerhorn, *Management* 11e, (Hoboken: John Wiley & Sons, 2011), p. 451.

52. T. Salvo, "Practical Tips for Successful Progressive Discipline," *SHRM White Paper*, (July 1, 2004), online at www.shrm.org accessed July 8, 2011.

53. See, for instance, G. A. Bielous, "Five Worst Disciplinary Mistakes (and How to Avoid Them)," *Supervision*, (March 2003), pp. 16–19.

54. G. Harrison, "Understanding Labor-Management Relations," Harrison, Moreland and Webber, PC. SHRM Collective Bargaining and Operating in a Union Environment Seminar, February 14, 2011.

55. It is true that two other disciplinary actions may be used—pay cuts or demotion—but they are rare.

56. D. Welch, D. Kiley, and M. Ihlwan, "My Way Or The Highway At Hyundai," *BusinessWeek*, (March 17, 2008), p. 48.

57. M. Chafkin, "Meet Rebecca. She's Here to Fire You," *Inc.*, (November 2007) pp. 25–26.

58. C. Pintella, "Buh Bye, Say Hello to a Better Way to Fire Employees," *Entrepreneur Magazine*, (September 2007), p. 28.

59. NJBIZ Staff, "Hire Slow . . . Fire Fast: The Complex Personnel Game," *NJBIZ* (November 19, 2007), online at http://www.njbiz.com/article/20071119/NJBIZ01/311199993/0/SEARCH.

60. R. T. Whipple, "Stop the Enabling," *HR Magazine*, (September 2010), p. 114–115.

61. S. Reeves, "Firing a Worker," *Forbes*, (April 27, 2006) online at http://www.forbes.com/2006/04/25/business-basics-firing-cx_sr_0427fire.html accessed September 14, 2012.

62. J. Bucking, "Employee Terminations," *Supervision*, (May 2008), pp. 11–13.

63. Case is based on C. Hirschman, "Off Duty, Out of Work," *HR Magazine*, (February 2003). Available online at www. shrm.org/hrmagazine/articles/0203/0203 hirschman.asp.

64. Adapted from S. P. Robbins and P. L. Hunsaker, *Training in Interpersonal Skills*, 3rd ed. (Upper Saddle River: Prentice Hall, 2003), chapter 5; Commerce Clearing House, "The Do's and Don'ts of Confronting a Troubled Employee," *Topical Law Reports* (Chicago: Commerce Clearing House, October 1990), pp. 4359–4360; G. D. Cook, "Employee Counseling Session," *Supervision*, (August,1989), p. 3; and A. E. Schuartz, "Counseling the Marginal Performer," *Management Solutions*, (March 1988), p. 30.

CHAPTER **5**
Human Resource Planning and Job Analysis

1. G. Sunseri, "Space Shuttle Atlantis: Now, the Layoffs," ABC News online at http://abcnews.go.com/Technology/space-shuttle-atlantis-layoffs-follow-florida-texas/story?id=14119413, (July 21, 2011) accessed July 22, 2011.

2. C. Moskowitz, "NASA in Transition as Congress OKs New Direction," (September 30, 2010), online at http://www.space.com/9233-nasa-transition-congress-oks-direction.html accessed July 22, 2011.

3. B. M. Testa, "New Workforce Orbit-Relaunch at NASA," *Workforce Management*, (August 17, 2009), pp. 16-20.

4. D. Moss, "Mission Critical HR," *HR Magazine*, (September 2010), pp. 32–33.

5. G. Sunseri, "Space Shuttle Atlantis: Now, the Layoffs," ABC News online at http://abcnews.go.com/Technology/space-shuttle-atlantis-layoffs-follow-florida-texas/story?id=14119413, (July 21, 2011) accessed July 22, 2011.

6. See "The 2002 SOTA/P Report Draws the Map for Achieving Customer Satisfaction Through the Integration of HR Practices and Policy with Business Strategy," *Human Resource Planning*, (March 2002), p. COV3; and B. Roberts, "Pick Employees' Brains," *HR Magazine*, (February 2000), p. 175.

7. "What Do CEOs Want from the HR Department?" *Human Resource Department Management Report*, (December 2002), p. 1.

8. P. M. Wright, D. L. Smart, and G. C. McMahan, "Matches Between Human Resources and Strategy Among NCAA Basketball Teams," *Academy of Management Journal*, Vol. 38, No. 4, (Winter 1995), pp. 1052–1074; and M. J. Plevel, S. Nells, F. Lane, and R. S. Schuler, "AT&T Global Business Communications Systems: Linking HR with Business Strategy," *Organizational Dynamics*, (1994), pp. 59–71.

9. G. Kesler, "Four Steps to Building an HR Agenda for Growth: HR Strategy Revisited," *Human Resource Planning*, (September 2000), p. 24.

10. As previous users have concurred, although strategic planning cannot be oversimplified in a two-page discussion, a quick overview is in order. With respect to the strategic nature of business, we recommend, for a comprehensive review of strategic planning, T. Whelan and J. D. Hunger, *Strategic Management and Business Policy* (Upper Saddle River: Prentice Hall, 2004).

11. "A Restatement of Purpose," *Fast Company*, (October 2001), p. 2.

12. Established goals are a function of various factors. The economy, government influences, market maturity, technological advances, company image, location, and other such issues will factor into the analysis.

13. C. LeBeau, "He's LEEDing the Way," *Workforce Management,* (September 2008,) online at http://www.workforce.com/apps/pbcs.dll/article?AID=/20080831/NEWS02/308319978&template=printarticle accessed July 19, 2011.

14. E. Binney, "Companies Making Jobs 'Green' but Not Creating Many Green Jobs," SHRM, (August 23, 2010), online at http://www.shrm.org/hrdisciplines/staffingmanagement/articles/pages/companyjobsnotgreenones.aspx accessed July 19, 2011.

15. "CI and Starbucks," Conservation International, (October 2010), online at http://www.conservation.org/campaigns/starbucks/Pages/default.aspx accessed July 19, 2011.

16. D. Jolly, "McDonald's to Serve Sustainable Fish in Europe," *New York Times,* (June 8, 2011) online at http://www.nytimes.com/2011/06/09/business/global/09fish.html accessed July, 19, 2011.

17. See C. Lachnit, "A People Strategy That Spans the Globe: Human Resources Is Key to the Success of a Company That Is 'Only World Famous in Denmark,'" *Workforce,* (June 2003), p. 76.

18. J. Spiro, "How to Improve Employee Retention," Inc. (April 7, 2010), online at http://www.inc.com/guides/2010/04/employee-retention.html accessed July 17, 2011.

19. B. Patterson and S. Lindsey, "Mining the Gold," *HR Magazine,* (September 2003), pp. 131–136; and "HRIS for the HR Professional: What You Need to Know," *HR Focus,* (June 2005), pp. 10–11.

20. H. O'Neil, "Focusing on the Core," *Workforce Management,* (April 2011), online at http://www.workforce.com/article/20110408/NEWS02/304089997 accessed July 19, 2011.

21. B. Roberts, "In Harsh Times, Software as a Service Gains Popularity," SHRM, (May 4, 2009), online at http://www.shrm.org/hrdisciplines/technology/articles/pages/softwareasaservicepopular.aspx accessed July 19, 2011.

22. SHRM and AARP, "SHRM - AARP Strategic Workforce Planning Poll," (November 17, 2010), online at http://www.shrm.org/research/survey-findings/articles/pages/shrmaarpstrategicworkforceplanning.aspx accessed July 19, 2011.

23. M. V. Rafter, "Shareholders Demand Better Window Into Succession," *Workforce Management,* (June 2010), p. 14.

24. K. Ellis, "Making Waves: With a Leadership Crisis on the Horizon, Organizations Are Looking Within to Build Talent Pools of Their Own," *Training,* (June 2003), pp. 16–22; and J. Jusko, "Unplanned Future: Private Company CEOs Give Little Thought to Succession Planning," *Industry Week,* (March 2005), p. 20.

25. F. Hansen, "Kick-Starting the Planning Process," *Workforce Management,* (April 18, 2008), p. 18.

26. ManpowerGroup, "Annual Survey Shows More than Half of U.S. Employers Cannot Find the Right Talent for Open Positions," (May 19, 2011), online at http://www.manpowergroup.com/investors/releasedetail.cfm?ReleaseID=579117 accessed July 19, 2011.

27. "Layoffs: Consider Other Options Before Reducing Full-Time Staff," *Fair Employment Practice Guidelines,* (April 15, 2003), pp. 1–3; and C. Huff, "With Flextime, Less Can Be More," *Workforce Management,* (May 2005), pp. 65–70.

28. "Right Management Survey Reveals Over 50% of Employees Have Been Involuntarily Separated During Their Careers," *Right Management,* (May 27, 2008), online at http://www.right.com/news-and-events/current-releases/2008-press-releases/item869.aspx accessed September 14, 2012.

29. R. Galbreath, "What Role Does Job Analysis Play in Defining a Job's Scope and Responsibilities?" *Workforce Management,* (February 2010), online at http://www.workforce.com/article/20100202/DEAR_WORKFORCE/302029991/dear-workforce-what-role-does-job-analysis-play-in-defining-a-jobs-scope-and-responsibilities, accessed July 19, 2011.

30. "Job Analysis: How do I conduct a job analysis to ensure the job description actually matches the duties performed by the employee in the job," SHRM, (October 15, 2010), online at http://www.shrm.org/TemplatesTools/hrqa/Pages/conductjobanalysis.aspx accessed July 19, 2011.

31. "The O*NET Content Model," O*NET Resource Center online at http://www.onetcenter.org/content.html accessed July 19, 2011.

32. "Job Analysis Questionnaire" PAQ Services, Inc. online at http://www.paq.com/index.cfm?FuseAction=bulletins.job-analysis-questionnaire accessed July 19, 2011.

33. "Ohio Court Analyzes Essentials of Essential Functions," SHRM, (November 16, 2010), online at http://www.shrm.org/LegalIssues/StateandLocalResources/Pages/OhioCourtAnalyzesEssential.aspx accessed July 19, 2011.

34. See also C. Joinson, "Refocusing Job Description," *HR Magazine,* (January 2001), pp. 65–70.

35. S. E. Humphrey, Florida State University, J. D. Nahrgang and F. P. Morgeson, Michigan State University, "Integrating Motivational, Social and Contextual Work Design Features: A Meta-Analytic Summary and Theoretical Extension of the Work Design Literature," *Journal of Applied Psychology,* 2007, Vol. 92, No. 5, 1332–1356.

36. J. Schermerhorn, *Management,* 11th ed. (Hoboken: John Wiley & Sons, 2011), p. 376.

37. R. Vance "Employee Engagement and Motivation," White Paper, SHRM Foundation, 2006.

38. American Sociological Association. "Flexible schedules, results-oriented workplaces reduce work-family conflict and turnover." *ScienceDaily,* (April 2011), online at http://www.sciencedaily.com/releases/2011/04/110406122219.htm accessed July 22, 2011.

39. C. Ressler and J. Thompson, *Why Work Sucks and How to Fix It,* (New York: Penguin Group, 2008), p. 63.

40. D. Woodward, "Beat the Clock," *Director,* (May 2010), pp. 42–44.

41. P. J. Kiger, "Flexibility to the Fullest," *Workforce Management,* (September 25, 2006), p. 1–23.

42. Ibid.

43. Planning Enhances the Potential of Telecommuting Success," *HR Focus: Special Report on Telecommuting,* (April 2008), pp. S1–S4.

44. S. Barr, "Rate Stabilizes at Homeland Security," *Washington Post,* (July 26, 2007), p. D4.

45. T. Frank, "Report: TSA screeners' low morale may hurt airport security," *USA Today,* (June 24, 2008), p. 3.

46. T. Frank, "Bonuses don't cut turnover for TSA," *USA Today,* (November 26, 2006), p. 1.

47. The Associated Press, "Screeners For T.S.A. Select Union," *New York Times,* (June 24, 2011) page B4.

CHAPTER 6
Recruiting

1. "The Container Store's employee focused culture," CBS News, (March 6 2011), online at http://www.cbsnews.com/video/watch/?id=7358608n accessed July 27, 2011.

2. Ibid.

3. "Solving the Riddle of Recruiting and Retention," *HR Focus,* (April 2008), p. 1.

4. A. Fox, "Mixing it Up," *HR Magazine,* (May 1, 2011), online at http://www.shrm.org/publications/hrmagazine/editorialcontent/2011/0511/pages/0511fox.aspx accessed July 27, 2011.

5. T. Chapelle, "Merrill Rolls Out New Recruiting Deals," *On Wall Street* (September 1, 2003), p. 1.

6. See, for instance, "Executive Hires and Compensation: Performance Rules," *HR Focus* (July 2003), p. 1.

7. "Benchmark Report: Focusing Attention on Talent," Staffing.org, online at http://www.staffing.org/library_ViewArticle.asp?articleid=384 accessed July 27, 2011.

8. L. Adler "Answers from Lou Adler, Interviews, Employee Referrals and Job Branding" *Workforce Management,* (June 9, 2004), online at http://www.workforce.com/article/20040609/NEWS01/306099996/answers-from-lou-adler-interviews-employee-referrals-and-job-branding accessed June 2, 2009.

9. J. Marquez, "When Brand Alone Isn't Enough," *Workforce Management,* (March 13, 2006), pp. 39–41.

10. T. Minton-Eversole, "Time is Right for Employment Brand 'Renovation'," SHRM, (April 20, 2011), online at http://www.shrm.org/hrdisciplines/ staffingmanagement/articles/pages/employmentbrandrenovation. aspx accessed August 9, 2011.

11. Ibid.

12. "How to Get Hired by a 'Best' Company," *Fortune,* (February 4, 2008), p. 96.

13. C. Gabor and M. King, "The Art and Science of Executive Recruiting," *Workforce Management,* (March 2010), online at http://www.workforce. com/article/20100324/NEWS02/303249990 accessed August 9, 2011.

14. E. Glazer, "Virtual Fairs Offer Real Jobs," *Wall Street Journal,* (October 31, 2011), p. B9.

15. G. Ruiz, "Job Fairs Find a New Home Under a Virtual Roof," *Workforce Management,* (May 21, 2008), online at http://www.workforce.com/ apps/pbcs.dll/article?AID=/20080521/NEWS02/305219990&template= printarticle accessed June 2, 2008.

16. "Even CEOs Use the Internet for Recruiting," *HR Magazine,* (March 2003), p. 14; M. N. Martinez, "Get Job Seekers to Come to You," *HR Magazine,* (August 2000), pp. 42–52; M. Frase-Blunt, "Make a Good First Impression," *HR Magazine,* (April 2004), pp. 81–86; D. Robb, "Career Portals Boost Online Recruiting," *HR Magazine,* (April 2004), pp. 111–115; and J. Marshall, "Don't Rely Exclusively on Internet Recruiting," *HR Magazine,* (November 2003).

17. Leah McKelvey, Marketing Manager at CareerBuilder.com, Chicago, IL. presentation July 15, 2011.

18. Ibid.

19. Compiled from surveys conducted by CareerXroads (2011) and JobVite (2011) online at http://www.ere.net/2011/03/17/referrals-lead-social-media-thrives-job-boards-survive-as-hiring-source/print/ http://recruiting.jobvite.com/resources/social-recruiting-charts.php accessed August 6, 2011.

20. See also A. E. Schultz, "Beware the Legal Risks of Hiring Temps: When Hiring Stalls and Stops, It 's Tempting to Hire Contingent Workers. To Avoid a Microsoft-sized Lawsuit, Understand the Critical Legal Issues Involving Temporary Workers," *Workforce,* (October 2002), pp. 50–58.

21. "How Well Are You Treating Your Temporary Workers?" *HR Briefing,* (January 15, 2003), pp. 6–8; and M. Frase-Blunt, "A Recruiting Spigot," *HR Magazine,* (April 2003), pp. 71–79.

22. D. Fenn, "Respect Your Elders," *Inc.,* (September 2003), pp. 29–30.

23. Reasons cited by the American Association of Retired Persons include the need to make money, to obtain health insurance coverage, to develop skills, to use time more productively, to feel useful, to make new friends, to provide some structure to daily lives, or to have a sense of achievement.

24. "8 Interview Questions for Older Workers to Anticipate," *AARP Bulletin,* (September 2002), online at http://www.aarp.org/bulletin/yourmoney/ Articles/0905_sidebar_4.html. Also see Robert Half International Inc., (2005), www.rhii.com.

25. Caution is warranted regarding for whom an individual works. Although the employee usually is the leasing company's responsibility, under certain circumstances, such as long-term duration of the lease, the acquiring organization may be the employer of record. The leasing company may only handle HRM-associated paperwork.

26. The U.S. Equal Employment Opportunity Commission, Best Practices Presented by Companies in Recruitment and Hiring, (February 28, 2002).

27. See, for instance, S. Cuthill, "Guest Column: Managing HR Across International Borders," *Compensation and Benefits,* (Summer 2000), pp. 43–45; and "Global Recruiting," *Practical Accountant,* (October 2000), p. 6.

28. "Ensure You Don't Make a Bad Expat Investment," *Personnel Today,* (August 19, 2003), p. 15.

29. See, for example, J. A. Volkmar, "Context and Control in Foreign Subsidiaries: Making a Case for the Host Country National Manager," *Journal of Leadership and Organizational Studies,* (Summer 2003), pp. 93–106.

30. Economist Intelligence Unit, *Global Firms in 2020: The Next Decade of Change for Organisations and Workers,* "Tapping into the global Talent Pool," *Economist,* (2010), online at http://www.shrm.org/research/sur- veyfindings/articles/documents/economist%20research%20-%20 global%20firms%20in%202020.pdf accessed August 9, 2011.

31. H. O'Neill, "Job Market Slowly Easing as College Grads Trade Books for Briefcases," *Workforce Management,* (June 2011), online at http://www. workforce.com/article/20110621/NEWS02/306219997 accessed August 6, 2011.

32. "Career Development," *HR Magazine,* (April 2008), p. 129.

33. "Networking Do's and Dont's," *Jobology,* CareerBuilder, online at http:// www.careerbuildercommunications.com/pdf/jobology.pdf accessed September 14, 2012, p. 13.

34. Case adapted from: K. Regan, "Recruiting for Paradise," *Workforce Management,* (September, 2004); and Honolulu Police Department, Career Center at www.honolulupd.org. Updated with an interview with HPD Recruiter, Officer Julie Kusuda on August 6, 2008.

35. Case is based on J. H. Coplan, "Se Habla Temp," *BusinessWeek Small Business,* (April 2, 2001), p. 42; and Priority Staffing Solutions (2005), online at www.prioritystaff.com/index.html.

36. This skill vignette is based on information provided in CCC Business Owner's Toolkit, "Information To Include in Job Ads," *SOHO Guidebook* (2003), online at http://www.toolkit.cch.com/text/P05_0673.asp, p. 1.

CHAPTER 7
Foundations of Selection

1. F. Soltes, "Grooming Great Sales People," National Retail Federation *Stores Magazine,* (April 2011) online at http://www.stores.org/ STORES%20Magazine%20April%202011/grooming-great-salespeople- accessed August 10, 2011.

2. B. Roberts, "Hire Intelligence," *HR Magazine,* (May 2011), pp. 63-67.

3. "Bon-Ton Stores Achieve Greater Sales Performance with Kenexa Custom Assessments," Kenexa, (February 2, 2011), online at http:// www.kenexa.com/aboutkenexa/mediaroom/ctl/detail/mid/667/ itemid/361 accessed August 10, 2011.

4. This story was influenced by an example in Arthur Sloan, *Personnel: Managing Human Resources* (Englewood Cliffs: Prentice Hall, 1983), p. 127.

5. See I. Kotlyar and L. Karakowsky, "If Recruitment Means Building Trust, Where Does Technology Fit In?" *Canadian HR Reporter,* (October 7, 2002), p. 21.

6. A. L. Rupe, "Facebook Faux Pas," *Workforce Management,* (March 2007), online at http://www.workforce.com/article/20070322/NEWS02/ 303229997# accessed June 2, 2009.

7. K. Dunn, "The Five New Rules of Using Social Media to Evaluate Candidates," *Workforce Management,* (January 2011), online at http://www. workforce.com/article/20110112/NEWS02/301129996 accessed July 23, 2011.

8. R. Kethley and D. E. Terpstra (2005). An Analysis of Litigation Associated with the Use of the Application Form in the Selection Process. *Public Personnel Management,* 34(4), 357. Retrieved from EBSCO*host* August 10, 2011.

9. J. C. Scott and D. H. Reynolds, *Handbook of Workplace Assessment,* (San Francisco Jossey-Bass, 2010), pp. 324-330.

10. See, for instance, S. R. Kaak, H. S. Field, W. F. Giles, and D. R. Norris, "The Weighted Application Blank," *Cornell Hotel and Restaurant Administration Quarterly,* (April 1998), pp. 18–24. The seven items were not specifically identified so that the competitive edge the hotel had in hiring practices would not be weakened.

11. T. A. Daniel, "Screening and Evaluating Candidates," SHRM, (November 11, 2011), online at http://www.shrm.org/templatestools/toolkits/ pages/screeningandevaluatingcandidates.aspx accessed August 6, 2012.

12. See, for example, J. H. Prager, "Nasty or Nice: 56-Question Quiz," *Wall Street Journal,* (February 22, 2000), p. A-4.

13. G. Nicholsen, "Screen and Glean: Good Screening and Background Checks Help Make the Right Match for Every Open Position," *Workforce,* (October 2000), pp. 70, 72.

14. S. Bates, "Personality Counts," *HR Magazine,* (February 2002), pp. 27–34.

15. See F. Lievens, "Trying to Understand the Different Pieces of the Construct Validity Puzzle of Assessment Centers: An Examination of Assessor and Assessee Effects, *Journal of Applied Psychology,* (August 2002), pp. 675–687; and D. J. Schleicher, B. T. Mayes, D. V. Day, and R. F. Riggio, "A New Frame of Reference Training: Enhancing the Construct of Validity of Assessment Centers," *Journal of Applied Psychology,* (August 2002), pp. 735–747.

16. "Mind Your P's and Q's," *Successful Meetings,* (February 2000), p. 33.

17. "Pepsi Beverages pays $3.1 million to settle federal race discrimination charges," *Washington Post,* (January 11, 2012), online at http://www.washingtonpost.com/business/industries/pepsi-beverages-pays-313-million-to-settle-federal-race-discrimination-charges/2012/01/11/gIQAHtgyqP_story.html accessed January 21, 2012.

18. Table compiled from information from: T. H. Nail, D. Scharinger "Guidelines on Interview and Employment Questions" SHRM Information White Paper (Reviewed 2002) and R. Sinha "Questions You Cannot Ask in Job Interviews," Bizcovering.com, (April 15, 2008), and Joyce Walker-Jones, Senior Attorney Advisor, ADA Policy Division "ADA: Disability-Related Inquiries and Medical Examinations" EEOC.gov (February 22, 2005).

19. J. Blau, "At Nokia Temperament Is a Core Competency," *Research Technology Management,* (July/August 2003), p. 6; and R. A. Posthuma, F. P. Morgeson, and M., A. Campion, "Beyond Employment Interview Validity: A Comprehensive Narrative Review of Recent Research and Trends Over Time," *Personnel Psychology,* (Spring 2002), pp. 1–80.

20. "Job Interviews Reveal Trouble Later On," *HR Briefing,* (January 15, 2003), p. 8.

21. "It's Not Your Grandfather's Hiring Interview," *Supervision,* (May 2003), pp. 21–23.

22. For a more detailed discussion of impression management, see N. L. Vasilopoulos, R. R. Reilly, and J. A. Leaman, "The Influences of Job Familiarity and Impression Management on Self-Report Measure Scales and Response Latencies," *Journal of Applied Psychology,* (February 2000), pp. 50–64; and D. R. Pawlowski and J. Hollwitz, "Work Values, Cognitive Strategies, and Applicant Reactions in a Structured Pre-Employment Interview for Ethical Integrity," *Journal of Business Communication,* (January 2000), pp. 58–76.

23. J. Silvester, F. M. Anderson-Gough, N. R. Anderson, and A. R. Mohamed, "Locus of Control, Attributions and Impression Management in the Selection Interview," *Journal of Occupational and Organizational Psychology,* (March 2002), pp. 59–77; and L. G. Otting, "Don't Rush to Judgement," *HR Magazine,* (January 2004), pp. 95–98.

24. C. H. Middendorf and T. H. Macan, "Note-Taking in the Employment Interview: Effects on Recall and Judgment," *Journal of Applied Psychology,* (April 2002), pp. 293–304.

25. See, for instance, "Recruitment: Job Seekers Take Offense at Interview Blinders," *Personnel Today,* (July 1, 2003), p. 3. See also M. Knudstrup, S. L. Segrest, and A. E. Hurley, "The Use of Mental Imagery in the Simulated Employment Interview Situation," *Journal of Managerial Psychology,* (June 2003), pp. 573–591.

26. W. Poundstone, "Beware the Interview Inquisition," *Harvard Business Review,* (May 2003), pp. 18–19; and T. Raz, "How Would You Design Bill Gates's Bathroom?" *Inc.,* (May 2003), p. 29.

27. "Focus on Ethics Includes Honest Interviews," *HR Briefing,* (April 1, 2003), p. 7.

28. See P. J. Taylor and B. Small, "Asking Applicants What They Would Do Versus What They Did Do: A Meta-Analysis Comparison of Situation and Past Behavior Employment Interview Questions," *Journal of Occupational and Organizational Psychology,* (September 2002), pp. 277–294; J. Merritt, "Improve at the Interview," *BusinessWeek,* (February 3, 2003), p. 63; S. D. Mauer, "A Practitioner-Based Analysis of Interviewer Job Expertise and Scale Format as Contextual Factors in Situational Interviews," *Personnel Psychology,* (Summer 2002), pp. 307–328; J. M. Barclay, "Improving

Selection Interviews with Structure: Organizations' Use of Behavioural Interviews," *Personnel Review,* Vol. 30, Issue 1 (2001), pp. 81–95; K. Tyler, "Train for Smarter Hiring," *HR Magazine,* (May 2005), pp. 89–93; A. C. Poe, "Graduate Work," *HR Magazine,* (October 2003), pp. 95–100; and "Using Behavioral Interviewing to Help You Hire the Best of the Best," *HR Focus,* (August 2004), p. 5.

29. J. Merrit, "Improve at the Interview," *BusinessWeek,* (February 3, 2003), p. 63; and P. J. Taylor and B. Small, "Asking Applicants What They Would Do Versus What They Did Do: A Meta-Analysis Comparison of Situation and Past Behavior Employment Interview Questions," *Journal of Occupational and Organizational Psychology,* (September 2002), pp. 277–294.

30. A. Phillips and R. L. Dipboye, "Correlation Tests of Predictions from a Process Model of the Interview," *Journal of Applied Psychology,* Vol. 74 (1989), pp. 41–52; M. Ronald Buckley and R. W. Edner, "B. M. Springbett and the Notion of the 'Snap Decision' in the Interview," *Journal of Management,* Vol. 14, No. 1, (March 1988), pp. 59–67.

31. See, for instance, R. Buda, "The Interactive Effect of Message Framing, Presentation Order, and Source Credibility on Recruitment Practices," *International Journal of Management,* (June 2003), pp. 156–164.

32. S. A. Larson, K. C. Lakin, American Association on Mental Retardation, R. H. Bruininks, D. L. Braddock, American Association on Mental Retardation, Staff Recruitment and Retention: Study Results and Intervention Strategies, AAMR, 1998. pp. 30–31.

33. For an interesting discussion on this topic, see P. G. Irving and J. E. Meyer, "On Using Residual Differences Scores in the Measurement of Congruence: The Case of Met Expectations Research," *Personnel Psychology,* (Spring 1999), pp. 85–95; and R. D. Bretz Jr., and T. A. Judge, "Realistic Job Previews: A Test of Adverse Self-Selection Hypothesis," *Journal of Applied Psychology,* (April 1998), pp. 330–337.

34. S. Bates, "Tight-Knit Reference Checks Rise," *HR News,* (February 2002), pp. 1, 4; V. Tsang, "No More Excuses," *CHRR Report on Recruitment and Staffing,* (May 23, 2005), available online at www.hrreporter.com; "Liar, Liar, Pants on Fire," *HR Magazine,* (September 2005), p. 16; "Cost of Poor People Management Is High," *HR Magazine,* (August 2004), p. 18; and J. George and K. Marett, "The Truth About Lies," *HR Magazine,* (May 2004), pp. 87–91.

35. N. A. Prall, "Global Immigration Blog," Jackson Lewis Law Firm, LLP, (April 15, 2011) online at www.globalimmigrationblog.com accessed May 2, 2011. "E-Verify" U.S. Citizenship and Immigration Services online at www.uscis.gov accessed September 3, 2011.

36. C. Garvey, "Outsourcing Background Checks," *HR Magazine,* (March 2001), pp. 95–103.

37. M. Mayer, "Background Checks in Focus," *HR Magazine,* (January 2002), pp. 59–62; J. H. Maxwell, "Of Resumes and Rap Sheets," *Inc.,* (June 13, 2000), p. 94; C. Mason-Draffen, "Resume Lies Are on the Rise," *Baltimore Sun,* (June 10, 2004) online at www.baltimoresun.com/business; and P. Babcock, "Spotting Lies," *HR Magazine,* (October 2003), pp. 46–52.

38. M. N. Le and B. H. Kleiner, "Understanding and Preventing Negligent Hiring," *Management Research News,* Vol. 23, No. 7/8 (2000), pp. 53–56.

39. J. Mullich, "Cracking the ex-files," *Workforce Management,* (September, 2003) online at http://www.workforce.com/apps/pbcs.dll/article?AID=/20030902/NEWS02/309029986&template=printarticle accessed September 14, 2012.

40. "Wishum v. RiteAid Los Angeles Superior Court BC 209910 (California), online at www.intelifi.com. accessed September, 3, 2011.

41. Bill Roberts, "Backgrounds to the Foreground," *HR Magazine,* (December 2010), Pages 46-51.

42. D. Lacy, S. Jackson, and A. St. Martin, "References, Cafeteria Changes, Smokers," *HR Magazine,* (April 2003), p. 37.

43. See, for example, S. L. Rynes, R. D. Bretz, and B. Gerhart, "The Importance of Recruitment in Job Choice: A Different Way of Looking," *Personnel Psychology,* Vol. 44, No. 3, (Autumn 1991), pp. 487–521.

44. For an interesting review of self-managed team behavior when evaluating one another, see C. P. Neck, M. L. Connerly, C. A. Zuniga, and S. Goel, "Family Therapy Meets Self-Managing Teams: Explaining Self-Managing

Team Performance Through Team Member Perception," *Journal of Applied Behavioral Science,* (June 1999), pp. 245–259; G. A. Neuman, S. H. Wagner, and N. D. Christiansen, "The Relationship Between Work Team Personality Composition and the Job Performance of Teams," *Group & Organization Management,* (March 1999), pp. 28–45; and V. U. Druskat and S. B. Wolff, "Effects and Timing of Developmental Peer Appraisals in Self-Managing Work Groups," *Journal of Applied Psychology,* (February 1999), pp. 58–74.

45. M. Frase-Blunt, "Peering Into an Interview" *HR Magazine,* (December 2001), pp. 71–77.

46. See C. Hymowitz, "In the Lead: How to Avoid Hiring the Prima Donnas Who Hate Teamwork," *Wall Street Journal,* (February 15, 2000), p. B-1.

47. Based on "Mistakes and Problems: Things Not to Do in an Interview," *Pagewise* (2005), online at www.pagewise.com/things-do-interview. htm; "What Are Some Applicants Thinking," *HR Briefing,* (January 15, 2003), p. 5; H. Delozalek, "Behavioral Blunders," *Training,* (January 2003), p. 1; and "Interview Blunders Can Close the Door," *Westchester County Business Journal,* (December 16, 2002), p. 17.

48. There are several methods of determining reliability. These include equivalent form, test-retest method, and internal consistency forms of reliability. Their discussion, however, goes well beyond the scope of this text. "Reliability vs. Validity: When a Company Overstresses the Former, the Opportunity to Exploit Design to Create Something New and Better Can Easily Be Missed," *BusinessWeek,* (September 2005), p. 1.

49. See, for example, R. E. Riggio, *Introduction to Industrial/Organizational Psychology,* 4th ed. (Upper Saddle River: Prentice Hall, 2003).

50. For an interesting perspective on the use of construct validity, see J. M. Hunthausen, D. M. Truxillo, T. N. Bauer, and L. B. Hammer, "A Field Study Frame of Reference Effects on Personality Test Validity," *Journal of Applied Psychology,* (June 2003), pp. 545–552; C. C. Hoffman, L. M. Holden, and K. Gale, "So Many Jobs, So Little 'N': Applying Expanded Validation Models to Support Generalization of Cognitive Test Validity," *Personnel Psychology,* (Winter 2000), p. 955; and L. Van Dyne and J. A. LePine, "Helping and Voice Extra-Role Behaviors: Evidence of Construct and Predictive Validity," *Academy of Management Journal,* (February 1998), pp. 108–119.

51. A limitation of concurrent validity is the possibility of restricting the range of scores in testing current employees. This occurs because current employees may have been in the upper range of applicants. Those not hired were undesirable for some reason. Therefore, these scores theoretically should represent only the top portion of previous applicant scores. W. Arthur, E. A. Day, T. L. Mcnelly, and P. S. Edens, "A Meta-Analysis of the Criterion-Related Validity of Assessment Center Dimensions," *Personnel Psychology,* (Spring 2003), pp. 125–154.

52. A specific correlation coefficient for validation purposes is nearly impossible to pinpoint. Many variables will enter into the picture, such as the sample size, the power of the test, and what is measured. However, for EEO purposes, correlation coefficients must indicate a situation where the results are predictive of performance greater than one where chance alone dictated the outcomes.

53. Cut scores are determined through sets of mathematical formulas—namely, a regression analysis and the equation of a line. We refer you to any good introductory statistics text for a reminder of how these formulas operate.

54. F. L. Schmidt and J. E. Hunter, "Developing a General Solution to the Problem of Validity Generalization," *Journal of Applied Psychology,* Vol. 62, No. 5, (October 1977), pp. 529–539.

55. See, for instance, C. O. and D. A. Harrison, "Meta-Analysis, Level of Analysis, and Best Estimates of Population Correlations: Cautions for Interpreting Meta-Analytic Results in Organizational Behavior," *Journal of Applied Psychology,* (April 1999), pp. 260–270; C. C. Hoffman, "Generalizing Physical Ability Test Validity: A Case Study Using Test Transportability, Validity Generalization, and Construct-Related Validation Evidence," *Personnel Psychology,* (Winter 1999), pp. 1019–1041; and N. S. Raju, T. V. Anselmi, J. S. Goodman, and A. Thomas, "The Effect of Correlated Artifacts and True Validity on the Accuracy of Parameter Estimation in Validity Generalization," *Personnel Psychology,* (Summer 1998), pp. 453–465.

56. See F. L. Oswald, S. Saad, and P. R. Sackett, "The Homogeneity Assumption in Differential Prediction Analysis: Does It Really Matter?" *Journal of Applied Psychology,* (August 2000), p. 536; J. N. Farrell and M. A. McDaniel, "The Stability of Validity Coefficients Over Time: Ackerman's (1988) Model and the General Aptitude Test Battery," *Journal of Applied Psychology,* (February 2001), p. 60; P. R. Jeanneret and M. H. Strong, "Linking O*Net Job Analysis Information to Job Requirement Predictors: An O*Net Application," *Personnel Psychology,* (Summer 2003), p. 465; and F. L. Schmidt, K. Pearlman, J. E. Hunter, and H. R. Hirsh, "Forty Questions About Validity Generalization and Meta-Analysis," *Personnel Psychology,* Vol. 38, No. 4, (Winter 1985), pp. 697–822.

57. M. T. Brannick, "Implications of Empirical Bayes Meta-Analysis for Test Validation," *Journal of Applied Psychology,* (June 2001), p. 468.

58. See, for instance, I. F. H. Wong, and L. Phooi-Ching, "Chinese Cultural Values and Performance at Job Interviews: A Singapore Perspective," *Business Communication Quarterly,* (March 2000), pp. 9–22.

59. G. Thornton, International, "Four in ten businesses worldwide have no women in senior management," online at http://www. gti.org/Press-room/Press-archive/2007/women-in-management. asp accessed February 1, 2009.

60. M. A. O'Neil, "How to Implement Relationship Management Strategies," *Supervision,* (July 2000), p. 3.

61. K. Gurchiek, "Some Addresses Raise a Red Flag," *HR Magazine,* (May, 2011), p. 16.

62. A. Kristof-Brown, M. R. Barrick, and M. Franke, "Applicant Impression Management: Dispositional Influences and Consequences for Recruiter Perceptions of Fit and Similarity," *Journal of Management,* (January 2002), pp. 27–46.

63. See, for example, K. J. Dunham, "Career Journal: The Jungle," *Wall Street Journal,* (May 21, 2002), p. B-10.

64. P. L. Lail and K. D. Kale, "Post-Offer Medical Exam Was Premature," *HR Magazine,* (June 2005), p. 163.

CHAPTER 8
Socializing, Orienting, and Developing Employees

1. Compiled from: K. Tyler, "From Dependence to Self-Sufficiency," *HR Magazine,* (September 2010), pp. 35–39; T. Fernholz, "Best Practices: Cascade Engineering Makes Welfare-to-Career a Reality," GOOD Business, (September 27, 2011), www.good.is/best-pratices-cascade-engineering-makes-welfare-to-career-a-reality accessed September 28, 2011; R. V. Habeck, Ph.D., and C. H. Rachel, Ph.D., "Organizational Factors at Cascade Engineering that Facilitate Successful Job Retention," Virginia Commonwealth University (March 2008, revised January 2010), www.worksupport.com/documents/CascadeEngineer.pdf accessed September 28, 2011; and Adam Bluestein, "Regulate Me. Please.," *Inc.,* (May, 2011): pp. 72–80.

2. "Organizational Entry: Onboarding, Orientation and Socialization" SHRM, online at http://www.shrm.org/Research/Articles/Articles/Pages/OrganizationalEntryOnboarding,OrientationAndSocialization. aspx accessed January 21, 2012.

3. T. N. Bauer, "Onboarding New Employees: Maximizing Success," *SHRM Foundation,* (2010), online at http://www.shrm.org/about/foundation/products/Pages/OnboardingEPG.aspx accessed September 25, 2011.

4. Ibid.

5. For a thorough review of this topic, see C. M. Riordan, E. W. Weatherly, R. J. Vandenberg, and R. M. Self, "The Effects of Pre-Entry Experiences and Socialization Tactics on Newcomer Attitudes and Turnover," *Journal of Managerial Issues,* (Summer 2001), pp. 159–173.

6. See, for example, S. L. Robinson and E. Wolfe, "The Development of Psychological Contract Breech Violation: A Longitudinal Study," *Journal of Organizational Behavior,* (August 2000), pp. 525–546.

7. J. Van Maanen and E. H. Schein, "Career Development," in J. R. Hackman and J. L. Suttle (eds.), *Improving Life at Work,* (Santa Monica: Goodyear Publishing, 1977), pp. 58–62. See also J. P. Wanous, A. E. Reichers, and S. D. Malik, "Organizational Socialization and Group Development," *Academy of Management Review* 9, (1992), pp. 670–683.

8. D. C. Feldman, "The Multiple Socialization of Organization Members," *Academy of Management Review,* (April 1981), pp. 310.

9. For a thorough discussion of these issues, see J. A. Chatman, "Matching People and Organizations: Selection and Socialization in Public Accounting Firms," *Administrative Science Quarterly,* (September 1991), pp. 459–485.

10. For example, see G. Blau, "Early-Career Job Factors Influencing the Professional Commitment of Medical Technologies," *Academy of Management Journal,* (December 1999), pp. 687–699; and C. R. Wanberg, "Unwrapping the Organizational Entry Process: Disentangling Multiple Antecedents and Their Pathways to Adjustment," *Journal of Applied Psychology,* (October 2003), pp. 779–794.

11. See T. J. Fogarty, "Socialization and Organizational Outcomes in Large Public Accounting Firms," *Journal of Managerial Issues,* (Spring 2000), pp. 13–33. See also T. Y. Kim, D. M. Cable, and S. P. Kim, "Socialization Tactics, Employee Proactivity, and Person-Organization Fit," *Journal of Applied Psychology,* (March 2005), pp. 232–241.

12. Compiled from: Tony Hsieh, "Your Culture Is Your Brand," *Zappos Blogs: CEO and COO Blog,* (January 3, 2009), online at http://blogs.zappos.com/blogs/ceo-and-coo-blog/2009/01/03/your-culture-is-your-brand accessed April 12, 2012; Interview with Tony Hsieh, Episode 191, *net@night with Amber MacArthur,* (June 9, 2010), online at http://twit.tv/show/netnight-amber-and-leo/191 accessed April 12, 2012; "Best Companies to work for: Happy Campers Zappos," *Fortune,* (April 2011).

13. See, for instance, T. G. Reio Jr., and A. Wiswell, "Field Investigations of the Relationship Among Adult Curiosity, Workplace Learning, and Job Performance," *Human Resource Development Quarterly,* (Spring 2000), p. 5.

14. M. Messmer, "Orientation Programs Can Be Key to Employee Retention," *Strategic Finance,* (February 2000), pp. 12–14; and H. J. Klein and N. A. Weaver, "The Effectiveness of an Organizational-Level Orientation Training Program in the Socialization of New Hires," *Personnel Psychology,* (Spring 2000), pp. 47–60.

15. Based on Catherine D. Fyock, "Managing the Employee Onboarding and Assimilation Process," SHRM, (Revised September 9, 2010), online at http://www.shrm.org/templatestools/toolkits/pages/onboardingandassimilationprocess.aspx accessed September 15, 2011.

16. C. Garvey, "The Whirlwind of a New Job," *HR Magazine,* (June 2001), pp. 110–117; and C. A. Hacker, "New Employee Orientation: Make It Pay Dividends for Years to Come," *Information Systems Management,* (Winter 2004), pp. 89–92.

17. See, for example, R. L. Robbins, "Orientation: Necessity or Nightmare?" *Supervision,* (October 2002), pp. 8–10.

18. "American Family Insurance Takes Employee Orientation Online," *Human Resource Department Management Report,* (February 2002), p. 9. See also C. W. Autry and A. R. Wheeler, "Post-Hire Human Resource Management Practices and Person-Organization Fit: A Study of Blue-Collar Employees," *Journal of Managerial Issues,* (Spring 2005), pp. 58–77.

19. L. Mallak, "Understanding and Changing Your Organization's Culture," *Industrial Management,* (March/April 2001), pp. 18–24.

20. W. W. Jones and N. Macris, "Where Am I and Where Do I Go from Here?" *Planning,* (June 2000), pp. 18–21.

21. See S. P. Robbins, *Business Today: The New World of Business,* (New York: Harcourt, 2001), pp. 317–318.

22. M. Boyle, "Just Right," *Fortune,* (June 10, 2002), pp. 207–208; and T. Davis and M. Landa, "The Story of Mary? How 'Organization Culture' Can Erode Bottom-Line Profitability," *Canadian Manager,* (Winter 2000), pp. 14–17.

23. See, for example, S. Hicks, "Successful Orientation Programs," *Training and Development,* (April 2000), pp. 59–60.

24. C. Garvey, "The Whirlwind of a New Job," *HR Magazine,* (June 2001), pp. 110–117; and C. A. Hacker, "New Employee Orientation: Make It Pay Dividends for Years to Come," *Information Systems Management,* (Winter 2004), pp. 89–92.

25. P. Harris, "Outsourced Learning: A New Market Emerges: The Lure of Cost-Savings and Other Incentives Are Prompting More Organizations to Outsource Their Entire Learning Function, or Large Portions of It. But Trainers Shouldn't Feel Threatened, Say Insiders, They Figure That Within 10 Years, Half of Them Will Be Working for Outsourcing Partners," *Training and Development,* (September 2003), pp. 30–39.

26. S. F. Del Brocco and R. W. Sprague, "Getting Your Supervisors and Managers in the Right Team," *Employment Relations Today,* (Autumn 2000), pp. 13–27; and D. L. Barrette, "What's New," *HR Magazine,* (November 2000), pp. 185–188.

27. "Virtual HR," *Business Europe,* (March 8, 2000), p. 1; "The Payoffs of Self-Service HR Are Significant," *HR Focus,* (January 2001), p. 10; and D. L. Prucino and C. M. Rice, "Point-and-Click Personnel Policies: State Laws May Affect Electronic Employee Handbooks," *Employment Relations Today,* (Autumn 2000), p. 111.

28. "Are Your Training Programs Legal Time Bombs?" *HR Focus,* (July 2000), pp. 6–7.

29. "Employers worldwide lack a strategy for developing women leaders, new Mercer survey shows," Mercer, (March 3, 2011), online at http://www.mercer.com/press-releases/1409145 accessed September 25, 2011.

30. C. Tuna, "Even in HR, Women's Pay Lags Men's," *Wall Street Journal,* (October 23, 2008), online at http://online.wsj.com/article/SB12246282036-7156127.html accessed January 21, 2012.

31. See, for instance, E. G. Tripp, "Aging Aircraft and Coming Regulations, Political and Media Pressures Have Encouraged the FAA to Expand Its Pursuit of Real and Perceived Problems of Older Aircraft and their Systems. Operators Will Pay," *Business and Commercial Aviation,* (March 2001), pp. 68–75.

32. C. S. Duncan, J. D. Selby-Lucas, and W. Swart, "Linking Organizational Goals and Objectives to Employee Performance: A Quantitative Perspective," *Journal of American Academy of Business,* (March 2002), pp. 314–318; and "Goal Seekers," *Training Magazine,* (September 7, 2005), p. 12.

33. R. Langlois, "Fairmont Hotels: Business Strategy Starts with People," *Canadian HR Reporter,* (November 5, 2001), p. 19; and "Line Manager Skills Top List of Learning Needs," *Personnel Today,* (May 24, 2005), p. 46.

34. See K. Ellis, "Top Training Strategies: New Twists on Familiar Ideas," *Training,* (August 2003), pp. 30–36.

35. See, for instance, "6 Ways to Transform Your 'See-Level' Employees Into Leaders," *Human Resource Department Management Report,* (September 2003), p. 5.

36. B. Pfau and I. Kay, "HR: Playing the Training Game and Losing," *HR Magazine,* (August 2002), pp. 49–53.

37. See D. Forman, "Eleven Common-Sense Learning Principles: Lessons from Experience, Sages, and Each Other," *Training and Development,* (September 2003), pp. 39–47.

38. Michael Gaynor, "Could You Drive A UPS Truck?" *Washingtonian,* (December 2010), online at http://www.washingtonian.com/articles/people/could-you-drive-a-ups-truck/ accessed October 3, 2011.

39. K. Ellis, "Making Waves: With a Leadership Crisis on the Horizon, Organizations Are Looking Within to Build Talent Pools of Their Own," *Training,* (June 2003), pp. 16–22; and "The Changing Face of Talent Management," *HR Focus,* (May 2003), p. 1.

40. H. Dolezalek, "Pretending to Learn: Training Professionals Are Using Games and Simulations in Complex Ways to Help Employees Understand Business Concepts and Uncover Millions in Cost Savings," *Training,* (July–August 2003), pp. 20–26.

41. N. H. Woodward, "Make the Most of Team Building," *HR Magazine,* (September, 2006), pp. 72–76.

42. Adventure Associates, www.adventureassoc.com (August 19, 2008).

43. "ASTD 2011 State of the Industry Report," American Society for Training and Development (2011), pp. 4–5.

44. S. Hicks, "What Is Organization Development?" *Training and Development,* (August 2000), p. 65.

45. R. Morgan, "Employers Must Prepare Staff for Change in Uncertain Times," *HR Briefing,* (May 15, 2003), pp. 2–4.

46. The idea for these metaphors came from P. Vaill, *Managing as a Performing Art: New Ideas for a World of Chaotic Change,* (San Francisco: Jossey-Bass, 1989).

47. K. Lewin, *Field Theory in Social Science,* (New York: Harper & Row, 1951).

48. K. Lewin, *Field Theory in Social Science,* (New York: Harper & Row, 1951).

49. See, for instance, C. R. Leana and B. Barry, "Stability and Change as Simultaneous Experiences in Organizational Life," *Academy of Management Review,* (October 2000), pp. 753–759.

50. A. E. Christopher and G. F. Worley, "Reflections on the Future of Organization Development" *Journal of Applied Behavioral Science,* (March 2003), pp. 97–115; H. Hornstein, "Organizational Development and Change Management: Don't Throw the Baby Out with the Bath Water," *Journal of Applied Behavioral Science,* (June 2001), pp. 223–227; and S. "What Is Organization Development?" *Training and Development,* (August 2000), p. 65.

51. M. J. Austin, "Introducing Organizational Development (OD) Practices into a Country Human Service Agency," *Administration in Social Work,* (Winter 2001), p. 63.

52. See, for instance, H. B. Jones, "Magic, Meaning, and Leadership: Weber's Model and the Empirical Literature," *Human Relations,* (June 2001), p. 753.

53. G. Akin and I. Palmer, "Putting Metaphors to Work for a Change in Organizations," *Organizational Dynamics,* (Winter 2000), pp. 67–79.

54. J. Grieves, "Skills, Values or Impression Management? Organizational Change and the Social Processes of Leadership, Change Agent Practice, and Process Consultation," *Journal of Management Development,* (May 2000), p. 407.

55. M. McMaster, "Team Building Tips," *Sales and Marketing Management,* (January 2002), p. 140; and "How To: Executive Team Building," *Training and Development,* (January 2002), p. 16.

56. Initial work on the learning organization is credited to P. M. Senge, *The Fifth Discipline: The Art and Practice,* (New York: Doubleday, 1990); C. Kontoghiorghes, S. M. Awbre, and P. L. Feurig, "Examining the Relationship Between Learning Organization Characteristics and Change Adaptation, Innovation, and Organizational Performance," *Human Resource Development Quarterly,* (Summer 2005), pp. 185–212; and P. Tosey, "The Hunting of the Learning Organization: A Paradoxical Journey," *Management Learning,* (September 2005), pp. 335–353.

57. B. Raabe and T. A. Beehr, "Formal Mentoring Versus Supervisor and Co-Worker Relationships: Differences in Perceptions and Impact," *Journal of Organizational Behavior,* (May 2003), pp. 271–294.

58. "Or Do You?" *Training and Development,* (June 2003), p. 6.

59. R. Ruggless, "Rewarding Excellence," *Restaurant News,* (December 19, 2011), online at http://nrn.com/article/rewarding-excellence accessed January 21, 2012.

60. "How to Measure 'Softer' Results," *HR Focus,* (April 2001), pp. 5–7; and A. Putra, "Evaluating Training Programs: An Exploratory Study of Transfer of Learning Onto the Job at Hotel A and Hotel B, Sydney, Australia," *Journal of Hospitality and Tourism Management,* (April 2004), pp. 77–87.

61. See, for example, D. L. Gay and T. J. LaBonte, "Demystifying Performance: Getting Started: This Conclusion to Article 1 (May) Spells Out How to Build Confidence and Credibility," *Training and Development,* (July 2003), pp. 40–451; and R. E. Catalano and D. L. Kirkpatrick, "Evaluating Training Programs—The State of the Art," *Training and Development Journal,* (May 1968), pp. 2–9. See also "Why a Stakeholder Approach to Evaluating Training," *Advances in Developing Human Resources* 7, no. 1 (2005), pp. 121–134. For another perspective, see D. L. Bradford and W. W. Burke, "Introduction: Is OD in Crisis?," *Journal of Applied Behavioral Science,* (December 2004), pp. 369–373.

62. M. A. Shaffer and D. A. Harrison, "Forgotten Partners of International Assignments: Developments and Test of a Model of Spouse Adjustment," *Journal of Applied Psychology,* (April 2001), p. 238.

63. J. Selmer, "The Preference for Pre-Departure or Post-Arrival Cross-Cultural Training: An Exploratory Approach," *Journal of Managerial Psychology,* (January 2001), p. 50; N. Zakaria, "The Effects of Cross-Cultural Training on the Acculturation Process of the Global Workforce," *International Journal of Manpower,* (June 2000), pp. 492–511; and F. Lievens, E. Van Keer, M. M. Harris, and C. Bisqueret, "Predicting Cross-Cultural Training Performance: The Validity of Personality, Cognitive Ability, and Dimensions Measured by an Assessment Center and a Behavior Description Interview," *Journal of Applied Psychology,* (June 2003), pp. 76–89.

64. See, for example, D. M. Eschbach, G. E. Parker, and P. A. Stoeberl, "American Repatriate Employees' Retrospective Assessments of the Effects of Cross-Cultural Training on the Adaptation to International Assignments," *International Journal of Human Resource Management,* (March 2001), p. 270. See also S. Taylor and N. K. Napier, "An American Woman in Turkey: Adventures Unexpected and Knowledge Unplanned," *Human Resource Management,* (Winter 2001), pp. 347–365; and R. C. May, S. M. Puffer, and D. J. McCarthy, "Transferring Management Knowledge to Russia: A Culturally Based Approach," *Journal of Management Executive,* (May 2005), pp. 24–35.

65. See, for instance, A. Yan, G. Zhu, and D. T. Hall, "International Assignments for Career Building: A Model of Agency Relationships and Psychological Contracts," *Academy of Management Review,* (July 2002), pp. 373–392; and D. Beadles, "An American Expat View," *Training and Development,* (July 2001), pp. 76.

66. K. Kingsbury, "The 2008 Time 100," *Time Magazine,* (April 25, 2008), p. 14.

67. D. Heath and C. Heath, "The Heroic Checklist," *Fast Company,* (March 2008), pp. 66–68.

68. L. Lavelle, "For UPS Managers, a School of Hard Knocks," *BusinessWeek,* (July 22, 2002), pp. 58–59; UPS, "Community Internship Program" (2005), http://www.community. ups.com/diversity/workplace/intern. html.

69. UPS Pressroom, UPS Community Internship Program (CIP) Fact Sheet. www.ups.com (August 19, 2008).

70. Statement of Lisa Hamilton, President, UPS Foundation, Before the Committee on Education and Labor, U.S. House of Representatives, (February 25, 2009), online at http://www.voicesforservice.org/Testimony/20090225LisaHamiltonTestimony.pdf accessed January 21, 2012; Ryan Wenzel, "43rd year of UPS Community Program Draws to Close," Henry Street Settlement, (August 11, 2011), online at http://www.henrystreet.org/news.

CHAPTER **9**
Managing Careers

1. J. Light, "Even Hints of Layoffs Decay Morale," *Wall Street Journal,* (September 19, 2011), online at http://online.wsj.com/article/SB10001424053111904491704576573273683844308.html accessed October 4, 2011.

2. See "Career Development Ranks Among the Most Demanded Content Areas Across Industries Worldwide," *Training and Development,* (September 2003), p. 18. See also P. Kaihla, "How to Land Your Dream Job," *Business 2.0,* (November 2004), pp. 103–108.

3. D. T. Hall, *Careers in Organizations,* (Santa Monica: Goodyear Publishing, 1976); and J. Van Maanen and E. H. Schein, "Career Development," in J. R. Hackman and J. L. Suttle (eds.), *Improving Life at Work: Behavioral Sciences Approaches to Organizational Change,* (Santa Monica: Goodyear Publishing, 1977), pp. 341–355.

4. M. Tight, *Key Concepts in Adult Education and Training,* (London and New York: Routledge, 2002), p. 85.

5. See, for instance, R. MacLean, "My Start-Up, Myself," *Inc,* (October 17, 2000), pp. 210–211. See also J. Goodman and S. Hansen, "Career Development and Guidance Programs Across Cultures: The Gap Between Policies and Practices," *Career Development Quarterly,* (September 2005), pp. 57–65.

6. "Career Development: Employers Urged to Act to Retain Key Workers," *Personnel Today,* (January 28, 2003), p. 7. See also J. Sturges, N. Conway,

D. Guest, and A. Liefooghe, "Managing the Career Deal: The Psychological Contract as a Framework for Understanding Career Management, Organizational Commitment, and Work Behavior," *Journal of Organizational Behavior,* (November 2005), p. 821; and R. Van Esbroeck, E. L. Herr, and M. L. Savickas, "Introduction to the Special Issue: Global Perspectives on Vocational Guidance," *Career Development Quarterly,* (September 2005), pp. 8–11.

7. G. Ruiz, "Keeping Young Talent Won't Be Easy," *Workforce Management,* (October 22, 2007), p. 14.

8. J. Hempel, "In the Land of Women," *Fortune,* (February 4, 2008), p. 69.

9. J. Van Maanen and E. H. Schein, "Career Development," in J. R. Hackman and J. L. Suttle (eds.), *Improving Life at Work: Behavioral Sciences Approaches to Organizational Change.* (Santa Monica: Goodyear Publishing, 1977), p. 343.

10. Ibid.; D. T. Hall, *Careers in Organizations* (Santa Monica: Goodyear Publishing, 1976); and M. London and S. A. Stumpf, *Managing Careers.* (Reading: Addison Wesley, 1982).

11. B. Morris, "So You're a Player: Do You Need a Coach?," *Fortune,* (February 21, 2000), pp. 144–154.

12. J. J. Sosik and V. M. Godshalk, "Leadership Styles, Mentoring Functions Received, and Job-Related Stress: A Conceptual Model and Preliminary Study," *Journal of Organizational Behavior,* (June 2000), p. 365; and K. Tyler, "Find Your Mentor," *HR Magazine,* (March 2004), pp. 89–93.

13. N. Richmond, "Mentoring for Success," NASA, online at http://www.nasa.gov/devguide/devprograms/mentor/mentorsuccess.ppt accessed October 15, 2011.

14. A. Kamentz, "Life in Beta," *Fast Company,* (May 2011), p. 56.

15. T. D. Allen and L. M. Finkelstein, "Beyond Mentoring: Alternative Sources and Functions of Development Support," *Career Development Quarterly,* (June 2003), pp. 346–356; and L. M. Finkelstein, T. D. Allen, and L. A. Rhoton, "An Examination of the Role of Age in Mentoring Relationships," *Group and Organization Management,* (June 2003), pp. 249–281.

16. B. Raabe and R. A. Beehr, "Formal Mentoring Versus Supervisory and Coworker Relationships: Differences in Perceptions and Impact," *Journal of Organizational Behavior,* (May 2003), pp. 271–294.

17. C. M. Solomon, "Cracks in the Glass Ceiling," *Workforce,* (September 2000), p. 86.

18. J. A. Segal, "Mirror-Image Mentoring," *HR Magazine,* (March 2000), pp. 157–165. For another view on this topic, see T. Allen, M. L. Poteet, and J. E. A. Russell, "Protege Selection by Mentors: What Makes the Difference?" *Journal of Organizational Behavior,* (May 2000), pp. 271–282.

19. J. A. Segal, "Mirror-Image Mentoring," *HR Magazine,* (March 2000), p. 158.

20. See M. C. Higgins, L. Trotter, S. L. Ablon, S. Pearson, and M. Mohan, "What Should C. J. Do?" *Harvard Business Review,* (November–December 2000), pp. 43–52; J. Hutchins, "Getting to Know You," *Workforce,* (November 2000), pp. 44–48; R. Sharpe, "As Leaders, Women Rule," *BusinessWeek,* (November 20, 2000), pp. 74–84; C. Benabou and R. Benabou, "Establishing a Formal Mentoring Program for Organizational Success," *National Productivity Review,* (Autumn 2000), pp. 1–8; and D. Zeilinski, "Mentoring Up," *Training,* (October 2000), pp. 136–140.

21. For an interesting perspective on this matter, see S. J. Armstrong, C. W. Allinson, and J. Hayes, "Formal Mentoring Systems: An Examination of the Effects of Mentor/Protege Cognitive Styles on the Mentoring Process," *Journal of Management Studies,* (December 2002), pp. 1111–1127.

22. See, for example, D. E. Super, *The Psychology of Careers,* (New York: Harper & Row, 1957); E. Schein, *Career Dynamics: Matching Individual and Organizational Needs,* (Reading: Addison Wesley, 1978); and D. J. Levinson, C. N. Darrow, E. B. Klein, M. H. Levinson, and B. McKee, *A Man's Life,* (New York: Knopf, 1978). Also see C. P. Chen, "Integrating Perspectives in Career Development Theory and Practice," *Career Development Quarterly,* (March 2003), pp. 203–217.

23. See M. Messmer, "Moving Beyond a Career Plateau," *National Public Accountant,* (September 2000), pp. 20–21; and J. Blenkinsopp and K. Zdunczyk, "Making Sense of Mistakes in Managerial Careers," *Career Development International* 10, no. 5 (2005), pp. 356–359.

24. S. Miller, "Benefits and Perks Keep Older Workers Working," SHRM, (April 2008), online at http://www.shrm.org accessed October 9, 2011.

25. "The 'Silver Tsunami': Why Older Workers Offer Better Value than Younger Ones," *Knowledge@Wharton,* Wharton School University of Pennsylvania, (December 2010), online at http://knowledge@wharton.upenn.edu accessed October 9, 2011.

26. K. Dychtwald, T. Erickson, and R. Morrison, *Workforce Crisis: How to Beat the Coming Shortage of Skills & Talent,* (Boston: Harvard Business School Press, 2006), p. 51.

27. "30 Occupations with the fastest projected growth," Bureau of Labor Statistics, online at http://www.bls.gov/news.release/ecopro.t07.htm accessed September 15, 2012.

28. D. E. Super, "A Life-Span Life Space Approach to Career Development," *Journal of Vocational Behavior* 16, (Spring 1980), pp. 282–298.

29. O*NET Online, www.onetonline.org accessed October 9, 2011.

30. J. Holland, *Making Vocational Choices,* 2nd ed. (Englewood Cliffs: Prentice Hall, 1986).

31. P. B. Robinson, D. V. Simpson, J. C. Huefner, and H. K. Hunt, "An Attitude Approach to the Prediction of Entrepreneurship," *Entrepreneurship Theory and Practice,* (Summer 1991), pp. 13–31.

32. B. M. Davis, "Role of Venture Capital in the Economic Renaissance of an Area," in R. D. Hisrich (ed.), *Entrepreneurship, Intrapreneurship, and Venture Capital* (Lexington: Lexington Books, 1986), pp. 107–118.

33. J. M. Crant, "The Proactive Personality Scale as a Predictor of Entrepreneurial Intentions," *Journal of Small Business Management,* (July 1996), pp. 42–49; J. D. Kammeyer-Mueller and C. R. Wanberg, "Unwrapping the Organizational Entry Process: Disentangling Multiple Antecedents and Their Pathways to Adjustment," *Journal of Applied Psychology,* (October 2003), pp. 779–794; J. A. Thompson, "Proactive Personality and Job Performance: A Social Capital Perspective," *Journal of Applied Psychology,* (September 2005), pp. 1011–1017; and D. G. Allen, K. P. Weeks, and K. R. Moffitt, "Turnover Intentions and Voluntary Turnover: The Moderating Roles of Self-Monitoring, Locus of Control, Proactive Personality, and Risk Aversion," *Journal of Applied Psychology,* (September 2005), pp. 980–990.

34. For an interesting discussion of Schein anchors, see E. H. Schein, "Career Anchors Revisited: Implications for Career Development in the 21st Century," *Academy of Management Journal* 10, no. 1 (January 1996), pp. 80–88; and D. C. Feldman and M. C. Bolino, "Career Patterns of the Self-Employed: Career Motivations and Career Outcomes," *Journal of Small Business Management,* (July 2000), pp. 53–67.

35. See, for example, J. Michael, "Using the Myers-Briggs Type Indicator as a Tool for Leadership Development? Apply with Caution," *Journal of Leadership and Organizational Studies,"* (Summer 2003), pp. 68–82; R. Badham, V. Morrigan, W. Rifkin, and M. Zanko, "The Use of Personality Typing in Organizational Change, Discourse, Emotions, and the Reflective Subject," *Human Relations,* (February 2003), pp. 211–235; and D. P. Shuit, "At 60, Myers-Briggs Is Still Sorting Out and Identifying People's Types; Demand for the Venerable Personality Test Remains Strong, Even Though the World Has Changed," *Workforce Management,* (December 2003), pp. 72–73.

36. Consulting Psychologists Press, Myers-Briggs Type Indicator® (MBTI)®, wwwl.cpp.com/products/mbti/index.asp (2000); R. B. Kennedy and D. A. Kennedy, "Using the Myers-Briggs Type Indicator® in Career Counseling," *Journal of Employment Counseling,* (March 2004), pp. 38–44; and J. Sample, "The Myers-Briggs Type Indicator and OD: Implications for Practice From Research," *Organization Development Journal,* (Spring 2004), pp. 67–75.

37. P. Moran, "Personality Characteristics and Growth-Orientation of the Small Business Owner Manager," *Journal of Managerial Psychology,* (July 2000), p. 651; and M. Higgs, "Is There a Relationship Between the Myers-Briggs Type Indicator and Emotional Intelligence?" *Journal of Managerial Psychology,* (September–October, 2001), pp. 488–513.

38. D. Richards, "Invaluable Experience and an Inside Track to Permanent Employment," *Job Journal* XXIX, no. 1261, (February 6–19, 2011), p. 7.

39. K. Gurchiek, "Older, Experienced Workers Applying for Internships," *HR Magazine,* (October 2010), p. 14.

40. Debbie Fischer, Interview at Campbell Mithun Headquarters, Minneapolis, MN October 13, 2011.

41. S. Elliott, "Competing for Summer Internships, Using a Twitter Contest," *New York Times,* (March 24, 2011), online at http://www.nytimes.com/2011/03/25/business/media/25adco.html accessed October 15, 2011.

42. See also M. Ligos, "Turning Down a Transfer Can Freeze a Career," *New York Times,* (September 28, 2003), p. B-8.

43. G. Kranz, "Newell Rubbermaid Aspires to Grow Leaders," *Workforce Management,* (July 24, 2011), online at http://www.workforce.com/article/20110724/NEWS02/307249994/newell-rubbermaid-aspires-to-grow-leaders accessed October 9, 2011.

44. Ibid.

45. "Newell Rubbermaid," The Ken Blanchard Companies, http://www.kenblanchard.com/leaders/newell/ accessed October 9, 2011.

46. I. R. Schwartz, "Self-Assessment and Career Planning: Matching Individuals and Organizational Goals," *Personnel,* (January-February 1979), p. 48.

CHAPTER **10**
Establishing the Performance Management System

1. "It's All Happening at the Zoo," Halogen Software (2010), online at http://www.halogensoftware.com accessed October 29, 2011.

2. "The Zoological Society of San Diego Redefined its Corporate Culture With its New Employee Performance Management System," Halogen Software, online at http://www.halogensoftware.com/customers/case-studies/services-manufacturing/study_sandiegozoo.php accessed June 14, 2012.

3. T. Henneman, "Employee Performance Management: What's Gnu at the Zoo," *Workforce Management,* (September 2006), online at http://www.workforce.com/article/20060911/NEWS02/309119997 accessed June 14, 2012.

4. K. J. Hatten and S. R. Rosenthal, "Why and How To Systemize Performance Measurement," *Journal of Organizational Excellence,* (Autumn 2001), pp. 59–74.

5. H. Levinson, "Management by Whose Objectives?" *Harvard Business Review,* (January 2003), pp. 107–110; and M. D. Cannon and R. Witherspoon, "Actionable Feedback: Unlocking the Power of Learning and Performance," *Academy of Management Executive,* (May 2005), pp. 120–134.

6. See also "Companies Appraise to Improve Development," *Personnel Today,* (February 25, 2003), p. 51.

7. C. Joinson, "Making Sure Employees Measure Up," *HR Magazine,* (March 2001), pp. 36–41.

8. R. Williams, "It's time to abolish the employee performance review," *Psychology Today,* (June 27, 2010), online at http://www.psychologytoday.com/blog/wired-success/201006/its-time-abolish-the-employee-performance-review accessed October 30, 2011.

9. E. Van Slyke, "An Alternative to Performance Appraisal," SHRM, (June 2, 2010), online at http://www.shrm.org/hrdisciplines/employeerelations/articles/pages/analternativetoperformanceappraisal.aspx accessed October 22, 2011.

10. J. Pfeffer, "Low Grades for Performance Reviews," *BloombergBusinessWeek,* (July 23, 2009), online at http://www.businessweek.com/magazine/content/09_31/b4141080608077.htm accessed October 30, 2011.

11. H. M. Findley, K. W. Mossholder, and W. F. Giles, "Performance Appraisal Process and System Facets: Relationships with Contextual Performance," *Journal of Applied Psychology,* (August 2000), pp. 634–640.

12. See, for example, S. Wilmer, "The Dark Side of 360-Degree Feedback," *Training and Development,* (September 2002), pp. 37–44.

13. See, for instance, M. S. Taylor, S. S. Masterson, M. K. Renard, and K. B. Tracy, "Managers' Reactions to Procedurally Just Performance Management Systems," *Academy of Management Journal,* (October 1998), pp. 568–678.

14. S. S. K. La, M. S. M. Yik, and J. Schaubroeck, "Responses to Formal Performance Appraisal Feedback: The Role of Negative Affectivity," *Journal of Applied Psychology,* (February 2002), pp. 192–202.

15. A. DelPo, *The Performance Appraisal Handbook,* 2nd ed. (Berkeley, Nolo Publishing, 2007).

16. E. Van Slyke, "An Alternative to Performance Appraisal, *SHRM,* (June 2, 2010), online at http://www.shrm.org/hrdisciplines/employeerelations/articles/pages/analternativetoperformanceappraisal.aspx accessed October 30, 2011.

17. T. Parker-Pope, "Time to Review Workplace Reviews?" *New York Times,* (May 17, 2010), online at http://well.blogs.nytimes.com/2010/05/17/time-to-review-workplace-reviews/ accessed October 22, 2011.

18. D. C. Martin, K. M. Bartol, and P. E. Kehoe, "The Legal Ramifications of Performance Appraisal: The Growing Significance," *Public Personnel Management,* (Fall 2000), pp. 379–406.

19. D. Pink, "Think Tank: Fix the workplace, not the workers," *The Telegraph,* (November 6, 2010), online at http://www.telegraph.co.uk/finance/jobs/8113600/Think-Tank-Fix-the-workplace-not-the-workers.html accessed October 30, 2011.

20. "The Rypple effect," *The Economist,* (December 30, 2008), online at http://www.economist.com/node/12863565 accessed October 30, 2011.

21. R. Pyrillis, "Is Your Performance Review Underperforming?" *Workforce Management,* (May 2011), pp. 20–22, 24–25.

22. Readers might find the following article of interest: J. Park and J. K. S. Chong, "A Comparison of Absolute and Relative Performance Appraisal Systems," *International Journal of Management,* (September 2000), pp. 423–429.

23. For an overview of appraisal methods, see A. Tziner, C. Joanis, and K. R. Murphy, "A Comparison of Three Methods of Performance Appraisal with Regard to Goal Properties, Goal Perception, and Ratee Satisfaction," *Group and Organization Management,* (June 2000), pp. 175–191; and G. J. Yun, L. M. Donahue, D. M. Dudley, and L. A. McFarland, "Rater Personality, Rating Format, and Social Context: Implications for Performance Appraisal Ratings," *International Journal of Selection and Assessment,* (June 2005), p. 97.

24. See R. I. Henderson, *Compensation Management in a Knowledge-Based World,* 9th ed. (Upper Saddle River: Prentice Hall, 2003), Ch. 13.

25. A. Tziner and R. Kopelman, "Effects of Rating Format on Goal-Setting: A Field Experiment," *Journal of Applied Psychology,* (May 1988), p. 323.

26. M. L. Tenopyr, "Artificial Reliability of Forced-Choice Scales," *Journal of Applied Psychology,* (November 1988), pp. 750–751.

27. See, for example, A. Tziner, C. Joanis, and K. R. Murphy, "A Comparison of Three Methods of Performance Appraisal with Regard to Goal Properties, Goal Perception, and Ratee Satisfaction," *Group and Organization Management,* (June 2000), pp. 175–190; K. R. Murphy and V. A. Pardaffy, "Bias in Behaviorally Anchored Rating Scales: Global or Scale Specific," *Journal of Applied Psychology,* (April 1989), pp. 343–346; and M. J. Piotrowski, J. L. Barnes-Farrell, and F. H. Esris, "Behaviorally Anchored Bias: A Replication and Extension of Murphy and Constans," *Journal of Applied Psychology,* (October 1988), pp. 827–828.

28. A. Tziner, C. Joanis, and K. R. Murphy, "A Comparison of Three Methods of Performance Appraisal with Regard to Goal Properties, Goal Perception, and Ratee Satisfaction," *Group and Organization Management,* (June 2000), pp. 175–190; and R. B. Kaiser, and R. E. Kaplan, "Overlooking Overkill? Beyond the 1-to-5 Rating Scale," *Human Resource Planning* 28, no. 3 (2005), pp. 7–11.

29. M. J. de la Merced, "AIG will use a grading system for bonuses," *New York Times,* (February 11, 2010), p. B6.

30. K. Holland, "Performance Reviews: Many Need Improvement" *New York Times,* (September 10, 2006), p. 3; L. Rivenbark, "Forced Ranking," *HR Magazine,* (November 2005), p. 131; G. Johnson, "Forced Rankings: The Good, the Bad, and the Alternative," *Training,* (May 2004), pp. 24–30; "Why HR Professionals Are Worried About Forced Rankings," *HR Focus,* (October 2004), p. 8; "Performance Management Systems Are Quickly Becoming More Popular," *HR Focus,* (August 2003), p. 8; and D. Grote, "Forced Ranking," *Executive Excellence,* (July 2003), p. 6.

31. The concept of management by objectives is generally attributed to Peter F. Drucker, *The Practice of Management,* (New York: Harper & Row, 1954). See also J. F. Castellano and H. A. Roehm, "The Problem with

Managing by Objectives and Results," *Quality Progress,* (March 2001), pp. 39–46; J. Loehr and T. Schwartz, "The Making of a Corporate Athlete," *Harvard Business Review,* (January 2001), pp. 120–128; and A. J. Vogl, "Drucker, of Course," *Across the Board,* (November/December 2000), p. 1.

32. M. Green, J. Garrity, and B. Lyons, "Pitney Bowes Calls for New Metrics," *Strategic Finance,* (May 2002), pp. 30–35.

33. See, for example, I. M. Jawahar and G. Salegna, "Adapting Performance Appraisal Systems for a Quality Driven Environment," *Compensation and Benefits Review,* (January–February 2003), pp. 64–71.

34. See, for example, E. A. Locke, "Toward a Theory of Task Motivation and Incentives," *Organizational Behavior and Human Performance,* (May 1968), pp. 157–189; E. A. Locke, K. N. Shaw, L. M. Saari, and G. P. Latham, "Goal Setting and Task Performance: 1969–1980," *Psychological Bulletin,* (July 1981), pp. 12–52; E. A. Locke and G. P. Latham, *A Theory of Goal Setting and Task Performance,* (Upper Saddle River: Prentice Hall, 1990); P. Ward and M. Carnes, "Effects of Posting Self-Set Goals on Collegiate Football Players' Skill Execution During Practice and Games," *Journal of Applied Behavioral Analysis,* (Spring 2002), pp. 1–12; D. W. Ray, "Productivity and Profitability," *Executive Excellence,* (October 2001), p. 14; D. Archer, "Evaluating Your Managed System," *CMA Management,* (January 2000), pp. 12–14; and H. Levinson, "Management by Whose Objectives?" *Harvard Business Review,* (January 2003), p. 107.

35. L. Weatherly, "Management by Objectives," SHRM Research, (May 2004), online at http://www.shrm.org/research/articles/articles/pages/performance_20management_20series_20part_20iii__20management_20by_20objectives.aspx accessed June 15, 2012.

36. See, for instance, J. R. Crow, "Crashing with the Nose Up: Building a Cooperative Work Environment," *Journal for Quality and Participation,* (Spring 2002), pp. 45–50; and E. C. Hollensbe and J. P. Guthrie, "Group Pay-for-Performance Plans: The Role of Spontaneous Goal Setting," *Academy of Management Review,* (October 2000), pp. 864–972.

37. "Should Performance Review Be Fired?," *Knowledge at Wharton,* (April 27, 2011), http://knowledge.wharton.upenn.edu accessed October 22, 2011.

38. See E. McMullen, J. Chrisman, and K. Vesper, "Some Problems in Using Subjective Measures of Effectiveness to Evaluate Entrepreneurial Assistance Programs," *Entrepreneurship Theory and Practice,* (Fall 2001), pp. 37–55. See also K. Tyler, "Performance Art," *HR Magazine,* (August 2005), pp. 58–63; and R. F. Martell and D. P. Evans, "Source-Monitoring Training: Toward Reducing Rater Expectancy Effects in Behavioral Measurements," *Journal of Applied Psychology,* (September 2005), pp. 956–963.

39. For an interesting discussion of leniency errors, see J. S. Kane, H. J. Bernardin, P. Villanova, and J. Peyrefitte, "Stability of Rater Leniency: Three Studies," *Academy of Management Journal* 38, no. 4, (November 1995), pp. 1036–1051.

40. L. Miller, "Dear Workforce," *Workforce Management,* (February 15, 2011), online at http://www.workforce.com accessed October 22, 2011. S. Garr, "Challenged to Create Consistency? Consider Performance Calibration Meetings," Bersin & Associates, (January 13, 2011), www.bersin.com accessed October 23, 2011.

41. "Should Performance Reviews Be Fired?," *Knowledge@Wharton,* (April 27, 2011), online at http://knowledge.wharton.upenn.edu accessed October 23, 2011.

42. "Performance Appraisal Consistency Is a Rare and Wonderful Thing," *Pay for Performance Report,* (December 2002), p. 8.

43. D. Kipnis, K. Price, S. Schmidt, and C. Stitt, "Why Do I Like Thee: Is It Your Performance or My Orders?" *Journal of Applied Psychology,* (June 1981), pp. 324–328. See also P. A. Heslin, D. Vande Walle, and G. P. Latham, "The Effect of Implicit Person Theory on Performance Appraisals," *Journal of Applied Psychology,* (September 2005), pp. 842–856.

44. Ibid.

45. "Online Objectivity," *Training,* (July 2004), p. 18.

46. M. Rafter, "Now Showing on the Small Screen," *Workforce Management,* (March 2008) http://www.workforce.com/article/20080313/NEWS02/303139986 accessed June 15, 2012.

47. An assumption has been made here. That is, these raters have specific performance knowledge of the employee. Otherwise, more information may not be more accurate information. For example, if the raters are from various levels in the organization's hierarchy, these individuals may not have an accurate picture of the employee's performance; thus, quality of information may decrease. See also C. Fletcher and C. Baldry, "A Study of Individual Differences and Self-Awareness in the Context of Multi-Source Feedback," *Journal of Occupational and Organizational Psychology,* (September 2000), pp. 303–319.

48. See, for example, H. R. Rothstein, "Interrater Reliability of Job Performance Ratings: Growth to Asymptote Level with Increasing Opportunity to Observe," *Journal of Applied Psychology,* (June 1990), pp. 322–327. See also M. D. Zalesny, "Rater Confidence and Social Influence in Performance Appraisals," *Journal of Applied Psychology,* (June 1990), pp. 274–289.

49. For an interesting perspective on aspects to avoid when using multiple raters, see A. H. Church, S. G. Rogelberg, and J. Waclawski, "Since When Is No News Good News? The Relationship Between Performance and Response Rates in Multirater Feedback," *Personnel Psychology,* (Summer 2000), pp. 435–451; and E. J. Inderrieden, R. E. Allen, and T. J. Keaveny, "Managerial Discretion in the Use of Self-Ratings in an Appraisal System: The Antecedents and Consequence," *Journal of Managerial Issues,* (Winter 2004), pp. 460–483.

50. J. S. Miller, "Self-Monitoring and Performance Appraisal Satisfaction: An Exploratory Field Study," *Human Resource Management,* (Winter 2001), pp. 321–333.

51. "Feedback, Feedback Everywhere. But How Effective Is the 360-Degree Approach?" *Training Strategies for Tomorrow,* (November/December 2002), pp. 19–23. See also B. I. J. M. Van Der Heiden and A. H. J. Nijhof, "The Value of Subjectivity: Problems and Prospects for 360-Degree Appraisal System," *International Journal of Human Resource Management,* (May 2004), pp. 493–511.

52. J. F. Brett and L. E. Atwater, "360-Degree Feedback: Accuracy, Reactions, and Perceptions of Usefulness," *Journal of Applied Psychology,* (October 2001), pp. 930–942; and P. Googe, "How to Link 360-Degree Feedback and Appraisal," *People Management,* (January 27, 2005), pp. 46–47.

53. M. Debrayen and S. Brutus, "Learning from Others' 360-Degree Experiences," *Canadian HR Reporter,* (February 10, 2003), pp. 18–20. See also "Performance Appraisals," *Business Europe,* (April 3, 2002), p. 3.

54. T. J. Maurer, D. R. D. Mitchell, and F. G. Barbeite, "Predictors of Attitudes Toward a 360-Degree Feedback System and Involvement in Post-Feedback Management Development Activity," *Journal of Occupational and Organizational Psychology,* (March 2002), pp. 87–107.

55. A. Evans, "From Every Angle," *Training* (September 2001): 22.

56. P. Kamen, "The Way That You Use It: Full Circle Can Build Better Organizations with the Right Approach," *CMA Management,* (April 2003), pp. 10–13.

57. J. F. Brett and L. E. Atwater, "360-Degree Feedback: Accuracy, Reactions, and Perceptions of Usefulness," *Journal of Applied Psychology,* (October 2001), p. 930; M. Kennett, "First Class Coach," *Management Today,* (December 2001), p. 84; and T. A. Beehr, L. Ivanitsjaya, C. P. Hansen, D. Erofeev, and D. M. Gudanowski, "Evaluation of 360-Degree Feedback Ratings: Relationships with Each Other and with Performance and Selection Predictors," *Journal of Organizational Behavior,* (November 2001), pp. 775–788. For an opposing view on the benefits of 360-degree feedback, see B. Pfau, I. Kay, K. M. Nowack, and J. Ghorpade, "Does 360-Degree Feedback Negatively Affect Company Performance," *HR Magazine,* (June 2002), pp. 54–60.

58. S. P. Robbins, *Organizational Behavior,* 10th ed. (Upper Saddle River: Prentice Hall, 2004), p. 494.

59. J. Day, "Simple, Strong Team Ratings," *HR Magazine,* (September 2000), pp. 159–161.

60. W. C. Borman, "The Rating of Individuals in Organizations: An Alternative Approach," *Organizational Behavior and Human Performance,* (August 1974), pp. 105–124.

61. C. P. Neck, G. L. Stewart, C. C. Manz, "Thought Self-Leadership as a Framework for Enhancing the Performance of Performance Appraisers," *Journal of Applied Behavior Science,* (September 1995).

62. See S. J. Reinke, "Does the Form Really Matter?" *Review of Public Personnel Administration*, (March 2003), pp. 23–38.

63. See W. R. Boswell and J. W. Boudreau, "Employee Satisfaction with Performance Appraisals and Appraisers: The Role of Perceived Appraisal Use," *Human Resource Development Quarterly*, (Fall 2000), pp. 283–299.

64. D. Briscoe, R. Schuler, and I. Tarique, *International Human Resource Management*, 4th edition, (New York: Routledge, 2012), pp. 341–352.

65. D. Chernovitskaya, "Culturally Sensitive Performance Appraisal Forms," *SHRM*, (February 26, 2010), online at http://www.shrm.org/hrdisciplines/diversity/articles/pages/culturallysensitiveperformance.aspx accessed October 29, 2011.

66. J. Shen, "International Performance Appraisals: Policies, Practices and Determinants in the Case of Chinese Multinational Companies," *International Journal of Manpower* 25, no. 6 (2004), pp. 547–556.

CHAPTER **11**
Establishing Rewards and Pay Plans

1. S. Taylor, "The Lowdown on Unpaid Internship Programs," *HR Magazine*, (November 2010), pp. 46–48.

2. R. Perlin, "Unpaid Interns, Complicit Colleges," *New York Times*, (April 2, 2011), online at http://www.nytimes.com/2011/04/03/opinion/03perlin.html?pagewanted=all accessed May 11, 2011.

3. L. Seasholtz, "Unpaid Internships: No Pay, No Gain?" *Wetfeet*, online at http://www.wetfeet.com/advice-tools/internships/unpaid-internships-no-pay-no-gain accessed November 13, 2011.

4. U.S. Department of Labor Wage and Hour Division "Fact Sheet #71: Internship Programs Under the Fair Labor Standards Act," online at http://www.dol.gov/whd/regs/compliance/whdfs71.htm accessed November 11, 2011.

5. U.S. Department of Labor Wage and Hour Division "Fact Sheet #71: Internship Programs Under the Fair Labor Standards Act," online at http://www.dol.gov/whd/regs/compliance/whdfs71.htm accessed November 11, 2011.

6. S. Greenhouse, "The Unpaid Intern, Legal or Not," *New York Times*, (April 3, 2010), online at http://www.nytimes.com/2010/04/03/business/03intern.html?pagewanted=all accessed November 11, 2011.

7. See, for example, C. Ginther, "Incentive Programs that Really Work," *HR Magazine*, (August, 2000), pp. 117–120; A. Drach-Zahavy, "The Proficiency Trap: How to Balance Enriched Job Designs and the Team's Need for Support," *Journal of Organizational Behavior*, (December 2004), pp. 980–997. See also D. R. May, R. L. Gilson, and L. M. Harter, "The Psychological Conditions of Meaningfulness, Safety, and Availability and the Engagement of Human Spirit at Work," *Journal of Occupational and Organizational Psychology*, (March 2004), pp. 11–37.

8. "Dissatisfaction with Salary Review," Report on Salary Surveys, (June 2002), p. 8.

9. F. Hansen, "Compliance Pitfalls Arise in Negotiations on Starting Salaries," *Workforce Management*, (October 16, 2008), online at http://www.workforce.com/apps/pbcs.dll/article?AID=/20081016/NEWS02/310169991# accessed June 18, 2009.

10. See, for example, D. W. Organ, "What Pay Can and Can't Do," *Business Horizons*, (September, 2003), p. 1.

11. R. L. Heneman, J. M. Werner, "Merit Pay: Linking Pay to Performance in a Changing World," (Charlotte: *Information Age Publishing*, 2005.)

12. L. Wolgemuth, "Why Do You Keep Your Salary Secret?," *U.S. News and World Report*, (June 19, 2008), online at http://money.usnews.com/money/careers/articles/2008/06/19/why-do-you-keep-your-salary-secret accessed June 17, 2009.

13. Supreme Court of the U.S.: *Ledbetter v. Goodyear Tire & Rubber Co* at http://www.supremecourtus.gov/opinions/06pdf/05-1074.pdf.

14. M. Marcus, "Starbucks Tips Baristas $100 Million," *Forbes Magazine*, (March 21, 2008), online at http://www.forbes.com/2008/03/21/starbucks-barista-tip-markets-equity-cx_mlm_0321markets08.html accessed June 17, 2009.

15. M. Bustillo, " Wal-Mart to Settle 63 Suits Over Wages," *Wall Street Journal*, (December 24, 2008), p. B1.

16. G. Kranz, "Training to Short-Circuit Wage Disputes," *Workforce Management*, (July 22, 2008), online at http://www.workforce.com/apps/pbcs.dll/article?AID=/20080722/NEWS02/307229995&template=print article accessed June 17, 2009.

17. U.S. Wage and Hour Division, U.S. Department of Labor at www.dol.gov/esa.

18. K. Filion, "Minimum Wage anniversary: Still helping millions of workers get by, but just barely," Economic Policy Institute, (July 23, 2010), online at http://www.epi.org/publication/minimum_wage_anniversary_still_helping_millions_of_workers_get_by_but_/ accessed September 14, 20212; and U.S. Bureau of Labor Statistics, "Characteristics of Minimum Wage Workers: 2010," (modified February 25, 2011), online at http://www.bls.gov/cps/minwage2010.htm accessed September 14, 2012.

19. U.S. Equal Employment Opportunity Commission, "The Equal Pay Act of 1963," online at http://www.eeoc.gov/laws/statutes/epa.cfm

20. National Committee on Pay Equity, "Wage Gap Statistically Unchanged," www.pay-equity.org accessed November 6, 2011

21. C. Banks, "How to Recognize, Avoid Errors in the Job Evaluation Rating Process," *Canadian HR Reporter*, (February 24, 2003), pp. 17–19; M. J. Ducharme, P. Singh, and M. Podolsky, "Exploring the Links Between Performance Appraisals and Pay Satisfaction," *Compensation and Benefits Review*, (September–October 2005), pp. 46–52; and S. Watson, "Is Job Evaluation Making a Comeback—Or Did It Never Go Away?" *Benefits and Compensation International*, (June 2005), pp. 8–13.

22. J. J. Martocchio, *Strategic Compensation: A Human Resource Management Approach*, 3rd ed. (Upper Saddle River: Prentice Hall, 2004), p. 202.

23. Ibid.

24. For a thorough discussion of various methods of determining the pay structure, see Martocchio, Part III, "Design a Compensation Systems."

25. Office of Personnel Management, November 8, 2011, online at http://www.opm.gov.

26. D. L. Gallant, "Compensation Strategies for a Dynamic Environment," presented September 8, 2008 at Vermont SHRM Conference.

27. N. Cossack, "HR Solutions" *HR Magazine*, (January, 2008), p. 42.

28. Consumer Price Index at http://www.bls.gov/cpi/.

29. T. Satterfield, "Speaking of Pay," *HR Magazine*, (March, 2003), pp. 99–101.

30. J. A. Ross, "Five Ways to Boost Retention," *Harvard Management Update*, (April 2008), pp. 3–4.

31. See D. Lewin, "Incentive Compensation in the Public Sector: Evidence and Potential," *Journal of Labor Research*, (Fall 2003), pp. 597–621; and S. J. Wells, "No Results, No Raise," *HR Magazine*, (May 2005), pp. 77–80.

32. "Companies More Cautious Over Pay Practices," *Benefits and Compensation International*, (September 2002), p. 34.

33. For an interesting article on this topic, see L. R. Gomez-Mejia, T. M. Welbourne, and R. M. Wiseman, "The Role of Risk Sharing and Risk Taking Under Gainsharing," *Academy of Management Review*, (July 2000), pp. 492–507.

34. Lincoln Electric at http://www.lincolnelectric.com accessed November 7, 2011.

35. R. J. Long, "Gainsharing and Power: Lessons from Six Scanlon Plans," *Industrial & Labor Relations Review*, (April 2000), pp. 533–535.

36. J. J. Martocchio, *Strategic Compensation: A Human Resource Management Approach*, 3rd ed. (Upper Saddle River: Prentice Hall, 2004), p. 148.

37. M. Figueroa, "3 Executives Share 'Little Bets' That Paid Off," Vistage International, American Express Open Forum, November 3, 2011 online at http://www.openforum.com/articles/3-executives-share-little-bets-that-paid-off accessed November 12, 2011.

38. See, for example, J. Wells, "Stock Incentives Remain Preferred Compensation Option," *HR News*, (September 2000), p. 17; and K. Kroll, "Benefits: Paying for Performance," *Inc.*, (November 2004), p. 46. See also J. Bowley and D. A. Link, "Supporting Pay for Performance with the Right Technology," *Compensation and Benefits Review*, (September–October 2005), pp. 36–41.

39. D. Cadrain, "Put Success in Sight," *HR Magazine* (May 2003), pp. 85–92; and J. Pfeiffer, "Sins of Commission," *Business 2.0* (May 2004), p. 56.

40. T. J. Hackett and D. G. McDermott, "Seven Steps to Successful Performance-Based Rewards," *HR Focus* (September 2000), pp. 11–13; "PFP Plans Tied to Lower Health Costs," *HR Focus* (September 2005), p. 12; and D. Adler, "P4P in Maine: Local Pilot Teaches Global Lessons," *Employee Benefits News* (October 1, 2005), p. 1.

41. L. Haun, "Survey: As Pay-For-Performance Goes Up, Forced Ranking Is Going Down," *TLNT*, (November 8, 2011), online at http://www.tlnt.com/2011/11/08/survey-pay-for-performance-goes-up-forced-ranking-gets-pushed-down/ accessed November 12, 2011.

42. M. Henricks, "Pay for Performance," *Entrepreneur Magazine*, (November 2008), pp. 77–78.

43. "Competency-Based Pay Programs: Too Hard to Live With or the Right Stuff?" *Pay for Performance Report*, (May 2002), p. 6; and R. K. Zingheim and J. R. Schuster, "The Next Decade for Pay and Rewards," *Compensation and Benefits Review*, (January–February 2005), pp. 26–32.

44. K. Ellis, "Developing for Dollars," *Training*, (May 2003), pp. 34–39.

45. "Is Broadbanding an Administrative Nightmare Worse than That of Any Grading System?" *Pay for Performance Report*, (August 2002), p. 8.

46. "Is Broadbanding an Administrative Nightmare Worse than That of Any Grading System?" *Pay for Performance Report*, (August 2002), p. 8.

47. Essential Role of Rewarding Teams and Teamwork," *Compensation & Benefits Management*, (Autumn 2000), pp. 15–27.

48. "Team Compensation: Compensation Is the Hot Button of Teaming: Learn How to Do It Right," *On Wall Street*, (October 1, 2003), p. 1.

49. M. Krantz and Barbara H., "CEO pay soars while workers' pay stalls," *USA Today*, (April 4, 2011), online at http://www.usatoday.com/money/companies/management/story/CEO-pay-2010/45634384/1 accessed November 12, 2011.

50. J. Liberto, "CEOs earn 343 times more than typical workers," CNN Money, (April 20, 2011), online at http://money.cnn.com/2011/04/19/news/economy/ceo_pay/index.htm accessed November 12, 2011.

51. "Top 200 U.S. CEOs," Equilar, online at www.equilar.com/ceo-compensation/2011/index.php accessed November 12, 2011.

52. D. Costello, "The Drought Is Over (At Least for CEOs)," *New York Times*, (April 9, 2011), online at http://www.nytimes.com/2011/04/10/business/10comp.html?pagewanted=all accessed November 12, 2011.

53. See, for example, S. Bates, "Piecing Together Executive Compensation," *HR Magazine* (May 2002), pp. 60–68.

54. See, for example, G. Colvin, "The Great CEO Pay Heist," *Fortune* (June 25, 2001), pp. 64–70; L. Lavelle, "The Artificial Sweetener in CEO Pay," *BusinessWeek*, (March 26, 2001), p. 53.

55. "Executive Hires and Compensations: Performance Rules," *HR Focus*, (July 2003), p. 1.

56. M. A. Carpenter and W. G. Sanders, "Top Management Team Compensation: The Missing Link Between CEO Pay and Firm Performance," *Strategic Management Journal*, (April 2002), pp. 367–376.

57. A. R. Hunt, "Letter from Washington: As U.S. rich-poor gap grows, so does public outcry," *Bloomberg News*, (February 18, 2007).

58. H. B. Herring, "At the Top, Pay and Performance Are Often Far Apart," *New York Times*, (August 17, 2003), p. B-9.

59. E. Tahmincioglu, "Can wild CEO pay be tamed? Probably not," MSNBC, (October 1, 2008), online at http://www.msnbc.msn.com/id/26963309/ns/business-stocks_and_economy/t/can-wild-ceo-pay-be-tamed-probably-not/ accessed September 14, 2012.

60. "Executive Compensation," *Forbes*, (April 25, 2011), p. 80.

61. Ibid. Under IRS regulations, beginning in 1994, annual salaries paid to a company's five top officers in a publicly held firm are not tax deductible if the salaries are over $1 million. Most companies have simply ignored this new ruling, while others are deferring the excess income for these executives until retirement.

62. G. Strauss, "CEOs' Golden Parachute exit packages pass $100 million," *USA Today*, (November 8, 2011), online at http://www.usatoday.com/money/companies/management/story/2011-11-07/100-million-dollar-chairmen/51116304/1 accessed November 12, 2011.

63. S. Thurm, "Mergers Open 'Golden Parachutes'," *Wall Street Journal*, (November 1, 2011), online at http://online.wsj.com/article/SB10001424052970204394804577010000947986974.html accessed November 12, 2011.

64. For further reading on international compensation, see K. B. Lowe, J. Millman, H. DeCeiri, and P. J. Dowling, "International Compensation Practices: A Ten-Country Comparative Analysis," *Human Resource Management*, (Spring 2002), pp. 45–67; "How Do Your Peers Handle International Compensation and Benefits?" *HR Focus*, (July 2001), p. S-4; E. Ng, "Executive Pay in Asia—The Stock Option Game," *Benefits & Compensation International*, (September 2000), pp. 3–6; S. Overman, "In Sync," *HR Magazine*, (March 2000), pp. 25–27; C. Reynolds, "Global Compensation and Benefits in Transition," *Compensation and Benefits Review*, (January–February 2000), pp. 28–38; and J. E. Richard, "Global Executive Compensation: A Look at the Future," *Compensation and Benefits Review*, (May–June 2000), pp. 35–38.

65. U.S. Bureau of Public Affairs, Department of State (2008), www.state.gov.

66. "Quality of Living worldwide city rankings 2010," Mercer Consulting, Marsh & McLennan Companies, (May 26, 2010), online at http://www.mercer.com/press-releases/quality-of-living-report-2010 accessed November 13, 2011.

67. A. Kantaria, "Dubai: hardship posting or golden opportunity?," Telegraph.co.uk, (September 24, 2010), online at http://my.telegraph.co.uk/expat/annabelkantaria/10140035/dubai-%E2%80%9Chardship%E2%80%9D-posting-or-golden-opportunity/ accessed November 12, 2011.

68. H. Adrion, "Rewarding the International Executive Using Stock Options: Part 2," *Benefits & Compensation International*, (December 2000), pp. 13–128.

CHAPTER **12**
Employee Benefits

1. M. Naughton, "Michelle Morse, 22; sought to alter insurance law," *Boston Globe*, (November 14, 2005), online at http://www.boston.com/news/globe/obituaries/articles/2005/11/14/michelle_morse_22_sought_to_alter_insurance_law/ accessed June 21, 2009.

2. A. Smith, "Michelle of 'Michelle's Law' Never Wanted To Be in Limelight," SHRM Online at www.shrm.org (November 6, 2008).

3. R. Alonzo-Aaldivar, "Survey: Significant drop in uninsured young adults," Associated Press, (September 21, 2011), online at http://www.usatoday.com/news/health/healthcare/health/healthcare/story/2011-09-21/Survey-Significant-drop-in-uninsured-young-adults/50491646/1 accessed November 26, 2011.

4. Employee Benefits Security Administration, Department of Labor "Young Adults and the Affordable Care Act: Protecting Young Adults and Eliminating Burdens on Families and Businesses," online at http://www.dol.gov/ebsa/newsroom/fsdependentcoverage.html accessed December 11, 2011.

5. A. Smith, "Michelle of 'Michelle's Law' Never Wanted To Be in Limelight," SHRM, (November 6, 2008), online at http://www.shrm.org/LegalIssues/FederalResources/Pages/MichelleofMichellesLaw.aspx accessed September 14, 2012.

6. L. A. Weatherly, "Voluntary Employee Benefits Series Part I," SHRM White Paper, (December 2005), online at http://www.shrm.org/research/articles/articles/pages/voluntary_20employee_20benefits_20series_20part_20i__20voluntary_20benefits_20_26_20job_20satisfaction.aspx accessed December 7, 2011.

7. C. Ryan, "Employee Retention—What Can the Benefits Professional Do?" *Employee Benefits Journal*, (December 2000), p. 18.

8. F. Herzberg, *Work and the Nature of Man*, (New York: World, 1966).

9. Bureau of Labor Statistics, "Employer Costs for Employee Compensation," retrieved at http://www.bls.gov/news.release/ecec.toc.htm (December 7, 2011).

10. This assumes that the insurance policy is part of a group term plan. If it were a single policy, other than term insurance, or if the plan discriminated in favor of the more highly paid employees, the entire benefit would be taxable. See E. E. Vollmar, Term Life Insurance," *Employee Benefits Journal*, (June 2000), pp. 36–41.

11. "More Employers Offer Benefits to Workers' Domestic Partners," *HR Focus*, (September 2005), p. 12; S. Moon, "Making a Business Case for Domestic Partner Benefits," *Employee Benefit News*, (July 1, 2005), p. 1; and "How HR Is Addressing Domestic Partner Benefits," *HR Focus*, (July 2004), p. S-1.

12. Domestic Partner Benefits: Facts and Background," Employee Benefits Research Institute at www.ebri.org.

13. Social Security here refers to FICA taxes for old age, survivors, and disability insurance (OASDI).

14. "Social Security Administration Summary of Performance & Financial Information FY 2010," Social Security Administration, online at http://www.socialsecurity.gov/pgm/FY2010SummaryOfPerformanceAndFinancialInformation-508Final.pdf accessed December 11, 2011.

15. Social Security Administration, "How Credits are earned," (December 2011), online at http://www.ssa.gov/retire2/credits1.htm.

16. Social Security Administration online at http://www.ssa.gov/policy/docs/chartbooks/fast_facts/2011/fast_facts11.html accessed December 11, 2011.

17. D. Smith, "First U.S. baby boomer applies for Social Security," Reuters, (October 15, 2007), online at http://www.reuters.com/article/2007/10/15/us-usa-retirement-idUSN1538350920071015 accessed September 14, 2012.

18. J. Rutherford, "America's first 'baby boomer' files for Social Security," NBC News Field Notes, online at http://fieldnotes.msnbc.msn.com/archive/2007/10/15/412037.aspx accessed October 15, 2007.

19. Social Security Administration, "Status of the Social Security and Medicare Programs, A Summary of the 2011 Annual Reports," www.ssa.gov accessed December 15, 2011.

20. See U.S. Department of Labor, Employment and Training Administration, "Unemployment Insurance Tax Topic," (2009), p. 1. Available online at http://workforcesecurity.doleta.gov/unemploy/uitaxtopic.asp.

21. Wage bases for unemployment insurance vary. Some states follow the federal $7,000 base, while others vary, to a maximum of $37,800 in Hawaii.

22. See, for instance, U.S. Department of Labor, Office of Workforce Security, "Unemployment Insurance Extended Benefits" (January 2009) at http://workforcesecurity.doleta.gov/unemploy/extenben.asp.

23. See, for instance, J. Romeu, "Worldwide Business Trends Create New Leverage for Voluntary Benefits," *Employee Benefits Journal*, (December 2000), p. 24; B. Liddick, "Voluntary Benefits Go by the Wayside Amid an Uncertain Economy," *Workforce Management*, (April 2005), pp. 68–69; and D. Woolf, "Voluntary Benefits Can Beef up Total Rewards," *Canadian HR Reporter*, (February 14, 2005), available online at www.hrreporter.com.

24. "Employer Health Benefits Survey," Kaiser Family Foundation and Health Research & Educational Trust, (September 27, 2011), online at http://ehbs.kff.org/pdf/2011/EHBS%202011%20Chartpack.pdf accessed December 19, 2011.

25. Bureau of Labor Statistics, "Employer Costs for Employee Compensation," BLS News Release, (December 7, 2011), online at http://www.bls.gov/news.release/pdf/ecec.pdf accessed December 19, 2011.

26. BlueCross BlueShield Association, "Medical Cost Reference Guide, adapted from The Henry J. Kaiser Family Foundation and Health Research and Educational Trust, September 2007," online at http://www.horizon-bcbsnj.com/pdf/med_cost_ref_guide.pdf accessed January 17, 2009.

27. S. Miller, "Employers Accelerate Efforts to Control Health Plan Costs," SHRM, (November 21, 2011), online at http://www.shrm.org/hrdisciplines/benefits/articles/pages/costcontrol.aspx accessed December 19, 2011.

28. "Employer Health Benefits Survey," Kaiser Family Foundation and Health Research & Educational Trust, (September 27, 2011), online at http://ehbs.kff.org/pdf/2011/EHBS%202011%20Chartpack.pdf accessed December 19, 2011.

29. BlueCross BlueShield Association, "Medical Cost Reference Guide, adapted from The Henry J. Kaiser Family Foundation and Health Research and Educational Trust, September 2007," online at http://www.horizon-bcbsnj.com/pdf/med_cost_ref_guide.pdf accessed January 17, 2009.

30. "Framing the Picture: Access to Health Insurance Often Defines the Employment Relationship," *HR Magazine*, (August 2008), pp. 62–70.

31. It also should be noted that in some self-funding cases, organizations seek assistance from another company commonly referred to as a third-party administrator (TPA). The TPA's role is simply to process health-care forms.

32. U.S. Department of Labor, "FAQs about COBRA Continuation Health Coverage," Employee Security Benefits Administration online at http://www.dol.gov/ebsa/faqs/faq_consumer_cobra.html, accessed January 12, 2009.

33. Ibid.

34. It may also be interesting to note that in early 2003, an IRS ruling mandated that continuation of medical coverage is required in the case of a divorce. The organization must, then, make health insurance coverage available to the divorced spouse as of the date of the divorce. See "Spouse Gets COBRA at the Time of Divorce," *HR Focus*, (March 2003), p. 2.

35. See "12 Steps to Ensure Your HR Department Meets HIPAA's April 14 Date," *Human Resource Department Management Report*, (February 2003), p. 7; M. Kolton, M. Costa, and D. B. Spanier, "The Effect of HIPAA Privacy Rules on Personal Medical Records," *Journal of Compensation and Benefits*, (July–August 2002), pp. 5–16; J. Plavner, "A Regulatory Surprise," *HR Magazine*, (May 2003), pp. 127–131; J. A. Brislin, "HIPAA Privacy Rules and Compliance with Federal and State Employment Laws: The Participant Authorization Form," *Employee Benefits Journal*, (March 2003), p. 51–64; M. Verespej, "HR Should Set High Standards on Privacy," *HR Magazine*, (August 2005), p. 32; K. Gurchiek and M. Verespej, "HIPAA Violation Liability Narrowed," *HR Magazine*, (July 2005), p. 36; and B. D. Annulis, "Identity Theft Case Creates HIPAA Concerns for Hospitals," *Health Care Strategic Management*, (January 2005), pp. 11–12.

36. "Patient Protection and Affordable Care Act of 2010," SHRM, online at http://www.shrm.org/LegalIssues/FederalResources/FederalStatutes-RegulationsandGuidanc/Pages/PatientProtecionandAffordableCare-Act.aspx accessed January 28, 2012. L. K. Horn, "Health Reform is a Reality: The Patient Protection and Affordable Care Act," SHRM, online at http://www.shrm.org/multimedia/webcasts/Documents/10healthcare2.pdf accessed January 28, 2012. "The Healthcare Law and You," U.S. Department of Health & Human Services, online at http://www.healthcare.gov/law/index.html accessed January 28, 2012.

37. The Retirement Equity Act of 1984 and the Tax Reform Act of 1986 modified participation ages, minimum vesting age, and vesting rights, requiring full vesting after five years, partial vesting after three years, and seven-year full vesting with plan years beginning after December 1, 1988. Companies with a retirement plan year prior to that date were not required to go to the new lower vesting rules until December 1, 1989. It is also important to note that any monies contributed by employees toward their retirement are immediately 100 percent vested.

38. Portability of pension rights is a complex issue beyond the scope of this book. However, depending on the company, employees may receive a permanent right to their monies, receiving a pension from the organization at retirement age or receiving a check that allows them to reinvest those monies on their own.

39. L. Bivins, "Pension Treasure," *Wall Street Journal*, (June 5, 2000), p. A-4.

40. P. G. Lester, "A Checklist for Disability Plan Design," *Compensation and Benefits Review*, (September–October 2000), pp. 59–61.

41. "The End of Pensions?" Fox Business interview at http://www.foxbusiness.com/video-search/m/20583297/the-end-of-pensions.htm, (August 4, 2008).

42. "Who We Are," Pension Benefit Guaranty Corporation, online at http://www.pbgc.gov/about/who-we-are.html accessed December 20, 2011.

43. U.S. Department of Labor, "Retirement Plans, Benefits and Savings," online at http://www.dol.gov/dol/topic/retirement/typesofplans.htm accessed January 4, 2008.

44. Ibid.

45. Profit-sharing plans require profits before a contribution can be made. When the period shows no profits, no contributions need be made. The only partial exception is that contributions can be made in a year in which there are no profits if there are accumulated profits from prior years. However, should this occur, further restrictions apply. See also J. Marquez, "Firms Replacing Stock Options with Restricted Shares Face a Tough Sell to Employees," *Workforce Management,* (September 2005), pp. 71–73.

46. U.S. Department of Labor Employee Benefits Security Administration, "SIMPLE IRA Plans for Small Businesses," online at https://www.dol.gov/ebsa/publications/simple.html accessed December 20, 2011.

47. E. Brandon, "Planning to Retire: FedEx eliminates 401k match for employees," *U.S. News and World Report,* (January 17, 2009).

48. M. Bruno, "Building a Better 401k," Workforce Management, (August 2008), online at http://www.workforce.com/article/20080805/NEWS02/308059992 accessed September 14, 2012.

49. Mayo Clinic "Summary of Benefits," at www.mayoclinic.org updated January, 2009.

50. See, for instance, "Survey Updates National Norms for Bonuses, Paid Leave, and Vacation Days," Report on Salary Surveys, (June 2003), p. 1.

51. Based on information provided by *Economic Policy Institute World Almanac,* 2001.

52. P. Koepp, "Most employees take a vacation from taking vacation in 2011," *Kansas City Business Journal* (December 23, 2011), online at http://www.bizjournals.com/kansascity/news/2011/12/23/most-employees-take-a-vacation-from.html accessed January 20, 2012.

53. K. Gurchiek, "Vacationing Workers Find It Hard To Let Go," *HR Magazine,* (August 2005), p. 30.

54. Survey Updates National Norms for Bonuses, Paid Leave, and Vacation Days," *Report on Salary Surveys,* (June 2003), p. 1, Table 2. IOMA at www.IOMA.com.

55. Based on articles found on HRM.Guide.com.uk, "3-Million Not Entitled to Easter Bank Holiday," (April 16, 2003); and "Call for More Public Holidays, (May 3, 2002), www.hrmguide. co.uk/rewards/public_holidays.htm.

56. "Global Benefits: Mandated Paid Vacation," SHRM, online at http://www.shrm.org/Publications/hrmagazine/EditorialContent/2011/0511/Documents/Global%20Benefits.pdf accessed January 28, 2012.

57. "Absence Makes the Workplace Grow Poorer," *Fair Employment Practices Guidelines,* (April 15, 2003), p. 8.

58. Short-term disability programs may be provided through commercial carriers or through self-funding arrangements. The more popular of the two is purchased coverage.

59. Before we proceed, an important piece of federal legislation warrants mentioning. Based on the 1978 Pregnancy Discrimination Act, employers that offer short-term disability insurance to their employees must include pregnancy as part of the policy's coverage. This means that in whatever capacity employers cover disabilities such as an extended illness, coverage for disability due to pregnancy must be the same (see Chapter 3).

60. The number of sick days offered to employees generally varies according to their position in the organization and their length of service. Many organizations require a waiting period, approximately six months, before sick leave kicks in.

61. See, for example, S. Armour, "Faced With Less Time Off, Workers Take More," *USA Today,* (October 29, 2002), p. 1A.

62. P. Robinson, "Bank Launches Pooled Sick Leave Plan," *Australian Business Intelligence,* (November 12, 2003), p. 1.

63. Business and Legal Reports, "Should You Offer a Paid Time Off Bank?" online at http://compensation.blr.com/display.cfm/id/154821 accessed January 17, 2009; and International Foundation of Employee Benefit Plans online at www.ifebp.org.

64. S. Kelly, "Life Insurance Most Widespread Voluntary Benefit," *Workforce Management,* (August 2, 2007).

65. J. J. Meyer, "The Future of Flexible Benefit Plans," *Employee Benefits Journal,* (June 2000), pp. 3–7.

66. J. A. Fraser, "Stretching Your Benefits Dollar," *Inc.,* (March 2000), pp. 123–126.

67. Abbott Laboratories, "U.S. Benefits" online at http://www.abbott.com/careers/experience/benefits/us.htm, accessed January 18, 2009.

68. "Healthcare Flexible Spending Accounts Facts and Figures," Consumer Healthcare Products Association online at http://www.chpa-info.org/pressroom/FSAs_FactsFigures.aspx accessed January 18, 2009.

69. R. M. McCaffery, *Employee Benefit Programs: A Total Compensation Perspective* (2nd ed.), (Boston: PWS-Kent, 1992), p. 197.

70. Compiled by Lisbeth Claus, professor of global HR, Willamette University, Portland, Ore. (2011), with the assistance of the following global HR experts: Loretta F. Pardo, vice president, human resources, Caribbean and Latin America, Assurant Solutions (Brazil, Mexico); Gerlinde Herrmann, director, The Herrmann Group Ltd. (Canada); Jeffrey Wilson, counsel, Jun He Law Offices (China); Jean-Louis Mutte, managing director, Amiens School of Management (France); Thomas Belker, managing director of human resources, OBI Group Holding (Germany); Brad Boyson, head of HR and corporate services, Hamptons MENA, in collaboration with SHRM Member Forum/UAE (UAE); SHRM Learning System (2010) (USA).

71. D. Briscoe, R. Schuler, and I. Tarique, I, *International Human Resource Management: Policies and Practices for Multinational Enterprises (4e),* (New York: Routledge, 2012).

72. D. Tobenkin, "Learn the Landscape," *HR Magazine,* (May 2011), pp. 51–54.

73. Genetech, "About Us," online at http://www.gene.com/gene/about/corporate/awards accessed January 25, 2009.

74. "100 Best Companies to Work For," *Fortune,* (February 2, 2009), p. 71.

75. J. M. O'Brien, "Zappos Knows How to Kick It," *Fortune,* (February 2, 2009), pp. 55–58.

76. This example was directly influenced by a similar example given in J. S. Rosenbloom and G. V. Hallman, *Employee Benefits Planning,* 3rd ed. (Englewood Cliffs: Prentice Hall, 1991), p. 225. See also J. S. Rosenbloom, *Handbook of Employee Benefits Design, Funding, and Administration,* 4th ed., (New York: McGraw-Hill Professional Book Group, 1996). Actual benefits under SSDI vary according to family status, average annual income, and the consumer price index. Therefore, SSDI given in this example is only an estimate.

CHAPTER 13
Ensuring a Safe and Healthy Work Environment

1. U.S. Department of Labor Bureau of Labor Statistics, "Occupational Injuries and Illnesses by Selected Characteristics," http://www. bls.gov/news.release/osh2.t14.htm Accessed November 9, 2011.

2. B. Poovey, "Volkswagen trains 'industrial athlete' for new U.S. plant," Associated Press, MSNBC.com, (June 6, 2010), online at http://www.msnbc.msn.com/id/37514219/ns/business-careers/t/vw-trains-industrial-athlete-new-us-plant/ accessed November 27, 2011.

3. Ibid.

4. U.S. Department of Labor, Bureau of Labor Statistics, "Workplace Illnesses and Injury Summary," (October 20, 2011), online at http://www.bls.gov/news.release/osh.nr0.htm accessed December 20, 2011.

5. Compiled from: V. VanKooten, "The Fire That Changed History," *Des Moines Register,* (March 25, 2011); p. 14; J. Greenwald, "Triangle Shirtwaist fire brought safety changes," Business Insurance, (March 13, 2011), online at http://www.businessinsurance.com/article/20110313/ISSUE01/303139973 accessed December 10, 2011; K. E. Boroff, "Triangle Waist Company Fire—Lessons and legacy," North Jersey.com, (March 14, 2011), online at http://www.northjersey.com/news/opinions/boroff_032511.html accessed December 10, 2011.

6. "Introduction to OSHA, Instructor Guide," *U.S. Department of Labor, Occupational Safety & Health Administration,* (April, 2011), online at http://www.osha.gov/dte/outreach/intro_osha/intro_to_osha_guide.html accessed November 28, 2011.

7. "Imminent Danger," OSHA Fact Sheet (2002) online at http://www.osha.gov/OshDoc/data_General_Facts/factsheet-imminent-danger.pdf accessed November 28, 2011.

8. In the Supreme Court case of *Whirlpool Corporation v. Marshall* [445 U.S. 1(1980)], employees may refuse to work if they perceive doing so can cause serious injury. This case has weakened termination for insubordination when the refusal stems from a safety or health issue. This refusal was further clarified in *Gateway Coal v. United Mine Workers* [94 S. Ct. 641(1981)], where a three-part test was developed. This was where (1) the refusal is reasonable; (2) the employee was unsuccessful in getting the problem fixed; and (3) normal organizational channels to address the problem haven't worked.

9. *Marshall v. Barlow, Inc.,* 436 U.S., 307 (1978).

10. United Stated Department of Labor, "OSH Act, OSHA Standards, Inspection, Citations and Penalties," online at http://www.osha.gov/doc/outreachtraining/htmlfiles/introsha.html accessed November 28, 2011.

11. The number 3,600,000 is determined as follows: 1,800 employees, working 40-hour weeks, for 50 weeks a year [1,800 3 40 3 50]. U.S. Department of Labor, "Occupational Safety and Health Administration," *OSHA Facts—December 2004* (2004), pp. 1–5. Available online at www.osha.gov. It's also important to note that in addition to federal inspections, state inspectors conducted nearly another 58,000 inspections in 2004, bringing the total of inspections by federal and state inspectors to nearly 100,000 per year.

12. U.S. Bureau of the Census, "Statistical Abstracts of the United States, 2005," (Washington, DC: Government Printing Office, 2005), p. 417.

13. For willful violation the minimum penalty is $5,000; other fines levied for violations other than those willful and repetitive carry a $7,000 maximum. R. Ilaw, "When OSHA Comes Knocking: Give 'Em the Facts, Just the Facts," *Industrial Safety and Hygiene News,* (September 2005), pp. 50–51.

14. U.S. Department of Labor, Occupational Safety and Health Administration, "OSHA Enforcement, Committed Safe and Healthful Workplaces," (November 28, 2011), online at http://www.osha.gov/dep/2010_enforcement_summary.html access November 28, 2011.

15. United States Department of Labor, Occupational Safety & Health Administration, "Small Business Handbook," online at http://www.osha.gov/publications/smallbusiness/small-business.html accessed November 28, 2011.

16. "What are the essential elements of an effective safety and health program?," SHRM, (April 2, 2008), online at http://www.shrm.org/TemplatesTools/hrqa/Pages/safetyandhealthprogram.aspx accessed November 22, 2011.

17. United States Department of Labor, Occupational Safety and Health Administration, "Most Frequently Cited Standards, 2008," (November 23, 2008), online at http://www.osha.gov/dcsp/compliance_assistance/frequent_standards.html accessed November 18, 2011.

18. U.S. Department of Labor, "Most Frequently Cited Standards, fiscal year 2011," online at http://www.osha.gov/dcsp/compliance_assistance/ frequent_standards.html accessed December 11, 2011.

19. National Institute for Occupational Safety and Health (NIOSH), "Preventing Deaths and Injuries of Adolescent Workers," http://www.cdc.gov/niosh/childlab.html accessed March 26, 2009.

20. J. Casale, "OSHA Safety Equipment Standard Done," *Workforce Management,* (November 20, 2007), online at http://www.workforce.com/apps/pbcs.dll/article?AID=/20071120/NEWS01/311209998&template=print article accessed June 21 2009.

21. D. Costello, "Stressed Out: Can Workplace Stress Get Worse?—Incidents of 'Desk Rage' Disrupt America's Offices—Long Hours, Cramped Quarters Produce Some Short Fuses; Flinging Phones at the Wall," *Wall Street Journal,* (January 16, 2001), p. B-1.

22. U.S. Department of Labor, Occupational Safety and Health Administration (2009), http:// www.osha.gov accessed November 11, 2011.

23. U.S. Department of Justice, "Special Report: Workplace Violence, 1993–2009," (March 2011), online at http://bjs.ojp.usdoj.gov/content/pub/pdf/wv09.pdf accessed December 10, 2011.

24. H. C. Adams, "Dealing with Violence in the Workplace," Dickinson, Mackaman, Tyler & Hagen, P.C. (2009).

25. U.S. Department of Labor, Occupational Safety and Health Administration, "OSHA Fact Sheet: Workplace Violence," (2002), online at http://www.osha.gov/OshDoc/data_General_Facts/factsheet-workplace-violence.pdf accessed December 10, 2011.

26. T. Anderson, "Training for Tense Times," *Security Management,* (March 2002), pp. 68–75.

27. See P. M. Buhler, "Workplace Civility: Has It Fallen by the Wayside?" *Supervision,* (April 2003), pp. 20–22.

28. "How Can HR Help Address the Threat of Workplace Violence," *HR Focus,* (October 2003), p. 8; L. Stack, "Employees Behaving Badly," *HR Magazine,* (October 2003), pp. 111–115; "The Most Effective Tool Against Workplace Violence," *HR Focus,* (February 2003), p. 11; and "How to Predict and Prevent Workplace Violence," *HR Focus,* (April 2005), pp. 10–11.

29. P. Falcone, "Dealing with Employees in Crisis: Use this Blueprint for Proactive Management Intervention," *HR Magazine,* (May 2003), pp. 117–122; and "How Can HR Help Address the Threat of Workplace Violence?" *HR Focus,* (October 2003), p. 8. For another insight into this matter, see E. Roche, "Do Something—He's About to Snap," *Harvard Business Review,* (July 2003), pp. 23–30.

30. See S. G. Minter, "Prevention to Solution to Workplace Violence," *Occupational Hazards,* (August 2003), p. 22; L. R. Chavez, "10 Things Healthy Organizations Do to Prevent Workplace Violence," *Occupational Hazards,* (August 2003), p. 22; and "Is Your Lobby Ripe for Violence?" *HR Focus,* (September 2003), p. 5.

31. R. J. Grossman, "Bulletproof Practices," *HR Magazine,* (November 2002), pp. 34–42.

32. J. I. Pasek, "Crisis Management for HR," *HR Magazine,* (August 2002), p. 111.

33. P. Temple, "Real Danger and 'Postal' Myth," *Workforce,* (October 2000), p. 8.

34. National Institute for Occupational Safety and Health, "Indoor Environmental Quality," online at http://www.cdc.gov/niosh/topics/indoorenv/accessed December 11, 2011.

35. A. Underwood, "A Hidden Health Hazard," *Newsweek,* (December 4, 2000), p. 74; and M. Conlin and J. Carey, "Is Your Office Killing You?," *BusinessWeek,* (June 5, 2000), pp. 114–128.

36. See Conlin and Carey, "Is Your Office Killing You?," *BusinessWeek,* (June 5, 2000), pp. 114–128.; and R. Schneider, "Sick Buildings Threaten Health of Those Who Inhabit Them," *Indianapolis Star,* (September 23, 2000).

37. A. G. Sulzberger, "Hospitals Shift Smoking Bans to Smoker Ban," *New York Times,* (February 10, 2011), online at http://www.nytimes.com/2011/02/11/us/11smoking.html?pagewanted=all accessed December 3, 2011.

38. American Cancer Society, "The Effects of Secondhand Smoke on Worker Health," (August 2010), online at http://www.acscan.org/content/wp-content/uploads/2010/09/smokefree-worker-health.pdf accessed December 3, 2011.

39. M. Conlin, "Get Healthy or Else," *BusinessWeek,* (February 26, 2007), online at http://www.businessweek.com/stories/2007-02-25/get-healthy-r-else accessed December 3, 2011.

40. U.S. Department of Labor, "Ergonomics: The Study of Work," OSHA 3125, (Washington, DC: Government Printing Office, 2000), p. 4.

41. K. J. DiLuigi, "Help for the Overworked Wrist," *Occupational Hazards,* (October 2000), pp. 99–101.

42. OSHA Issues Final Ergonomics Standards," *Healthcare Financial Management,* (January, 2001), p. 9; G. Flynn, "Now Is the Time to Prepare for OSHA's Sweeping New Ergonomic Standard," *Workforce,* (May 2001), pp. 76–77; C. Haddad, "OSHA New Regs Will Ease the Pain—For Everybody," *BusinessWeek,* (December 4, 2000), pp. 90–91; and Y. J. Dreazen, "Ergonomic Rules Are the First in a Wave of Late Regulations," *Wall Street Journal,* (November 14, 2000), p. A-41. For another view on these standards, see P. Kuntz, "What a Pain: Proposed OSHA Rules for Workplace Injuries Make Companies Ache—Agency Stretches Data to Fit Burgeoning Mission; Cost of Compliance Debated—Looking for 10 Pallbearers," *Wall Street Journal,* (September 18, 2000), p. A-1.

43. See, for example, S. Bates, "Industry Ergonomic Guidelines 'Not Standards in Disguise,' OSHA Official Says," *HR Magazine*, (September 2003), p. 34.

44. See Occupational Safety and Health Administration, *OSHA's Ergonomics Enforcement Plan*, (Washinton, D.C.: Government Printing Office, 2003).

45. U.S. Department of Labor, "Ergonomics: The Study of Work," OSHA 3125, (Washington, DC: Government Printing Office, 2000), p. 1; and R. Kaletsky, "Beyond Musculoskeletal Disorders: Subtle Aspects of Ergonomics," *Safety Compliance Letter*, (November 2005), pp. 4–5.

46. F. M. Spina, "Ergonomically Correct," *Risk Management*, (December 2000), pp. 39–41; and L. Eig and J. Landis, "MSDs and the Workplace: EA Professionals Can Work with Ergonomists to Identify Jobs and Workstations That Place Employees at Risk for Musculoskeletal Disorders," *Journal of Employee Assistance*, (September 2004), pp. 12–14.

47. J. Perkins, "Finding spirituality amid slaughter," *The Des Moines Register*, (June 5, 2006).

48. J. Russell, "Chaplains Join 'Faith Friendly' Workplace," *Morning Edition*, National Public Radio, (January 10, 2007). Originally broadcast by Iowa Public Radio, http://www.npr.org/templates/story/story.php?storyId=6777784 accessed November 28, 2011.

49. "HR Execs Polled About Stress," *Work and Family* Newsbrief, (May 2002), pp. 2–4.

50. R. R. Hastings, "Find the Right Balance Between Stress and Results," SHRM, (April 13, 2010), online at http://www.shrm.org/hrdisciplines/employeerelations/articles/Pages/FindtheRightBalance.aspx accessed December 4, 2011.

51. P. Babcock, "Workplace Stress? Deal with it!," *HR Magazine*, (May 2009), online at http://www.shrm.org/Publications/hrmagazine/EditorialContent/Pages/0509babcock.aspx accessed December 4, 2011.

52. "Japan Asks If It Works Too Hard," *Christian Science Monitor* (Tokyo), (April 6, 2000), p. 4. See also "When Heartache May Bring on a Heart Attack," *BusinessWeek*, (May 6, 2002), p. 97.

53. For some interesting reading on organizational stress, see E. Wethington, "Theories of Organizational Stress," *Administrative Science Quarterly*, (September 2000), p. 640; and T. Beehr, "Consistency of Implications of Three Role Stressors Across Four Countries," *Journal of Organizational Behavior*, (August 2005), pp. 467–487.

54. K. Tyler, "Cut the Stress," *HR Magazine*, (May 2003), pp. 101–106.

55. See, for example, "Stressed Out: Extreme Job Stress: Survivors' Tales," *Wall Street Journal*, (January 17, 2001), pp. B-1; M. C. Bolino and W. H. Turnley, "The Personal Costs of Citizenship Behavior: The Relationship Between Individual Initiative and Role Overload, Job Stress, and Work-Family Conflict," *Journal of Applied Psychology*, (July 2005), pp. 740–748; and "Stressed Out," *Training*, (December 2004), p. 16.

56. C. Goggi, "Internet Monitoring Software: A happy employee means better productivity," GFI Software, (April 12, 2011), online at http://www.letsgeek.net/2011/04/internet-monitoring-software-a-happy-employee-means-better-productivity/ accessed December 4, 2011.

57. "Internet Usage Statistics," (2004), www.n2h2.com/about/press/usage_stats.php accessed; V. K. G. Lim, "The IT Way of Loafing on the Job: Cyberloafing, Neutralizing, and Organizational Justice," *Journal of Organizational Behavior*, (August 2002), pp. 675–694; "Control Your Internet Destiny," (2005), www.2watch.com accessed; and M. Conlin, "Workers Surf at Your Own Risk," *BusinessWeek*, (June 12, 2000), p. 106.

58. "Employee Assistance Programs," *HR Magazine*, (May 2003), p. 143.

59. N. Schutte, S. Toppinen, R. Kalimo, and W. Schaufeli, "The Factorial Validity of the Maslach Burnout Inventory—General Survey (MBI–GS) Across Occupational Groups and Nations," *Journal of Occupational and Organizational Psychology*, (March 2000), pp. 3–66.

60. See, for instance, S. Vanheule, A. Lievrouw, and P. Verhaeghe, "Burnout and Intersubjectivity: A Psychoanalytical Study from a Lacanian Perspective," *Human Relations*, (March 2003), pp. 321–339; and D. Wise, "Employee Burnout Taking Major Toll on Productivity," *Los Angeles Times*, (July 9, 2001), p. 29.

61. B. Perlman and E. A. Hartman, "Burnout: Summary and Future Research," *Human Relations* 25, no. 4 (1982), p. 294.

62. See, for instance, S. Bates, "Expert: Don't Overlook Employee Burnout," *HR Magazine*, (August 2003), p. 14.

63. "EAPs: They're Well Intentioned, But Also Risky," *HR Briefing*, (May 1, 2002), pp. 2–3; and F. Hansen, "Employee Assistance Programs (EAPs) Grow and Expand Their Reach," *Compensation and Benefits Review*, (March/April 2000), p. 13.

64. Employee rights legislation mandates that any activity in an EAP remains confidential. This means records of who is visiting the EAP, the problems, and intervention, must be maintained separately from other personnel records. Also, HIPAA regulations (see Chapter 12) may also mandate confidentiality of EAP activities.

65. "EAPs with the Most," *Managing Benefits Plans*, (March 2003), p. 8; K. Tyler, "Helping Employees Cope with Grief," *HR Magazine*, (September 2003), pp. 55–58; and "EEOC Considers EAPs a 'Best' Practice," *HR Briefing*, (April 1, 2003), p. 5.

66. F. Phillips, "Employee Assistance Programs: A New Way to Control Health Care Costs," *Employee Benefit Plan Review*, (August 2003), pp. 22–24.

67. W. Atkinson, "Wellness, Employee Assistance Programs: Investments, Not Costs," *Bobbin*, (May 2000), pp. 42–48.

68. K. Lee, "EAP Diversity Detracts from Original Focus, Some Say," *Employee Benefits News*, (July 1, 2003), p. 1.

69. K.M. Quinley, "EAPs: A Benefit That Can Trim Your Disability and Absenteeism Costs," *Compensation and Benefits Report*, (February 2003), pp. 6–7.

70. "EAPs Flounder Without Manager Support," *Canadian HR Reporter*, (June 2, 2003), p. 7.

71. See, for instance, M. Derer, "Corporate Benefits Take Aim Against Obesity," *USA Today*, (September 1, 2003), p. A1; P. Petesch, "Workplace Fitness or Workplace Fits?" *HR Magazine*, (July 2001), pp. 137–140; and J. L. Barlament, "Disease Management: Legal Implications," *Benefits and Compensation Digest*, (November 2005), pp. 32–36.

72. C. Petersen, "Value of Complementary Care Rises, But Poses Challenges," *Managed HealthCare*, (November 2000), pp. 47–48; T. Anderson, "Employers Boost Financial Incentives for Disease Management," *Employee Benefit News*, (October 1, 2005), p. 1; and "43% of Companies Have Adopted 'Formal' Disease-Management/Wellness Programs," *Managing Benefits Plans*, (August 2005), p. 9.

73. S. Coffey, "Wellness at Work," America's Best Companies, (July 22, 2008), online at http://www.americasbestcompanies.com/blog/wellnessatwork.aspx accessed September 14, 2012.

74. A. E. Chernov, "Weight Discrimination: The Effects of Obesity in Employment," *Hohonu: Journal of Academic Writing* 4, no.1, (2006).

75. See, for example, K. Greco, R. Paul, and B. Pawlecki, "Promoting Healthy Weight: With Obesity on the Rise, Eaps Can Take Advantage of Their Assessment, Referral, and Case Management Skills to Help Employers Keep Healthcare Costs under Control and Encourage Employees to Maintain Healthy Lifestyles," *Journal of Employee Assistance*, (December 2004), pp. 14–16; and K. Merx, "The Rising Cost of Fat; Business Is Finding out That Obesity Drives up Costs for More than Just Health Insurance," *Crain's Detroit Business*, (September 13, 2004), p. 11.

76. K. Sweeney, "Wellness Programs Must Be Properly Constructed and Marketed for Maximum Return on Investment," *Employee Benefit News*, (March 1, 2005), p. 1.

77. Vignettes for this case were found at the U.S. Department of Labor, Occupational Safety and Health Administration, "Making a Positive Difference: OSHA Saves Lives," (November 27, 2005), www.osha.gov/as/opa/oshasaveslives.html.

CHAPTER **14**
Understanding Labor Relations and Collective Bargaining

1. R. J. Burnette, "Walking Out on Wages," *Workforce Management*, (August 2005), pp. 12–13.

2. "Labor Unions: Good for Workers, Not for U.S. Competitiveness," Pew Research Center Publications, (February 17, 2011), http://pewresearch.org/pubs/1897/favorability-labor-unions-salary-american-worker-productivity-public-sector accessed January 2, 2012.

3. "Union Members Summary," Bureau of Labor Statistics, (January 27, 2012), online at http://www.bls.gov/news.release/union2.nr0.htm accessed January 29, 2012.

4. AFL-CIO, "Union Membership by Industry" www.aflcio.org/aboutunions/joinunions/whyjoin/uniondifference/uniondiff11.cfm accessed December 29, 2011.

5. D. B. Klaff and R. G. Ehrenberg, "Collective Bargaining and Staff Salaries in American Colleges and Universities," *Industrial and Labor Relations Review,* (October 2003), pp. 92–104.

6. U.S. Department of Labor Bureau of Labor Statistics "Union affiliation of employed wage and salary workers by occupation and industry 2010," (December 2011), online at http://www.bls.gov/cps/tables.htm#union accessed December 29, 2011.

7. J. Bladen and S. Machin, "Cross-Generation Correlations of Union Status for Young People in Britain," *British Journal of Industrial Relations,* (September 2003), p. 391; and R. J. Grossman, "Unions Follow Suit," *HR Magazine* (May 2005), pp. 47–51.

8. "Why you need a Union," AFL-CIO, online at http://www.aflcio.org/joinaunion/why accessed February 14, 2009.

9. Readers should recognize that although the closed shop (compulsory union membership before one is hired) was declared illegal by the Taft-Hartley Act, a modified form still exists today. That quasi-closed shop arrangement is called the hiring hall and is found predominantly in the construction and printing industries. However, a hiring hall is not a form of union security because it must assist all members despite their union affiliation. Additionally, the hiring hall must establish procedures for referrals that are nondiscriminatory.

10. There are, however, exceptions to this in the construction industry.

11. See, for instance, M. Romano, "Hospital Accused of Iron-Fist Tactics," *Modern Hospital,* (January 8, 2001), p. 16.

12. L. Stein, "Ports of Call," *U.S. News and World Report,* (October 21, 2002), p. 14.

13. B. Feldacker, *Labor Guide to Labor Law,* 4th ed., (Upper Saddle River: Prentice Hall, 2004), p. 5.

14. The Railway Labor Act created the National Mediation Board, which works on matters of recognition, dispute resolution, and unfair labor practices in the railroad and airline industries only. The National Railroad Adjustment Board was also part of the Railway Labor Act, and this body arbitrated disputes between railroads and unions.

15. W. Zellner and M. Arndt, "Concession at the Bargaining Table, Too," *BusinessWeek,* (March 19, 2001), p. 46.

16. It is also important to note that the Wagner Act was amended in 1974 with the Health Care Amendments. These brought both nonprofit hospitals and healthcare organizations under the jurisdiction of the Wagner Act.

17. M. J. Goldberg, "An Overview and Assessment of the Law Regulating Internal Union Affairs," *Journal of Labor Research,* (Winter 2000), pp. 15–36.

18. It must be noted that when one discusses government labor relations, two categories emerge. One is the federal sector, the other the public sector. In a brief discussion of government labor relations, the focus is on the federal sector due to its federal legislation. However, one must realize that state or municipal statutes do define practices for labor-management relationships for state, county, and municipal workers (typically police officers, fire fighters, and teachers). Because these laws differ in the many jurisdictions, it goes beyond the scope of this text to attempt to clarify each jurisdiction's laws.

19. Although government employees often face a no-strike clause, with the exception of the air traffic controllers' case, such restrictions are generally ineffective. Working to rules, "blue flues," and recorded sanitation, nursing, and teacher strikes across this country support the contention that a no-strike clause is weak.

20. United States Code Annotated, Title 18, Section 1961, (St. Paul: West Publishing, 1984), p. 6.

21. Ibid., p. 228.

22. United States Code Annotated, Title 29, Section 186, (St. Paul, MN: West Publishing, 1978), p. 17.

23. U.S. Department of Labor, Office of the Inspector General, *Semiannual Report to the Congress April 1, 2002–September 30, 2002,* (Washington, DC: Government Printing Office, 2002).

24. Only pure grievance awards can be solely determined by the FLRA.

25. M. M. Clark, "NLRB Still Unsure How 'To Define' Supervisor," *HR Magazine,* (September 2003), pp. 23–24; J. E. Lyncheski and R. J. Andrykovitch, "Who's a Supervisor?" *HR Magazine,* (September 2001), pp. 159–168; and D. Foust, "The Ground War at FedEx," *BusinessWeek,* (November 28, 2005), pp. 42–43.

26. Elections may not be the only means of unionizing. In cases where a company has refused to recognize a union because of a past unfair labor practice, the NLRB may certify a union without a vote.

27. Adapted from S. P. Robbins and D. A. DeCenzo, *Supervision Today,* 4th ed. (Upper Saddle River: Prentice Hall, 2004), p. 434; M. K. Zachary, "Labor Law for Supervisors: Union Campaigns Prove Sensitive for Supervisory Employees," *Supervision,* (May 2000), pp. 23–26; S. Greenhouse, "A Potent, Illegal Weapon Against Unions: Employers Know It Costs Them to Fire Organizers," *New York Times,* (October 24, 2000), p. A-10; and J. E. Lyncheski and L. D. Heller, "Cyber Speech Cops," *HR Magazine,* (January 2001), pp. 145–150.

28. D. C. Bok and J. T. Dunlop, "Collective Bargaining in the United States: An Overview," in W. Clay Hammer and Frank L. Schmidt (eds.), *Contemporary Problems in Personnel,* (Chicago: St. Clair Press, 1997), p. 383.

29. An international union, in this context, refers to a national union in the United States that has local unions in Canada.

30. M. H. Bowers and D. A. DeCenzo, *Essentials of Labor Relations,* (Englewood Cliffs: Prentice Hall, 1992), p. 101.

31. For a thorough explanation of the grievance procedure, see ibid., pp. 109–114.

32. See also M. I. Lurie, "The 8 Essential Steps in Grievance Processing," *Dispute Resolution Journal,* (November 1999), pp. 61–65.

33. S. Shellenbarger, "Companies Are Finding Real Payoffs in Aiding Employee Satisfaction," *Wall Street Journal,* (October 11, 2000), p. B-1.

34. To be accurate, a strike vote is generally held at the local union level in which the members authorize their union leadership to call the strike.

35. U.S. Department of Labor, Bureau of Labor Statistics, "Work Stoppages Summary," (February 8, 2011), online at http://www.bls.gov/news.release/wkstp.nr0.htm accessed February 8, 2011.

36. S. Greenhouse, "More Lockouts as Companies Battle Unions," *New York Times,* (January 22, 2012), online at http://www.nytimes.com/2012/01/23/business/lockouts-once-rare-put-workers-on-the-defensive.html?pagewanted=all accessed January 31, 2012.

37. C. Tejada, "Graduate Students at Private Universities Have Right to Unionize, Agency Rules," *Wall Street Journal,* (November 2, 2000), p. B-22; and A. Bernstein, "Big Labor's Day of Reckoning," *BusinessWeek,* (March 7, 2005), pp. 65–66.

38. U.S. Department of Labor, Bureau of Labor Statistics, "Union Members Summary," (January 2012), online at http://www.bls.gov/news.release/union2.nr0.htm accessed January 20, 2012.

39. K. Maher, "Big Union to Step Up Recruiting," *Wall Street Journal,* (February 11, 2011), online at http://online.wsj.com/article/SB10001424052748703716904576134243686318466.html?mod=googlenews_wsj accessed December 30, 2011.

40. This section based on G. R. King, "New Guidelines From the National Labor Relations Board Regarding Participative Management Initiatives and Employee Committee," *SHRM Legal Report,* (August 2001).

41. J. Smerd, "Union Membership Rises, but Quality of Jobs has Changed," *Workforce Management,* (February 7, 2008).

42. R. C. Kearney, "Patterns of Union Decline and Growth: An Organizational Ecology Perspective," *Journal of Labor Research,* (Fall 2003), p. 561.

43. Bureau of Labor Statistics, "Union Membership Annual News Release," (January 21, 2011).

44. Ibid.

45. An extensive discussion of Sunshine Laws can be found at Sunshine Review, at http://sunshinereview.org/index.php/State_sunshine_laws.

46. U.S. Department of Labor, Employment and Earnings, (January 2001), and AFL-CIO, www.aflcio.org/uniondifference/uniondiff5.html.

47. International Labour Organization Statistics, and P. Hall-Jones, "Unionism and Economic Performance" *New Unionism 2007*, www.newunionism. net accessed February 21, 2009.

48. "National Industrial Relations," Worker-Participation.eu, http://www.worker-participation.eu/National-Industrial-Relations accessed January 1, 2012.

49. Organisation for Economic Cooperation and Development, "Trade Union Density," OECD, StatExtracts Data (extracted January 1, 2012), http://stats.oecd.org/Index.aspx?DataSetCode=UN_DEN. Trade union density corresponds to the ratio of wage and salary earners that are trade union members, divided by the total number of wage and salary earners (OECD *Labour Force Statistics*). Density is calculated using survey data, wherever possible, and administrative data adjusted for non-active and self-employed members otherwise.

50. See, for example, R. Harbridge, R. May, and G. Thickett, "The Current State of Play: Collective Bargaining and Union Membership Under the Employment Relations Act of 2000," *New Zealand Journal of Industrial Relations*, (September 2003), p. 140.

51. "Chinese Trade Unions Makes [sic] Progress in 2010," All-China Federation of Trade Unions, online at http://english.acftu.org/template/10002/file.jsp?cid=63&aid=622 accessed January 2, 2012.

52. QI Dongtao, "Progress and Dilemmas of Chinese Trade Unions," *East Asian Policy*, (June 24, 2010), online at http://www.eai.nus.edu.sg/Vol2No3_QiDongtao.pdf accessed January 2, 2012.

53. Gong Wen, "ACFTU Maps Out Tasks for 2011," *Chinese Trade Unions*, (January 2011), p. 4.

54. L. Lin and S. Ozasa, "LG Display China Strike Ends as Fresh Labor Protest Reported," Bloomberg Businessweek, (December 29, 2011), online at http://www.businessweek.com/news/2011-12-29/lg-display-china-strike-ends-as-fresh-labor-protest-reported.html accessed January 2, 2012.

55. Based on R. Fisher and W. Ury, *Getting to Yes: Negotiating Agreement Without Giving In*, (Boston: Houghton Mifflin, 1981); J. A. Wall Jr., and M. W. Blum, "Negotiations," *Journal of Management*, (June 1991), pp. 295–96; M. H. Bazerman and M. A. Neale, *Negotiating Rationally*, (New York: Free Press, 1992); and D. A. DeCenzo and S. P. Robbins, *Fundamentals of Management*, 5th ed., (Upper Saddle River: Prentice Hall, 2006), pp. 413–416.

Glossary

360-degree appraisals Performance evaluations in which supervisors, peers, employees, customers, and the like evaluate the individual.

4/5ths rule A rough indicator of discrimination, this rule requires that the number of minority members a company hires must equal at least 80 percent of the majority members in the population hired.

absolute standards Measuring an employee's performance against established standards.

acquisition The transfer of ownership and control of one organization to another.

adverse (disparate) impact A consequence of an employment practice that results in a greater rejection rate for a minority group than for the majority group in the occupation.

adverse (disparate) treatment An employment situation where protected group members receive treatment different from other employees in matters such as performance evaluations and promotions.

affirmative action A practice in organizations that goes beyond discontinuance of discriminatory practices to include actively seeking, hiring, and promoting minority group members and women.

Age Discrimination in Employment Act (ADEA) This act prohibits arbitrary age discrimination, particularly among those over age 40.

agency shop A union security arrangement whereby employees must pay union dues to the certified bargaining unit even if they choose not to join the union.

Albemarle Paper Company v. Moody Supreme Court case that clarified the methodological requirements for using and validating tests in selection.

Americans with Disabilities Act of 1990 This act extends employment protection to most forms of disability status.

application form Company-specific employment form used to generate specific information the company wants.

apprenticeships Combine instruction with coaching from an experienced mentor.

assessment center A facility where performance simulation tests are administered. These include a series of exercises used for selection, development, and performance appraisals.

attribution theory A theory of performance evaluation based on the perception of who is in control of an employee's performance.

authorization card A card signed by prospective union members indicating that they are interested in having a union election held at their work site.

baby boomers Individuals born between 1946 and 1965.

background investigation The process of verifying information job candidates provide.

behavioral interview Observing job candidates not only for what they say but for how they behave.

behaviorally anchored rating scales (BARS) A performance appraisal technique that generates critical incidents and develops behavioral dimensions of performance. The evaluator appraises behaviors rather than traits.

blind-box ad An advertisement that does not identify the advertising organization

bona fide occupational qualification (BFOQ) Job requirements that are "reasonably necessary to meet the normal operations of that business or enterprise."

broad-banding Paying employees at preset levels based on their level of competency.

burnout Chronic and long-term stress.

career The sequence of employment positions that a person has held over his or her life.

carpal tunnel syndrome A repetitive-motion disorder affecting the wrist.

central tendency The tendency of a rater to give average ratings.

change agent Individual responsible for fostering the change effort and assisting employees in adapting to changes.

checklist appraisal A performance evaluation in which a rater checks off applicable employee attributes.

Civil Rights Act of 1964 Outlawed racial segregation and discrimination in employment, public facilities, and education.

Civil Rights Act of 1991 Employment discrimination law that nullified selected Supreme Court decisions. It reinstated burden of proof by the employer and allowed for punitive and compensatory damage through jury trials.

Civil Service Reform Act Replaced Executive Order 11491 as the basic law governing labor relations for federal employees.

classification method Evaluating jobs based on predetermined job grades.

classroom lectures Training in a traditional classroom setting.

code of ethics A formal document that states an organization's primary values and the ethical rules it expects organizational members to follow.

collective bargaining The negotiation, administration, and interpretation of a written agreement between two parties, at least one of which represents a group that is acting collectively, and that covers a specific period of time.

communications programs   HRM programs designed to provide information to employees.

comparable worth   Equal pay for jobs similar in skills, responsibility, working conditions, and effort.

compensation administration   The process of managing a company's compensation program.

compensation and benefits   HRM function concerned with paying employees and administering the benefits package.

compensation surveys   Used to gather factual data on pay practices among firms and companies within specific communities.

competency-based compensation   Organizational pay system that rewards skills, knowledge, and behaviors.

comprehensive interview   A selection device used to obtain in-depth information about a candidate.

comprehensive selection   Applying all steps in the selection process before rendering a decision about a job candidate.

compressed work week schedules   Employees work longer days in exchange for longer weekends or other days off.

conciliation and mediation   Impasse resolution techniques using an impartial third party to help management and the union to resolve the conflict.

concurrent validity   Validating tests by using current employees as the study group.

conditional job offer   A tentative job offer that becomes permanent after certain conditions are met.

Consolidated Omnibus Budget Reconciliation Act (COBRA)   Provides for continued employee benefits up to three years after an employee leaves a job.

constraints on recruiting efforts   Factors that can limit recruiting outcomes.

construct validity   The degree to which a particular trait relates to successful job performance, as in IQ tests.

consumer driven health plan (CDHP)   Combines a health plan with a high deductible with a health savings account that the insured uses to pay for deductibles and medical care.

content validity   The degree to which test content, as a sample, represents all situations that could have been included, such as a typing test for a clerk typist.

contingent workforce   The part-time, temporary, and contract workers used by organizations to fill peak staffing needs or perform work not done by core employees.

continuous improvement   Organizational commitment to constantly improving quality of products or services.

controlling   A management function concerned with monitoring activities to ensure that goals are met.

core competency   Organizational strengths that represent unique skills or resources.

core employees   An organization's full-time employee population.

criterion-related validity   The degree to which a particular selection device accurately predicts the important elements of work behavior, as in the relationship between a test score and job performance.

critical incident appraisal   A performance evaluation that focuses on key behaviors that differentiate between doing a job effectively or ineffectively.

cut score   A scoring point below which applicants are rejected.

decline or late stage   The final stage in one's career, usually marked by retirement.

defined benefit plan   A retirement program that pays retiring employees a fixed retirement income based on average earnings over a period of time.

defined contribution plan   No specific benefit payout is promised because the value of the retirement account depends on the growth of contributions of employee and employer.

diary method   A job analysis method requiring job incumbents to record their daily activities.

discipline   A condition in the organization when employees conduct themselves in accordance with the organization's rules and standards of acceptable behavior.

dismissal   A disciplinary action that results in the termination of an employee.

documentation   A record of performance appraisal process outcomes.

domestic partner benefits   Benefits offered to an employee's live-in partner.

downsizing   An activity in an organization aimed at creating greater efficiency by eliminating certain jobs.

drug testing   The process of testing applicants/employees to determine if they are using illicit.

Drug-Free Workplace Act   Requires specific government-related groups to ensure that their workplace is drug free.

dues check-off   Employer withholding of union dues from union members' paychecks.

Dukes v. Walmart Stores   Lawsuit brought on behalf of 1.6 million women who have worked at Walmart since 1998 claiming discrimination in pay and promotions.

economic strike   An impasse that results from labor and management's inability to agree on the wages, hours, and terms and conditions of a new contract.

employee assistance programs (EAPs)   Specific programs designed to help employees with personal problems.

employee benefits   Membership-based, nonfinancial rewards offered to attract and keep employees.

employee development   Future-oriented training that focuses on employee personal growth.

employee handbook   A booklet describing important aspects of employment an employee needs to know.

employee monitoring   An activity whereby the company keeps informed of its employees' activities.

employee referral   A recommendation from a current employee regarding a job applicant.

employee relations function   Activities in HRM concerned with effective communications among organizational members.

Employee Retirement Income Security Act (ERISA)   Law passed in 1974 designed to protect employee retirement benefits.

employee training   Present-oriented training that focuses on individuals' current jobs.

employment agencies   Assists in matching employees seeking work with employers seeking workers.

employment-at-will doctrine   Nineteenth-century common law that permitted employers to discipline or discharge employees at their discretion.

encounter stage   The socialization stage where individuals confront the possible dichotomy between their organizational expectations and reality.

Equal Employment Opportunity Act (EEOA)   Granted enforcement powers to the Equal Employment Opportunity Commission.

Equal Employment Opportunity Commission (EEOC)   The arm of the federal government empowered to handle discrimination in employment cases.

Equal Pay Act of 1963   This act requires equal pay for equal work.

essential functions   Activities that are core to a position and cannot be modified.

establishment period   A career stage in which one begins to search for work and finds a first job.

ethics   A set of rules or principles that defines right and wrong conduct.

executive search firms   Private employment agency specializing in middle- and top-management placements.

exempt employees   Employees in positions that are exempt from most employee protection outlined in the Fair Labor Standards Act, especially overtime pay.

expatriate   An individual who lives and works in a country of which he or she is not a citizen.

exploration period   A career stage that usually ends in the mid-twenties as one makes the transition from school to work.

external career   Attributes related to an occupation's properties or qualities.

extrinsic rewards   Benefits provided by the employer, usually money, promotion, or benefits.

fact-finding   The technique whereby a neutral third party conducts a hearing to gather evidence and testimony from the parties regarding the differences between them.

Fair Credit Reporting Act   Requires an organization to notify job candidates of its intent to check into their credit.

Fair Labor Standards Act (FLSA)   Passed in 1938, this act established laws outlining minimum wage, overtime pay, and maximum hour requirements for most U.S. workers.

Family and Medical Leave Act of 1993   Federal legislation that provides employees with up to 12 weeks of unpaid leave each year to care for family members or for their own medical reasons.

Federal Mediation and Conciliation Service (FMCS)   A government agency that assists labor and management in settling disputes.

flex time   An alternative to traditional "9 to 5" work schedules allows employees to vary arrival and departure times.

flexible benefits   A benefits program in which employees pick benefits that most meet their needs.

flexible spending accounts   Allow employees to set aside money before payroll taxes to pay for healthcare or dependent care.

forced-choice appraisal   A performance evaluation in which the rater must choose between two specific statements about an employee's work behavior.

General Duty Clause   Covers any potentially dangerous or unhealthy workplace condition that isn't covered by specific OSHA industry regulation.

Genetic Information Nondiscrimination Act (GINA)   Prohibits employers from making employment decisions based on information about an employee's genetic information.

glass ceiling   The invisible barrier that blocks females and minorities from ascending into upper levels of an organization.

globalization   A process of interaction and integration among the people, companies, and governments of different nations, driven by international trade and investment, accelerated by information technology.

golden parachute   A financial protection plan for executives in case they are severed from the organization.

graphic rating scale   A performance appraisal method that lists traits and a range of performance for each.

grievance procedure   A complaint-resolving process contained in union contracts.

Griggs v. Duke Power Company   Landmark Supreme Court decision stating that tests must fairly measure the knowledge or skills required for a job.

group incentive   Motivational plan provided to a group of employees based on their collective work.

group interview method   Meeting with a number of employees to collectively determine what their jobs entail.

halo error   The tendency to let our assessment of an individual on one trait influence our evaluation of that person on other specific traits.

Hawthorne studies   A series of studies that provided new insights into group behavior and motivation.

Health Insurance Portability and Accountability Act of 1996 (HIPAA)   Ensures confidentiality of employee health information.

health maintenance organization   Provide comprehensive health services for a flat fee.

Holland vocational preferences model   Represents an individual occupational personality as it relates to vocational themes.

honesty test   A specialized question-and-answer test designed to assess one's honesty.

host-country national (HCN)   A citizen of the host country hired by an organization based in another country.

hostile environment harassment   Offensive and unreasonable situations in the workplace that interfere with the ability to work.

hot-stove rule   Discipline, like the consequences of touching a hot stove, should be immediate, provide ample warning, be consistent, and be impersonal.

HR generalist   Position responsible for all or a large number of HR functions in an organization.

human resource information system (HRIS)   A computerized system that assists in the processing of HRM information.

human resource planning   Process of determining an organization's human resource needs.

imminent danger   A condition where an accident is about to occur.

implied employment contract   Any organizational guarantee or promise about job security.

impression management   Influencing performance evaluations by portraying an image desired by the appraiser.

IMPROSHARE   An incentive plan that uses a specific mathematical formula for determining employee bonuses.

incidence rate   Number of injuries, illnesses, or lost workdays as it relates to a common base of full-time employees.

individual incentive plans   Motivation systems based on individual work performance.

individual interview method   Meeting with an employee to determine what his or her job entails.

individual ranking   Ranking employees' performance from highest to lowest.

individual retirement accounts   A type of defined contribution plan with employer contributions.

initial screening   The first step in the selection process whereby job inquiries are sorted.

interest arbitration   An impasse resolution technique used to settle contract negotiation disputes.

intergroup development   Helping members of various groups become a cohesive team.

internal search   A promotion-from-within concept.

internships   Structured program for students to gain employment experience in their area of study

interviewer bias   Image created by reviewing materials such as the résumé, application, or test scores prior to the actual interview.

intrinsic rewards   Satisfactions derived from the job itself, such as pride in one's work, a feeling of accomplishment, or being part of a team.

job analysis   Provides information about jobs currently being done and the knowledge, skills, and abilities that individuals need to perform the jobs adequately.

job description   A statement indicating what a job entails.

job design   Refers to the way the position and the tasks within that position are organized, including how and when the tasks are done and any factors that affect the work, such as in what order the tasks are completed and the conditions under which they are completed.

job enrichment   Enhancing jobs by giving employees more opportunity to plan and control their work.

job enrichment   Expanding job content to create more opportunities for job satisfaction.

job evaluation   Specifies the relative value of each job in the organization.

job fairs   Events attended by employer representatives or recruiters with the goal of reaching qualified candidates.

job rotation   Moving employees horizontally or vertically to expand their skills, knowledge, or abilities.

job sharing   Two people share one job by splitting the work week and the responsibilities of the position.

job specification   Statements indicating the minimal acceptable qualifications incumbents must possess to successfully perform the essential elements of their jobs.

kaizen   The Japanese term for an organization's commitment to continuous improvement.

karoshi   A Japanese term meaning death from overworking.

Kirkpatrick's model   Evaluates the benefits of training for skills that are hard to quantify, such as attitudes and behaviors.

knowledge workers   Individuals whose jobs are designed around the acquisition and application of information.

labor union   Acts on behalf of its members to secure wages, hours, and other terms and conditions of employment.

Landrum-Griffin Act of 1959   Also known as the Labor and Management Reporting and Disclosure Act, this legislation protected union members from possible wrongdoing on the part of their unions. It required all unions to disclose their financial statements.

late-career stage   A career stage in which individuals are no longer learning about their jobs nor expected to outdo levels of performance from previous years.

leading   A management function concerned with directing the work of others.

learning organization   An organization that values continued learning and believes a competitive advantage can be derived from it.

leased employees   Individuals hired by one firm and sent to work in another for a specific time

legally required benefits   Employee benefits mandated by law.

leniency error   Performance appraisal distortion caused by evaluating employees against one's own value system.

lockout   A situation in labor-management negotiations whereby management prevents union members from returning to work.

maintenance function   Activities in HRM concerned with maintaining employees' commitment and loyalty to the organization.

maintenance of membership   Requires an individual who chooses to join a union to remain in the union for the duration of the existing contract.

management   The process of efficiently completing activities with and through people.

management by objectives (MBO) A performance appraisal method that includes mutual objective setting and evaluation based on the attainment of the specific objectives.

management thought Early theories of management that promoted today's HRM operations.

Marshall v. Barlow's, Inc. Supreme Court case that stated an employer could refuse an OSHA inspection unless OSHA had a search warrant to enter the premises.

material safety data sheet (MSDS) Employers with hazardous chemicals in the workplace are required to label them clearly and provide material safety data sheets (MSDS). Complete MSDS forms are usually made available by the manufacturer of the chemical product.

medical/physical examination An examination to determine an applicant's physical fitness for essential job performance.

merger Joining ownership of two organizations.

merit pay An increase in pay, usually determined annually.

metamorphosis stage The socialization stage during which the new employee must work out inconsistencies discovered during the encounter stage.

McDonnell-Douglas Corp. v. Green Supreme Court case that led to a four-part test used to determine if discrimination has occurred.

mid-career stage A career stage marked by continuous improvement in performance, leveling off in performance, or beginning of deterioration in performance.

mission statement A brief statement of the reason an organization is in business.

motivation function Activities in HRM concerned with helping employees exert themselves at high energy levels.

multimedia learning Videos, simulations and games are used for learning and training.

multinational corporations (MNCs) Corporations with significant operations in more than one country.

musculoskeletal disorders (MSDs) Continuous-motion disorders caused by repetitive stress injuries.

National Institute for Occupational Safety and Health (NIOSH) The government agency that researches and sets OSHA standards.

National Labor Relations Board (NLRB) Established to administer and interpret the Wagner Act, the NLRB has primary responsibility for conducting union representation elections.

nonexempt employees Employees who are covered by the Fair Labor Standards Act, including overtime pay and minimum wage provisions.

observation method A job analysis technique in which data are gathered by watching employees work.

offshoring The process of moving jobs out of one country and in to another country.

on-the-job training Trainee works with more experienced employee in the actual work environment.

online résumés Résumés created and formatted to be posted on online résumé or job sites.

open shop Employees are free to join the union or not, and those who decline need not pay union dues.

opportunities External environmental factors that can be used for the organization's advantage.

ordering method Ranking job worth from highest to lowest.

organization culture The system of sharing meaning within the organization that determines how employees act.

organization development (OD) The part of HRM that addresses system-wide change in the organization.

organization-wide incentive A motivation system that rewards all facility members based on how well the entire group performed.

organizing A management function that deals with determining what jobs are to be done and by whom, where decisions are to be made, and how to group employees.

orientation Activities that introduce new employees to the organization and their work units.

outsourcing Contracting with a company to handle one or more HR functions.

outsourcing Sending work "outside" the organization to be done by individuals not employed full time with the organization.

paired comparison Ranking individuals' performance by counting the times any one individual is the preferred member when compared with all other employees.

Patient Protection and Affordable Care Act Reforms the healthcare insurance system in the U.S. by expanding the availability and regulation of health insurance coverage and making significant changes to how health insurance coverage is provided and paid for.

pay-for-performance programs Rewarding employees based on their job performance.

peer evaluation A performance assessment in which coworkers provide input into the employee's performance.

Pension Benefit Guaranty Corporation (PBGC) The organization that lays claim to corporate assets to pay or fund inadequate pension programs.

performance simulation tests Work sampling and assessment centers evaluate abilities in actual job activities.

performance-based rewards Rewards exemplified by the use of commissions, piecework pay plans, incentive systems, group bonuses, or other forms of merit pay.

perquisites Attractive benefits, over and above a regular salary, granted to executives, also known as "perks."

planning A management function focusing on setting organizational goals and objectives.

plateaued mid-career Promotion beyond one's current job becomes less likely.

point method Breaking down jobs based on identifiable criteria and the degree to which these criteria exist on the job.

point-of-service (POS) Healthcare plan that includes primary care physicians but allows greater flexibility for using services out of the network.

Polygraph Protection Act Prohibits the use of lie detectors in screening all job applicants.

Position Analysis Questionnaire (PAQ)   A job analysis technique that rates jobs on elements in six activity categories.

post-training performance method   Evaluating training programs based on how well employees can perform their jobs after training.

pre-arrival stage   This socialization process stage recognizes that individuals arrive in an organization with a set of organizational values, attitudes, and expectations.

pre–post-training performance method   Evaluating training programs based on the difference in performance before and after training.

pre–post-training performance with control group method   Evaluating training by comparing pre-and post-training results with individuals.

predictive validity   Validating tests by using prospective applicants as the study group.

preferred provider organizations (PPOs)   Organization that requires using specific physicians and healthcare facilities to contain the rising costs of healthcare.

Pregnancy Discrimination Act of 1978   Law prohibiting discrimination based on pregnancy.

Privacy Act   Requires federal government agencies to make information in an individual's personnel file available to him or her.

proactive personality   Describing those individuals who are more prone to take actions to influence their environment.

professional employer organization   Assumes all HR functions of a client company by hiring all of its employees and leasing them back to the company.

progressive discipline   A system of improving employee behavior that consists of warnings and punishments that gradually become more severe.

qualified privilege   The ability for organizations to speak candidly to one another about employees or potential hires.

quality management   Organizational commitment to continuous process of improvement that expands the definition of customer to include everyone involved in the organization.

quid pro quo harassment   Some type of sexual behavior is expected as a condition of employment.

Racketeer Influenced and Corrupt Organizations Act (RICO)   Law passed to eliminate any influence on unions by members of organized crime.

Railway Labor Act   Provided the initial impetus to widespread collective bargaining.

realistic job preview (RJP)   A selection device that allows job candidates to learn negative as well as positive information about the job and organization.

reasonable accommodations   Changes to the workplace that allow qualified workers with disabilities to perform their jobs.

recruiter   Represents employer to prospective applicants at colleges and job fairs.

recruiting   The process of seeking sources for job candidates.

relative standards   Evaluating an employee's performance by comparing the employee with other employees.

reliability   A selection device's consistency of measurement.

repetitive stress injuries   Injuries sustained by continuous and repetitive movements of the hand.

replacement chart   HRM organizational charts indicating positions that may become vacant in the near future and the individuals who may fill the vacancies.

representation certification (RC)   The election process whereby employees vote in a union as their representative.

representation decertification (RD)   The election process whereby union members vote out their union as their representative.

reverse discrimination   A claim made by white males that minority candidates are given preferential treatment in employment decisions.

right to work laws   Prohibit union membership as a condition of employment.

rightsizing   Linking employee needs to organizational strategy.

role ambiguity   When an employee is not sure what work to do.

role conflicts   Expectations that are difficult to reconcile or achieve.

role overload   When an employee is expected to do more than time permits.

Sarbanes-Oxley Act   Established procedures for public companies regarding how they handle and report their finances.

Scanlon Plan   An organization-wide incentive program focusing on cooperation between management and employees through sharing problems, goals, and ideas.

scientific management   A set of principles designed to enhance worker productivity.

seniority systems   Decisions such as promotions, pay, and layoffs are made on the basis of an employee's seniority or length of service.

sexual harassment   Anything of a sexual nature that creates a condition of employment, an employment consequence, or a hostile or offensive environment.

shared services   Sharing HRM activities among geographically dispersed divisions.

sick building   An unhealthy work environment.

similarity error   Evaluating employees based on the way an evaluator perceives himself or herself.

simulation   Any artificial environment that attempts to closely mirror an actual condition.

social media   Websites and mobile applications that facilitate interactive communication.

Social Security   Retirement, disability, and survivor benefits paid by the government to the aged, former members of the labor force, the disabled, or their survivors.

socialization or onboarding   A process of adaptation that takes place as individuals attempt to learn the values and norms of work roles.

staffing function Activities in HRM concerned with seeking and hiring qualified employees.

strategic human resource management Aligning HR policies and decisions with the organizational strategy and mission.

strengths An organization's best attributes and abilities.

stress A dynamic condition in which an individual confronts an opportunity, constraint, or demand related to a desire and perceives the outcome both uncertain and important.

stressor Something that causes stress in an individual.

structured questionnaire method A specifically designed questionnaire on which employees rate tasks they perform in their jobs.

summary plan description (SPD) An ERISA requirement of explaining to employees their pension program and rights.

survey feedback Assessment of employees' perceptions and attitudes regarding their jobs and organization.

suspension A period of time off from work as a result of a disciplinary process.

SWOT analysis A process for determining an organization's strengths, weaknesses, opportunities, and threats.

Taft-Hartley Act Amended the Wagner Act by addressing employers' concerns in terms of specifying unfair union labor practices.

team-based compensation Pay based on how well the team performed.

technical conference method A job analysis technique that involves extensive input from the employee's supervisor.

telecommuting Using technology to work in a location other than the traditional workplace.

threats External environmental factors that present challenges to the organization.

Title VII The most prominent piece of legislation regarding HRM, it states the illegality of discriminating against individuals based on race, religion, color, sex, or national origin.

training and development function Activities in HRM concerned with assisting employees to develop up-to-date skills, knowledge, and abilities.

type A behavior Personality type characterized by chronic urgency and excessive competitive drive.

type B behavior Personality type characterized by lack of either time urgency or impatience.

unemployment compensation Employee insurance that provides some income continuation in the event an employee is laid off.

Uniformed Services Employment and Reemployment Rights Act of 1994 (USERRA) Clarifies and strengthens the rights of veterans to return to their jobs in the private sector when they return from military service.

union Organization of workers, acting collectively, seeking to protect and promote their mutual interests through collective bargaining.

union security arrangements Labor contract provisions designed to attract and retain dues-paying union members.

union shop Any nonunion workers must become dues-paying members within a prescribed period of time.

upward appraisal Employees provide frank and constructive feedback to their supervisors.

validity The proven relationship of a selection device to relevant criterion.

vestibule training Using actual work tools or equipment in a training situation.

vesting rights The permanent right to pension benefits.

wage structure A pay scale showing ranges of pay within each grade.

Wagner Act Also known as the National Labor Relations Act of 1935, this act gave employees the right to form and join unions and to engage in collective bargaining.

Wards Cove Packing Company v. Atonio A notable Supreme Court case that had the effect of potentially undermining two decades of gains made in equal employment opportunities.

weaknesses Resources an organization lacks or activities it does poorly.

weighted application form A special type of application form that uses relevant applicant information to determine the likelihood of job success.

wellness programs Organizational programs designed to keep employees healthy.

whistle-blowing A situation in which an employee notifies authorities of wrongdoing in an organization.

wildcat strike An unauthorized and illegal strike that occurs during the terms of an existing contract.

work process engineering Radical, quantum change in an organization.

work sampling A selection device requiring the job applicant to perform a small sampling of actual job activities.

Worker Adjustment and Retraining Notification (WARN) Act Specifies employers' notification requirements when closing down a plant or laying off large numbers of workers.

workers' compensation Employee insurance that provides income continuation if a worker is injured on the job.

workforce diversity The varied personal characteristics that make the workforce heterogeneous.

workplace romance A personal relationship that develops at work.

written verbal warning Temporary record that a verbal reprimand has been given to an employee.

written warning First formal step of the disciplinary process.

Company Index

Subject Index